Asset and Liability Management Handbook

Asset and Liability Management Handbook

Edited by

Gautam Mitra
Chairman and Managing Director of OptiRisk Systems
Distinguished Professor and Director of CARISMA, Brunel University, UK

and

Katharina Schwaiger
Quantitative Analyst at OptiRisk Systems and a Postdoctoral Knowledge
Transfer Partnership (KTP) Associate at CARISMA, Brunel University, UK

First published 2011 by
PALGRAVE MACMILLAN

Palgrave Macmillan in the UK is an imprint of Macmillan Publishers Limited,
registered in England, company number 785998, of Houndmills, Basingstoke,
Hampshire RG21 6XS.

Palgrave Macmillan in the US is a division of St Martin's Press LLC,
175 Fifth Avenue, New York, NY 10010.

Palgrave Macmillan is the global academic imprint of the above companies
and has companies and representatives throughout the world.

Palgrave® and Macmillan® are registered trademarks in the United States,
the United Kingdom, Europe and other countries.

ISBN: 978–0–230–27779–3 hardback

This book is printed on paper suitable for recycling and made from fully
managed and sustained forest sources. Logging, pulping and manufacturing
processes are expected to conform to the environmental regulations of the
country of origin.

A catalogue record for this book is available from the British Library.

Library of Congress Cataloging-in-Publication Data

    Asset and liability management handbook / [edited by] Gautam Mitra,
Katharina Schwaiger.
       p. cm.
    Includes index.
    Summary: "Recent years have shown an increase in development and
acceptance of quantitative methods for asset and liability management
strategies. This book presents state of the art quantitative decision models for
three sectors: pension funds, insurance companies and banks, taking into
account new regulations and the industries risks" – Provided by publisher.
    ISBN 978–0–230–27779–3 (hardback)
    1. Asset-liability management. 2. Asset-liability management –
Mathematical models. I. Mitra, Gautam. II. Schwaiger, Katharina, 1983–

HG1615.25.A73 2011
332.068'1—dc22   2011001649

Contents

Part IV   ALM Models Applied to Other
Areas of Financial Planning

Illustrations

Tables

Figures

Foreword

It is a long-established truth that the stability of financial institutions depends crucially on the matching of assets and liabilities. However, there has been great invention in recent decades by financial markets seeking to meet the needs of both wholesale and retail consumers. As a result, today, the agility and dynamics of both assets and liabilities challenge the ALM skills of every institution. The complexity of the issues is further complicated by the greater range and speed of market movements and the increasing sophistication of consumers. Good ALM creates real, competitive advantage. Naïve or clumsy ALM can and does lead to disaster.

This book is therefore ideally timed. It collects together some of the best thinkers working in ALM currently, mixing leading edge academic work with practitioner insights. The focus by industry sector allows experts to enjoy comparing best practice in their own sectors with the frontiers of knowledge in allied disciplines. It also makes a valuable additional resource for trainee actuaries. For those less familiar with the subject, the format gives an appreciation of the range of innovation that ALM is driving across the financial sector.

As events in the past three years have proved, financial instability creates fundamental stresses for governments, society and individuals. Financial risk managers bear a heavy responsibility to ensure strong institutions. This must be based on clear understanding and effective management of the interaction of assets and liabilities. This book makes an important contribution to that understanding and management.

NIGEL MASTERS
Immediate Past President
Institute and Faculty of Actuaries
January 2011

About the Editors

Gautam Mitra is an internationally renowned research scientist in the field of operational research in general and computational optimization and modelling in particular. He has developed a world-class research group in his area of specialization with researchers from Europe, the United Kingdom and the United States. He has published three books and over 100 refereed research articles. He was head of the Department of Mathematical Sciences, Brunel University, London, from 1990 to 2001. In 2001 he established CARISMA, the Centre for the Analysis of Risk and Optimisation Modelling Applications. CARISMA specializes in research into risk and optimization and their combined paradigm in decision modelling. Mitra is a director of OptiRisk Systems UK and OptiRisk India. Many of the research results of CARISMA are exploited through these companies.

Katharina Schwaiger is a KTP post-doc associate at OptiRisk Systems. She received her PhD in operational research from the Centre for the Analysis of Risk and Optimisation Modelling Applications (CARISMA), Brunel University, London, in 2009. Prior to this she gained a BSc in financial mathematics from Brunel University. Her work experience includes internships in applied research, equities and asset management at Metzler Investments and Metzler Asset Management, Frankfurt; sponsored research on liability-driven investment at Insight Investments, London; and an Engineering and Physical Sciences Research Council-funded research internship at ACE Ltd, London.

Notes on Contributors

Sarp Kaya Acar finished his BSc in mathematics at the Middle East Technical University, Ankara. Afterwards, he graduated from the Technical University, Kaiserslautern, with an MSc and PhD in financial mathematics. From 2003 to 2005, he worked as a scientific researcher at the Technical University, Kaiserslautern, and he joined Fraunhofer ITWM in 2005. His main areas of interest include Levy processes, credit risk and interest rate models.

Wan Kamaruzaman Wan Ahmad has been the general manager of the Employees' Provident Fund at the Treasury Department in Malaysia since 2007. Prior to this he served as finance director at Izoma Sdn. Bhd. and at Kemuncak Facilities Management Sdn. Bhd. From March 1981 to November 2005, Wan Kamaruzaman worked in various positions and institutions in the financial markets. He started his career with Malayan Banking Bhd. From 1994 to 2005, he served as CEO and director of several companies within the Affin Group. He was then CEO for Affin Moneybrokers Sdn. Bhd., and he was CEO and director for Affin Trust Management Bhd. and Affin Fund Management Sdn. Bhd. Wan Kamaruzaman received his BSc in analytical economics from the University of Malaya in 1981.

Noël Amenc is Professor of Finance at EDHEC Business School, Nice, France and the director of EDHEC-Risk Institute. He holds a master's degree in economics and a PhD in finance, and has conducted research in the fields of quantitative equity management, portfolio performance analysis and active asset allocation, resulting in numerous academic and practitioner articles and books. He is a member of the editorial board of the *Journal of Portfolio Management*, associate editor of the *Journal of Alternative Investments* and a member of the scientific advisory council of the AMF (the French financial regulatory authority).

Arjan Berkelaar is Head of Asset Allocation and Risk Management at Kaust Investment Management Company, which performs advisory and investment services to the King Abdullah University of Science and Technology Trust, Washington D.C. Before joining Kaust Investment Management Company, he was a principal investment officer and head of multi-asset class investment strategies at the World Bank Treasury. Berkelaar holds a PhD in finance from Erasmus University, Rotterdam, and an MSc in mathematics (summa cum laude) from Delft University of Technology. He is both a CFA and a CAIA charter holder.

David Blake is Professor of Pension Economics and director of the Pensions Institute at Cass Business School, London; chairman of Square Mile Consultants, a training and research consultancy; and co-founder with JP Morgan of the LifeMetrics Index. He is a consultant to many organizations, including JP Morgan, Merrill Lynch, Deutsche Bank, Union Bank of Switzerland, Paribas Capital Markets, Prudential UK, AXA, Aegon, Friends Provident, McKinsey & Co., the Office for National Statistics, the Financial Services Authority, the Department for Work and Pensions, HM Treasury, the Bank of England, the Prime Minister's Policy Directorate, the OECD, the International Monetary Fund and the World Bank. In June 1996, he established the Pensions Institute, which undertakes high-quality research on all pension-related issues and publishes details of its research activities online at www.pensions-institute. org. His recent books include *Pension Schemes and Pension Funds in the United Kingdom* (Oxford University Press, 2003) and *Pension Economics and Pension Finance* (Wiley, 2006). David is also a member of the academic advisory board of the Behavioral Finance Forum founded by Professor Shlomo Benartzi of UCLA.

Andrew Cairns is Professor of Financial Mathematics at Heriot-Watt University, Edinburgh. He is well known internationally for his research in financial risk management for pension plans and life insurers, with particular focus on asset liability modelling and long-term interest rate risk management. More recently he has been working on the modelling of longevity risk: how this can be modelled, measured and priced, and how it can be transferred to the financial markets. In this field, he has developed a number of innovative stochastic mortality models – work that has established him as one of the world's leading experts on the modelling of longevity risk. He is an active member of the UK and international actuarial profession in both research and education. He qualified as a fellow of the Faculty of Actuaries in 1993; since 1996 he has been editor of the leading international actuarial journal *ASTIN Bulletin*, and in 2005 he was elected as a corresponding member of the Swiss Association of Actuaries.

Moorad Choudhry has over 21 years of experience in investment banking in the City of London and was most recently Head of Treasury at Europe Arab Bank Plc. He was previously Head of Treasury at KBC Financial Products, and Vice President in Structured Finance Services at JP Morgan Chase Bank. Moorad is a visiting professor in the Department of Economics, London Metropolitan University; a senior research fellow at the ICMA Centre, University of Reading; a fellow of the ifs-School of Finance, London; and a fellow of the Chartered Institute for Securities and Investment. He is on the editorial board of the *Journal of Structured Finance* and the editorial advisory board of the *American Securitization Forum*. He is also visiting professor at CARISMA, Brunel University.

Michael Dempster is emeritus professor at the Centre for Financial Research, University of Cambridge. He has taught and researched in leading universities on both sides of the Atlantic and is founding editor-in-chief of *Quantitative Finance*. Consultant to many global financial institutions and governments, he is regularly involved in executive education worldwide. He is the author of over 100 research articles in leading international journals and 12 books, and his work has won several awards. He is an honorary fellow of the UK Institute of Actuaries and managing director of Cambridge Systems Associates Ltd., a financial analytics consultancy and software company.

Dan diBartolomeo is president and founder of Northfield Information Services, Inc. Before starting Northfield, he held the position of director of research at a New York investment firm, where he was responsible for investment strategy and equity, fixed-income and derivatives research. Dan writes and lectures extensively and frequently presents papers at academic and industry meetings. He serves on the boards of the Chicago Quantitative Alliance, Woodbury College, the American Computer Foundation and the Boston Committee on Foreign Relations. He is an active member of the Financial Management Association, QWAFAFEW, the Southern Finance Association and the International Association of Financial Engineers. He has published numerous articles in a variety of journals, has contributed chapters to several finance textbooks and recently finished his first book, on investment management for high-net-worth individuals, published by the CFA Research Foundation. He received his degree in applied physics from Cornell University. He is also visiting professor at CARISMA, Brunel University.

Steward Doss is an assistant professor at the National Insurance Academy, Pune, and is involved in training, teaching, research and consultancy in insurance. He specializes in business intelligence, CRM, marketing, market research, actuarial risk modelling, quality management, organizational studies and quantitative techniques, including multivariate analysis. He has 18 years of experience in research and teaching at the National Insurance Academy. He was a consultant for a World Bank project on portfolio risk management in agricultural insurance. He has developed a dynamic financial analysis for the

Agricultural Insurance Corporation of India. He co-authored a book on *Personal Financial Planning* (Cengage India, 2009) and has contributed more than 20 research papers to national and international journals and conference proceedings.

Kevin Dowd is a visiting professor at the Pensions Institute, Cass Business School, London, and Emeritus Professor of Financial Risk Management at Nottingham University Business School, where he worked in the Centre for Risk and Insurance Studies. He has written widely in the fields of financial and monetary economics, political economy, financial regulation, financial risk management, pensions and, more recently, mortality modelling. His books include *Competition and Finance: A New Interpretation of Financial and Monetary Economics* (Macmillan, 1996), *Beyond Value at Risk: The New Science of Risk Management* (Wiley, 1998) and *Measuring Market Risk* (2nd edn, Wiley, 2005). He is also affiliated to the Institute of Economic Affairs. He is one of the co-authors of the Cairns-Blake-Dowd (CBD) mortality model.

Robert Ferstl received his MSc and doctorate in economics from the Vienna University of Economics and Business, in 2004 and 2008, respectively. Currently, he is a postdoctoral researcher in the Department of Finance, University of Regensburg. His principal research interests include financial econometrics, computational finance, fixed income and stochastic optimization.

Jacek Gondzio is Professor of Optimization in the School of Mathematics, University of Edinburgh. His research interests include the theory, implementation and applications of optimization techniques, and in particular the development of theory and practical algorithms based on interior point methods for optimization. The algorithms and software he has developed (HOPDM and OOPS) have been used to solve some large-scale optimization problems, including those arising in financial applications. He has published more than 50 articles in leading optimization journals.

Andreas Grothey has been a lecturer in operations research in the School of Mathematics, University of Edinburgh, since 2005. He holds an MSc in numerical analysis from the University of Dundee and a PhD in optimization from the University of Edinburgh. His main research interests are interior point methods and stochastic programming.

David Hand is an enrolled actuary and has served in the past as chairman of the American Society of Pension Professionals and Actuaries (ASPPA). He has been CEO of Hand Benefits & Trust since 1991, a firm his grandfather founded.

Siti Sheikh Hussin is a PhD student in the Centre for the Analysis of Risk and Optimisation Modelling Applications (CARISMA), Brunel University, London, under the supervision of Professor Gautam Mitra and Dr Diana Roman. She is a recipient of the Lecturer Scheme Scholarship awarded by Universiti Teknologi MARA (UiTM), Malaysia, and the Malaysian government. She holds a degree in chemical engineering from Universiti Putra, Malaysia, and an MSc in quantitative sciences from UiTM. She worked for seven years in a manufacturing company prior to becoming a management trainee (production) and trainee in an oil and gas consulting firm. Siti worked as a lecturer from March 2007 to December 2007 before accepting the Lecturer Scheme Scholarship offered by UiTM. Her research interests include asset liability management, stochastic programming, and pension fund and financial risk assessment and modelling.

Garud Iyengar is an associate professor in the Industrial Engineering and Operations Research Department, Columbia University, New York. He has a PhD in electrical engineering from Stanford University and an undergraduate degree in electrical engineering from the Indian Institute of Technology, Kanpur. Iyengar's research interests include convex optimization, robust optimization, combinatorial optimization, mathematical and computational finance, mathematical biology, and communication and information theory. His research has been published in the *IEEE Transactions on Information Theory, Mathematical Finance, Computational Finance, Mathematics of Operations Research* and *Mathematical Programming*.

Stuart Jarvis is a member of the BlackRock Multi-Asset Client Solutions Group, which is responsible for developing, assembling and managing investment solutions involving multiple strategies and asset classes. He joined Barclays Global Investors (BGI) in 2004, which merged with BlackRock in 2009. At BGI, he led the research effort behind the solutions and strategies created to address a wide range of client investment problems. Jarvis developed rigorous techniques for analysing potential solutions to these problems, exploring ways to measure the associated risks and providing robust optimization tools. In addition to specific client projects, he was heavily involved in the analysis of clients' asset/ liability profiles, to help clients looking to put in place liability-driven investment strategies, and in developing techniques to create multi-asset diversified portfolios. Prior to joining BGI, he worked as a pensions consultant at Hewitt Bacon & Woodrow. Jarvis earned a BA in mathematics from Cambridge University in 1990 and a D.Phil. from Oxford University in 1994. He is also a qualified actuary.

Con Keating is Head of Research at BrightonRock Group, UK. Con, a chemist and economist by training, is perhaps best known for his quantitative work in investment performance measurement and forecasting with techniques such as the Omega function and metrics. He has also been involved with pensions as a fund manager and trustee since the early 1970s, when he managed the NATO provident fund. His professional career has included periods as an analyst with INA on P&C and large risk insurance, and subsequently with CIGNA in life, pensions and health care. He chaired the European Federation of Financial Analysts Societies' committee on methods and measures from 1994 to 2001. He is a member of the steering committees of the Finance Research Institute and the Financial Econometrics Research Centre, University of Warwick, and a member of the Société Universitaire Européene de Recherche en Finance and of the American Finance Association. He was also an advisor to the World Bank and to the OECD's working party on private pensions.

Woo Chang Kim is an assistant professor in the Industrial and System Engineering Department, Korea Advanced Institute of Science and Technology (KAIST), Daejeon, Korea. He received his PhD from Princeton University in operations research and financial engineering.

Ralf Korn is Professor of Financial Mathematics, University of Kaiserslautern. He also heads the Financial Mathematics group at the Fraunhofer Institute for Industrial Mathematics ITWM, Kaiserslautern, which collaborates in numerous projects with the finance and insurance industries. He has written five books (the most recent one on *Monte Carlo Methods and Models in Finance and Insurance*, Chapman & Hall/ CRC, 2010) and has published over 50 articles in refereed journals.

Roy Kouwenberg is chair of the PhD program at Mahidol University College of Management and a visiting faculty member in the Finance Department at Erasmus University, Rotterdam. Earlier he worked as a postdoctoral fellow at the University of British Columbia and as a quantitative analyst at AEGON Asset Management. Kouwenberg holds a PhD in finance from Erasmus University and is a CFA charter holder. His research on investment and financial risk management has been published in the *Review of Economics and Statistics* and the *Journal of Banking and Finance*, among other journals.

Cormac Lucas is Senior Lecturer in the Centre for the Analysis of Risk and Optimisation Modelling Applications (CARISMA), Brunel University, London, and a director of OptiRisk Systems. He has researched optimization in relation to scheduling applications and finance. He has published in journals such as *Operational Research, Quantitative Finance* and *IMA* and has worked on a number of large industrial projects, such as those of the US Coast Guard and UBS, as well as research council grants. Currently, he is involved in PhD research projects on metaheuristics for portfolio planning and supply-chain planning optimization.

Alfred Ka Chun Ma is an assistant professor in the Department of Finance, Chinese University of Hong Kong. He obtained his PhD from the Industrial Engineering and Operations Research Department, Columbia University, and his BSc and MPhil in mathematics from the Chinese University of Hong Kong. He has worked at Goldman Sachs in New York as a summer associate and is an associate of the Society of Actuaries.

Yi Ma is a PhD student in the Department of Operations Research and Financial Engineering, Princeton University. Her current research interests include stochastic volatility models and asset allocation. She received her BE and MS in electrical engineering from Tsinghua University, Beijing.

Lionel Martellini is Professor of Finance at EDHEC Business School, Nice, France and the scientific director of the EDHEC-Risk Institute. He holds graduate degrees in economics, statistics and mathematics, as well as a PhD in finance from the University of California, Berkeley. Lionel is a member of the editorial board of the *Journal of Portfolio Management* and the *Journal of Alternative Investments*. An expert in quantitative asset management and derivatives valuation, Lionel has published widely in academic and practitioner journals and has co-authored textbooks on alternative investment strategies and fixed-income securities.

Elena Medova is a senior research associate at the Judge Business School, University of Cambridge. Her research focuses on stochastic optimization techniques for dynamic systems, in particular for long-term asset liability management, and credit, market and operational risk integration and capital allocation. She has published extensively in leading journals, including *RISK, Quantitative Finance*, the *Journal of Banking and Finance*, the *Journal of Portfolio Management* and the *British Actuarial Journal*. Medova has managed industry-sponsored projects, advised governments, and trained professional risk managers globally and is managing director of Cambridge Systems Associates Ltd, a financial analytics consultancy specializing in optimal risk managed investment strategies.

Vincent Milhau holds master's degrees in statistics from ENSAE, Paris (France), and financial mathematics from Université Paris VII, as well as a PhD in finance from Université de Nice – Sophia-Antipolis. He is currently a senior research engineer at EDHEC-Risk Institute. His research focus is on dynamic asset allocation, portfolio choice over long horizons, and asset-liability management.

John M. Mulvey is Professor of Operations Research and Financial Engineering and a founding member of the Bendheim Center for Finance, Princeton University. His specialty is large-scale optimization, with applications to strategic financial planning. He has implemented asset liability management systems for many companies. His current research looks at the role of alternative investments for institutional investors, with an emphasis on approaches for optimizing performance and protecting investor wealth over time. He has invented a systematic approach to investing, called dynamic portfolio tactics, emphasizing flexibility and responsiveness, especially during periods of high turbulence.

Kalina Natcheva-Acar graduated with a BBA from Sofia University, with a major in management information systems. She continued her education with an MSc and PhD in financial mathematics at the Technical University of Kaiserslautern. Since 2002, she has worked as an associate Researcher at Fraunhofer ITWM. Her area of scientific interest is the enhancement of numerical methods for stochastic differential equations, credit risk, and interest rate and equity models.

Diana Roman obtained her PhD from Brunel University, London, in 2006. The following year she worked as a research assistant in a knowledge transfer partnership project between Brunel Business School and OptiRisk Systems, a London-based company specializing in optimization software and consultancy. Since 2007, she has been a lecturer at the School of Information Systems, Computing and Mathematics, Brunel University. Her research interests include decision making in finance, financial optimization, risk modelling and asset pricing. Prior to starting a PhD, Roman obtained a BSc in mathematics and an MSc in applied statistics and optimization from the University of Bucharest. Her work experience includes several years of teaching in the Department of Mathematics at the Technical University of Civil Engineering, Bucharest.

Hira Sadhak is a well-known economist, fund manager and financial sector expert. Before joining LIC Pension Fund Ltd as the CEO in 2007 he was an executive director with Life Insurance Corporation of India and fund manager with LIC Mutual Fund. Prior to that he served as an officer with Union Bank of India and as a lecturer in economics. He has authored five books and more than 100 articles and research papers. His books include *Life Insurance in India: Opportunities, Challenges* *and Strategic Perspective* (Response/SAGE, 2009), *Mutual Funds in India: Marketing Strategies and Investment Practices* (Response/SAGE, 2008), *Role of Entrepreneurs in Backward Areas* (Daya, 1989) and *Impact of Incentives on Industrial Development in Backward Regions* (Chugh, 1987). His forthcoming book is *Pension Reform and New Pension System in India*. Sadhak has been associated with many working groups and technical committees of the government of India, including the Technical Committee on Accounting Policy for NPS and working groups on household savings, the 11th and 10th five-year plans, the real estate price index and the fifth economic census. Sadhak holds a PhD in industrial finance, an MA in economics and a diploma in operations research for management.

Frank Sortino is Emeritus Finance Professor at San Francisco State University and director of the Pension Research Institute, which he founded in 1981. For ten years he wrote a quarterly analysis of mutual funds for *Pensions and Investments Magazine*, and he has written two books on the subject of post-modern portfolio theory. He has been a featured speaker at many conferences in the United States, Europe, South Africa and the Pacific Basin. Sortino is now working with a team of financial experts to offer a defined benefit approach to managing 401(k) plans.

Michael Villaverde is principal of BlueCrest Capital Management, London, and the product manager of the BlueCube Fund. Before joining BlueCrest in April 2008, Michael developed and managed quantitative portfolios and headed a research group at Marshall Wace Asset Management. Before that, he worked as a quantitative analyst for the Emerging Markets Special Opportunities Fund at Citigroup Alternative Investments. Villaverde received his PhD in quantitative finance from Cambridge University, and an MSc in financial engineering and a BA in mathematics from the University of Michigan at Ann Arbor.

Alexander Weissensteiner received his MSc and PhD in social and economic sciences from Leopold Franzens University, Innsbruck, in 1998 and 2003, respectively. Since 2010 he has been an assistant professor at the Free University of Bozen-Bolzano. His research interests include stochastic (linear) programming, control theory, neural networks and financial risk management.

Jörg Wenzel is deputy head of the Financial Mathematics Department of Fraunhofer Institute for Industrial Mathematics (ITWM) in Kaiserslautern. He received his PhD in mathematics from the Friedrich-Schiller-University Jena. He is co-author of a book on orthonormal systems and Banach spaces and has published many research articles. At ITWM, he is responsible for managing projects in option pricing and interest rate derivatives valuation and works on problems in stochastic analysis.

Xi Yang was awarded a PhD in optimization at the University of Edinburgh. She received her BSc in computational mathematics in China, and subsequently graduated with an MSc in Financial Mathematics from the University of Edinburgh. Her main research interests are risk measures and management, stochastic dominance and stochastic programming.

Volker Ziemann holds a master's degree in statistics from ENSAE (Paris, France) and a PhD in finance from Paul Cézanne Université – Aix-Arseille III. He is now an economist at the French Ministry of Economy, Industry and Employment and was a senior research engineer at EDHEC-Risk Institute when this research was conducted. His research focus is on the econometrics of financial markets and optimal asset allocation decisions involving nonlinear payoffs.

Chapter Abstracts

2 Bank Asset-Liability and Liquidity Risk Management

Moorad Choudhry

Asset-liability management (ALM) for banking institutions is defined as the high-level management of a bank's assets and liabilities. ALM is conducted at a group aggregate balance sheet level. The principal objective of the ALM function is to manage interest-rate risk and liquidity risk. This chapter describes the essential principles of the ALM responsibility of a bank, and the function of the guardians of ALM at a bank, the asset-liability committee or ALCO. Liquidity risk management concerns the discipline of ensuring that a bank remains liquid at all times and under all market conditions. This chapter reviews the principal requirements of maintaining funding liquidity, the key management risk reporting metrics and a sample framework for a bank's internal funding rate policy.

3 A Two-Factor HJM Interest Rate Model for Use in Asset Liability Management

Sarp Kaya Acar, Ralf Korn, Kalina Natcheva-Acar and Jörg Wenzel

This chapter proposes a Gaussian two-factor Heath–Jarrow–Morton (HJM) model as an alternative to popular short rate models for use in asset liability management. It will prove to be efficient and realistic, and offers the possibility to set up a generic pricing tool that allows for the valuation of a wide range of structured products.

4 Long-Term Interest Rates and Consol Bond Valuation

Michael Dempster, Elena Medova and Michael Villaverde

This chapter presents a Gaussian three-factor model of the term structure of interest rates which is Markov and time-homogeneous. The model captures the whole term structure and is particularly useful in forward simulations for applications in long-term swap and bond pricing, risk management and portfolio optimization. Kalman filter parameter estimation uses EU swap rate data and is described in detail. The yield curve model is fitted to data up to 2002 and assessed by simulation of yield curve scenarios over the next two years. It is then applied to the valuation of callable floating rate consol bonds, as recently issued by European banks to raise Tier 1 regulatory capital over the period from 2005 to 2007.

5   Asset Liability Management Modelling with Risk Control by Stochastic Dominance

Xi Yang, Jacek Gondzio and Andreas Grothey

An asset liability management model with a novel strategy for controlling the risk of underfunding is presented in this chapter. The basic model involves multiperiod decisions (portfolio rebalancing) and deals with the usual uncertainty of investment returns and future liabilities. Therefore, it is well suited to a stochastic programming approach. A stochastic dominance concept is applied to control the risk of underfunding through modelling a chance constraint. A small numerical example and an out-of-sample backtest are provided to demonstrate the advantages of this new model, which includes stochastic dominance constraints, over the basic model and a passive investment strategy. Adding stochastic dominance constraints comes with a price. It complicates the structure of the underlying stochastic program. Indeed, the new constraints create a link between variables associated with different scenarios of the same time stage. This destroys the usual tree structure of the constraint matrix in the stochastic program and prevents the application of standard stochastic programming approaches, such as (nested) Benders decomposition and progressive hedging. Instead, we apply a structure-exploiting interior point method to this problem. The specialized interior point solver, an object-oriented parallel solver, can deal efficiently with such problems and outperforms the industrial strength commercial solver CPLEX on our test problem set. Computational results on medium-scale problems with sizes reaching about one million variables demonstrate the efficiency of the specialized solution technique. The solution time for these non-trivial asset liability models appears to grow sublinearly with the key parameters of the model, such as the number of assets and the number of realizations of the benchmark portfolio, which makes the method applicable to truly large-scale problems.

6   The 401(k) Retirement Income Risk

Frank Sortino and David Hand

The essence of PMPT is to identify the return needed to accomplish a financial goal and measure risk and reward relative to that Desired

Target Return®. The goal is what one wants one's money to accomplish – for example, retirement. In this chapter we apply the principles of PMPT to the task of helping participants in a defined contribution plan to accomplish their retirement goals. Further information on this application is provided at www.definedtargetreturn.com.

7 Pensions, Covenants and Insurance

Con Keating

This chapter considers asset liability management in the context of pension indemnity assurance. The problem is uniquely long in duration – from inception to final discharge the term could be 150 years. The problem is compound – risk management of a long corporate credit risk exposure and subsequent management of a pension annuity book. This requires the analysis and risk management to proceed from first principles, separating short-term considerations from those important to long-term security and performance. This chapter discusses a number of current problems in UK pensions practice, such as the accounting standards and regulatory regime. The asset strategy that follows differs markedly from the market-based liquidity and short-term performance model of the traditional third-party investment manager.

8 Employees' Provident Funds of Singapore, Malaysia, India and Sri Lanka: A Comparative Study

Siti Sheikh Hussin, Gautam Mitra, Diana Roman and Wan Kamaruzaman Wan Ahmad

In this chapter we describe the structure of employees' provident funds (EPFs), which are the main retirement schemes for private sector employees of the four countries discussed: Singapore, Malaysia, India and Sri Lanka. We compare the EPF plans for these four countries and describe the similarities and differences in terms of contributions and accounts, dividend withdrawals and annuities, minimum sum, health benefits, investments and also performance. In addition we discuss the challenges faced by EPFs and possible ways to overcome them. The phenomenon of the 'aging population', which is occurring even faster in Asia than in the Western countries, is the biggest challenge. EPFs are defined contribution pension schemes; thus, an increase in life expectancy brings the risk that participants could outlive their savings. Lastly, we discuss the EPF framework from an asset liability management perspective.

9   Dynamic Risk Management: Optimal Investment with Risk Constraints

Stuart Jarvis

This chapter examines a trade-off between utility and downside risk in a dynamic context. A standard CRRA utility function is used and downside risk tolerance is described by a tail value at risk (CVaR) measure. The optimal strategy is derived using elementary variational techniques in a continuous-time framework. In a discrete-time framework, numerical techniques are applied to find a solution. In both cases, the optimal strategy involves an increase in instantaneous portfolio risk if returns are either good or very poor. While the former is similar to dynamic strategies such as CPPI, the time inconsistency of the CVaR risk measure is highlighted as explaining the latter feature.

10   Optimal Investment Strategies in Defined Contribution Pension Plans

David Blake, Andrew Cairns and Kevin Dowd

Many, if not most, individuals cannot be regarded as 'intelligent consumers' when it comes to understanding and assessing different investment strategies for their defined contribution pension plans. This gives very little incentive to plan providers to improve the design of their pension plans. As a consequence, pension plans and their investment strategies are still currently in a very primitive stage of development. In particular, there is very little integration between the accumulation and decumulation stages. It is possible to produce well-designed defined contribution plans, but these need to be designed from back to front (that is, from desired outputs to required inputs) with the goal of delivering an adequate targeted pension with a high degree of probability. We use the analogy of designing a commercial aircraft to explain how this might be done. We also investigate the possible role of regulators in acting as surrogate 'intelligent consumers' on behalf of plan members.

11   Duration-Enhancing Overlay Strategies for Defined Benefit Pension Plans

John M. Mulvey, Woo Chang Kim and Yi Ma

Many large corporate and public pension trusts remain underfunded since the 2001–2002 recessionary periods. These plans are challenged by global demographic trends and the recent slowing economic conditions.

We show that a special overlay strategy can improve performance and reduce risks by adding duration to the portfolio. The approach combines elements of liability-driven investing and asset liability management. Versions of the strategy are evaluated via historical data. In addition, the strategy is tested with a widely employed, forward-looking economic projection system.

12 A Robust Optimization Approach to Pension Fund Management

Garud Iyengar and Alfred Ka Chun Ma

In this chapter, we propose a robust optimization-based framework for defined benefit pension fund management. We show that this framework allows one to flexibly model many features of the pension fund management problem. Our approach is a computationally tractable alternative to the stochastic programming-based approaches. We illustrate the important features of the robust approach using a specific numerical example.

13 Alternative Decision Models for Liability-Driven Investment

Katharina Schwaiger, Cormac Lucas and Gautam Mitra

Asset liability management (ALM) models have been recently recast as liability-driven investment (LDI) models for making integrated financial decisions in pension schemes investment, matching and outperforming a pension plan's liabilities. LDI has become extremely popular as the decision tool of choice for pension funds. Market developments and recent accounting and regulatory changes require a pension fund to adopt a new view on its asset allocation decision. We present a generic ALM problem cast as an LDI, which we represent through a family of four decision models: a deterministic linear programming model, a two-stage stochastic programming (SP) model incorporating uncertainty, a chance-constrained SP model and an integrated chance-constrained SP model. In the deterministic model, we study the relationship between $PV01$ matching and the required funding. In the model, we have two sources of randomness: liabilities and interest rates. We generate interest rate scenarios using the Cox, Ingersoll and Ross model and investigate the relationship between funding requirements and minimize the absolute deviation of the present value matching of the assets and liabilities over time. In the chance-constrained programming model, we limit the number of future deficit events by introducing binary variables and a user-specified reliability level. The fourth model has integrated chance constraints, which limits not only the events of underfunding but also the amount of underfunding relative to the liabilities. All models employ a buy-and-hold strategy in a fixed-income portfolio, and recourse actions are taken only in borrowing and lending.

14   A Liability-Relative Drawdown Approach to Pension Asset Liability Management

Arjan Berkelaar and Roy Kouwenberg

Defined benefit pension schemes accumulate assets with the ultimate objective of honouring their obligation to the beneficiaries. Liabilities should be at the centre of designing investment policies and serve as the ultimate reference point for evaluating and allocating risks and measuring performance. The goal of the investment policy should be to maximize expected excess returns over liabilities subject to an acceptable level of risk that is expressed relative to liabilities. In this chapter, we argue for the use of a liability-relative drawdown optimization approach to construct investment portfolios. Asset and liability returns are simulated using a vector autoregressive process with state variables. We find that drawdown optimal portfolios provide better downside protection, are better diversified and tend to be less equity centric while providing higher expected returns than surplus variance portfolios.

15   Asset-Liability Management in Defined Contribution Pensions: A Stochastic Model with Reference to Auto Choice Portfolios in the New Pension System in India

Hira Sadhak and Steward Doss

In this chapter we examine the implication of asset liability management (ALM) in a defined contribution pension plan where investment risks are transferred to the members of the fund. An ALM model has been developed with the help of Monte Carlo simulation, and future liability and cash flow have been projected, which can guide the fund managers to design an appropriate asset allocation and reallocation strategy for managing an auto choice life-cycle fund under the investment regulation norms. Pension fund investment return and risks will be largely influenced by the market environment – availability of financial instruments, market volatility, liquidity. We briefly discuss the prevailing situation in the Indian market to identify opportunities and constraints.

16   Planning for Retirement:
Asset Liability Management for Individuals

Michael Dempster and Elena Medova

This chapter gives a non-technical introduction to a goal-oriented system developed to help middle-class families and their advisors plan for their future lifestyle choices, including retirement and bequests, through management of their financial and other assets. The user-friendly system described – iALM for 'individual asset liability management' – brings institutional ALM techniques to bear on planning over a household's lifecycle. However, prospective solutions are designed to be easily revised in light of a household's changed personal or market circumstances and iALM also supports the rapid 'what-if' exploration of alternative future choices. Fully developed UK and US versions of iALM are currently available. This chapter illustrates the UK system's capabilities.

17   The Discretionary Wealth Hypothesis in
an Arbitrage-Free Term Structure Approach to
Asset-Liability Management

Dan diBartolomeo

Traditional approaches to asset-liability management have evolved substantially in recent years. Unfortunately, even the sophisticated, multi-period approaches in common use neglect important features of the underlying economic problem. This chapter describes a new approach to asset-liability management that combines four key elements, one of which is quite new to the finance literature. There are several key benefits to this technique. First, it estimates the present value of future consumption liabilities in a fashion that is consistent with current market conditions, is arbitrage free, yet does not imply an absolute guarantee of liability fulfilment in cases where no such guarantee is desired. The second key benefit of this technique is that it dynamically reallocates assets over time in a sensible way, based on the Discretionary Wealth Hypothesis of Wilcox (2003), yet is mean-variance optimal as defined in Markowitz (1952) at each moment in time. This approach maximizes the median, rather than the expected value of surplus in a way that more realistically represents investor utility. Finally, we show that our combined technique is equally suitable as an ALM technique for both institutions and households. This technique also explicitly addresses the existence of transaction costs, and other frictions within the multi-period process, as opposed to the single-period assumptions underlying Markowitz.

18   Exploiting Asset-Liability Management Concepts in Private Wealth Management

Noël Amenc, Lionel Martellini, Vincent Milhau and Volker Ziemann

This chapter sheds light on the potential benefits of the use of asset-liability management techniques in a private wealth management context. Our main contribution is to show that a significant fraction of the complexity of optimal asset allocation decisions for private investors can be captured through the introduction of a single additional state variable, the liability value, which can account in a parsimonious way for investors' specific constraints and objectives. Taking an ALM approach to private wealth management has a direct impact on the selection of asset classes, in that it leads to a focus on the liability-hedging properties of various asset classes, a focus that would, by definition, be absent from an asset-only perspective. It also leads to using the liability portfolio as a benchmark or numeraire, hence recognizing that what matters for private investors is not so much terminal wealth per se as ability to achieve such goals as preparing for retirement or buying property.

19   Backtesting Short-Term Treasury Management Strategies Based on Multi-Stage Stochastic Programming

Robert Ferstl and Alexander Weissensteiner

We show the practical viability of a short-term treasury management model which is formulated as a multi-stage stochastic linear program. A company minimizes the conditional value at risk of final wealth, subject to given future cash flows and the uncertain future development of interest rates and equity returns, choosing an asset allocation among cash, several bonds and an equity investment. The scenario generation procedure includes an estimation of the market price of risk and a change of the underlying probability measure. We provide an out-of-sample backtest for the proposed policy and compare the performance to alternative strategies. Our approach shows a better risk-return trade-off for different aggregated risk measures. Further, we perform several numerical studies based on a real market data set to test for the sensitivity to changes in the input parameters – for example, shifts of the yield curve, or changes in the equity spread or the cash flows. The resulting portfolios are well diversified and the impact on the asset allocation follows economic intuition.

1
Introduction

Gautam Mitra and Katharina Schwaiger

Asset and liability management (ALM) is a financial (analytic) tool for decision making that sets out to maximize stakeholder value. Its overall objective is to make judicious investments that increase the value of capital, match liabilities and protect from disastrous financial events. An integrated asset and liability management model sets out to find the optimal investment strategy by considering assets and liabilities simultaneously. Simply stated, the purpose of such an approach is to reduce risk and increase returns; ALM models have been used successfully for banks, pension funds and insurance companies, university endowments, hedge funds, mutual funds and wealthy individuals. Risks that can be addressed are interest rate risk, market risk, credit risk, liquidity risk and financial risk. In effect, a financial institution that applies ALM can operate more soundly and profitably. The decision maker under the ALM approach needs to have a good understanding of the financial markets in which the institution operates. ALM is interpreted differently among practitioners from different sectors.

Quantitative models for ALM are gaining acceptance at different stages across Europe, America and Asia. It is expected that these quantitative models will be used more frequently and across different industries.

In this book we aim to shed light on how ALM is understood in various application areas, what the current models available from academia and industry are, and which external factors affect the decisions obtained from ALM models. We present a collection of chapters contributed by high calibre academics and leading industry experts. Some of the chapters have previously been featured as papers in a special issue of the *Journal of Asset Management* (Volume 11, Numbers 2/3), and we bring them together here with additional new chapters.

We begin with a review of existing ALM models applied to a series of areas followed by an overview of the book. Subsequent chapters then bring together the latest research and thinking from leading academics and industry professionals

1

to bring you a balanced picture from both sides. The book is divided into five sections: the first three sections look at ALM applied to banks, insurance companies and pension funds. The fourth section gives insight into new application areas of ALM, namely for wealthy individuals and private wealth management. The last section is an ALM service provider directory, with companies stating their products, services, prices and contact details. We hope that this will be a useful reference source for practitioners, scholars and researchers alike.

Since the mid 1990s ALM models have been applied to pension funds, and a number of leading researchers have contributed to this domain – a selection of models are set out here: Cees Dert (1995) wrote his PhD thesis on an ALM model for a Dutch pension fund, and his model was built using chance constraints. Boender et al. (in Ziemba and Mulvey, 1998) developed and described the ORTEC model, which used multistage stochastic programming. The ALM system for Towers Perrin-Tillinghast by Mulvey (2000) has three components: a scenario generator (CAP:Link), an optimization simulation model (OPT:Link), and a liability- and financial-reporting module (FIN:Link). It is a system used by a financial firm that makes use of multistage stochastic programming. Kouwenberg (2001) focuses on comparing scenario generation methods for a multistage stochastic programming model of a Dutch pension fund. InnoALM by Geyer (2006) is an ALM model for the largest corporate pension plan in Austria of Siemens Österreich. It is a multiperiod stochastic linear programming model with the aim to maximize the expected present value of terminal wealth.

One of the areas in which ALM is widely applied is the banking sector. In particular, ALM models for banks are implemented to comply with the Basel II accord. Pioneering work includes Kusy and Ziemba (1986), in which they introduce a multiperiod stochastic linear programming ALM model for the Vancouver City and Savings Credit Union. The goal is to maximize expected income minus expected costs. The drawback is that the model is not truly dynamic, and the method of describing uncertainties is kept simple. Oğuzsoy and Güven (1997) present a multiperiod stochastic linear ALM model with simple recourse for a Turkish bank. It is important to meet regulations and policies while allowing depositors' withdrawals at any time. Banks are affected by credit, liquidity, capital and interest rate risk.

Recently, new applications of ALM models for hedge funds and mutual funds have emerged. A detailed introduction is given in Ziemba (2003), in which stochastic programming is used for risk control and optimal betting strategies. When added to a portfolio, hedge funds significantly improve the trade-off between risk and return.

A fourth application field of ALM is for insurance companies, which can be further divided into life and non-life (property/casualty) insurers. One of the most famous implemented models for insurance companies is the Russell-Yasuda Kasai model (Carino et al., 1994); it is a large-scale multiperiod stochastic programming model. The objective is to maximize discounted expected wealth minus discounted expected penalty costs, while meeting regulatory requirements, keeping enough cash reserves and offering competitive insurance policies. Consigli and Dempster (1998) designed the multistage-stochastic-programming-based computer-aided asset/liability management (CALM) model, which maximizes terminal wealth at the end of the time horizon. The Watson model (named after Watson & Sons Consulting Actuaries) is a specific instance of the CALM model for a pension fund, in which the scenarios are generated using the Wilkie investment model. The CALM model has also been used for Pioneer (Dempster, 2003). Hoyland et al. (2001) analyze the implications of regulations on Norwegian life insurance companies using a multistage stochastic ALM model. Their results show that some regulations (the annual guaranteed rate of return, for example) do not coincide with the insurance holders' best interests. Frangos et al. (2004) propose a discrete time model of an insurance company incorporating transaction costs, nonlinear financial constraints and feasible portfolio control strategies. Within the rebalancing constraints, the monetary value of assets sold is equal to the monetary value of assets bought plus transaction costs. To calculate a time-dependent portfolio strategy, feasible control is applied. Rudolf and Ziemba (2004) presented a continuous-time four-fund capital asset pricing model. The associated asset returns and liability returns followed an Itô process as functions of a risky state variable. The Prometeia model by Consiglio et al. (2005) is an example of a multiperiod stochastic programming ALM for an Italian insurance company: the model has multiperiod guarantees with bonuses paid at each subperiod; the bonus is a fraction of the portfolio's excess return above the guaranteed rate during each subperiod.

Further ALM models have been created for University Endowment Funds: in Merton (1991) the author sets out that universities offer education, training, research and storage of knowledge and that all of these activities incur a specific cost. University inflows consist of business income, property and grants. The corresponding ALM problem has been formulated and solved as a stochastic dynamic programming model. Ziemba (2003) has extensively explained ALM for wealthy individuals and families. Especially if high taxes apply and the income depends only on assets, a stochastic programming model might reallocate the assets while reducing the risk of unfavourable outcomes. A computer-based solution for individual financial planning is introduced via iALM by Cambridge Systems Associates (see Medova, 2008), which uses dynamic multistage stochastic programming. The aim is to optimize individuals' future goals, while taking into account their individual risks and their future liabilities. Some factors that need to be considered are tax levels; current assets, including real estate properties; future goals; and age of the individual. Major impacts are caused by eventual long-term care and death.

ALM models for banks, insurance companies and pension funds need to specify regulatory requirements, such as the Basel II Accord, Solvency II and FRS 17. The Basel Committee on Banking Supervision introduced the Basel Accords. The Capital Adequacy Accord (Basel I) from 1988 provided a risk-based framework for assessing the capital adequacy of banks to cover credit risks. This accord was then replaced in 1999 with Basel II, which requires banks to improve risk management and corporate governance in conjunction with improved supervision and transparency. The aim was to improve and create good risk management by tying regulatory capital requirements to the results of internal systems and processes. Basel II is a three-pillar system: the first pillar is on Minimum Capital Requirements, the second pillar is on the Supervisory Review Process and the third pillar is on Market Discipline. The first pillar deals with the calculation of regulatory capital of three risks that banks face: credit risk, operational risk and market risk. The Basel II framework allows banks to either use a standardized approach to calculate these risks using specified risk factors or an internal ratings based (IRB) system for these risks due to explicit approval by bank supervision. The preferred method for market risk is Value at Risk (VaR). The second pillar is the internal regulatory response to the first pillar, and the third pillar increases the disclosures that banks must make, which allows the market to have a better view on the overall risk position of the banks.

Most banks worldwide are required to adopt these rules. The Basel II rules of calculating credit risk can be implemented under three alternative approaches: the standardized, foundation IRB and advanced IRB approaches. The standardized approach is the most straightforward one to apply, where risk-weights are assigned according to asset class or formal credit rating. Under the foundation IRB, the capital calculation is made after the bank itself sets default probabilities (PD) to each asset class. Using Basel II guidelines, it then sets the loss-given-default (LGD), exposure-at-default (EAD) and maturity (M) parameters. These inputs are then used to calculate risk-weights for each asset class using the Basel II capital calculation formula. Under advanced IRB, a bank will calculate risk-weights using its own parameters, which are derived from its own default data and internal models. To calculate operational risk, three methods are specified: basic indicator approach (BIA), standardized approach (SA) and advanced measurement approach (AMA).

The International Association of Insurance Supervisors (IAIS) is developing a common international framework for assessing the solvency of insurers: Solvency II. Sometimes colloquially called Basel II for insurance companies, Solvency II also operates on a three-pillar system. Solvency II seeks to incorporate risk management techniques to provide all policyholders across the EU with the same levels of protection. The aims are to enhance policy protection, modernize supervisory bodies, avoid significant market disruptions caused by adverse events and develop a more competitive EU insurance market.

Pension funds are affected by FRS17 (replacing SSAP 24) implemented by the Accounting Standards Board, which requires the following: (a) pension scheme assets to be measured at market values, (b) pension scheme liabilities to be measured using the projected unit method (using discount rates on then AA-rated bonds), (c) pension scheme surplus or deficit to be explicitly mentioned on the sponsoring company's balance sheet and (d) the movement in the scheme's surplus or deficit to be analyzed into the current service cost, any past service cost, interest cost, expected returns on assets and actuarial gains or losses.

Solvency II also has effects on pension fund supervision: occupational pension funds and life insurers are pension providers; however, Solvency II applies only to life insurers, giving individuals with pensions provided by life insurers a higher protection than individuals with pensions from occupational pension funds. The European insurance and reinsurance federation believes that the proposed framework under Solvency II is flexible enough to enable it to take into account the specificities of different pension providers, the schemes they offer and EU member states. The aim of Solvency II should be in the interest of the consumers, both beneficiaries of pension funds and beneficiaries of pensions provided by life insurance companies. The application of Solvency II to occupational pension funds would lead to efficient and consistent supervision of pensions across the EU, better overall risk management, improved mobility of workers and healthy competition between pension providers (see the European Commission, http://ec.europa.eu).

The International Organization of Pension Supervision (IOPS) and the World Bank are working together on an international risk-based supervision of pension funds project (see www.iopsweb.org for more information). Leading countries that have already developed these methods include the Netherlands, Denmark, Australia and Mexico. The utilization of risk-based methods originates mainly in the supervision of banks, that is, Basel I and Basel II.

There are various techniques to solve ALM problems; these include deterministic linear programming, dynamic programming and stochastic programming. Depending on the desired decision-making outcome, one of those techniques can be used. Most ALM models have as decision variables the amount of assets to be bought, sold and held in the portfolio in order to match or outperform the liabilities. Other decision variables can be the rate of increase or decrease of contributions in a pension fund context, cash injected by the sponsoring company in a pension fund context or how much to borrow from or reinvest at the bank. A set of constraints are common within all of those solution techniques: the *asset balance constraint* defines the amount of each asset within the portfolio to be made up of the holding of the previous time period, plus any new amount bought, minus an amount sold. For the first time period there are no previous time period holdings; instead the opening position is used. The *funding constraint* ensures that no more assets can be bought than were liquidated, and there cannot be more assets sold than the amount in the portfolio (which is equal to prohibiting short selling; however, long-short models (see, for example, Kumar et al., 2010) relax this assumption). The *cash flow constraint* equates the portfolios inflows (for example, any inflows from held assets, liquidated assets or cash borrowed) to the outflows (for example, any assets bought, cash lent or the liabilities). Additional constraints include regulatory requirements, *holding limit constraints* and *risk constraints*, such as VaR or CVaR (Bogentoft et al., 2001). The objective function, and if it is maximization or minimization, varies the most. The most classical objective functions are to maximize utility or to maximize return (in the mean-variance context, this is equated to minimize risk), to maximize expected present value of terminal wealth or to minimize expected discounted penalty costs for shortfalls. Another common type of objective function is to minimize any deviation mismatch between assets and liabilities. And then there are application-specific objective functions, for example, to minimize the volatility of contributions increase or decrease for pension fund plan members, or to meet withdrawal requests of depositors at all times in the case of a bank ALM model.

Since the mid 1980s the use of stochastic programming (SP) models for the asset and liability management problem have been widely advocated, and it has been applied in banks (see Kusy and Ziemba, 1986), insurance companies (Carino et al., 1998), hedge and mutual funds (Ziemba, 2003), university endowments (Merton, 1991), applied to wealthy individuals (Medova et al., 2008) and pension funds (Consigli and Dempster, 1998, and Mulvey et al., 2000). In the late 1990s, a book by Ziemba et al. (1998) described case studies and applications. SP models are classified as single-stage optimization models, two-stage optimization models, multistage optimization models and chance constrained optimization models. The most frequently used mean-variance approach falls under the single-stage model category. A recent survey by Fabozzi et al. (2007, and its update in 2008) showed that quantitative fund management is now widely used in industry. Although optimization is used, the most applied is mean-variance optimization, with stochastic programming being applied only in one case out of 36 survey participants. Measuring risk is also widely employed, but variance and value at risk (VaR) are the most frequently used measures, with conditional value at risk (CVaR) being one of the least used techniques. We note in this context that scenario-based stochastic programming models allow the inclusion of VaR and CVaR constraints.

Recent advances have increased the user-ability of ALM models: technological progress enables the capture, transfer and use of large data sets; computational resources make large models solvable within a reasonable time; and acceptance of quantitative models with quality assurance and testing have proved the stability of these models. ALM models are available from a wide range of sources: stand-alone products for specific application areas can be bought, consultancies offer tailor-made solutions and external consultants offer regular ALM reporting on site. A few of these providers are listed in the back of this handbook with contact details and product/service specifications.

Application areas discussed in this book are banks, insurances, private wealth management and individuals. The industry and academic lead articles are followed by a directory of service providers, mainly from the United Kingdom and the United States, with a short description of services and software provided by each company, followed by contact details.

The demographics of the global community of working people are moving in a clear direction; essentially we are living longer. The requirement of financial care through pensions for this ageing population is becoming an important problem not only in the advanced economies, but also in the emerging economies. The third section of this book brings together a collection of chapters by a number of experts who have studied different facets of the pension problem. In recent years the pension fund industry has adopted tailor-made asset and liability management strategies, also called Liability Driven Investment. One focus of this section is on quantitative methods for Asset and Liability Management (ALM) – Liability Driven Investment (LDI) for Pensions Funds. The aim of LDI strategies is to match and outperform a pension fund's liability stream and at the same time take into account country-specific regulations. The decision models as well as simulation/evaluation models which take into consideration stochastic asset price dynamics and stochastic behaviour of the liabilities are covered. Inflation risk, interest rate risk, contribution risk of the pension plan's sponsor and no doubt the longevity risk of its members are examples of additional risk, some or all of which are measured and managed by these models. The academic-led chapters in this book address a number of interrelated themes including pricing of assets, models for ex ante financial decision making and strategies of asset allocation, including overlays, while the industry-led chapters give insight into ALM approaches with banks and insurance companies which can be applied to other areas, too.

1.1 Overview of chapters

Choudhry discusses the principles of asset and liability management in a bank via examples and case studies. He also mentions the important roles of the asset-liability committee (ALCO). He starts his chapter with an introduction to basic concepts of bank asset and liability management, in which the main risks a bank faces are interest rate risk and liquidity risk. He sets out to explain the notions of liquidity gap and interest rate gap on a bank's balance sheet. The most common approach in managing liquidity and interest rate risk is the so-called matched book approach (also known as cash matching). The next part of his chapter illustrates a case study of a derivatives-trading house ALM policy and profile. He then highlights the importance of the ALM reporting process (overseen by the asset-liability management committee, ALCO) and the associated features and missions of the ALCO procedures.

Acar, Korn, Natcheva-Acar and Wenzel describe a Two-Factor Heath-Jarrow Morton interest rate model. Interest rate scenario generation is indeed a very important input in any asset and liability management model. In particular for banks that look at interest rate risk, such a pricer plays a key role. It can also be used for insurance ALM or pension fund ALM alike when assets and liabilities need to be valued (and discounted). Classical short rate models include Vasicek, Cox-Ingersoll-Ross or Hull-White. The authors describe the criteria for choice among models and propose a Two-Factor Heath-Jarrow Morton model that fits these criteria. They conclude the chapter with examples of interest rate products and a generic pricing of CMS/LIBOR structured products.

Asset pricing is the focus of the chapter by Dempster, Medova and Villaverde. The authors present a three-factor term structure interest rate model for consol bond valuation. The authors discuss a detailed computational study and simulation results and present a detailed analysis of the yield curves. Given that almost all pension funds include fixed income assets in one form or another this chapter clearly makes a very important contribution to the valuation of this class of assets.

Yang, Gondzio and Grothey also investigate the issue of the computational tractability of an asset allocation model which is based on second-order stochastic dominance for the purpose of risk control. Their computational study underlines how exploitation of structure and use of interior point optimization can lead to efficient solution of the computational decision models.

Sortino and Hand discuss 401(k) plans and risks associated with the inclusion of Qualified Default Investment Alternatives, Age 50 Catch-up Provisions, Pending Bills on Plan Fees, and Qualified Automatic Contribution Arrangements. Another area they cover is performance measurement and the fact that 401(k) participant portfolios should not be measured the same way as money manager portfolios. They then give recommendations for regulators, plan sponsors and consultants.

Keating discusses the ALM problem for UK-defined benefit pension schemes and describes the principal terms of the optimal pension indemnity assurance policy. He sets the scene by explaining how to define assets and liabilities, risk and return, and diversification, which all play a key role in pension schemes. He then continues with the (real) pension problem and the UK Pension Protection Fund (PPF). Finally, he introduces an insurance of pension schemes against sponsor insolvency – which is aimed to be the solution to the fundamental problem of defined benefit schemes. Such an insurance has clear advantages on the balance sheet of the sponsor.

Hussin, Mitra, Roman and Ahmad introduce the concepts of Employees' Provident Funds (EPFs) in Asian countries, such as Singapore, Malaysia, India and Sri Lanka. Its main purpose is to provide retirement income, but it has been adjusted to also give members the option to withdraw funds to cover homeownership, education and healthcare. The authors discuss the differences among EPFs in various countries, challenges faced by them and how to overcome those challenges. The chapter concludes with an Asset and Liability Management model for EPFs.

Stuart Jarvis discusses the multiperiod investment strategy of assets that shall meet future liabilities. Depending on the investor, different risk return profiles occur; a set of risk measures is explained, but tail value at risk is used for the computational study. He states the importance of dynamic optimization as opposed to the (more commonly known to the finance industry) mean-variance Markowitz approach. In the computation study, optimal portfolios with CVaR constraints are compared to optimal portfolios with CVaR constraints and portfolio-level constraints. A combined tree approach and lattice approach is used to analyse the latter problem numerically.

Blake, Cairns and Dowd use an analogy of designing a commercial aircraft to explain how to produce a well-designed defined contribution (DC) pension plan. They need to be designed from back to front, starting from the desired outputs and working backwards to the required inputs. The authors discuss the inadequacy of the current design of DC plans in great detail and offer solutions to plan members, including annuitisation and drawdown programmes. They also investigate the important role of regulators who need to act as 'intelligent consumers' on behalf of plan members.

Mulvey, Kim and Ma present a chapter in which they first highlight the present situation in which large corporate and public funds have become underfunded and thereby mismatched during the recent prolonged recessionary period. Their contribution is in proposing a strategy of incorporating a duration-enhancing overlay to the pension fund assets, thereby controlling the underlying risk.

Iyengar and Ma have applied robust optimization for the asset allocation model of a pension fund in which the uncertainty set is ellipsoidal. The authors formulate their model with a second-order cone programming constraint and report that the corresponding model is computationally tractable. They illustrate an example of a frozen pension fund (its liabilities are known) and formulate the optimization problem that computes the optimal contribution schedule and portfolio holdings.

Schwaiger, Lucas and Mitra have a set of four alternative models addressing the question of optimum fund allocation in the face of future uncertainties: deterministic linear programming, two-stage stochastic programming, chance-constrained programming and integrated chance-constrained programming. Their models include PV01/PV sensitivities and trade-off between cash input required and PV01/PV mismatch. The fixed income portfolio is suitable for a defined benefit pension plan with a long time horizon.

Berkelaar and Kouwenberg address the question of asset allocation from an extremely novel perspective. They state that the goal of the investment policy should be to maximize expected excess returns over liabilities subject to an acceptable level of risk expressed relative to liabilities. Their asset allocation is based on drawdown risk optimization, and through simulation studies they show that their strategy leads to better downside protection. Asset and liability returns are simulated using a vector autoregressive approach with state variables. Their conclusions are that drawdown optimal portfolios offer better downside protection for pension funds while at the same time being more diversified and less equity centric.

Sadhak and Doss discuss the implication of ALM in a defined contribution pension plan. As opposed to defined benefit plans, in a defined contribution plan the member bears the investment risks. In India the New Pension System (NPS) was introduced in 2004; the accumulation and investment of pension assets are being managed by fund managers approved by the pension fund regulator. Regulations and asset allocation options of the NPS are introduced, followed by the affecting risks. The author then introduces an ALM model for the NPS Auto Choice Fund (Default Option of NPS).

Individuals have future income prospects, future liabilities, life goals and desired consumption levels. Medova et al. try to meet these by introducing a new solution called iALM, which determines the optimal asset allocation strategies for individuals.

DiBartolomeo proposes an approach to ALM that takes the following into account: arbitrage-free discounting process of assets and liabilities, existence of transaction costs and maximization of the median of surplus to reflect investor utility. This approach follows the discretionary wealth hypothesis by Wilcox while at the same time being Markowitz mean-variance efficient. He then explains an algorithm to model the probability distributions of funding surpluses (deficits) over time.

Amenc, Martellini, Milhau and Ziemann apply ALM to a new area: private wealth management. The authors introduce a formal stylized model of asset-liability management for household-financial decisions, where they introduce a single additional state variable – the liability value – into the optimal asset allocation decision-making model. As an example, they focus on a pension objective. To reflect uncertainty affecting asset returns and liabilities they use a vector-autoregressive (VAR) approach similar to Berkelaar and Kouwenberg (Chapter 14) for modelling the joint asset and liability return dynamic distributions.

Ferstl and Weissensteiner have studied short-term treasury management strategies. They have developed a multistage stochastic programming model which in turns uses a scenario generator, with no arbitrage interest rate model, with market price estimation and change of measure. As an objective function they minimize the coherent risk measure Conditional Value at Risk (CVaR) of final wealth subject to given future cash flows and the uncertain future developments of interest rates and equity returns. Finally, they carry out extensive back testing to validate their model. Their results offer a better risk-return trade-off for different aggregate risk measures, while the optimal portfolios are well-diversified portfolios and the impact on the asset allocation follows economic intuition.

References

Altenstedt, F. and M. Patriksson. 'Policy optimization: Parameterized decision rules vs. stochastic programming for asset liability management'. Department of Mathematics, Chalmers University of Technology, Goteborg,Sweden, 2003.

Bogentoft, E., H. E. Romeijn and S. Uryasev. 'Asset/liability management for pension funds using CVaR constraints'. *Journal of Risk Finance*, 3(1):57–71, 2001.

Carino, D. R., T. Kent, D. H. Myers, C. Stacy, M. Sylvanus, A. L. Turner, K. Watanabe and W. T. Ziemba. 'The Russell-Yasuda Kasai model: An asset/liability model for a Japanese insurance company using multistage stochastic programming'. *Interfaces*, 24(1):29–49, 1994.

Consigli, G. and M. A. H. Dempster. 'Dynamic stochastic programming for asset-liability management'. *Annals of Operations Research*, 81:131–162, 1998.

Consiglio, A., F. Cocco and S. A. Zenios. 'The Prometeia model for managing insurance policies with guarantees'. *Handbook of Asset and Liability Management, Handbooks of Finance*. North-Holland, Amsterdam, The Netherlands, 2005.

Daellenbach, H. G. and S. H. Archer. 'The optimal bank liquidity: A multi-period stochastic model'. *The Journal of Financial and Quantitative Analysis*, 4(3):329–343, 1969.

Dempster, M. A. H., M. Germano, E. A. Medova and M. Villaverde. 'Global asset liability management'. *British Actuarial Journal*, 9:137–216, 2003.

Dert, C. L. *Asset liability management for pension funds. A multistage chance-constrained programming approach*. PhD thesis, Erasmus University, Rotterdam, The Netherlands, 1995.

Fabozzi, F., S. Focardi and C. Jonas. 'Trends in quantitative equity management: survey results'. *Quantitative Finance* 7(2):115–122, 2007.

Fabozzi, F., S. Focardi and C. Jonas. 'On the challenges in quantitative equity management'. *Quantitative Finance* 8(7):647–665, 2008.

Fabozzi, F. J. and A. Konishi. *The handbook of asset/liability management: state-of-the-art investment strategies, risk controls and regulatory requirements*. Irwin Professional Pub., Chicago, Ill., 1996.

Frangos, C., S. A. Zenios and Y. Yavin. 'Computation of feasible portfolio control strategies for an insurance company using a discrete time asset/liability model'. *Mathematical and Computer Modelling*, 40(3–4):423–446, 2004.

Gaivoronski, A. A. and P. E. de Lange. 'An asset liability management model for casualty insurers: complexity reduction vs. parameterized decision rules'. *Annals of Operations Research*, 99(1):227–250, 2000.

Geyer, A. and W. T. Ziemba. 'The innovest Austrian pension fund financial planning model InnoALM'. *Operations Research*, 56(4):797–810, 2008.

Haneveld, W. K. K., M. H. Streutker and M. H. van der Vlerk. 'An ALM Model for Pension Funds using Integrated Chance Constraints'. University of Groningen, Research Institute SOM (Systems, Organisations and Management), 2005.

Hilli, P., M. Koivu, T. Pennanen and A. Ranne. 'A stochastic programming model for asset liability management of a Finnish pension company'. *Annals of Operations Research*, 152:115–139, 2007.

Holmer, M. R. 'The asset-liability management strategy system at Fannie Mae'. *Interfaces*, 24(3):May–June, 3–21, 1994.

Hoyland, K. and S. W. Wallace. 'Analyzing legal regulations in the Norwegian life insurance business using a multistage asset-liability management model'. *European Journal of Operational Research*, 134(2):293–308, 2001.

Kouwenberg, R. 'Scenario generation and stochastic programming models for asset liability management'. *European Journal of Operational Research*, 134(2):279–292, 2001.

Kumar, R. G. Mitra and D. Roman. 'Long-short portfolio optimisation in the presence of discrete asset choice constraints and two risk measures'. *Journal of Risk* (Forthcoming),13(2):Winter 2010/11.

Kusy, M. I., and W. T. Ziemba. 'A bank asset and liability management model'. *Operations Research*, 34(3):356–376, 1986.

Medova, E. A., J. K. Murphy, A. P. Owen and K. Rehman. 'Individual asset liability management'. *Quantitative Finance*, 8(6):547–560, 2008.

Merton, R. (1993) Optimal Investment Strategies for University Endowment Funds. In: C.T. Clotfelter and M. Rothschild (eds.) Studies of Supply and Demand in Higher Education. USA: NBER, 211–236.

Moynihan, G. P., P. Purushothaman, R. W. McLeod and W. G. Nichols. 'DSSALM: a decision support system for asset and liability management'. *Decision Support Systems*, 33(1):23–38, 2002.

Mulvey, J. M., G. Gould and C. Morgan. 'An asset and liability management system for Towers Perrin-Tillinghast'. *Interfaces*, 30(1):96–114, 2000.

Oguzsoy, C. B., and S. Guven. 'Bank asset and liability management under uncertainty'. *European Journal of Operational Research*, 102(3):575–600, 1997.

Rudolf, M., and W. T. Ziemba. 'Intertemporal surplus management'. *Journal of Economic Dynamics and Control*, 28(5):975–990, 2004.

van der Vlerk, M. H. *Integrated Chance Constraints in an ALM Model for Pension Funds.* University of Groningen, University Library Groningen Host, The Netherlands, 2003.

Winklevoss, H. E. 'Plasm: pension liability and asset simulation model'. *The Journal of Finance*, 37(2):585–594, 1982.

Zenios, S. A. 'Asset/liability management under uncertainty for fixed-income securities'. *Annals of Operations Research*, 59(1):77–97, 1995.

Zenios, S. A. *Financial Optimization*. Cambridge University Press, Cambridge, UK, 1996.

Zenios, S. A., and W. T. Ziemba. *Handbook of Asset and Liability Management: Applications and Case Studies*. North Holland, Amsterdam, The Netherlands, 2007.

Zenios, S. A., and W. T. Ziemba. *Handbook of Asset and Liability Management: Theory and Methodology*. North Holland, Amsterdam, The Netherlands, 2007.

Ziemba, W. T. *The Stochastic Programming Approach to Asset, Liability, and Wealth Management*. CFA Institute, USA, 2003.

Ziemba, W. T., and J. M. Mulvey. *Worldwide Asset and Liability Modeling*. Cambridge University Press, Cambridge, UK, 1998.

Part I
ALM Models Applied to Banks

2
Bank Asset-Liability and Liquidity Risk Management
Moorad Choudhry

Asset-Liability Management is a generic term that is used to refer to a number of things by different market participants. We define it as the high-level management of a bank's assets and liabilities; as such it is a strategy-level discipline and not a tactical one. It may be set within a bank's Treasury division or by its asset-liability committee (ALCO). The principal objective of the ALM function is to manage interest-rate risk and liquidity risk. It also sets overall policy for credit risk and credit risk management, although tactical-level credit policy is set at a lower level within credit committees. Although the basic tenets of ALM would seem to apply more to commercial banking, rather than investment banking, in reality it is important that it is applied to both functions. A trading desk still deals in assets and liabilities, and these must be managed for interest-rate risk and liquidity risk. In a properly integrated banking function, the ALM desk will have a remit covering all aspects of a bank's operations.

In this chapter we describe the essential principles of the asset-liability management responsibility of a bank. This is illustrated using examples and an investment bank case study. We also look at the function of the guardians of ALM at a bank, the asset-liability committee or ALCO. The remainder of the chapter looks at liquidity management, the key liquidity risk reporting metrics and a sample framework for a bank's internal funding rate policy.

2.1 Basic concepts of bank asset-liability management

In financial markets, the two main strands of risk management are interest-rate risk and liquidity risk. ALM practice is concerned with managing these risks. Interest-rate risk exists in two strands. The first strand is the more obvious one, the risk of changes in asset-liability value due to changes in interest rates. Such a change impacts the cash flows of assets and liabilities, or their present value, because financial instruments are valued with reference to market interest rates. The second strand is that associated with optionality, which arises with

15

products such as early redeemable loans. The other main type of risk that ALM seeks to manage is liquidity risk, which refers to both the liquidity of markets and the ease with which assets can be translated into cash.

ALM is conducted primarily at an overview, balance sheet level. The risk that is managed is an aggregate, group-level risk. This makes sense because one could not manage a viable banking business by leaving interest-rate and liquidity risk management at individual operating levels. We illustrate this in Figure 2.1, which shows the cornerstones of ALM. Essentially, interest-rate risk exposure is managed at the group level by the Treasury desk. The drivers are the different currency interest rates, with each exposure being made up of the net present value (NPV) of cash flow as it changes with changes in interest rates. The discount rate used to calculate the NPV is the prevailing market rate for each time bucket in the term structure.

The interest-rate exposure arises because rates fluctuate from day to day and continuously over time. The primary risk is that of interest-rate reset, for floating rate assets and liabilities. The secondary risk is liquidity risk: unless assets

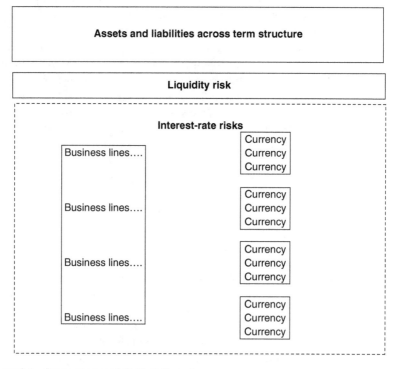

Figure 2.1   Cornerstones of ALM philosophy

and liabilities are matched by amount and term, assets must be funded on a continuous, rolling basis. Equally, the receipt of funds must be placed on a continuous basis. An asset's exposure to interest-rate fluctuations will determine whether it carries a fixed or floating rate reset. Where an asset is marked at a fixed rate, a rise in rates will reduce its NPV and so reduce its value to the bank. This is intuitively easy to grasp, even without recourse to financial arithmetic, because we can see that the asset is now paying a below-market rate of interest. Or we can think of it as a loss due to opportunity cost foregone, since the assets are earning below what they could earn if they were employed elsewhere in the market. The opposite applies if there is a fall in rates: this causes the NPV of the asset to rise. For assets marked at a floating rate of interest, the exposure to fluctuating rates is much less, because the rate receivable on the asset will reset at periodic intervals, which will allow for changes in market rates.

We speak of risk exposure as being for the group as a whole. This exposure must therefore aggregate the net risk of all of the bank's operating business. Even for the simplest banking operation, we can see that this will produce a net mismatch between assets and liabilities, because different business lines will have differing objectives for their individual books. This mismatch will manifest itself in two ways:

1. the mismatch between the different terms of assets and liabilities across the term structure
2. the mismatch between the different interest rates at which each asset or liability contract has been struck.

This mismatch is known as the ALM *gap*.[1] The first type is referred to as the *liquidity gap*, while the second is known as the *interest-rate gap*. We value assets and liabilities at their NPV; hence we can measure the overall sensitivity of the balance sheet NPV to changes in interest rates. Thus, ALM is an art that encompasses aggregate balance sheet risk management at the group level.

Figure 2.2 shows the aggregate group-level ALM profile for a derivatives-trading house based in London. There is a slight term mismatch as no assets are deemed to have 'overnight' maturity, whereas a significant portion of funding (liabilities) is in the overnight term. One thing we do not know from looking at Figure 2.2 is how this particular institution is defining the maturity of its assets.[2] To place these in the relevant maturity buckets, one can adopt one of two approaches, namely

- the actual duration of the assets
- the 'liquidity duration', which is the estimated time it would take the firm to dispose of its assets in an enforced or 'firesale' situation, such as a withdrawal from the business.

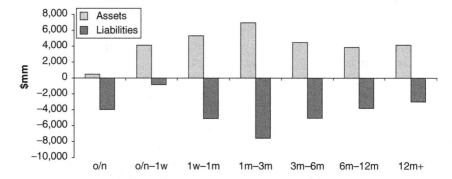

Figure 2.2   Derivatives trading house ALM profile

Each approach has its adherents, and we believe that there is no 'right' way. It is up to the individual institution to adopt one method and then consistently adhere to it. The second approach has the disadvantage, however, of being inherently subjective – the estimate of the time taken to dispose of an asset book is not an exact science and is little more than educated guesswork. Nevertheless, for long-dated or illiquid assets, it is at least a workable method that enables practitioners to work around a specified ALM framework with regard to structuring the liability profile.

2.2   Liquidity gap

There is an obvious risk exposure arising because of liquidity mismatch of assets and liabilities. The maturity terms will not match, which creates the liquidity gap. The number of assets and liabilities maturing at any one time will also not match (although overall, by definition, assets must equal liabilities). Liquidity risk is the risk that a bank will not be able to refinance assets as liabilities become due, for any reason.[3] To manage this, the bank will hold a large portion of assets in very liquid form.[4] A surplus of assets over liabilities creates a funding requirement. If there is a surplus of liabilities, the bank will need to find efficient uses for those funds. In either case, the bank has a liquidity gap. This liquidity can be projected over time, so that one knows what the situation is each morning, based on net expiring assets and liabilities. The projection will change daily of course, due to new business undertaken each day.

We could eliminate liquidity gap risk by matching assets and liabilities across each time bucket. Actually, at the individual loan level this is a popular strategy: if we can invest in an asset paying 5.50% for three months and fund this with a three-month loan costing 5.00%, we have locked in a 50 basis point gain that is interest-rate risk free. However, while such an approach can be undertaken at the individual asset level, it would not be possible at an aggregate level, or at least not possible without imposing severe restrictions on the business. Hence liquidity risk is a key consideration in ALM. A bank with a surplus of long-term assets over short-term liabilities will have an ongoing requirement to fund the assets continuously, and there is the ever-present risk that funds may not be available as and when they are required. The concept of a future funding requirement is itself a driver of interest-rate risk, because the bank will not know what the future interest rates at which it will deal will be.[5] So a key part of ALM involves managing and hedging this forward liquidity risk.

2.2.1 Definition and illustration

To reiterate, then, the liquidity gap is the difference in maturity between assets and liabilities at each point along the term structure. Because for many banks ALM concerns itself with a medium-term management of risk, this will not be beyond a five-year horizon, and in many cases will be considerably less than this. Note from Figure 2.2 how the longest-dated time bucket in the ALM profile extended out to only '12-month plus', so that all liabilities longer than one year were grouped in one time bucket. This recognizes that most liabilities are funded in the money markets, although a material proportion of funding should be much longer term, and up to the maximum tenor that the bank is able to obtain.

For each point along the term structure at which a gap exists, there is (liquidity) gap risk exposure. This is the risk that funds cannot be raised as required, or that the rate payable on these funds is prohibitive.[6] To manage this risk, a bank must perforce

- disperse the funding profile (the liability profile) over more than just a short period of time. For example, it would be excessively risky to concentrate funding in just the overnight to one-week time bucket, so a bank will spread the profile across a number of time buckets. Figure 2.3 shows the liability profile for a European multi-currency asset-backed commercial paper programme, with liabilities extending from one-month to one-year;
- manage expectations such that large-size funding requirements are diarised well in advance, as well as not planned for times of low liquidity such as the Christmas and New Year period;
- hold a significant proportion of assets in the form of very liquid instruments, such as very-short-term cash loans, Treasury bills and high-quality short-term bank Certificates of Deposit (CDs).

The last can act as a reserve of liquidity in the event of a funding crisis, because they can be turned into cash at very short notice.

The size of the liquidity gap at any one time is never more than a snapshot in time, because it is constantly changing as new commitments are entered into on both the asset and liability side. For this reason some writers speak of

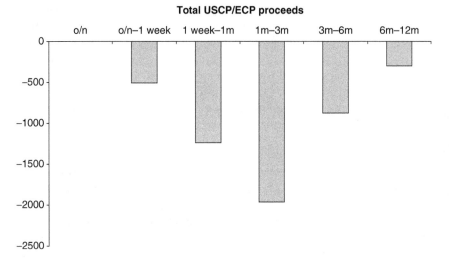

Figure 2.3   Commercial paper programme liability profile

a 'static' gap and a 'dynamic' gap, but in practice one recognizes that there is only ever a dynamic gap, because the position changes daily. Hence we will refer only to one liquidity gap.

A further definition is the 'marginal' gap, which is the difference between the change in assets and change in liabilities during a specified time period. This is also known as the 'incremental' gap. If the change in assets is greater than the change in liabilities, this is a positive marginal gap, while if the opposite applies this is a negative marginal gap.[7]

We illustrate these values in Table 2.1. This is a simplified asset-liability profile from a regional European bank, showing gap and marginal gap at each time period. Note that the liabilities have been structured to produce an 'ALM smile', which is recognized to follow prudent business practice. Generally, no more than 20% of the total funding should be in the overnight to one-week time bucket, and similarly for the 9–12 month bucket. The marginal gap is measured as the difference between the change in assets and the change in liabilities from one period to the next.

Figure 2.4 shows the graphical profile of the numbers in Table 2.1.

2.2.2   Liquidity risk

Liquidity risk exposure arises from normal banking operations. That is, it exists irrespective of the type of funding gap, be it excess assets over liabilities for any particular time bucket or an excess of liabilities over assets. That is, there is a

Table 2.1   Simplified ALM profile for regional European bank

	One week	One month	3–month	6–month	9–12 month	>12 months	Total
Assets	10	90	460	710	520	100	1890
Liabilities	100	380	690	410	220	90	1890
Gap	−90	−290	−230	300	300	10	
Marginal gap		200	−60	−530	0	290	

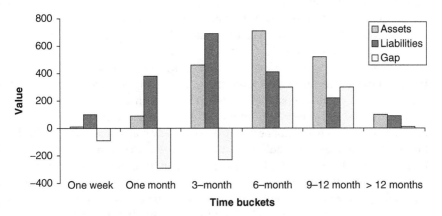

Figure 2.4   ALM time profile

funding risk in any case; either funds must be obtained or surplus assets laid off. The liquidity risk in itself generates interest-rate risk, due to the uncertainty of future interest rates. This can be managed through hedging.

If assets are floating rate, there is less concern over interest-rate risk because of the nature of the interest-rate reset. This also applies to floating-rate liabilities, but only insofar that these match floating-rate assets. Floating-rate liabilities issued to fund fixed-rate assets create forward risk exposure to rising interest rates. Note that even if both assets and liabilities are floating-rate, they can still generate interest-rate risk. For example, if assets pay six-month Libor and liabilities pay three-month Libor, there is an interest-rate spread risk between the two terms. Such an arrangement has eliminated liquidity risk, but not interest-rate spread risk.

Liquidity risk can be managed by matching assets and liabilities, or by setting a series of rolling term loans to fund a long-dated asset. Generally, however, banks will have a particular view of future market conditions, and manage the ALM book in line with this view. This would leave in place a certain level of liquidity risk.

2.2.3   Matched book

The simplest way to manage liquidity and interest-rate risk is the matched book approach, also known as cash matching. This is actually very rare to observe in practice, even among conservative institutions such as the smaller UK building societies. In matched book, assets and liabilities, and their time profiles, are matched as closely as possible. This includes allowing for the amortization of assets.[8] As well as matching maturities and time profiles, the interest-rate basis for both assets and liabilities will be matched. That is, fixed loans to fund fixed-rate assets, and the same for floating-rate assets and liabilities. Floating-rate instruments will further need to match the period of each interest-rate reset, to eliminate spread risk.

Under a matched book or *cash flow matching*, in theory there is no liquidity gap. Locking in terms and interest-rate bases will also lock in profit. For instance, a six-month fixed-rate loan is funded with a six-month fixed-rate deposit. This would eliminate both liquidity and interest-rate risk. In a customer-focused business it will not be possible to precisely match assets and liabilities, but from a macrolevel it should be possible to match the profiles fairly closely, by netting total exposure on both sides and matching this. Of course, it may not be desirable to run a matched book, as this would mean the ALM book was not taking any view at all on the path of future interest rates. Hence a part of the book is usually left unmatched, and it this part that will benefit (or lose out) if rates go the way they are expected to (or not!).

2.2.4   Managing the gap with undated assets and liabilities

We have described a scenario of liquidity management in which the maturity date of both assets and liabilities is known with certainty. A large part of retail and commercial banking operations revolves around assets that do not have an explicit maturity date, however. These include current account overdrafts and credit card balances. They also include drawn and undrawn lines of credit. The volume of these is a function of general economic conditions, and can be difficult to predict. Banks will need to be familiar with their clients' behaviour and their requirements over time to be able to assess when and for how long these assets will be utilized.

Undated assets are balanced on the other side by nondated liabilities, such as noninterest bearing liabilities (NIBLs) which include cheque accounts and instant-access deposit accounts. The latter frequently attract very low rates of interest, and may be included in the NIBL total. Undated liabilities are treated in different ways by banks; the most common treatment places these funds in the shortest time-bucket, the overnight to one-week bucket. However, this means the firm's gap and liquidity profile can be highly volatile and unpredictable, which places greater strain on ALM management. For this reason some banks take the opposite approach and place these funds in the longest-dated bucket, the greater-than-12-month bucket. A third approach is to split the total undated liabilities into a 'core' balance and an 'unstable' balance, and place the first in the long-date bucket and the second in the shortest-dated bucket. The amount recognized as the core balance will need to be analysed over time, to make sure that it is accurate.

2.3 Managing liquidity

Managing liquidity gaps and the liquidity process is a continuous, dynamic one, because the ALM profile of a bank changes on a daily basis. Liquidity management is the term used to describe this continuous process of raising and laying-off funds, depending on whether one is long or short on cash that day.

The basic premise is a simple one: the bank must be 'squared off' by the end of each day, which means that the net cash position is zero. Thus liquidity management is both very short term as well as projected over the long term, because every position put on today creates a funding requirement in the future on its maturity date. The ALM desk must be aware of their future funding or excess cash positions and act accordingly, whether this means raising funds now or hedging forward interest-rate risk.

2.3.1   The basic case: The funding gap

A funding requirement is dealt on the day it occurs. The decision on how it will be treated will factor the term that is put on, as well as allowing for any new assets put on that day. As funding is arranged, the gap at that day will be zero. The next day, there will be a new funding requirement, or surplus, depending on the net position of the book.

This is illustrated in Figure 2.5. Starting from a flat position on the first day (t_0) we observe a gap (the dotted line) on t_1, which is closed by putting on funding to match the asset maturity. The amount of funding to raise, and the term to run it to, will take into account the future gap as well as that day's banking activities. So at t_2 we observe a funding excess, which is then laid off. We see at t_3 that the assets invested in run beyond the maturity of the liabilities at t_2, so we have a funding requirement again at t_3. The decision on the term and amount will be based on the market view of the ALM desk. A matched book approach may well be taken where the desk does not have a strong view, or if its view is at odds with market consensus.

There are also external factors to take into account. For instance, the availability of funds in the market may be limited, due to both macrolevel issues and to the bank's own ability to raise funds. The former might be during times of market correction or recession (a 'credit crunch'), while the latter includes the bank's credit lines with market counterparties. Also, some funds will have been raised in the capital markets, and this cash will cover part of the funding

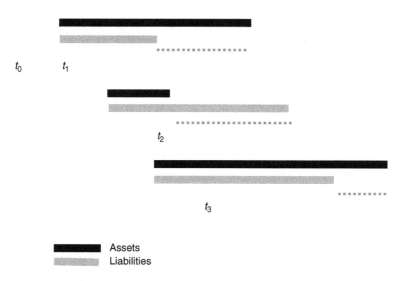

t_0 t_1

t_2

t_3

■■■■■■ Assets
▨▨▨▨▨▨ Liabilities

Figure 2.5   Funding position on a daily basis

requirement. In addition, the ALM desk must consider the cost of the funds it is borrowing; if, for example, it thought that interest rates in the short-term, and for short-term periods, were going to fall, it might cover the gap with only short-term funds, so it can then refinance at the expected lower rates. The opposite might be done if the desk thought rates would rise in the near future.

Running a liquidity gap over time, beyond customer requirements, would reflect a particular view of the ALM desk. So maintaining a consistently under-funded position suggests that interest rates are expected to decline, at which longer-term funds can be taken at cost. Maintaining an overfunded gap would imply that the bank thinks rates will be rising, and so longer-term funds are locked in now at lower interest rates. Even if the net position is dictated by customer requirements (for example, customers placing more on deposit than they take out in loans), the bank can still manage the resultant gap in the wholesale market.

Having excess liabilities generally is a rare scenario at a bank and is not, under most circumstances, a desirable position to be in. This is because the bank will have target return on capital ratios to achieve, and this requires that funds be put to work, so to speak, by acquiring assets. In the case of equity capital, it is imperative that these funds are properly employed.[9] The exact structure of the asset book will depend on the bank's view on interest rates and the yield curve generally. The shape of the yield curve and expectations on this will also influence the structure and tenor of the asset book. The common practice is to spread assets across the term structure, with varying maturities. There will also be investments made with a forward start date, to lock in rates in the forward curve now. Equally, some investments will be made for very short periods, so that if interest rates rise, when the funds are reinvested they will benefit from the higher rates.

2.3.2 The basic case: Illustration

The basic case is illustrated in Table 2.2, in two scenarios. In the first scenario, the longest-dated gap is -130, so the bank puts on funding for $+130$ to match this tenor of three periods. The gap at period t_2 is -410, so this is matched with a 2-period tenor funding position of $+280$. This leaves a gap of -180 at period t_1, which is then funded with a 1-period loan. The net position is zero at each period ('squared off'), and the book has been funded with three bullet fixed-term loans. The position is not a matched book as such, although there is now no liquidity risk exposure.

In the second case, the gap is increasing from period 1 to period 2. The first period is funded with a 3-period and a 2-period borrow of $+50$ and $+200$, respectively. The gap at t_2 needs to be funded with a position that is not needed

Table 2.2 Funding the liquidity gap: two examples

Time	t_1	t_2	t_3
(i)			
Assets	970	840	1250
Liabilities	380	430	1120
Gap	−590	−410	−130
Borrow 1: tenor 3 periods	130	130	130
Borrow 2: tenor 2 periods	280	280	
Borrow 3: tenor 1 period	180		
Total funding	+590	+410	+130
Squared off	0	0	0
(ii)			
Assets	970	840	1250
Liabilities	720	200	1200
Gap	−250	−640	−50
Borrow 1: tenor 3 periods	50	50	50
Borrow 2: tenor 2 periods	200	200	
Borrow 3: tenor 1 period	0	390	
Total funding	+250	+640	+50
Squared off	0	0	0

now. The bank can cover this with a forward-start loan of $+390$ at t_1 or can wait and act at t_2. If it does the latter it may still wish to hedge the interest-rate exposure.

2.3.3   The liquidity ratio

The *liquidity ratio* is the ratio of assets to liabilities. It is a short-term ratio, usually calculated for the money market term only, that is, up to one year. Under most circumstances, and certainly under a positive yield curve environment, it would be expected to be above 1.00, however this is less common at the very short end, because the average tenor of assets is often greater than the average tenor of liabilities. So in the one-month to three-month period, and perhaps out to the six-month, the ratio may well be less than one. This reflects the fact that short-term borrowing is used to fund longer-term assets.

A ratio of below one is inefficient from a Return on Equity (RoE) point of view. It represents an opportunity cost of return foregone. To manage it, banks may invest more funds in the very short term, but this also presents its own problems, because the return on these assets may not be sufficient. This is especially true in a positive yield curve environment. This is one scenario in which a matched book approach will be prudent, because the bank should be able to lock in a bid-offer spread in the very short end of the yield curve.[10] A more risky approach would be to lend in the short term and fund these in the long term, but this would create problems because the term premium in the yield curve will make borrowing in the long term expensive relative to the return on short-dated assets (unless we have an inverted yield curve). There is also the liquidity risk associated with the more frequent rolling-over of assets compared to liabilities. We see then, that maintaining the liquidity ratio carries something of a cost for banks.

2.4   Case Study: Derivatives trading House ALM policy and profile

I illustrate the basic concept of ALM with a look at the ALM policy and profile of a derivatives trading house, which we will call XYZ Securities Limited. The business is a financial institution based in London, with a number of business lines in Foreign Exchange (FX), equity, and credit derivatives trading and market making. We outline the various firm-wide policies on ALM, cash management, liquidity and investment formalized at XYZ Securities.

2.4.1   XYZ securities limited

2.4.1.1   *Funding and asset-liability management*

This note outlines the approach to managing the asset-liability profile that is generated by the funding requirements of XYZ Securities Limited ('XYZ').

The principal source of funding is the parent bank. Funds are also taken from a variety of external sources (prime brokerage, bank lines, Total Return Swap (TRS) and repo lines and an asset-backed commercial paper programme.). The overall management of the ALM profile is centralized within the XYZ Treasury desk.

The key objective of the Treasury desk is to undertake prudent management of XYZ's funding requirement, with regard to liquidity management, interest-rate management (gap profile) and funding diversification. This process includes management information and reporting. The primary Management Information (MI) deliverable of the Treasury desk is the ALM report. This is presented at Figure 2.6.

2.4.1.2 ALM report

The asset-liability profile (ALM) of all combined XYZ business lines is shown at Figure 2.6. The report is comprised of the following segments:

- ALM report
- asset liquidity profile
- liabilities.

I consider each part next.

2.4.1.3 ALM report

This report summarizes the total funding requirement of each of XYZ's business lines. The business lines are: FX, interest-rate and credit derivatives market making; equity derivatives proprietary trading, asset management and equity brokerage. The funding is profiled against the asset profile to produce the firm-wide ALM profile. Liability represents the funding taken by each business line. They are set out in accordance with the maturity term structure of each constituent loan of the total funding requirement. The maturity buckets used are

- overnight
- overnight – one week
- one week – one month
- one month – three months
- three months – six months
- six months – 12 months
- over 12 months.

The asset pool is distributed along the same maturity buckets, in accordance with certain assumptions. These assumptions are concerned with the expected turnover of assets in each business, and the time estimated to liquidate the business under enforced conditions.[11] Underneath the ALM profile is shown the gap profile. Gap is defined as the difference between assets and liabilities per maturity bucket; it shows how the liability profile differs from the asset profile. It is also a snapshot that reflects where the forward funding requirement lies at the time of the snapshot.

2.4.1.4   Asset liquidity profile

This report is a detailed breakdown of the funding requirement of each business line. Assets and liabilities are split according to desk within each business line, set out by maturity profile.

2.4.1.5   Liabilities

This is the detailed liability profile breakdown of all the business lines. Funding is split into term structure of liabilities. A separate table is given for each business line. There is also a detailed breakdown of use of funds from each source of funds.

2.4.1.6   Aims and objectives

Historically, the funding of XYZ business was concentrated overwhelmingly on a very short-term basis. The motivation for this was primarily the short-term trading nature of XYZ's assets, which meant that the asset profile was effectively changing on a high frequency. Over time, XYZ's business evolved into dealing in longer-term asset classes, and as a consequence XYZ is in the process of rolling out funding into longer tenors to more adequately match its asset profile. The Treasury aim going forward is based on the following reasoning:

- As much as possible, to match asset profile with liability profile and to minimise forward gap.
- To term out the funding away from the very short-dated tenors used hitherto.
- To construct an ALM profile that recognises the differing requirements of individual business lines. For example, the market making businesses are expected to have a more flexible liquidity profile than the asset management business. Hence the liability profile of the former will be concentrated along the short end of the funding term structure when compared to the latter.
- To even out the liability profile such that no one maturity bucket contains more than 20% of the total funding requirement. This will be treated as a funding limit.

The 20% limit will apply to the overall XYZ funding requirement.

2.4.1.7 Application of cost of funds

The effect of terming out funding is to produce a cost of funds that is not explicitly observable without calculation. That is, the cost of funds must be determined as a pooled or weighted-average cost of funds (WAC). XYZ uses a simplified version of this calculation that is essentially the interest charged on each loan as a proportion of the total borrowing, or, put another way, the daily interest payable on all loans divided by the total notional amount. This is standard market practice and is used, for example, at a number of European investment banks. Treasury applies the WAC to each business line.

2.4.1.8 Summary

The objective of ALM policy is to apply market-standard guidelines to the business and to follow prudent market practice. It is also to make the whole funding process more transparent with regard to management reporting and to centralize funding onto one desk within the group.

2.4.2 XYZ securities limited ALM and funding report

The firm-wide ALM report is shown in Figure 2.6(i) and (ii). From Figure 2.6(i) we observe the following:

- The 'gap' is defined as the absolute value of the assets and liabilities added together, which, because liabilities are reported as negative numbers, is essentially assets minus liabilities.
- The funding within each time bucket is reported as a per cent of total funding. This is a key control measure, as prudent ALM policy suggests that the liability profile should be humped in shape (the 'ALM Smile'), so that each bucket should not hold more than approximately 15–20% of the total funding.
- The next control value is the 'gap as per cent of total gap'. This is noted to prevent excessive forward gap developing in one time bucket.
- The key control measure is the gap as per cent of total funding, which at XYZ is set at a 20% limit. We see that on this date there was no breach of this limit in any of the time buckets.
- The report also lists cumulative assets and liabilities, as well as the 'net gap', which is the sum of the two cumulative values for each time bucket.

We observe that the ALM profile at XYZ follows roughly the 'ALM Smile' shape that is recommended as the ideal profile over the term structure.

The firm-wide funding report is shown in Figure 2.7. This is reported in graphical form to observe adherence to funding limits and indicate breaches. Unlike the ALM report, which is produced by Treasury (a front-office function), the funding report is produced by the Middle Office. Figure 2.8 shows the breakdown by business line.

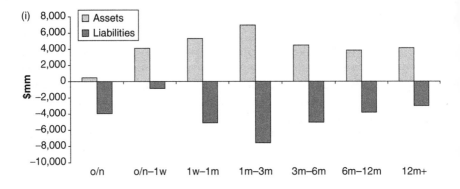

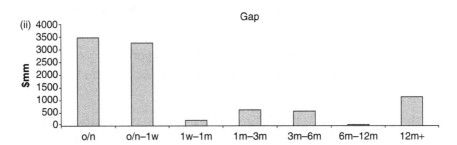

Figure 2.6   (i) XYS Securities Limited ALM report and profile. (ii) XYZ Securities Limited gap profile

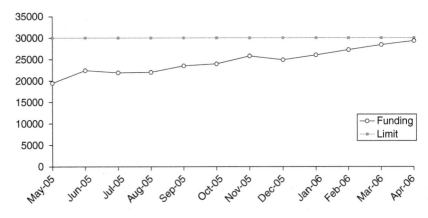

Figure 2.7   XYZ Securities Limited funding usage and limit report

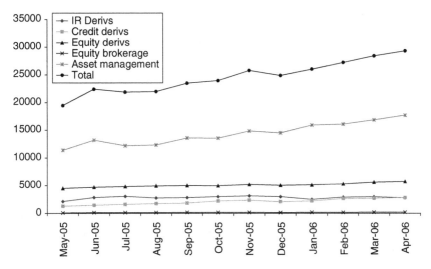

Figure 2.8 XYZ Securities Limited funding usage by business line

2.4.2.1 Asset-liability management reporting

XYZ Treasury follows the asset-liability management (ALM) policy previously described to and approved by senior management. One strand of the ALM discipline is the regular reporting of the firm's ALM profile, by means of the ALM report. This is produced by Treasury using data recorded by itself as well as data from Middle Office (MO).

2.4.3 XYZ securities liquidity portfolio: UK gilt portfolio

Commercial banks and building societies are natural holders of government bonds such as gilts, for the following reasons:

- for liquidity purposes, as gilts are the most liquid instruments in the UK market
- as an instrument in which to invest the firm's capital reserves
- for income generation purposes, given the favourable funding costs of gilt repo and the zero credit and liquidity risk
- to intermediate between gilt, stock loan and interbank markets in CDs
- to benefit from being long in gilts that go 'special' and can be funded at anything from 25 bps to 2–3% cheaper than 'general collateral' (GC) repo
- to establish an asset pool that receives favourable capital treatment (0% risk-weighted under Basel I and Basel II).

The benefits to XYZ of holding such a portfolio include some of the above, as well as the following:

- earning the spread between yield and funding cost
- using the business to set up dealing relationships with bank counterparties that could then be used as sources of additional funding if required, adding to the diversity of funding (required as part of the Treasury remit)
- assisting Treasury in undertaking ALM objectives.

2.4.3.1   *Portfolio makeup*

The UK government bond portfolio managed by XYZ Securities Treasury was ramped up as follows:

- A portfolio of very short-dated gilts and gilt strips on the balance sheet (maximum maturity recommended one year, majority in three to six months). The expected make-up of the book might be
  - 125m 3m
  - 200m 6m
  - 25m 1 year
  - average maturity of portfolio in the first year would be around the six-month tenor.
- Funding these in gilt repo, under the Global Master Repurchase Agreement (GMRA) agreement and also funding using TRS under International Swaps and Derivatives Association (ISDA) if required.
- The repo funding margin for gilts in the wholesale market is often 0%. With zero or very low margin or 'haircut', all positions will be virtually fully funded.
- Holding gilts and gilt strips to maturity to generate a steady income stream. With ultra-short-dated strips, we also benefit from the pull-to-par effect.

2.4.3.2   *Market rates*

Table below shows income yields and funding rates as of 2 June 2004. This shows where value was obtained from holding a book of gilts in the first instance. For example, all the following positions yielded funding profit:

- Hold gilts and fund in GC; depending on the specific stock and the term of funding arranged, a gain ranging from 15 to 50–60 basis points.
- Hold strips to maturity; for example, gain of approximately 35 bps for Dec 04 Principal strip at 1w or 2w funding. Locked-in funding gain (buy 6-m strip and fund in 6-m) of 9 bps for Dec 04 strip – this is risk free income.

- Hold strips at 3-, 6- and 9-month maturities as longer-dated Bills and hold to maturity. Funding will be locked in if available or rolled:
  - For example, as of 2 June 2004, XYZ purchased the Sep 04 coupon strip at 4.34% and funded in the one-week term at 4.15% (and ran the resultant funding gap risk – but this gilt had a strong pull-to-par effect. If funding is no longer profitable in the short dates, XYZ would have sold the gilt for a probable realised mark-to-market profit).
  - Coupon strips are bid for in repo by the main market makers, thereby reducing liquidity risk in these products.
- take advantage of special rates for stocks XYZ is long in. On 2 June 2004, a position in 9.5% 2005 gilt was funded cheaper due to special status, from 35 bps (down from 50 bps the week before). The 6.75% 2004 gilt was being funded at 100 bps cheaper than GC. So the gain on holding that stock would be significant, as the funding cost in repo would be very low. It would be an objective of the Treasury desk to be aware of stocks expected to go special and act accordingly.

2.4.3.3   Risks

The principle risk is funding roll-over (gap risk). Where possible one will lock in funding that matches the expected holding period of positions, but will also look to take advantage of markets rates as appropriate and roll over funding. Gap risk will be managed in the normal way as part of overall Treasury operations. Gaps will be put on to reflect the interest-rate and yield curve view of the desk.

There is no credit risk.

The interest-rate risk and gap risk are managed as a standard Banking ALM or cash book. The objective is to set up an income stream position at low risk, but if necessary DV01 risk would be managed where deemed necessary using 90-day sterling futures, Overnight-Index Swap (OIS) or short-dated swaps. XYZ can also sell out of positions for which it expects significant market movement (for example, a central bank base rate hike). The main objective, however, is to establish an income stream, in line with a view on short-term interest rates. Hedging would only be carried out when necessary for short-term periods (say, ahead of a data release or anticipated high volatility).

As the positions would be on the Trading book, not Banking book, they will be marked-to-market. The desk expects volatility in short-dated gilts to be considerably lower than for medium- and long-dated gilts, but volatility is a risk exposure and there may be periods when the desk will experience mark-to-market losses.

The interest-rate risk for longer-dated stocks is shown in the Table below measured as DV01 (dollar-value of loss for a 1 bp rise in yields). Longer-dated stocks expose FP to greater interest-rate risk position when marking-to-market.

2.4.3.4   Market rates

GC Rates 2 Jun		
1w	4.15	4.10
2w	4.25	4.15
3w	4.25	4.15
1m	4.25	4.15
2m	4.28	4.18
3m	4.32	4.22
4m	4.40	4.30
5m	4.43	4.33
6m	4.50	4.40
9m	4.67	4.57
1y	4.78	4.68

Source: HBOS Screen

	Gilt yields 2 Jun		Special rates
	GRY %	DV01	
5% Jun 04	4.05		
6T Nov 04	4.33	0.00416	100 bps
9H Apr 05	4.668	0.00817	35 bps cheaper than GC
8H Dec 05	4.818	0.014	25 bps cheaper, down from1.5%
7T Sep 06	4.945	0.02141	
7H Dec 06	4.966	0.02364	10 bps

Source: Butler Securities / KSBB screens

	Gilt strip yields 2 Jun	
	GRY %	DV01
P Jun 04	3.78	
C Sep 04	4.342	0.00195
C Dec 04	4.509	0.00432
C Mar 05	4.633	0.00664
C Jun 05	4.744	0.00888
C Sep 05	4.829	0.01107
P Dec 05	4.85	0.01321

Source: Bloomberg

2.5 Asset and liability management: The ALCO

The ALM reporting process is often overseen by the bank's asset-liability management committee (ALCO). The ALCO will have a specific remit to oversee all aspects of asset-liability management, from the front-office money market function to back-office operations and middle-office reporting and risk management. In this section we consider the salient features of ALCO procedures.

2.5.1 ALCO policy

The ALCO is responsible for setting and implementing the ALM policy. Its composition varies in different banks, but usually includes heads of business lines as well as director-level staff, such as the finance director. The ALCO also sets hedging policy. Typical membership of ALCO is as follows:

Members
    CFO (Chairman); Deputy (Head of Financial Accounting)
    CEO (Deputy Chairman)
    Head of Treasury; Deputy (Head of Money Markets)
    MD Commercial Banking
    MD Retail banking
    Chief Risk Officer
Guests
    Head of Market and Liquidity Risk
    Head of Product Control
    Head of ALM/Money Markets
    Head of Financial Institutions
Secretary
    PA to the Head of Treasury

The ALM process may be undertaken by the Treasury desk, ALM desk or other dedicated function within the bank. In traditional commercial banks it will be responsible for management reporting to the asset-liability management committee (ALCO). The ALCO will consider the report in detail at regular meetings, usually weekly. Main points of interest in the ALCO report include variations in interest income, the areas that experienced fluctuations in income and what the latest short-term income projections are. The ALM report will link these three strands across the group entity and also to each individual business line. That is, it will consider macrolevel factors driving variations in interest income as well as specific desk-level factors. The former includes changes in the shape and level of the yield curve, while the latter will include new business, customer behaviour and so on. Of necessity the ALM report is a detailed, large document.

Figure 2.9   ALCO main mission

Bank ALM strategic overview	
Mission	**Components**
ALCO management and reporting	Formulating ALM strategy Management reporting ALCO agenda and minutes Assessing liquidity, gap and interest-rate risk reports Scenario planning and analysis Interest income projection
Asset management	Managing bank liquidity book (CDs, Bills) Managing FRN book Investing bank capital
ALM strategy	Yield curve analysis Money market trading
Funding and liquidity management	Liquidity policy Managing funding and liquidity risk Ensuring funding diversification Managing lending of funds
Risk management	Formulating hedging policy Interest-rate risk exposure management Implementing hedging policy using cash and derivative instruments
Internal Treasury function	Formulating transfer pricing system and level Funding group entities Calculating the cost of capital

Figure 2.9 is a summary overview of the responsibilities of ALCO.

The ALCO will meet on a regular basis; the frequency depends on the type of institution, but is usually once a month. The composition of the ALCO also varies by institution, but the norm is as described above. Representatives from the credit committee and loan syndication may also be present. A typical agenda would consider all the elements listed in Figure 2.9. Thus the meeting will discuss and generate action points on the following:

- Management reporting: this will entail analysing the various management reports and either signing off on them or agreeing on items for action-ing. The issues to consider include lending margin, interest income, vari-ance from last projection, customer business and future business. Current business policy with regard to lending and portfolio management will be reviewed and either continued or adjusted.
- Business planning: existing asset (and liability) books will be reviewed, and future business direction drawn up. This will consider the performance of

existing business, most importantly with regard to return on capital. The existing asset portfolio will be analysed from a risk-reward perspective, and a decision taken to continue or modify all lines of business. Any proposed new business will be discussed, and if accepted in principle, will be moved on to the next stage.[12] At this stage any new business will be assessed for projected returns, revenue and risk exposure.

- Hedging policy: overall hedging policy will consider the acceptability of risk exposure, existing risk limits and use of hedging instruments. The latter also includes use of derivative instruments. Many bank ALM desks find that their hedging requirements can be met using plain vanilla products such as interest-rate swaps and exchange-traded short-money futures contracts. The use of options, and even more vanilla derivative instruments, such as Forward Rate Agreement (FRAs), is much less common than one might think. Hedging policy takes into account the cash book revenue level, current market volatility levels and the overall cost of hedging. On occasion certain exposures may be left unhedged because the costs associated with hedging them is deemed prohibitive (this includes the actual cost of putting on the hedge as well as the opportunity cost associated with expected reduced income from the cash book). Of course, hedging policy is formulated in coordination with overall funding and liquidity policy. Its final form must consider the bank's views of the following:

- expectations on the future level and direction of interest rates
- the need to manage and control risk exposure balanced against the need to maximise revenue and income
- level of risk aversion, and how much risk exposure the bank is willing to accept.

The ALCO is dependant on management reporting from the ALM or Treasury desk. The reports may be compiled by the Treasury middle office. The main report is the overall ALM report, showing the composition of the bank's ALM book. Other reports will look at specific business lines, and will consider the return on capital generated by these businesses. These reports will need to break down aggregate levels of revenue and risk by business line. Reports will also drill down by product type, across business lines. Other reports will consider the gap, the gap risk, the VaR or DV01 report and credit risk exposures. Overall, the reporting system must be able to isolate revenues, return and risk, by country sector, business line and product type. There is usually also an element of scenario planning, that is, expected performance under various specified macro- and microlevel market conditions.

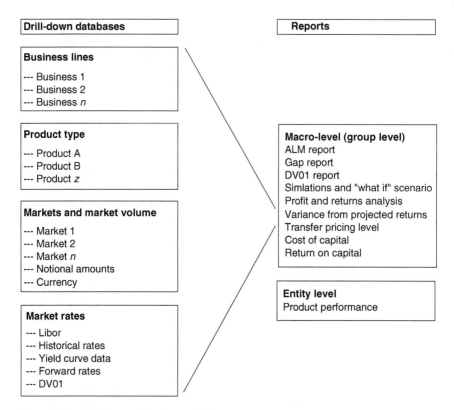

Drill-down databases

Business lines
--- Business 1
--- Business 2
--- Business *n*

Product type
--- Product A
--- Product B
--- Product *z*

Markets and market volume
--- Market 1
--- Market 2
--- Market *n*
--- Notional amounts
--- Currency

Market rates
--- Libor
--- Historical rates
--- Yield curve data
--- Forward rates
--- DV01

Reports

Macro-level (group level)
ALM report
Gap report
DV01 report
Simlations and "what if" scenario
Profit and returns analysis
Variance from projected returns
Transfer pricing level
Cost of capital
Return on capital

Entity level
Product performance

Figure 2.10   ALCO reporting input and output

Figure 2.10 illustrates the general reporting concept.

2.6   ALCO reporting

I now provide a flavour of the reporting that is provided to, and analysed by, the ALCO. This is a generalization; reports will, of course, vary by the type of the institution and the nature of its business.

Earlier we showed an example of a macrolevel ALM report. The ALCO will also consider macrolevel gap and liquidity reports compiled for product and market. The interest-rate gap, being simply the difference between assets and liabilities, is easily set into these parameters. For management reporting purposes, the report will attempt to show a dynamic profile, but its chief limitation is that it is always a snapshot of a fixed point in time, and therefore, strictly speaking, will always be out of date.

Figure 2.11 shows a typical dynamic gap, positioned in a desired 'ALM smile', with the projected interest-rate gaps based on the current snapshot profile. This report shows future funding requirements, on which the ALCO can give direction that reflects their view on future interest-rate levels. It also shows where the sensitivity to falling interest rates, in terms of revenue, lies because it shows the volume of assets. Again, the ALCO can give instructions on hedging if they expect interest income to be affected adversely. The x-axis represents the time buckets from overnight out to two years or beyond. Banks use different time buckets to suit their own requirements.[13]

Figure 2.12 shows the same report with a breakdown by product (or market– the report would have a similar layout). We use a hypothetical sample of different business lines. Using this format, the ALCO can observe which assets and liabilities are producing the gaps, which is important because it shows if products (or markets) are fitting into overall bank policy. Equally, policy can be adjusted if required in response to what the report shows. So the ALCO can see what proportion of total assets is represented by each business line, and which line has the greatest forward funding requirement. The same report is shown again in Figure 2.13, but this time with the breakdown by type of interest rate, fixed or variable.

Another variation of this report that will be examined by ALCO is a breakdown by income and margin, again separated into business lines or markets as

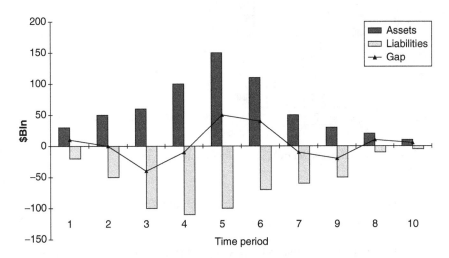

Figure 2.11   ALM and expected liquidity and interest-rate gap, snapshot profile

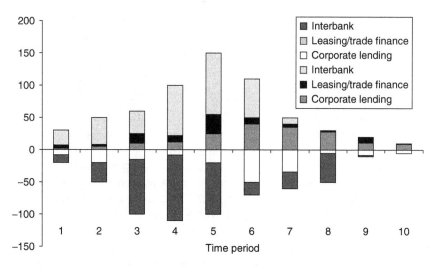

Figure 2.12   ALM breakdown by product (or market) segment

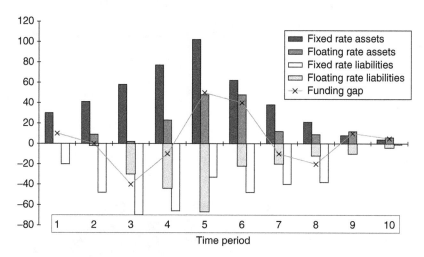

Figure 2.13   ALM breakdown by type of interest rate

required. In a pure commercial banking operation the revenue type mix will comprise the following (among others):

- the bid-offer spread between borrowing and lending in the interbank market
- corporate lending margin, that is, the loan rate over and above the bank's cost of funds

- trading income
- fixed fees charged for services rendered.

The ALCO will receive an income breakdown report, split by business line. The x-axis in such a report would show the margin level for each time period, that is, it shows the margin of the lending rate over the cost of funds by each time bucket. Figure 2.14 is another type of income report, which shows the volumes and income spread by business line. The spread is shown in basis points and is an average for that time bucket (across all loans and deposits for that bucket). The volumes will be those reported in the main ALM report (Figure 2.11), but this time with the margin contribution per time period. As we might expect, the spread levels per product across time are roughly similar. They will differ more markedly by product time. The latter report is shown in Figure 2.15. Figure 2.15 is more useful because it shows the performance of each business line. In general, the ALCO will prefer low volumes and high margin as a combination, because lower volumes consume less capital. However some significant high volume business (such as interbank money market operations) operates at relatively low margin.

The income and return reports viewed by ALCO will be required by it to enable it to check if lending and money market trading adheres to bank policy. Essentially, these reports are providing information on the risk-return profile of the bank. The ideal combination is the lowest possible risk for the highest possible return, although of course low risk business carries the lowest return. The level of trade-off that the bank is comfortable with is what the ALCO will set in its direction and strategy. With regard to volumes and bank business,

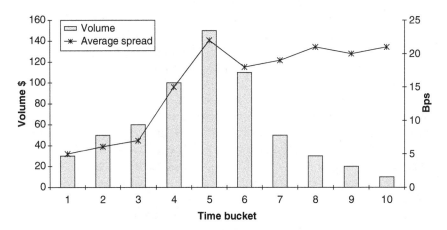

Figure 2.14   Asset profile volume and average income spread

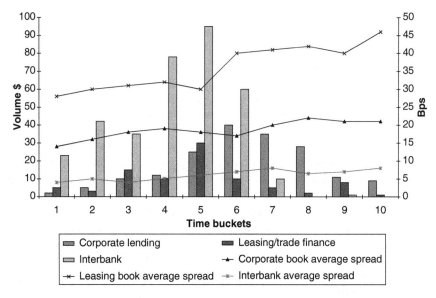

Figure 2.15   Business lines and average income spread

it might be thought that the optimum mix is high volume mixed with high income margin. However high volume business consumes the most capital, so there will be another trade-off with regard to use of capital.

2.7   Principles of bank liquidity risk management[14]

At a conference hosted by the UK Financial Services Authority (FSA) on 9 October 2009, there was significant focus given to the UK bank HSBC's model of liquidity management. Given that, rare amongst large Western banks, HSBC did not suffer a liquidity crisis in 2007 and 2008, observers commented on the efficacy of the HSBC model, and on what lessons could be learned for banks in general.

In truth, a close look at HSBC's approach to liquidity and asset generation shows that it is neither unique nor proprietary to the bank. The 'HSBC model' would have been the norm, rather than the exception, amongst banks as recently as 10 or 15 years ago. In an era of excess, the basic tenets of the approach were applied by fewer and fewer banks, to the extent that they were no longer seen as an essential ingredient of prudent bank risk management at the time of the 2007–2008 financial crash.

These principles represent basic principles of banking, and not a specific response to the events of 2007 and 2008. They can be taken to be general principles of banking liquidity management, and ones that more banks will readopt as they return to a more conservative business model, either though choice or because the requirements of the national banking regulator insist upon a more robust approach to risk management.

This section considers the most important principles of what should be taken to be the cornerstone of banking and liquidity management.

2.7.1   Fund illiquid assets with core customer deposits

In hindsight, this looks an eminently sensible guideline, but during the bull-market build-up of 2001 to 2007 it was not applied universally. The best example of this was Northern Rock plc, which built an asset book that far exceeded its retail deposit base in size, but this pattern was observed with many banks in Western Europe. It is not difficult to ascertain the logic behind this principle: core customer deposits are generally more stable than wholesale funds and also at lower risk of withdrawal in the event of a downturn in economic conditions (an apparent paradox is that they may actually increase as customers seek to deleverage and also hold off committing to cash-rich expenditure). Therefore, funding illiquid assets with core customer deposits is prudent banking practice.

2.7.2   Where core customer deposits are not available, use long-term wholesale funding sources

This follows on naturally from the first principle. Where there are insufficient core deposits available, and banks resort to the wholesale funding market, banks should ensure that only long-dated wholesale funds are used to fund illiquid assets. Generally 'long-dated' means over one year in maturity, although of course the appropriate tenor to source is a function of the maturity of the asset. This approach reduces rollover liquidity risk in the event of a crisis.

2.7.3   No over-reliance on wholesale funding.
Run a sensible term structure wherever this is used:
More of funding should be in long term (>5 Years) than in short term

This follows on from the primary dictum of not building up the asset base using wholesale funds unless absolutely necessary. Where recourse is made to wholesale funds, as much of this should be in the long-term as possible, so as to minimize exposure to frequent short-term rollover risk to wholesale funds.

2.7.4   Maintain 'liquidity buffers' to cater for stresses, both firm-specific and market-wide stresses

The UK FSA has stipulated, in its *Policy Statement 09/16* published in October 2009, that this will be a requirement. However, only 10 or 15 years ago it was quite common for banks to hold some of their assets in the form of liquid risk-free government bonds. Traditionally a bank's capital was always invested in such securities or in shorter-dated government bills, but beyond this it was accepted good practice for banks to have a proportion of their balance sheet assets in sovereign securities. For the FSA to make it a requirement under law demonstrates the extent to which this practice fell into disuse.

It is evident that banks reduced their holdings of government bonds so they could deploy more of their funds in higher-paying risky assets. But the logic of holding a liquidity buffer is irrefutable: in periods of stress or illiquidity, government bonds are the only assets that remain liquid. As such, if need be they can be sold to release liquidity. Even hitherto highly liquid assets such as high-rated bank CDs or short-dated Medium Term Notes (MTN)s became illiquid virtually overnight in the immediate aftermath of the Lehman collapse in 2008. This demonstrates that the liquidity buffer should be comprised of sovereign risk-free securities only.

2.7.5 Establish a liquidity contingency plan

A well-managed liquidity operation recognizes that bank funding should be sourced from multiple origins, and that 'concentration risk' should be avoided, both in any specific sector and to any one lender. However, even without excess concentration, at any time particular sectors or lenders may become unavailable, for either exogenous or endogenous reasons.

Given this risk, banks needs to have contingencies to fall back on whenever particular sources of funding dry up. This may include applying for and setting up facilities at the central bank, or establishing relationships with particular sectors that, for reasons of cost or convenience, the bank does not customarily access. The contingency plan needs to be tested regularly and kept updated.

2.7.6 Know what central bank facilities the bank can assess and test access to them

This follows logically from the requirement to have a contingency funding plan in place. Once a bank has established borrowing facilities at its central bank, it needs to be aware exactly how they function and what the requirements to access them are, so that if necessary it can benefit from them without delay.

2.7.7 Be aware of all the bank's exposures (on the liability side, not credit side)

For example, sponsoring an asset-backed commercial paper (ABCP) conduit creates a reputational, rather than contractual, obligation to provide funding. Therefore be aware of reputational obligations, especially if it means the bank has to lend its name to another entity.

This is fairly straightforward to understand, but in a bull market when credit spreads are tight it was frequently forgotten. Banks may desire the fee-based income, at favourable capital levels, that comes with sponsoring a third-party entity or providing a line of liquidity, but in a stress situation that line will be drawn on. Is the bank prepared to take on this additional liquidity risk exposure to an entity that it might not normally, in a bear market, wish to lend funds to?

2.7.8 Liquidity risk is not a single metric

It is an array of metrics, and a bank must calculate them all in order to obtain the most accurate picture of liquidity. This is especially true for multinational banks or banks with multiple business lines.

Smaller banks often rely on just one or two liquidity indicators, such as loan-to-deposit ratio. Given that bank asset-liability management is more an art than a science, it is vital that banks use a range of liquidity measures for risk estimation and forecasting. We will address the different metrics required in the next section.

2.7.9 The internal transfer pricing framework must be set correctly and adequately

An artificial internal lending rate to business lines can drive inappropriate business decision-making and was a factor behind the growth in risky assets during the build-up to the US sub-prime crisis.

The business of banking is, if nothing else, the business of managing the gap between assets and liabilities. In the history of banking, banks have never matched their asset maturity with their funding liability maturity. But it is the management of this gap risk that should be the primary concern of all banks. The basic principles we have discussed above represent business best practice, evolved over centuries of modern banking, in mitigating gap risk.

2.8 Measuring bank liquidity risk: Key metrics

As noted above, given that bank asset-liability management is as much an art as a science, it is vital that banks use a range of liquidity measures for risk estimation and forecasting. In this section we list six baseline liquidity metrics, which all banks, irrespective of their size or line of business, should adopt and monitor as a matter of course. These are

1. loan-to-deposit ratio
2. 1-week and 1-month liquidity ratios
3. cumulative liquidity model
4. liquidity risk factor
5. concentration report
6. inter-entity lending report.

These reports measure and illustrate different elements of liquidity risk. For consolidated or group banking entities, reports must be at country level, legal entity level and Group level. Taken together, on aggregate the reports provide detail on

- the exposure of the bank to funding rollover or 'gap risk
- the daily funding requirement, and what it is likely to be at a forward date
- the extent of 'self-sufficiency' of a branch or subsidiary.

Liquidity reports also help in providing early warning of any likely funding stress points. We next examine them individually.

2.8.1   Loan-to-deposit ratio (LTD)

This is the standard and commonly used metric, typically reported monthly. It measures the relationship between lending and customer deposits, and is a measure of the self-sustainability of the bank (or the branch or subsidiary). A level above 100% is an early warning sign of excessive asset growth; of course a level below 70% implies excessive liquidity and implies a potentially inadequate return on funds.

The LTD is a good measure of the contribution of customer funding to the bank's overall funding, however it is not predictive and does not account for the tenor, concentration and volatility of funds. As such it is insufficient as a liquidity risk measure on its own and must be used in conjunction with the other measures.

2.8.2   1-Week and 1-month liquidity ratios

These are standard liquidity ratios that are commonly measured against a regulatory limit requirement. An example of a report for a Group-type entity comprised of four subsidiaries is shown in Figure 2.16.

Liquidity ratios are an essential measure of 'gap' risk. They show net cash flows, including the cash effect of liquidating 'liquid' securities, as a percentage

Figure 2.16   Sample liquidity ratio report

Country	1–week Gap	1–week Liquidity		1–month Liquidity	
	USD mm	This week limit	Excess	This week limit	Excess
F	−1586	−22.83%	−30.00%	−39.11%	−50.00%
D	188	15.26%	0.00%	1.62%	25.00%
H	786	22.57%	0.00%	19.12%	25.00%
G	550	53.27%	25.00%	69.83%	25.00%
Regional total	−62	−0.48%		−10.64%	

of liabilities, for a specific maturity 'bucket'. These are an effective measure of structural liquidity, with early warning of likely stress points.

A more detailed liquidity ratio report is shown in Figure 2.17. This shows the breakdown of cash inflows and outflows per time bucket, and also the liquidity ratio. The ratio itself is calculated by dividing the selected time bucket liability by the cumulative liability. So in this example the 30-day ratio of 17.3% is given by [781,065/4,511,294].

2.8.3   Cumulative liquidity model

This is an extension of the liquidity ratio report and is a forward-looking model of inflows, outflows and available liquidity, accumulated for a 12-month period. It recognizes and predicts liquidity stress points on a cash basis. A report such as this, like the liquidity ratios, will be prepared daily at legal entity level and Group level.

Figure 2.18 is an example of a cumulative outflow output graph rising from the cumulative liquidity model. This gives a snapshot view of forward funding stress points.

2.8.4   Liquidity risk factor (LRF)

This measure shows the aggregate size of the liquidity gap: it compares the average tenor of assets to the average tenor of liabilities. It is also known as a 'maturity transformation report'. The ratio can be calculated using years or days, as desired. For example, Figure 2.19 is an example of the risk factor for an hypothetical bank, for which the unit of measurement is days. In this example, (262/19) is slightly below 14.

The higher the LRF, the larger the liquidity gap, and the greater the liquidity risk. It is important to observe the trend over time and the change to long-run averages, so as to get early warning of the build-up of a potentially unsustainable funding structure.

2.8.5   Concentration report and funding source report

Figure 2.21 shows the extent of reliance on single sources of funds. An excess concentration to any one lender, sector or country is an early warning sign of potential stress points in the event of a crash event.

An example of a concentration report is shown in Figure 2.20. In this example, Customer 1 is clearly the focus of a potential stress point, and a bank would need to put in a contingency in the event that this source of funds dried up.

A related report is the funding source report, an example of which is shown in Figure 2.21. This is a summary of the share of funding obtained from all the various sources, and should be used to flag potential concentration risk by sector.

Figure 2.17 Liquidity report and liquidity ratio calculation

E U R O ' s
XYZ Bank, London – Liquidity Report
28-Nov-08

	Sight	2–8 Days	9 Days–1 Month	1–3 Months	3–6 Months	6 Mths to 1 Yr	1–3 Years	3–5 Years	+5 Years	Total
Corporate current / call	24,289	0	0	0	0	0	0	0	0	24,289
Corporate time loan	28,433	14,203	151,471	106,637	98,959	47,608	357,872	573,993	642,563	2,021,738
Government current/call	342	0	0	0	0	0	0	0	0	342
Government time loan	250	3	805	63	3,383	2,942	12,656	7,016	76,853	103,971
Interbank current / call	41,752	0	0	0	0	0	0	0	0	41,752
Interbank time loan	339,276	201,745	6,251	31,906	18,704	28,428	11,971	0	0	638,281
Repos	0	0	0	47,500	0	0	0	0	0	47,500
Intergroup current / call	4,445	0	0	0	0	0	0	0	0	4,445
Intergroup time loan	210,177	348,414	277,964	76,268	13,981	30,047	156	101	0	957,108
Marketable secs & CDs – <1Mth to Mat	5,009	0	55,358	0	0	0	0	0	0	60,367
Retail current / call	8,215	0	0	0	0	0	0	0	0	8,215
Retail time loan	238	41	w221	2,643	2,427	310	6,294	38,755	10,204	61,133
Additional corporate time lending	0	8	1,313	43	624	0	21,608	7,857	75,724	107,177
Receivables	0	0	0	0	0	0	0	0	0	0
Total assets	**662,426**	**564,414**	**493,383**	**265,060**	**138,078**	**109,335**	**410,557**	**627,722**	**805,344**	**4,076,318**
Corporate current / call	51,033	0	0	12,758	0	0	0	0	0	63,791
Corporate time deposit	32,303	122,955	114,627	299,551	28,387	928	0	0	0	598,751
Government current / call	1,946	0	0	0	0	0	0	0	0	1,946
Government time deposit	2,056	8,112	24,391	23,503	22,687	1,200	0	0	0	81,949
Interbank current / call	82,087	0	0	0	0	0	0	0	0	82,087
Interbank time deposit	83,898	83,684	349,461	86,979	23,967	1,205	0	0	0	629,194
Repos	0	0	0	50,000	0	0	0	0	0	50,000
Intergroup current / call	47,095	0	0	0	0	0	0	0	0	47,095
Intergroup time deposit	302,879	418,383	629,809	225,314	88,464	78,769	375	0	0	1,743,993
Retail current / call	65,273	0	0	16,318	0	0	0	0	0	81,591

Retail time deposit	203	54,128	167,090	683,288	27,925	13,273	9,224	0	955,131
Additional govt / local authority time deposits	8,656	9,319	50,508	82,531	15,252	8,500	1,000	0	175,766
Share capital	0	0	0	0	0	0	0	0	0
Payables	0	0	0	0	0	0	0	0	0
Total liabilities	**677,429**	**696,581**	**1,335,886**	**1,480,242**	**206,682**	**103,875**	**10,599**	**0**	**4,511,294**

Ratio Calculation	Sight	Sight–8 Days	Sight–1 M
Marketable Securities	0	630,536	630,536
Repos Adj	0	0	0
CD'S	39,000 0	353,219	353,219
Unutilised Commitments	(55,520)	(55,520)	(55,520)
Liquidity Gap	(15,003)	(147,170)	(989,673)
Total Available Funds	(70,523)	781,065	(61,438)
Total Liabilities	4,511,294	4,511,294	4,511,294
Liquidity Ratio	**-1.56%**	**17.31%**	**-1.36%**
	45	45	45
Internal Limit	3.00%	3.00%	-3.00%
FSA Limit	0.00%	0.00%	-5.00%
Stress testing 10% Fall in Marketable Securities	15.13%	15.13%	-3.54%
Stress testing 10% Fall in Stickiness		17.32%	-2.79%
Stress testing Combined Effect of above		15.14%	-4.97%

Liquidity gap is assets minus liabilities in relevant tenor bucket

Total available funds is liquidity gap, plus marketable securities (FRNs), CDs and committed facilities that are as yet undrawn (which is subtracted)

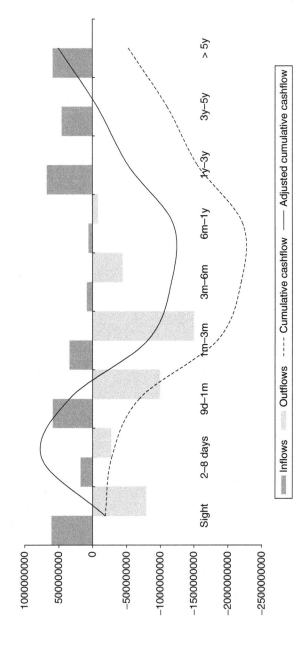

Figure 2.18 Cumulative liquidity model

Figure 2.19 Liquidity risk factor

Report date	Average liabilities tenor (days)	Average assets tenor (days)	Maturity transformation effect	Limit
30/09/2009	19	262	14	24

Figure 2.20 Large depositors as percentage of total funding report

Customer	Deposit Amount 000s	Percentage of Bank Funding (%)	Percentage of Group External Funding (%)
Customer 1	836,395	17.1	2.6
Customer 2	595,784	7.9	1.8
Customer 3	425,709	5.8	1.3
Customer 4	241,012	0.6	0.7
Customer 6	214,500	1.2	0.7
Customer 21	190,711	4.5	0.6
Customer 17	123,654	2.9	0.4
Customer 18	97,877	2.3	0.3
Customer 14	89,344	2.1	0.3
Customer 15	88,842	2.1	0.3
Customer 31	83,272	2.0	0.3
Customer 19	74,815	0.5	0.2
Customer 10	64,639	1.5	0.2
Customer 29	59,575	1.4	0.2
Customer 16	58,613	1.4	0.2
Total	6,562,116	53.3	20.1

2.8.6 Inter-entity lending report

This report is relevant for Group and consolidated banking entities. As intra-group lending is common in banking entities, this report is a valuable tool used to determine how reliant a specific banking subsidiary is on Group funds. An example of a report for a Group entity is shown in Figure 2.22.

We have described the range of reports that represent essential metrics in the measurement of liquidity risk. They are the minimum management information that banks and group Treasuries will wish to prepare, both as business best practice and as part of adherence to new regulatory standards.

2.9 Internal funding rate policy

I define liquidity risk as the risk of being unable to (a) raise funds to meet payment obligations as they fall due and (b) fund an increase in assets. Funding risk is the risk of being unable to borrow funds in the market. The United Kingdom regulatory authority, the Financial Services Authority, has prescribed a mechanism to mitigate liquidity and funding risk that is notable for its focus

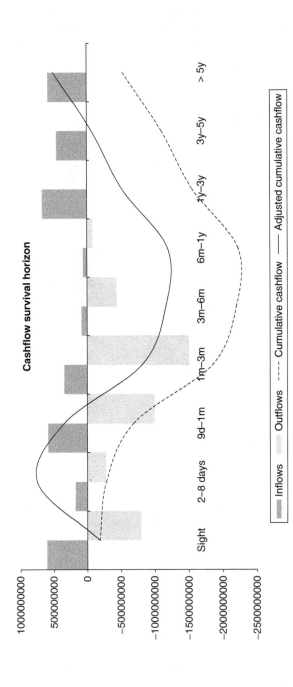

Cashflow survival horizon

Inflows   Outflows   ---- Cumulative cashflow   — Adjusted cumulative cashflow

	Sight	2–8 days	9d–1m	1m–3m	3m–6m	6m–1y	1y–3y	3y–5y	>5y
Inflows ("Assets")	607,358,152	177,828,693	587,128,345	342,080,905	83,708,732	57,945,513	669,190,119	452,116,938	580,149,786
Outflows ("Liabilities")	(792,700,834)	(272,356,971)	(993,857,612)	(1,498,903,403)	(437,080,965)	(81,984,848)	(3,155,014)	0	(7,451,508)
Net mismatch	(185,342,681)	(94,528,278)	(406,729,267)	(1,156,822,497)	(353,372,233)	(24,039,335)	666,035,105	452,116,938	572,698,278
Cumulative cashflow	(185,342,681)	(279,870,959)	(686,600,226)	(1,843,422,724)	(2,196,794,956)	(2,220,834,291)	(1,554,799,186)	(1,102,682,247)	(529,983,969)
Adjustments	1,031,223,663	1,031,223,663	1,031,223,663	1,031,223,663	1,031,223,663	1,031,223,663	1,031,223,663	1,031,223,663	1,031,223,663
Adjusted cumulative cashflow	(185,342,681)	751,352,704	344,623,437	(812,199,061)	(1,165,571,293)	(1,189,610,628)	(523,575,523)	(71,458,584)	501,239,694

Report date	Average liabilities tenor (days)	Average assets tenor (days)	Maturity transformation effect	Limit
10/30/2009	20	248	12	24

Source	Balance (€000,000's)	% Funding	Limit	Limit Breach (Y/N)
Corporate and retail customer	1,891	46	>40%	Y
Institutional - financial institutions	675	17	<25% or 1bn	Y
Interbank	301	7	<25% or 1bn	Y
Inter-Group (NET balance)	400	10	<25% or 1bn	Y
Other	20	0	<25% or 1bn	Y
Total liabilities	4,087			

Top 5 counterparties	Balance (€000,000's)	% Funding	Limit (%)
Commercial bank	491	12.0	10
Central bank ABC	227	5.5	10
Central bank XYZ	167	4.1	10
Defence office	129	3.2	10
State Bank	87	2.1	10
		26.9	

Figure 2.21 Funding source report

Figure 2.22   Sample inter-company lending report

Group treasury			
As at (date)	Total borrowing	Total lending	Net intergroup lending
London	1,713,280	883,133	−830,157
Paris	3,345,986	978,195	−2,367,617
Frankfurt	17,026	195,096	178,089
Dublin	453,490	83,420	−370,070
HK	0	162,000	162,000
NY	690,949	1,516,251	825,302

on the type, tenor, source and availability of funding, exercised in normal and stressed market conditions.[15]

This emphasis on liquidity is correct, and an example of a return to the roots of banking, when liquidity management was paramount. While capital ratios are a necessary part of bank risk management, they are not sufficient. Northern Rock and Bradford & Bingley were more a failure of liquidity management than capital erosion. Hence it is not surprising that there is now a strong focus on the extraneous considerations to funding.

However, the use of that funding within banks, including the price at which cash is internally lent or transferred to business lines, has not been as closely scrutinized by the FSA. This issue needs to be addressed by regulators because it is a driver of bank business models, which were shown to be flawed and based on inaccurate assumptions during 2007 and 2008.

2.9.1   An effective internal funding framework

While the FSA does touch on bank internal liquidity pricing,[16] the coverage is peripheral. This is unfortunate, because it is a key element driving a bank's business model. Essentially, the price at which an individual bank business line raises funding from its Treasury desk is a major parameter in business decision making, driving sales, asset allocation, and product pricing. It is also a key hurdle rate behind the product approval process and in an individual business line's performance measurement. Just as capital allocation decisions affecting front office business units need to account for the cost of that capital (in terms of return on regulatory and economic capital), so funding decisions exercised by corporate treasurers carry significant implications for sales and trading teams at the trade level.

In an ideal world, the price at which cash is internally transferred within a bank should reflect the true economic cost of that cash (at each maturity band), and its impact on overall bank liquidity. This would ensure that each business aligns the commercial propensity to maximize profit with the correct maturity profile of associated funding. From a liquidity point of view, any mismatch between the asset tenor and funding tenor, after taking into account the 'repo-ability' of each asset class in question, should be highlighted and acted upon as a matter of priority, with the objective to reduce recourse to short-term, passive funding as much as possible. Equally, it is important that the internal funding framework is transparent to all trading groups.

A measure of discipline in business decision-making is enforced via the imposition of minimum return-on-capital (ROC) targets. Independent of the internal cost of funds, a business line would ordinarily seek to ensure that any transaction it entered into achieved its targeted ROC. However, relying solely on this measure is not always sufficient discipline. For this to work, each business line should be set ROC levels that are commensurate with its (risk-adjusted) risk-reward profile. However, banks do not always set different target ROCs for each business line, which means that the required discipline breaks down. Second, a uniform cost of funds, even allowing for different ROCs, will mean that the different liquidity stresses created by different types of asset are not addressed adequately at the aggregate funding level.

For example, consider the following asset types:

- a 3-month interbank loan
- a 3-year floating rate corporate loan, fixing quarterly
- a 3-year floating-rate corporate loan, fixing weekly
- a 3-year fixed-rate loan
- a 10-year floating-rate corporate loan fixing monthly
- a 15-year floating-rate project finance loan fixing quarterly.

We have selected these asset types deliberately, to demonstrate the different liquidity pressures that each places on the Treasury funding desk (listed in increasing amount of funding rollover risk). Even allowing for different credit risk exposures and capital risk weights, the impact on the liability-funding desk is different for each asset. We see then the importance of applying a structurally sound transfer pricing policy, dependent on the type of business line being funded.

2.9.2 Cost of funds

As a key driver of the economic decision-making process, the cost at which funds are lent from central Treasury to the bank's businesses needs to be set at a rate that reflects the true liquidity risk position of each business line. If it is unrealistic, there is a risk that transactions are entered into that produce an unrealistic profit. This profit will reflect the artificial funding gain, rather than the true economic value-added of the business.

There is empirical evidence of the damage that can be caused by artificially low transfer pricing. In a paper from 2008, Adrian Blundell-Wignall and Paul Atkinson[17] discuss the losses at UBS AG in its structured credit business, which originated and invested in collateralized debt obligations (CDO). Quoting a UBS shareholder report,

> internal bid prices were always higher than the relevant London inter-bank bid rate (LIBID) and internal offer prices were always lower than relevant London inter-bank offered rate (LIBOR). (p. 97)

In other words, UBS structured credit business was able to fund itself at prices better than in the market (which is implicitly inter-bank risk), despite the fact that it was investing in assets of considerably lower liquidity (and credit quality) than inter-bank risk. There was no adjustment for tenor mismatch, to better align term funding to liquidity. A more realistic funding model was viewed as a 'constraint on the growth strategy'.

This lack of funding discipline undoubtedly played an important role in the decision-making process, because it allowed the desk to report inflated profits based on low funding costs. As a stand-alone business, a CDO investor would not expect to raise funds at sub-Libor, but rather at significantly over Libor. By receiving this artificial low pricing, the desk could report super profits and very high return-on-capital, which encouraged more and more risky investment decisions.

Another example involved banks that entered into the 'fund derivatives' business. This was lending to investors in hedge funds via a leveraged structured product. These instruments were illiquid, with maturities of two years or longer. Once dealt, they could not be unwound, thus creating significant liquidity stress for the lender. However, banks funded these business lines from central Treasury at Libor-flat, rolling short term. The liquidity problems that resulted became apparent during the 2007–2008 financial crisis, when inter-bank liquidity dried up.

Many banks operate on a similar model, with a fixed internal funding rate of Libor plus (say) 15 bps for all business lines, and for any tenor. But such an approach does not take into account the differing risk-reward and liquidity profiles of the businesses. The corporate lending desk will create different liquidity risk exposures for the bank compared to the CDO desk or the project finance desk. For the most efficient capital allocation, banks should adjust the basic internal transfer price for the resulting liquidity risk exposure of the business. Otherwise they run the risk of excessive risk-taking, heavily influenced by an artificial funding gain.

2.9.3 Business best practice

It is important that the regulatory authorities review the internal funding structure in place at the banks they supervise. An artificially low funding rate can create as much potentially unmanageable risk exposure as an risk-seeking loan origination culture. A regulatory requirement to impose a realistic internal funding arrangement will mitigate this risk. We recommend the following approach:

A fixed add-on spread over Libor for term loans or assets over a certain maturity, say one year, where the coupon re-fix is frequent (such as weekly or monthly), to compensate for the liquidity mismatch. The spread would be on a sliding scale for longer-term assets.

Internal funding discipline is as pertinent to bank risk management as capital buffers and effective liquidity management discipline. As banks adjust to the new liquidity requirements soon to be imposed by the FSA, it is worth looking beyond the literal scope of the new supervisory fiat to consider the internal determinants of an efficient, cost effective funding regime. In this way they can move towards the heart of this proposition, which is to embed true funding cost into business-line decision-making.

2.9.4 Funds transfer pricing policy: Liquidity premium framework

This policy framework has been introduced to better reflect the usage and provision of funds that flow through Treasury as a result of the business undertaken by the individual bank business lines ('SBUs'). It is meant to be reflective of market conditions and is separate to any Treasury margin that may be applied.

It is also a requirement of the UK FSA, under PS 09/16, that the cost of liquidity should be included as part of the internal pricing of funds within an entity. We refer to this internal funding rate as the 'transfer price' (TP).

TP does not in any way reflect credit spread or credit premium. It is a pure liquidity premium.

2.9.5 Scope

This policy applies to all interest-bearing assets and liabilities on the bank's balance sheet, effective from 1 January 2010 onwards. It includes

- All interest-bearing assets and liabilities that are 'live', that is, legacy transactions, as of 1 January 2010.
- The separate trading desks within Treasury.

- The gross cash flows of each SBU/Trading desk; as per existing transfer pricing rules for interest-rate risk, there is no netting allowed by the SBUs.
- Non–interest-bearing assets and liabilities are covered under a separate policy.

2.9.6   Framework

The TP policy applies equally to both sides of the balance sheet.

2.9.6.1   Assets

The framework for the pricing of assets is as follows:

- Libor will be used as the basis for funding as per existing transfer pricing rules.
- The final maturity date for assets is to be determined by reference to the shorter of economic life or legal maturity date; economic life, in the case of corporate lending/securities, is to be determined on a case by case basis, although legal maturity date is to be used as the default end point.
- This applies to legacy trades as set out under Scope in Section 2.
- The pricing framework has been set by Treasury and agreed by the bank's ALCO as below:

Period to Maturity	<6 mths	6 mths–12 mths	1 yr–5 yr	>5 yr
Assets	Libor	Libor + 4 bps	Libor + 8 bps	Libor + 12 bps

2.9.6.2   Liabilities

The proposed framework for the pricing of liabilities is as follows:

- Libor will be used as the basis for funding as per existing transfer pricing rules.
- The final maturity date for liabilities is to be determined by reference to the longer of economic life or final maturity date; economic life will be determined with reference to the stickiness rate allowed by the FSA under current reporting rules:

Corporate Deposits	50%
Retail Deposits	60%

- For the purposes of this framework, deposits that have had stickiness applied will be treated as having an economic life of 1yr–5yr. Stickiness is applied on a portfolio basis.
- This applies to legacy trades as set out under Scope in Section 2.

- The pricing framework has been set by Treasury and agreed by ALCO as below:

Period to Maturity	<6 mths	6 mths–12 mths	1 yr–5 yr	>5 yr
Liabilities	Libor	Libor + 4 bps	Libor + 8 bps	Libor + 12 bps

2.9.7   Implementation

2.9.7.1   Transitional arrangements

The implementation of this policy will take effect from 1 January 2010. It is not intended to phase the implementation process and therefore it will be applied to all existing interest-bearing assets and liabilities as of the effective date, that is, 1 January 2010.

It will not be possible to systemically capture the liquidity premium from 1 January 2010. A temporary process will be adopted to calculate the premium until such time as the systemic solution can be implemented. A working group will be established and tasked with ensuring that the premium is captured systemically as soon as possible in 2010.

The 2010 budget will be updated to reflect the impact of the liquidity framework.

2.9.7.2   Ongoing

On an ongoing basis

- ALCO is responsible for ensuring that this policy is maintained.
- A review of the pricing framework is to be undertaken by ALCO every six months.
- Pricing can be updated more frequently should market conditions require it.

2.9.8   Calculation methodology: The liquidity premium

The TP rate will be reviewed every six months to ensure that it is realistic to the market. There is no universal method to calculate the liquidity premium that should be added to the Libor funding cost. Approaches include the following:

- the difference between ASW and CDS of the banks (where this is negative) for each tenor maturity
- the difference between the funding spread over a bank of the same credit rating
- a subjective add-on based on what ALCO believes the bank will pay to raise longer-dated funds, separate to the credit risk perception of the bank.

2.10   Conclusion

In this chapter we considered the essential principles of bank asset-liability management, and the main tenets of bank liquidity risk management. The events of 2007 and 2008 served to reiterate the importance of sound ALM practice in banks. For this reason it is important that a bank's ALCO be set up as an effective management entity at every bank, empowered to ensure correct business practice for asset-liability management. The framework set out in this chapter can be viewed as the best-endeavours approach to the operation of the ALCO function at a bank.

Notes

1. In continental European banks, they appear to prefer retaining the term *mismatch* rather than gap.
2. This report is discussed in full in the case study later in the chapter.
3. The reasons can be macrolevel ones, affecting most or all market participants, or more firm or sector specific. The former might be a general market correction that causes the supply of funds to dry up, and would be a near-catastrophic situation. The latter is best illustrated with the example of Barings plc in 1995: when it went bust overnight due to large, hitherto covered-up losses on the Simex exchange, the supply of credit to similar institutions was reduced or charged at much higher rates, albeit only temporarily, as a result.
4. Such assets would be very short-term, risk-free assets, such as Treasury bills.
5. It can, of course, lock in future funding rates with forward-starting loans, which is one way to manage liquidity risk.
6. Of course the opposite also applies: the gap risk refers to an excess of liabilities over assets.
7. Note that this terminology is not a universal convention.
8. Many bank assets, such as residential mortgages and credit card loans, are repaid before their legal maturity date. Thus the size of the asset book is constantly amortizing.
9. The firm's capital will be invested in risk-free assets such as government Treasury bills or, in some cases, bank CDs. It will not be lent out in normal banking operations because the ALM desk will not want to put capital in a credit-risky investment.
10. In addition, the bank will be able to raise funds at LIBID, or at worst at Li-mid, while it should be able to lend at Libor in interbank credit quality assets.
11. The percentage breakdown that reflects senior management assumptions of the maturity profile of assets is an input into the ALM report.
12. New business will follow a long process of approval, typically involving all the relevant front-, middle- and back-office departments of the bank and culminating in a 'new products committee' meeting at which the proposed new line of business will be approved, sent back to the sponsoring department for modification or rejected.
13. For example, a bank may have the 'overnight' time bucket on its own, or incorporate it into an 'overnight to one-week' period. Similarly, banks may have each period from one month to 12 in their own separate buckets, or may place some periods into combined time periods. There is no 'correct' way.

14. This section is an extract from Chapter 5 of *Bank Asset and Liability Management*, written by Moorad Choudhry and published by John Wiley & Sons (Asia) Pte Lt in 2007. Reproduced with permission.
15. FSA, *Policy Statement 09/16*, October 2009.
16. See page 23, FSA CP 08/22, *Strengthening Liquidity Standards*, December 2008.
17. Blundell-Wignall, A., and Atkinson, P., *The Sub-Prime Crisis: Causal Distortions and Regulatory Reform*, Working Paper, OECD, July 2008.

3
A Two-Factor HJM Interest Rate Model for Use in Asset Liability Management

Sarp Kaya Acar, Ralf Korn, Kalina Natcheva-Acar and Jörg Wenzel

3.1 Managing interest rate risk: Choice of an appropriate interest rate model

3.1.1 Why use an interest rate model at all?

With regard to asset liability management (ALM), the future evolution of the interest rate market plays a major role. This is natural, as with a deterministic evolution of the interest rate (in fact, only in a deterministic setting we could speak of **the** interest rate!), interest rate risk would not play a role in ALM. However, as the main objective of ALM is to relate payments occurring at different times in a suitable way, especially when the time horizon is large, assuming a deterministic interest rate evolution is absolutely inappropriate. Thus, finding a good model for the evolution of the term structure of interest rates is one of the main obstacles to overcome for successful ALM.

Moreover, due to the volume of the trades related to various types of interest rates in banks, the interest rate risk plays a major role in the ALM of banks. For life insurance companies and pension funds, the interest risk is the major source of uncertainty of their ALM due to their typical investment strategies, while they can control the biometrical risk in a much better way. Furthermore, as the ALM of insurance companies also hinges on the reinvestment risk (there are no bonds covering the usual investment horizon of life insurance or pension-related products!), modeling the evolution of the future term structure of interest rates is, again, a most important issue.

Valuation of structured interest rate products and the simulation of their future prices as part of the whole portfolio also require the use of an interest rate model.

3.1.2   Which type of interest rate model to choose?

As there is not yet agreement on a standard reference model, the choice of a particular interest rate model (class) has to be a compromise between desirable theoretical aspects and practicability. We will not discuss possible model classes or aspects, but will concentrate on some popular models, particularly short rate models and LIBOR market models.

In the industry and in the literature of established short rate models, one can distinguish between one-factor short rate models (such as Vasicek, CIR, Black-Karasinski, Black-Derman-Toy, and so on), two-factor Hull-White type models (such as G2++ by Brigo and Mercurio; see Brigo and Mercurio (2006) also as a reference for most of the interest rate models mentioned in this article), and two-factor CIR++ models. Although one can think of models with more factors, we will limit ourselves to at most two-factor ones. A popular alternative derived from the class of forward rate models are the LIBOR market models (with/without stochastic volatility).

Important criteria for the choice among those models are

- a good explanation of observable market prices ('a good fit')
- the possibility to calibrate the model efficiently to the market
- the possibility of an efficient simulation of the evolution of the relevant interest rate
- the possibility of an efficient valuation of important interest rate products.

These criteria can be specified even further when the model should be flexible enough to deal with a wide variety of structured products:

1. The model should admit closed-form valuation formulae for caps/floors or swaptions (needed for a fast calibration).
2. The model should allow for a flexible numerical pricing of American and strongly path-dependent types of options.
3. The model should allow for a complex correlation structure between forward rates.

The one-factor short rate models fulfill the first two criteria but fail the last one, which leads to unsatisfactory calibration. On its turn, this often results in strong mispricing of volatility-sensitive claims (see Section 3.2.2.3).

The LIBOR market models satisfy the first and the last criteria, but are very cumbersome when pricing generic payoffs with both American/Bermudan options and path-dependence. Numerical methods such as the Longstaff and Schwarz algorithm for pricing American options with Monte Carlo simulation can be applied to Bermudan payoffs in this case, but they tend to be very slow when applied to American options.

The two-factor short rate models satisfy all the criteria. The Gaussian models produce short rates which could become negative with very small probability. The two-factor CIR++ model does not allow for negative rates but assumes the correlation between the factors to be zero in order to preserve some tractability. This limits the ability of the CIR++ model to fit swaption prices.

In the literature, there are at least two equivalent two-factor Gaussian models for the instantaneous short rate with perfect initial fit: the two-factor Hull White model (see Hull and White, 1994) and the G2++ model by Brigo and Mercurio (see Brigo and Mercurio, 2006). Both these models first specify time homogeneous two-factor short rate dynamics. Then, by adding a deterministic shift function $\varphi(\cdot)$ exact fit of the initial term structure of interest rates is obtained. However, the obtained results are rather clumsy and not intuitive, which means that special care has to be taken for their correct numerical implementation.

On the other side, as noted by Heath-Jarrow-Morton (1992, HJM), virtually any exogenous short rate model can be derived within the HJM framework by choosing the class of the forward rate volatilities. By starting within the HJM framework and limiting the forward rate volatility to a deterministic, exponentially decaying one, we derive another two-factor Gaussian short rate model which has a very simple and intuitive form. Moreover, by its construction the model has a perfect fit of the initial term structure. Additionally, the dynamics of the underlying factors under the forward risk-neutral measure is a very simple one, which facilitates the derivation of closed-form solutions. We call this construction the HJM−G2++ model due to its similarity to the G2++ model of Brigo and Mercurio.

3.2   The HJM−G2++ model

In this section, we set up the HJM−G2++ model and present closed-form expressions for the prices of the standard options needed for calibration purposes (caps, floors, bond options and swaptions). Further, we calibrate the model parameters to at-the-money (ATM) caps market volatilities and ATM swaption volatility surfaces and comment on the ability of the model to fit real market data. For derivations and proofs we refer to Acar and Natcheva-Acar (2009).

3.2.1   Definition of the HJM−G2++ model

We consider a two-factor HJM model with deterministic volatility given by

$$\sigma(t,T) = \sigma_1 e^{-\kappa_1(T-t)} + \sigma_2 e^{-\kappa_2(T-t)}$$

with $\kappa_i \in \mathbb{R}^+$, $\kappa_i \neq 0$, $\sigma_i \in \mathbb{R}^+$, $i = 1,2$. Then, following Cheyette (see Cheyette and Markov, 1996), the forward rate equation with the so-defined volatility can be written as

$$f(t,T) = f(0,T) + \sum_{i=1}^{2} e^{-\kappa_i(T-t)} \left[X_i(t) + \sum_{k=1}^{2} b_k(t,T) Z_{ik}(0,t) \right] \tag{3.1}$$

for state variables $X_1(t)$ and $X_2(t)$,

$$b_1(t,T) = \frac{1 - e^{-\kappa_1(T-t)}}{\kappa_1}, \quad b_2(t,T) = \frac{1 - e^{-\kappa_2(T-t)}}{\kappa_2},$$

and cumulative quadratic variation that is defined as

$$Z_{11}(u,t) = \int_u^t cov(X_1(s), X_1(s)) ds = \int_u^t \sigma_1^2 e^{-2\kappa_1(t-s)} ds = \frac{\sigma_1^2 (1 - e^{-2\kappa_1(t-u)})}{2\kappa_1}$$

$$Z_{12}(u,t) = \int_u^t cov(X_1(s), X_2(s)) ds = Z_{21}(u,t) = \frac{\rho \sigma_1 \sigma_2}{\kappa_1 + \kappa_2} \left(1 - e^{-(\kappa_1 + \kappa_2)(t-u)} \right)$$

$$Z_{22}(u,t) = \int_u^t cov(X_2(s), X_2(s)) ds = \int_u^t \sigma_2^2 e^{-2\kappa_2(t-s)} ds = \frac{\sigma_2^2 (1 - e^{-\kappa_2(t-u)})}{2\kappa_2}.$$

The state variables $X_1(t)$ and $X_2(t)$ are defined under an equivalent martingale measure Q as

$$dX_1(t) = \left(-\kappa_1 X_1(t) + \sum_{k=1}^{2} Z_{1,k}(0,t) \right) dt + \sigma_1 d\tilde{W}_1^Q(t), \quad X_1(0) = 0 \tag{3.2}$$

$$dX_2(t) = \left(-\kappa_2 X_2(t) + \sum_{k=1}^{2} Z_{2,k}(0,t) \right) dt + \sigma_2 d\tilde{W}_2^Q(t), \quad X_2(0) = 0 \tag{3.3}$$

with correlation $d\langle \tilde{W}^1, \tilde{W}^2 \rangle_t = \rho dt$ (see Cheyette and Markov, 1996). By $r(t) = f(t,t)$, the short rate is thus of the form

$$r(t) = f(0,t) + X_1(t) + X_2(t). \tag{3.4}$$

The price of a zero coupon bond $P(t,T)$ at time t can easily be calculated via

$$P(t,T) = E\left(e^{-\int_t^T r(s)ds} \,|\, F_t \right) = e^{-\int_t^T f(t,u)du}$$

$$= \frac{P(0,T)}{P(0,t)} \exp(-b_1(t,T)X_1(t) - b_2(t,T)X_2(t) - \frac{1}{2} \sum_{i,j=1}^{2} b_i(t,T) b_j(t,T) Z_{ij}(0,t)).$$

3.2.2 Closed-form solutions and parameter calibration

3.2.2.1 Caplet and swaption formulas

The two important building blocks for an efficient parameter calibration are the closed pricing formula for a caplet and the semi-closed formula for a swaption in our model (see Brigo and Mercurio, 2006 for the caplet and Acar and Natcheva-Acar, 2009 for the swaption case).

Theorem 3.1 (the price of a caplet) *Using the short rate dynamics of Equation (3.4), the price* **Caplet**(*t,T,S,K*) *at time t of a* **caplet** *resetting at time T > t, with payoff at time S > T and strike K is calculated to*

$$
\mathbf{Caplet}(t,T,S,K) = P(t,T)\Phi\left(\frac{ln\left(\dfrac{K^{*}\,P(t,T)}{P(t,S)}\right) + \dfrac{1}{2}\Sigma^{2}(t,T,S)}{\Sigma(t,T,S)}\right)
$$

$$
-\frac{1}{K^{*}}P(t,S)\Phi\left(\frac{ln\left(\dfrac{K^{*}\,P(t,T)}{P(t,S)}\right) - \dfrac{1}{2}\Sigma^{2}(t,T,S)}{\Sigma(t,T,S)}\right)
$$

with $K^{*} = \dfrac{1}{1 + K(S-T)}$, $\Phi(\cdot)$ denoting the cumulative standard normal distribution function and

$$
\Sigma^{2}(t,T,S) := b_{1}(T,S)^{2}Z_{11}(t,T) + b_{2}(T,S)^{2}Z_{22}(t,T) + 2b_{1}(T,S)b_{2}(T,S)Z_{12}(t,T).
$$

Theorem 3.2 (the price of a swaption) *Consider a European option, giving the right at time $t_{0} = T$ (maturity) to enter an interest rate swap with payment times $T = \{t_{1},...,t_{n}\}$ (reset times $\{t_{0},...,t_{n-1}\}$), fixed leg rate X and notional N. Let further $\tau_{i} = t_{i} - t_{i-1}$. Then, the arbitrage-free price at time 0 of a European payer swaption is then given by*

$$
ES_{p}(0) = N \cdot P(0,T)\frac{1}{\sqrt{2\pi z_{11}}} \int_{-\infty}^{+\infty} \exp\left(\frac{-x^{2}}{2z_{11}}\right)
$$

$$
\left(\Phi(-h_{0}(x,y)) - \sum_{i=1}^{n}\lambda_{i}(x)\Phi(-h_{i}(x,y))\right)dx. \tag{3.5}
$$

Here, we have used

$$\lambda_i(x) := c_i A_i \exp\left(-b_1(T,t_i)x - b_2(T,t_i)\frac{z_{12}}{z_{11}}x + \frac{b_2(T,t_i)^2}{2}\frac{z_{22}}{z_{11}}\kappa^2 \right),$$

$$h_0(x,y) := \frac{yz_{11} - xz_{12}}{\sqrt{z_{11}}\kappa}, \qquad h_i(x,y) := h_0(x,y) + \frac{b_2(T,t_i)}{\sqrt{z_{11}}}\kappa,$$

and $y = y(x)$ denotes the unique solution of the equation

$$\sum_{i=1}^{n} c_i A_i \exp(-b_1(T,t_i)x - b_2(T,t_i)y) = 1. \tag{3.6}$$

Moreover, the following abbreviations are used:

$$\kappa := \sqrt{z_{11}z_{22} - z_{12}^2},$$
$$c_i := X\tau_i, \quad i = 1,\dots,n-1, \quad c_n := 1 + X\tau_n,$$
$$A_i := \exp\left(-\int_T^{t_i} f(0,u)du - \frac{1}{2}\Sigma(0,T,t_i) \right),$$
$$Z_{kl} := Z_{kl}(0,T).$$

A similar formula holds for the receiver swaption.

3.2.2.2 *Implementation of the swaption semi-closed-form formula*

In this section, we shall devote some attention to the implementation of the semi-closed formula for the payer (respectively receiver) swaption price given by Equation 3.5, since it requires numerical procedures of root finding and integration.

To do this, the integral in Equation 3.5 is computed numerically. After intensive tests (see Table 3.1) we have chosen the 20-point Gaussian quadrature rule,

$$\int_{-\infty}^{\infty} g(x)dx \approx \sum_{j=0}^{19} w_j g(x_j)$$

where the weights and abscissas are set according to the Gauss-Legendre polynomials (see Press et al., 2002). The limits of the integration are set observing that the integrand in formula 3.5 is actually a bounded function against a normal distribution (see Figure 3.1). Hence, one can truncate the domain of integration to the interval $\lfloor \mu_{x_1} - N\sigma_{x_1}, \mu_{x_1} + N\sigma_{x_1} \rfloor$, where $N \in \mathbf{N}$.

Since the precision of the integral approximation is affected by the integral bounds, by keeping in mind that the integrand is monotone at the left and right wings, we have chosen the constant N adaptively, according to the following algorithm.

Table 3.1   Comparison of the sum of squared errors of the swaption surface calculated by different numbers of Gauss-Legendre polynomials (rows) and different precisions of the root-finding algorithm (columns)

	$10e^{-05}$	$10e^{-07}$	$10e^{-09}$	$10e^{-11}$
10	0.023053435634 00:00:01.79	0.023053435640 00:00:02.34	0.023053435634 00:00:02.90	0.023053435634 00:00:03.46
20	0.023073833332 00:00:02.48	0.023073766462 00:00:03.26	0.023073766455 00:00:04.04	0.023073766455 00:00:04.82
30	0.023073835520 00:00:03.17	0.023073766434 00:00:04.20	0.023073766427 00:00:05.21	0.023073766427 00:00:06.25
40	0.023073834632 00:00:03.87	0.023073766434 00:00:05.15	0.023073766427 00:00:06.39	0.023073766427 00:00:08.18

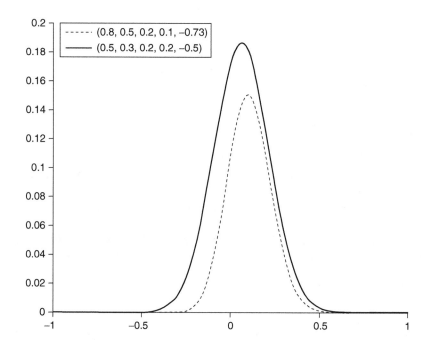

Figure 3.1   Plot of the integrand

Plot of the integrand in formula 3.5 for a 1Y-swaption with an underlying 1Y swap and the underlying process has the parameters ($\kappa_1 = 0.8$, $\kappa_2 = 0.5$, $\sigma_1 = 0.2$, $\sigma_2 = 0.1$, $\rho = -0.73$), ($\kappa_1 = 0.5$, $\kappa_2 = 0.3$, $\sigma_1 = 0.2$, $\sigma_2 = 0.2$, $\rho = -0.5$).

Compute lower and upper bounds for $N=1$: $l = -N\sigma_{x_1}$, $u = N\sigma_{x_1}$
Compute the integrand at l and u
If *Integrand(l)* $< 10^{-8}$, set lower bound as l. Else increase N and go to step 1.
If *Integrand(u)* $< 10^{-8}$, set lower bound as u. Else increase N and go to step 1.

Now, let us consider Equation 3.6. We have to find the root of this equation. First, we bracket the root in an interval $[x_2^l, x_2^r]$ and then use a hybrid root-finding algorithm, which is a combination of Newton-Raphson and bisection algorithms. The numerical procedures that we used can be found in Press et al., 2002.[1] The precision for the root-finding algorithm is set to be 10^{-7} (see Table 3.1).

Looking at Table 3.1, one can observe a trade-off between the precision of the results and computing time. As a reasonable trade-off, we have chosen the **20-point Gauss-Legendre** and **precision 10^{-7} for the root-finding algorithm.**

3.2.2.3 Some notes on the calibration results

A few words are due on the calibration properties of the offered model. The standard products to which the parameters of the short rate model are calibrated are caps/floors and swaptions. As far as the caps and floors are concerned, it is important to note (see, for example, Brigo and Mercurio (2006) for a detailed explanation) that the correlation between the forward LIBOR rates plays no role in the closed-form solution, and thus typically a one-factor model should be used. This also reflects our observation of obtained calibrated correlation coefficients of around 96%−98%. However, in the case of a strongly humped curve, as in the times of the credit crunch, a two-factor model produced a better fit due to five parameters it uses for the calibration (see Tables 3.2 and 3.3).

Concerning the calibration to swaption data, it is a well-known fact that a model with two or more stochastic factors allows for a more general form for the correlation between the forward LIBOR rates. In turn, the correlation between the forward rates plays a role in the swaption closed-form solution

Table 3.2 Fitted ATM cap/floor volatilities using Hull-White Vasicek model and data from 6 August 2008

Maturity	Market volatility	Model volatility	Rel. perc. error (%)	Abs. error
1y	13.1	16.22	−3.82	3.12
2y	19.3	18.00	−6.72	1.30
3y	19.4	17.69	−8.79	1.71
4y	18.5	17.40	−5.95	1.10
5y	17.8	17.13	−3.74	0.67
6y	17.15	16.82	−1.93	0.33
7y	16.58	16.49	−0.52	0.09
8y	16.02	16.15	0.80	0.13
9y	15.52	15.79	1.71	0.26
10y	15.02	15.42	2.69	0.40
12y	14.8	14.73	−0.47	0.07
15y	13.9	13.91	0.08	0.01
20y	13.1	13.04	0.42	0.06

The market and model volatilities and abs. errors are given in percentages.

Table 3.3 Fitted ATM cap/floor volatilities using 2FHW and data from 6 August 2008

Maturity	Market volatility	Model volatility	Rel. perc. error (%)	Abs. Error
1y	13.1	19.57	49.35	6.46
2y	19.3	20.21	4.69	0.91
3y	19.4	19.12	−1.44	0.28
4y	18.5	18.25	−1.34	0.25
5y	17.8	17.59	−1.18	0.21
6y	17.15	17.01	−0.80	0.14
7y	16.58	16.52	−0.37	0.06
8y	16.02	16.07	0.33	0.05
9y	15.52	15.66	0.90	0.14
10y	15.02	15.28	1.73	0.26
12y	14.8	14.61	−1.31	0.19
15y	13.9	13.86	−0.27	0.04
20y	13.1	13.12	0.17	0.02

The market and model volatilities and abs. errors are given in percentages.

and logically leads to the conclusion that a two- or multi-factor model is more suitable for fitting swaption prices.

In these points we notice that both one- and two-factor Gaussian models are able to produce a slight smile for both cases of fixed swaption maturity and changing the swap maturities, and for a fixed swap maturity and changing the swaption maturity. The limitation of both the one- and two-factor Gaussian model is that the smile they produce is too slight to match the hump of the market data, especially the one for short swaption maturities. When the surface is well behaved or smoothed, the models are able to fit the data well. As soon as we try to fit an irregular swaption volatility surface, for example, one with multiple humps, the Gaussian models fail to fit it in a sufficient way.

After calibrating several surfaces we observed that the HJM−G2++ model always outperforms the Hull-White Vasicek model. It is also able to reproduce a more pronounced smile in the implied volatilities than a one-factor Vasicek model. A limitation of both models is that they cannot reproduce two peaks in the implied volatilities as well as a very sharp one, as the one in the short maturities ATM caps/floor volatilities and the ATM swaption volatility. For several calibration results see Figures 3.2 and 3.3.

3.2.3 Numerical pricing methods for general products

Having now calibrated all the necessary input parameters, we can turn to the task of pricing more general (structured) products with no closed-form valuation formula. For that purpose, in our HJM−G2++ framework we offer a Monte Carlo simulation scheme and a lattice approximation with a construction

a

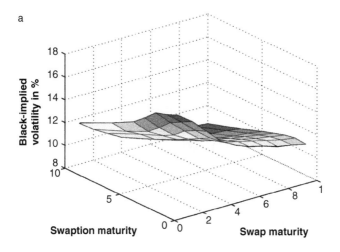

b

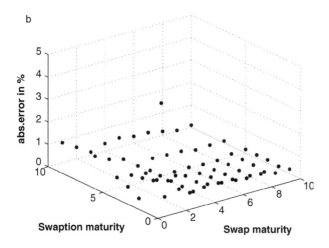

Figure 3.2 Swaption market data and swaption calibration error from 13 March 2001

similar to the one of Li, Ritchken and Sankarasubramanian Li, Ritchken and Sankarasubramanian (1954).

While the Monte Carlo approach is straightforward (but can, of course, make use of the usual variance reduction techniques), the construction of the two-dimensional pricing tree is more involved. The details of setting it up can be found in Acar and Natcheva-Acar (2009).

a

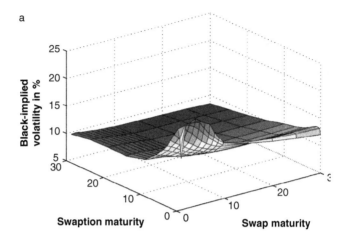

b

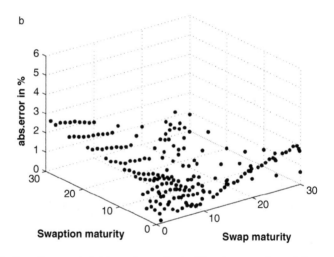

Figure 3.3   Swaption market data and swaption calibration error from 6 August 2008

3.3   Examples of interest rate products used in ALM

In this section, we describe some interest rate products commonly used by insurance companies with their ALM strategy. These products share the feature that the actual nominal value increases over time, thus making the products particularly sensitive to interest rate changes. In particular, this implies a high sensitivity to volatility and to credit spreads of the debitor. Moreover, these products are usually very long running.

3.3.1 Multitranche products

This type of product includes the right for the debitor to offer further tranches of a product with the same features as the mother tranche typically at multiple future times. Through this feature, the leverage of the creditor increases dramatically.

3.3.2 Accruing products

In this type of product, the coupons (fixed or floating) are not paid out during the lifetime of the product, but at the end, together with the nominal. If the coupon is fixed, this can be seen as a zero coupon bond with nominal equal to the initial nominal plus the accrued interest. For a floating accruing bond, however, the nominal is usually the nominal at inception and increases over time.

3.3.3 Steepener

In times of low interest rates the prospect of steepening yield curves leads to a high popularity of leveraged Steepener products. A CMS steepener pays coupons based on the difference between two CMS rates. The coupons of such a structure depend on the slope of the yield curve. The steeper the yield curve, the greater the coupon.

3.3.4 Structured products prices: One- vs. two-factor models

Nowadays structured interest rate products are becoming more and more important for the investment, risk management, and ALM of both banks and insurance companies. To price them and to simulate their price evolution in an ALM study one needs an interest rate model that should allow for an efficient valuation of those products.

To demonstrate the differences in valuation and calibration between a one- and a two-factor model, we will use a steepener as an example. The product under consideration pays the difference between the 30- and 1-year CMS rate multiplied by a leverage of 30. Starting in 2008 and running over 20 years, the steepener is capped at 12% and floored at 0%.

Valuing the steepener on 9 February 2010, we get a price of 118.55% with the two-factor Hull-White model, compared to 122.97% with the one-factor model. The difference becomes even more pronounced if one looks at the values of the cap and floor.

For the two-factor model, the cap's value is 150.52%, compared to 155.73% for the one-factor model. The floor's value is 127.01% for the two-factor model, while the one-factor model only gives a floor price of 103.53%.

Even though one can argue whether the two-factor Hull-White model is appropriate at all for valuing a steepener, it becomes clear that it can better fit a volatility smile and thus yield more reliable pricing.

3.4   Generic pricing of CMS/Libor structured products

Although it might look like a tremendous task, building up an own valuation framework for interest rate products pays out as it results in independence from black box software. Furthermore, own software allows enlargement when new products enter the scene. However, there has to be a good concept for its development and implementation. We will cover how to combine this with the HJM−G2++ model framework.

The pricing of a wide variety of structured interest rate notes can be done efficiently via the development of a generic pricing tool for the most common CMS/Libor-dependent products. It is one of our main aims to describe the construction and the use of such a tool.

The first essential part of a generic framework has already been dealt with – the possibility of efficiently calibrating the necessary input parameters from a given term structure. This has been ensured by the (semi-)closed pricing formulae for bonds, call, caps, and swaptions.

The next step is to set up a concept that allows for a generic description of the interest rate products that should be priced. Such a description has to cope with at least the following features:

Fixed coupon payments defined as $f\% \times Notional$ at payment times $T_1,...,T_k$
Floating coupon payments with a generic structure at coupon payment times $T_{k+1},...,T_n$. The fixing of the floating coupons should be allowed to be **'in advance'** or **'in arrear'.**
Call feature at $c\% \times Notional$ and **Put feature** at $p\% \times Notional$.

Here, we suggest a general coupon structure for the coupon times $T_{k+1},...,T_n$ such as a capped and floored linear combination $(c_1 u_1^j + c_2 u_2^j + c_3)$ of two underlying interest rates, x_1^j and x_2^j, fixed at t_{j-1} (in advance) or t_j (in arrears). We also allow for a digital part paying a linear combination of the two underlying interest rates $(p_1 x_1^j + p_2 x_2^j + p_3)$ if another linear combination of the underlying interest rates is below a barrier $(l_1 x_1 + l_2 x_2 \leq l_3)$ and the same for an upper barrier. Formally, the payoff can thus be written as

$$coupon_j = linear \ payoff_j + digital \ payoff_j, \tag{3.7}$$

with

$$linear \ payoff_j = \max(cap, \min(floor, c_1 u_1^j + c_2 u_2^j + c_3)),$$

$$digital \ payoff_j = (p_1 x_1^j + p_2 x_2^j + p_3) \cdot 1 \ \ 1_{l_1 x_1 + l_2 x_2 \leq l_3} + (q_1 x_1^j + q_2 x_2^j + q_3) \cdot 1 \ \ 1_{u_1 x_1 + u_2 x_2 \leq u_3}.$$

Note that the interest rates u_1^j and u_2^j can be any CMS or LIBOR rates.

To demonstrate how to use this generic formulation, we give the following example of a floored **CMS Steepener** with leverage M and base margin m:

$$Floating\ coupon = M \cdot \max\left(CMS_k - CMS_l + m, 0\right) \tag{3.8}$$

where we have **no digital part** and

$$x_1^j = CMS_x, \quad x_2^j = CMS_y,$$
$$c_1 = M, \quad c_2 = -M, \quad c_3 = mM,$$
$$Floor = 0, \quad Cap = \infty.$$

Using this general description of the floating coupons, we have developed a Generic Pricing Tool which in addition allows a flexible call/put structure. The tool can price a wide variety of Libor/CMS-structured notes based on the HJM−G2++ model. In addition, the model parameters are calibrated to the actual market data of cap/floor prices and ATM swaption prices. The extension of the Generic Pricing Tool for the pricing of products with new (not described above) features or path-dependent products is straightforward due to the flexibility of the applied numerical algorithms (lattices).

3.5   Conclusion

In this chapter, we presented a new class of a two-factor Gaussian short rate model that has an intuitive form of the forward rate volatility, allows for closed formulae for the price of the most liquid standard products (and thus for an efficient calibration of the input parameters), and offers an easy way to value more exotic structured products via Monte Carlo or via tree methods.

Furthermore, we suggested a generic framework for an interest rate product pricer based on the new HJM−G2++ model. Such a pricer can be implemented in a modular way and would greatly enhance the tool box of a company for performing ALM analyses.

Notes

The authors thank the Rheinland-Pfalz Research Center (CM)^2 for support .

1. Bracketing algorithm (zbrac) is on page 356 and root-finding algorithm (rtsafe) is on page 370.

References

Acar, S. K., and K. Natcheva-Acar. 'A guide on the implementation of the Heath-Jarrow-Morton Two Factor Gaussian Short Rate Model (HJM-G2++)'. *Berichte des Fraunhofer ITWM*, (170), 2009.

Brigo, D., and F. Mercurio, *Interest Rate Models – Theory and Practice*. Springer-Verlag, Berlin, Second edition, 2006. With smile, inflation and credit.

Cheyette, O., and Markov. 'Representation of the Heath-Jarrow-Morton Model'. Presented at the UCLA Workshop on the Future of Fixed Income Financial Theory, 1996.

Hull, J. C., and A. White. 'Numerical procedures for implementing term structure models II: two-factor models'. *The Journal of Derivatives*, 2:37–47, 1994.

Li., A., P. Ritchken. and L. Sankarasubramanian. 'Lattice models for pricing American interest rate claims'. *The Journal of Finance*, 50(2):719–737, 1954.

Press, W. H., S. A. Teukolsky, W. T. Vetterling, and B. P. Flannery. *Numerical Recipes in C++*. Cambridge University Press, Cambridge, Second edition , 2002.

Part II
ALM Models Applied to Insurance Companies

4
Long-Term Interest Rates and Consol Bond Valuation

Michael Dempster, Elena Medova and Michael Villaverde

4.1 Introduction

The literature in the area of interest rate modelling is extensive. Traditional term structure models, such as Vasicek (1977) and Cox *et al* (1985) specify the short rate process. As short-term and long-term rates are not perfectly correlated, the data are clearly inconsistent with the use of one-factor time-homogeneous models. Chan *et al* (1992) demonstrate the empirical difficulties of one-factor continuous-time specifications within the Vasicek and Cox-Ingersoll-Ross (CIR) class of models using the generalized methods of moments.

Litterman and Scheinkman (1991) find that 96 per cent of the variability of the returns of any risk-free zero-coupon bond can be explained by three factors: the *level, steepness* and *curvature* of the yield curve. They also point out that the 'correct model' of the term structure may involve unobservable factors. For instance, it is widely believed that changes in the Federal Reserve policy are a major source of changes in the shape of the US yield curve. Even though the Federal Reserve policy is itself observable, it is not clear how to measure its effect on the yield curve. Litterman and Scheinkman (1991) themselves used unobservable factors in their approach by applying principal component analysis.

Most term-structure models, such as those of Ho and Lee (1986), Hull and White (1990) and Heath *et al* (1992), are specified using the risk-neutral measure corresponding to a complete market. This makes them appropriate for relative-pricing applications, but inappropriate for forward simulations, which needs to take place under the market measure in an incomplete market. An exception is Rebonato *et al* (2005) who focus on yield curve evolution under the market measure and present a semi-parametric method to explain the yield curve evolution. Ho and Lee (1986) and Heath *et al* (1992) introduced a new approach to interest rate modelling in which they fit the initial term structure exactly. Duffie and Kan (1996) developed a general theory for multifactor affine versions of these models with coefficients obtained analytically. The book by James and Webber (2000) gives a comprehensive summary of development to 2000. See also Brigo and Mercurio (2007) and Wu (2009) for more recent summaries.

In spite of significant theoretical achievements, there are still difficulties with the long-term forecasting of future yields. The affine arbitrage-free version of the Nelson-Siegel (1987) model by Christensen *et al* (2007) investigates the gap between the theoretically rigorous risk-neutral models used for pricing and the empirical tractability required by econometricians for forecasting and offers some improvements in forecasting performance.

In our research, we focus on the development of a model that allows simulation of long-term scenarios for the yield curve, which include the market prices of risk in the dynamics (Medova *et al*, 2006). Historically low interest rates in recent years have emphasized the importance of accurately valuing long-term guarantees (Wilkie *et al*, 2004; Dempster *et al*, 2006). The asset liability management of funds behind the guaranteed return products offered by pension providers must be based on yield curve modelling (Dempster *et al*, 2007, 2009). Banks also face new pricing challenges because of the increased demand for long-maturity derivatives to hedge insurance and pension liabilities (for liability-driven investment) and therefore require good long-term interest rate models.

Figure 4.1 shows the development over time of short- and long-term interest rates in the Eurozone for the period 1997–2002. Figure 4.2 plots the weekly standard deviations of the yields over the same period.

In this article, we focus on a term structure model with the following characteristics:

• The model is set in a continuous-time framework. This allows implementation in discrete time with any length of time step Δt without the need to construct a new model each time we change Δt. This is an important requirement for the flexibility of forward simulations.
• Interest-rate dynamics are consistent with what we observe in historical data.
• The affine class model has a closed-form solution for bond pricing, permitting straightforward analytical calculation of bond prices in forward simulation.
• The short rate is mean-reverting.
• The model permits a tractable method of estimation and calibration.
• The model is flexible enough to give rise to a range of different yield curve shapes and dynamics (steepening, flattening, yield curve inversion and so on).

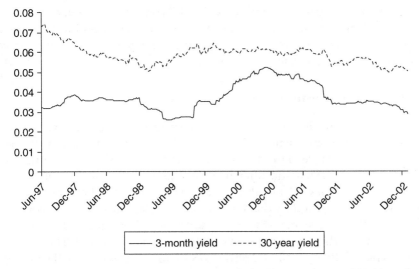

Figure 4.1 Three-month and thirty-year EU yields for the period June 1997–December 2002

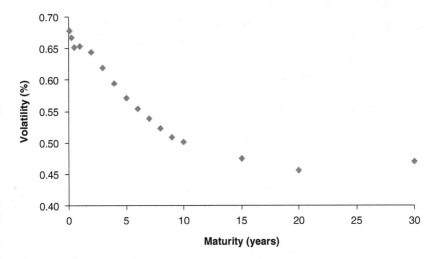

Figure 4.2 Weekly standard deviation of yields for the period June 1997–December 2002

The remainder of the article is structured as follows. In the next section, the three-factor Gaussian term structure model is introduced and a closed-form solution for bond prices is derived. The section after that discusses the state-space formulation of the model and the estimation of its parameters using the Kalman filter and numerical likelihood maximization. The data and empirical analyses, focussing on fitting the data as well as on the simulation potential of the model, are presented in the subsequent section. The penultimate section applies the three-factor model to the pricing of a representative consol bond and the final section concludes the article.

4.2   Three-factor term structure model

The term structure model presented in this article is driven by three factors and can be viewed as an extension to the generalized Vasicek model of Langetieg (1980), which includes a third factor. The first two factors[1] X and Y satisfy the standard Vasicek stochastic differential equations with *mean reversion rates* λX and λY and *levels* $\mu X/\lambda X$ and $\mu Y/\lambda Y$, respectively. The innovation of our model is in the treatment of the instantaneous short rate **R**. The mean reversion of **R** with rate k has a level that is *stochastic* rather than deterministic and depends on the level of the other two factors **X** and **Y** driving the model. The **X** and **Y** factors may be interpreted, respectively, as a long rate and (minus) the slope of the yield curve from a perceived (instantaneous) short rate **R*:=X+Y**.

4.2.1   Risk-neutral measure

Starting from the formulation of the model under the risk-neutral measure Q, we have the following three stochastic differential equations (SDEs) for the factors

$$dX_t = (\mu_X - \lambda_X X_t)dt + \sigma_X d\tilde{W}_t^X, \tag{4.1}$$

$$dY_t = (\mu_Y - \lambda_Y Y_t)dt + \sigma_Y d\tilde{W}_t^Y, \tag{4.2}$$

$$dR_t = k(X_t + Y_t - R_t)dt + \sigma_R d\tilde{W}_t^R, \tag{4.3}$$

where the dW terms are correlated. Factoring the covariance matrix of the dW terms using a Cholesky decomposition into the product of a transposed upper and a lower triangular square root matrix results in a new formulation of the form

$$dX_t = (\mu_X - \lambda_X X_t)dt + \sum_{i=1}^{3} \sigma_{X_i} dZ_t^i, \tag{4.4}$$

$$dY_t = (\mu_Y - \lambda_Y Y_t)dt + \sum_{i=1}^{3} \sigma_{Y_i} dZ_t^i, \tag{4.5}$$

$$dR_t = k(X_t + Y_t - R_t)dt + \sum_{i=1}^{3} \sigma_{R_i} dZ_t^i, \tag{4.6}$$

where the dZ terms are uncorrelated.

4.2.2 Closed-form solution

The solution follows the usual steps. We first solve the SDEs for X, Y and R to obtain the price of a zero-coupon bond at time t paying 1 at time T

$$P(t,T) = \mathbb{E}_t^Q \left\{ \exp\left(-\int_t^T R_s \, ds \right) \right\}, \tag{4.7}$$

where $\mathbb{E}_t^Q$ denotes the expectation under the risk-neutral measure Q conditional on the information at time t. As R_s is normally distributed in our model, we can use the moment-generating function for the normal distribution to rewrite (4.7) as

$$P(t,T) = \exp\left\{ \mathbb{E}_t^Q \left(-\int_t^T R_s \, ds \right) + \frac{1}{2} \mathrm{var}_t^Q \left(-\int_t^T R_s \, ds \right) \right\}, \tag{4.8}$$

where var_t^Q denotes the conditional variance under Q. Integrating the solution of the SDE for R and taking the expectation and variance of the result gives expressions for the two terms in (4.8) involving (to simplify notation) the parameters

$$m_{X_i} := -\frac{k\sigma_{X_i}}{\lambda_X(k - \lambda_X)},$$
$$m_{Y_i} := -\frac{k\sigma_{Y_i}}{\lambda_Y(k - \lambda_Y)},$$
$$n_i := \frac{\sigma_{X_i}}{k - \lambda_X} + \frac{\sigma_{Y_i}}{k - \lambda_Y} - \frac{\sigma_{R_i}}{k},$$
$$p_i := -(m_{X_i} + m_{Y_i} + n_i). \tag{4.9}$$

Hence (see for example, Medova *et al*, 2006),

$$P(t,T) = e^{-\gamma_{t,T}(T-t)}$$
$$= \exp\{ -A(t,T)R_t - B(t,T)X_t - C(t,T)Y_t - D(t,T) \} \tag{4.10}$$

with corresponding yield to maturity

$$y_{t,T} = \frac{A(t,T)R_t + B(t,T)X_t + C(t,T)Y_t + D(t,T)}{T - t}, \tag{4.11}$$

where

$$A(t,T) = \frac{1}{k}(1 - e^{-k(T-t)}), \tag{4.12}$$

$$B(t,T) = \frac{k}{k-\lambda_X}\left\{\frac{1}{\lambda_X}(1 - e^{-\lambda_X(T-t)}) - \frac{1}{k}(1 - e^{-k(T-t)})\right\}, \tag{4.13}$$

$$C(t,T) = \frac{k}{k-\lambda_Y}\left\{\frac{1}{\lambda_Y}(1 - e^{-\lambda_Y(T-t)}) - \frac{1}{k}(1 - e^{-k(T-t)})\right\}, \tag{4.14}$$

$$
\begin{aligned}
D(t,T) = {} & \left(T - t - \frac{1}{k}(1 - e^{-kT})\right)\left(\frac{\mu_X}{\lambda_X} + \frac{\mu_Y}{\lambda_Y}\right) - \frac{\mu_X}{\lambda_X}B(t,T) - \frac{\mu_Y}{\lambda_Y}C(t,T) \\
& - \frac{1}{2}\sum_{i=1}^{3}\left\{\frac{m_{X_i}^2}{2\lambda_X}(1 - e^{-2\lambda_X(T-t)}) + \frac{m_{Y_i}^2}{2\lambda_Y}(1 - e^{-2\lambda_Y(T-t)})\right. \\
& + \frac{n_i^2}{2k}(1 - e^{-2k(T-t)}) + p_i^2(T-t) + \frac{2m_{X_i}m_{Y_i}}{\lambda_X+\lambda_Y}(1 - e^{-(\lambda_X+\lambda_Y)(T-t)}) \\
& + \frac{2m_{X_i}n_i}{\lambda_X+k}(1 - e^{-(\lambda_X+\kappa)(T-t)}) + \frac{2m_{X_i}p_i}{\lambda_X}(1 - e^{-\lambda_X(T-t)}) \\
& + \frac{2m_{Y_i}n_i}{\lambda_Y+k}(1 - e^{-(\lambda_Y+\kappa)(T-t)}) + \frac{2m_{Y_i}p_i}{\lambda_Y}(1 - e^{-\lambda_Y(T-t)}) \\
& \left. + \frac{2n_ip_i}{k}(1 - e^{-k(T-t)})\right\}.
\end{aligned}
\tag{4.15}
$$

4.2.3   Market measure

Bond pricing is achieved under the *risk-neutral* measure Q. However, for the model to be used for forward simulations, we need to adjust the set of SDEs so that we capture the model dynamics under the *market* (or real-world) measure P by adding a *risk premium* to each drift term. The risk premium is given by the *market price of risk* γ times the quantity of risk, and it is generally assumed in a Gaussian specification that the quantity of risk is given by the *volatility* of each factor. We assume that the market prices of risk are independent of the time to maturity of the bond and are not functionally dependent on the factor being modelled.

The set of processes under the market measure thus satisfy

$$dX_t = (\mu_X - \lambda_X X_t + \gamma_X \sigma_X)dt + \sigma_X d\widetilde{W}_t^X, \tag{4.16}$$

$$dY_t = (\mu_Y - \lambda_Y Y_t + \gamma_Y \sigma_Y)dt + \sigma_Y d\widetilde{W}_t^Y, \tag{4.17}$$

$$dR_t = \{k(X_t + Y_t - R_t) + \gamma_R \sigma_R\}dt + \sigma_R d\widetilde{W}_t^R, \tag{4.18}$$

where all three factors contain a market price of risk γ in volatility units.

4.3 Estimation procedure

The estimation of affine term structure models is known to be problematic because of the existence of numerous model likelihood maxima with essentially identical fit to the data (Kim and Orphanides, 2005). Babbs and Nowman (1999) applied the Kalman filter to estimate the two-factor generalized Vasicek model. Some other examples of the literature on filtering methods are Chen and Scott (1993), De Jong (2000), De Jong and Santa-Clara (1999), Geyer and Pichler (1999) and Duffee (2002). Most of these papers analyse multi-factor versions of the CIR model using mutually independent factors. De Jong (2000) extends this approach to the more general class of affine models proposed by Duffie and Kan (1996).

4.3.1 Kalman filter

Here we describe in detail the Kalman filter estimation procedure (Harvey, 1989), for our three-factor yield curve model in state-space form, which simultaneously integrates time series and cross-sectional aspects of the model. It also allows the identification of the market prices of interest rate risk critical for forward simulation.

The general state-space form applies to multivariate time series. The N observable variables y_t at time t (here, zero-coupon bond yields of various maturities) are related to a vector α_t known as the *state vector* (here our three yield curve factors) via a *measurement equation*

$$y_t = Z\alpha_t + d + \varepsilon_t, \qquad t = 1,...,T, \tag{4.19}$$

where Z is an $N \times m$ matrix, α_t is an $m \times 1$ vector, d and ε_t are $N \times 1$ vectors and the error term is assumed to consist of serially uncorrelated disturbances with mean zero and covariance matrix H, that is,

$$\mathbb{E}(\varepsilon_t) = 0 \qquad \text{var}(\varepsilon_t) = H. \tag{4.20}$$

In general, Z, d and H may depend on t.

Even though the elements of the state α_t are unobservable, they are known to follow a first-order Markov process specified by the *transition equation*

$$\alpha_t = A\alpha_{t-1} + c + S\eta_t, \quad t = 1,...,T \tag{4.21}$$

where A is an $m \times m$ matrix, c an $m \times 1$ vector, S an $m \times g$ matrix and η_t a $g \times 1$ vector of serially uncorrelated disturbances with mean zero and covariance matrix Q, that is,

$$\mathbb{E}(\eta_t) = 0, \qquad \text{var}(\eta_t) = Q. \tag{4.22}$$

Again, in general, A, c and S may depend on t, however, we will treat here the *time-homogeneous* case appropriate to the long term.[2]

Two further assumptions will be required to complete the state-space formulation:

- The initial state vector α_0 has mean a_0 and covariance matrix P_0, that is

$$\mathbb{E}(\alpha_0) = a_0, \quad \text{var}(\alpha_0) = P_0. \tag{4.23}$$

- The disturbance terms ε_t and η_t are uncorrelated with each other in all time periods and uncorrelated with the initial state, that is,

$$\mathbb{E}(\varepsilon_t \eta_s') = 0, \quad \text{for all} \quad s,t = 1,...,T \tag{4.24}$$

and

$$\mathbb{E}(\varepsilon_t \alpha_0') = 0 \quad \mathbb{E}(\eta_t \alpha_0') = 0 \quad t = 1,...,T \tag{4.25}$$

The important concept behind the state-space formulation is this separation of the noise driving the system dynamics η_t and the observational noise ε_t.

The *Kalman filter* is applied recursively in order to compute the optimal estimator of the state vector at time t given all the information currently available, which consists of the observations up to and including yt. Assuming a Gaussian state space, the disturbances and the initial state vector will be normally distributed.

In a state-space model, the system matrices depend on a set of unknown parameters (in our case 14) referred to as *hyper-parameters* and defined in Table 4.1. Using the Kalman filter to construct the likelihood function and then maximizing it using a suitable numerical optimization procedure, we can carry out maximum likelihood estimation of the hyper-parameters. The joint probability of a set of T observations can be expressed in terms of conditional distributions. For a multivariate normal distribution we have

$$L(y;\varphi) = \prod_{t=1}^{T} p(y_t \mid Y_{t-1}), \tag{4.26}$$

where $p(y_t \mid Y_{t-1})$ is the distribution of $\mathbf{y}_t$ conditional on the information at time $t-1$, that is $Y_{t-1} = (y_{t-1}, y_{t-2}, ... , y_1)'$. As we have a Gaussian model, we can write the log-likelihood function in *prediction error decomposition form* as

$$\log L(\varphi) = -\frac{NT}{2} \log 2\pi - \frac{1}{2} \sum_{t=1}^{T} \log|F_t| - \frac{1}{2} \sum_{t=1}^{T} v_t' F_t^{-1} v_t, \tag{4.27}$$

Table 4.1   Estimated parameters using the Kalman filter

Euro data		Estimated value	SE
Long-term risk-neutral mean X	μ_X/λ_X	0.199	1.69E-04
Long-term risk-neutral mean Y	μ_Y/λ_Y	−0.134	1.69E-04
Speed of mean reversion X	λ_X	0.161	1.03E-03
Speed of mean reversion Y	λ_Y	1.332	6.87E-03
Speed of mean reversion R	k	0.117	1.64E-03
Volatility X	σ_X	0.030	1.89E-04
Volatility Y	σ_Y	0.186	9.80E-04
Volatility R	σ_R	0.006	2.26E-04
Correlation X and Y	ρ_{XY}	−0.642	6.94E-03
Correlation X and R	ρ_{XR}	0.177	1.82E-02
Correlation Y and R	ρ_{YR}	−0.540	1.81E-02
Market price of risk for X	γ_X	0.556	3.91E-03
Market price of risk for Y	γ_Y	−1.017	5.50E-03
Market price of risk for R	γ_R	0.096	1.65E-02

where F_t is estimated by the covariance matrix obtained from the Kalman filter as

$$F_t = ZP_{t|t-1}Z' + H \tag{4.28}$$

and v_t is the vector of *prediction errors* given by

$$v_t = y_t - \bar{y}_{t|t-1} = Z(\alpha_t - \alpha_{t|t-1}) + \varepsilon_t. \tag{4.29}$$

Together with the following two equations, (4.28) and (4.29) form the *measurement update equations*

$$a_t = a_{t|t-1} + P_{t|t-1}Z'F_t^{-1}v_t, \tag{4.30}$$

$$P_t = P_{t|t-1} - P_{t|t-1}Z'F_t^{-1}P_{t|t-1}. \tag{4.31}$$

Therefore, first we specify starting values for the parameters. With these starting values, we run the Kalman filter to obtain estimated yields and a time series for the unobserved state variables. Next, the parameters are estimated by maximizing the log-likelihood using the state variable path estimates as observations. The optimized parameter values are then used as the starting values for the next iteration of the Kalman filter. This loop continues until we obtain the optimal parameter estimates by this generalized EM algorithm (Dempster *et al*, 1977). The calibration code is implemented in C++ and the optimization is performed using a combination of global (Direct, see Jones *et al*, 1993) and local (approximate) conjugate direction (Powell, 1964) or derivative-free quasi-Newton (NAG BFGS, used in the section 'Pricing consol bonds') numerical algorithms.

The starting values for the Kalman filter are given by the mean and the covariance of the unconditional distribution of the stationary state vector. The state vector is stationary if c and A are time invariant and $|\lambda(A)| < 1$, where $\lambda(A)$ is the leading eigenvalue of A. In this case, the mean a_0 is given by the unique solution to

$$a_0 = Aa_0 + c \quad \text{given by} \quad a_0 = (I - A)^{-1}c \tag{4.32}$$

and the covariance matrix P_0 will be given by the unique solution to the *Riccati equation*

$$P_0 = AP_0A' + SQS' \quad \text{given by} \quad \text{vec}(P_0)$$
$$= (I - A \otimes A)^{-1}\text{vec}(SQS'). \tag{4.33}$$

4.3.2   State-space form

In our case, the observable variables are given by risk-free (Treasury) yields of different maturities, and are related to the vector of unobservable state variables (X, Y, R) via the measurement equation. The measurement equation is obtained using (4.11) and adding serially and cross-sectionally uncorrelated disturbances with mean zero to take into account non-simultaneity of the observations, errors in the data and so on. The unobservable state variables are generated via the transition equations, which in our case are given by the discretized versions of (4.1), (4.2) and (4.3), using Euler's first-order approximation,[3] that is

$$X_{t+\Delta t} = X_t + (\mu_X - \lambda_X X_t + \gamma_X \sigma_X)\Delta t + \sigma_X \sqrt{\Delta t}\eta_{t,X}, \tag{4.34}$$

$$Y_{t+\Delta t} = Y_t + (\mu_Y - \lambda_Y Y_t + \gamma_Y \sigma_Y)\Delta t + \sigma_Y \sqrt{\Delta t}\eta_{t,Y}, \tag{4.35}$$

$$R_{t+\Delta t} = R_t + (k(X_t + Y_t - R_t) + \gamma_R \sigma_R)\Delta t + \sigma_R \sqrt{\Delta t}\eta_{t,R}. \tag{4.36}$$

In matrix form, the transition equations can be written as

$$\begin{pmatrix} X_t \\ Y_t \\ R_t \end{pmatrix} = A \begin{pmatrix} X_{t-\Delta t} \\ Y_{t-\Delta t} \\ R_{t-\Delta t} \end{pmatrix} + c + S\eta_t, \tag{4.37}$$

where

$$A := \begin{pmatrix} 1 - \lambda_X \Delta t & 0 & 0 \\ 0 & 1 - \lambda_Y \Delta t & 0 \\ k\Delta t & k\Delta t & 1 - k\Delta t \end{pmatrix}, \tag{4.38}$$

$$
c := \begin{pmatrix} (\mu_X + \gamma_X \sigma_X)\Delta t \\ (\mu_Y + \gamma_Y \sigma_Y)\Delta t \\ \gamma_R \sigma_R \Delta t \end{pmatrix},
\tag{4.39}
$$

$$
s := \begin{pmatrix} \sigma_X \sqrt{\Delta t} & 0 & 0 \\ 0 & \sigma_Y \sqrt{\Delta t} & 0 \\ 0 & 0 & \sigma_R \sqrt{\Delta t} \end{pmatrix}
\tag{4.40}
$$

and $\boldsymbol{\eta}_t$ is a vector with serially uncorrelated disturbances satisfying

$$
\mathbb{E}(\boldsymbol{\eta}_t) = 0
$$

$$
\mathrm{var}(\boldsymbol{\eta}_t) = \begin{pmatrix} 1 & \rho_{XY} & \rho_{XR} \\ \rho_{XY} & 1 & \rho_{YR} \\ \rho_{XR} & \rho_{YR} & 1 \end{pmatrix}.
\tag{4.41}
$$

In the current literature, several approaches have been adopted to estimate the covariance matrix of the measurement errors. For example, De Jong and Santa Clara (1999) used a spherical covariance matrix, $H = hI$, whereas Babbs and Nowman (1999) use a diagonal matrix. De Jong (2000) uses a full covariance matrix. We adopt a diagonal covariance matrix approach, optimizing likelihood using one-at-a-time search with the parameters divided into two groups: in the first search, the model parameters are optimized followed by the minimization of the measurement errors in the second search. This process is repeated until convergence. The one-at-a-time search method is preferred over the full optimization with 14 model parameters and 16 measurement errors because of the scale of the optimization problem in the combined case. Even though the full covariance matrix is to be highly preferred, we have avoided this specification, because using yields of 16 different maturities would result in 136 noise parameters to be estimated.

4.3.3 Estimation results

For our empirical analysis, yields on ordinary (par) fixed-for-floating rate Euro swap contracts[4] are used as data. As the swap market is highly liquid with many par swaps traded every day, it is possible to obtain rates for a set of swaps with *constant* maturities from 1 to 30 years from the market. From the market swap rates, a swap curve that gives the rates for constant maturity swaps (CMS) of *all* durations may be constructed each day. Dai and Singleton (2000) point out that these yields are preferable for analysis for the following reasons. The swap markets provide 'constant maturity' yield data, whereas in the Treasury market the maturities of 'constant maturity' yields are only approximately constant or the data represent interpolated series. In addition, the on-the-run (that is, just purchased at auction) treasuries that are often used in empirical studies are typically on 'special' (haircut) in the repo market to which they are immediately (although temporarily) sold. Therefore, strictly speaking, the Treasury data should be adjusted for repo specials before any empirical analysis. Unfortunately, the requisite data for making these adjustments are not readily available, and consequently such adjustments are rarely made.

For estimation and calibration purposes, we first use weekly 1-, 3- and 6-month EU LIBOR and Euro swap data for the period from June 1997 to December 2002 (a total of 292 time points) for 16 different yields with maturities equal to 1, 3 and 6 months and 1, 2, 3, 4, 5, 6, 7, 8, 9, 10, 15, 20 and 30 years. The sample period was determined on one end by the unavailability of reliable long-term swap data for years before 1997 and on the other end by its use for backtests over the difficult 2003–2004 period in the bond markets.[5] We interpolate the swap curve linearly to obtain swap rates at all maturities and then use the data recursively from the 1-month rate to back out a zero-coupon bond yield curve from the basic swap pricing equation for each week.[6] This derived data is the input for model calibration. The estimation results are presented in Table 4.1 all have plausible values. Bearing in mind that the factor **y** is a *negative* yield curve slope, between a market expected short rate and the long rate, all the signs in Table 4.1 are as expected. All parameter estimates are statistically significant at the 1 per cent level, unlike the estimates found by Babbs and Nowman (1999), who looked at Kalman filtering generalized Vasicek models. However, they only used yields of eight different maturities and Geyer and Pichler (1999) show that a larger number of maturities is important to improve the precision of the parameter estimates. Shocks to the long rate and the expected yield curve slope decay here with half lives over 4 years and about 6 months, respectively.

Table 4.2 provides the estimated standard deviations $\sqrt{h_i}$ of the measurement errors, where h_i is the ith diagonal element of the covariance matrix H. In particular, these standard deviations range from less than 1 basis point for the 7-year yield to 24 basis points for the 30-year yield. These measurement errors are all significant at the 1 per cent level and compare in magnitude to those in Babbs and Nowman (1999) and very favourably to studies by, for example Chen and Scott (1993) and Geyer and Pichler (1999), who both estimate the multifactor CIR model on US data.

A general limitation of affine yield curve models with mean reversion is that the volatility of long rates tends to decay too rapidly with maturity relative to that exhibited by market data. Our use of maturity-specific volatilities for the measurement errors compensates for this effect. Indeed, the standard deviation of the measurement errors for the 15, 20 and 30 years' rates shown in Table 4.2 are significantly greater than those for the other maturities. More generally, and similar to Geyer and Pichler (1999), the error standard deviations exhibit a

Table 4.2 Measurement errors

	Maturity	Estimated value	Standard error
$3\sqrt{h_1}$	1 month	1.57E-03	6.63E-05
$3\sqrt{h_2}$	3 months	8.64E-04	3.81E-05
$3\sqrt{h_3}$	6 months	1.55E-04	3.19E-05
$3\sqrt{h_4}$	1 year	6.71E-04	2.96E-05
$3\sqrt{h_5}$	2 years	5.08E-04	2.15E-05
$3\sqrt{h_6}$	3 years	2.85E-04	1.21E-05
$3\sqrt{h_7}$	4 years	1.49E-04	7.03E-06
$3\sqrt{h_8}$	5 years	4.96E-05	4.59E-06
$3\sqrt{h_9}$	6 years	6.58E-05	2.89E-06
$3\sqrt{h_{10}}$	7 years	1.00E-05	3.83E-06
$3\sqrt{h_{11}}$	8 years	9.44E-05	4.1E-06
$3\sqrt{h_{12}}$	9 years	1.75E-04	7.63E-06
$3\sqrt{h_{13}}$	10 years	2.94E-04	1.28E-05
$3\sqrt{h_{14}}$	15 years	7.45E-04	3.14E-05
$3\sqrt{h_{15}}$	20 years	1.23E-03	5.32E-05
$3\sqrt{h_{16}}$	30 years	2.37E-03	1.03E-04

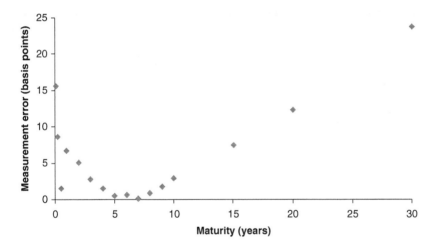

Figure 4.3 Measurement error of the fitted yields

distinct U-shaped pattern as depicted in Figure 4.3. A possible explanation for this might be that the observed data for medium range maturities are highly correlated and therefore easier to fit. The short rate behaviour in Figure 4.3 also indicates that the use of the 1-month yield as a proxy for the instantaneous short rate is likely to give rise to problems. In general, 1-month and 6-month LIBOR rate measurement errors appear inconsistent with those for rates derived from the swap data for maturities in years, probably because of liquidity factors.

4.3.4 Factor loadings

Similar to Babbs and Nowman (1999), we also look at the factor loadings of our three-factor model as a function of maturity to determine the nature of the factors calculated by the Kalman filter. The resulting curve for each factor represents the change in yield caused by a shock to that factor of one standard deviation magnitude so that all shocks are equally likely events (Litterman and Scheinkman, 1991). As factor loadings correspond to orthogonal Brownian motions, rather than those with correlated innovations, we first use Cholesky decomposition, as described in the section 'Three-factor term structure model', to transform the SDEs. For comparison with Babbs and Nowman (1999), we also impose the following three additional restrictions: the second factor has zero impact on the term structure at approximately the 5-year maturity and the third factor loading disappears at about 2 and 12 years. This gives a set of nine equations in the nine volatility parameters of (4.4), (4.5) and (4.6).

Figure 4.4 plots the factor loadings for the three-factor model. Although Babbs and Nowman found that their third factor loading had a negligible effect, we find all three factors have a significant impact on the yields of all maturities. We also find that the range of the impact of the factors **R**, **Y** and **X** on the yields is similar to that found by Litterman and Scheinkman (1991), using principal component analysis on weekly US data with these three factors interpreted as *level*, *curvature* and *steepness*, respectively.

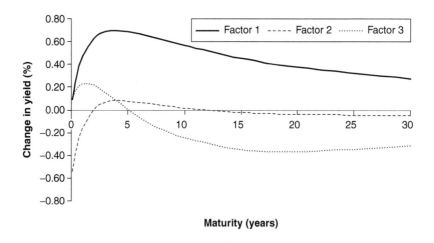

Figure 4.4 Factor loadings of the three-factor model

4.4   Simulation

One of the objectives of this article is to propose a term structure model that is tractable in forward simulations of closed form yields through its factors but can still capture the salient features of the yield curve.

4.4.1   Yield curve statistics

To evaluate our model initially, we performed an out-of-sample backtest over 2003. Using the historical 52 weekly data points for the yields in 2003, we calculated the mean level and the weekly standard deviation for each of the 16 maturities. We then simulated forward from January 2003 to beginning January 2004 using the parameter estimates given in Table 4.1. In total, 500 scenarios were generated and for each scenario the mean and standard deviation, over time for the 16 maturities, was calculated. Averaging over all scenarios finally gives an average mean and standard deviation for the simulated yields.

Figure 4.5 plots the mean levels of the yields for both the historical and the simulated data and Figure 4.6 similarly plots the standard deviations. As can be observed from Figure 4.5, the two sets of means closely match each other. Figure 4.6 shows that the simulated standard deviations slightly overestimate the historical ones. However, yields were considerably less volatile in 2003 than over the 1997–2002 in-sample period (cf. Figure 4.2), which would explain this discrepancy.

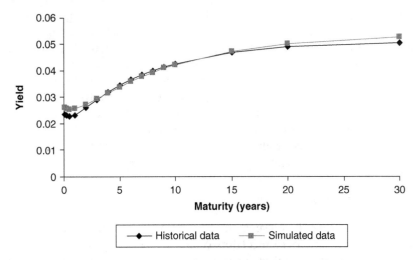

Figure 4.5   Mean level of yields over 2003 for historical and simulated data

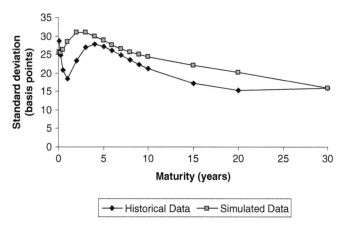

Figure 4.6   Weekly standard deviation of yields over 2003 for historical and simulated data

4.4.2   Yield curve dynamics

Another objective of this work was to develop a model that is able to simulate the various yield curve dynamics encountered in practice, for example steepening, flattening and inversion. Figures 4.7 and 4.8 show historical yields up to 2002, followed by simulated yields for 2 years to end 2004 on specific yield curve scenarios selected from the 500 simulated scenarios.[7] Figure 4.7 demonstrates that the model can simulate yield curve steepening and flattening, whereas Figure 4.8 demonstrates that it can simulate yield curve inversion. Indeed, both visual and statistical analysis of the 500 simulated scenarios (not presented here in the interests of brevity) demonstrate that the model's simulated dynamic behaviour is consistent with the historical behaviour of the yield curve over the out-of-sample period. This has been true for the many different applications with different time steps for which we have used it.

   Application of the yield curve model to the risk management of portfolios of guaranteed investment products involving simulations with a monthly time step may be found in Dempster *et al* (2006, 2007, 2009).

4.5   Pricing consol bonds

In 2005, a number of European banks[8] issued floating rate callable *consol* bonds as a means of raising Tier 1 regulatory capital. In the absence of the exercise of the call option by the bank at any time after a specified number of fixed interest payments, these bonds are *perpetual*, that is, they have an infinite maturity,

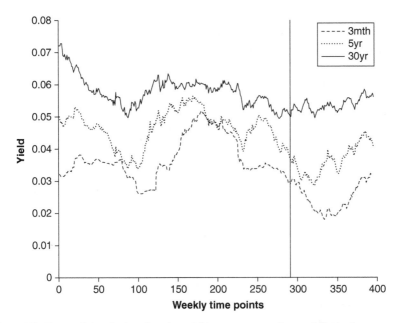

Figure 4.7 Forward simulation showing yield curve steepening and flattening

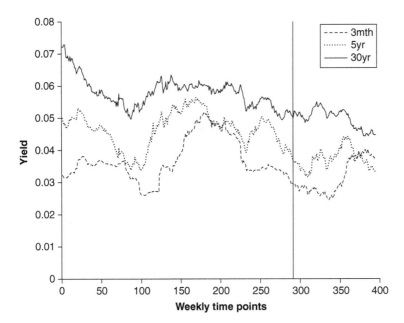

Figure 4.8 Forward simulation showing yield curve inversion

and their holders have purchased an indefinite income stream in exchange for their capital. After the period specified, the fixed rate payable by the banks to the holder on the nominal face value of the bond is converted to a floating rate, which is a multiple of the CMS-spread, usually the difference between the 10 and 2 year CMS rates, on the interest payment fixing date. In addition, these bonds' payments normally have a cap and a floor, possibly in terms of another floating money market rate, such as 3-month EURIBOR. In the *worst* case, when the swap curve is flat (see Figure 4.10) and the spread negligible, the bond holder will receive the floor rate.

The details of *over-the-counter* contracts are important and we present here a representative example of a callable CMS-spread consol hybrid product used to generate Tier 1 capital by the issuing bank.

4.5.1   Example

Nominal (face) value	€1.5 million
Commencement date of contract	28 January 2005
Maturity	perpetual (unless called at 5 years or after)

The bank pays a fixed rate of 6 per cent per annum in arrears for 5 years. The interval between payments on 28 January each year is 1 year. At these dates, the annual floating rate payments in arrears are calculated as

$$4(CMS10_i - CMS2_i \quad i = 6,7,...,$$

where CMS10 is the 10 year swap rate (base rate 10) and CMS2 is the 2 year swap rate (base rate 2) and $(CMS10_i - CMS2_i)$ is referred to as the *spread*. This floating rate coupon is capped at 10 per cent per annum and floored at 3.5 per cent per annum. As the spread decreases to 0, the bondholder receives only the floor rate of 3.5 per cent per annum.

The expected value of this bond for the purchaser (that is, investor) is embedded in their belief about future movements of the swap curve over time. Historical swap curves illustrate that the expected and realized market rates may differ significantly. Figure 4.9 shows the movements of swap curves in 2005 and 2006.

It is obvious that interest rate and, more generally, swap curve forecasting rests at the centre of CMS-spread instrument pricing for both seller and purchaser. Analysis of the risk of the proposed bond depends upon the counterparties' abilities to model and simulate forward the yield and swap curves at the payment dates under the market measure. The broad movements of the spreads between 10 and 2 year maturities for the yield curve (for zero-coupon Treasury bonds) and the swap curve are similar. However, the swap curve spread has extra volatility because of the market's changing views on general counterparty creditworthiness – essentially AA credit rating spread volatility.

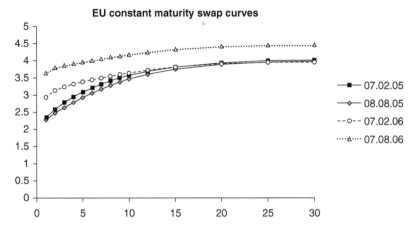

Figure 4.9 Illustrative swap curve movements

Depending on the market conditions, the credit spreads of consols, similar to our example, appear to be associated with credit ratings which vary between A and BB in Standard and Poor's (S&P) terms. However, some of this market spread may be mainly because of the individual investors who bought and are currently trading these perpetual securities, evaluating them as relatively long but *finite* lived bonds. For example, currently valuing the perpetual bond as having a 25 year maturity *without* credit risk produces a discount to face value of about 30 per cent, near the current trading range.

The holder of a CMS-spread consol bond is in effect giving the issuer a levered call option on the flattening of the yield curve – that is, the *decrease* of the spread – which normally follows sharp rises in short term rates. Global macroeconomic conditions, in the late 2004 to early 2005 period, in which these contracts were issued clearly indicated sharply increasing short rates, a process that had already begun in the United States at the time and followed in the EU only shortly thereafter. Moreover, this was recently the situation because of credit market turmoil, with short rates extremely high. However, the situation from January 2011 forward is naturally unclear at this point. There exists considerable asymmetry of information between issuer and bondholder and the latter may genuinely be convinced that 'the yield curve will not become significantly flatter' in the long run to yield around 6 per cent in perpetuity.

4.5.2 Calibration

The data used to calibrate the model consist of freely available *daily* euro 3-and 6-month LIBOR and Euro swap data with the same maturities as in the section 'Estimation procedure' from the start of 1999 to the end of 2007, a total of 2133 observations.[9] Although the historical EU data often used by banks go back to 1992, these data have had to be constructed before the introduction of the euro in 1999. In any event, missing the sharp short rate rises of the early 1990s in our data will tend to make our valuation estimates conservative. We again interpolate the swap curve linearly to obtain swap rates at all maturities, then use the 3- and 6-month EU LIBOR rates and the swap curve to recursively back out a risk-free zero-coupon bond yield curve from the basic par swap pricing equation for each day. These derived data are the input data for estimation of the parameters of our three-factor yield curve model (which we shall do at the date of bond issue and a more recent date). From this, we can compute the yield curve based on the posterior mean for the three factors R, X and Y at historical dates in our data and compare this to the actual yield curve deduced from the (linearly interpolated) historical swap curve on that day. This is shown in Figure 4.10 for a representative date, 28 July 2003, after calibration to the data up to consol bond inception at 28 January 2005.[10]

For such calibrations on daily data, the parameter estimates for the model have similar characteristics to those given for weekly data in Tables 4.1 and 4.2 in the section 'Estimation procedure'. Although long run means and mean reversion speeds are quite stable, market prices of risk and volatilities vary with calibration end date. Moreover, as we shall see below, the resulting consol bond Monte Carlo valuations vary considerably with the initial yield, and corresponding swap, curves – actually their model approximations at the calibration end date – from which forward simulation paths for valuation on that date begin.

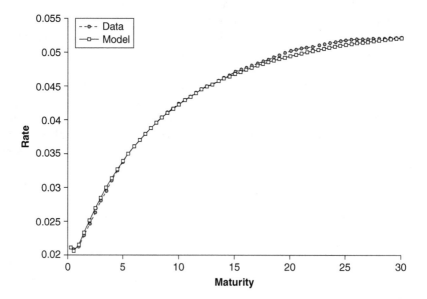

Figure 4.10   Yield curve fit for 28 July 2003

Ignoring for the moment the ability of the bank to call (cancel) the bond to find its fair price in the absence of credit risk, we simulate the swap curve forward under the risk adjusted probabilities (that is, with factor market prices of risk set to 0) using our interest rate model.

We compute the floating payment on each simulated scenario at each payment date and average across scenarios the total of the discounted payments along each random scenario. This is the standard Monte Carlo pricing methodology for European-style financial instruments. We used 50 000 paths for pricing the contract.

Clearly, the present value of an infinite stream of payments from this consol cannot be obtained mathematically and must be valued numerically over a finite horizon. We chose this horizon by the criterion of the maturity at which the present value at inception of the remaining coupon payments thereafter (assumed to be at the 10 per cent cap and discounted conservatively at 2.5 per cent per annum) is less than 1 per cent of face value, which occurred at 241 years.

With the right to cancel in place, the fair value is given by the expected discounted value of the sum of the coupon payments with the risk-neutral probabilities under the assumption that the bank uses an optimal call strategy. As determining the exact optimal cancellation rule is computationally difficult, we use a sub-optimal cancellation rule derived using the popular method of Andersen (1999). Owing to the fact that only the bank has the right to cancel, the sub-optimality of our cancellation strategy may lead to an *overestimation* of the value of contract from the viewpoint of the bondholder.

In brief, Andersen's method relies on a *score* function $st(r, x, y)$, which should be low if cancellation is likely to be correct and seeks a cancellation rule of the form: cancel if $s_t < s_t^*$. The exercise thresholds s_t^* are determined recursively based on a *separate* set of random paths for (R, X, Y). We used 10 000 paths to estimate the optimal cancellation thresholds. Andersen proposed a simple method for determining good values for s_t^*. For our calculations, we take s_t^* to be the discounted value of all the remaining swap payouts to the bank under the assumption that (R, X, Y) evolves according to its expected path.

We further improve the cancellation strategy as follows. Before evaluating the score function, we compute an accurate approximation to the expected value of the next payout (as this is the payment committed to by opting not to cancel the contract at this time) by linearizing the expression for the spread (CMS10–CMS2) at the end of the next period as a function of (R, X, Y). This leads to an integral involving two correlated Gaussian random variables, which can be evaluated in closed form. If the expected next net return to the bank on the face value, relative to the coupon paid to the bondholder, is positive, it cannot be correct to call the bond and it is better to wait for at least one more coupon payment.

To handle the credit spread because of the creditworthiness of these subordinated consol bonds, we assume a *constant* per annum default rate appropriate to the credit class. This class could possibly be defined from market conditions (current yield curve) and similar instruments trading at different discounts because of different terms (nominal rates over 3-month euro LIBOR or EURIBOR). We might therefore have chosen to use the corresponding default rate at a constant 2.3 per cent per annum, which represents the margin over EURIBOR of the interest rate paid for similar consol bonds issued at par but on more favourable terms – and currently trading near par – by other institutions than our issuing bank in the same period. This corresponds to a S&P BB credit rating historical default rate. However, this default rate is inconsistent with the A credit rating initially assigned to this bond, and below we shall actually approximate the credit discount *implied* by the market for a 241 year maturity bond.

4.5.3 NPV value at risk

Value at risk (VaR) can be computed at any point in time for the bondholder from a *simulated distribution* of the *present value* (PV) of all future (*net*) payments of the deal treating the initial face value payment as a sunk cost to the bond holder. We compute VaR for the deal at inception and about 3 years later using exactly the same Monte Carlo methodology as that used for pricing, except that the market probabilities, involving estimates of the constant market prices of risk for the three factors, are used. We then compute normalized histograms of deal PVs and find the 99 per cent VaR level (relative to 1 representing par or face value) for both the issuing bank and the bondholder. As the factor market prices of risk are in fact *processes*, the standard deviations of their *constant* estimates are high relative to those of other parameters. Moreover, the estimates of the deal present value distributions are sensitive to the estimated value of the market price of risk for the short rate used to discount future payments (Cairns, 2004). We have attempted to overcome this effect in the estimation procedure by penalizing deviations from the (estimated) long run (asymptotic) short rate, which can be obtained in closed form as a function of the model parameters and is estimated from the historical 3-month EURIBOR and euro LIBOR rates.

4.5.4 Cash flow analysis

The swap rates for CMS2 and CMS10 (Figure 4.11) evolved significantly over the 2 years 2005 and 2006, which moved the spread beyond (that is, to 0.006 on 21 December 2006) its historical minimum value up to 2004 of 0.3250 per cent. This has had a dramatic effect on the forecast floating rate coupon payments to the bondholder after the 5-year 6 per cent fixed rate period (see Figure 4.13).

Figure 4.12 presents the results of simulation of the coupon payments with the mean and range given by one standard deviation, which seems beneficial

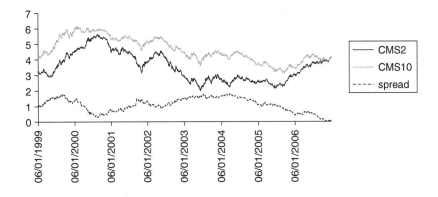

Figure 4.11   Base rate and spread evolution

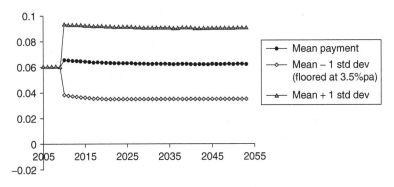

Figure 4.12   View of forward coupon payment distribution on 28 January 2005

for the bondholder at inception on 28 January 2005, assuming *no bond call or default* by the bank. Our model predicts that the evolution of this distribution of net payments from inception is not symmetrical about its mean, which falls slightly over the life of the bond. Note that the first five points in Figure 4.12 represent the first five fixed annual payments to the bondholder.

Figure 4.13 shows the simulation of the coupon payments for the bond, assuming no call or default by the bank, from the model calibrated on data to 20 December 2007 – a year when significant changes in the spread occurred (see Figure 4.11). In fact, the long-run stationary distribution of the spread under the market probabilities is 1.03 per cent per annum with corresponding 3-month short rate of 3.11 per cent per annum. This spread is similar to the 1.47 per cent historical average spread from 1995 to 2005 but lower because

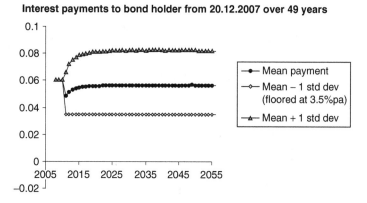

Figure 4.13   View of forward coupon payment distribution on 20 December 2007

of more recent history in which short rates were rising and long rates were depressed by global liquidity before the credit crisis. Under the risk discounted (pricing) probabilities (risk-neutral measure), the spread becomes −3.3 basis points with short rate 8.42 per cent per annum. Market moves over the 2 years from inception have been in a direction, which has made the non-credit-risk adjusted CMS-spread bond deal costly in the outcome for the bondholder at 20 December 2007 at now less than 6 per cent per annum in expectation.

4.5.5   Deal valuations and values at risk

Market price of bond at inception (8 January 2005)	86.05 per cent of face value or *€1.291 million*
Six standard deviation pricing uncertainty (99.7 per cent confidence interval):	85.57–86.53 per cent of nominal or €1.284–€1.298 million
The *call option* at inception is *always used* prospectively	
Value at risk at inception to investor at the 99 per cent level:	46.27 per cent of face value recovered, that is 53.73 per cent or *€806 k* lost
Market price of bond (20 December 2007) after two 6 per cent coupon payments	80.06 per cent of face value or *€1.207 million*
Six standard deviation pricing uncertainty (99.7 per cent confidence interval):	79.67–80.44 per cent of face value or €1.195– €1.206 million
Value at risk on 20 December 2007 to investor at 99 per cent level:	48.97 per cent of face value recovered, that is 51.03 per cent or *€765 k* lost

A number of observations are immediate. First, the deal was not initially fairly priced at par. Approximately 14 per cent of face value of €1.5 million or €210 k was collected up front from the bond holder by the bank. The initial fair price of 86 per cent of face value is a higher than current market prices for these bonds, which are currently in the range of 60–65 per cent – perhaps because of higher credit risk or the individual investor finite horizon effect discussed above.

Second, in the absence of default, the bank's call (cancellation) option is optimally *always used*. The call date varies by scenario from 5 to 224 years from inception with an average of about 18 years.

Third, the 99 per cent VaR to the bondholder involves considerable losses and depends critically on market conditions. Note, however, that 30 per cent of the face value is recovered in the five fixed payments before discounting. The situation is illustrated graphically in Figures 4.14 and 4.15, which give the distributions of PV of future payments as a proportion of nominal (1 represents face value). These figures show the asymmetry in these distributions with a long, thin upside tail in favour of the bondholder and a significantly *probable downside* in favour of bank. From inception at 28 January 2005 to 20 December 2007, the expected PV has been reduced significantly from 1.154 (115.4 per cent of face value) to 1.055 (105.5 per cent), although the more appropriate median present value has been reduced somewhat less.

4.5.6   Comparison with risk-free bonds

By comparison with the 115.4 per cent PV of future payments at inception of the actual contract on 28 January 2005 (Figure 4.14), the corresponding figure for an 18-year maturity 6 per cent fixed coupon risk-free bond (with no call option) is 120.6 per cent. The 5.2 per cent reduction for the consol bond represents the balance between the average effects of the call option and the potential for coupon payments near the floor (reducing) and the potential for higher coupon payments of up to 10 per cent over periods when the bank optimally calls the perpetual bond later than the average 18 years (enhancing). Nearly 3 years later, on 20 December 2007 (Figure 4.15) when the PV of future payments is only 105.5 per cent, the corresponding reduction relative to a 15-year maturity 6 per cent risk-free bond exceeds 15 per cent. At this date, the likelihood of the bondholder not even recovering the original investment has risen to nearly 50 per cent.

4.5.7   Credit risk analysis

Finally, let us consider the effects of credit risk on the current market price of this consol bond. Taking account of credit risk for such a perpetual bond from a necessarily (short) finite amount of historical default data is fraught with error. We have chosen to use the maturity of 241 years of our finite maturity approximation to obtain at least a plausible value for the credit risk discount. The difference between our market risk valuation of 80 per cent of face value on 20 December 2007 and the market value of the bond on that day of 60 per cent allows 20 per cent of face value as credit risk discount and/or behavioural finite horizon and tax effects. Assuming that this figure is essentially because of *pure credit risk* implies that the market on that day was assuming approximately a default discount rate of 8.3 bp per annum,[11] which would lead to a credit risk discount over 241 years of 20.1 per cent.

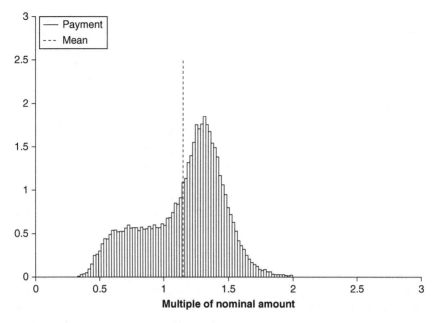

Figure 4.14   Distribution of total discounted payments to investor in multiple of face value at 28 January 2005

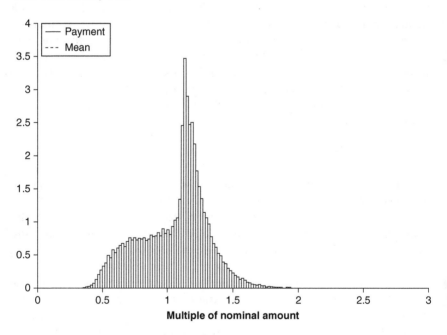

Figure 4.15   Distribution of total discounted payments to investor at 20 December 2007

The only rational explanation for the purchase of this representative consol is that bondholders believed that their coupon payments would genuinely not be significantly reduced from the first five at 6 per cent. As we have seen (in Figure 4.12), this would have been a reasonable expectation based on history at inception, but actual market outcomes – possibly revealed to the issuing bank in the forward economic and market views at inception – have further moved strongly against the bondholders (see Figure 4.13). The result is that an investor is left holding an illiquid credit risky perpetual bond, which is currently trading at a 30 per cent to 40 per cent loss on their investment with the prospect in 2 years time of possibly receiving only 3.5 per cent annual coupons because of CMS-spreads of only a few basis points.

Obviously, these credit risky structural floating rate consol bonds provide investors with returns far inferior to risk-free fixed rate bonds of comparable expected maturities issued in the same period. However, the complexity of these instruments, which require sophisticated Monte Carlo analysis to price, has by and large been ignored by investors. Indeed, initially investors appear to have treated these securities naively, and sub-optimally, as short maturity risk-free fixed rate bonds that would be called by banks soon after all their initial fixed rate payments were made.

4.6 Conclusion

The objective of this article is to specify a model that captures the salient features of the whole term structure, rather than one that just focuses on the short-term interest rate. It also has to be tractable in order to form a basis for asset pricing applications and forward simulations for asset liability management. To this end, we consider a Gaussian three-factor continuous-time model within the affine class with a closed-form solution for bond prices.

For our empirical analysis, the model is expressed in a state-space formulation, which allows us to take into account both the cross-sectional and time-series information contained in the term structure data and to use the Kalman filter and numerical likelihood maximization recursively to estimate the parameters.

The model explains the cross-section of interest rates well with reasonably small yield errors. We also show that in forward simulations this model gives rise to a wide and realistic range of future interest rate scenarios, as shown by both backtest and simulation results, involving flattening/steepening/inversion of the yield curve.

We apply the model to pricing perpetual callable consol bonds with structured floating coupon payments, based on the 10–2 year CMS-spread, using forward simulations over a 241-year horizon with a daily time step. As a result, we find these credit risky floating rate consol bonds issued by banks to raise

Tier 1 capital in the 2004–2005 period to be initially mispriced and with lower expected yields than comparable finite horizon sovereign fixed coupon bonds.

Acknowledgements

We thank Drs Yee Sook Yong, Muriel Rietbergen and Giles Thompson for analytical and computational assistance on the research reported herein. We also acknowledge helpful comments from Julian Roberts, Cambridge Finance Seminar participants and anonymous referees, which materially improved the paper.

Notes

1. We use boldface throughout the paper to denote random or conditionally random entities.
2. This assumption implies that the conditional variance of yield changes is constant over time. A number of studies concerned with the relatively short term have found that yield changes are conditionally heteroscedastic, cf. Ball and Torous (1996). Fong and Vasicek (1991) introduced stochastic volatility to represent this situation, whose relevance to the long run is questionable, for pricing (see also Litterman *et al*, 1991 and Andersen *et al*, 2004).
3. Alternatively, De Jong (2000) presents a general way to obtain the exact discrete-time state distributions in affine class models. As the benefits are unclear for our purposes and simulation complexity increases, we have not pursued this approach here.
4. A *par interest rate swap* is a standard contract between two counterparties to exchange cash flows. At set time intervals termed *reset dates*, one pays a predetermined fixed rate of interest on the *nominal value*, the other a *floating rate*, until the maturity date of the contract. The floating leg of swap fixes the interest rates for each payment at the rate of a published interest rate. The fixed rate, known as the *swap rate*, is that interest rate, which makes the fair value of the par swap 0 at inception. Thus, the cash flows of the two legs of a par swap are those of a pair of bonds with face value the swap nominal, one fixed rate and the other floating rate.
5. But, see the section 'Pricing consol bonds' in which more recent data up to 2008 are used.
6. We also evaluated the quadratic interpolation but deemed the negligible improvement in accuracy not worth the considerable increase in computational burden.
7. Given the relatively low yield volatilities depicted in Figure 4.6 and the yield levels in Figure 4.5 we concluded that the probability of negative yields with our Gaussian model under the market measure is negligible. Using values from the data of Figure 4.5 and 4.6, these correspond to a minus 10 standard deviation event. Our decision is borne out by the representative paths in Figures 4.7 and 4.8 and, in fact, none of the 500 scenarios simulated produced negative yields over the out-of-sample period. However, see Abu-Mostafa (2001) for a technique for reducing this probability over longer simulation horizons.
8. For example, in 2005 Deutsche Bank issued a €900 million tranche of bonds at par to *face value* or *nominal*. This revives an instrument that has not been in favour since the Russian Revolution, when Tsar Nicholas' consols became worthless, although UK

consols initiated in the eighteenth century are still in existence (with reduced fixed coupon). There is little current literature on their pricing when coupon rates are floating.

9. We use daily data for consol bond valuation to conform to market practice by issuers who value fixed income instruments incorporating yield curve data on (or just before) the day of sale. Our example here is representative of a number of consol bonds we have valued initially on different dates in the period 2004–2006.

10. Note that these fits on representative days do not always accurately capture the long end of the yield curve, which might require a fourth factor. They are, however, acceptably accurate up to 10-year maturity and in any event generally err on the conservative side, by producing lower discount rates.

11. This corresponds to the historical *4-year* S&P cumulative default rate for the bond's A rating which suggests that the market was optimistic regarding the bank's possible default on the contract over possibly nearly two and a half centuries.

References

Abu-Mostafa, Y.S. (2001) Financial model calibration using consistency hints. *IEEE Transactions on Neural Networks* 12(4): 191–223.

Andersen, L. (1999) A Simple Approach to Pricing Bermudan Swaptions in the Multi-Factor LIBOR Market Model. Geneva Re Financial Products. Working Paper.

Andersen, T.G., Benzoni, L. and Lund, J. (2004) Stochastic Volatility, Mean Drift, and Jumps in the Short-term Interest Rate. Minneapolis: Carlson School of Management, University of Minnesota. Working Paper.

Babbs, S.H. and Nowman, K.B. (1999) Kalman filtering of generalized Vasiçek term structure models. *Journal of Financial and Quantitative Analysis* 34(1): 115–130.

Ball, C.A. and Torous, W.N. (1996) Unit roots and the estimation of interest rate dynamics. *Journal of Empirical Finance* 3: 215–238.

Brigo, D. and Mercurio, F. (2007) *Interest Rate Models – Theory and Practice*, 2nd edn. Berlin: Springer.

Cairns, A.J.G. (2004) A family of term-structure models for long-term risk management and derivative pricing. *Mathematical Finance* 14(3): 415–444.

Chan, K.C., Karolyi, G.A., Longstaff, F.A. and Sanders, A.B. (1992) An empirical comparison of alternative models of the short-term interest rate. *Journal of Finance* 47(3): 1209–1227.

Chen, R. and Scott, L. (1993) ML estimation for a multifactor equilibrium model of the term structure. *Journal of Fixed Income* 3: 14–31.

Christensen, J.H.E., Diebold, F.X. and Rudebusch, G.D. (2007) PIER Working Paper 07–029. University of Pensylvania http://www.econ.upenn.edu/pier.

Cox, J.C., Ingersoll, J.E. and Ross, S.A. (1985) A theory of the term structure of interest rates. *Econometrica* 53(2): 385–407.

Dai, Q. and Singleton, K.J. (2000) Specification analysis of affine term structure models. *Journal of Finance* 55(5): 1943–1978.

De Jong, F. (2000) Time-series and cross-section information in affine term-structure models. *Journal of Business and Economic Statistics* 18(3): 300–314.

De Jong, F. and Santa-Clara, P. (1999) The dynamics of the forward interest rate curve: A formulation with state variables. *Journal of Financial and Quantitative Analysis* 34(1): 131–157.

Dempster, A.P., Larid, N.M. and Rubin, D.B. (1977) Maximum likelihood from incomplete data via the EM-algorithm. *Journal of the Royal Statistical Society: Series B* 39: 1–38.

Dempster, M.A.H., Germano, M., Medova, E.A., Rietbergen, M.I., Sandrini, F. and Scrowston, M. (2006) Managing guarantees. *Journal of Portfolio Management* 32(2): 51–61.

Dempster, M.A.H., Germano, M., Medova, E.A., Rietbergen, M.I., Sandrini, F. and Scrowston, M. (2007) Designing minimum guaranteed funds. *Quantitative Finance* 7(2): 245–256.

Dempster, M.A.H., Mitra, M. and Pflug, G. (eds.) (2009) *Quantitative Fund Management*, Financial Mathematics Series, Boca Raton, FL: Chapman & Hall CRC.

Duffee, G.R. (2002) Term premia and interest rate forecasts in affine models. *Journal of Finance* 57: 405–443.

Duffie, D. and Kan, R. (1996) A yield-factor model of interest rates. *Mathematical Finance* 6(4): 379–406.

Fong, G. and Vasicek, O. (1991) Fixed income volatility management. *Journal of Portfolio Management* 17(4): 41–46.

Geyer, A.L.J. and Pichler, S. (1999) A state-space approach to estimate and test Cox-Ingersoll-Ross models of the term structure. *Journal of Financial Research* 22(1): 107–130.

Harvey, A.C. (1989) *Forecasting, Structural Time Series Models and the Kalman Filter.* Cambridge, UK: Cambridge University Press.

Heath, D., Jarrow, R. and Morton, A. (1992) Bond pricing and the term structure of interest rates: A new methodology for contingent claims valuation. *Econometrica* 60(1): 77–105.

Ho, T.S.Y. and Lee, S. (1986) Term structure movements and pricing interest rate contingent claims. *Journal of Finance* 41(5): 1011–1029.

Hull, J.C. and White, A.D. (1990) Pricing interest rate derivative securities. *Review of Financial Studies* 3(4): 573–592.

James, J. and Webber, N. (2000) *Interest Rate Modelling.* Chichester, UK: Wiley.

Jones, D.R., Perttunen, C.D. and Stuckmann, B.E. (1993) Lipschitzian optimization without the Lipschitz constant. *Journal of Optimization Theory and Applications* 79(1): 157–181.

Kim, D.H. and Orphanides, A. (2005) Term Structure Estimation with Survey Data on Interest Rate Forecasts. Board of Governors of the Federal Reserve System. Finance and Economics Discussion Series, No. 48.

Langetieg, T.C. (1980) A multivariate model of the term structure. *Journal of Finance* 35(1): 71–97.

Litterman, R. and Scheinkman, J. (1991) Common factors affecting bond returns. *Journal of Fixed Income* 1: 54–61.

Litterman, R., Scheinkman, J. and Weiss, L. (1991) Volatility and the yield curve. *Journal of Fixed Income* 1: 49–53.

Medova, E.A., Rietbergen, M.I., Villaverde, M. and Yong, Y.S. (2006) Modelling the Long-term Dynamics of Yield Curves. Centre for Financial Research, Judge Business School Working Paper WP24/2006 http://www.cfr.statslab.cam.ac.uk.

Nelson, C.R. and Siegel, A.F. (1987) Parsimonious modelling of yield curves. *Journal of Business* 60: 473–489.

Powell, M.J.D. (1964) An efficient method of finding the minimum of a function of several variables without calculating derivatives. *Computer Journal* 11: 302–304.

Rebonato, R., Mahal, S., Joshi, M., Buchholz, L.-D. and Nyholm, K. (2005) Evolving yield curves in the real-world measures: A semi-parametric approach. *Journal of Risk* 7(3): 29–61.

Vasicek, O. (1977) An equilibrium characterization of the term structure. *Journal of Financial Economics* 5(2): 177–188.

Wilkie, A.D., Waters, H.R. and Yang, S. (2004) Reserving, pricing and hedging for policies with guaranteed annuity options. *British Actuarial Journal* 10(1): 101–152.

Wu, L. (2009) *Interest Rate Modelling: Theory and Practice*, Financial Mathematics Series, Boca Raton, FL: Chapman & Hall CRC.

5
Asset Liability Management Modelling with Risk Control by Stochastic Dominance

Xi Yang, Jacek Gondzio and Andreas Grothey

5.1 Introduction

The Asset Liability Management (ALM) problem has crucial importance for pension funds, insurance companies and banks whose business involves a large amount of liquidity. Indeed, these financial institutions apply ALM to guarantee meeting their liabilities while pursuing profit. The liabilities may take different forms: pensions paid to the members of the scheme in a pension fund, savers' deposits paid back in a bank or benefits paid to insurers in an insurance company. A common feature of these problems is the uncertainty of liabilities and asset returns and the resulting risk of underfunding. This constitutes a non-trivial difficulty in managing risk in any model applied by the financial institution. The need for multi-period planning additionally complicates the problem.

The paradigm of stochastic programming (Kall and Wallace, 1994; Birge and Louveaux, 1997) is well suited to tackle these problems and has already been applied in this context as shown in (Ziemba and Mulvey, 1998) and in the many references therein. One of the first industrially applied models of this type was the stochastic linear program with simple recourse developed in Kusy and Ziemba (1986). This model captured certain characteristics of ALM problems: it maximized revenues for the bank in the objective under legal, policy, liquidity, cash flow and budget constraints to make sure that deposit liabilities were met as closely as possible. Under the computational limits at the time when it was developed, this model took advantage of stochastic linear programming so as to be practical even for the large problems faced in banks. It was shown to be superior to a sequential decision theoretical model in terms of maximizing both the initial profit and the mean profit. However, risk management was not considered in this work: only expected penalties of constraint violation were taken into account.

A major difficulty in ALM models consists in risk management. One may follow the Markowitz risk-averse paradigm (Markowitz, 1959) and trade off multiple contradictory objectives: maximize the return and minimize the associated risk (for example Pyle, 1971). A successful example of optimization-based ALM modelling, which took risk management issues into account, was the Russell–Yasuda Kasai model, for a Japanese insurance company by the Frank Russell consulting company, which used multi-stage stochastic programming (Cariño *et al*, 1994; Cariño and Ziemba, 1998). This dynamic stochastic model took into account multiple accounts, regulatory rules and liabilities to enable the managing of complex issues arising in the Yasuda Fire and Marine Insurance company. Expected shortfall, that is the expected amount by which the goals were not achieved, was applied to measure risk more accurately than the calculation of expected penalties and it was easy to handle in the solution process. Moreover, the model proved to be easy to understand for decision makers. The implementation results showed the advantages of the Russell–Yasuda model over the mean-variance model in multi-period and multi-account problems.

There are various ways to control risk in addition to those mentioned above, such as variance and value at risk. Stochastic dominance leads to an alternative tool and it has recently gained substantial interest from the research community. It has several attractive features, of which two are particularly important: stochastic dominance is consistent with utility functions and it considers the whole probability distribution. We will discuss these issues in detail in the section 'Stochastic Dominance'. The stochastic dominance concept dates from the work of Karamata in 1932 (see (Levy, 1992) for a survey). Subsequently, stochastic dominance has been applied in statistics (Blackwell, 1951), economics (Hadar and Russell, 1969; Hanoch and Levy, 1969) and finance. However, stochastic dominance involves the comparison of (nonlinear) probability distribution functions, which makes its straightforward application difficult.

The inclusion of first-order stochastic dominance (FSD), within the stochastic programming framework, leads to a non-convex mixed integer programming formulation. By contrast, second-order stochastic dominance (SSD) can be incorporated in the form of linearized constraints (Dentcheva and Ruszczyński, 2003) that makes it a more attractive option. In a series of papers, Dentcheva and Ruszczyński analysed several aspects of the use of stochastic dominance, such as its optimality and duality (Dentcheva and Ruszczyński, 2003), applications to nonlinear dominance constraints (Dentcheva and Ruszczyński, 2004) and an application to static portfolio selection (Dentcheva and Ruszczyński, 2006). The introduction of non-convex constraints by the use of FSD introduces serious complications into optimization models and makes their solution difficult. Relaxations of these problems were analysed in Noyan *et al* (2006); stability and sensitivity of FSD with respect to general perturbation of the underlying probability measures were studied in Dentcheva *et al* (2007). Noyan *et al* (2006) also introduced interval SSD, which is equivalent to FSD, and generated a mixed integer problem based on this dominance relation. Roman *et al* (2006) proposed a multi-objective portfolio selection model with SSD constraints and Fábián *et al* (2009) developed an efficient method to solve this model based on a cutting-plane scheme. The application of stochastic dominance in dispersed energy planning and decision problems has been illustrated in (Gollmer *et al*, 2007, 2008, 2009), including both first-order and SSD. The use of multivariate stochastic dominance to measure multiple random variables jointly was discussed in Dentcheva and Ruszczyński (2009).

To the best of our knowledge, stochastic dominance has not yet been applied in the ALM context; and, in this article, we demonstrate how this can be done. Further, we introduce relaxed interval SSD, which is a dominance constraint intermediate between first-order and second-order, in a problem with discrete probability distributions, and demonstrate how it can be used to model chance constraints. By combining SSD and relaxed interval SSD, the model can help generate portfolio strategies with better management of risk and better control of underfunding. We illustrate this issue with a small example and an out-of-sample backtest analysed in the sections 'Model Example' and 'Backtesting', respectively.

Owing to the uncertainties of asset returns and liabilities, the resulting stochastic programming formulation involves many scenarios corresponding to the Monte Carlo simulation of realizations of the random factors. As a result, the problem grows to a large size, especially when the problem has multiple stages, and this leads to difficulties in the solution process. Consigli and Dempster (1998) proposed the Computer-aided Asset/Liability Management model as a multi-stage model and solution. Of the simplex method including the interior point method and nested Benders decomposition, the latter is shown to be the most efficient with regard to both solution time and memory requirements.

Stochastic dominance constraints link variables that are associated with different nodes at the same stage in the event tree. Adding such constraints to the linear stochastic programming problem destroys the usual tree structure of the problem and prevents the effective use of direct Benders decomposition or the progressive hedging algorithm (Rockafellar and Wets, 1991). See Fábián and Veszpremi (2008) for a solution based on dual decomposition. We discuss this issue further in the section 'Numerical Efficiency'. Instead, we apply the specialized structure-exploiting parallel interior point solver, object-oriented parallel solver (OOPS), to the structure of our ALM model with stochastic dominance constraints, to take advantage of such information in the solution process. OOPS is an interior point solver, which uses object-oriented programming techniques and treats each sub-structure of the problem as an object carrying its own dedicated linear algebra routines (Gondzio and Grothey, 2009). This design allows OOPS to deal with complicated ALM problems that contain stochastic dominance constraints. The computational results confirm that, by exploiting the structure, OOPS outperforms the commercial optimization solver CPLEX 10.0 on these problems.

The basic multi-stage stochastic programming model used for ALM is discussed in the next section. The theoretical issues of stochastic dominance are discussed in the section after that, with an emphasis on SSD and relaxed interval SSD. The practical aspects of the application of different stochastic dominance constraints in the ALM model (second-order and relaxed interval SSD) are covered in the subsequent section. These are followed, in the penultimate section, by an analysis of a small example of the model proposed and a backtest and discussion of computational results for a selection of realistic medium scale problems. The final section concludes the article.

5.2   Asset liability management

ALM models assist financial institutions in decision making on asset allocations, considering full use of the fund and resources available. The model aims to maximize the overall revenue, sometimes as well as revenue at intermediate stages, while controlling risk. Risk in ALM problems is present in two aspects: a possible loss of investment value and the inability to meet liabilities. The returns of assets and the liabilities are both uncertain. It is essential in ALM modelling to deal with these uncertainties as well as with the resulting risks. The stochastic programming approach is naturally applicable to problems that involve basic uncertainties; an approach to deal with risk management is discussed in the next section.

5.2.1   Multi-stage ALM modelling

Suppose a financial institution plans to invest in assets from a set $I=\{1,...,m\}$, with x_i denoting the investment in asset i. The return r of assets is uncertain, but we assume that it has a known probability distribution, which can be deduced from historical data, and the total return of the portfolio is $R = r^T x$. Then, we can calculate the expected return of the portfolio:

$$E[R] = \sum_i E[x_i * r_i]$$
$$= \sum_i x_i E[r_i]. \tag{5.1}$$

Considering a risk function $\phi(x)$, measuring the risk incurred by decision $x \in \mathbb{R}^m$, a general portfolio selection problem, without taking the liabilities into account, can be formulated in one of the following three ways:

$$\min_{x} - E[r^T x] + \phi(x), \quad x \in X, \tag{5.2}$$

$$\min_{x} \phi(x), \quad E[r^T x] \geq \alpha, \quad x \in X, \tag{5.3}$$

$$\min_{x} - E[r^T x], \quad \phi(x) \leq \beta, \quad x \in X. \tag{5.4}$$

Suppose that constraints $E[r^T x] \geq \alpha$, $\phi(x) \leq \beta$ have strictly feasible points. It can be proven (Krokhmal *et al*, 2001) that these three problems are equivalent in the sense that they can generate the same efficient frontier, given a convex set X and a convex risk measure function $\phi(x)$. The best-known example of formulation (5.2) is the Markowitz mean-variance multi-objective model (Markowitz, 1959), which considers both return and risk in the objective. In formulation (5.3), risk is minimized with acceptable returns, whereas in formulation (5.4), the return is maximized subject to risk being kept at an acceptable level. The constraint in (5.4) defines the feasible set with feasible risk, so that, in the objective, the decision maker can focus on maximizing the return. In this article, we will use formulation (5.4).

Besides return and risk control, the ALM model considered has also the following features:

1. Transaction costs; each transaction will be charged a certain percentage of total transaction value, and different transaction costs may apply to purchases and sales.
2. Cash balance; liabilities should be paid to clients, meanwhile there is an inflow in terms of deposits or premiums; the model should make sure there is outflow and inflow match.
3. Inventories of assets and cash, which are essential in a dynamical system of 2- or even a multiple-stage problem.
4. Legal and policy constraints should be aligned with the financial sector's requirements.

This work considers the first three points.

It is important for the decision makers to rebalance the portfolio during the investment period as they may wish to adjust the asset allocations according to updated information on the market. The strategy that is currently optimal may not be optimal any more as the situation changes. Taking this into account, the problem is a multi-period problem and at the beginning of each period in the model, new decisions are made.

We denote the time horizon by T, and decision stages by $t = 0, ..., T$. At each time stage t, a decision is made on the units of each asset to be invested in and amount of cash held, based on the state of the total wealth and the forecast of

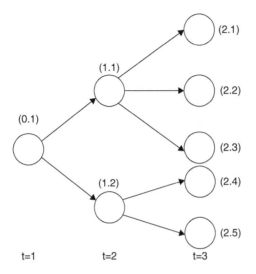

Figure 5.1   An example event tree describing different return states of nature

prospective performance of the assets at that particular time. When the random factors follow discrete distributions, the resulting decision process can be captured by an event tree, as shown in Figure 5.1. Each node is labelled with (i,j) denoting node j at stage i. Each node represents a possible future event. Asset returns, liabilities and cash deposits are subject to uncertain future evolution. Meanwhile, asset rebalancing is done after knowing the values that the asset returns and liabilities take at each node.

The notation of the model is given first:

5.2.1.1   Parameters:

W_i price of asset i

G total initial wealth

λ the penalty coefficient of underfunding

γ the transaction fee, which is proportional to trading volume (assumed to be equal for purchases and sales)

β upper bound on acceptable risk

ψ funding ratio, showing the percentage of liabilities to be satisfied

5.2.1.2   Random data:

$R_{i,j}^t$ the return of asset i in node j at stage t

$R_{c,j}^t$ the interest rate in node j at stage t

A_j^t the outflow of resources, for example liabilities

D_j^t the inflow of resources, for example. Contributions

π the joint probability distribution of above uncertain factors

5.2.1.3   Decision variables:

$xh_{i,j}^t$ units of asset i held in node j at stage t

$xs_{i,j}^t$ units of asset i sold in node j at stage t

$xb_{i,j}^t$ units of asset i bought in node j at stage t

c_j^t units of cash held in node j at stage t

b_j^T the amount of underfunding in node j at the terminal stage that cannot be satisfied

5.2.1.4   Indexes and sets:

t the stage index, with $t = \{1,..., T\}$

i the asset index, with $i \in I = \{1,..., m\}$

n_t the number of nodes at stage t

j the node index, with $j \in N_t = \{1,..., n_t\}$, $t = \{1,..., T\}$

$a_{(j)}$ the ancestor of node j

Then the multi-stage ALM problem concerning the investment strategy can be represented as:

$$\max \sum_{j \in N_T} \pi_j^T \left(\sum_{i \in I} (1-\gamma) W_i x h_{i,j}^T \right) + c_j^T - \lambda b_j^T \tag{5.5a}$$

s.t.

$$(1+\gamma)\sum_{i \in I} W_i x h_{i,0}^0 + c_0 = G - A_0 + D_0 \tag{5.5b}$$

$$(1+\gamma)\sum_{i \in I} W_i x b_{i,j}^t + c_j^t = (1-\gamma)\sum_{i \in I} W_i x s_{i,j}^t + (1 + R_{c,j}^t)c_{a(j)}^{t-1} - A_j^t + D_j^t, \tag{5.5c}$$

$$(1 + R_{i,j}^t)x h_{i,a(j)}^{t-1} + x b_{i,j}^t - x s_{i,j}^t = x h_{i,j}^t, \tag{5.5d}$$

$$\sum_{i \in I} (1-\gamma) W_i x h_{i,j}^T + c_j^T + b_j^T \geq \psi A_j^T, \tag{5.5e}$$

$$\phi(x h_j^t, c_j^t) \leq \beta, \tag{5.5f}$$

$$x h_{i,j}^t \geq 0, \ x s_{i,j}^t \geq 0, \ x b_j^t \geq 0, \ b_j^T \geq 0$$

$$x h_j^t, \ x s_j^t, \ x b_j^t \in \mathbb{R}^m$$

$$i \in I = \{1,...,m\}, \quad j \in N_t = \{1,...,n_t\}, \quad t = 1,...,T,$$

where $\phi(\cdot)$ gives the risk associated with position (xh, c).

The decision maker does not seek a strategy to strictly satisfy the liability at the horizon of the problem, but penalizes the underfunding. The objective (5.5a) aims to maximize the final wealth of the fund taking into account the penalties of underfunding. Equation (5.5b) balances the initial wealth at the first stage, whereas (5.5c) are cash balances for the following stages, both taking into account transaction costs, proportional to the total trade volume. The inventories of each asset at each stage are captured in (5.5d). (5.5e) defines the underfunding level b_j at the terminal stage. Risk control is expressed in (5.5f) with the risk measure function $\phi(\cdot)$ and the maximum acceptable level of risk β. This constraint will be discussed in greater detail in the following section. If the risk constraint is linear, the model (5.5) is a linear program.

Risk control in an ALM problem involves many aspects. Two of the most important aspects are overall performance and underfunding. The overall performance is analysed considering all possible outcomes of the portfolio, for example variance. We will use stochastic dominance to control the risk of overall performance and discuss the modelling issues involved in the section 'Linear formulation of SSD'. Underfunding concerns the possibility of unsatisfied liabilities only. To avoid underfunding completely is expensive to implement and in many situations impossible. We will control underfunding through the stochastic dominance constraints discussed in the section 'Interval SSD and chance constraints'.

5.3   Stochastic dominance

Stochastic dominance, as a risk control tool, has been considered in reference to certain risk measures in Ogryczak and Ruszczyński (2002) and Ruszczyński and Shapiro (2006). Below, we demonstrate how it can be incorporated into our ALM model. First, we briefly recall the definitions of stochastic dominance, following closely the exposition in Ogryczak and Ruszczyński (2002). The reader familiar with these definitions may skip the section 'Definition and properties of stochastic dominance'.

5.3.1   Definition and properties of stochastic dominance

Given a random variable ω, we consider the first performance function, which is actually the probability distribution function, as:

$$F^1_\omega(\eta) = P(\omega \le \eta). \tag{5.6}$$

Then we say that random variable Y dominates L by FSD if:

$$F^1_Y(\eta) \le F^1_L(\eta), \quad \forall \eta \in \mathbb{R}, \tag{5.7}$$

denoted as

$$Y \succeq_1 L. \tag{5.8}$$

Next, we define the second performance function as:

$$F_\omega^2(\eta) = \int_{-\infty}^{\eta} F_\omega^1(\zeta)d\zeta, \quad \forall \eta \in \mathbb{R}.$$ (5.9)

Then we say that random variable Y dominates L by SSD if:

$$F_Y^2(\eta) \leq F_L^2(\eta), \quad \forall \eta \in \mathbb{R},$$ (5.10)

denoted as

$$Y \geq_2 L.$$ (5.11)

Hence, if Y and L are returns of two portfolio strategies satisfying (5.7) (or (5.10)), then Y dominates L and Y is preferable. Iteratively, we can define higher-order stochastic dominance. And, it has also been proven that the lower-order dominance relations imply the dominance of higher orders (Ogryczak and Ruszczyński, 2002; Ruszczyński and Vanderbei, 2003).

Stochastic dominance has been used up to the present in decision theory and economics. The most important reason for this is its consistency with utility theory. Utility measures a degree of satisfaction. The value of a portfolio depends only on itself and is equal for every investor; the utility, however, is dependent on the particular circumstances of the person making the estimate. Investors seek to maximize their utilities. In general, utility functions are non-decreasing, which means that most people prefer more fortune to less. It is known that $X \geq_1 Y$, if and only if $E[U(X)] \geq E[U(Y)]$ for any non-decreasing utility function U for which these expected values are finite. And, $X \geq_2 Y$, if and only if $E[U(X)] \geq E[U(Y)]$ for any non-decreasing and concave utility function U for which these expected values are finite. A non-decreasing and concave utility function reflects that the investor prefers more fortune but that the speed of increase in satisfaction decreases. Details of stochastic dominance and utility theory can be found in Levy (1992). Generally, a reasonable risk-averse investor has a non-decreasing and concave utility function. Hence, we will incorporate SSD in ALM models because of its computational advantage, as we will show later, whereas FSD leads to a mixed-integer formulation that can be found in Noyan *et al* (2006) and Gollmer *et al* (2008).

5.3.2   Linear formulation of SSD

For a general probability distribution, the evaluation of the integral in the definition of SSD can lead to considerable computational difficulty. However, if the distribution is discrete, then this term can be simplified as is shown next.

Changing the interval of integration in (5.9), we obtain

$$F_\omega^2(\eta) = E[(\eta - \omega)_+].$$ (5.12)

Hence, inequality (5.10) can be written as

$$E[(\eta - Y)_+] \le E[(\eta - L)_+], \quad \eta \in \mathbb{R}.$$ (5.13)

To make the problem easier for modelling and computation, consider a relaxed formulation of this constraint valid in the interval $[a, b]$:

$$E[(\eta - Y)_+] \le E[(\eta - L)_+], \quad \eta \in [a, b].$$ (5.14)

Denote the shortfall as $\nu \in \mathbb{R}$, and observe that (5.14) is equivalent to:

$$\begin{cases} Y + \nu \ge \eta, \\ E[\nu] \le E[(\eta - L)_+], \quad \eta \in [a, b] \\ \nu \ge 0. \end{cases}$$ (5.15)

If L has a discrete probability distribution with realizations $l_k, \; k = 1, \ldots, K,$ $a \le l_k \le b$, then (5.14) can be rewritten as

$$E[(l_k - Y)_+] \le E[(l_k - L)_+], \quad \forall k = 1, \ldots, K.$$ (5.16)

Furthermore, if Y has a discrete distribution with realizations $y_m, \; m = 1, \ldots, M,$ $a \le y_m \le b$ (5.15) becomes

$$\begin{cases} y_m + \nu_{m,k} \ge l_k, \\ \sum_m \pi_m \nu_{m,k} \le \hat{l}_k, \\ \nu_{m,k} \ge 0, \end{cases}$$ (5.17)

where $\hat{l}_k = E[(l_k - L)_+]$. It is easy to see that the inequalities of (5.17) are linear.

5.3.3 Interval SSD and chance constraints

Interval SSD was first introduced by Noyan *et al* (2006) and demonstrated to be a sufficient as well as a necessary condition for FSD. Here, we will consider a relaxed interval SSD in the discrete case as an intermediate stochastic dominance relation between FSD and SSD, that is a weaker condition than FSD, but stronger than SSD.

We say that a random variable Y dominates another L by interval second-order stochastic dominance (ISSD) if:

$$E\left[(\eta_2-Y)_+\right] - E\left[(\eta_1-Y)_+\right] \leq E\left[(\eta_2-L)_+\right] - E\left[(\eta_1-L)_+\right],$$
$$\eta_1, \quad \eta_2 \in \mathbb{R}, \quad \eta_1 \leq \eta_2. \tag{5.18}$$

The proposition below establishes a relation between FSD and ISSD, which was first proven in Noyan *et al* (2006) for the case of discrete probability distributions. We shall prove it in the general form.

Proposition 1: $Y \geq_1 L$ if and only if Y dominates L by ISSD.

Proof: The proof of necessity is simple. If $Y \geq_1 L$, then for any given $\eta_1 \leq \eta_2$ and t, $\eta_1 \leq t \leq \eta_2$,

$$0 \leq F_Y^1(t) \leq F_L^1(t).$$

Hence, integrating

$$\int_{\eta_1}^{\eta_2} F_Y^1(t)\,dt \leq \int_{\eta_1}^{\eta_2} F_L^1(t)\,dt. \tag{5.19}$$

Using (5.12), (5.19) is equivalent to the definition of ISSD, that is inequality (5.18). We prove sufficiency by contradiction. Suppose there exists t^* such that

$$F_Y^1(t^*) > F_L^1(t^*).$$

Let $[a^*, b^*]$ be an interval such that $t^* \in [a^*, b^*]$ and

$$a^* = \inf\left[a : F_Y(t) > F_L(t), \quad t \in [a, t^*]\right]$$
$$b^* = \sup\left[b : F_Y(t) > F_L(t), \quad t \in [t^*, b]\right].$$

As both distribution functions F_Y and F_L are semi-continuous, it follows that $a^* < b^*$. Then, we have

$$\int_{a^*}^{b^*} F_Y^1(\alpha)\,d\alpha > \int_{a^*}^{b^*} F_L^1(\alpha)\,d\alpha$$

which violates the definition of ISSD. The sufficiency is proved.   □

If Y and L both have discrete probability distributions with realizations $y_1 < y_2 < \cdots < y_M$, and $l_1 < l_2 < \cdots < l_K$, the ISSD condition in this case can be written as:

$$E\big[(l_k - Y)_+\big] - E\big[(y_m - Y)_+\big] \le E\big[(l_k - L)_+\big] - E\big[(y_m - L)_+\big], \qquad (5.20)$$

for all $m \in \{1, ..., M\}$ and $k \in \{1, ..., K\}$ such that $l_k \ge y_m$ and

$$\{l_1, ..., l_K, y_1, ..., y_M\} \cap (y_m, l_k) = \varnothing, \qquad (5.21)$$

where (y_m, l_k) is the open interval with endpoints y_m and l_k (Noyan *et al*, 2006).

Incorporating the ISSD constraints (5.20) into a linear optimization model could lead to a mixed-integer formulation. The integer variables are induced by the dependence of y_m on the decision variables in the model Noyan *et al* (2006). Hence, we consider a relaxed form of ISSD in the situation with a discrete distribution:

$$E\big[(l_k - Y)_+\big] - E\big[(l_{k-1} - Y)_+\big] \le E\big[(l_k - L)_+\big] - E\big[(l_{k-1} - L)_+\big], \quad k = 1, ..., K, \qquad (5.22)$$

where l_k, $k = 1, ..., K$ are the realizations of L and l_0 is any real number such that $l_0 < l_1$, and denote the above relation of Y and L as

$$Y \succeq_{1\frac{1}{2}} L. \qquad (5.23)$$

It is easy to prove that this relaxed ISSD is weaker than FSD but stronger than SSD, that is

$$FSD \Rightarrow \text{Relaxed } ISSD \Rightarrow SSD. \qquad (5.24)$$

The first implication was proven in Noyan *et al* (2006). We give a full picture of these three dominance relations in the following proposition.

Proposition 2: If Y dominates L by FSD, then $Y \succeq_{1\frac{1}{2}} L$; If $Y \succeq_{1\frac{1}{2}} L$, then Y dominates L by SSD.

Proof: By Proposition 1, if FSD is true, ISSD is satisfied, which is sufficient for relaxed ISSD.

If relaxed ISSD is satisfied, we have

$$\int_{l_{k-1}}^{l_k} F_Y^1(t)\,dt \le \int_{l_{k-1}}^{l_k} F_L^1(t)\,dt,$$

for $k = 1,..., K$. As $F_L^l(t) = 0$, for any t such that $l_0 < t < l_1$,

$$\int_{l_0}^{l_1} F_Y^1(t)\,dt \le \int_{l_0}^{l_1} F_L^1(t)\,dt = 0$$

and we have $F_Y^l(t) = 0$, a.e., for $t < l_1$. Hence, for any real number $\eta \le l_1$,

$$\int_{-\infty}^{\eta} F_Y^1(t)\,dt \le \int_{-\infty}^{\eta} F_L^1(t)\,dt = 0. \tag{5.25}$$

Also,

$$\int_{-\infty}^{l_k} F_Y^1(t)\,dt = \int_{-\infty}^{l_1} F_Y^1(t)\,dt + \sum_{j=1,...,k-1} \int_{l_j}^{l_{j+1}} F_Y^1(t)\,dt \le 0 + \sum_{j=1,...,k-1} \int_{l_j}^{l_{j+1}} F_L^1(t)\,dt$$

$$= \int_{-\infty}^{l_k} F_Y^1(t)\,dt,$$

$k = 1,..., K$. Suppose there exists $\eta \in [l_k, l_{k+1}]$ such that

$$\int_{-\infty}^{\eta} F_Y^1(t)\,dt > \int_{-\infty}^{\eta} F_L^1(t)\,dt.$$

As

$$\int_{-\infty}^{l_k} F_Y^1(t)\,dt \le \int_{-\infty}^{l_k} F_L^1(t)\,dt,$$

we have

$$\int_{l_k}^{\eta} F_Y^1(t)\,dt > \int_{l_k}^{\eta} F_L^1(t)\,dt. \tag{5.26}$$

In addition, for $t \in [l_k, l_{k+1})$, $F_L^l(t) = F_L^l(l_k)$. From (5.26), using monotonicity of F_Y^1,

$$F_Y^1(\eta) > F_L^1(l_k). \tag{5.27}$$

As a result,

$$\int_{\eta}^{l_{k+1}} F_Y^1(t)\,dt > \int_{\eta}^{l_{k+1}} F_L^1(t)\,dt. \tag{5.28}$$

Inequalities (5.26) and (5.28) together imply

$$\int_{l_k}^{l_{k+1}} F_Y^1(t)\,dt > \int_{l_k}^{l_{k+1}} F_L^1(t)\,dt, \tag{5.29}$$

which contradicts the relaxed ISSD condition. Therefore, for all $\eta \in [l_1, l_K]$, SSD is satisfied. For $\eta > l_K$,

$$\int_{-\infty}^{\eta} F_L^1(t)\,dt = \int_{-\infty}^{l_K} F_L^1(t)\,dt + \int_{l_K}^{\eta} F_L^1(t)\,dt$$

$$= \int_{-\infty}^{l_K} F_L^1(t)\,dt + \int_{l_K}^{\eta} 1\,dt$$

$$\geq \int_{-\infty}^{l_K} F_Y^1(t)\,dt + \int_{l_K}^{\eta} F_Y^1(t)\,dt.$$

The sufficiency of SSD is proved.   □

An interesting question arises as to whether any reverse implication to (5.24) holds. Two examples are given below to illustrate that the opposite implications of these relations are not true. The first demonstrates that the relaxed ISSD does not imply FSD and the second shows that SSD does not imply the relaxed ISSD.

Example 1:   Consider two assets L and Y with the following probability distributions of returns: $P(L = 100) = \frac{1}{3}$, $P(L = 200) = \frac{1}{3}$, $P(L = 300) = \frac{1}{3}$; $P(Y = 150) = \frac{1}{2}$, $P(Y = 300) = \frac{1}{2}$. For these distributions, we find:

$$E\big[(\eta - L)_+\big] = \begin{cases} 0, & \eta \leq 100 \\[2mm] \dfrac{1}{3}(\eta - 100), & 100 < \eta \leq 200 \\[2mm] \dfrac{2}{3}(\eta - 200) + \dfrac{1}{3}(200 - 100), & 200 < \eta \leq 300 \\[2mm] (\eta - 300) + \dfrac{2}{3}(300 - 200) + \dfrac{1}{3}(200 - 100), & 300 < \eta \end{cases}$$

$$E\big[(\eta - Y)_+\big] = \begin{cases} 0, & \eta \leq 150 \\[2mm] \dfrac{1}{2}(\eta - 150), & 150 < \eta \leq 300 \\[2mm] (\eta - 300) + \dfrac{1}{2}(300 - 150), & 300 < \eta \end{cases}$$

and collect the values of $E[(l_k - X)_+] - E[(l_{k-1} - X)_+]$ for both variables L and Y for all intervals $(l_{k-1}, l_k]$ in Table 5.1.

Table 5.1   The relaxed ISSD values of assets L and Y

$E[l_k{-}X]_+{-}E[l_{k-1}{-}X]_+$	[0, 100]	[100, 200]	[200, 300]
$X{=}L$	0	33.3	66.7
$X{=}Y$	0	25	50

Obviously, inequality (5.22) is always satisfied hence the relaxed ISSD is satisfied, that is $Y \succeq_{1\frac{1}{2}} L$. However, $P(L \le 150) < P(Y \le 150)$, which means FSD is violated.   □

Example 2:   Consider two assets L and Y, where L is the same as in Example 1. Asset Y has three possible returns: $P(Y = 150) = \frac{1}{2}$, $P(Y = 200) = \frac{1}{4}$ and $P(Y = 300) = \frac{1}{4}$. Y dominates L by SSD but Y does not dominate L by relaxed ISSD, because

$$F_\omega^2 = E[(\eta - \omega)_+] = \int_{-\infty}^{\eta} F_\omega(\xi)d\xi,$$

$$F_L^2(\eta) = E[(\eta - L)_+] = \begin{cases} 0, & \eta \le 100 \\ \frac{1}{3}(\eta - 100), & 100 < \eta \le 200 \\ \frac{2}{3}(\eta - 200) + \frac{1}{3}(200 - 100), & 200 < \eta \le 300 \\ (\eta - 300) + \frac{2}{3}(300 - 200) + \frac{1}{3}(200 - 100), & 300 < \eta \end{cases}$$

$$F_Y^2(\eta) = E[(\eta - Y)_+] = \begin{cases} 0, & \eta \le 150 \\ \frac{1}{2}(\eta - 150), & 150 < \eta \le 200 \\ \frac{3}{4}(\eta - 200) + \frac{1}{2}(200 - 150), & 200 < \eta \le 300 \\ (\eta - 300) + \frac{3}{4}(300 - 200) + \frac{1}{2}(200 - 150), & 300 < \eta \end{cases}$$

illustrating that $E[(\eta - L)_+] \ge E[(\eta - Y)_+]$, whereas

$$E[(300 - L)_+] - E[(200 - L)_+] = \frac{200}{3} \le E[(300 - Y)_+] - E[(200 - Y)_+] = 75. \qquad □$$

Below, we prove one more technical result regarding relaxed ISSD, which has important consequences for a practical way of modelling relaxed ISSD constraints as stated in the rest of this section.

Proposition 3:   Let Y and L be random variables, whose probability distributions are discrete with realizations $y_1, ..., y_M$ and $l_1, ..., l_K$, respectively. Let Y

dominate L by relaxed ISSD. If there exists $k \in \{1,...,K-1\}$, such that

$$\{y_1,...,y_M\} \cap (l_k, l_{k+1}) = \varnothing, \tag{5.30}$$

then $F_Y^1(t) \le F_L^1(t)$ for all $t \in [l_k, l_{k+1}]$

Proof: For any k such that

$$\{y_1,...,y_M\} \cap (l_k, l_{k+1}) = \varnothing, \tag{5.31}$$

$F_Y^1(t) \le F_Y^1(l_k)$, $t \in [l_k, l_{k+1}]$. Then by the relaxed ISSD relation,

$$\int_{l_k}^{l_{k+1}} F_Y^1(t) dt = F_Y^1(l_k)(l_{k+1} - l_k) \le \int_{l_k}^{l_{k+1}} F_L^1(t) dt$$
$$= F_L^1(l_k)(l_{k+1} - l_k) \Rightarrow F_Y^1(l_k) \le F_L^1(l_k). \qquad \square$$

Remark 4: By comparing relaxed ISSD and ISSD, which is equivalent to FSD, we can see the relaxation is at the points of y_m. Assume that the relaxed ISSD is true. From the above proposition, $F_Y^1(t) \le F_L^1(t)$ holds in any interval $[l_k, l_{k+1})$, which does not contain any ym. Actually, even if y_m appears in this interval, $F_Y^1(t) \le F_L^1(t)$ still holds if $F_Y^1(y_m) \le F_L^1(l_k)$. Such a relation is violated only in the interval in which the probability of Y jumps over the probability of the benchmark L. This violation will not transfer to the next interval because of relaxed ISSD.

Proposition 3 opens a way to express chance constraints in the LP form by imposing relaxed ISSD constraints. Assume that L is a benchmark with discrete distribution and the portfolio Y dominates L by relaxed ISSD, and let $l_k < l_{k+1}$ be two neighbouring realizations of the benchmark. If $[l_k, l_{k+1}]$ is such that the portfolio will not have any realization in this interval, then

$$P(Y \le t) \le P(L \le t), \quad \forall t \in [l_k, l_{k+1}].$$

Hence, the probability of the portfolio can be constrained for those values in such an interval. There is an issue of how to guarantee the existence of such intervals. We address this problem below.

The risk control in ALM modelling reflects concerns about underfunding, which is the amount of unsatisfied liability. Bogentoft *et al* (2001) applied Conditional Value at Risk (CVaR) to control the return of the pension fund with a certain percentage to cover the liability. Although it is difficult and costly to avoid any underfunding, it seems highly desirable to limit the probability that any underfunding happens. We will show how to express such probability constraints in an LP form. Suppose the portfolio is expected to satisfy the following chance constraint:

$$P(\text{final wealth} - \text{liability} < 0) \leq \alpha, \tag{5.32}$$

where α is a given threshold. An interval $[\theta_1, \theta_2]$ is assumed to exist such that the following two equations

$$\text{final wealth} - \text{liability} < \theta_1 \tag{5.33}$$

$$\text{final wealth} - \text{liability} < \theta_2 \tag{5.34}$$

are equivalent to

$$\text{final wealth} - \text{liability} < 0. \tag{5.35}$$

For example, it is the same to the fund manager in practice to have either no underfunding or an underfunding of £1. Then this interval can be $[-1, 0]$. We assume that such an interval always exists. Suppose the return of the portfolio is modelled by M scenarios. A benchmark L can be constructed satisfying the following conditions:

- The benchmark value has K realizations and $K > M+1$.
- Among the K realizations, at least $M+1$ are allocated in the interval $[\theta_1, \theta_2]$, with θ_1 and θ_2 defined as above.
- Last but most important, $P(L - \text{Liability} < 0) \leq \alpha$.

If a portfolio outperforms such a benchmark by relaxed ISSD, there must be an interval $[l_k, l_{k+1}) \subset [\theta_1, \theta_2]$, where the portfolio value has no realization. Then by Proposition 3, this portfolio has return below l_{k+1} with probability less than α. Although there is no difference to the fund manager to have an underfunding of l_{k+1} or 0, the chance constraint of the underfunding is successfully satisfied. For multiple chance constraints, separate relaxed ISSD constraints can be applied and the derivation is the same as in the single case.

5.4 Multi-stage alm model with SSD and relaxed ISSD constraints

Now, we will apply SSD and relaxed ISSD in the multi-stage ALM model to control risk. Either SSD or relaxed ISSD can be independently incorporated in the model. Both SSD and relaxed ISSD constraints are set at each stage: overall portfolio returns are required to dominate a benchmark by SSD and relaxed ISSD constraint guarantees that the portfolio value minus liabilities dominates a benchmark by relaxed ISSD.

In addition to the notation listed in the section 'Asset Liability Management', new notation is introduced to construct the stochastic dominance constraints in the model as follows:

τ_l the values of benchmark performance used for the SSD constraint, $l = 1, ..., L$

μ_k the values of benchmark performance used for the relaxed ISSD constraint, $k = 1, ..., K$. These values are set such that the probability of this benchmark being negative is equal to α, that is we want the probability of underfunding to be less than or equal to α

$$\hat{\tau}_l = E[(\tau_l - \tau)_+], \quad l = 1, ..., L$$

$$\hat{\mu}_k = E[(\mu_k - \mu)_+], \quad k = 1, ..., K$$

$s_{j,t}^l$ shortfall of the portfolio in node j at stage t compared to lth value of the benchmark in the SSD constraint

$v_{j,t}^k$ shortfall of the portfolio in node j at stage t compared to kth value of the benchmark in the relaxed ISSD constraint

In the following model (5.36), we can find that (5.36f) and (5.36g) are SSD constraints that the return of the portfolio is restricted to dominate the benchmark τ by SSD; whereas (5.36h), (5.36i) and (5.36j) are relaxed ISSD constraints that guarantee that the value of the portfolio minus the amount of the liability dominates the benchmark μ by relaxed ISSD, so as to control the probability of underfunding:

$$\max \sum_{j \in N_T} \pi_j^T \times \left(\sum_{i \in I} (1 - \gamma) W_i x h_{i,j}^T + c_j^T - \lambda b_j^T \right) \tag{5.36a}$$

$$s.t.$$

$$(1 + \gamma) \sum_{i \in I} W_i x h_{i,0}^0 + c_0 = G - A_0 + D_0 \tag{5.36b}$$

$$(1 + \gamma) \sum_{i \in I} W_i x b_{i,j}^t + c_j^t = (1 - \gamma) \sum_{i \in I} W_i x s_{i,j}^t + (1 + R_{c,j}^t) c_{a(j)}^{t-1} - A_j^t + D_j^t, \tag{5.36c}$$

$$(1 + R_{i,j}^t) x h_{i,a(j)}^{t-1} + x b_{i,j}^t - x s_{i,j}^t = x h_{i,j}^t, \tag{5.36d}$$

$$\sum_{i \in I} (1 - \gamma) W_i x h_{i,j}^T + c_j^T + b_j^T \geq \psi A_j^T, \tag{5.36e}$$

$$\sum_{i \in I} (1 + R_{i,j}^t) W_i x h_{i,a(j)}^{t-1} + (1 + R_{c,j}^t) c_{a(j)}^{t-1} + s_{j,t}^l \geq \tau_l, \qquad (5.36\text{f})$$

$$\sum_{j \in N_t} \pi_j^t s_{j,t}^l \leq \hat{\tau}_l, \quad l = 1, \dots, L, \qquad (5.36\text{g})$$

$$\sum_{i \in I} (1 + R_{i,j}^t) W_i x h_{i,a(j)}^{t-1} + (1 + R_{c,j}^t) c_{a(j)}^{t-1} - \psi A_{j,t} + v_{j,t}^k \geq \mu_k, \qquad (5.36\text{h})$$

$$\sum_{j \in N_t} \pi_j^t v_{j,t}^k - \sum_{j \in N_t} \pi_j^t v_{j,t}^{k-1} \leq \hat{\mu}_k - \hat{\mu}_{k-1}, \quad k = 2, \dots, K, \qquad (5.36\text{i})$$

$$\sum_{j \in N_t} \pi_j^t v_{j,t}^1 \leq \hat{\mu}_1, \quad x h_{i,j}^t \geq 0, \quad x s_{i,j}^t \geq 0, \quad x b_j^t \geq 0, \quad b_j^T \geq 0 \qquad (5.36\text{j})$$

$$x h_j^t, \quad x s_j^t, \quad x b_j^t \in \mathbb{R}^m$$

$$i \in I = \{1, \dots, m\}, \quad j \in N_t = \{1, \dots, n_t\},$$

$$t = 1, \dots, T, \quad l = 1, \dots, L, \quad k = 1, \dots, K.$$

Now we can see that, by incorporating SSD in the ALM model, the risk incurred by overall performance is controlled by requesting that our portfolio outperforms the benchmark by SSD in (5.36f) and (5.36g); by incorporating relaxed ISSD, the risk of underfunding is controlled in terms of chance constraints (5.36h), (5.36i) and (5.36j).

5.5   Numerical results

The models discussed in this article are applicable in practice. We first demonstrate the advantages of taking stochastic dominance constraints into account using a small example, followed with an out-of-sample backtest. Then, we will show how real-world problems can be solved. We use the structure-exploiting interior point solver OOPS (Gondzio and Grothey, 2009) to solve these problems and compare its performance with that of the general-purpose commercial optimizer CPLEX 10.0 on a number of medium-scale test examples.

5.5.1   A model example

Consider a small investment problem with two stages and four stocks to be chosen from. One stage corresponds to 1 day. There are four branches in the first stage and two branches from each node of the second stage. Both asset returns and liabilities are random. The returns in per cent of the four stocks are shown in Table 5.2, with the probabilities in brackets and the other parameters are presented in Table 5.3.

We generate the optimal investment strategy using three models. In the first one, (i), the underfunding is penalized in the objective without any SD constraint. In the second one, (ii), an SSD constraint is added to the first model, (i), to restrict the portfolio to outperform a benchmark at the first stage. As the third model, (iii), we apply the full model (5.4) for this problem, in which the probability of underfunding at the final (second) stage is restricted to be less than 5 per cent by relaxed ISSD constraints, with all other features the same as for the second model.

Results are summarized in Table 5.4. Model (i) suggested investing only in assets A and D, whereas both models (ii) and (iii) include also asset B with slight differences in the weights of each asset, respectively. Assets A and D have better

Table 5.2 Returns of the assets (%)

	A	B	C	D
1st stage				
1 (0.5)	0.0145	−0.1020	−0.0305	0.2299
2 (0.2)	0.0056	0.2050	0.1041	−0.0236
3 (0.2)	−0.0113	0.0007	−0.0287	0.1658
4 (0.1)	0.1573	−0.0286	0.0645	−0.0742
2nd stage				
1 (0.40)	0.1145	−0.2020	−0.0305	0.0299
2 (0.10)	−0.1060	0.2450	0.0341	0.0167
3 (0.16)	0.1145	−0.2020	−0.0305	0.0299
4 (0.04)	−0.1060	0.2450	0.0341	0.0167
5 (0.16)	0.1145	−0.2020	−0.0305	0.0299
6 (0.04)	−0.1060	0.2450	0.0341	0.0167
7 (0.08)	0.1145	−0.2020	−0.0305	0.0299
8 (0.02)	−0.1060	0.2450	0.0341	0.0167

Table 5.3 Typical parameter values

	Parameter	Value
No. of assets	m	4
No. of leaf nodes	n_T	8
No. of SSD benchmarks	K_1	1
No. of rISSD benchmarks	K_2	1
Length of investment horizon	T	2
Penalty coefficient for underfunding at horizon	λ	2
Lower bound of funding ratio	ϕ	1.01
Transaction fee ratio	γ	0.03

Table 5.4 Portfolio properties generated from three models: portfolio composition, expected return and the probability of underfunding

Model	Portfolio				Return (%)	Prob(underfunding) (%)
	A (%)	B (%)	C	D (%)		
(i) No SD	26.6	0	0	73.4	11	22
(ii) SSD	39.3	18.2	0	42.5	6	6
(iii) SSD + rISSD	41.5	15.6	0	42.9	6	2

performance in terms of expected return compared with the other two. However, the inclusion of asset B can lead to better diversification. From the results presented in Table 5.4, we can see that taking SSD constraints into account can half the risk of underfunding, whereas the expected return is reduced by 45 per cent. Relaxed ISSD together with SSD can effectively reduce the probability of underfunding to merely 2 per cent, whereas the return is the same.

5.5.2   Backtesting

Assume a fund management project with the initial wealth of £100 000 that can be invested in the stocks in the FTSE100 and as deposits in the money market with certain interest. Benchmarks are constructed as the worst portfolio that can be accepted. All the parameters in the backtest are the same as in Table 5.3, except the number of assets and the number of nodes, which are 102 and 80, respectively. The backtest is run with 80 rolling time windows. The model first learns from 80 days of market data to generate the optimal portfolio, and then we apply this portfolio strategy for the next 80 days and compare its performance with a passive investment strategy, only following the FTSE100 Index and the investment strategy generated from a Markowitz model. Then we roll this 160-day time window by one day to the next and repeat the above computations. For example, in the first window, we run the model with market data from 09 October to 16 February 2008 (80 days), to generate an optimal portfolio strategy; then we see how this portfolio performs from 19 February to 11 June 2008 (the following 80 days, 17 February and 18 February 2008 are weekends). In Figure 5.2, the results are shown with a thick solid line for the portfolio, a dotted line for the FTSE100 Index and a thin solid line for the strategy generated by the Markowitz model, where the value of the portfolio is generally above those of the Index and the Markowitz strategy.

For each time window, we count the percentage of the 80 days that underfunding occurs as an indicator of the possibility of underfunding. Figure 5.3 shows for the 80 time windows the percentage of days of the 80 that underfunding over 5 per cent occurs for both the portfolio and the FTSE100 Index. The percentage of days of the 80 that underfunding over 10 per cent occurs are shown in Figure 5.4. In Figure 5.3, we can see that until 04 April 2008, the underfunding of the portfolio by over 5 per cent appeared less frequently than that of the Index, which is below 10 per cent of 80 days. Then the curve of the portfolio jumped above the Index, which was because of the big recession of the market starting from 19 May 2008. Figure 5.5 shows the performance of the portfolio, the Index and the Markowitz strategy over those 80 days from 04 April 2008. The portfolio performs relatively steadily compared with the Index, that is the underfunding is below 10 per cent, although underfunding exists through the whole period. The worst performance of the portfolio in both Figures 5.3 and 5.4 appears around 20 May 2008, similarly to the Index,

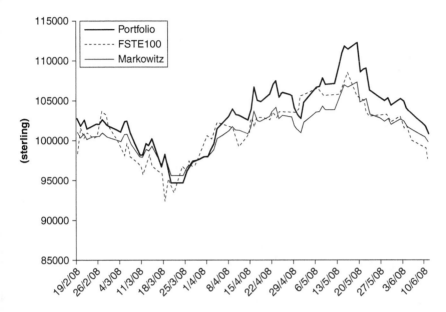

Figure 5.2 Value of the portfolio and FTSE100 Index in first time window (19 February–11 June 2008)

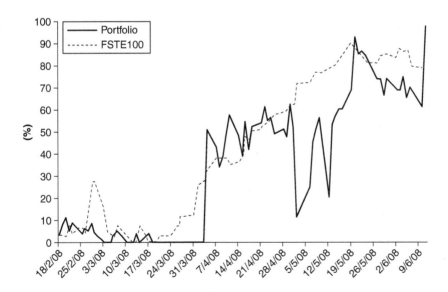

Figure 5.3   Percentage of days with underfunding over 5 per cent

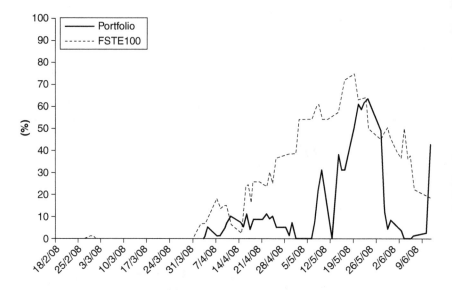

Figure 5.4   Percentage of days with underfunding over 10 per cent

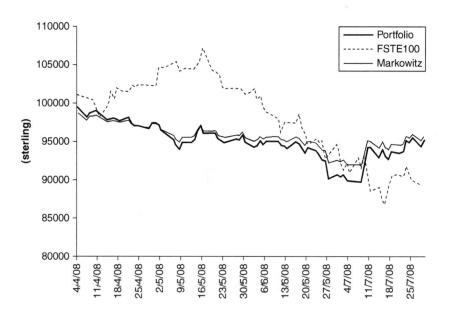

Figure 5.5   Value of the portfolio and FTSE100 Index over 4 April–29 July 2008

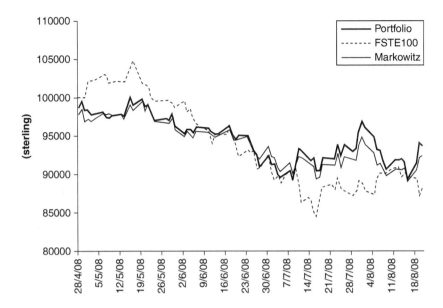

Figure 5.6 Value of the portfolio and FTSE100 Index over 28 April–20 August 2008

when the market was at a turning point and started to decrease along the way until touching a 21-month low on 15 July 2008.

Through the whole test, the portfolio generated by the model presents a relative steady performance compared with FTSE100 Index. For example, on 28 April 2008, the two curves in Figure 5.3 cross, which means the percentages of days with underfunding over 5 per cent are the same for both the portfolio and the Index investment. However, the possibility of the portfolio under-funding over 10 per cent corresponding to that day is 5 per cent as shown in Figure 5.4, significantly smaller than the 37.5 per cent of the Index. That 80-day performance is illustrated in Figure 5.6. Among the 80 time windows, there are 58 windows (72.5 per cent) when the percentage of days with portfolio underfunding over 5 per cent is smaller than that of the Index, as illustrated in Figure 5.3, and 75 windows (93.75 per cent) for underfunding over 10 per cent, as is shown in Figure 5.4.

5.5.3 Numerical efficiency

The ALM stochastic programming model (5.36) proposed in the previous section has the constraint matrix structure shown in Figure 5.7 for a two-stage problem. Each diagonal block composed of small *A* and *B* matrices corresponds to an initial branch in the event tree. The inventory, cash balance and underfunding constraints are at the last stage. The left column contains the coefficients of the first

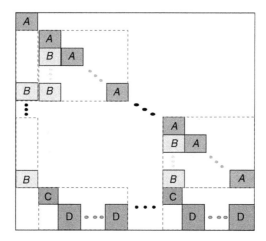

Figure 5.7   The constraint matrix structure of the two-stage ALM stochastic programming model with SSD constraints

stage variables and the left-top diagonal block contains the initial budget constraint. The bottom border corresponds to the stochastic dominance constraints linking all the nodes of a given stage together. For multi-stage problems, the small diagonal A-blocks are themselves structured. This nested bordered block-diagonal structure can be efficiently exploited by OOPS (Gondzio and Grothey, 2007a, 2009), whereas traditional approaches for linear stochastic programming, such as Benders decomposition and progressive hedging (Rockafellar and Wets, 1991), will have difficulties with the SSD constraints.

The computational tests were performed using stocks in the FTSE100 and FTSE250 daily data from 01 January 2003 to 01 January 2008 to construct the scenarios of portfolio return. Table 5.5 summarizes the statistics of the ALM problems tested. All the problems are modelled following expression (5.36) and are linear programs. 'Stages' and 'Total Nodes' refer to the geometry of the event tree for these problems. As this section is more concerned with numerical efficiency, 'Stages' here is not assigned with any specific meaning. 'Blocks' is the number of second-stage nodes. All problems have a number of branches different from stage to stage. There are more branches at the second stage than in the following stages, for example 80 branches at the second stage and two branches for all later stages (see Dempster *et al*, 2007). 'Assets' is the number of assets that can be invested in, which are the FTSE stocks. 'Bnmk' is the number of realizations of each benchmark portfolio.

The size of ALM problems grows exponentially with the number of stages. There are two sets of SSD constraints (5.36f), (5.36g) and three sets of ISSD constraints (5.36h), (5.36i), (5.36j) for each benchmark at each stage. Suppose

Table 5.5   Problems scales for comparison of OOPS with CPLEX

Problem	Stages T	Blocks B	Assets I	Bnmk L	Total Nodes $\lvert N \rvert = \sum_{t=0}^{T-1} N_t$	Constraints $(I+L+2)\lvert N \rvert$	Variables $(3I+L+2)\lvert N \rvert$
ALM1a	2	80	64	20	81	6966	17334
ALM1b	2	40	128	20	41	6150	16646
ALM1c	2	80	128	20	81	12150	32886
ALM1d	2	160	128	20	161	24150	65366
ALM2a	2	80	64	40	81	8586	18954
ALM2b	2	40	128	40	41	6970	17466
ALM2c	2	80	128	40	81	13770	34506
ALM2d	2	160	128	40	161	27370	68586
ALM3a	2	80	64	80	81	11826	22194
ALM3b	2	40	128	80	41	8610	19106
ALM3c	2	80	128	80	81	17010	37746
ALM3d	2	160	128	80	161	33810	75026
ALM4a	3	40	128	10	201	28140	79596
ALM4b	3	80	128	10	241	33740	95436
ALM5a	4	40	128	10	1641	229740	649836
ALM5b	4	40	128	10	2921	408940	1156716
ALM5c	4	80	128	10	1681	235340	665676
ALM5d	4	80	128	10	3281	459340	1299276

there are T stages, N nodes, A_1 and A_2 benchmarks in total for SSD and relaxed ISSD, respectively, and each benchmark a_1 (or a_2) has K_{a1} (or K_{a2}) realizations, $a_1=1,...,A_1$ and $a_2=1,...,A_2$. SSD requirements are captured by $(N+T)\Sigma_{a1}K_{a1}$ linear constraints and relaxed ISSD requirements are taken into account by means of $(N+T)\Sigma_{a2}K_{a2}$ linear constraints. The presence of these stochastic dominance constraints makes the problem very difficult for standard optimization approaches. For example, it makes the application of Benders decomposition impossible (which is otherwise a powerful method for stochastic programming (Birge and Louveaux, 1997; Consigli and Dempster, 1998)).

All computations were done on the Intel Core2 Duo machine. This machine features two 2.66 GHz processors and a total of 2 GB memory.

The numerical results are collected in Table 5.6. We report the solution time, number of iterations and memory requirements for CPLEX 10.0 barrier (ILOG) and OOPS (Gondzio and Grothey, 2007a, 2007b, 2009) for each problem. Most of the problems can be solved within reasonable time and barrier iterations. Both solvers did very well for small problems. Although CPLEX ran out of memory for problems ALM5b and ALM5d, OOPS could solve them within half an hour. For most of the problems, OOPS was faster than CPLEX, although CPLEX generally took fewer iterations. The solution time of OOPS increases steadily with the scaling of problems. When the number of assets is doubled, the solution time of OOPS increases by a factor smaller than three, which can be seen from the comparison of solution statistics of ALM1a and ALM1c, ALM2a

Table 5.6   Comparing solution time in seconds of CPLEX and OOPS

Problem	CPLEX 10.0			OOPS		
	Time(s)	Itr	MEM(Mb)	time(s)	Itr	MEM(Mb)
ALM1a	53.47	14	100.3	19.93	24	38.9
ALM1b	26.73	20	55.3	21.05	27	38.9
ALM1c	133.91	19	184.3	41.467	26	75.8
ALM1d	9.72	42	106.5	104.132	33	147.5
ALM2a	95.07	18	114.7	37.59	28	61.4
ALM2b	63.29	18	92.2	51.16	25	59.4
ALM2c	447.85	20	335.9	111.695	27	114.7
ALM2d	5021.74	35	1265.7	316.92	39	223.3
ALM3a	124.23	19	147.5	61.49	25	102.4
ALM3b	138.89	25	143.4	92.99	29	98.3
ALM3c	1072.28	30	421.9	180.91	28	190.5
ALM3d	7709.53	28	1316.9	593.562	47	376.8
ALM4a	96.89	15	196.6	72.179	28	133.1
ALM4b	588.11	15	536.6	160.20	30	262.1
ALM5a	1291.18	29	1357.8	890.44	41	1075.2
ALM5b	–	–	–	1557.15	41	1843.2
ALM5c	1542.12	20	1597.4	589.65	26	1118.2
ALM5d	–	–	–	1140.16	25	1822.7

and ALM2c, ALM3a and ALM3c. By comparing solution statistics of problems ALM1a, ALM2a and ALM3a, we can observe the influence of the number of benchmark realizations on the efficiency of both solvers compared. The solution statistics of ALM1b/c/d, ALM2b/c/d and ALM3b/c/d demonstrate that the solution time of CPLEX increases with the number of blocks much faster than that of OOPS. Both CPLEX and OOPS solution times are badly affected by the increase of the number of benchmark realizations. The memory requirements of OOPS are generally smaller than those of CPLEX.

5.6   Conclusions

In addition to the operational constraints, that is inventory and cash balance, ALM models require sophisticated risk control to ensure that liabilities are met. As a consequence, underfunding, which measures the amount of non-satisfied liabilities, is expected to be zero. Stochastic dominance as a reference to efficient risk control can manage the risk in ALM problems effectively by its consistency with utility theory. Furthermore, the concept of relaxed ISSD is developed and used to model chance constraints in linear form, which can manage underfunding in line with other stochastic dominance constraints. OOPS (Gondzio and Grothey 2007a, 2009) can handle such problems efficiently in terms of both storage requirements and solution time.

Acknowledgements

We are grateful to Dr Marco Colombo for help with the efficient set up of the problem in OOPS. We are also grateful to two anonymous referees whose comments helped us to improve the presentation.

References

Birge, J.R. and Louveaux, F. (1997) *Introduction to Stochastic Programming*. New York: Springer-Verlag.

Blackwell, D. (1951) Comparison of experiments, in J. Neyman (ed) *Second Berkeley Sympos. Math. Statist. and Probability*. Berkeley, California: University of California Press, pp. 93–102.

Bogentoft, E., Romeijn, H.E. and Uryasev, S. (2001) Asset/liability management for pension funds using CVaR constraints. *The Journal of Risk Finance* 3(1): 57–71.

Cariño, D.R. *et al* (1994) The Russell–Yasuda Kasai model: An asset/liability model for a Japanese insurance company using multistage stochastic programming. *Interfaces* 24: 29–49.

Cariño, D.R. and Ziemba, W.T. (1998) Formulation of the Russell–Yasuda Kasai financial model. *Operations Research* 46(4): 433–449.

Consigli, G. and Dempster, M.A.H. (1998) Dynamic stochastic programming for asset-liability management. *Annals of Operation Research* 81: 131–161.

Dempster, M.A., Germano, M., Medova, E.A., Rietbergen, M.I., Sandrini, F. and Scrownston, M. (2007) Designing minimum guaranteed return funds. *Quantitative Finance* 7: 245–256.

Dentcheva, D., Henrion, R. and Ruszczyński, A. (2007) Stability and sensitivity of optimization problems with first order stochastic dominance constraints. *SIAM Journal of Optimization* 18(1): 322–337.

Dentcheva, D. and Ruszczyński, A. (2003) Optimization with stochastic dominance constraints. *SIAM Journal of Optimization* 14(2): 548–566.

Dentcheva, D. and Ruszczyński, A. (2004) Optimality and duality theory for stochastic optimization problems with nonlinear dominance constraints. *Mathematical Programming* 99: 329–350.

Dentcheva, D. and Ruszczyński, A. (2006) Portfolio optimization with stochastic dominance constraints. *Journal of Banking Finance* 30: 433–451.

Dentcheva, D. and Ruszczyński, A. (2009) Optimization with multivariate stochastic dominance constraints. *Mathematical Programming* 117: 111–127.

Fábián, C.I. and Veszpremi, A. (2008) Algorithms for handling CVaR constraints in dynamic stochastic programming models with applications to finance. *Journal of Risk* 10(3): 111–131.

Fábián, C.I., Mitra, G. and Roman, D. (2009) Processing second-order stochastic dominance models using cutting-plane representations. *Mathematical Programming* 1–25, doi: 10.1007/s10107-009-0326-1.

Gollmer, R., Gotzes, U., Neise, F. and Schultz, R. (2007) Risk Modeling Via Stochastic Dominance in Power Systems With Dispersed Generation. Department of Mathematics, University of Duisburg-Essen. Technical report.

Gollmer, R., Gotzes, U. and Schultz, R. (2009) A note on second-order stochastic dominance constraints induced by mixed-integer linear recourse. *Mathematical Programming*, published online February 2009, 1–12.

Gollmer, R., Neise, F. and Schultz, R. (2008) Stochastic programs with first-order dominance constraints induced by mixed-integer linear recourse. *SIAM Journal on Optimization* 19: 552–571.

Gondzio, J. and Grothey, A. (2007a) Parallel interior point solver for structured quadratic programs: Application to financial planning problems. *Annals of OR* 152(1): 319–339.

Gondzio, J. and Grothey, A. (2007b) Solving nonlinear portfolio optimization problems with the primal-dual interior point method. *European Journal of Operational Research* 181(3): 1019–1029.

Gondzio, J. and Grothey, A. (2009) Exploiting structure in parallel implementation of interior point methods for optimization. *Computational Management Science* 6: 135–160.

Hadar, J. and Russell, W.R. (1969) Rules for ordering uncertain prospects. *American Economic Review* 59: 25–34.

Hanoch, G. and Levy, H. (1969) The efficiency analysis of choices involving risk. *Review of Economics Studies* 36: 335–346.

ILOG. Ilog cplex 10.0. http://www.ilog.com.

Kall, P. and Wallace, S.W. (1994) *Stochastic Programming.* Chichester: John Wiley & Sons.

Krokhmal, P., Palmquist, J. and Uryasev, S. (2001) Portfolio optimization with conditional value-at-risk objective and constraints. *Journal of Risk* 4(2): 43–68.

Kusy, M.I. and Ziemba, W.T. (1986) A bank asset and liability management model. *Operations Research* 34(3): 356–376.

Levy, H. (1992) Stochastic dominance and expected utility: Survey and analysis. *Management Science* 38(4): 555–593.

Markowitz, H.M. (1959) *Portfolio Selection, Efficient Diversification of Investments.* New York: John Wiley&Sons.

Noyan, N., Rudolf, G. and Ruszczyński, A. (2006) Relaxations of linear programming problems with first order stochastic dominance constraints. *Operations Research Letters* 34: 653–659.

Ogryczak, W. and Ruszczyński, A. (2002) Dual stochastic dominance and related mean-risk models. *SIAM Journal of Optimization* 13(1): 60–78.

Pyle, D.H. (1971) On the theory of financial intermediation. *Journal of Finance* 26: 737–747.

Rockafellar, R.T. and Wets, R.J.-B. (1991) Scenarios and policy aggregation in optimization under uncertainty. *Mathematics of Operations Research* 16(1): 119–147.

Roman, D., Darby-Dowman, K. and Mitra, G. (2006) Portfolio construction based on stochastic dominance and target return distributions. *Mathematical Programming* 108: 541–569.

Ruszczyński, A. and Shapiro, A. (2006) Optimization of convex risk functions. *Mathematics of Operation Research* 31(3): 433–452.

Ruszczyński, A. and Vanderbei, R.J. (2003) Frontiers of stochastic nondominated portfolios. *Econometrica* 71(4): 1287–1297.

Ziemba, W.T. and Mulvey, J.M. (1998) *Worldwide Asset and Liability Modeling,* Publications of the Newton Institute Cambridge: Cambridge University Press.

Part III

ALM Models Applied to Pension Funds

6
The 401(k) Retirement Income Risk

Frank Sortino and David Hand

6.1 Introduction

In the last few years there has been a push from the Department of Labor (DOL), IRS, SEC and Congress to change 401(k) plans from savings plans at the full discretion of the employee to retirement plans with legislative requirements to target retirement income. Many practitioners are saying we are moving quickly to a 401(k) plan that looks like a 'Defined Benefit plan at the participant level.' In effect, everything is changing except that the participant must accept the risk. This puts a burden on all parties to understand and manage the true risks involved.

The QDIA provisions set new fiduciary standards that allow plan sponsors to default participants into certain types of investment options under the safe harbor protection of section 404(c).

This chapter will look at the 'true risk' and the high points of legislation affecting 401(k) plans to include

- Qualified Default Investment Alternative (QDIA)
- Age 50 Catch-Up Provisions
- Pending Bills on 'Plan Fees'
- Qualified Automatic Contribution Arrangement (QACA)

The basic problem is that too many employees are waiting too long to start investing, investing without the proper knowledge and putting too little aside each month to fund a decent level of retirement income. According to a DOL report on retirement adequacy, U.S. workers retiring in the 2050s will have saved only enough money in their 401(k)-style accounts to replace an average of 22% of their pre-retirement income, and 37% will have no savings at all. Representative George Miller has said, 'Unless we act now, too many workers just starting their careers today will unfortunately face a less secure retirement than did many of their parents.'

This led Congress to pass the Pension Protection Act (PPA), which was signed into law in 2006. 'The PPA directed the Department of Labor to issue a regulation to assist employers in selecting default investments that *best serve the retirement needs of workers* who do not direct their own investments.'[1] While the final regulation issued by the DOL provides the conditions that must be satisfied in order to obtain safe harbor relief, it offers no advice on how one should go about determining the 'best' option from those available. As part of the congressional effort to encourage more individual savings, companies may automatically enrol employees in the employer 401(k) plan, starting with a minimum of 3% of gross income, increasing to 6% after three years. The DOL estimates that the QDIA could result in $134 billion in additional retirement savings by 2034.[2]

6.2   QDIA options

There are three types of long-term QDIAs:

1. target maturity funds, sometimes called target dated funds or life cycle funds
2. risk-based or lifestyle funds (including balanced funds)
3. managed accounts.

The preamble to the regulation states, 'The Department believes that each of these qualified default investment alternatives is appropriate for participants and beneficiaries who fail to provide investment direction; accordingly, the rule does not require a plan fiduciary to undertake an evaluation as to which of the qualified default investment alternatives is the most prudent for a participant or the plan.'[3]

The regulation *does not require* an evaluation as to which type is best, but neither does it preclude an evaluation. Indeed the regulation goes on to say that once a type is chosen, the fiduciary must engage in a prudent process to select and monitor the QDIA. Why, then, wouldn't it be prudent to engage a consultant to evaluate the different types of QDIAs before making a selection?

The GAO report on retirement adequacy released on 11 December 2007 noted that many economists and financial advisors only consider retirement income adequate if it replaces 65% to 85% of pre-retirement income. The Harken & Kohl bill (H&K), now pending, provides a clear path to achieving that objective by requiring the plan administrator to provide a quarterly notice of 'the estimated amount that the participant needs to save each month to retire at 65.'[4] The Aon Consulting/Georgia State University's 'income replacement ratio' is an example of the growing recognition that this is the proper investment objective for 401(k) participants. For this reason, we believe retirement income replacement should be a criterion for evaluation of QDIAs.

6.3   Goals and objectives

Much has been written about goals, objectives and investment policy and there is very little agreement on what these terms mean. What some call goals, others call objectives, and there are some who use them interchangeably.[5] The Pension Research Institute (PRI) offers the following:[6]

- The goal is the end toward which effort is directed. It is the broadest generalization of what one is trying to accomplish.
- The objectives translate the goal into more specific language leading to a definite and measurable standard of performance. The objective must support the goal so that, if the objectives are achieved, the goal will be accomplished.

PIMCO executives have called for plan sponsors to look beyond the asset-only-based approach of modern portfolio theory and move toward a 'needs-based' optimization to maximize the probability of an income replacement ratio.[7] This agrees with the GAO reference above that retirement with dignity is related to replacing some percentage of pre-retirement income. In 1995, Andrew Rudd, cofounder of BARRA, the leading proponent of Capital Asset Pricing Model (CAPM) applications, founded Advisor Software (www.advisorsoftware.com) to offer a new goals-based software program that considers both assets and liabilities. Dr. Rudd said, 'What clients really want is to know that they are able to meet a range of financial goals given their current and future assets and liabilities.' He went on to say that risk budgets should be 'determined by the potential impact of a shortfall on goals.'[8] Sortino Investment Advisors (www.sortinoia.com) takes a similar approach, but measures risk and reward relative to a Desired Target Return (DTR) needed to achieve a desired retirement income. All of the above discuss goals and objectives in terms of an asset and liability framework. Therefore, we believe that **the goal of retirement with dignity and the investment objective of replacing pre-retirement income is reasonable and appropriate.**

6.4   Potential conflicts

The goal for an individual 401(k) participant is not the same goal that portfolio theory would claim is proper for investors as a whole under certain restrictive conditions. It also may not be the same goal a money manager has. Therefore, it is important to recognize potential conflicts of interests:

- Portfolio theory describes how investors who make their decisions based solely on expected return (the mean or average return) and volatility (standard deviation) should make rational choices. Each investor chooses a portfolio from the efficient frontier[9] based on their tolerance for risk. Textbooks in finance do not discuss goals. Instead, they assume everyone has the same investment objective, to maximize expected return for an acceptable level of risk (risk is measured as volatility around the mean). The Capital Asset Pricing Model (CAPM) proposed by William Sharpe extends the theory of Harry Markowitz to say, if there exists a risk-free asset then everyone should want some combination of the risk-free asset and the market portfolio. Risk becomes the risk of being in the market and is called Beta. In equilibrium, one should not be able to beat the market. Neither the Markowitz nor the Sharpe models recognize cash outflows in the future as a liability that must be dealt with. They are asset management models, not asset/liability models. How does portfolio theory fit the PRI definition of goals and objectives? It is possible to earn the highest return for a given level of volatility or beta and not accomplish the goal of retirement with dignity. Also, one could beat a market index but not accomplish the goal of retirement with dignity. The concept of 'market indexes' being a standard for 401(k) plan investment performance is reinforced by recent bills proposing that all investment options have an index to which to compare; one bill even mandates a low-cost index fund as an investment fund of choice. Indeed, even those who beat the market index between 2000 and 2004 lost a substantial part of their income-producing assets and may have had to postpone retirement. **Therefore, neither beating a market index nor maximizing expected return for a given level of volatility is a proper investment objective for a 401(k) participant.** 401(k) plans are not about how everyone in general should invest to get the highest expected return for a given level of risk. They are about how individual participants should invest to achieve their investment objective of replacing a specified percentage of their salary at retirement.

- The future income streams of participants are not on most money managers' radar screens and are therefore not the investment objective of most money managers. Money managers are usually hired based on their demonstrated ability to 'beat the market' on a risk-adjusted basis. To do what theory says they cannot do in the long run. **Their goal is to get hired.** If they beat the market they promote that fact in the expectation of being hired. Therefore, **the investment objective of most money managers is to beat the market index.**

6.5   Performance measurement

Performance measurement of money managers is different than measuring the performance of a 401(k) participant's portfolio. Whether the participant's portfolio beats some index or some other participant's portfolio is irrelevant.

The critical question for a participant at any point in time is, am I on the path, below the path, or above the path to my goal? An employee who has not been putting in enough money monthly and has 25 years to go should not compare portfolio performance with an employee who has five years to retirement and is overfunded.

If beating an index is not the objective, then it is also not the proper benchmark to use for performance measurement of 401(k) plans. **The participant's portfolio performance should be related to the funding status of the individual participant's account balance and future savings for secure retirement income.** This can be done in the traditional manner of showing the present value of the liabilities versus the present value of the assets. We think it is helpful to view retirement as a future value problem. The question to be answered is, what rate of return do I need to earn on my contributions in the future in order to accumulate a level of assets that will provide a desired retirement income? This desired target return (DTR) could be estimated and used in a similar manner to the assumed actuarial return for DB plans. The DTR could then be used as a benchmark (see Figure 6.1 below).

The example in Figure 6.1 depicts a DTR of 10% when the participant was 30 years old. Returns above the DTR would be desirable and provide the potential to exceed the desired income at retirement. Returns below the DTR (see * at age 40) would incur the risk of not achieving the investment objective. **That is the True Risk!** The participant's portfolio in this example has declined and

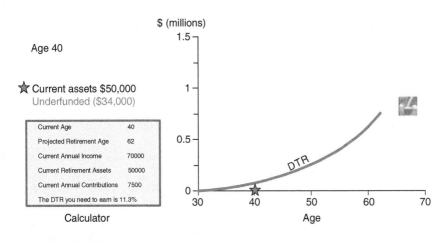

Desired Target Return (DTR) = 12%

Figure 6.1 Participant's 401(k) performance

now requires a new DTR of 11.3% to achieve the investment objective of 75% of pre-retirement income projected to age 65. The participant should be made aware that he or she is below the path. To maintain the current equity exposure, the participant should be allowed to make a catch-up contribution. **If a DB plan is required to increase contributions when underfunded, why shouldn't a participant be allowed the same opportunity?** The current position of the participant's 401(k) plan (*) is shown relative to the original DTR of 10%. All that is needed to calculate the DTR is shown in the blue box to the left and is readily available from the record keeper.

6.6   QDIA evaluation

The DOL, by not allowing fixed income funds to be used as a long-term QDIA, implicitly recognized that fixed income funds are not a risk-free investment. This in spite of the fact that fixed income funds are currently the most popular default option in 401(k) plans. This action on the part of the DOL also implicitly recognizes that the goal is not preservation of capital but retirement with dignity, because **investing everything in a fixed-income fund or stable value fund literally guarantees an insufficient income stream at retirement for most participants.**[10]

Let us now examine each QDIA option and see how well they meet the basic criterion of future income replacement:

- Target dated funds: The single determinant for selecting the optimal target dated fund is the participant's age. Is that all that is needed to determine the future cash flow required? Doesn't the participant need to know how much to contribute each month? Doesn't the proper contribution schedule depend on the participant's salary and how much money is currently invested? Target dated funds are a simplistic way of getting participants to invest for their future without regard to adequacy. **In short, target dated funds ignore anything to do with the replacement of pre-retirement income.**
- Lifestyle funds: Ask a participant how much risk they want to take and they will probably say, 'as little as possible.' This is why so many participants defaulted into fixed income or stable value funds. They don't realize that preservation of capital is not the goal. To have some chance at retiring with dignity they will have to take some loss-of-principle risk in order to reduce the true risk of failure to achieve the goal. How much risk they need to take depends on their financial profile, not their risk profile. **The same argument about target dated funds ignoring future cash flows applies to lifestyle funds.**

- Managed accounts: Many managed account services provide some type of financial planning tool that attempts to project future cash inflows to the 401(k) plan and subsequent cash outflows at retirement. On that basis alone, **the managed account option holds the greatest promise of achieving a participant's goal.** It then behooves the plan sponsor to find the managed account service that best fulfills this goal of income replacement.

6.7 Recommendations for regulators

We believe regulators are on the right track in their efforts to improve retirement results for 401(k) participants. However, much of the proposed legislation on plan fees includes significant legislation on plan investments, index funds, bench marking, and additional required plan administration and employee communications that need to be reviewed carefully. Another area for consideration in future revisions is to provide a new catch-up provision to participants who can show they will be less than 65% funded at age 65. The way the law currently reads, a participant who is 50 years old would be allowed to make catch-up contributions of $5000 per year. Unfortunately, this is right at the time that the 'glide path rule' encourages the QDIA to be reducing equity exposure, resulting in lower and lower returns. Research shows that most participants are not contributing enough, and the younger they are, the worse it is. If participants were aware of their current funding status and what it would take to get them back on a fully funded path, a new 'catch-up provision' for them could allow the power of compound interest to work wonders on their behalf.

For example, most baby boomers now in their mid 50s would be defaulted under the QDIA and typical 'lifestyle' fund into a fund earning a lower rate of return, say, 7%. This would reduce the risk of loss of principle in 10 years, but increase the risk of not achieving the desired retirement income (see Figure 6.1). True, a participant who is, say, 55 years old could be allowed under the 'catch-up provisions' to make an additional $5000 contribution per year in the 401(k) plan to offset the lower return. However, the combination of lower return, a relatively short time to invest and only $5000 per year still yields a lower retirement income than desired.

Yet, take that same $50,000 total investment for a participant who is 30 years old and contributions of only $2000 for 25 years with the opportunity to be defaulted into an investment product with higher returns, say, at 11%, then significant retirement income can be obtained. True, the risk of loss of principle is increased in any given year, but the true risk of not achieving a desired retirement income is actually reduced over a 35-year interval.

In the above examples (given the same $50,000 investment in a 401(k) plan), the difference is outstanding. The 55-year-old baby boomer has only approximately $74,000 at retirement, and the 30-year-old participant has over

$700,000–nearly ten times the dollar amount at retirement and, adjusting for inflation, over four times the retirement income.

From a tax policy point of view it is less costly to allow 'catch-up provisions' at early ages at lower amounts. Yet, this would provide the longer-term retirement security so greatly needed to ensure the success of 401(k) plans.

6.8   Recommendations for plan sponsors

Plan sponsors should adopt a policy statement for their 401(k) plan that clearly states the goal and investment objectives in terms of income replacement. They should hire a consultant to evaluate all available QDIA options and provide this information to all participants. Plan sponsors should make participants aware of the different types of risks they must manage.

6.9   Recommendations for consultants

Consultants should develop new performance measurement standards that specifically take into consideration the liability element of future income replacement for participants. They should consider both assets and liabilities when making asset allocation recommendations.

6.10   Summary and conclusions

We believe that a 401(k) default option should be constructed for the sole benefit of the participant and for the exclusive purpose of providing retirement benefits. This necessitates an investment strategy affecting future cash inflows in the form of contributions prior to retirement, followed by cash outflows sufficient to provide a desired retirement income. The result may be thought of as a personalized defined benefit plan in which the participant assumes the role of the plan sponsor. This chapter has attempted to develop guidelines for plan sponsors desiring to establish the best default option for their 401(k) plan. **The single most important criterion for selecting a default option is the potential to replace a designated percentage of the participant's income at retirement.**

6.11   Highlights

- The goal is retirement with dignity.
- The investment objective that supports the goal is to replace a stipulated percentage of the participant's gross income at retirement.
- Participants need to know if they are on track toward their goal.
- True risk is that the participant does not achieve their goal.

- Catch-up provisions and glide path rules should be revised.
- Proposed legislation on 'Plan Fees' that include investment provisions need to be reviewed carefully.

Notes

1. DOL Fact Sheet relating to QDIAs, October 2007. Emphasis is ours.
2. DOL Fact Sheet, Regulation Relating to Qualified Default Investment Alternatives in Participant-Directed Individual Account Plans, October 2007.
3. DOL Issues the Final QDIA Regulation, Fred Reish and Stephanie Bennett, November 2007 Bulletin.
4. Harkin and Kohl, p. 18, section (ii).
5. The Pension Research Institute has published several articles on this subject.
6. These definitions are based on research carried out at PRI and the textbook, *Principles of Management*, Harold Koontz and C. O'Donnell, McGraw-Hill, 1968.
7. PIMCO DC Dialogue, October 2007.
8. Keynote address at the World Series of ETF's Conference, 31 March 2005.
9. The efficient frontier consists of those portfolios with the highest expected return for a given level of standard deviation.
10. The preamble states, 'It is the view of the Department that investments made on behalf of defaulted participants ought to and often will be long-term investments and that investment of defaulted participants' contributions and earnings in money market and stable value funds will not over the long term produce rates of return as favorable as those generated by products, portfolios and services included as qualified default investment alternatives, thereby decreasing the likelihood that participants invested in capital preservation products will have adequate retirement savings.'

7
Pensions, Covenants and Insurance
Con Keating

7.1 Preamble

Before moving to consider the ALM problem for UK defined benefit pension schemes or, more correctly, voluntary self-administered pension schemes, and their corporate sponsors, we shall first address briefly a few elementary issues relevant to the subsequent analysis. We omit any consideration of local authority and quasi-government schemes, though it should be realized that the term 'corporate' encompasses many 'not-for-profit' and charitable concerns, as well as many other companies, such as the Bank of England, that are popularly believed to be part of government. This is broadly the population of companies, currently some 18,000 or so, whose schemes are required to subscribe to the United Kingdom's Pension Protection Fund (PPF). We shall describe the principal terms of the optimal pension indemnity assurance policy that in turn facilitates optimal pension management by the sponsor employer and scheme, together with the ALM overview of that assurer. In this chapter, the central thrust may be acquired by reading just the bold body text. Footnotes contain illustrations and peripheral arguments and information. The boxes contain explanations and illustrations of theoretical concepts.

7.2 Introductory issues in analysis

7.2.1 Liabilities

A liability is, of course, some other party's asset, as is recognized by the elementary accounting identity. As such, there is little or nothing that can be done by the obligor to alter or manage it; **it is**, above all, **someone else's property**. We **cannot alter this without** the **consent** of the asset's owner; this is a fundamental tenet of the law of property.

Pension liabilities represent commitments (promises) to perform at future times; in the case of pensions, to make cash payments to scheme members over their lifetime in retirement. It is this futurity which introduces the possibility of a form of management; **we can manage our estimates of the present value of the future liabilities,**[1] the cash payments promised to retirees. As these are estimates, the very idea that there is a single 'correct' value is flawed; the best which can be achieved is a value which is most likely, and that, of course, has to be derived recursively.

An asset and its corresponding liability are mirror images of one another; mathematically this is a rigid rotation about zero, multiplication by minus one. In the context of price (or probability) distributions, the symmetries reverse and all odd moments alter their sign. An asset is not well defined in the domain of negative values; a contract which requires us to make payments rather than receive them is a liability. This, of course, does not mean that assets will not from time to time produce negative returns, only that on average the expected return must be positive.

This relation between an asset and its corresponding liability carries some consequences, most notably that **the uncertainty or risk which lowers the value of our asset also lowers the value of our current liability.**[2] The effect of uncertainty is to diminish the amount of each – they both move towards the zero origin. Moreover, if we have a preference for positive skewness in asset price distributions, we will also have a preference for positive skewness in the liability price distributions.

The consequence for pensions is that **effective regulatory interventions which seek to increase the security of a scheme member's pension,** by reducing the uncertainty associated with it, will **inevitably raise the current cost estimate of provision of those benefits.** To the extent that regulation[3] requires intervention in the financing process it will also increase the ultimate cost of provision of that benefit. This is an introduction of path dependency to the funding process. Ineffective regulation merely introduces deadweight costs of compliance and administration.

The **regulatory interventions of the 1970s and 1980s raised the total amount of pensions ultimately payable** through measures such as compulsory limited price inflation and preservation of former employees' benefits: **a shift of responsibility from the public to private sector.** The **regulatory interventions in the period since have raised the costs of the corporate sponsor, but not improved the ultimate benefits payable** – and it is debatable whether they have raised the true or perceived security for members. In economic terms, **in the first period the costs represent capital formation,** while **in the second they are an element of consumption.**

The taxation concessions[4] for pension schemes, in which contributions and investment accruals are exempt from income and capital gains taxation but pensions in payment are subject to income tax, were originally justified on the basis that this arrangement was intertemporally fiscally neutral. If this were true historically, it can no longer be so – the distinction between capital formation for ultimate post-tax consumption and immediate tax-advantaged consumption is material. This aspect and its consequences for social welfare policy have not been widely discussed.

There are, of course, many assets for which there is no corresponding liability; gold and many physical commodities are immediate examples. It is also worth considering some distinctions among assets. **A capital asset is distinguished by its generation of a productive return;**[5] the farm (capital asset) which produces barley (asset) is an illustration.

Today, we may correctly refer to investing in capital assets, but only to speculating[6] in (commodity) assets. It is necessary to suspend belief in the rational expectations model of markets to justify such speculation and that, perhaps, places this at odds with prudential principles, if we define those as codification of rational and well-informed behaviour.[7] It is disappointing to so regularly see practitioner asset allocation analyses, performed in a capital asset pricing framework, that contain commodities which purport to show positive expected returns (see Box 7.1).

Box 7.1   Risk and Return

Perhaps the easiest way to demonstrate the effect of uncertainty, or its subset risk, in a financial context, and on pensions in particular, is to consider long multi-period returns which are stochastic or random in nature. If we received returns which (arithmetically) averaged on a single-period basis, say, 5% and their volatility or variability was 10% on average, then we observe, in the asymptotic limit, that the geometric achieved return was 4.5% per period. If the volatility was 20%, then we observe the geometric achieved return was just 3%. The adjustment here is well known and is equal to one-half of the variance of the distribution of returns.

The geometric return can be considered as a post-risk experienced return. This is also the Achilles' heel of the latest regulatory fad, 'outcomes'-based supervision. As we move to consider the future, it is feasible, with plausible expectations of arithmetic return and volatility, to derive in this way the implicit full-term geometric return – this is a forecast risk-adjusted return. This adjustment is nonlinear in volatility; in the earlier illustration we saw that doubling the volatility increased the realised return penalty fourfold. The preference for low volatility of assets is rationally based.

Preferences over asymmetry (negative skewness) are a little more difficult to illustrate, but rest upon consideration of the value of the asset in intervening periods of finite terms. If we begin by considering a solitary, large negative return and a commensurately higher average return from all other periods in a finite term, such that the returns average (arithmetically) again, say, 5%, then the consequences for the asset's value vary with the timing of the occurrence of the large negative event. If this occurs in the first period, the asset's value and realised geometric return only slowly recover, and indeed, estimates of the volatility of the asset also only slowly decline to its full-term value. If the negative result occurs in the last period, the geometric return is radically lowered at this late date, and the sample volatility jumps. All intermediate occurrences show variations of these two extremes; there is a new uncertainty introduced as to the accuracy of our sample estimates. It is rational to avoid this uncertainty, and, of course, it is widely observed empirically. This is actually the heart of the Ellsberg 'paradox'. Uncertainty aversion is also rational, since uncertainty lowers the level of trade exchange; for example, without a need to reduce the uncertainties arising from the double coincidence of wants required for barter exchange, even money, as a medium of exchange, would be unnecessary.

Only too many hedge fund strategies, for example, those which are intrinsically option-writing strategies, possess the inherent asymmetry of many small gains and occasional large losses. When that is combined with a manager compensation schedule which effectively taxes positive returns, the investor is materially disadvantaged, as is obvious from consideration of the manager incentives. After the occurrence of the large negative event, the presence of a high-water rule removes all manager incentive until the asset's prior high value is fully regained. Prior to the event, the manager collects performance fees for returns which are, in fact, risk compensation premia; when the event occurs, it becomes obvious that the fund is deficient by at least the amount of performance fees previously deducted.

Perhaps the best way to evaluate alternate investments is to consider them as if they are impaired assets. The asset's full value is the sum of all future returns, so a 20% performance fee immediately reduces the value of the asset by that amount, with fixed *ad valorem* fees further compounding the decline in value.

The attraction of diversification among many assets is that this reduces the idiosyncratic risk, lowering the overall volatility of the portfolio, relative to one containing a small number of securities.

7.2.2   Diversification

Diversification is the key to stable long-term investment performance. These concepts and some of their consequences are discussed and illustrated in Box 7.2, Elements of Diversity.[8]

7.2.3   Risk and DB pension schemes

In DB arrangements, the employer sponsor underwrites the scheme; provided the sponsor exists and is solvent, it will ensure that all payments due to members are made on time and in full. This underwriting[9] covers all liabilities, including those financed by members' contributions. The investment and biometric risks associated with any and all members' lifetime retirement incomes are collectively borne by the sponsor employer. The sole risk faced by members is sponsor insolvency, and at that point the employees face the compound risk of unemployment and pension uncertainty.

The organization of a DB scheme, in which the pension entitlement is set by years of service and a final or career-average salary, while contributions are fixed as a proportion of salary received for both employee and employer sponsor, is a highly efficient risk pooling and sharing mechanism. To illustrate

---

Box 7.2   Elements of Diversity

We begin by considering two independent assets having expected returns of 10% and volatility of 20%, and construct from these two portfolios, A and B. For portfolio A, we choose to invest €100 in one asset; we therefore have an expected return of €10 and volatility of €20. For portfolio B, we wish to limit our risk to be less than or equal to €20, while investing equally in both assets; we may now invest €70 in each, which results in a volatility which satisfies the constraint by having a value of €19.8. The expected return of portfolio B is €14, which compares most favourably to portfolio A's return of just €10 for broadly the same risk.

Let us next consider a two-period setting for the two assets and again construct two portfolios, C and D. In portfolio C, we again place €100 in one asset for just the first period, resulting in an expected return of €10 and a risk of €20. In portfolio D, however, we place €70 in either one of the two assets, but the investment is now for the two-year period. Provided the asset's returns are serially independent, this results in an income of €14 and risk of €19.8.

These simple examples are very powerful illustrations of the difficulty of adding value to portfolios by active investment management, by the techniques of either stock selection, which involves reduced diversification, or by market timing, which involves reduced intertemporal diversity. The fact that security returns are usually positively correlated across securities, together with the observation that security returns are largely uncorrelated with their own past serial histories (autocorrelation), suggests that it is more difficult to add value through market-timing than through stock selection.

Returns forecasting also brings with it further complications. This can be illustrated by considering an asset whose return distribution is well characterised as normal (10, 20). If we now forecast a return of 30%, a situation which is exceeded in just 16% of outcomes, we can no longer use the 20% volatility figure, as this is calculated about the mean of the distribution, a return of 10%. We now need to consider the volatility about the projected return, and that has a value of 28.3%. In other words, it is necessary to consider the entire volatility function across the range of return support in order to select the correct risk-return parameter couplet. If we wish to retain the €20 risk constraint from earlier, we may invest just €70 in this security – and if we have higher returns forecasts, we must invest even less in the security.

This process is central to any form of risk budgeting, but has never been observed in practice by the author. Moreover, it appears to be standard practice, when using mean variance portfolio optimisation tools, for investment managers to use forecast returns while retaining empirical historic volatilities and correlations. It should not surprise anyone that the resultant allocations of these tools have greatly disappointed their users in terms of their performance. The estimation of noncentral correlations among securities is also not trivial, though it would be necessary for coherent completion of optimisation input parameters. The problems of mean-variance optimisation extend well beyond the usual, and correct, criticism that these tools maximise estimation errors in their resultant asset allocations. There have been a number of empirical studies conducted which show that even naive equal weighting among assets frequently outperforms these more complex strategies in practice; this would be expected when the noise in parameter estimates exceeds the information.

just a few of these, the longevity risk for a young man is much higher than that of an employee approaching retirement, while the potential investment gain is much higher for the young man's contributions than the mature employee. At the same time, the salaries and actual cash contributions of senior employees are higher than those of younger members. These and other more complex elements serve to limit the risks faced by the employer sponsor as underwriter of the collective scheme. The risk-pooling in DB schemes brings the law of large numbers to bear, lowering the uncertainty associated with longevity esti-mates[10] and similar risk factors applicable to scheme liabilities.[11]

The true risks faced by a DB scheme are slow to materialize. Inflation raises more time-remote payments by more than the immediate. Increases in longevity only become relevant once the current life expectations of members have been reached. The effect of discounting to present values can also have material effects; for example, in one recent analysis an increase in life expectation that increased total ultimate payments by 42% resulted in an increase of just 12% in the present value of those payments. We shall discuss later in Section 7.5, the meaning and problems of current values in pension management.

There are two dimensions to the risk of a DB pension scheme: the likeli-hood of sponsor insolvency and the consequence arising from insolvency, and the degree of scheme funding relative to its liabilities. Risk is properly defined as the product of these two elements.

These are not independent of each other; clearly the amounts contributed to pension schemes usually differ in terms of their effect upon the scheme and sponsor balance sheets. The relation between funding contributions[12] and sponsor insolvency likelihood is markedly nonlinear in practice and generates a complex risk function.

There is a causal order in the elements of the risk of a scheme; in the absence of sponsor insolvency the degree of scheme underfunding is immaterial. There are many circumstances in which the correct risk manage-ment practice would be for the scheme to support its sponsor's commercial activities,[13] since this lowers the likelihood of their failure, rather than to seek to improve its level of funding.

Unfortunately, UK pension legislation places emphasis upon the consequence part of this risk relationship, on scheme funding rather than the insolvency likelihood.[14,15] This focus, of course, places scheme trustees in a position of potential conflict with the financial management of the sponsor employer.

7.3   The pension problem

The time frame over which pensions are promised is very long.[16] Contributions are made at many points over a working lifetime,[17] and pen-sions are paid in small amounts at many times over the life in retirement. It is self-evident that the descriptive statistics of these processes are not those of markets or bank risk management. The investment and disinvestment profiles are intrinsically smooth. In the accumulation phase, a form of dollar cost-averaging is evident.

Contrary to popular belief, DB schemes in the United Kingdom are still growing in aggregate;[18] this is true even after the many, much publicized sponsor failures, scheme closures through 'bulk annuitisation' and lowering of the terms of new awards. The measure of scheme growth here is their aggregate liabilities rather than funding; this is the economically important capital formation. This occurs with the creation of the pension liability, not their funding in markets or elsewhere; schemes may be underfunded, but the extent of any underfunding forms part of the capital base of the sponsor firm. We shall return to consider these issues in some detail later in Section 7.6.

There is a caution here for pension legislators, which arises from consideration of repeat games. The incentive to cooperate and perform today for the rationally self-interested player is calculated by reference to the sum of all future exchanges; if this does not outweigh today's costs, defection is the justified strategy. **Excessively onerous regulation which raises future costs will result rationally in scheme closure**; it is as well to remember that these schemes were initially created and offered voluntarily on the basis that they represented good or at least fair value for money. Many sponsor surveys have indicated that were it not for the barrier to exit introduced by the Pensions Act 2004 they would have discharged their obligations to their scheme and ceased offering DB pensions. The barrier to exit is the need to fully annuitise a scheme with an insurance company in order to discharge the liabilities; this has a cost typically of around 140% of the technical best estimate of those liabilities.

Liquidity is not a prime consideration of pension scheme management. The words of John Maynard Keynes on this subject[19] are worth recalling: 'Of the maxims of orthodox finance none, surely, is more anti-social than the fetish of liquidity, the doctrine that it is a positive virtue on the part of investment institutions to concentrate their resources upon the holding of 'liquid' securities. It forgets that there is no such thing as liquidity of investment for the community as a whole. The social object of skilled investment should be to defeat the dark forces of time and ignorance which envelop our future.' For the growing scheme, in which contributions exceed pension payments, the liquidity available from the pension fund investments, and even its income, are currently immaterial.

Many have expressed reservations about the inclusion of consideration of future contributions in analysis, and in result most pension analysis is conducted on the basis of the projected benefit obligation, the best estimate of the future value of currently awarded pensions payable, and financial assets presently held in the pension fund, which as we shall see later, can be misleading in the extreme. This reservation is unfounded and inconsistent with other financial practice. For example, the value of equity capital derives solely from the promise of future dividends. In fact, all of the capital and operating funds of any company arise from promises to perform specified acts at later dates and to make future payments.

The real problem of DB schemes lies in the dependence upon the sponsor employer's solvency. Prior to an event of insolvency, it would be inequitable to demand that a pension scheme be funded at anything greater than 100% of the true, technical liabilities. (This is something of a theoretical abstraction, since the technical liabilities are estimated on the basis of many assumptions.) However, **once the sponsor is insolvent**, it can no longer act as underwriter of the scheme; in this situation, **the pension scheme needs additional capitalization**, in excess of 100% of technical liabilities, as it faces considerable risk and uncertainty over the time to full discharge of its liabilities.[20] The scheme, post-insolvency, is now functioning as if it is an insurance company, and would require capitalization in similar fashion to reflect that; **this is the principal risk management problem** with DB pensions schemes.[21]

There is a debate in Europe on this topic, where regulators favour the presence of capital buffers at all times; this may be appropriate for a stand-alone ongoing pension scheme which lacks any recourse to its sponsor employers, but it is inappropriate where the scheme has recourse to an employer sponsor underwriter.[22]

Perhaps the greatest failing of historic pension regulation was that it did not consider the credit standing of the sponsor employer at the time of the creation of the pension scheme; any sponsor could, by agreement with the tax authorities, create an authorized scheme. The Pensions Regulator does now concern itself with the sponsor employer's finances and activities, which it refers to as the corporate covenant, but it cannot determine which companies may or may not establish pension schemes.

The real problem of DB pensions can, in fact, be fully addressed by insurance, and the optimal form of this is pension indemnity assurance. The potential role of insurance was recognized at the time of the major reforms of DB regulation that resulted in the Pensions Act of 2004; this legislation created the Pension Protection Fund, which has on occasion referred to its activities as insurance.

7.4   Pensions and insurance

Insurance fulfils many roles[23] in the world of pensions. The most promoted insurance solution for DB schemes in the United Kingdom is bulk annuitisation, which crystallizes the risk exposure of the sponsor as underwriter of the scheme at the time of annuitisation, and defines a termination cost. It effectively terminates the scheme, since no new pension entitlements can be created; the liabilities of the scheme are fully discharged and assumed by the insurer. This is known as 'buy-out'.

There is a variant, known as 'buy-in', where some class of liabilities, usually pensioners in payment, are covered by an annuity contract; this annuity contract is an asset of the scheme which matches that portion of the scheme's total liabilities. This serves, in many circumstances, to lower the volatility of the funding ratio since it is partial matching of assets to liabilities. However, it also lowers the diversification and risk-pooling benefits of the larger scheme. The scheme can continue to offer pension benefits to current and future employees; the sponsor continues to underwrite the scheme in its entirety.

The optimal insurance solution, pension indemnity assurance, allows the scheme to continue to offer new benefits; the economic good of future capital formation is preserved. Pension indemnity assurance supplements the sponsor underwriting commitment to the scheme; the sponsor covenant is augmented. As an asset of the scheme, it also alters the optimal asset allocation and management of the scheme; the scheme and sponsor have more degrees of freedom in this regard. The most notable is elimination of the myopic tyranny of present values and current funding ratios.

7.4.1   The pension protection fund

This was created by the Pensions Act of 2004.[24] It is a classic illustration of inept and inappropriate institutional design. **The PPF is not an insurer but a mutual compensation fund; its costs are borne entirely by pension schemes and their sponsors.**

The PPF does not pay the full benefit entitlements of members who enter after their sponsor has failed. It pays a maximum pension slightly in excess of £27,000 per annum and pays a maximum of 90% to members who have not yet retired at normal retirement age.[25] The PPF has estimated that these rules meant that they would pay approximately 83% of members' accrued entitlements under schemes' rules.

The sole justification for these lowered benefits is that they reduce the potential exposure of the PPF. This can be illustrated most forcefully by consideration of the pathological case of the last man standing, the scheme which outlives all others. It will have made contributions to the costs of all other prior failures, in increasingly large proportions of those failure costs, but there is no surviving scheme to cover its shortfalls.

The lowered benefits introduce a new sunk cost to the administration of pension schemes; the need to produce periodic actuarial valuations in which the liabilities are based upon the PPF reduced benefit rules. This is known as a Section 179 valuation. **Properly designed insurance would pay full benefits to members**, and, inter alia, obviate any need for such valuations.

The PPF is funded by a levy[26] upon pension schemes; the levy[27] is partly a fixed sum based upon scheme size and partly risk-based. The legislation requires that the risk-based element be at least 80% of the total levy amount. The risk-based element uses estimates of the sponsor insolvency likelihood, currently supplied by Dun & Bradstreet,[28] and the level of funding[29] relative to the section 179 reduced benefits valuation to determine an individual scheme's levy payment liability.[30] Many schemes have introduced new contingent assets, such as guarantees, into their pension schemes in order to reduce levy demands.

It is important to realize that the levies paid by schemes cover the costs of other schemes, whose sponsor has failed; it is not provision for their own ultimate failure. Unfortunately, it cannot be argued that this form of risk-based arrangement of levy is equivalent to a provision. The schemes which fail in the early decades of the PPF's existence will not have contributed adequate sums to offset their deficits. With a declining population of schemes, as is the case in the United Kingdom, this levy arrangement will prove profoundly inequitable among schemes.[31] There is even one class of failing scheme which is disadvantaged in a particularly pernicious way; those schemes which are funded at levels above the PPF section 179 valuation, but below the cost of buying improved annuities in the commercial market, lose that excess value to the PPF. This subsidy will serve to extend the PPF's survival time.[32]

The PPF is a creditor of the failed sponsor. It seeks to recover the difference between the level of scheme funding at the time of application to the PPF and an amount which is a calculation of the cost of full annuitisation, known as the section 75 valuation.[33] In the United Kingdom, the pension scheme is currently a general unsecured creditor in its sponsor insolvency; there are suggestions in Europe[34] that this should be improved to give the scheme preferred status.

By virtue of the fact that the PPF levies meet the costs of other scheme failures, **these levies are sunk costs**. In late 2009 the UK High Court reinforced this sunk cost aspect with a ruling that schemes may not rely upon the presence of the PPF when determining their investment strategy. By contrast **if the levies represented insurance premium provisions against their own future failure, they would create an asset for the scheme**. This difference requires consideration of the accounting principles in effect for pension schemes and their sponsors.

7.5 Accounting for pensions

In terms of the distinction made at the beginning of this chapter between liabilities and current estimates of those liabilities, **the accounting treatment generates and considers current estimates**.

Assets are valued at market prices. The projected benefits obligation, the future pension sums payable based upon current entitlements projected forward to members' retirement dates and expected lifetimes in retirement (**liabilities**), is **discounted** using a AA corporate bond rate **to arrive at a present value. This combination of techniques is known as mixed attribute accounting.** Unfortunately **it is inherently biased**[35] **and distorts reality,** creating a false and weaker appearance for the pension scheme. As we shall see, this distortion is then transmitted to the sponsor's reported accounts.

Technically, the problem is that this standard uses different measures[36] for assets and liabilities. Moreover, in the case of equity assets, we do not even know and cannot observe the measure, the implicit discount function of future equity dividends and cash flows, since these are not known with certainty.

Attempts are often made to justify this accounting treatment on the basis that it is in some way consistent and facilitates comparison. This is simply untrue.[37] The use of market prices[38] is particularly suspect; the central question is quite simple to ask: what is the value relevance of the market price of an asset today with respect to a pension payment cash flow occurring 50 years in the future? But the obvious answer is most unsatisfactory.

These effects result in the present value of liabilities being overstated relative to assets by a substantial amount, of the order of 30% or so in recent times. Moreover, a spurious volatility is introduced into statements of surplus or deficit, and transferred to sponsor accounts.

This accounting induces some perverse behaviour into pension fund management. Notwithstanding the fact that the ultimate liabilities are not determined by interest rates, we see many schemes entering into interest rate swaps in order to 'hedge' the volatility introduced by the discount rate function. The hedge consists of a long-term swap where the scheme receives fixed rate and pays Libor. Contrary to popular belief, this actually introduces a real dependency for the scheme on interest rates. In particular, it induces a short-term potential for liquidity demands, as the Libor rate increases. This institutionalizes myopia, while the scheme in reality is concerned with the long term. The presence of credit support agreements with their collateral provision protocols can compound these liquidity calls. The use of swaps in this way is a central element to the management strategy known as liability-driven investment.[39] One criticism of this technique is that there is a very substantial basis risk associated with it.[40]

In the United Kingdom legislation was specifically introduced in 2003 to ensure that the treatment of pension funding shortfalls is as debt on the employer. The deficit (or surplus) of scheme assets to liabilities is reported as a net liability (surplus) in the sponsor balance sheet and equity adjusted accordingly.[41] It passes through the statement of total recognized losses and gains (STRGL). Contributions and levies pass through the scheme and the sponsor's cash flow and income and expenditure accounts. In recent times it has become standard to treat the net liabilities of pension schemes in similar fashion to debt securities.[42]

It is important to realize that **a pension obligation lacks some of the usual properties of a commercial debt**; no rational scheme is likely to induce sponsor failure by enforcement or collection efforts, since this triggers both the prospect of immediate unemployment for some of its active members and crystallizes the pension deficit.[43] It should also be realized that the effective term of pension liabilities, where payments may extend to 75 years or more, far exceeds the effective term[44] of market-traded corporate debt or even equity for most companies, even though this is permanent capital. This question of the term of assets or liabilities is important in another context – the holding period experienced volatility.[45] For pension schemes, the effective holding period can be very long; for a growing scheme, it is perpetual.

7.6   The corporate sponsor perspective

Historically, the corporate sponsor had an incentive to create and underwrite DB pensions for its employees; the value for money here exceeded that of a simple cash payment of higher wages. The effect of new legislation has been to raise the cost inexorably. Where these costs represent enhanced pensions received in retirement, they are additional compensation for the employee and can be factored into wage-setting negotiations, but where they are deadweight costs,[46] they are deeply problematic.

The **new regulations**, in Europe and domestically, all place emphasis upon the level of scheme funding; the **objective now is clear – full funding at all times. This is very costly, as it makes the funding process path dependent**; it is simply inefficient myopic investment. The scheme specific funding regime,[47] under which the Pensions Regulator and schemes agree on deficit repair and special contribution schedules, is less draconian than this, but still inefficient and costly. Simple calculations indicate that the system is fundamentally both sound and affordable, even with longevity at retirement of 30 years, without these costs and special contributions.[48]

The question for the corporate sponsor, the employer, is whether these contributions are valued by employees as equivalent to or higher than wages at that amount.[49] Their alternative, to provide a DC scheme, is far cheaper.[50]

The question of scheme funding also needs a little thought. The sole risk faced by an employee with DB is, as was noted earlier, insolvency of the sponsor employer. In this situation, the active scheme member loses both his or her job and, to the extent that the scheme is unfunded, some, or all, of the accumulated pension. This double risk exposure can be mitigated by funding the scheme and buying investments unrelated to the sponsor employer;[51] the investment fund is serving as collateral security to lower the consequence of sponsor insolvency. **If an award of pension is not funded**, that is, the sponsor does not make any contribution to the scheme in respect of the award, then **this represents new capital funding for the sponsor employer**. This capital does not come without cost – that is determined by the returns which could have been earned in markets if the awards had been funded and invested. The presence of a DB scheme as a potential source of capital funding[52] was historically a significant incentive to the sponsor in their creation.

In fact, with correctly designed pension indemnity assurance it is unnecessary for the scheme ever to fully fund an insured scheme. This situation arises because the insurance policy is an asset of the scheme – one which capitalizes the sponsor's covenant, their promise to pay future premiums until insolvent.

In the past five years, sponsor employers have made total special contributions which have ranged from £12.3 billion to £6.9 billion. These **special contributions** are, perhaps, a measure of the risk which they have underwritten; at 35% to 65% of normal contributions this **implies that pensions are very risky** indeed. However, if we examine the **pension liabilities ultimately payable**, it is clear that they **have not** unexpectedly **altered in amount by anything like this extent. The uncertainty and expense introduced** by these payments, the result of the estimation process, into the sponsor's wage costs is substantial, **at 5% to 10% of wages**, which **is sufficiently large that it may have a material effect upon a company's competitive position.** This is a real effect of poor regulation and inadequate pension accounting.

The Pensions Act of 2004 placed a new emphasis upon the corporate affairs[53] of the sponsor. The expression 'the corporate covenant' was coined by the Pensions Regulator to cover this. The Regulator is, in essence, concerned only with any corporate actions which may weaken the security of the pension scheme and has introduced elaborate clearance mechanisms which serve to offer sponsors comfort that the Regulator will not use any of its statutory powers in this regard. This adds a new complexity to, and **reduces the flexibility of, the management of corporate finances and strategies,** which is often clearly resented by sponsor management.

The ethos has changed from the voluntary, cooperative and perhaps paternalistic motivation under which schemes were originally established to one in which compliance dominates. **No new DB schemes are being created;** the liabilities of existing schemes are being eliminated or reduced going forward. The **economic impact of this reduced capital formation will, in time, prove economically significant.**

The central issue is that there are really **no remaining incentives** for the sponsor to offer this form of pension, relative to some well-defined alternative fixed cost arrangement, such as DC or simply increasing wages. It is possible with **pension indemnity assurance to capitalize the sponsor covenant, reinstating incentives for the sponsor** to offer DB pensions.

7.7 Pension indemnity assurance

Insurance of the scheme against sponsor insolvency is an obvious solution to the fundamental problem of DB of schemes. The details of the policy design are important. In consideration of an annual premium, the policy contracts to issue (or procure the issuance of) annuities paying the benefit entitlements due to members under scheme rules, in full and on time. This annual premium is set at initiation of the policy as a fixed proportion of liabilities, and this rate prevails for the life of the policy.[54] **This allows the sponsor employer full flexibility in its compensation policy; it may increase or decrease awards as their commercial objectives dictate.** The policy is assurance in form, as it exists for the life of the sponsor, or the scheme if that proves shorter.

The premiums may be paid by either the sponsor or the scheme, but would usually be paid by the sponsor employer. This annual premium,[55] being based upon the present value of liabilities, is eminently forecastable for the sponsor's budgetary purposes. The premium is set by reference to the marginal contribution of a particular scheme and sponsor to the assurer's aggregate risk. This is feasible as insolvency rates in the corporate sector overall lie below 1% p.a.; in fact, companies with DB schemes over the long term have been more likely to cease trading through merger, acquisition or solvent liquidation than they are to fail insolvent.

This sponsor commitment to pay annual premiums creates an asset for the assurer, the present value of future premiums payable to it. It is an interesting form of credit, unusual in that there is no initial exchange of principal. In addition, the assurer receives the annual cash premiums, which pass through income and expenditure and cash-flow accounts in the usual manner. This value of the asset is derived using standard IAS 39 accounting techniques and actually required under the latest draft of Solvency 2 insurance regulations. This credit exposure is substantial and will have profound implications for the asset allocation of the assurer. The assurer also records, as a liability provision, the expected policy loss.

The sponsor records in its balance sheet a liability for future premiums payable. Again, this is IAS 39 accounting. This entry is explicit capitalization of its covenant. The premium paid in any year passes through income and expenditure and cash-flow statements in the usual way.

The pension scheme now has a new asset, the assurance policy. The present value of this is entered alongside its investments. Once again, IAS 39 is the relevant accounting standard for valuation. The present value of this asset will usually exceed the corresponding liability reported in the sponsor accounts. This arises because the assurer's premium-setting process considers estimated recoveries from the insolvent sponsor, as well as some more complex risk-sharing aspects, when fixing that premium. As this is perhaps a little difficult to comprehend, we quote from the pension indemnity assurer, BrightonRock: 'BrightonRock bases its premium on our loss expectation, which is its fully loaded cost of production of the bulk annuity less the expected funding level; our loss expectation is our best estimate of the actuarial liabilities (usually in the range 105–110% of FRS/IAS) loaded for the cost of capital of the reserves we need to carry for the risk factors affecting the value of the best estimate. BrightonRock has certain advantages with respect to most of these risk factors, most notably longevity and limited price inflation. This means that we can produce, because of the policy form, annuitisation at prices materially below the market price – as this gain arises principally from risk-sharing among policyholders we choose to rebate it to them by lowering the initial premium fixing.'

The policy pay-off value is based upon the future levels of funding relative to liabilities, the deficit at insolvency. In this estimation, it is necessary to consider contributions made between the current date and that estimated time of insolvency. The policy explicitly considers an aspect which is entirely absent from the regulatory view of pensions schemes, future contributions.

If we consider an open ongoing scheme, with contributions at around 5% of the present asset portfolio value, and interest rates at 4.00%, then we observe that **the present value of these future contribution payments exceeds the value of actual assets currently held.** This has consequence for the investment strategy of the fund. It should be obvious that when making future investments we would like to see those future prices low – we are consuming investments in the future. The investment objective should no longer rely solely on improvements to the level of market prices, the beta of the capital asset pricing model. Investments which generate returns independent of the level of capital asset market prices, the alpha of financial theory, are most attractive.

It is immediately obvious that **this policy asset has not been fully funded by the sponsor employer**; for example, in the first year, the employer may have paid only 0.5% of liabilities while creating an asset for the scheme with a value of perhaps 12% or 15% of liabilities. The **capitalization of the sponsor covenant**, afforded by pension indemnity assurance, clearly **provides an incentive for the company to offer DB benefits.**

This is an illustration of a positive externality; by assuring the excess funding required post-insolvency, the sponsor creates an asset today for the pension scheme, which in turn lowers its current aggregate funding requirement. This deserves some elaboration and a simplified example. Consider a scheme which is fully funded, today and at the point of future insolvency. The pension indemnity assurance policy has a present value to the scheme equal to the product pay-off at insolvency, discounted to the present at the risk-free rate. Suppose, then, that this pay-off (the S75 value – the required capitalization that would allow the scheme to continue to meet its liabilities in the face of uncertainty) is 45%, that insolvency is predicted to occur 30 years in the future, and that interest rates for this term are 4% p.a.; the present value of this policy is 13.87% as an asset of the scheme.[56] In turn this means that, if full funding of the scheme is the desired objective, only 86.13% of liabilities are required. The true situation is a little more complex than this simplified illustration, since with funding at 86.13%, the pay-out at insolvency increases and becomes 58.87%, which has a present value to the scheme of 18.15%, implying a yet lower funding requirement, and the pricing/funding process continues iteratively.

The incentive available to the sponsor for offering this form of pension is the **difference between this value of the assurance asset to the scheme and the cost of provision of the assurance policy**, the present value of the future premiums payable by it. The demands upon the sponsor's cash flows are also obviously much lower than under traditional funding arrangements.[57]

7.7.1   Term of the pension indemnity assurance policy

Neither the sponsor nor the assurer can cancel the policy during its term. However, the **sponsor may, at any time, with the agreement of the trustees, discharge the liabilities of the scheme by transfer of the liabilities** and assets to a new scheme, which effectively ends the existing pension indemnity policy. This action has only minor cost, and might be appropriate when the credit standing of the sponsor has improved markedly and existing policy terms are no longer justified.

The assurer may call for immediate full annuitisation of the scheme (at the sponsor's expense) in the event that new unfunded liabilities are added, without agreement, to the scheme. In fact, such an action, if unresolved by negotiation between the parties, would likely result in transfer of the scheme in the manner described above; in practice, enforcement of this term would prove most unlikely.

It is important to recognize that **the term of the policy is the source of most of its benefits to the sponsor, scheme and assurer.** This is rather more than the potential problem that may occur with fixed-term assurance, that cover may be unavailable or excessively expensive at a renewal date, though that prospect is eliminated by this policy contract design. **It is capitalization of long-term promises.**

The **trigger contingency of the pension indemnity assurance policy is sponsor insolvency,** the point in time at which this occurs is not, however, the point at which a loss is realized by the pension assurance group, if they are the writer of the annuities issued to scheme members. Of course, this is the point in time at which asset transfers between group companies occur and annuities are issued; these transfers utilize standard insurance valuation and accounting methods. As scheme assets are transferred into the pension indemnity assurance group at the point of sponsor insolvency, the actual loss on any policy is not realized until those assets have been fully expended in pension payments – and, even then, it occurs over the remaining life of the scheme. The result is a much-reduced dependency on or sensitivity to the timing of sponsor insolvency than is the case with, for example, credit default swaps or trade credit insurance. The true investment horizon of premiums received is not the point of insolvency, but the times at which pensions in excess of scheme assets are ultimately paid. **Technically, losses are incurred at the point of sponsor insolvency, but not realized for many decades**; this admits a role for risk and performance management both before and after sponsor insolvency.

7.7.2   Incentives

The sole covenant necessary to support the policy is that new awards of benefits should be funded at the time of award, unless the scheme is in surplus. It should be realized that **the moral hazard arising from sponsor and scheme behaviour once the policy is written is quite limited**. Unless or until the sponsor is insolvent, the costs of the pension scheme will ultimately be borne by the sponsor employer, which will, under normal circumstances, act to discipline both the financial management of the sponsor and the trustees. Of course, even though insured, the scheme still has to comply with all other UK pension legislation in effect.

The policy is an interesting **asset of the scheme that serves to supplement and complement the underwriting commitment of the sponsor firm**. If the sponsor's credit standing worsens, the value of the policy as an asset of the scheme increases. If the level of scheme funding declines, the value of the policy as an asset of the scheme also increases. These **contra-cyclical policy properties remove the need for any special contributions arising from the underwriting commitment of the sponsor firm**. The policy reduces both the requirement for full funding of the scheme and eliminates the need to make special contributions when investment market developments prove adverse. **Members' security is substantially enhanced** as now the requirement is one of double default, sponsor and assurer in sequence, before they experience harm to their pensions. And in the unlikely event of default of the pension indemnity assurer, the Financial Services Compensation Scheme will compensate annuity holders at the level of 90% of their benefits.

More importantly, there is a correct alignment of incentives between all parties. **Should an assured sponsor employer find itself in difficulty and distress, it is in the assurer's interest to assist in avoiding the occurrence of**

this risk event. At the simplest level the assurer may convert its debt asset, the future premiums owed to it, to equity – this can be structured such that new money, new working capital is advanced to the sponsor. In more advanced situations, the assurer may encourage the sponsor to take pension contribution holidays from which the resultant increased loss in default is more than offset by the lowered likelihood of insolvency. **Unusually for an insurance contract, the assurer may materially affect the timing of default, the assured risk.**

The assurer need not concern itself in any way with the investment strategy of the scheme. This **allows the sponsor and trustees full freedom to pursue asset allocations** which reflect the realities of the scheme and the commercial prospects of the sponsor. The assurer needs only to know what these allocations are; any which constitute excessive risk for it can be hedged in markets and contained within the asset allocation of its own investment portfolio.

In fact, with the assurance in place, sponsor and scheme trustees may pursue more aggressive asset allocation strategies in the attempt to further lower funding costs, or even to increase benefits. These riskier strategies are only of marginal consequence for the assurer.

7.7.3 The pension indemnity assurer

The asset and liability management problem for the assurer is most interesting. It is unique among insurance companies in that **the risk event which generates a claim does not require the payment of a substantial cash sum;** the claim payment is the issuance of annuities, which in turn pay cash over the remaining lives of the pension scheme members, which may be 75 years or longer. **The claim event actually generates an inflow to the pension indemnity assurer as the scheme's funding, the assets of a scheme whose sponsor has failed, are transferred to the pension indemnity assurer.** The effective life of a policy is unusually long; it is the sum of the expected life of the sponsor and the residual life of the scheme when that event has occurred. This may easily exceed 100 years. **Liquidity needs in any period are small and highly predictable.**

The **pension indemnity assurer is a creditor of the failed sponsor**, in an amount which equals the difference between the scheme funding and the full market cost of annuitisation at that time, the section 75 debt mentioned earlier. It will seek recovery of this debt and also be deeply involved in rescue and restructuring of the sponsor employer. This rescue and recovery process, of course, will typically have begun prior to the formal insolvency of the sponsor – insolvency only rarely arrives as a complete surprise.

The **pension indemnity assurer also possesses some unique risk sharing and hedging characteristics.** For example, increases in life expectation will increase the liabilities of the scheme and increase both the premium revenues of the assurer and its assets. Similarly, increased inflation will raise scheme liabilities and the revenues and assets of the assurer. In the early years of its life, the assurer will be uniquely positioned to bear longevity and inflation risk.

The pension indemnity assurer has a **substantial credit exposure to the UK corporate sector** arising from the future premiums payable to it; in consequence, it should limit its investment portfolio exposure to the equity and debt of the UK corporate sector. Where it chooses to invest internationally, **it should, in principle, not hedge the currency risk exposure**; over the time horizons of the policy, hedging costs would prove extremely costly, and the evidence is that purchasing power parity applies at these long horizons. This currency exposure, of course, may also **substitute for inflation hedging.**

The future cash flows of the liabilities of the assurer may be projected using standard actuarial and econometric techniques. Cash flows from assets are also projected.[58] The asset problem then becomes one of ensuring adequate cash flows from these assets for the assurer to meet these future liability cash flows and its operating costs. There is **no reliance** here **on asset realizations at uncertain market values**. The horizon to which it is necessary to assure cash sufficiency is determined by the significance of those cash flows in present value terms; if, say, the first 30 years contribute 90% of the present value of the current liability cash flows, the asset portfolio cash generation must cover those 30 years. This confidence level is chosen such that it is strictly less than the current capital and reserves of the pension indemnity assurer in overall capitalization.[59]

This calculation is the principal dependency upon interest rates for the assurer's asset and liability management strategy. When interest or discount rates are low, coverage to far horizons is required, and when rates are high, shorter horizons suffice. When rates are low, asset values tend to be high, and the assurer has a higher capacity to write more new business.

Diversity in the asset portfolio is a prime concern. However, this is not a question of returns being uncorrelated, as correlation is simply a measure of association. The question is one of **causal independence of cash flows** generated. This can be determined by using Bayesian network modelling. The caution must be added that these financial networks have grown in complexity over time and the interdependencies between economies and financial markets have increased markedly with financial globalization – the real world is not stationary in this regard.

The **asset portfolio** chosen is therefore **dominated by long-term investments of limited marketability.** Government securities, sufficient to meet **three years' cash-flow** uncertainty on realization, should be held as a contingent **liquidity buffer.** This is relatively unimportant within the overall allocation. **Internationally,** the investment may be foreign **direct investment, corporate participations,** but limited to countries where dividend repatriation is explicitly permitted, **rather than portfolio investment** in a local stock or bond market. **Infrastructure** such as roads, railways, airports, hospitals and schools, all **figure prominently** as investments. In general, amortizing asset finance, such as capital equipment leasing, should also be present. In addition, residential rental property, such as university accommodation, will be used. **Commercial and industrial property** will be **limited to the international** context.

For the reasons outlined at the beginning of this chapter, the diminution of diversity, **opportunistic investment management is avoided.**

Asset specificity, the characteristic that the **difference in value between first best and second best use** is large, is potentially a problem for all of these investments; this is **limited by causal independence among asset cash flows,** diversity among assets. All of these investments have the characteristic that they should prove productive for the economy in a broad sense and generate low but sustainable long-term real returns for the assurer.

Hedge funds will not be utilized; the problem here is the dependence upon specific human capital, which is ill advised at investment terms as long as those of the assurer. Similarly, **venture capital and private equity funds will be avoided;** in addition to the human capital problem, there are both **cash-flow drawdown concerns and an absence of control over realizations and returns of investment capital.** Commodities will also not be utilized, though related infrastructure such as pipelines, mining equipment and grain elevators would be eligible.

In general, the assurer will **avoid the use of derivatives contracts,** even for hedging purposes. In the case of OTC products, there is an **unacceptable credit exposure**[60] and when this is collateralized, **an undesired resultant emphasis on the short term.**

7.7.4 Portfolio optimization

The **portfolio asset allocation** is optimized in a gain and loss framework, in which the **risk measure is loss rather than variance** or some more complex risk measure; this is achieved utilizing the Omega functions of Keating and Shadwick.[61] These have the advantage of considering the entire distribution function of outcomes and may be used in a global and local manner considering both the immediate and long-term outcomes. In this framework, illiquidity of investments is not problematic. The ethos, however, is one of satisficing in a precautionary manner, rather than maximizing return outcomes.

7.7.5 Sources and uses of funds

Table 7.1 shows the sources and uses of funds of the pension indemnity assurer. With the exception of the items 'Assets Received' and 'Assets Transferred', all are cash items. The table refers to a credit insurer and a life assurer; this form of organization of the pension indemnity assurer, though principally one of

Table 7.1 Sources and uses of funds for a pension indemnity assurer

Sources	Uses
Credit insurer	
Premiums received	Operating expense
Assets received	Assets transferred
Investment income	Intra-group Compensation
Recoveries	
Life assurer	
Assets received	Operating expense
Investment income	Pensions paid
Intra-group Compensation	

administrative and regulatory convenience, serves to segregate the principal risk-taking activities of the group and facilitate management of the cash flows. Each element of the table has a distinct model, though causal linkages between the items are retained. For example, an event of default will lower future premium income and it will also create an asset receipt of the failing sponsor's scheme funding and a recovery on the section 75 debt. On the debit side, it will create an asset transfer to the Life Assurer, the cost of the annuitisation which pays members' pensions. The table also shows entries 'Intra-Group Compensation'; these are entries arising from intra-group risk transfer and equalization.

The life assurer is effectively a mono-line annuity writer. It receives assets from the credit insurer, which may include cash, in consideration of its cost of production, including margins, of the annuities written. It should be noted that this is not equal in amount to the assets received from the pension scheme of a failed sponsor by the credit insurer. The credit insurer assumes long-term corporate insolvency risk. This risk is not new; it is borne by almost all insurance companies within their asset portfolios.

In all of the discussion of annuitisation and its costs, including the regulatory debates, one simple fact has tended to get lost. If **the technical best estimate of liabilities is soundly based, that should ultimately prove the true cost of providing those pensions**; the capital buffers which offer comfort against adverse developments of risk and uncertainty are freed over time and become available to the shareholders of the life assurer. In popular parlance, one might almost say that the capital has merely been rented in this situation.

7.7.6 Regulation of the pension indemnity assurer

Pension indemnity assurance is not some clever form of **regulatory arbitrage** between pensions and insurance. Far from it, the capital requirements of the assurance structure are substantially more onerous than pension regulation. The value of the pension indemnity assurance is derived from an element which is unrecognized by regulation – the sponsor's commitment to make future contributions and pay future assurance premiums. By insuring against the harm of its insolvency to its scheme, the sponsor company reduces its funding costs and reinstates incentives for DB provision.

Like all European insurance companies, the **pension indemnity assurer** will be **subject to the Solvency 2** insurance regulations. Given the mixed nature of its business lines, credit insurance of the sponsor companies, and annuity writing for scheme members, it turns out that two distinct companies, one general insurer and one life assurer, are the optimal structure from a regulatory standpoint, as well as operationally.

The general insurer writes the pension indemnity assurance policy with the sponsor and scheme, and also has an agreement in place with its life assurer under which it is assured availability of the annuities required on commercial agreed terms. Absent this agreement, further risk provisions would be needed. In addition, there are risk-sharing agreements, which offset risk exposures to, for example, longevity and inflation, in place between the two companies. These contracts allow the life assurer to write annuities on very competitive terms. The life assurer is simply a bulk annuity writer, such as Paternoster or the Prudential; it is unusual only in having a sole source of pension schemes for annuitisation, the credit or general insurer, which also offsets some of its risk exposures.

The usual Solvency 2 'own funds' and liquidity regulations apply, as well as the standard stress tests. This subject alone could occupy a complete book; suffice it to say that everything described here is fully compliant with the latest draft of those regulations.

7.7.7 Business strategy

In the case of BrightonRock, rather than adopting an approach which is capital efficient, the pension indemnity assurer will emphasize its own security and excessive capital adequacy, reflecting this in policy pricing. It will, as a result, operate at between two and three times the regulatory capital minima specified. This is a significant departure from recent market practice, in which the ambition was typically to maximize the premium revenue for a given level of capital by underwriting the maximum possible volume of risk. In turn, this practice requires the use of reinsurance to limit excessive losses. The pension indemnity assurer should write only that business which it can cover comfortably from its own resources; it should not use reinsurance.

In terms of the risk management of the pension indemnity assurer, this self-reliance is sound; the cost of reinsurance can be remarkably volatile and need not be available at future dates when required. This is conservative and, perhaps, old-fashioned management. However, it is not economically inefficient.

7.8 Conclusion

DB pension analysis, accounting and regulation as currently practised in the United Kingdom are all deeply flawed. These are point in time analysis of a complex ongoing multiple-period risk-sharing arrangement. The role of the sponsor as underwriter of the scheme is recognized only in its negative sense, and no incentives remain for the sponsor to offer this form of pension. **There is no consideration of the future contributions.**[62]

The single-period analysis of Markowitz or Sharpe is inappropriate in this situation, as the long-run optimal strategy is only the sequence of successive short-run optimal strategies in exceptional circumstances which are most unlikely to be met in practice.[63]

The accounting standards, through their use of a mixed attribute standard, **distort reality.** It is simple enough to produce unbiased estimates; this would involve no more than projecting the cash flows of both assets and liabilities and then using a common discount function.[64]

DB pension schemes are highly efficient risk sharing and pooling arrangements, in which scheme members face just one risk, sponsor insolvency.

The **real problem for DB pensions** comes with **the extra capital funding requirement that arises** for the scheme **after sponsor insolvency.** This can be completely resolved by the use of pension indemnity assurance.

This assurance lowers the **scheme funding requirement for the sponsor employer.** It also displaces the intermediate special contribution claims arising from the regulation in effect that penalizes the sponsor as underwriter of the scheme. **The effect of the policy is to capitalize the sponsor covenant. This restores incentives for DB scheme provision by a corporate sponsor.**

Though this chapter has focussed on the traditional DB scheme, the use of pension indemnity assurance could be far broader than this and encompass, with minor modification, many of the newer ideas circulating for alternative pension risk-sharing arrangements; all that is required is that a set of liabilities are well defined. Pension indemnity assurance could be used more broadly, for example, to enhance local authority schemes, but it should be recognized that the regulation, costs and incentives for these differ from those for the corporate sector. The international dimension to this form of assurance is, of course, dominated of the minutiae of local regulation.[65]

The asset and liability management problem for the pension indemnity assurer is unique. It is extremely long term. Its **liability cash flows are highly predictable and small in any one period; its liquidity demands are predictable.** As its insurance risk is primarily corporate insolvency, and as one of its principal assets is corporate indebtedness under the assurance policy, **it must avoid further corporate debt and equity exposure in its investment portfolio.**

The result is a cash-flow projection and sufficiency form of asset and liability management, with no dependence upon future sale of assets in capital markets.[66] Market values determine only the horizon to which cash-flow sufficiency is desired.

The emphasis for the pension indemnity assurer here is not upon maximizing the volume of business written for a given level of capital, but rather upon self-sufficiency ensuring a steady, and predictable long-term profitability from a stable and secure business, even in the face of adverse development of its covered risks.

Notes

1. Much of the discussion of pension risk management in recent times has confused this estimate aspect by confounding it with actions which limit the benefits arising from future employment service. Closure to new members, movement from a final salary to a career average basis for future accruals and changes in service entitlements (say, from one-sixtieth to one-eightieth of final salary per year of employment service) are all examples of these latter changes. A change in the discount rate applied to the future cash flows, though, is a change in our estimate, not the actual liabilities ultimately payable.

2. This shift of risk preference, between assets and liabilities, and positive and negative returns, is widely observed and reported as 'anomalous' by behavioural economists in empirical and experimental studies, but unaccountably and illogically, they regard it as evidence of irrationality on the part of individuals. For the avoidance of any doubt, we shall emphasise this – it is perfectly rational to dislike uncertainty or risk in our assets and also to like uncertainty or risk in the corresponding liability.

3. It is interesting to note that the regulation of pensions in the United Kingdom changed character in the wake of the Maxwell Mirror Group Newspapers scandal in the early 1990s. Prior to this it was economic in nature, serving to transfer ever more of the liability for pension provisions from the public to the private sector; now it is overwhelmingly social in nature, seeking to protect scheme members from perceived risks. The UK legislation, its subsequent modification and its implementation exhibit and create an aura of distrust, with the predictable effect that sponsors and schemes now comply rather than cooperate–a situation which is economically suboptimal.

4. Of the two tax concessions offered to pension schemes in the United Kingdom, deductibility of contributions and exemption of investments from income and capital gains taxes, it is the latter which is usually the more significant determinant of the cost of pension provision.

5. This distinction also has important historic antecedents in, for example, the definition and prohibition of usury. Scholars and theologians distinguished between loans for subsistence and loans of capital, and usury, the charging of interest, was prohibited only for subsistence loans. Bernardino of Siena, a student of Thomas Aquinas, expounded this well: 'Money has not only the character of money, but it has beyond this a productive character which we commonly call capital.' This distinction is also prominent in Hyman Minsky's analysis of financial instability.

6. Certainly in a UK context, there is also a potential taxation issue, as speculation and trading are close bedfellows. This arises from the prohibition of trading by schemes in order to qualify for exemption of investment income and capital gains from taxation;

simply put, schemes may invest, buying and selling securities, but systematic dealing or trading for profit is prohibited. The intention behind this prohibition was to remove the possibility that businesses might assume the form of pension schemes in order to operate and gain commercial advantage from the tax concessions.

7. In respect of UK regulations, the Pensions Regulator interprets 'prudential' as meaning conservative – estimates are biased by further 'safety' margin provisions under their interpretation. Such a practice greatly compounds the actuarial and statistical difficulties in scheme valuation and risk management. This is counterproductive in terms of the regulator's mandated objectives and the maintenance of affordable DB provision.

8. Another criticism of these traditional diversified asset allocation programmes is that they all consider the investment horizon to be known with certainty in advance; the reality, of course, is that few investors know their investment horizon with great precision, for a very wide range of reasons. The issue of the effective action of accounting and regulation in shortening horizons to the myopic immediate is also relevant.

9. The scheme member is in a risk-neutral position from the standpoint of the sponsor.

10. It is worth noting that the average longevity estimate in use within pension schemes has been increased in each of the last four years by about one year in each period. The latest evidence, by contrast, suggests that actual mortality experience in the United Kingdom is now falling within the actuarial long cohort projection; that is to say, there is some recent evidence of moderation in the rates of improvement of longevity.

11. It should be noted that the pension liabilities of a DB scheme are not sensitive to interest rates; they do not enter any of the calculations determining the pensions ultimately payable. By contrast, there is a dependence on future interest rates for the DC member intending to purchase annuities to generate retirement income, as the payment rates of annuities are in large part determined by the future yields available on government securities.

12. The amounts contributed to the funding of the scheme are not directly available to the sponsor to reinforce its balance sheet in times of distress. UK regulations do not allow the removal of surpluses until they exceed the full cost of bulk annuitisation with an insurance company. In a situation where the scheme is funded at above 100% of the level of the best technical estimate of liabilities but below the level of full annuitisation costs, it may take contribution holidays.

13. Such behaviour has been historically evident; the resolution of New York City's mid-1970s financial crisis involved that city's DB pension schemes investing in significant amounts of the debt issued under the financial reorganisation. This was the episode which spawned the NY Daily News headline, 'Ford to City: Drop Dead', and led the creation of the Municipal Acceptance Corporation (Big MAC), which, together with budgetary reforms, successfully resolved the financial issues and was finally dissolved in 2008.

14. This should not surprise anyone, since government support or enhancement intervention in any particular company's affairs is neither natural nor politically acceptable. Delegation of such activity to government's administrative agencies is clearly anathema to the body politic. Supporting one company inevitably disadvantages some other; the competition policy aspects are obvious, and would doubtless also raise issues in a European competition context. Practically, then, regulation and supervision has to focus on the secondary risk element, the level of scheme funding.

15. The UK Pensions Regulator and the PPF have from time to time become involved in corporate restructurings where sponsors were distressed, and they have presented their actions as active corporate finance. The reality is that in all cases, the pension scheme has received additional contributions, rather than made contributions to the sponsor employer's operating capital. In these arrangements, we have never seen explicit worsening of funding security in order to improve the sponsor insolvency likelihood. Regardless of this criticism, these are a welcome, if imperfect, development.

16. A rather extreme example is appropriate: soldiers in the United States who fought for either the North or South in the American Civil War were awarded pensions which included surviving spouses' benefits. In the hardship of the 1930s recession, because of the security of this income, these former soldiers became very attractive marriage propositions, notwithstanding their advanced ages. The last pensioner spouse from the Union side, Gertrude Janeway, died in 2003 and the last Confederate pensioner, Alberta Martin, died in 2004 – that's 140 years after the war service.

17. Commitments of a repeated nature are well understood and central to finance and commerce; for example, trust and reputation are devices of repetition to facilitate trade and exchange. These remove the effort and expense of attempting to write complete contracts. It may even be argued that private free market law, *lex mercatoria*, arose from the need to resolve problems arising from nonrepeated elements in international trade.

18. Until the removal in 1997 of the credits to pension schemes under advanced corporation tax, schemes in the United Kingdom were almost without exception still growing; their annual contribution receipts exceeded their annual pension payments. Liquidations and reliance upon the market were unnecessary. This tax change had a capital cost to schemes at the time estimated at some £67 billion; its more pernicious cost lay in the removal of the repetitive characteristic of those tax credits, and their portfolio value smoothing benefits. It has clearly contributed to the lowering of pension fund holdings of UK equity and preferred stock.

19. The second sentence of this quotation has gained direct relevance in the context of the recent financial crisis, but it is also a profound criticism of the current mark-to-market accounting standard for assets.

20. The separate trust structure in the United Kingdom ensures that scheme assets are in essence remote and unavailable to creditors in the insolvency process, but if a scheme is funded at greater than 100% of the technical best estimate of liabilities at the time of insolvency, this surplus could be subject to challenge and reclaim by the receiver or liquidator for the benefit of other creditors.

21. There is a further issue if a scheme is capitalized such that it can cope with uncertainty; when liabilities are measured as the best technical estimates, this additional capital is not expected to be consumed by pensions paid. It is expected to survive the discharge of liabilities, so the question of ownership of that excess must arise.

22. The related financial analyst's favourite of comparing pension scheme deficits and the market capitalization of the sponsor also deserves some thought. It may grab headlines to describe British Airways as a pension scheme deficit with an airline attached, and to show that the scheme deficit is far larger than the market capitalization, but this is an incorrect analysis. The market is well aware that the company has a pension deficit – in the efficient markets form, this deficit is, in theory, fully incorporated into the valuation of the company's stock. The market capitalization of the company is then the extent of the capital buffer (in excess of full technical level funding) which permits it to fulfill its role as underwriter of the scheme – but that is far less newsworthy.

23. There are other forms of insurance that exist, such as Trustee Indemnity and Insurance Company provided pensions, which are not covered in this chapter.

24. The debates which led to its formation included elements of concern that European rulings would introduce significant liabilities for government arising from sponsor failures and harm to members' pensions. In fact, European employment legislation enacted in 2008 did introduce a requirement for support provision. This legislation is the basis of current proceedings in Strasbourg against the Irish Government in the case of the Waterford Wedgewood pension schemes. It was also evident that HM Treasury was most unwilling to assume any such contingent liabilities.

25. This has been presented as a form of insurance 'deductible', which is nonsense. The purpose of an insurance deductible is to limit problems of moral hazard which may arise from the changing behaviour of the insured once the policy has been written. In the case of DB schemes, members cannot influence the likelihood of sponsor insolvency or the level of scheme funding, the two risk elements. High and differential deductibles can also be used as a filtering device in insurance, for which there is the potential of adverse selection. But this is also irrelevant, as all corporate schemes are required to participate in the fund.

26. In total this levy is currently estimated to raise £720 million in 2010. In addition, schemes faced other administrative costs, such as those for the production of S179 valuations, which are estimated to add a further £250 million to their expenses. In total this amounts to almost £1 billion of new costs. This compares badly with the £300 million annual cost that was presented to Parliament in the course of the Pensions Act debates; it also does not compare favourably to the 2008 ONS estimate of £20.2 billion of normal employer contributions made by public and private sector schemes combined.

27. There is a cap on the total levy payable by a scheme – this is set to subsidize and reduce the levies paid by the weakest 10% of schemes.

28. The Dun & Bradstreet evaluations of sponsor insolvency likelihood have proved most contentious and there has been considerable alteration of estimates – this looks likely to continue.

29. Scheme deficits are difference statistics, and as such, are inherently unstable; it is a poor choice as a determinant of the levy amount calculation in consequence.

30. The PPF has consulted on adding further complexities to this formula, such as including a further term based upon the asset allocation of the fund.

31. This can be illustrated most forcefully by consideration of the pathological case of the last man standing, the scheme which outlives all others. It will have made contributions to the costs of all other prior failures, in increasingly large proportions of those failure costs, but there is no surviving scheme to cover its shortfalls.

32. At its March 2009 year-end, the PPF reported an accumulated deficit from operations of $1.2 billion, and the recession has so far proved rather benign in terms of major corporate insolvencies. The PPF has, with the appropriate government consents, the ability to lower the benefits it pays to pensioners; it seems obvious that this will, in the fullness of time, become necessary. Many trade associations, such as the National Association of Pension Funds and the Confederation of British Industry, have explicitly called for the PPF to carry a government guarantee; this has been dismissed.

33. The PPF managed to achieve some impressive recoveries on these debts in the early years of its existence. It seems possible, though, that this aspect of the Pensions Act of 2004 could be subject to challenge in the courts by the receiver of a failed sponsor,

since the PPF does not pay the full benefits on which it is based. This is now an issue in the US and Canadian court proceedings over the Nortel insolvency.

34. In addition, there is currently a UK Insolvency Service consultation which is considering enhancing the position of new creditors in rescue and recovery; it appears likely that new super-senior priorities will be permitted.

35. If this accounting were unbiased, we would be able to produce the returns and prices of equities and bonds perfectly at all times, using only the other asset, and this we know has never been the historic case. In fact, the most elementary bond and equity portfolio management relies upon the diversity of bond and equity characteristics.

36. However, there is substantial historic evidence that, over the long term, equity returns exceed those of corporate and government bonds, which implies a higher discount function for those future dividends and cash flows than is implicit for bonds.

37. Even the meaning of a deficit varies with the level of the discount function under which it was derived; for any specified deficit, the lower interest rates and the liability discount function are, the longer the scheme and sponsor have to repair those deficits. This aspect of deficit repair plans seems to be entirely ignored by the Pension Regulator when agreeing scheme specific deficit repair plans.

38. In addition to the problem of implicit discount functions, the volatilities of equities and corporate bonds differ, with consequence for the resultant realised geometric returns, as was demonstrated earlier.

39. This strategy, with its implicit borrowing and lending legs, is, perhaps, in breach of the 2003 European Directive which prohibits borrowing other than for liquidity purposes. The provision of collateral to swap counterparties is also suspect, in as much as this may be considered to be a payment in preference to the priority of scheme members.

40. The extent of this may be judged from the results of the PPF's use of swaps in its liability-driven investment strategy. It reported investment portfolio returns for its year ended March 2009 of 13.4% including swaps and of −3.4% ex swaps. In that year long dated (25 year) government bond yields declined by just three basis points, but the spread of swaps to governments moved from 16 basis points positive to 45 basis points negative, some 61 basis points in total. At one point in the course of the year, this spread approached 100 basis points negative. It is difficult not to conclude that the PPF's positive result was a fortuitous result derived from the basis risk introduced; clearly the 'hedge' is now a source of risk and volatility in its own right. In terms of the earlier analysis this strategy is hedging the measure, not the ultimate liabilities.

41. Note that these are not realised gains or losses, but simply changes in estimates.

42. It should be recognized that this classification is arbitrary. Historically, at least one major credit rating agency partitioned scheme deficits between sponsor debt and equity for the purpose of credit analysis.

43. In addition, it would trigger the need for funding at the level of full annuitisation since it would have lost the sponsor as underwriter – perhaps equivalently, this action might reduce all members' benefits to those payable by the PPF.

44. The effective term of equity, the time to recover the principal invested, is determined by its earnings and dividend policy.

45. Campbell and Viceira produced the classic study of this, showing that the volatility of equity declines with the holding period, while the volatility of debt securities

increases with both the term and the holding period. In their data sample, the volatility of bonds can even exceed that of equity at long holding periods. The principal reason for this is the uncertainty surrounding the reinvestment of principal repayments in the case of bonds or other debt instruments.

46. In 1990 the costs of scheme administration and compliance were around 2.5% of pensions in payment, by the early 2000s this had risen to 6.5% of pensions in payment. It is simply not possible to overcome this level of deadweight frictional costs with any plausible, prudent investment policy. More importantly, over this time no new benefits have been added which might account for this cost increase.

47. Special contributions from sponsors, a measure of the significance of the scheme specific funding regime, were some £11.9 billion in 2007, a year in which normal contributions were just £19.8 billion. This special contribution figure appears to have stabilized at around £7 billion in the years since. By contrast, members' contributions are now around £4.9 billion, some 4.9% of salaries. On top of the normal contributions, which at 15.6% of salaries are already high, these special contributions are very onerous indeed.

48. Based on full (45-year) career membership, contributions at normal levels (15.9% company and 4.9% employee) can support pensions of two-thirds of the final salary, indexed at 3% inflation, for 30 years in retirement, if real investment returns are just 2%. Without the members' contributions, only 50% of final salary can be offered under these conditions. If the scheme member were to take the full 25% cash commutation (pension scheme members may withdraw up to 25% of the value of their pension fund at retirement) of the pension fund permitted, a pension of 50% of final salary could still be achieved from the scheme.

49. The survey evidence on this is mixed.

50. However, it is obvious that DC contribution rates, at just 6.5% for employers and 2.7% for employees, are woefully inadequate for any meaningful level of retirement income.

51. One of the great surprises at the time of the Enron failure was that employees had material holdings of Enron equity in their 401(k) pension plans, which they directed. This was a self-evident concentration of risk. This investment was in stock which was already issued and trading, and as such, it did not represent new capital funding for Enron. Similarly, a pension scheme, which buys the equity or debt securities of its sponsor employer from capital markets, does not create new capital for that sponsor. Clearly these purchases will influence the prices of those securities, but there is no new money for the sponsor. Only if the purchase is a subscription to a new issue does this become capital for the sponsor – this was the case with the New York 'Big MAC' issues mentioned earlier.

52. The idea of operating pension schemes as sources of capital funding is not new. The spectacular post-war revival of German industrial activity, the Wirtschaftwunder, was financed to a very large extent by the book-entry, unfunded pension schemes of small- and medium-sized enterprises, the Mittelstand, which drove it. These schemes are insured against sponsor insolvency by the Pensions-Sicherungs-Verein.

53. The emphasis of pension regulation in practice, though, remains upon scheme funding, the consequence of insolvency, rather than upon the primary risk, insolvency.

54. If the scheme finds itself, under the standard accounting conventions, funded at greater than 115%, the premium becomes a nominal sum, but reinstates at the prior level when the funding position deteriorates. This concession can be offered as the scheme constitutes no risk to the assurer at this level of funding.

55. Premiums would typically lie below 0.5% of liabilities per annum.
56. This asset is not subject to the securities investment limits of 5% in any security or 10% in any Group, contained in the 2003 EU Directive, since, in common with bank deposits, it is not a security.
57. In addition, in order to ensure that premiums paid cannot possibly become sunk costs, the policy can offer to credit all premiums paid, but not the investment income arising from them, towards the cost of any elective bulk annuitisation effected with the assurer. In fact, the only circumstance in which the value of the policy could decline to this minimum value would be one in which the scheme was significantly overfunded.
58. The volatility of dividend and related cash flows is far lower and more predictable than the volatility of equity or bond prices; this result has been known since the work of Schiller and others in the early 1980s, which resulted in the 'fundamentals' valuation debate. The cash-flow projection problem is, in fact, simpler than the price problem, in large part because it abstracts from the question of market liquidity and the role of 'animal spirits'.
59. This paragraph has abstracted from the fact that the pension indemnity assurer has other sources of revenue, such as premiums and recoveries from insolvent sponsors.
60. The nature of the problem here is explored in Keating and Marshall, 2010.
61. Keating C. and Shadwick, W., 'A Universal Performance Measure', *Journal of Performance Measurement*, Spring 2002.
62. Let us demonstrate one aspect of this problem simply: Consider, say, a 10% coupon bond, with a two-year term, and suppose we had bought this at par to yield 10% to maturity. The total value of this at maturity is 121%. Now let us suppose that one-year rates rise to 15% just at the coupon payment, then the 10% coupon is reinvested not at 10% but at 15% to yield a total value at maturity of 121.5%, a higher realised return. At the same time the market price of the bond has declined to 95.65%. New contributions compound these effects.
63. The intertemporal capital asset pricing model due to Merton is an attempt to overcome the shortcomings of these single-period models. In this, the investor holds both a Markowitz/Sharpe optimal portfolio and a second portfolio, which hedges against the uncertainty of future events. Unfortunately, this model expressly excludes future contributions, which in the case of pensions is a material concern.
64. This mark-to-market issue is confounded by the fact that we do not know how likely a particular set of market price outcomes in fact were. We are, for example, accustomed to conducting performance attribution analyses relative to a benchmark, such as an index, when it is clear that the likelihood of that particular outcome for that benchmark is a determinant of the absolute skill or value added of a portfolio manager. It is trivial, in that case, to assess, *ex post* the *ex ante* likelihood of a particular asset price outcome. The equivalent position for pension scheme funding is to assess and report the likelihood of current funding, calculated under the accounting rules, proving sufficient to discharge the scheme's liabilities.
65. This is appropriate as the element of a scheme which justifies national approval is driven by the nature of the tax concessions. This aspect is evident in the United Kingdom inasmuch as it is possible for a company to create an unapproved scheme (EFRBS), under which it receives tax relief only as the pensions are paid.
66. This is analogous to the traditional banking practice of advancing loans only to those who can generate the cash flows to pay the interest and amortise the principal; in Minsky's terminology this is hedge finance, when 'hedge' had the meaning 'to take precautions'.

References

Campbell J., and L. Viceira. 'Strategic Asset Allocation: Portfolio Choice for Long-Term Investors', Clarendon Lectures in Economics, Oxford University Press, New York, 2002.

Keating C., and B. Marshall. 'The Nature of Banking: Liquidity & Collateral', 2010, available from: www.BrightonRockGroup.co.uk.

Keating C., and W. Shadwick. 'A Universal Performance Measure', *Journal of Performance Measurement*, Spring 2002.

Minsky H. *Stabilising an Unstable Economy*, McGraw Hill, 2008.

8

Employees' Provident Funds of Singapore, Malaysia, India and Sri Lanka: A Comparative Study

Siti Sheikh Hussin, Gautam Mitra, Diana Roman and
Wan Kamaruzaman Wan Ahmad

8.1 Introduction

Demographic changes affect social and economic performance all over the world. Current demographic trends, such as declining fertility rates, declining mortality rates and increasing life expectancies, are causing an aging population, in which the proportion of elderly people to the total population is increasing (Long, 2008). In 2000, less than one in ten people were over 60 years old, but estimates indicate that by year 2050 one in every five people will be over 60 years old (United Nations, 2000). As an example, in Japan, which is one of the fastest aging nations in the world, there were 9.3 people under 20 for every person over 65 in 1950; for 2025, this ratio is forecasted to be 0.59 people under 20 for every person older than 65 (United Nations, 2000).

In Asia, the process of population aging occurs even faster than in Western countries, according to several sources, including Creighton et al. (2005). Table 8.1 shows the geographic distribution of the population aged 60 and above in 2000 and the estimated distribution for 2050.

Caring for the aging population requires massive public expenditures on pensions – both state (public) and private pensions – and health care. Most of the pension plans introduced were based on the idea that the government or employers would be able to support the pension benefits or payments as and when they were due. However, most pension schemes did not consider the impact of longevity risk. This will be a big burden to government budgets and will threaten the continuous long-term fiscal sustainability of governments. Longevity has resulted in a higher number of retirees withdrawing pension benefits from money collected from working persons, and has caused deficits, especially in Defined Benefits (DB) pension plans. A DB plan, also known as a final salary scheme, is a retirement account that defines the amount of

Table 8.1   Geographic distribution of population aged 60 and above

	Year 2000 (%)	Year 2050 (%)
Asia	54	62
Europe	24	11
Latin America/Caribbean	7	9
North America	8	6
Africa	6	11
Oceania	1	1
Total/Estimated Population	605 million	1970 million

Table adapted from figure 1, Creighton et al., 2005.

retirement income based on the length of service and the final salary at retirement; the life annuity is paid monthly, from the time of retirement until the death of the retiree.

In many countries, pension plans are shifting from DB plans toward defined contribution (DC) schemes, due to the challenges of implementing DB pension funds. A DC pension plan, also known as a 'money purchase' scheme, is a pension plan in which contributions are fixed as a percentage of the salary, determined by contractual agreement between employees and employers; however, the benefits or the amount of income received on retirement varies, depending on the accumulated contributions and the returns generated from investments in various assets. Some DC schemes guarantee annual minimum returns or dividends. Although a DC scheme could address the issue of sustainability, DC schemes do not provide benefit payments throughout the lives of retirees. In some DC plans, the benefits are paid to participants as a lump sum at retirement, placing the pensioners at risk of outliving their retirement savings.

Some of the most important challenges that governments around the world need to address with respect to pension funds are (a) finding the best way to meet the needs of the elderly and (b) ensuring that the pension strategies implemented will not burden the younger generation and weaken the economic growth of the country (Rozinka and Tapia, 2007). In order to address the above challenges, it is important to understand and compare pension systems and practices of other countries.

8.1.1   Guided tour

The rest of this chapter is organized as follows. Section 8.2 gives a background of EPFs (Employee Provident Funds): the historical perspective, features of EPFs, challenges faced by EPFs, and possible strategies to overcome the challenges.

Sections 8.3, 8.4, 8.5 and 8.6 describe the EPFs of Singapore, Malaysia, India and Sri Lanka, respectively, in terms of contributions and accounts, dividends, withdrawals, annuities, health benefits and investments.

In Section 8.7, we discuss and compare the magnitude and ranking of CPF Singapore, EPF Malaysia, EPF India and EPF Sri Lanka. We consider some relevant aspects of the ALM framework within the EPF plan.

Section 8.8 presents the conclusions.

The similarities as well as the differences between the Provident Funds of Singapore, Malaysia, India and Sri Lanka are tabulated in a summarized form in the Appendix.

8.2 Background

This chapter concentrates on the Employees' Provident Funds of Singapore, Malaysia, India and Sri Lanka. In these countries, EPFs are DC pension funds, except in India, where the EPF Organization combined both DC and DB schemes. The main objective of an EPF is to provide for post-retirement assurance through compulsory savings for participants. This scheme has been a very important source of retirement remuneration since it was introduced in the 1950s. Over the years, other benefits in addition to retirement were added for participants, such as homeownership, education and healthcare withdrawal schemes.

8.2.1 Historical perspective and features of EPFs

Britain introduced the pension concept in its former colonies in Asia. There were two different types: one was a DB pension scheme for government workers, and the other was a provident fund (PF) for those in the private sector (Lindeman, 2002). The first mandatory EPF was originally introduced and implemented in Malaysia in 1951 (Thillainathan, 2000).

Three features define the traditional provident funds (Lindeman, 2002):

1. central management: all funds are collected, invested and paid out by a central financial agency (statutory body appointed by the Government)
2. a formal structure of individual accounts, to which contributions as well as dividends are credited
3. lump sum withdrawals at retirement.

These features are shown in Figure 8.1. The countries that still maintain provident funds similar to those with the above-mentioned features are Singapore, Malaysia, India and Sri Lanka (Lindeman, 2002). In other Asian countries, new types of PFs were introduced. For example, in Hong Kong the Mandatory Provident Fund (MPF) works on a decentralized basis and encourages workers to make their own investment choices through their employers (Lindeman, 2002).

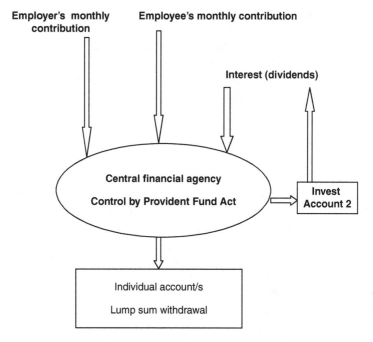

Figure 8.1 The common features of provident funds

Besides the three traditional features described above, there are other important features of the EPFs, such as the following:

- It is mandatory for targeted participants, that is, private sector employees.
- Both employers and employees need to contribute certain percentages of the
  employees' wages to the financial agency on a monthly basis. The benefits
  depend on the asset returns of the fund, except in India, where there is a mix
  of DB and DC.
- Withdrawals prior to retirement are allowed; however, only participants eligible under certain rules and regulations can make them.
- Provident Fund Acts exist and are enacted by the Parliament in each country.

The core functions of the PFs or the Central Financial Agency appointed by
the government are the following:

- the collection of monthly contributions from both employers and
  employees
- payment of both pre-retirement and retirement benefits

- evaluation of the eligibility of applicants to withdraw the nonretirement benefits, based on supporting documents
- investments of the provident fund's assets.
- tracing and taking action against employers that try to avoid contributing to the provident fund.

8.2.2   Life cycle benefits

EPFs provide social security benefits to participants not only during the decumulation phase (retirement), but also during the accumulation phase (pre-retirement). Active participants are allowed to make withdrawals for purposes such as homeownership or mortgage, children's education, health benefits and other reasons, depending on the regulations in each country. Withdrawals are allowed from EPFs, so that participants can balance their income to consumptions, especially during critical times in life. These early withdrawal schemes are 'Life Cycle' benefits – a lifetime budget constraint problem, in which individuals need to make the decision to withdraw from EPF, when the need arises, in light of their expected income, retirement age and life expectancy (Adams and Prazmowski, 2003).

Most people rely on monthly salaries as their main source of income; however, income varies and typically grows with age and experience. There are times when individuals needs to protect their households from unexpected emergencies, especially during the initial phase in adult life during which consumptions are higher than incomes. Unlike income, expenditures generally decline with age. For employees with an uninterrupted career, their expenditures decline especially when their children start to leave home (Adams and Prazmowski, 2003). Based on this idea, EPFs allow members to withdraw from their own account, subject to their eligibility and the regulations. However, participants have to remember that the main purpose of contributing to an EPF is to ensure post-retirement security, and pre-retirement withdrawals are not encouraged unless necessary, as they may lead to insufficient retirement wealth balance to last throughout retirement.

8.2.3   Challenges faced by administrators of EPFs

The main challenge faced by administrators of EPFs is to provide members with a sufficient balance to last throughout retirement. The value of the accumulated wealth in participants' accounts at retirement determines the retirement income. Inadequacy arises because of many factors. One of them is the current system that allows pre-retirement withdrawals for benefits such as mortgage, education and health. Another factor is the low investment returns. EPF ratios of assets to Gross Domestic Product (GDP) for each country are high due to the high monthly contributions from participants; however, the domestic financial markets are quite limited, and the capital markets in Asia are underdeveloped

(Thillainathan, 2004). In most countries, EPFs only invest locally. The investments of EPFs are strictly regulated, and a high percentage of the investments go to public sector products and the country's developments; this causes low rates of return. Most provident funds pay out a lump-sum benefit at retirement, leaving the retirees at risk of outliving their incomes. Based on a survey done in Malaysia, most retirees, especially those in the lower income group, spent the total lump sum withdrawn at retirement within 5 to 10 years. In fact, 60% of respondents had to depend on their children in order to survive during retirement (Ibrahim, 2004).

Another challenge is altering the structure of Provident Funds in order to include a scheme for informal (casual workers), especially in India and Sri Lanka (Rannan, 2006). As Provident Funds and their participants are based on a full-time employment model, casual workers and workers with interrupted careers will not be able to contribute to EPFs or any other retirement schemes. Administrators of EPFs need to consider ways for the self-employed, those with interrupted careers and temporary workers to contribute to EPFs in order to reduce the risk of individuals with insufficient savings and facing poverty in old age.

EPFs are state mandated and managed. It is difficult for the state to separate the conflicting roles of being the service provider, the supervisor and the regulator, with the result that the policy formulation, oversight and implementation of EPFs are not being separated (Asher, 2005). With the absence of a single independent regulatory body to oversee EPF functions, the effectiveness of investment decisions, performances and strategies that will benefit all stakeholders are not closely monitored, which impedes the development of market infrastructure (Abdul Ghani, 2007).

8.2.4   Possible strategies to overcome the challenges

There has been a need to amend and improvise the strategies and regulations in response to factors like changing demographics, economic conditions and expectations of EPF stakeholders (Asher, 2003).

In order to finance pension benefits in European countries, large tax increases were introduced; however, this method has not always been successful in overcoming the problem (Abdul Ghani, 2007). Government could help the demand for financial instruments in order to hedge the long-term pension liabilities by the issuance of large amounts of long dated bonds and index-linked bonds (Abdul Ghani, 2007). This is a way to reduce risks associated with the duration gaps of asset against liability. Asher (2002) suggested investment companies be more transparent; he also encouraged international diversification of provident fund assets, since in Asian countries domestic financial and capital markets are quite limited.

There is a need to review policies concerning withdrawals from the accumulated balances and possibly set a minimum sum, as introduced by CPF Singapore in 2003. Having a target for the minimum sum in individual accounts during the accumulation phase ensures that participants have the minimum income necessary to live on during retirement (http://mycpf.cpf.gov.sg/). The present system of nonreturnable lump-sum withdrawal often results in insufficient reserves during old age. Apart from limiting withdrawal facilities, mandatory annuitization for EPF participants needs to be given serious consideration.

Another way to provide members with a sufficient balance to last during retirement is to introduce reverse mortgages for PF members. Reverse mortgages allow an elderly person who owns a house to borrow cash against the value of the property. A monthly annuity can be arranged, and this annuity is considered an amount borrowed that will accumulate with interest rates until the death of the homeowner. Following the homeowner's death, the property will be sold to pay off the debt to the agency (Tse, 1995). The remaining amount, if any, will be given to the descendant. This concept is new to the Asian region, compared to the developed countries. It should be looked into especially to help the 'asset-rich cash-poor' EPF members mitigate longevity risk and live comfortably during retirement.

The absence of a formal system for retirement income support for unorganized and informal workers has resulted in a high percentage of elderly having to work even after retirement in order to survive (Rannan, 2006). A strategy is required to strengthen and expand the coverage of the pension system. Pension coverage for informal workers can be introduced through individual account-based or voluntary retirement saving schemes, as the government alone will not be able to afford and subsidize such program. In May 2009 India, under PFRDA (Pension Fund Regulatory and Development Authority), extended the New Pension Scheme (NPS) to all citizens of India on a voluntary basis (http://www.pfrda.org.in). Under this scheme, participants can deposit their contributions in banks and post offices all over the country. Fund managers will charge a very low fund management charge (0.0009%), as compared to mutual funds (http://www.indianstocksnews.com/2009/05/nps-new-pension-scheme-from-pfrda-ndia.html). Participants are given the freedom to choose from equity, government securities and debt/fixed income based investments. Since NPS is still new, we are unable to see the performance or the response of informal workers towards this scheme.

According to Facer (2009), improvements are required regarding the education of individuals on adequate retirement provisions and on how to manage their investments. In Asia, retirees have always depended on their children for support during retirement. However, low birth rates and fewer children staying with their parents mean that this tradition will soon diminish. Hence, there is a need to prepare individuals to be responsible for their own retirement (Goswami, 1997). One of the options is to educate individuals to practice Individual Asset and Liability Management (iALM). iALM influences optimal investment and savings decisions as well as individual attitudes towards risk (Medova et al., 2008). iALM helps individuals and families to identify feasible spending levels for retirement and plan the investment strategy that ensures obligations and goals during retirement can be achieved with the available assets (Medova et al., 2008). Government bodies and EPFs should encourage and educate individuals about iALM.

In India, the Pension Fund Regulatory and Development Authority (PFRDA) was set up by the Government as the regulator for the New Pension Scheme (NPS) to promote income security during retirement by establishing, developing and regulating pension funds and to safeguard and protect the interests of participants. Even though the Provident Fund Act governs EPFs, there is still a need for a singular independent regulatory body to oversee the functions of EPFs and other pension schemes that are available in each country.

8.3   Central Provident Fund (CPF) Singapore

In Singapore, the provident fund was introduced in 1955 and is known as the Central Provident Fund (CPF). As at 30 September, 2009, the CPF has 3.28 million members, of which 1.63 million are active participants, with total assets of S$163 billion (http://mycpf.cpf.gov.sg). The CPF falls under the scope of the Ministry of Manpower. Board members appointed by the Minister from the Ministry of Manpower include representatives from the government, employers, employees and professionals. Board members do not hold any policy-making or investment responsibilities (Asher, 2002). The Government of Singapore Investment Corporation (GSIC) and other government investment holding companies perform investment responsibilities (Asher, 2002).

8.3.1   Contributions and accounts

Besides being a retirement scheme, CPF also allows participants to use their contributions to finance homeownership, medical expenses, education and investments. CPF contributions are divided into three different accounts, namely, the Ordinary Account (for homeownership, investments, tertiary education and topping-up of parents' Retirement Accounts), the Special Account (for old age, approved investments and CPF insurance), and the Medisave Account (for hospitalization and medical insurance; Asher, 2002). The percentage of contributions by employees is based on their age. Table 8.2 shows the percentages of contributions for employers and employees and the percentages of the amount allocated to the three accounts as at July 2007. The maximum contribution is calculated based on a salary ceiling of S$4500 (contributions for high-income earners are only up to the salary ceiling) for both employers and employees (http://mycpf.cpf.gov.sg/).

Table 8.2 The percentages of contributions for employers and employees and the percentages allocated to the three accounts as at July 2007

Employee age (years)	Contribution (% of wage)			Accounts and percentages of contributions		
	Employer	Employee	Total	Ordinary Account (%)	Special Account (%)	Medisave Account (%)
35 and below	14.50	20.00	34.50	66.67	14.49	18.84
35–45	14.50	20.00	34.50	60.88	17.39	21.73
45–50	14.50	20.00	34.50	55.09	20.28	24.63
50–55	10.50	18.00	28.50	45.62	24.56	29.82
55–60	7.50	12.50	20.00	57.50	0	42.50
60–65	5.00	7.50	12.50	28.00	0	72.00
Above 65	5.00	5.00	10.00	10.00	0	90.00

Table adapted from http://mycpf.cpf.gov.sg/.

8.3.2 Dividend withdrawals and annuity

Interest rates are fixed for all three accounts (Ordinary Account, Special Account and Medisave). The interest rate for the Ordinary Account is fixed at 2.5%. Both the Special Account and Medisave interest rates are fixed at 4%. At the age of 55, CPF savings can be withdrawn after setting aside the CPF Minimum Sum. CPF savings may also be withdrawn if one leaves Singapore permanently or becomes permanently disabled.

At retirement (age 62), Special Account savings are transferred to retirement accounts with fixed 4% interest rate, and annuities are paid to retirees for up to 20 years (age 82). If a participant chooses to purchase a life annuity, a monthly income for life will be paid. Participants also have the choice to leave the CPF minimum sum with a participating bank or with the CPF Board, from which monthly remuneration will be given until the accumulated sum is exhausted.

8.3.3 Minimum sum

The CPF minimum sum (amount essential to ensure members have the minimum income to survive during retirement) is set at S$99,600 as of 1 July 2007; this amount will be raised slowly until it reaches S$120,000 in 2013. Once the CPF minimum sum is met, a Medisave required amount also needs to be set aside. However, in the event that the Medisave required amount is not met, the Special Account and Ordinary Account may be used – provided that participants have put aside the minimum sum and still have excess (http://mycpf.cpf.gov.sg/). The Medisave required amount is set at S$14,000 as of 1 January 2008 and will increase by S$2500 each year until it reaches S$25,000 on 1 January 2013 (http://mycpf.cpf.gov.sg/).

8.3.4　Health benefits

The health insurance introduced by CPF of Singapore includes the Medisave saving, Medishield (catastrophic medical insurance), Medisave-Approved Integrated Shield Plans and Medifund to help the poor and needy (www.cpf. gov).

Medisave is considered to be the National healthcare savings scheme that can be used to cover medical expenses by individuals (CPF participants) as well as immediate family members. Medisave savings can also be used to cover the premiums for MediShield and Medisave-approved integrated plans, if the need arises.

Medishield is a catastrophic medical insurance scheme for participants and their dependents. Premiums for MediShield are kept low so that it is affordable to participate in the scheme. The annual premiums for MediShield range from S\$33 to S\$1123 (depending on age).

Medisave-approved Integrated Shield Plans are for members who can afford and require higher medical coverage. The Medisave-approved Integrated Shield Plan is actually a product that combines the benefits offered by private medical insurers and MediShield.

Medifund, an endowment fund, was set up by the Government to help the poor and needy who are unable to pay their medical bills and to ensure that Singapore citizens have access to medical care (Koh et al., 2007).

8.3.5　Investment

CPF funds are invested by the Singapore government through SGIC (the Singapore Government Investment Corporation). The operations of SGIC (and other government investment holding companies) do not have to be revealed (Asher, 2003). CPF members may invest their Ordinary Account (OA) balance under the CPF Investment Scheme [Ordinary Account (CPFIS-OA)] and their Special Account (SA) balance under the CPF Investment Scheme [Special Account (CPFIS-SA)]. Assets that may be invested include insurance, unit trusts, Exchange Traded Funds (ETFs), fixed deposits, bonds and Treasury bills, shares, Property Fund and gold.

Both contributions and returns of CPF are tax-free.

8.4　Employees' Provident Fund (EPF) Malaysia

The Employees' Provident Fund (EPF) of Malaysia was established in October 1951. The total number of members in 2007 amounted to 11.69 million, out of which 5.29 million members were active (EPF annual report 2007). The total assets as of 2007 were recorded at Ringgit Malaysia (RM) 318.29 billion. As of 31 December 2002, the EPF ranked as the 20th largest pension fund in the world and the eighth largest pension fund in Asia (Ibrahim, 2004). The

Employees' Provident Fund Act, 1991, governs the EPF. The EPF Board has representation from the government, employers, employees and professionals. The investment panel is separated from the board and reports directly to the Ministry of Finance. Investment panel members are the CEO of EPF, the chairman, one representative from the Ministry of Finance, one representative from the central bank and three experts in finance and investment.

8.4.1 Contributions and accounts

As of the end of 2008, the mandated contributions rate is within the range of 8% (minimum) to 11% of each member's monthly salary, while employers are obligated to add at least 12% of each employee's salary to the savings.

An EPF member's savings consist of two accounts. The first account, Account I, contains 70% of the member's monthly contribution, while the second account, Account II, stores 30%. Account I is for retirement; withdrawals are restricted until members have reached the retirement age (55 years old), are disabled, leave the country or pass away.

Pre-retirement withdrawals of savings from Account II are permitted for homeownership, education and medical expenses.

8.4.2 Dividend withdrawals and annuity

Besides pre-retirement withdrawals for homeownership, education finances and medical expenses, members are allowed to use Account II savings for their own investments. However, EPF does not cover the risk of the investments; members are to support any losses incurred. The EPF's annual dividend depends on the performance of investments; however, EPF is obligated to provide at least a 2.5% dividend every year.

On reaching retirement age (55 years), the balances in the two accounts are merged and can be withdrawn. The member can choose to receive the entire balance as a lump-sum payment, withdraw one portion as a lump sum and the rest as monthly installments, or receive the entire balance as monthly installments. However, the monthly installments (annuity) option is only available for contributors who have at least RM 12,000 in their accounts; the monthly amount payable must not be less than RM 200, and payments are made for at least 60 months (www.kwsp.gov.my). Should the contributor die prior to retirement, the named (legal) beneficiaries would receive the entire sum accumulated in both accounts. Full withdrawal is also permitted on account of permanent impairment and permanent emigration from the country.

8.4.3 Health benefits

In Malaysia, during pre-retirement, EPF members are allowed to withdraw from their own account in order to pay for medical bills. After retirement, members will have to use their own pocket money or their personal health insurance to pay for medical bills.

8.4.4   Investment

The EPF can only invest in instruments as stated in the EPF Act of 1991. The objective of the investments is to ensure a guaranteed return (at least 2.5% per annum) and to ensure that the fund has the financial capacity to meet withdrawals by members as and when they require them (Ibrahim, 2004). The EPF was overinvested in Malaysian Government Securities (MGS) during the 1980s and even during the early 1990s (Thillainathan, 2000). In the 1990s, when opportunities for investment in MGS declined because of public sector budget surpluses, the fund was invested in assets such as money and equity markets. The regulations for the investment of EPF assets specify that (a) at least 70% must be invested in low-risk fixed-income instruments, and (b) the amount invested in domestic equity must not exceed 25%.

Both contributions and returns are tax-free.

8.5   Employees Provident Fund (EPF) India

India's working population, from age 18 to 59 years, is estimated at 321 million people. Out of 321 million workers, it is estimated that only 11.53% (37 million) are covered under pensions (World Bank, 2007). 284 million workers do not have any formal retirement coverage (World Bank, 2007). The main reason for low coverage is the fact that 85% of the labor force is made up of self-employed or casual workers (World Bank). It is estimated that 15 million workers are to be covered under the EPF and Employee Pension Scheme (EPS) that are administered by the Employees' Provident Fund Organization (EPFO; Asher, 2000).

The Employees' Provident Fund and Miscellaneous Provisions (EPF & MP) Act of 1952 consists of three schemes and are a hybrid of DC and DB schemes. The three schemes are

1. Employees' Provident Fund (EPF) Scheme, 1952
2. Employees' Pension Scheme (EPS), 1995
3. Employees' Deposit Linked Insurance (EDLI) Scheme, 1976 (Asher, 2007).

The Central Provident Fund Commissioner (usually a civil bureaucrat) is appointed by the government and acts as the CEO of the EPF. The CEO is supported by Assistant and Regional Provident Fund Commissioners. The Central Board of Trustees acts as the supervisory authority and consists of the Minister of Labor as the Chairman, the Central Provident Fund Commissioner, federal government representatives, state government representatives, employer representatives and employee representatives. All trustees are appointed by federal government.

EPFO carries administrative and record-keeping responsibilities, whereas fund management duty is contracted out to a professional fund manager. The State Bank of India is the current fund manager.

8.5.1   Contributions and accounts

8.5.1.1   Employees' provident fund scheme, 1952

The EPF is a defined contribution (DC) scheme. Employees contribute 12% of their earnings, while employers contribute another 12% of employees' earnings to the EPF scheme. Out of the 12% of the employees' contributions, only 3.67% will remain in the EPF account: the remaining 8.33% will go to the EPS account as shown in Table 8.3.

8.5.1.2   Employees' pension scheme, 1995

The EPS is a defined benefit (DB) scheme run by the Employees' Provident Fund Organisation (EPFO) that is guaranteed by the government. The 8.33% from the employer's contribution (as mentioned above) is diverted to EPS, while the government contributes another 1.16% of the participant's salary to EPS. The

Table 8.3   Contribution rates for EPFO schemes

Contribution [% of wages]	EPF (1952)	EPF (1995)	EDLI (1976)	Total contribution rate
Employer	3.67	8.33	0.50	12.50
Employee	12.00	nil	nil	12.00
Government	nil	1.16	nil	1.16
Total contribution rate	15.67	9.49	0.5	25.66
Administrative charges paid by employer [un-exempted sector only]	1.10	Paid out of EPS fund	0.01	1.11
Insepection charges paid by employer [exempted sector only]	0.18	n.a	0.005	0.185
Benefits	Accumulation plus interest on retirement, resignation, death. Partial withdrawals permitted for specific purposes	Monthly pension on superannuation, retirement, disability, survivor, widow/ widower, children	Lump sum benefit on death while in service	

Source: Pension Reform in India (Asher, 2007)

scheme provides annuity payment for life to members. The amount received (annuity) is based on the following formula:

$$\frac{\text{Pensionable Salary} \times \text{Pensionable Service (Years)}}{70}$$

The maximum pensionable salary is limited to India Rupee INR 6500 (USD 163) per month (Kakar, 2008).

8.5.1.3   *Employees' Deposit Linked Insurance Scheme (EDLI), 1976*

The EDLI scheme is the insurance paid to descendants in the event of the death of the participant. The employer contributes 0.5% of individual's monthly earnings to fund an additional amount paid on death and subject to a ceiling of INR 60,000 (USD 1500).

8.5.2   Dividend withdrawals and annuities

Members are allowed to withdraw from the EPF for purposes that include housing, life insurance policies, health care and marriage. A full account balance can be withdrawn in the event of retirement, permanent disability, early retirement or death. The benefit is paid as a lump sum. EPF interest rates were fixed at 12% from 1991–1992 to 1999–2000. The interest rate was cut down to 11% in 2000–2001 and further reduced to 9.5% in 2001–2002 due to the fall of interest rates (Rao, N., 2001). In 2008 the dividend was fixed at 8.5%.

The EPS can be claimed as early as the age of 50, that is, after a member contributes to the scheme for at least ten years. The benefits are reduced by 3% for each year of early retirement. If a member contributes for less than ten years to EPS, he or she is still entitled to a withdrawal benefit; however, the amount that can be withdrawn is only a portion of the monthly salary at the date of retirement. The size of this portion depends on the number of years the participant is in service. No benefit can be claimed before five years of service.

8.5.3   Insurance

Under the Employees' Deposit Linked Insurance Scheme (EDLI), in the event of the death of an employee, the dependent(s) are paid the insurance linked to the accumulated wealth available in the employee's account.

8.5.4   Health benefits

EPF members can withdraw money for medical costs from their own accounts if the need arises before retirement. However, health insurance is not included in the EPF framework. After retirement, the monthly EPS pension can be used to cover medical bills.

8.5.5 Investment

Funds are entirely channeled to government or government enterprises for investment. No investments are allowed in international securities, stocks, real estate, gold, bank or corporate deposits (Rao, N., 2001). Investments are allowed only in marketable securities; no loans to individuals or corporations are allowed. The only exception is a loan to the federal government's Special Deposits. Contributions are invested in the bond market that consists of national government bonds, state government bonds and public enterprise bonds. Only recently, since 1998, investment in private sector bonds has been undertaken. Both contributions and returns are tax-free.

8.6 Employees' Provident Fund (EPF) Sri Lanka

The Employees' Provident Fund (EPF) is the largest pension scheme in Sri Lanka. The EPF was established under Act No. 15 of 1958 (www.epf.lk). As at December 2007, the EPF's assets amounted to Rs 560 billion, which is equivalent to 25% of the GDP (http://www.epf.lk/A_Fund_mgt_banner_content. htm). The EPF was established when the economy of Sri Lanka was confined to a small urban formal sector. Twenty years later, EPF membership expanded by 60%; this is due to the growth of the manufacturing and service sectors that are related to the agricultural sector. Even with this increase, by 1995 EPF memberships as a proportion of Sri Lanka's total workforce remained only around 10% (Kanakaratnam and Ya, 2004).

Central Bank of Sri Lanka manages and administers the EPF fund on behalf of the Department of Labor. The Monetary Board of Central Bank decides on investment decisions, reports and responds to the Minister of Labor. The Monetary Board is chaired by the governor of the Central Bank and the secretary to the Ministry of Finance and Planning.

8.6.1 Contributions and accounts

The mandatory contribution rate is 8% (minimum) of a member's monthly salary, while employers are obligated to contribute another 12% of the employee's salary to the savings. In Sri Lanka there is only one account. Withdrawals (including housing loans) can be made every five years.

8.6.2 Dividend withdrawals and annuities

The government determines dividends and they are taxed, therefore decreasing the net return. The entire lump sum is paid at the time of retirement. The retirement age is 55 for men and 50 for women. Withdrawal can also be made in the event that the government closes the place of employment, immigration, or (for employed women) marriage. There is no minimum rate or annuity plan offered in Sri Lanka. It is not possible to delay pension claims after the retirement age.

8.6.3 Health benefits

Health benefits are not included in the EPF framework. However, a free education and health care initiative was launched in 1930 (Rannan, 2006). Therefore, Sri Lanka's citizens are entitled to free medical treatment irrespective of age.

8.6.4 Investment

The investment portfolio includes investments in government securities (Treasury bonds and bills, Rupee loans), listed and unlisted equities and corporate debt instruments. Out of the total investments, 96.5% represent investments in government securities. The remaining 3.5% represent investment in corporate debt instruments.

The reasons for the high proportion of EPF investment in government debt instruments are as follows:

• Income tax enforcement in Sri Lanka has been weak; the average corporate and personal income taxes are only 1.7% and 0.8% of GDP, respectively, as at end of the 1980s.
• The government is responsible for the investment decisions of the EPF.
• The EPF represents the largest source of funds for government domestic borrowing (Kanakaratnam and Ya, 2004).

There is no income tax relief or reduction in work-related expenses for participants. Even the returns of EPF (dividends) are taxed.

The summary of the similarities and differences between the Provident Funds of Singapore, Malaysia, India and Sri Lanka is tabulated in the Appendix.

8.7 Magnitude and ranking of provident funds

Based on Pension and Investment (P&I), Watson Wyatt World 300 largest pension fund survey for year 2006 and 2007 (http://www.pionline.com/), Singapore, Malaysia and India Provident Funds were listed in the top 100. This survey is based on the asset value of the pension funds. The results of the survey for Singapore, Malaysia and India for 2006 and 2007 are tabulated in Table 8.4. As of 2007, Singapore's CPF was ranked 22nd with assets amounting to 94.9 billion USD, followed by Malaysia, 23rd, with assets amounting to 94.6 billion USD. India's EPF was ranked 64th with total assets amounting to 43.1 billion USD. Sri Lanka was not listed in the top 300 largest pension funds; however, its total assets as of 2007 were 4.8 billion USD.

Table 8.4   Results of Watson Wyatt top 300 pensions

	2006		2007	
	Rank	Total asset (Billion USD)	Rank	Total asset (Billion USD)
CPF Singapore	32	70,468	22	94.9
EPF Malaysia	21	82,256	23	94.6
EPF India	80	31,581	68	43.1

Table adapted from the P&I/Watson Wyatt 300: world's largest pension funds, http://www.pionline.com/apps/pbcs.dll/section?category=WWTOPFUNDS&Issue Date=20080901.

Table 8.5   Provident fund assets as percentage of GDP as of 2007

Country	Population size (million) 2008	GDP (million USD) 2007	GDP growth Rate (%) (2007)	Total PF assets (Billion USD) (2007)	Asset as percentage of GDP (2007)
Singapore	4.5	161,347	7.40	94.9	58
Malaysia	24.8	180,714	5.70	94.6	52
India	1129	1,170,968	8.50	43.1	4
Sri Lanka	20.9	32,354	6.00	4.8	14

Table adapted from http://www.photius.com/rankings/_2007_0.html.

It is difficult to compare and classify Provident Funds performance (based on annual dividends) in these four countries. For example, in Singapore and India, the returns earned on contributions are administered and do not reflect the real performance of assets. In Singapore, the dividends are fixed at 2.5% for the Ordinary Account and 4% for both the Special Account and Medisave. This is considered extremely low, as the contribution rate to the Provident Fund in Singapore is the highest among the four countries. As for India, the dividends used to be guaranteed at 12%, until the government decided to reduce it to 9% (between 2002 and 2007), and further decreased it to 8.5 % in 2008. Returns in India are still the highest among the four countries considered.

In Malaysia and Sri Lanka, the dividends are based on the asset returns. If we were to rank the performance of Provident Funds solely on dividends, the Employees' Provident Fund of India (even after the decrement of the guaranteed dividend) would be at the top spot, followed by the Employees' Provident Fund Malaysia with an average 5% dividend.

Based on the statistics tabulated in Table 8.5, it can be said that total savings in Employees' Provident Funds are high in Asia, ranging from 4% up to 58%

of GDP. Underdeveloped capital markets mean that returns are low. Normally the government manages national investment; however, government does not always invest the funds in the most economically productive opportunities. The purpose of retirement funds is to ensure that members are able to live comfortably on their EPF savings. Therefore, the replacement rate can be used to compare the performances of EPFs in these four countries. The replacement rate is the ratio of the pension over the last earned salary. In 2007 the World Bank considered the gross replacement rate as the benefits (retirement) as a share of individual lifetime average earning, while net retirement income takes into account the taxes and social security contributions paid on earnings and on retirement accounts. Based on the article 'Pension at a Glance' (World Bank, 2007), the net replacement rates by earning for average earners among the four countries considered are as follows: Singapore's net replacement rate by earning is the lowest, followed by Malaysia and India. Sri Lanka has the highest net replacement rate.

8.7.1   Matching perspective for Asset and Liability Management (ALM)

In this section we explain the general framework of the Asset and Liability Management (ALM) model using stochastic programming (SP) as a tool in the decision making applied to EPFs. ALM is a mathematical tool that is used to address the integrated management of the assets and liabilities of companies (Cornuejols and Tutuncu, 2007). Uncertainties impinge on both assets and liabilities. Due to the long-term obligations to the retirees, the planning horizons of pension funds are naturally long. The SP formulation for the underlying ALM model includes the stochastic parameters that describe the assets and liabilities. The investment decisions are made *ex ante* and the parameter values (realizations) are revealed in stages. The subsequent decisions at every stage depend on the observations at that particular time, and do not depend on future realizations.

Integrated ALM models are used to meet the objective of achieving optimal investment strategy, that is, to maximize wealth and minimize risk. ALM models have been formulated and applied in the context of pension funds, insurance companies, banks and also for individuals (Dupacová and Polívka, 2009). In Section 8.2.4, we briefly described the individual ALM (iALM) as a method that can be applied in educating individuals on how to manage their investments.

Most of the existing ALM models applied in pension funds are designed for DB funds. The liabilities (that is, benefits to participants) of DB plans are guaranteed prior to knowing the uncertain outcomes of the future long investment horizons. The employers are responsible to fulfil the agreement even if the assets are short of the promised benefits. Among ALM research applied to DC plans are the asset-liability management for Czech pension funds using stochastic programming formulated by Dupacová and Polívka (2009) and the

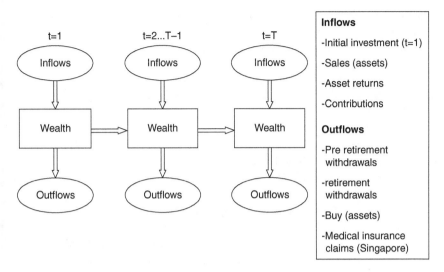

Figure 8.2   ALM framework

InnoALM model of Geyer and Ziemba (2008). The InnoALM model can also be applied for DB pension funds.

Figure 8.2 shows the ALM framework for EPFs. The inflows (assets) include the contributions from both employers and employees, assets sold, asset returns and the initial investment. The outflows (liabilities) include retirement withdrawals, pre-retirement withdrawals, assets bought and medical insurance claims (only applied to CPF Singapore).

8.7.1.1 Assets

Four different types of asset classes (bond, equity, property and money market instruments) are included in the generic model. The stochastic asset returns are included in the specification of the SP decision model. Contributions are computed based on a fixed fraction of the total participants' wages, which vary among employees.

8.7.1.2 Liabilities

The liabilities (outflows) are divided into two categories: the liability payment for the retirees during retirement and the pre-retirement withdrawals for active participants. In the case of CPF Singapore another outflow, medical insurance, needs to be taken into consideration. The future retirement liabilities depend on the accumulated wealth of retirees and the participants' option to receive the balance as a lump-sum payment, to purchase an annuity, to withdraw one portion as a lump sum and the rest as monthly instalments, or to receive the entire balance as monthly installments. The eligibility and purposes of pre-retirement liabilities for each country is different; the model of the pre-retirement withdrawal is based on the selected country. The liability side of the ALM model of the defined contribution pension plan is driven by several factors, such as demographic data of the country, plan regulations (retirement age, minimal required insured time) and the economy.

8.7.1.3 Uncertainties

In ALM, uncertainties are inherent in both assets and liabilities. These uncertainties are captured using discrete models of randomness known as scenario generators. Uncertainties formulation requires both demographic and economic data. Among the uncertainties considered are the earnings growth of active participants, asset return models, liabilities and the population model of EPF members.

This involves ongoing research; both the mathematical model and the scenario generation model for assets, liabilities and the population modeling are considered in detail in Siti Sheikh Hussin's forthcoming thesis.

8.8 Conclusions

EPFs are the general retirement schemes for private sector employees in Singapore, Malaysia, India and Sri Lanka. The main purpose of the EPF is to provide for post-retirement security through compulsory saving. We highlighted the challenges faced by EPFs systems and recommendations on ways to overcome these challenges and to increase awareness among members. In this chapter we presented the similarities and the differences of the EPF systems in the four countries in terms of contributions and accounts, dividends, withdrawals, annuities, health benefits, investments, and last but not least, rankings and performance.

The world, and especially the Asian region, is going through a demographic transition from high to low rates of fertility and mortality; as a consequence the percentage of the aging within the population is increasing. In this chapter we discussed the foreseeable future growth of Asia's elderly population, and the impact of demographic changes pertaining to financial security during retirement. Income provision for older people requires massive public expenditures. Governments need to find ways to meet the needs of the elderly, and at the same time ensure that the pension strategies implemented will not burden the younger generation and mitigate the economic growth of a country.

Appendix

Comparison Employees' Provident Fund (EPF) Malaysia, India, Sri Lanka and CPF Singapore

	EPF (Malaysia)	EPF (India)	CPF (Singapore)	EPF (Sri Lanka)
Managed by	Kewangan Wang Simpanan Pekerja (KWSP)	Employees Provident Fund Organisation (EPFO)	Central Provident Fund (CPF)	Central Bank of Sri Lanka on behalf of the government (department of Labor)
Total Assets as at 2007 (billion USD)	94 .6	43. 1	94 .9	4.8
Contribution (Percentage of employees salaries)	12% employers' share 8–11% employees' share as at 2008 Total – 20 to 23% of employees' salaries	12% employers' share 12% employees' share Government 1.16% Extra 0.50% from employers for Insurance (EDLI) Total – 25.66% of employees' salaries Basis salary ceiling of 6 500 rupee per month	Depending on age basic salary ceiling of S$4500 (see contribution table below) (source http//mycpf.cpf.gov.sg) Total: from 10 to 34.5% of employees' salaries.	12% employers' share 8% employees' share Total – 20% of employees' salaries
Dividends	Obligated at least 2.5% Fixed Dividend However based on performance of investments.	Fixed Dividend 2002 to 2007–9% 2008–8.5% EPS account does not give dividend.	Ordinary Account 2.5% (Fixed) Special Account 4% (Fixed) Medisave 4% (Fixed)	Based on the performance of investments, determined by the government. Will be taxed

CPF (Singapore) contribution table:

Employees Age (years)	Contribution By Employers (% of wages)	Contribution By Employees (% of wages)	Total Contribution (% of wages)
35 & below	14.5	20	34.5
Above 35–45	14.5	20	34.5
Above 45–50	14.5	20	34.5
Above 50–55	10.5	18	28.5
Above 55–60	7.5	2.5	20
Above 60–65	5	7.5	12.5
Above 65	5	5	10

Appendix Continued

	EPF (Malaysia)	EPF (India)	CPF (Singapore)				EPF (Sri Lanka)
Account	Account 1–70% of total contribution Account 2–30% of total contribution	Provident Fund 15.67% out of 24% of total contribution Pension Fund 8.33 % out of 24% of total contribution (EPS)	**Age**	**Account (ratio out of total contribution)**			Only one account, no separate account
				Ordinary	Special	Medisave	
			35 & below	0.6667	0.1449	0.1884	
			Above 35–45	0.6088	0.1739	0.2173	
			Above 45–50	0.5509	0.2028	0.2463	
			Above 50–55	0.4562	0.2456	0.2982	
			Above 55–60	0.575	0	0.425	
			Above 60–65	0.28	0	0.72	
			Above 65	0.1	0	0.9	
			35 & below	0.6667	0.1449	0.1884	
			(source http//mycpf.cpf.gov.sg)				
Retirement Age	56	58	62				Age 55 (men) and 50 (women)
Withdrawals	Account I–at retirement. Account II–can be withdrawn for the purpose of financing of house (monthly housing loan payment), Health and Education.	Provident Fund–can be withdrawn for the purpose of marriage, mortgage, education and health. Pension Fund Scheme–at retirement (non indexed-Defined Benefit). Employees' Deposit Linked Insurance (EDLI) Scheme for surviving relatives after the early death of an employee.	Ordinary Account–can be withdrawn for the purpose of mortgage, insurance, investment and education. Special account–for investment in retirement-related financial products. Medisave Account–for hospitalization and approved medical insurance				Fund members may withdraw funds from their individual account once every 5 years. Also able to withdraw for housing/ mortgage.

Investments	Malaysian Government Securities Loans and Bonds Equity Money Market Instruments Properties	Federal Government Bonds State Government Bonds Bonds of Public Enterprises Any Public category Private Sector Bonds	Government of Singapore Investment Corporation and other government holding companies are responsible for the investment. Ordinary account and special account-participants are allowed to invest in a wide range of capital market instruments (unit trust, equities, gold, fixed deposit and etc) if not government managed default fund.	Bonds Rupee Loans
Minimum sum at retirement	NA Only those with accumulated wealth of at least RM12 000 (minimum sum) at retirement are eligible to choose annuity.	NA	Minimum sum S$99 600 as at 1st July 2007 will be raised gradually until it reaches $120,000 in 2013. Medisave : minimum sum S$14 000 will increase by $2,500 (adjusted for inflation) each year until it reaches $25,000 on 1st January 2013.	NA
Health Benefits	If the need arises –withdraw from Account II during pre retirement. However post retirement health benefit is not covered.	Withdraw from EPF Account during pre retirement EPS–post retirement, monthly defined benefit pay can be used.	Medical Insurance–Medisave catastrophic medical insurance schemes for one and one's dependents.	Medical care is available free of charge in government health centres and hospitals.
Annuity	Annuity only eligible if one has the minimum amount RM12 000. Minimum annuity period (payment) is 60 months.	EPS–Monthly post retirement allowance.	At age 62, SA savings are transferred to a retirement account which can also earn 4% interest and pays an annuity over 20 years up to age 82. If life annuity had been purchased, a monthly income for life shall be given.	NA

Continued

Appendix Continued

	EPF (Malaysia)	EPF (India)	CPF (Singapore)	EPF (Sri Lanka)
Income tax	Both contributions and returns are tax free.	Both contributions and returns are tax free.	Both contributions and returns are tax free.	EPF Returns are taxed by the government.
Insurance	NA	EDLI–for surviving relatives after the early death of an employee.	Health insurance that include–Medisave saving, Medishield (catastrophic medical insurance), Medisave-Approved Integrated Shield Plans and Medifund to help the poor and needy.	NA
Investment decision by employees	Members are allowed to use their Account II EPF savings in their own investments.	NA	Individuals, have the option to place their moneys with one of a large number of outside investment managers within asset limits specified by the CPF.	NA

References

Abdul, Ghani Z. (2007) Bank Negara Malaysia. Deputy Governor's Keynote Address at the 4th Asian Conference on Pensions and Retirement Planning: Reinventing Retirement Strategies in the New World of Risks, Kualalumbur, Malaysia (26 November 2007). www.bnm.gov.my, accessed in June 2010.

Adams, F. G., and Prazmowski, P. A. (2003) Why are saving rates in East Asia so high? Reviving the life cycle hypothesis, *Empirical Economics* 28:275–289.

Asher, M. G. (2007) Pension Reform in India, paper presented at Conference on the Indian Economy at 60: Performance and Prospects, The Australian National University, 20–21 August.

Asher, M. G., and Nandy, A. (2005) Governance and Regulations of Provident and Pension Scheme in Asia, www.spp.nus.edu.sg/docs/wp/wp1405.pdf, accessed in June 2010

Asher, M. G. (2003) Governance and Investment of Provident and Pension Funds: The Case of Singapore and India, paper prepared for the Second Public Pension Fund Management Conference, World Bank Headquarters, Washington, DC, May 5–7.

Asher, M. G. (2004) Retirement Financing Dilemmas Facing Singapore, International Conference on Pension in Asia, Tokyo, Japan, 23–24 February.

Asher, Mukul G. (2001) The Case for a Regulatory Authority for India's Pension System, International Center for Pension Research, (ITAM), Mexico, Report No. 2.

Asher, Mukul G. (2002) The Role of The Global Economy in Financing Old Age: The Case of Singapore, International Center for Pension Research, (ITAM), Mexico, Report No. 2.

Charles, B., and Collins, P. (2005) Pensions in Asia: Potential becomes reality. Watson Wyatt's January 2005, www.watsonwyatt.com/asia-pacific/.../Pensions%20in%20Asia. pdf, accessed on 16 November 2010.

Cornuejols, G. and Tutuncu, R. (2007) *Optimizations Methods in Finance*, Cambridge University Press, New York, USA.

Central Provident Fund (CPF) Singapore website, http://mycpf.cpf.gov.sg/.

Creighton, A., Jin, H., Piggot, J., and Valdez, E. A. (2005) Longevity Insurance a Missing Market, *The Singapore Economic Review* 50 (1):417–435.

Crispin, S. W (March, 2009) Cracks appear in Lee's mantle, Asiatimes online http://www.atimes.com/atimes/Southeast_Asia/KC20Ae02.html, accessed in June 2010.

DiBiasio, J. (2000) Academic warns Singapore must overhaul CPF, http://www.singapore-window.org/sw00/000906fa.htm, accessed in June 2010.

Drijver, S. (2005) Asset Liability Management for Pension Funds using Multistage Mixed-Integer Stochastic Programming, PhD thesis, Rijksuniversiteit Groningen, Labyrint Publications, Ridderkerk, The Netherlands.

Dupacová, J., and Polívka, J. (2009) Asset-liability management for Czech pension funds using stochastic programming, *Annals of Operations Research* 165:5–28.

Employees' Provident Fund Malaysia website, www.kwsp.gov.my.

Employees' Provident Fund Organisation India website, http://epfindia.nic.in/epfbrief. htm.

Employees' Provident Fund Sri Lanka website, http://www.epf.lk/.

Facer, B. (2009) Lessons to learn from DC systems in the Asia Pacific region, MERCER www.mercer.com/referencecontent.htm?idContent=1350690, accessed in June 2010.

Geyer, A., and Ziemba, W. T. (2008) The Innovest Austrian Pension Fund Financial Planning Model InnoALM, Operations Research 56(4):797–810.

Goswami, R. (1997) Indian Pension System: Problems and Prognosis, Fellow, Indian Institute of Management Bangalore, *International Social Security Review*, 55, 95–121,

2002, available at SSRN: http:/ssrn.com/abstract=309077, accessed in 16 November 2010.

Ibrahim, R. (2004) Financing Challenges Facing Social Security Scheme: The Experience of the Employees' Provident Fund of Malaysia, International Social Security Association 13th Regional Conference for Asia and The Pacific, Kuwait, 8–10 March.

Kakar, G. (2008) Retirement in India Pension Benefits and Beyond, MERCER Retirement Perspective, http://www.mercer.com/referencecontent.htm?idContent=1303935, accessed in June 2010.

Kanakaratnam, A., Ya, P. Y. (2004) Reforming the Sri Lankan Employees' Provident Fund: A Historical and Counterfactual Simulation Perspective, University of Hertfordshire Business School, Presented at 7th Annual Conference on Global Economic Analysis, Washington, DC, 17–19 June.

Karunarathne, W. (2005) Mandatory Savings and Retirement Adequacy: Portfolio Simulation of EPF in Sri Lanka. Presented at Globalisation of Pension Fund Investments, 13th Australian Colloquium of Superannuation Researchers, Centre for Pensions and Superannuation, Australian School of Business at University of New South Wales (UNSW) Sydney Australia, http://www.business.unsw.edu.au/nps/servlet/portalservice?GI_ID=System.LoggedOutInheritableArea&maxWnd=_ResearchCentres_CPS_GlobalisationConference, accessed in 16 November 2010.

Koh, B. S. K., Mitchell, O. S., Tanuwidjaja, T., and Fong, J. (2007) Investment patterns in Singapore's Central Provident Fund System, *Journal of Pension Econamics and Finance*, 7:37–65, March, Cambridge University Press, UK.

Lindeman, D. C. (2002) Provident Funds in Asia: Some Lessons for Pension Reformers, *International Security Review* 55(4): 55–70.

Giang Thanh Long. (2008) Aging Population and the Public Pension Scheme in Vietnam: A Long-term Financial Assessment, East & West Studies, 20(1) (June 2008): 171–193.

Medova, E. et al. (2008) Individual Asset Liability Management, Centre for Financial Research, Judge Institute of Management, Quantitative Finance, 8(6): September 2008, 547–560, University of Cambridge.

Ngee, C. C., Tsu, A. K. C. (2003) Life annuities of Compulsory Saving and Income Adequacy of the Elderly in Singapore, Department of Economics, National University of Singapore, *Journal of Pension Economics and Finance*, 2:41-65, Cambridge University Press, UK.

NPS New Pension Scheme from PFRDA, 'What is it' and 'Analysis' accessed 15 May 2009, http://www.indianstocksnews.com/2009/05/nps-new-pension-scheme-from-pfrda-india.html.

PFRDA website, http://blish.in.com/atulkr4u/post/new_pensionscheme_nps-25985.html, http://www.pfrda.org.in.

P&I/Watson Wyatt 300: world's largest pension funds, http://www.pionline.com/apps/pbcs.dll/section?category=WWTOPFUNDS&IssueDate=20080901, accessed in June 2010.

Rannan, R. P. (2006) Sri Lanka's Schemes for Informal Sector Workers, Workshop on Extending Pension Coverage to Informal Sector Workers in Asia, Bangkok, 30 November–1 December.

Rao, N. (2001) Public Pension Fund Management in India, Conference on Public Pension Fund Management at World Bank, Washington, USA, 24–26 September. www1.world-bank.org/finance/assets/images/Nagashwar_Rao.ppt, accessed in June 2010.

Rozinka, E., and Tapia, W. (2007) Survey of Investment Choice by Pension Fund Members, OECD Working Papers on Insurance and Private Pensions, No. 7, OECD Publishing, Paris, France.

Sally (2008) 'CPF Act amended to help prepare for retirement' http://www.singaporedelivery.com/cpf-act-amendment-200809/.

Sane, R., and Harshankar, N. (2004) A Study of Exempt Funds in India, India Pension Research Foundation Working Paper Series, No. 08/04, New Delhi, India.

Thillainathan, R. (2004) Malaysia: Pension and Financial Market Reforms and Key Issues on Governance, paper presented at the Conference on Pensions in Asia: Incentives, Compliance and Their Role in Retirement, Hitotsubashi University, Tokyo, Japan, 23–24 February.

Thillainathan, R. (2000) The Employees Provident Fund of Malaysia: Asset Allocation Investment Strategy and Governance Issues Revisited, paper presented at Pension Fund Management Workshop organized by Employees Provident Fund Kuala Lumpur, 14–15 August, Kualalumpur, Malaysia.

Tse, Y. K. (1995) Modeling Reverse Mortgages, *Asia Pacific Journal of Management* 12(2):79–95.

United Nations (2000) 'World Population Ageing 1950–2050', www.un.org/esa/population/publications/worldageing19502050/pdf/80chapterii.pdf, accessed in June 2010.

World Bank and OECD (2008) Pension at a Glance: Asia Pacific www.apapr.ro/.../oecd%20 asia%20pacific%20at%20a%20glance%202008.pdf, accessed on 16 November 2010.

9
Dynamic Risk Management: Optimal Investment with Risk Constraints

Stuart Jarvis

9.1 Introduction

9.1.1 Quantifying the trade-off between risk and return

When choosing an investment strategy, investors select assets that are likely to meet their particular return goals while managing the likelihood or severity of returns falling short of these goals. Assessing the right trade-off between return and risk therefore requires the following:

- *Target outcome*: The investor's goals should be clear. This may be expressed in terms of a benchmark or a return target, for example. Ideally these goals will be embedded in the wider situation facing the investor – the investor's asset allocation is likely only one of several levers that can be adjusted to meet these goals. These goals then help determine the average return required of the investor's assets.
- *Risk tolerance:* A judgement of the extent to which the investor is prepared to tolerate the return falling short of this target return. In the simplest situation, this could be expressed as an aversion to volatility, although more explicitly focusing on the probability or severity of poor returns may be more appropriate.

With these in place, an investor will then seek to carry out a form of optimization – finding a strategy which gives as good a trade-off as possible between the average return and the variability relative to this average. In carrying out this optimization, further choices have to be made: What time horizon is relevant for the investor? What instruments are available in the investment universe? Is the strategy static or is it able to evolve dynamically in response to events?

9.1.1.1   Mean-variance approaches

The classic Markowitz approach involves trading the expected return outcome off against the volatility of returns around this outcome. This can be framed in multiple equivalent ways:

- maximize expected return for a given level of volatility
- minimize volatility for a given level of average return
- maximize risk-adjusted return, that is, return minus risk stated as a variance and weighted by an aversion parameter (5 return 2 aversion 3 variance).

These are equivalent approaches, thus varying the level of volatility, return or aversion, respectively, in the three versions above sweeps out the same 'efficient frontier' of portfolios that are mean-variance efficient.

9.1.1.2   Utility-based approaches

A utility function provides a way of doing both at the same time: a score can be applied to each consumption and wealth outcome; two strategies can then be directly compared by comparing the expected utility, using the distributions of outcomes from following the two strategies.

Alternatively, utility can be combined with a risk measure such as volatility: maximizing utility subject to a cap on the variance of outcomes provides a way to focus separately on the desired outcomes and the express tolerance for risk.

9.1.1.3   Asymmetric outcomes

Volatility is most useful if the underlying distributions are symmetrical. If the distributions have material skewness, for example, if options form part of the allowable investment universe or dynamic strategies could give rise to option-like payoffs, in such cases using a symmetric risk measure may give unappealing results. The average outcome plus dispersion around this may give a misleading sense of the real outcome distribution.

This re-emphasizes the point that the focus should be on the investor's goals – if these are properly captured by an average return, well and good. If not, an appropriately structured utility function and measure of tail risk may provide more control.

9.1.1.4   Tail-risk measures

Use of variance as a risk measure has the notorious implication that it penalizes above-average outcomes as much as below-average outcomes. Measures of risk that focus on the tail have been developed that focus instead on the 'left hand tail' of returns well below the average outcome. Value at risk (VaR) is such a measure that has been widely used for many years. More recently, academics have tended to use other risk measures, in a growing literature that was kick-started by the famous article of Artzner et al. on coherent risk measures, which pointed out the lack of coherence of VaR. Whereas VaR essentially reports quantiles such as the '1 in 200 event', 'conditional value at risk' (CVaR) looks at the average of the worst 0.5% of possible outcomes. Due to its coherence, it has attractive theoretical and analytical properties that make it more suitable for modern risk management.

Therefore, trading off the mean outcome against a tail risk measure, such as CVaR, or the mean utility against this measure can be an attractive means to compare tail-risk management procedures.

9.1.2   Which measure?

The particular choices of return and risk measure will vary according to the investor, or user, of the statistics. Some possible considerations include the following:

- Regulators are likely to focus on tail risk; the risks may be measured via deterministic stress tests in addition to more probabilistic measures such as value at risk.
- An investor with a longer-term perspective may be happier to focus on the dispersion of returns around the general level, rather than on the tail. This may lead to worse short-term performance, for example, if market liquidity dries up, but the investor will expect to get paid sufficient premium for bearing this risk.
- Particular portfolio characteristics may be more intuitive in specific circumstances. For example, active duration or PV01 would often be a more natural risk metric in a fixed income setting than a statistical measure such as tracking error.
- A risk metric agreed between an investor and an investment manager will need to be verifiable. *Ex ante* risk, used in portfolio construction, and *ex post* risk, derived from actual returns achieved, may both need to be tracked to ensure that they are compatible. The latter may be especially hard for some measures of tail risk (we don't want to wait 200 years[1] to see if a tail event only happened one year in 200) or for strategies where the risk budget varies dynamically, so some visibility into the *ex ante* risk methodology – and perhaps the use of a third party model – may be required.
- The time frame of the risk exposure, or in other words, the time period over which the risk is measured, should be clear, particularly for instruments or strategies whose exposures are not constant over time. For example, the characteristics of an option in a portfolio held for a short period would often be materially different if the option were held until maturity, and risk is measured over this longer timeframe.

9.1.3 Related work

In an asset-liability management (ALM) context, the investor's goal will often be framed in terms of generating sufficient return in the asset portfolio to pay the liabilities, while ensuring a minimum income level can be paid. This minimum liability level may be a hard floor (ensure with certainty that the minimum is always achievable) or may be soft (keep the likelihood of falling through the floor less than 5%, say). Hard floors lead fairly rapidly to options (for example, puts) or option-replication strategies (for example, CPPI) – the discussion in this chapter of CVaR shows the impact of using a 'soft' floor. We refer to Jarvis et al. (2010) for a fuller discussion of the hard floor case, and for a discussion of similar problems in an ALM context, we also refer to Dempster et al. (2009).

9.2 Optimal dynamic strategies

To the practising finance community, Markowitz is well known, but Bellman is not. The technology of efficient frontiers is a standard piece of financial training, and the resulting jargon, of betas, alphas, Sharpe ratios and information ratios, is extremely well established. Markowitz's mean-variance approach retains the focus on a single period – any portfolio is assumed to be put in place at the start of this period and then allowed to run until the end.

In practice, even if they have a fixed planning horizon, investors operate over a number of sub-periods, with opportunities to rebalance or reconfigure the portfolio at the end of each sub-period. For example, a portfolio might be rebalanced at the end of each month in a year, at the end of each day, or at irregular points based on particular triggers being breached.

9.2.1 Impact of dynamic policies

An investor seeking to optimize a risk/return trade-off has a much richer opportunity set available if dynamic policies are feasible strategies. At the risk of stating the obvious, their inclusion has several impacts:

- Better results are achievable. Since static strategies form a subset of dynamic ones, the best risk-return trade-off from the set of dynamic strategies must be at least as good as that available from static ones. The main caveat here is that there may be more model risk. If there are arbitrages or near-arbitrages ('good deals') available in a poorly constructed model, then a dynamic strategy often stands a better chance of finding them. (This is, of course, a challenge to construct more robust risk models or to test strategies on multiple models; not to ignore dynamic possibilities.)
- The optimization problem is much harder, at least on the face of it. A dynamic strategy is specified not just by the initial asset allocation, but also by rules

on how this allocation (and perhaps other things, such as contribution and bonus policies) will vary as a function of future unknown performance. The dimension of the set of such strategies is thus much greater (often, infinite dimensional). Finding an optimum feels like an impossible dream.

- The risk and return metrics or constraints may need more attention. The distribution of outcomes arising from a dynamic strategy can be more complex than the distributions available from static strategies. Typically, outcome distributions with more skew and fatter tails may become achievable via dynamic strategies. A metric that adequately reflected an investor's goals for a set of static strategies may no longer be fit for the purpose. Constraints that may not have been needed in a static model may become more important to keep the solution reasonable.

9.2.2   Example

Consider one of the most widely used toy investment models: a market with two assets – cash and stock – whose return follows a random walk (that is, the stock price is geometric Brownian motion). Suppose that we want to maximize the return subject to a constraint on CVaR. A static investor has one decision to make: the proportion invested in the stock at the outset. As this proportion increases, the expected return increases, but the CVaR also increases; so the optimal policy is given by the proportion that exactly meets the CVaR constraint.

In a dynamic context, this model is known to be 'dynamically complete'. This means that any well-behaved function of the final stock price is achievable as the payoff from a suitable dynamic strategy. An initial budget constraint, that the initial portfolio has a certain value, acts as the main restriction (scaling) on the set of possible payoffs. For any threshold stock price, we can consider a digital option payoff[2] which is equal to (minus) the CVaR constraint below this threshold, and a higher value above the threshold. As long as the threshold is above the quantile in the CVaR definition, the CVaR constraint will be exactly met. For a fixed budget constraint, this higher value increases as the threshold increases; and (provided stocks have a positive expected return over cash) the expected value also increases. Indeed, it increases without bound – that is, for a given constraint, we can obtain an expected value that is as high as we like.

Thus, in this example of mean-CVaR optimization, the simple static problem becomes an unbounded dynamic optimization problem. Constraints or adjustments to the problem are required in order to achieve a sensible outcome.

9.3   Utility-CVaR problem

This section focuses on a particular dynamic optimization problem, that of maximizing a utility function given a CVaR risk constraint, in a simple model. This problem has already been well studied, notably by Gandy (2005). We therefore leave many of the mathematical details unwritten and focus on the payoff, and the investment strategy, that results. This section is arranged as follows:

- To set notation, we define the CVaR risk constraint and define the CRRA utility function we will use.
- We illustrate the optimal payoff profile.
- We illustrate the strategy, and describe how it evolves over time.
- Finally, we discuss the likely impact of constraints and describe some ways in which the constrained optimization can be achieved in practice.

9.3.1 Tail risk metrics

Value at risk measures the potential loss over a particular time frame. The loss is stated at a particular probability level, for example, the loss will be less than the particular level 99.5% of the time. Although authors generally agree upon the meaning in practice, there is considerable scope for confusion: Do you think of the probability level as 0.5% or 99.5%? And is the focus on the portfolio return or the portfolio loss? For clarity, the definition we use here is as follows. Suppose X is a random variable representing the portfolio value at the time horizon we are interested in, and ε (for example, $\varepsilon = 5\%$) is the tail probability we are interested in:

$$VaR_\varepsilon(X) = -\inf\{x : P(X \le x) > \varepsilon\}.$$

This definition is illustrated in Figure 9.1, based on a Student t distribution. In this continuous-density example, the vertical red dotted line represents the point at which the 5% probability level is breached. The value at risk is -4.2 in this example.

The picture also shows the CVaR, the conditional or tail value at risk. This represents the average loss in the blue area shown: first define the quantile function

$$q_X(p) = F_X^{-1}(p) = \inf\{x : F_x(x) \ge p\} \in \mathbb{R} \cup \{-\infty, \infty\}$$

and then

$$CVaR_\varepsilon(X) = \alpha^{-1} \mathbb{E}\left[\left(F_X^{-1}(\varepsilon) - X\right)^+\right] - F_X^{-1}(\varepsilon)$$

In the intuitive case, when there are no jumps in the cumulative distribution function, the quantile function is, up to a sign, the same as the value at risk, and the CVaR is the expected loss in the tail bounded by the VaR. Where the portfolio can take particular values with positive probability (for example, the case for typical option payoffs or when working with simulations) slightly more care is required.

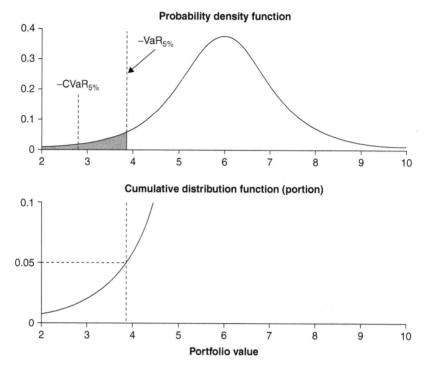

Figure 9.1   Relationship between value at risk (VaR) and conditional value at risk (CVaR or tVaR)

9.3.2 Utility objective

To keep things simple, we use a standard Constant Relative Risk Aversion (CRRA) utility function, that is, for some γ:

$$u(x) = \begin{cases} \dfrac{x^{1-\gamma}-1}{1-\gamma} & \gamma > 0, \gamma \neq 1 \\ \ln(x) & \gamma = 1 \end{cases}$$

9.3.3 Optimization problem and model

The objective is to find a strategy that maximizes utility, subject to the CVaR risk being below a limit:

$$\begin{cases} Max\ \mathbb{E}\big(U\big(X_T\big)\big) \\ CVaR_\varepsilon\big(X_T\big) \leq -c \end{cases} \tag{9.1}$$

We assume a geometric Brownian motion model for returns on assets, that is, the total return of the i'th asset evolves according to a stochastic differential equation of the form

$$S_i(t) = S_i(0)\exp\left(\left(\mu_i - \frac{1}{2}\Sigma_{ii}\right)t + A_i'W(t)\right).$$

Here $W(t)$ is a multivariate Brownian motion, A_i is a vector containing the (constant) exposures of asset i to each driver, and $\Sigma_{ij} = A_i'A_j$ is the covariance of assets i and j. To avoid arbitrage opportunities, the expected returns μ_i must be of the form

$$\mu_i = r + A_i'\lambda. \tag{9.2}$$

Here, $\lambda \geq 0$ is a vector, each of whose components is the market price of risk for the underlying drivers, and r is the (again, assumed constant) rate of interest on cash. The pricing kernel $m(t) = \exp(-rt - \lambda'\lambda t/2 - \lambda'W)$ is a key object of interest: the product of this kernel and any total return index will be a martingale (under the real-world measure). The existence of this pricing kernel, that is, the condition (Equation 9.2), is thus a familiar one on the existence of an equivalent martingale measure.

9.3.4 Optimal payoff

The model as described is dynamically complete, that is, any payoff at time T can be replicated using a suitable dynamic hedging strategy. This therefore allows us to use the martingale approach (rather than the more complicated Bellman approach) to solving the optimization problem (Equation 9.1). We can first derive the optimal payoff X_T and subsequently determine the investment strategy that supports it.

This is straightforward using standard variational calculus: the optimal payoff is of the form

$$X_T = \begin{cases} (\lambda_1 m_T)^{-1/\gamma} & \text{if } h < (\lambda_1 m_T)^{-1/\gamma} \\ h & \text{if } (\lambda_1 m_T)^{-1/\gamma} < h < (\lambda_1 m_T - \lambda_2)^{-1/\gamma} \\ (\lambda_1 m_T - \lambda_2)^{-1/\gamma} & \text{if } h > (\lambda_1 m_T - \lambda_2)^{-1/\gamma} \end{cases}$$

For clarity, in the absence of the risk constraint, the optimal payoff profile would simply be $X_T = (\xi m_T)^{-1/\gamma}$ for some constant ξ. These payoffs are all functions of the so-called 'growth-optimal' portfolio (GOP) $G_t = m_t^{-1}$ at time T. The typical structure of the payoff from the constrained problem (Equation 9.1)

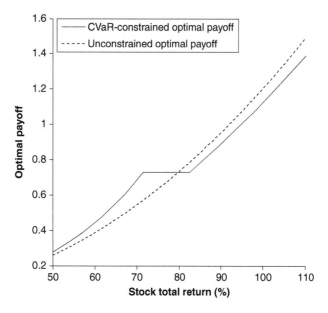

Figure 9.2 Impact of conditional value at risk constraint on optimal payoff at time horizon, one-asset case

is illustrated in Figure 9.2. (Special cases can arise from some constraints: if the constraint does not bite then $\lambda_2 = 0$ and the unconstrained-optimum applies; in other cases we can have $X_T \geq h$ everywhere or even $X_T \in \{0,h\}$ everywhere. The optimal X_T is always nondecreasing with the value of the GOP.)

The constants λ_1, λ_2, h must satisfy the budget constraint $\mathbb{E}(m_T X_T) = X_0$ and the shortfall constraint $\mathbb{E}\big((h - X_T)^+\big) = \varepsilon(h - c)$. The remaining degree of freedom can be found by maximizing the expected utility. Each of these constraints and operations are straightforward to carry out numerically.

9.3.5   Investment strategy example

The weights in each risky asset are always in the same relative proportions; for example, these can be identified with the weights in the growth-optimal portfolio, or equivalently the weights in the unconstrained optimal portfolio. The allocations thus vary over time along a single dimension, namely, the total exposure to risky assets can vary (with the balance made up with cash or bonds). The evolution of this exposure could equally be described as the variation of the risk budget, or return target of the portfolio over time. In Figures 9.3(a) and 9.3(b), we choose to show the total risky asset allocation as a percentage of the unconstrained asset allocation: where this percentage is above (below) one we are therefore taking more (less) risk than we would in the absence of a risk constraint.

There is, therefore, no additional complexity here with having more than one risky asset, so we keep things simple in the following example, which has one asset, with $\Sigma_{11} = (15\%)^2$, $\lambda = 1/3$, $r = 5\%$. The CVaR constraint we impose is $CVaR_{5\%} \leq -70\%$, that is, the average loss for the worst 5% of scenarios can be at most 30% over a one-year horizon. This is a fairly mild restriction, which allows Figures 9.3(a) and 9.3(b) to be easily readable. (The tail VaR for the unconstrained optimal portfolio is $CVaR_{5\%} = -57\%$.)

The evolution of the strategic allocation over time is illustrated in Figures 9.3(a) and 9.3(b).

Figure 9.3(a) shows how the risk level, as a proportion of that which would apply in the absence of a risk constraint, varies over time. Initially, when the portfolio value is 1, the optimal level of risk is below the unconstrained version. If the portfolio value stays around or above a threshold value, the risk remains below 1, but if the value falls too far below then it is optimal to take more risk. The highest possible level of risk is obtained if we are just below the threshold level very close to the time horizon.

Figure 9.3(b) illustrates this from a different perspective: the time zero and time 1 slice is given at the bottom, to make the structure of the surface in Figure 9.3(a) clearer; and on the right we also give the equivalent surface if

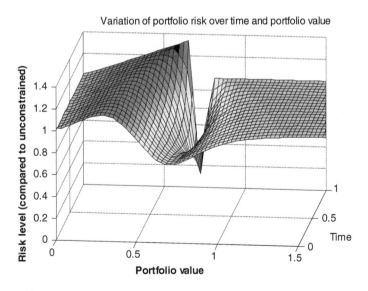

Figure 9.3(a) Optimal portfolio risk for Equation 9.1, as function of portfolio value

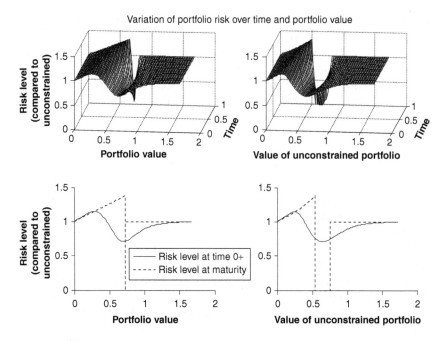

Figure 9.3(b)   Optimal portfolio risk for Equation 9.1, as function of unconstrained portfolio value

we plot against the unconstrained portfolio value rather than the constrained portfolio value. As the optimal constrained portfolio attains the threshold value with a strictly positive probability (see Figure 9.1), this gives a slightly smoother picture.

9.3.5.1   Comments

The evolution of the risk budget can be compared to the evolution that would have occurred if a put-option or CPPI strategy had been followed. Recall that these latter strategies enforce a 'hard floor' on the portfolio value, whereas here, the portfolio value can fall below any threshold, albeit with low probability. The evolution of the strategies if the portfolio value rises through time is similar: as the value increases, the risk budget is able to increase towards what it would have been in the absence of a risk constraint. If the portfolio value does not rise too much, or falls slightly, then again the strategies are similar: the risk budget falls. The main difference is in what happens if the portfolio value falls significantly (something which could not happen if a strategy was designed with a hard floor in mind). In this case, the risk budget can actually increase. This is due to the structure of the CVaR constraint – the scenarios where the portfolio falls materially in value lie within the '5% of outcomes' tail. CVaR continues to penalize risk-taking within this tail but there is also potential reward from the utility function. We note in passing that the increase in risk budget would have been greater for a VaR constraint.

The optimization process has, of course, traded off good outcomes in some scenarios with worse outcomes in others – but the structure of this trade-off results in paths that are quite different to those that an option replication strategy would produce. With a hard floor in place, the floor is 'ever present' along each path: if the portfolio value falls, the risk budget falls. In contrast, the dynamic strategy derived here leads to paths on which the floor becomes almost irrelevant: if the portfolio value falls too far, risk is ramped up. Risk is measured at time zero, using probabilities at time zero. It is not obviously consistent with a risk measurement that might be made halfway along a path, conditional on what has happened to date. We return to this issue of 'time consistency' and the related notion of a Bellman principle, at the end of this chapter.

9.4   Portfolio constraints

The previous section outlined the solution of the problem of optimizing utility subject to a risk constraint, with the specific example of a CVaR constraint. Although investors are often willing and able to use leverage or derivatives to gain the right risk exposures, this is not always the case, and they may be subject to *portfolio*-level constraints.

The classic example of this is a 'long only' investor, who is unable to create short, or leveraged, exposures to a basic set of asset classes. These constraints may well be binding even for our investor with no risk constraint in the previous section. There are at least three approaches to these kinds of problem:

1. Bellman equation. This approach is the most generic, and thus requires the most creativity, to solve. This typically works in special situations.
2. Duality approach. As described in Karatzas and Shreve (1998) and Rogers (2003), Lagrange multipliers (in fact, a Lagrange multiplier *process*) can be introduced to produce a modified optimization problem. A solution to the unconstrained modified problem is often a solution to the unmodified constrained problem, in the usual way, given appropriate Lagrange multipliers. Again, in some situations, the dual problem (effectively, finding the appropriate Lagrange multipliers) can be more readily solved and a solution then found for the original ('primal') problem.
3. Numerical approach. This is a brute force approach, using a discretization of the problem on a suitable tree. Care and attention is required to set up the algorithm to ensure that a solution can be found in reasonable time. Analytical work can sometimes be undertaken to simplify the problem

before resorting to the computer. For example, at each point the chosen portfolio will usually be mean-variance optimal and a parameterization of the mean-variance efficient frontier means that only a single parameter, rather than n portfolio holdings, need be found at each point of the tree. The parameter used can be thought of as a Lagrange multiplier, and thus this approach can be linked into the duality approach above.

Recently, there has been considerable interest in CVaR minimization as well as volatility minimization (see Roman et al., 2008). These authors have also investigated and report tail risk control through the use of second order stochastic dominance. Recent research results in this area (Fabian, et al., 2010) are also noteworthy.

9.5   Numerical approach

In order to determine an optimal dynamic strategy in the presence of constraints, an analytical approach has to be replaced with a numerical approach. We outline here a possible approach, following Jarvis et al. (2010).

The problems we are looking at are expressed in the continuous domain (continuous prices, continuous time), but a discrete form of the problem has to be created in order to analyse the problem numerically. A combined version of a tree approach and a lattice approach can be used.

9.5.1   Brief review of numerical techniques

9.5.1.1   Tree approaches

A classic approach that has been used in the option pricing literature (following Cox et al., 1979, for example) is to construct a tree. The tree encodes a simplified set of future paths for asset prices, starting with the current set of prices. A simple example of a recombining binomial tree is illustrated in Figure 9.4.

There is a single node at time 0, and the price of the (single) instrument being modelled can go either up or down. After one time step there are two possible future states. Over n time steps, there are 2^n possible paths for asset prices and either 2^n states at the end of these steps or, in a recombining tree (that is, a tree in which going up then down produces an identical situation as going down then up), $n + 1$ states.

Standard arbitrage arguments can be used to price any stochastic payoff payable at time $n\Delta t$ – the price is given by working backwards. That is, the price at the final set of nodes is known; the price one step back is given by constructing an appropriate hedge portfolio for the payoff at each node and then valuing this hedge portfolio. This gives the prices at each of the nodes at time $(n-1)\Delta t$. Iterating this procedure then produces a price at the initial node, time 0.

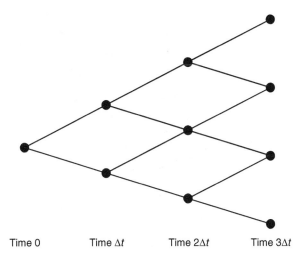

Time 0   Time Δ*t*   Time 2Δ*t*   Time 3Δ*t*

Figure 9.4   Binomial tree, with recombination

This approach works well if the final payoff is known and if the tree provides a good approximation to the set of future paths. For many standard models and options, this is indeed the case, and it can even be shown that the binomial tree approaches the continuous-time model as the step size tends to zero. (This is not surprising: it is well understood how the binomial distribution approaches the normal distribution in an example of the central limit theorem in action.) In a simple model, in which, for example, the mean and variance are constant over time, the calibration is straightforward: the size of the up and down moves can be set so that the distribution of outcomes at $n\Delta t$ matches the expected distribution.

In some circumstances, a trinomial tree approach may be preferred (for example, this helps the calibration when fitting 'implied volatility' surfaces) – in this case, there are three possible branches at each node. This is illustrated schematically in Figure 9.5.

In this case, with a recombining tree, after n steps there are $2n + 1$ nodes. The total number of nodes is 2^{n+1}.

9.5.1.2 Lattice approaches

To value an option, a more general alternative to building a tree involves using a lattice. Here, a subtly different perspective is taken. Given stochastic differential equations for a set of asset classes, a partial differential equation (PDE) can be written down which governs the evolution of the price of an option

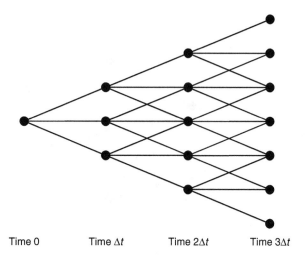

Time 0   Time Δ*t*   Time 2Δ*t*   Time 3Δ*t*

Figure 9.5   Trinomial tree, with recombination

over time. Now, rather than building a tree and arguing that the tree is a good approximation to the continuous limit, the goal is to find an approximation (in discrete time) to the solution to this PDE (in continuous time). The PDE has the generic form

$$\frac{\partial f}{\partial t} = a + b\frac{\partial f}{\partial x} + c\frac{\partial^2 f}{\partial x^2}$$

(Here a, b, c are usually functions rather than constant parameters.)

The numerical solution of PDEs, particularly PDEs of the form (parabolic) that arises in this context, is a subject that has garnered a lot of attention, for example in engineering contexts. The simplest approach, the finite difference (FD) approach, approximates the region over which the PDE is to be solved by a lattice (see Figure 9.6). The differentials that appear in the PDE are approximated by finite differences, for example:

$$\frac{\partial f}{\partial t}(x,t) \approx \frac{f(x,t+\Delta t)-f(x,t)}{\Delta t}$$

The differential equation then can be approximated by a set of difference equations, and these equations can be readily solved. A set of general results then provides confirmation that, under certain conditions, as the step sizes of the lattice $\Delta x, \Delta t \rightarrow 0$, the lattice values tend to the solution to the continuous PDE.

A number of choices can be made about the approximations used to define these derivatives. These are illustrated in Figures 9.6, through 9.8. If the derivatives in the x direction are estimated using values of the function at time t, then the explicit method results: the estimate of $f(x + \Delta x, t + \Delta t)$ depends on the three nearest values at time t. If the derivatives are estimated using time $t + 1$ values, then the implicit method results. Finally, using a weighted average of these leads to a 'theta' method (with theta being the relative weight).

The conditions for convergence in the limit as the step sizes go to zero for an implicit or theta method are less severe than in the explicit method, which runs the risk of magnifying any rounding errors that arise in the numerical approximation. The main example of a theta method is to set theta equal to

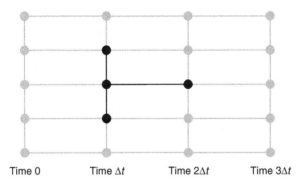

| Time 0 | Time Δt | Time $2\Delta t$ | Time $3\Delta t$ |

Figure 9.6   Finite difference lattice: explicit method

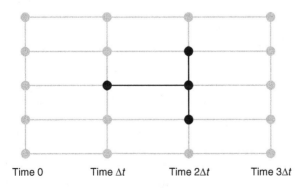

| Time 0 | Time Δt | Time $2\Delta t$ | Time $3\Delta t$ |

Figure 9.7   Finite difference lattice: implicit method

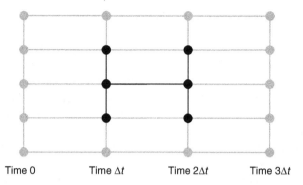

Time 0   Time Δ*t*   Time 2Δ*t*   Time 3Δ*t*

Figure 9.8   Finite difference lattice: theta method (for example, Crank-Nicolson)

one-half: this is usually the most accurate approximation that can be made (the order of the approximation is two rather than one). This method is due to Crank and Nicolson (1947).

These finite-difference approximation schemes can be applied to the (well-known) PDE arising in option pricing. The 'forward direction' in time for the PDE is actually backwards in time for the option. Just as in the tree approach, we start with a set of values at the terminal horizon and derive values for prior times by moving backwards one step at a time.

9.5.2   Suggested numerical approach

The problem we want to investigate is different to an option-pricing problem. With an option, the 'payoff' at the terminal horizon is known, and the tree or lattice approaches provide a means to divine a price and a hedging strategy that will produce this payoff. In contrast, we want to specify a function of the payoff (the mean minus a multiple of the CVaR) – and the goal is to find an asset strategy that maximizes this payoff.

We can make use of a PDE in a similar way to the option-pricing problem. Whereas the option price satisfied a PDE – essentially the backward Kolmogorov equation – it turns out that the probability distribution of outcomes (from which the mean and CVaR or any other statistic can be calculated) satisfies the forward Kolmogorov equation, also known as the Fokker-Planck equation. The coefficients in this equation depend on the asset strategy – solving this PDE approximately for a discrete version of the asset strategy thus provides an approximation to the function we want to optimise. A nonlinear optimization routine can then be applied to find the optimal (discrete) asset strategy, which should be close to the optimal (continuous) asset strategy.

9.5.2.1   The Fokker-Planck equation

A strategy for a dynamic optimization problem consists of a set of asset weights *w* at each time. In principle, the weights could depend upon the path taken up to that time. However, as the mean-CVaR objective function is defined in terms of statistics defined at the terminal time, the optimal weight at time *t* will depend only on this path via the portfolio value at time *t*. This assumes that the future opportunity set is homogeneous (otherwise, state variables that determine the regime at time *t* will need to be included alongside the portfolio value) and that transaction costs are negligible.

If the weights are functions of time *t* and portfolio value *Y* alone, then so are the drift and volatility of the strategy. Thus, the portfolio value satisfies a stochastic differential equation of the form

$$dY = Y\mu'\left(w(t,Y)\right)dt + Y\sigma\left(w(t,Y)\right)dW_t$$

The probability density function, $p_Y(y,t)$ (informally, $p_Y(y,t)dy = \mathbb{P}(Y(t) \in [y, y + dy])$) satisfies:

$$\frac{\partial p(y,t)}{\partial t} = -\frac{\partial}{\partial y}\left[x\mu'(y,t)p(y,t)\right] + \frac{1}{2}\frac{\partial^2}{\partial y^2}\left[x^2\sigma^2(y,t)p(y,t)\right].$$

This is the Fokker-Planck or forward-Kolmogorov equation.

In fact, it's simpler, and numerically more stable, to do a log-transformation and express the equation in terms of $p_X(x,t) = \exp(x)p_Y(\exp(x),t)$, the pdf of $X = \ln(Y)$. With a slight abuse of notation, Ito's formula leads us to set $\mu = \mu' - \sigma^2/2$, then giving:

$$dX = \mu\left(w(t,X)\right)dt + \sigma\left(w(t,X)\right)dW_t,$$

and so

$$\frac{\partial p_X(x,t)}{\partial t} = -\frac{\partial}{\partial x}\left[\mu(x,t)p_X(x,t)\right] + \frac{1}{2}\frac{\partial^2}{\partial x^2}\left[\sigma^2(x,t)p_X(x,t)\right]. \tag{9.3}$$

It is worth mentioning that, although we have stated the forward Kolmogorov equation for diffusions, that is, solutions of stochastic differential equations, a similar equation is valid in much more general contexts, the main requirement being the Markov property that the future depends on the past only via the current state. Thus, for example, a similar approach can be taken for regime models that depend on finite-state Markov chains, for jump process models and so forth.

9.5.2.2   Local efficient frontier

In principle, the weights at each time and portfolio value could take any value in a multidimensional space, where the number of dimensions equals the number of assets less 1 (the constraint that the asset proportions must total to 1). However, in the example here, where the underlying drivers are normal, the optimal weights will be locally efficient, that is, they will be on the mean-variance efficient frontier – if there is a portfolio with a higher mean and the same risk, this will be preferred.

It therefore makes sense to parameterize the efficient frontier, by a parameter α say, and seek to find the optimal $\alpha(x,t)$ rather than the weight-vector $w(x,t)$. In the time-homogeneous set-up, we can determine global functions $\mu(\alpha),\sigma(\alpha)$ for the corresponding (log) drift and volatility.

9.5.2.3   Combined lattice-and-tree approach

To make the numerical routine manageable, we would like to define the parameter function $\alpha(x,t)$ on a tree rather than a lattice. A straightforward mapping is required between the two – this is illustrated in Figure 9.9.

At each time, the x direction (the vertical direction here) can be broken into a series of intervals, with the interval boundaries set to the lattice points midway between each tree node. The number of intervals thus equals the number of nodes, and a function on the tree-nodes is mapped directly to a step function on the whole real line.

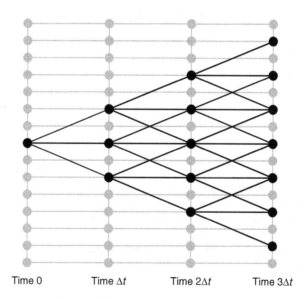

Time 0   Time Δt Time $2\Delta t$ Time $3\Delta t$

Figure 9.9   Combined lattice-and-tree mapping

More explicitly, but less clearly, suppose that there are M lattice points per node ($M-1$ lattice points between each node: $M=2$ in Figure 9.9) and $2N+1$ lattice points in total (N above and N below the initial node: $N=7$ in Figure 9.9). Then given a function $f(x)$ on the nodes $-t \leq x \leq t$ at time t, we can define a function $f(l)$ on the lattice points $-N \leq l \leq N$ via

$$
f(l) = \begin{cases}
f\left(\mathrm{int}\left(\dfrac{l}{2M}+\dfrac{1}{2}\right)\right) & \text{if } x-\dfrac{1}{2} < \dfrac{l}{2M} < x+\dfrac{1}{2} \\
& \text{\textit{for some integer }} x, -t < x < t \\[4pt]
\dfrac{1}{2}f\left(\dfrac{l}{2M}+\dfrac{1}{2}\right)+\dfrac{1}{2}f\left(\dfrac{l}{2M}-\dfrac{1}{2}\right) & \text{if } \dfrac{l}{2M} = x+\dfrac{1}{2} \\
& \text{\textit{for some integer }} x, -t < x < t \\[4pt]
f(t) & \text{if } t-\dfrac{1}{2} < \dfrac{l}{2M} \\[4pt]
f(-t) & \text{if } \dfrac{l}{2M} < -t+\dfrac{1}{2}
\end{cases}
$$

Here 'int' denotes 'nearest integer'. The idea is that node x gets mapped to the lattice points $(2M-1)x$ to $(2M+1)x$. It is worth pointing out that the number of lattice points, $2N+1$, should thus satisfy $N \geq 2MT$, where T is the number of time steps; in practice a larger N is often useful so that a boundary condition on $p(\pm N)$ can be imposed without hindering numerical stability.

9.5.2.4   Applying the Fokker-Planck equation

This therefore suggests the following algorithm, starting from a set of parameters α on the nodes of a tree:

1. Approximate $\alpha(t,x)$ by a step function, defined by values on the nodes of a tree.
2. This determines the corresponding drift and volatility functions, $\mu(t,x), \sigma(t,x)$.
3. Approximate the probability density function $p_X(x,t)$ the Fokker-Planck equation (9.3) using a numerical scheme such as Crank-Nicolson, starting from an initial delta function $p_X(x,0) = \delta_0(x)$ (corresponding to an initial portfolio value of 1).
4. Determine the mean and CVaR of the portfolio at time T using $p(x,T)$.

This therefore enables an objective function to be defined in terms of a set of tree-node parameters. An optimization routine (we have used Matlab here; similar results were obtained in Jarvis et al., 2010, using NAG) can then be applied to find the set of parameters that maximizes this objective function.

9.5.3   Numerical results

9.5.3.1   Simple example

This approach then leads to a strategy such as the one illustrated in Figure 9.10. The vertical axis, the risk budget (essentially, the parameter α) has been determined for each time and portfolio value.

Figure 9.10 results from numerically maximizing 'mean $-0.1 \times$ CVar' for a very simple model (a risk-free asset and a single risky asset with expected log-return 5% and volatility 15%). This can be compared to Figure 9.3(a): it can be seen that the granularity is much less. The time interval has been split into ten steps ($\Delta t = 0.1$) and the distance between lattice points is $\Delta x = 0.001$ with 20 lattice points between each tree node. At time $t = 0.9$ (the final decision point) there are 19 nodes, and so a minimum of around 400 lattice points is needed; however, extending much further than this (to 1200 lattice points) provides more numerical stability by allowing the probability density function to decay sufficiently before being cut off at zero.

The terminal probability density function is shown in Figure 9.11. Consistent with the analytical approach above, a large probability mass (though not a strict delta function, which we could not have in this discrete approximation) appears – the left-hand tail is strongly curtailed below this, with the right-hand tail much fatter above.

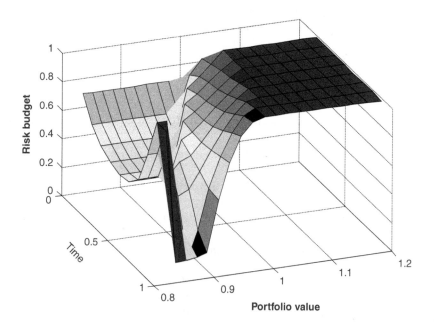

Figure 9.10   Optimal portfolio risk as function of portfolio value

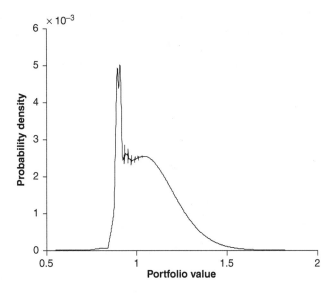

Figure 9.11 Terminal probability density of optimal strategy

9.5.3.2 Efficient frontier

Combining the results across many runs enables an efficient frontier to be shown in Figure 9.12. This can be compared with the risk and return characteristics that would be available if a static strategy is followed (that is, no rebalancing). In our simple example (single risky asset) the static efficient frontier is a straight line; in general the two lines will meet at the top and bottom (taking minimum and maximum risk throughout, respectively).

9.6 Time consistency

Although tail value at risk is an appealing risk measure in a single-period framework, it has theoretical shortcomings in the multi-period (that is, dynamic) context that we have been analysing here. This seems to have been first highlighted in Artzner (2002). Artzner et al. (2004) discuss the example illustrated in Figure 9.13.

9.6.1 Risk measures and capital requirements

A (coherent) measure $\rho(X)$ of the risk of a strategy's outcome X can be thought of as a capital requirement: the amount of capital required to make the portfolio 'acceptable'. Indeed, defining the set of outcomes X which would be acceptable (the set of X for which $\rho(X) \leq 0$) rather than the risk metric itself is a common approach to analysing risk measures in the substantial recent literature on risk measurement. To do this uses the apparently reasonable assumption that the capital required for a set of outcomes $X + m$, for any constant m, should be $\rho(X + m) = \rho(X) - m$; it is then easy to see that a risk measure can be defined

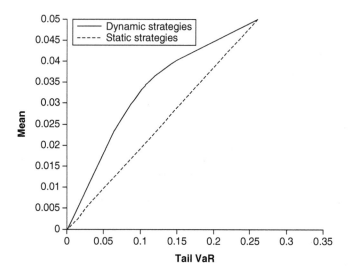

Figure 9.12 Efficient frontier

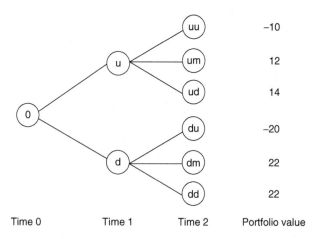

Figure 9.13 Multi-period tail VaR strategy problem from Artzner et al. (2004)

as the least capital that would need to be added to make the set of outcomes 'acceptable'.

In a multi-period setting, we need to make capital requirements not just at some initial time, but at subsequent times, too. These should be consistent in some sense. Some authors (for example, Kupper et al., 2009, and Boyle et al., 2005) frame this in terms of a recursion property, such as:

$$\rho_t(X) = \rho_t(-\rho_{t+1}(X)). \tag{9.4}$$

This says that the capital requirement at time t can be determined from the potential capital requirements at time $t+1$.

9.6.2 Tail value of risk is not dynamically consistent

To assess tail value at risk against this time-consistency requirement, consider the example illustrated in Figure 9.13 and tail VaR assessed at a 2/3 probability level. At time zero, the tail value of risk is +1 (minus the average of −10, 12, 14 and −20), while at time 1 it is −1 whichever outcome (u or d) occurs. In capital terms, this would mean that 1 unit of capital would be required at time 0 but 1 unit of capital could be released at time 1. This is clearly inconsistent with the recursion property (Equation 9.4) as well as with many weaker forms of time consistency.

9.6.3 Law invariance

A useful property of value at risk and tail value at risk are that they are 'law invariant' in the sense that the risk measure depends only on the set of possible outcomes and their probability distribution. It might be hoped that some suitably minor adjustment to one of these risk measures could be made to make them dynamically consistent. Kupper and Schachermayer (2009) show that, under apparently mild technical assumptions, this hope is misplaced – the only law-invariant dynamically consistent risk measures are of the form

$$\rho_t(X) = \frac{1}{\gamma} \log E_t\left(\exp(-\gamma X)\right). \tag{9.5}$$

These are the so-called 'entropic' risk measures. If the 'translation invariance' requirement $\rho(X+m) = \rho(X) - m$ is not required, then the slightly more general class

$$\rho_t(X) = u^{-1} E_t\left(u(X)\right) \tag{9.6}$$

of certainty-equivalent expected utility measures is obtained.

This leads to the more recent investigation as to whether weaker notions of time consistency could be used. Roorda and Schumacher (2005) propose two alternatives for dynamically-consistent versions of tail VaR.

9.6.4   Impact of time-inconsistency

In the specific optimization problems discussed above, the problem of dynamic inconsistency can be clearly seen: initially, a risk budget is set which offers a reasonable trade-off between risk and return. But this trade-off does not remain unchanged along each path – if things go 'well' then the risk budget can be increased, and the risk metric can become more and more irrelevant. In contrast, if things go sufficiently 'badly', then the ability to meet a risk constraint becomes more and more difficult – eventually, taking more risk becomes attractive, because de-risking offers no return *and* no help towards meeting the risk constraint. In both cases, the risk constraint is relative to the amount of risk that is deemed reasonable at the initial time – there is no opportunity or requirement to update this at subsequent times, in light of experience.

9.7   Final thoughts

This chapter has sought to illustrate the possibilities and challenges that arise in multi-period strategy optimization problems, by looking at an easily stated problem of trying to trade off return and risk, where risk is measured according to tail value at risk.

In rare circumstances, an analytical approach can be taken. While this is unlikely to be the case in practice, an analytical approach provides the security of knowing that an optimum has been obtained, and allows the optimal strategy to be studied from a number of angles. Here, for example, we have examined the evolution of the risk budget as a function of time, portfolio value and relative to a risk-neutral investor. For examples where an analytical approach is infeasible, we have also laid out a simple numerical approach which we have found to work in practice.

This chapter used independent identically-normally-distributed innovations throughout. Of course, asset returns are not so well behaved! They exhibit fat tails, and volatility tends to cluster over time. These are important aspects to consider in practice – although the main principles outlined here will remain valid, it is to be expected that optimal strategies should seek to manage such risks dynamically, and we leave the exploration of this to further research.

Finally, we have highlighted the need for risk measures to evolve sensibly over time. As Tail VaR fails this test, this feature of risk management which is clearly vital in practice is thus missing from the analysis. As this is a rapidly evolving area of current research, we hope that there will be more for future researchers to say on this very soon.

Notes

1. Even longer if we want to have some statistical significance!
2. There is nothing special about the payoff profile described here: we could have used a series of call options with increasing exercise prices. The optimization problem is unbounded and many sequences demonstrate this.

References

Artzner, P. (2002). Conditional value at risk: is it good in the multiperiod case? IIR Conference on Volatility and Risk, London, February.
Artzner, P., Delbaen, F., Eber, J.-M., Heath, D. and Ku, H. (2007). Coherent multiperiod risk adjusted values and Bellman's principle. *Annals of Operations Research* 152:5–22.
Artzner, P., Delbaen F., Eber, J.-M., Heath, D. (1999). Coherent risk measures. *Mathematical Finance* 9:203–228.
Boyle P., Hardy M. and Vorst T. (2005). Life after VaR. *Journal of Derivatives* 13:48–55.
Cheridito, P., Delbaen, F. and Kupper, M. (2006). Dynamic monetary risk measures for bounded discrete-time processes. *Electronic Journal of Probability* 11:57–106.
Cox, J. C., Ross, S. A. and Rubinstein, M. (1979). Option pricing: a simplified approach. *Journal of Financial Economics* 7:229–263.
Crank, J. and Nicolson, P. (1947). A practical method for numerical evaluation of solutions of partial differential equations of the heat conduction type. Proceedings of the Cambridge Philosophical Society 43:50–67.
Dempster, M. A. H., Pflug, G. and Mitra, G. (2009) *Quantitative Fund Management.* Chapman and Hall, London.
Fabian, C. I., Mitra, G., Roman, D., Zverovich, V. (2010) An Enhanced model of portfolio choice with SSD criteria: a constructive approach, to appear in *Quantitative Finance.*
Gabih, A. and Wunderlich, R. (2004). Optimal portfolios with bounded shortfall risks. In vom Scheidt, J. and Richter, M., editors, Tagungsband zum Workshop 'Stochastische Analysis', pages 21–42. TU Chemnitz, Fakultät für Mathematik.
Gandy, R. (2005). Portfolio Optimization with Risk Constraints. PhD Dissertation, Universität Ulm.
Jarvis, S., Lawrence, A. and Miao, S. (2010). Dynamic asset allocation techniques. *British Actuarial Journal,* forthcoming.
Karatzas, I. and Shreve, S. E. (1998). *Methods of Mathematical Finance,* Springer, New York.
Kupper, M. and Schachermeyer, W. (2009). Representation results for law-invariant time consistent functions. *Mathematics and Financial Economics* 2:189–210.
Rogers, L. C. G. (2003). Duality in constrained optimal investment and consumption problems: a synthesis. Paris-Princeton Lectures on Mathematical Finance 2002, (Springer Lecture Notes in Mathematics 1814), 95–131.
Roman, D., Darby-Dowman, K., Mitra, G. (2007), Mean-risk models using two risk measures: a multiobjective approach, *Quantitative Finance* 7(4):443–458.
Roorda, B. and Schumacher, J. M. (2007). Time consistency conditions for acceptability measures, with an application to tail value at risk. *Insurance: Mathematics and Economics* 40:209–230.
Roorda, B. and Schumacher, J. M. (2010). When can a risk measure be updated consistently? Preprint.
Seydel, R. (2009). *Tools for Computational Finance* (4th edition). Springer, Berlin.

10
Optimal Investment Strategies in Defined Contribution Pension Plans

David Blake, Andrew Cairns and Kevin Dowd

Many, if not most, individuals cannot be regarded as 'intelligent consumers' when it comes to understanding and assessing different investment strategies for their defined contribution pension plans. This gives very little incentive to plan providers to improve the design of their pension plans. As a consequence, pension plans and their investment strategies are still currently in a very primitive stage of development. In particular, there is very little integration between the accumulation and decumulation stages. It is possible to produce well-designed DC plans, but these need to be designed from back to front (that is, from desired outputs to required inputs) with the goal of delivering an adequate targeted pension with a high degree of probability. We use the analogy of designing a commercial aircraft to explain how this might be done. We also investigate the possible role of regulators in acting as surrogate 'intelligent consumers' on behalf of plan members.

10.1 Introduction

Currently, the design of defined contribution (DC) plans is inadequate for a number of reasons: (a) members are required to make very complex investment choices without having the skills to do so, and (b) during the accumulation stage, fund managers invest contributions taking into account the member's risk aversion, but without taking into account the decumulation stage and, in particular, the standard of living desired in the decumulation stage; in other words, fund managers have no target fund to accumulate.

Hence, there is a need to design plans recursively from back to front (this design strategy is known as dynamic programming).

In a sense, we can think of a well-designed DC plan as being like a defined benefit plan, offering a promised retirement pension, but without the guarantee implicit in the DB promise. In other words, a well-designed DC plan will try to target a particular pension by generating the lump sum needed on the retirement date to deliver that pension in the form of a life annuity, although it will not be able to guarantee delivery of that target pension. This is because guarantees over long investment horizons are very expensive to secure.

The academic literature tells us that when investment opportunities are time varying, fund managers should try to time the market. For example, when the equity premium is expected to rise, the fund manager should buy more equities, and when interest rates are expected to fall, the fund manager should buy more bonds. However, the empirical evidence shows that a market timing strategy cannot be implemented in practice with any degree of success. Hence, there is a need to tie the hands of fund managers. The way to do this is not through quantitative investment rules, but through setting target fund levels that managers need to meet. These should be designed using some form of lifestyling investment strategy during the accumulation stage, with a high initial weight in equities and with a switch to bonds as the retirement date approaches; in practice, the strategy is likely to be deterministic due to the information intensive nature of stochastic investment strategies, such as stochastic lifestyling. Lifestyling is justified by two properties of equity returns for which there appears to be strong empirical evidence, namely, mean reversion in equity returns and a positive equity premium. These two properties suggest that equities should play a large role in the portfolios of young pension plan members. Lifestyling is also justified by recognizing that human capital is an important bond-like asset of the plan member, which decays over the member's working life. As the time of annuitization approaches, bonds should play a greater role, in order to hedge the interest rate risk in the annuity purchase and to compensate for the decay of human capital. The purpose of lifestyling is to reduce the risk of falling short of the target and to reduce the variability of contributions into the plan during the accumulation stage. Given the nature of the target that the investment strategy is intended to achieve, members should be given only limited choice over which lifestyle fund to invest in. The annuitization and retirement ages do not need to be the same. This is especially so for richer individuals, who can afford to have some flexibility over both when they retire and when they begin to draw their pension.

The menu of retirement products can include flexible annuity vehicles that take into account the member's degree of risk aversion and the bequest motive of retirees. Individuals with a low degree of risk aversion might wish to consider an investment-linked retirement income programme, such as an investment-linked annuity. For poorer individuals, such choice flexibility is most likely not feasible. In fact, to avoid the potential moral hazard problem of individuals consuming their retirement pot too quickly and falling back on the state for support, there needs to be a minimal annuitization fund accumulated before any post-retirement investment flexibility should be permitted. Members with accumulated funds below the minimum annuitization fund level necessary to keep them off further state support should be required to purchase an index-linked life annuity with their accumulated fund.

We use the analogy of designing a commercial aircraft to illustrate the design issues, especially those related to risks. Flying, compared to other modes of transport, is the safest way to travel, and the reason it is so safe is that aircraft designers had to overcome people's fear of flying: it does not take long for an airline passenger to know whether they are using a safe means of travel or not. Aircraft designers also need to find out quickly when and how accidents happen. Why are pension plans not designed in the same way as commercial aircraft? At first sight, you might think that this is a strange question. It is, however, also a very instructive one. In fact, there are many similarities between pension plans and aircraft, and designers of pension plans have much to learn from aircraft designers. The purpose of this chapter is to spell out these lessons by using the framework of designing a commercial aircraft to illustrate how the investment strategy of a personal defined contribution (DC) pension plan should be designed if it is to achieve its objective of delivering an adequate and secure pension in retirement for the pension plan member. As in the design of a commercial aircraft, there are trade-offs to be made, but these trade-offs are much fewer and more clearly defined than you might have realized. More importantly, understanding the process of designing an aircraft will greatly improve our understanding of what an optimal DC pension plan might look like. It can also considerably simplify the work of pension regulators, whose task it is to oversee personal DC pension plans.

Pension planning execution can be compared to commercial airline design and operation.

10.2   How are DC pension plan investment strategies currently designed?

We can think of DC plans as having three stages – the initial marketing stage, the accumulation stage and the decumulation stage – and it is curious to note that there is currently very little connection between them. This is, in part, because the three stages are arranged by three different and disconnected groups of people: the sales agent of a pension plan provider, who competes against other providers; the fund manager appointed by the chosen provider; and the annuity seller, who often works for a life office that is not part of the same group as either the plan provider or the fund manager. The lack of connection between the three stages is also, in part, due to the fact that the customer, the potential pension plan member, generally has a very poor understanding of each stage and of the resources required and risks involved in delivering an adequate and reliable pension in retirement.

In terms of investment strategy, the one concern that the fund manager has about the customer or plan member is to invest the contributions in a portfolio of assets in accordance with the plan member's attitude to risk.

10.2.1 The plan member's attitude to risk

The member's attitude to risk is conventionally measured by the *coefficient of relative risk aversion* (γ). This is defined as the wealth elasticity of the marginal utility of wealth:

$$\gamma = -\frac{WU''(W)}{U'(W)} \tag{10.1}$$

where the member's pension wealth is denoted by W, the utility of (or welfare derived from) pension wealth is denoted by $U(W)$, the marginal utility of pension wealth (that is, the change in utility if pension wealth changes by \$1) is denoted by $U'(W)$, and the degree of curvature of the utility function of pension wealth (which measures the rate at which marginal utility changes if pension wealth changes by \$1) is denoted by $U''(W)$. For all investors, $U'(W) > 0$, utility is increasing in wealth: more wealth means higher utility. For risk averse investors, $U''(W) < 0$.

This means that investors who are risk averse will tend to have lower holdings of risky assets than risk-seeking investors. Risky assets, such as equities, have higher returns in boom conditions than conservative assets, such as bonds, but lower returns in slump conditions. Risk-averse investors are prepared to forego some of the upside potential of equities if the investment conditions turn out to be favourable, in order to avoid some of the downside losses on equities if investment conditions turn out to be unfavourable. It is conventional to classify as highly risk averse (or conservative), those investors with a γ value above unity, and to classify as moderately risk averse those investors with a γ value between zero and unity. Risk-neutral investors have a γ value of zero and risk-seeking investors have a negative γ value.

The plan member's attitude to risk will also have potential implications for the volatility of contributions into the pension plan. The lower the degree of risk aversion, the higher the optimal equity weighting in the pension fund, and hence the more potentially volatile the value of the pension fund over time. If the plan member has a target pension fund value (or a target annuity amount) for the retirement date, and the current value of the pension fund has fallen short of the level needed to reach that target, say as a result of poor equity returns, the only way to rectify this is to increase contributions into the plan, if the retirement date is not to be delayed. Some members might not welcome volatile contributions into the plan, since it implies a volatile pattern to consumption over time. Such individuals are said to have a low intertemporal elasticity of substitution (IES) in consumption[1] (Blake, 2006, p. 17) and will prefer a lower equity weighting in their pension fund and hence more stable contributions over time and, as a consequence, a more stable consumption pattern. The plan member's degree of risk aversion will indicate to the fund manager which way will be preferred by the member in question: one with a high equity weighting and lower average, but more volatile contributions, or one with a low equity weighting and higher average, but more stable contributions.

10.2.2   Single-period investment strategy

The simplest asset allocation model in the academic literature is the myopic or single-period portfolio choice model. This assumes that the pension plan member has a power utility function of wealth and that asset returns are lognormally distributed. The simplest power utility function has the property that the coefficient of relative risk aversion (γ) is constant both over time and for different wealth levels. We will allow for the fact that the individual has precautionary savings (which we assume are held in a risk-free asset, such as Treasury bills or a deposit account), but will assume that all long-term savings are held in the pension plan. To keep things simple, we will also assume, to begin with, that there are only two possible assets for the pension plan: a risk-free asset (which in line with standard financial market parlance we will refer to as 'cash') and a risky asset, equities.

The fund manager's objective is to choose the asset allocation that maximizes expected utility subject to the budget constraint. This is equivalent to maximizing:

$$ln\, E_t \frac{W_{t+1}^{1-\gamma}}{(1-\gamma)} = -ln(1-\gamma) + (1-\gamma)E_t w_{t+1} + \frac{1}{2}(1-\gamma)^2 \sigma_{wt}^2 \qquad (10.2)$$

where w_{t+1} is the log of pension wealth and σ_{wt}^2 is the conditional variance of the log of pension wealth, subject to the natural log of the budget constraint where $r_{p,t+1}$ is the log return on the portfolio in which pension wealth is held:

$$w_{t+1} = r_{p,t+1} + w_t \qquad (10.3)$$

If we now substitute (10.3) into (10.2) and recognize that w_t is predetermined at time t and so will not affect the optimal asset allocation and, further, that the optimal asset allocation does not depend on the size of the constant term in (10.2) or the common factor $(1-\gamma)$ in the other two right-hand side terms, then the fund manager's objective becomes:

$$max\left\{ ln E_t(1+R_{p,t+1}) - \frac{\gamma}{2}\sigma_{pt}^2 \right\} \qquad (10.4)$$

Equation (10.4) tells us that the fund manager chooses the investment strategy to maximize the risk-adjusted expected return on the accumulating pension fund. This risk-adjusted expected return is equal to the natural log of the arithmetic mean portfolio return $(lnE_t(1 + R_{p,t+1}))$ minus 50% of a *risk penalty*, where the risk penalty equals the product of the fund risk (as measured by the conditional variance of the return on the fund's assets (σ_{pt}^2)) and the coefficient of relative risk aversion of the plan member (γ).

10.2.3 Multi-period investment strategy

A pension fund is in existence for many periods. We therefore need to extend our analysis to a multi-period setting.

Suppose, then, the plan member intends to retire in K periods' time. The utility function over terminal wealth is $U(W_{t+k})$ and the budget constraint becomes:

$$W_{t+k} = (1 + R_{pK,t+K})W_t$$
$$= (1 + R_{p,t+1})(1 + R_{p,t+2})...(1 + R_{p,t+K})W_t \tag{10.5}$$

This implies that the cumulative log return over K periods is the sum of the K one-period log returns:

$$r_{pK,t+K} = r_{p,t+1} + r_{p,t+2} + ... + r_{p,t+K} \tag{10.6}$$

One special case of this problem that has received much attention is due to Samuelson (1969) and Merton (1969, 1971). They show that if two conditions hold, then it is optimal for a long-term investor, such as a pension plan member, to behave myopically in the sense of choosing the same portfolio as a short-term (that is, one-period) investor. The first condition is that the plan member has power utility. This implies that the asset allocation does not depend on current wealth, and hence, previous returns. The second condition is that asset returns are independent and identically distributed (i.i.d.). This implies that the mean log return on the risky asset (Er) is constant, so that the mean log K-period return on the risky asset is therefore KEr, the returns on the risky asset are serially independent ($E(r_{t+i} - Er)(r_{t+j} - Er) = 0, i \neq j$), the variance of the log return on the risky asset is constant (σ^2), and the variance of the log K-period return on the risky asset is

$$Var_t\, r_{K,t+K} = Var_t r_{t+1} + Var_t r_{t+2} + ... + Var_t r_{t+K} = K\sigma^2 \tag{10.7}$$

When asset returns are i.i.d., any news (that is, the unpredictable element) in asset returns ($r_{t+i} - Er$) is uncorrelated with any news from asset returns in previous periods (($r_{t+j} - Er$), $j < i$), so will not alter the optimal asset allocation.

Of course, in the real world, there are number of reasons why the myopic or constant-composition portfolio choice model might not be valid for long-term investors. The two main ones are the existence of time-varying investment opportunities and mean reversion in asset returns. In the real world, the risk-free rate, the excess returns on risky assets, the variances of the returns on risky assets, and the covariances between the excess returns on risky assets are time varying or stochastic. A stochastic investment opportunity set then creates *intertemporal hedging demands* for those assets that are capable of hedging against adverse movements in the investment portfolio (Merton, 1973).

The presence of time-varying interest rates will create a demand for a third class of asset, apart from cash and equities, namely bonds. For example, when interest rates are expected to fall, this will reduce the income generated by the portfolio. Since the prices of long-term bonds rise when interest rates fall, long-term bonds provide a better intertemporal hedge than Treasury bills, whose prices change very little when interest rates change. Only when interest rates are fixed over time is it the case that bonds are a redundant asset class: in this limited case, but only in this limited case, the optimal portfolio can be constructed exclusively using cash and equities.

10.2.4   Mean reversion in asset returns

There is also substantial evidence that asset returns (both the real risk-free component of the return and the risk premium) are mean-reverting. If equity returns are mean-reverting, then an unexpectedly high return today will be offset by lower expected returns in the future. There is therefore a benefit to investing in equities over long periods in terms of reduced total variance, a benefit known as *time diversification* (or the horizon effect). Time diversification is the equivalent of risk sharing with the future, since it implies that $Var_t\, r_{K,t+K} < K\sigma^2$, that is, that risk compounds less than linearly with time. This implies that long-horizon investors, such as pension funds, should have a 'positive hedging demand for risk (that is, equities) at the initial stage of the game' (Gollier, 2004, p. 2).

There is considerable evidence that equity returns are mean-reverting; see, for example, Poterba and Summers (1988), Fama and French (1988), Blake (1996) and Balvers et al. (2000). Figure 10.1 shows the variability of multi-period asset returns in the United States, and it is clear that over long investment horizons, equities are not much riskier than long-maturity bonds that are held to maturity (a view held by others, such as Siegel, 1997).

10.2.5   Multi-period investment strategy with
time-varying investment opportunities and mean reversion

Campbell and Viceira (1999) develop a model in which the return on the risk-free asset (r_f) is constant and the expected excess log return on equities is driven

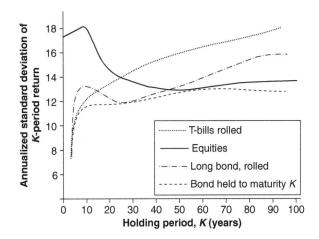

Figure 10.1   Variability of multi-period asset returns in the United States, 1890–1998
Source: Campbell and Viceira (2002, Fig. 4.2a)

by a mean-reverting state variable, x_t. Campbell and Viceira show that the optimal weight in equities is a linear function of the state variable $(a_0 + a_1 x_t)$.

Conservative long-term investors will hold equities in a multi-period setting, even when the expected excess return is zero. A conservative investor will want to hedge the risk of deteriorating investment opportunities by holding assets, such as equities, that deliver excess returns when investment opportunities deteriorate. Conservative investors will therefore have a positive intertemporal hedging demand for equities, even when their current forecast of the risk premium, and hence their myopic demand for equities, is zero. For conservative investors, the intertemporal hedging demand moves in the same direction as the state variable, x_t. This means that the optimal strategic asset allocation is no longer fixed, as it is for myopic investors. Rather, it is optimal for long-term investors to become strategic market timers and respond to forecast changes in investment opportunities.

This is shown in Figure 10.2. The horizontal line is the myopic buy-and-hold strategy in which the asset allocation is constant over time at a level consistent with a constant excess stock return set equal to the unconditional mean, μ. The tactical asset allocation line shows the optimal investment strategy for a myopic single-period investor who has no intertemporal hedging demand. For such an investor, $a_0 = 0$ and $a_1 = 1/\gamma\sigma_u^2$, where σ_u^2 is the variance in the innovation in equity returns. The tactical asset allocation line passes through both the origin (confirming that a single-period investor should not hold equities if the expected excess return is zero) and the myopic buy-and-hold line where the expected excess return equals the unconditional mean. The strategic

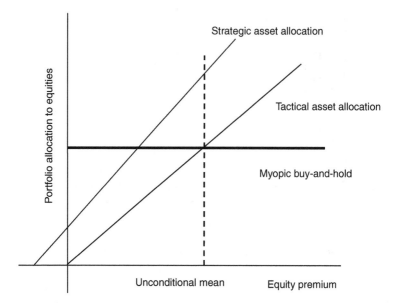

Figure 10.2   Alternative portfolio rules
Source: Campbell and Viceira (2002, Fig. 4.1)

asset allocation line shows the optimal investment strategy for a long-term investor. It is higher and steeper than the tactical asset allocation line because of the presence of an intertemporal hedging demand which leads to a positive intercept and a steeper slope than the case in which there is no intertemporal hedging demand.

There are two important lessons here: (a) equities appear to exhibit a positive long-run risk premium (although there is an ongoing debate as to its size and whether it is likely to be smaller in the future than the past), and (b) equity returns appear to be mean-reverting. These, in turn, have two important implications for the strategic asset allocation of long-term investors: the first is that equities have a definite place in the portfolios of such investors; the second is that equities should not be held passively, but should be actively managed (that is, investors should engage in market timing) in line with forecast changes in the mean-reverting state variables that drive excess returns. The most important state variables have been shown to be the short-term nominal interest rate (that is, the yield on Treasury bills which will include an inflation premium), the dividend-price ratio, the price-earnings ratio, and the term spread between the yields on long-term bonds and Treasury bills (Campbell and Viceira 2002). Given that these state variables are partly predictable, this implies that the excess returns on equities, and hence the returns on equities themselves, are (partly) predictable, and this generates market-timing opportunities.

Campbell and Viceira (1999) and Barberis (2000) estimate the orders of magnitude of the hedging demand when equity returns are predictable. For an investor with $\gamma = 10$ and a ten-year investment horizon, the optimal weighting in equities is 40% without predictability and 100% when there is mean reversion.

Equity returns are also predictable when the volatility of those returns is time-varying. A number of studies have shown that an increase in volatility is associated with large negative equity returns over long periods (for example, French et al., 1987, and Ghysels et al., 1996). Chacko and Viceira (2005) show that when $\gamma > 1$, there is a negative hedging demand when changes in volatility are negatively correlated with excess returns on equities. However, the hedging demand is only significant when the shocks to volatility are sufficiently persistent.

The investment strategies discussed above are certainly more sophisticated than the kind of headline investment advice bandied about in the professional pensions trade press. Professional fund managers have, by and large, tended to be ineffective in implementing the market timing strategies outlined above. Although there do exist a very small number of star fund managers who are skilled at picking winning equities (Kosowski et al., 2006), the evidence shows that the vast majority of professional fund managers produce negative returns from active fund management and, in particular, negative returns from market timing.

To illustrate, Blake et al. (1999, 2002) showed how well UK pension fund managers performed in comparison with other participants in the market over the period 1986 to 1994. The markets were UK equities, international equities, UK bonds, international bonds, UK index bonds, cash/other investments and UK property. The fund managers considered were managing defined benefit plans, rather than defined contribution plans. However, during the period under investigation, they were managing the assets of immature plans, and hence were largely unconstrained by plan liabilities. As a consequence, they were running portfolios with high equity weightings, similar in structure to the managed funds used by defined contribution pension plans. Furthermore, the UK pension fund industry was highly concentrated at the time, with the same fund management houses managing the assets of both defined benefit and defined contribution plans. The authors showed that the average UK pension fund underperformed the benchmark (that is, the market average represented by the market index) by 0.45% per annum; and this was *before* the fund manager's fee was taken into account. Furthermore, only 42.8% of funds outperformed the market average, even without taking account management fees. This underperformance in portfolio returns arises largely from underperformance in UK equities.

Blake et al. (1999, 2002) decomposed the total return generated by fund managers as follows (using the modelling framework of Brinson et al., 1986, 1991). Active fund managers attempt to beat the market in comparison with a myopic or passive buy-and-hold strategy (see Figure 10.2). They claim that they can 'add value' through the active management of their fund's assets. Blake et al. (1999, 2002) found that 99.47% of the total return generated by UK fund managers could be explained by the return on a passive portfolio invested in the market indices with the same average portfolio weights as in the studies (approximately 50% in UK equities, 20% in international equities, 10% in UK property and the rest in bonds and cash/other investments). The active components are stock picking and market timing. The average pension fund was unsuccessful at market timing, generating a negative contribution to the total return of −1.64%. The average pension fund was, however, more successful at security selection, making a positive contribution to the total return of 2.68%. But the overall contribution of active fund management was just over 1% of the average total return (or about 12 basis points), which is *less than the annual fee that active fund managers charge* (which range between 20 basis points for a £500m fund to 75 basis points for a £10m fund).

Active investment performance is even worse in international markets than in domestic markets, according to studies of UK pension funds' active management in international equity markets (Timmermann and Blake, 2005, Blake and Timmermann, 2005). Again, using the Brinson et al., (1986, 1991) decompositions of the investment performance of a large sample of UK pension funds between 1991 and 1997, these studies show that not only do the funds underperform substantially relative to regional benchmarks – that is, the FT/S&P indices for the four regions considered, namely Japan, North America, Europe (excluding the United Kingdom) and Asia-Pacific (excluding Japan) – but this underperformance is much larger than has been found in studies of performance in the domestic market. As with their UK investments, the results suggest that the pension funds earned negative returns from active management in their overseas portfolios (that is, from international market timing and from selecting stocks within individual foreign regions).

Even those pension fund managers who do generate superior performance in certain periods find it very hard to maintain that performance over time, with the exception, as mentioned above, of a very small number of stars. Evidence from a large number of UK defined benefit pension fund managers examined over five-year periods shows that only 4% of funds achieved above-average performance in each of the five years, while another 4% of funds underperformed in each of the five years. About half the funds had superior performance in three or more years and about half had below-average performance in three or more years. This distribution is almost exactly what would be expected if above- (or below-) average performance arose entirely by chance in each year. This pattern is found consistently across a number of five-year periods and is not affected by whether the investments considered are UK equities or more broadly based portfolios.

Other studies have found some limited evidence that consistency of performance was possible, particularly in the top and bottom performance quartiles, but only over very short horizons. For example, Blake et al. (1999) found that, in the case of UK defined benefit pension fund managers, UK equity managers in the top quartile of performance in one year had a 37% chance of being in the top quartile the following year, rather than the 25% that would have been expected if relative performance arose purely by chance. Similarly, there was a 32% chance of the UK equity managers in the bottom quartile for one year being in the bottom quartile the following year. There was also evidence of some consistency in performance in the top and bottom quartiles for cash/other investments, but there was no evidence of consistency in performance for any other asset category or for the portfolio as a whole. Nor was there evidence of any consistency in performance over longer horizons than one year in any asset category or for the whole portfolio. This evidence is consistent with the suggestion that so-called 'hot hands' in investment performance is a short-term phenomenon which does not persist for the extended periods.

What should the designer of the investment strategy of a DC pension plan make of this? On the one hand, in a multi-period setting, he is told that it is optimal to engage in strategic market timing. But, on the other, there is little evidence that professional pension fund managers have been successful at timing markets, either domestically or internationally. So we are left with a conundrum. We need to return to our airline analogy for guidance.

10.3 How similar are pension plans and commercial airline journeys?

When you think about it, there is much in common between a pension plan and a commercial airline journey. The strategic investment strategy of a pension plan is analogous to the aircraft. The aircraft operator is analogous to the pension plan provider. The contributions into a pension plan are analogous to the aircraft's fuel. The climb stage of an aircraft's journey is analogous to the accumulation stage of a pension plan, and the aircraft's descent stage is analogous to the pension plan's decumulation stage. The actions of the pilot in managing the progress of the flight (for example, in dealing with turbulence and cross winds) are analogous to the market timing or tactical asset allocation decisions of the fund manager. Air traffic controllers play the same role as pension regulators.

This comparison indicates some clear similarities between airline journeys and pension plans: (a) both seek to get you to a destination: in one case, a safe landing, in the other case, a comfortable retirement until death; (b) both involve the commitment of significant resources; (c) both involve managing risks; and (d) both involve a climb and a descent stage.

However, there are also some very significant differences, and these differences are also highly instructive. To start with, there is no uncertainty about the destination of an airline journey and the passenger does not – and indeed cannot – change his or her mind once the journey has started. By contrast, with a pension plan, both the destination of the journey (how much pension is desired in retirement) and the anticipated length of the journey (the member's retirement lifespan) are generally much less clearly formulated when the pension plan journey begins. This gives a greater opportunity for the member to change his or her mind regarding decisions such as the retirement date or whether a lump sum or annuity is required at retirement. The retirement and annuity decisions can also take place at different times. The need to accommodate this additional choice flexibility makes the design of the investment strategy much more complicated than the design of an aircraft.

The time horizon with an airline journey is also much shorter, typically a few hours, compared with the 70-year or so journey of a pension plan. Aircraft designers *must* get the design right *before* the aircraft ever takes off, otherwise they will lose their reputation, job or worse. By contrast, the designers of pension plans will have long departed the scene by the time the member discovers whether his plan was well designed.

Another important difference is that airline passengers know that they need to get to the airport by a certain time if they want to catch their plane and reach their destination in time. On the other hand, the much longer journey of a pension plan offers plenty of opportunities to delay the journey's start, and consequently to end up with a lower pension by the time the retirement date arrives. There are behavioural explanations for delaying pension saving (which we consider in Section 10.5), but there might also be rational reasons. For example, young people might have debts to pay off, mortgages to pay or children to bring up. They might also rationally anticipate higher income in middle age, which would enable saving for retirement to begin much later in the life cycle, or they might be willing to work longer before retiring if they discover that they would otherwise live in poverty. The pension plan is just one part of an individual's life cycle financial plan, and there are other factors to take into account, such as the desire to make a bequest to one's children (which influences the demand for life annuities in retirement) and the existence of social security (which influences the demand to save privately for retirement). In comparison, an airline journey is a one-off event that rarely impinges on other aspects of an individual's life.

Yet another difference lies in the fact that the laws of aerodynamics are known and unchanging, whereas the processes generating asset returns are still poorly understood. No one would expect an individual contemplating an airline journey to have a deep understanding of the laws of aerodynamics, yet individuals considering joining a defined contribution pension plan are expected to make very complex investment choices that implicitly presuppose a knowledge of asset return processes that even experts do not have.

There is also virtually no danger of an aircraft having insufficient fuel to reach its destination. Although there is a clear trade-off in the design of a commercial aircraft between fuel efficiency and gross takeoff weight (GTOW), there are very, very few cases of aircraft crashes caused by running out of fuel. And, of course, it is very obvious with a commercial airline flight that no improvement in fuel efficiency can compensate for insufficient fuel to reach the destination. Indeed, with an aircraft it is unthinkable to consider possible improvements in fuel efficiency in order to compensate for fundamentally inadequate fuel provision. For its part, a pension plan does involve an important trade-off between investment strategy and contributions: a low-risk investment strategy with high but stable contributions, on the one hand, or a higher-risk investment strategy with lower but more volatile contributions, on the other. Nevertheless, as with airline fuel, we would argue that no increase in investment risk can compensate for fundamentally inadequate contributions, if a particular target replacement ratio in retirement is desired. This, to us, is one of the key problems in the design of current pension plans: the misguided attempt to use investment strategy to compensate for fundamentally inadequate contributions.

Another subtle but important difference relates to economies of scale. Such economies are an integral feature of the design of a commercial aircraft: they are essential to keep prices down and demand high. While the super rich can afford their own jumbo jets, there is no feasible mass market for single individual commercial airline flights. With pensions, on the other hand, there is a large market for personal DC plans, but these plans are very expensive in terms of charge extraction via reduction in yield, especially if the plans are voluntary and have to be marketed directly to individuals, separately. Two ways around this are auto-enrolment in worked-based DC plans (discussed in more detail in Section 10.5) or mandatory participation in a government-sponsored plan, such as the Swedish Premium Pension System.

A final difference relates to the relationship between the climb and descent stages of an aircraft journey, on the one hand, and the accumulation and descent stages of a DC pension plan, on the other. Whereas the climb and descent stages of an aircraft journey make up a seamless whole, there is an almost complete lack of integration of the accumulation and decumulation stages in the current design of DC pension plans. We put this down to the absence of an effective target replacement ratio in a DC plan. Fund managers take whatever contributions they receive and invest them in line with the declared level of risk aversion they are told that the plan member has. They have no incentive to deliver any specific fund level, since they have been set no target to do so. At the start of the decumulation stage, the assets are typically handed over to life assurers and, depending on the size of this lump sum, the age and sex of the member and whether a spouse's pension is also required, the life assurers provide a life annuity to the member. Again, the life assurers have no incentive to deliver any specific replacement ratio in retirement, since again, they have been set no target to do so. All this contrasts markedly with an aircraft, for which the climb and descent stages are an integral part of the overall design because the aircraft is designed for the ultimate purpose of reaching a destination safely. Imagine being told by the captain of the 'climb plane' that it is time for you to transfer to the 'descent plane' as the 'climb plane' is running out of fuel and has to turn back, but that the 'descent plane' is 1000 metres above you!

Although there are clear differences between commercial airline journeys and pension plans, none of them seriously undermines the usefulness of the analogy, and even the differences are instructive for good pension plan design. A well-designed pension plan is, like a successful airline journey, one that is designed from back to front, with the destination – an adequate pension in retirement until death – being at the forefront of the design. Current pension plans are far from this ideal and are not currently designed at all well: they are currently 'designed' from front to back, beginning with the question 'how much would you like to contribute to your pension plan?' before going on to frighten off potential members with the next question 'what is your attitude to risk?' No wonder pension savings are so low!

10.4   How can we apply these lessons to the design of DC pension plans?

Of the two stages of a DC pension plan, it is the decumulation, or descent stage, of the pension plan journey that is – or should be – of most interest to pension plan members. It is on the descent journey that plan members discover whether they have been members of good pension plans. The test will be whether they enjoy a satisfactory standard of living in retirement.

If a pension plan is designed from back to front, then the following key factors need to be taken into account: the consumption profile desired by the plan member from his or her pension plan; the target date for drawing a pension from the plan (this might be, but need not be, the same date as the member's retirement date); the value of the fund needed to deliver the desired consumption profile at the target date; the vehicle for delivering the pensions (this can either be a life annuity or an income drawdown (or systematic withdrawal) facility from the fund which remains invested in the stock market); the contribution amount and investment strategy needed during the accumulation stage to build up the required lump sum, taking into account the plan member's attitude to risk; and the value of the plan member's human capital, which is defined as the discounted present value of lifetime labour income. An estimate of human capital is needed to determine both the required value of the fund at the retirement date and the required contribution amount during the accumulation stage.

The first question we need to ask, therefore, is what consumption profile do pension plan members desire in retirement? The expected present value of this consumption profile gives the value of the fund that needs to be accumulated by the retirement date. Then working backwards, we need to find the combination of plan contributions and investment strategy that are most likely to deliver that pension, taking into account the plan member's attitude to risk.

10.4.1 What type of consumption profile do members want from their pension plan?

The life cycle model (LCM) of Ando and Modigliani (1963) predicts that individuals prefer a smooth consumption profile over time and will plan to run down their assets to zero over the course of their life cycle. For example, if an individual retires at 65 and the pension wealth is converted into an index-linked lifetime annuity, then this provides for a retirement income that is initially lower than pre-retirement income, but gradually rises over time. Consumption during the period just after retirement is sustained by drawing down financial assets. The result is that consumption over the lifecycle is smoother than income over the lifecycle.[2]

But do individuals prefer a fairly steady profile over time, an upward sloping profile or a downward sloping profile? Frank and Hutchens (1993) and Matsumoto et al. (2000) offer evidence indicating that, during the working life, individuals tend to prefer a rising profile of consumption relative to wages. But what preferences do people expect to have when they are retired?

The answer varies with the individual. Some possible insights into this issue are suggested by Keasey et al. (2006), who present the results of a survey that specifically asks this question. Respondents came from all age and wealth levels and were shown three charts with (a) pension slowly rising in real terms, (b) pension remaining the same in real terms and (c) pension slowly falling in real terms. They were told that the income profile in each graph is inflation-adjusted and has the same discounted present value, and so would cost the same to purchase. They were asked to rate how attractive each option was to them: (a) was preferred to (b) which was preferred to (c). The main explanation given by those preferring a rising profile is the need for higher expenses when older, while the main explanation for preferring a falling profile is the desire to enjoy spending more money when younger. Those preferring a steady profile felt that it was easier to budget and plan with this profile.

10.4.2   The accumulation stage

Then there is the question of how contributions during the accumulation stage should be invested. The answer depends, in part, on issues such as the plan member's degree of risk aversion, as suggested earlier, but also on the riskiness of his or her labour income, and hence human capital; and it depends, too, on whether there are other *background risks* to take into account.

10.4.2.1   *Labour income*

A key factor ignored by the investment strategies discussed earlier is that the contributions into the plan must be paid out of labour income. This, in turn, raises the issue of the plan member's career salary profile. The shape of the career salary profile can have a dramatic effect on the size of the pension, as Blake et al. (2007) have documented. This study suggests that the career salary profile is driven by two key parameters, namely relative career average salary (RCAS) and peak salary age (PSA). The study shows that DC pension plans benefit most those workers who have the highest career average salary relative to final salary or those whose salary peaks earliest in their careers.

Thus low-skilled workers and women do *relatively* well from DC plans (that is, relative to final salary). Blake et al. (2007) show that, in the case of an equities-only investment strategy, the largest median pension-to-final-salary difference between occupations in the UK is 34% for men and 38% for women, for the same contribution rate as a proportion of salary. Male personal service workers have a 34% higher pension (relative to final salary) than male professionals, whose incomes peak much later in their careers. The largest median pension-to-final-salary difference between women and men in the same occupation (managerial workers) is 45%. The implication is that there are major differences across both occupation and gender, and this suggests that key aspects of a DC pension plan design (in particular contribution rates) should be occupation and gender specific.

10.4.2.2   *The optimal investment strategy with riskless labour income*

Now consider how the optimal asset allocation in the accumulation stage is determined when labour income is assumed to be riskless. In this case, human capital (H_t) is measured as the present value of future labour income discounted at the riskless rate.

Following Campbell and Viceira (2002, chapter 6), the plan member then treats human capital as one of his or her riskless assets. Total long-term assets are now the sum of financial assets (which are assumed to be held in the pension plan) and human capital ($W_t + H_t$). The optimal asset allocation in the presence of human capital is found by investing (in the case of unchanging investment opportunities) $\alpha(W_t + H_t)$ dollars in equities and $(1 - \alpha)(W_t + H_t) - H_t$ dollars in the riskless asset. This implies that the optimal share of equities in financial assets is (Campbell and Viceira, 2002, Equation (6.1)):

$$
\begin{aligned}
\hat{\alpha}_t &= \frac{\alpha(W_t - H_t)}{W_t} \\[2ex]
&= \frac{Er - r_f + \dfrac{\sigma^2}{2}}{\gamma \sigma^2} \left[1 + \frac{H_t}{W_t} \right]
\end{aligned}
\tag{10.8}
$$

It is possible that the optimal dollar investment in the riskless asset might be negative, which implies that the investor takes a leveraged position in equities, that is, he or she might borrow at the riskless rate to invest in the stock market. It is also clear from Equation (10.8) that $\hat{\alpha}_t \geq \alpha$, the optimal investment in equities, is higher when an investor has human capital than when he or she does not. It is also optimal for the weight in equities to decline over time as human capital is depleted and financial wealth grows. Early in adult life, the ratio (H_t/W_t) is likely to be very high, because the individual's human capital is high and his or her accumulated financial wealth is likely to be low. Over time, this ratio falls, and so does the optimal investment in equities. The move away from equities also accelerates as the performance of equities improves. The optimal strategy is therefore dynamic (with a trend decline in equities over time), but also contrarian (that is, the individual disinvests from equities the stronger the returns on equities). We can also see that the optimal allocation has two components, a myopic or static component and an intertemporal hedging component that depends on (H_t/W_t).

10.4.2.3 *The optimal investment strategy with risky labour income*

In reality, of course, future labour income is not riskless: rather, it is both volatile and correlated with the returns on risky financial assets. Risky labour income is an example of a *background risk*, that is, a risk that is not under the individual's control and which is not directly related to the investment strategy itself, but which nevertheless influences the outcome of the investment strategy.

Campbell and Viceira (2002, Equation (6.11)) show that the optimal share of equities in the portfolio when labour income risk is taken into account is given by:

$$\hat{\alpha}_t = \frac{1}{\rho}\left(\frac{Er - r_f + \frac{\sigma_u^2}{2}}{\gamma\sigma_u^2}\right) + \left(1 - \frac{1}{\rho}\right)\frac{\sigma_{ul}}{\sigma_u^2} \tag{10.9}$$

where σ_u^2 is the variance in the innovation in the risky asset return, and σ_{ul} is the conditional covariance between the return on the risky asset and the logarithm of labour income (that is, $Cov_t(r_{t+1}, l_{t+1}) = \sigma_{ul}$),

$$\frac{1}{\rho} = 1 + \overline{H/W} \tag{10.10}$$

where $\overline{H/W}$ is the average human capital to financial wealth ratio over the working life. Campbell and Viceira (2002, p.169) show that ρ has a natural interpretation as the elasticity of consumption with respect to financial wealth, while $(1-\rho)$ is the elasticity of consumption with respect to labour income.

Unfortunately, investors cannot trade away (that is, hedge) labour income risk for the simple reason that human capital is a nontradeable asset, that is, individuals cannot sell their human capital. One reason for this is the obvious one that this is tantamount to slavery, which is illegal. But a second reason is that there would be an immediate moral hazard problem if they did: having received the proceeds from the sale of their human capital, individuals would have a much reduced incentive to provide the future labour they have promised. This explains the additional hedging demand for equities given by the second term in Equation (10.9).

In any case, labour supply is not fixed over time, as implicitly assumed so far. People can choose how much labour to supply each year (N_{t+1}) in the light of the real wage that they are offered that year (Z_{t+1}). They also have some choice about how long to work. The choice of retirement date might be affected by both employment and portfolio developments, as emphasized by Bodie et al. (1992). For example, if the accruing pension fund is insufficient to support an adequate pension in retirement, say because of poor investment performance or because the plan member was unemployed for a significant period, a plan member might delay retirement and work longer. On the other hand, outstanding investment performance might induce earlier retirement. We shall come back to the timing-of-retirement issue shortly.

When labour supply is endogenous, Campbell and Viceira (2002, Equation (6.27)) go on to show that the optimal share of equities in the portfolio is given by:

$$\hat{\alpha}_t = \frac{1}{\beta_w} \left(\frac{Er - r_f + \frac{\sigma_u^2}{2}}{\gamma \sigma_u^2} \right) - \frac{\beta_z}{\beta_w} \frac{\sigma_{uz}}{\sigma_u^2} \tag{10.11}$$

where σ_u^2 is the variance in the innovation in the risky asset return, and σ_{uz} is the conditional covariance between the return on the risky asset and the logarithm of the real wage (that is, $Cov_t(r_{t+1}, z_{t+1}) = \sigma_{uz}$). In Equation (10.11),

$$\beta_w = \frac{\rho}{1 + (1 - \rho)\gamma\nu} \in (0, \rho) \tag{10.12}$$

$$\beta_z = \frac{(1 - \rho)(1 + \nu)}{1 + (1 - \rho)\gamma\nu} \tag{10.13}$$

where ν is the elasticity of labour supply with respect to the real wage.[3] Comparing Equations (10.11) and (10.9), and recognizing that $\beta_w \leq \rho$, it is clear that the flexibility to adjust labour supply over time increases the weight of equities in the portfolio if wages are uncorrelated with equity returns. However, if wages are positively correlated with equity returns, this flexibility will lead to a reduction in the weight of equities in the portfolio.

This analysis has been generalized by Cairns et al. (2006) to allow for annuity risk, which in their model arises from a time-varying riskless interest rate. Annuities will be discussed in more detail in Section 10.4.4, but for now the key point to take into account is that the price of annuities is inversely related to the interest rate. Annuity risk can be hedged using a third asset class, bonds, in addition to equities and cash: bonds are a good hedge for annuity risk because their values also vary inversely with interest rates.

This leads to an optimal strategy that Cairns et al. (2006) call *stochastic lifestyling*. This strategy requires three funds, an 'equities' fund, a 'bond' fund and a 'cash' fund.[4] Assuming a Vasicek (1977) model of stochastic interest rates with a mean reversion term given by $\kappa(Er_f - r_{f,t})$, where κ measures the speed of adjustment of the actual interest rate, $r_{f,t}$, back to the equilibrium rate, Er_f, Cairns et al. show that the optimal weight in the 'equities' fund at time t is

$$\bar{\alpha}_t = \frac{W_t + \Pi_t}{\gamma W_t} \tag{10.14}$$

where W_t is accruing pension wealth and Π_t is the present value of future contributions into the pension plan.[5] The weight in equities will start out very high, because W_t starts out very low and Π_t starts out very high. However, as Π_t falls over time relative to W_t, then $\bar{\alpha}_t$ will fall. For its part, the optimal weight in the 'bond' fund is given by

$$\bar{\alpha}_{Bt} = \frac{(\gamma-1)(W_t+\Pi_t)e^{-\kappa(T-t)}}{\gamma W_t} \qquad (10.15)$$

where T is the retirement date. Again this starts out very high, but falls very rapidly and then rises steadily over time. And, finally, the optimal weight in the 'cash' fund is given by

$$\bar{\alpha}_{Ct} = 1 - \bar{\alpha}_t - \bar{\alpha}_{Bt}$$
$$= -\frac{\Pi_t}{W} + \frac{(\gamma-1)(W_t+\Pi_t)\left(1-e^{-\kappa(T-t)}\right)}{\gamma W_t} \qquad (10.16)$$

As mentioned above, the optimal weight in the 'cash' fund can start out highly negative: cash is borrowed to finance highly leveraged positions in equities and bonds. The cash weighting then rises over time and becomes positive after a few years, before falling back to zero as the retirement date approaches.

Figure 10.3 depicts the optimal investment strategy for $\gamma = 6$ and for one possible random scenario. The figure shows the pattern of asset weights just described. The purpose of the 'equities' fund is to hedge human capital and to benefit from the equity premium in particular. The purpose of the 'cash' fund is first to finance the initial very high leveraged positions in equities and bonds, and then to hedge the inflation risk in labour income. An individual's labour income increases over time as a result of career progression, productivity improvements and expected inflation, and the nominal return on cash adjusts to reflect inflationary expectations. The purpose of the 'bond' fund is to hedge interest rate risk, given the inverse relationship between bond – and hence annuity – prices and interest rates. Towards the end of the investment horizon, annuity risk becomes a more important risk to hedge than inflation risk, so the weight in bonds rises and that in cash falls.

10.4.2.4 How investment strategy is influenced by other background risks

There are other background risks that might influence the investment strategy of the pension plan. The two most important ones are housing risk and entrepreneurial risk. A house is an asset that is lumpy and provides rental services

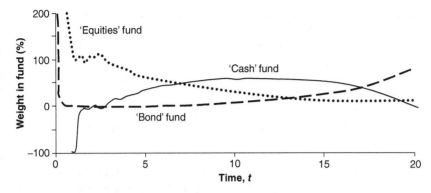

Figure 10.3 Stochastic lifestyling when $\gamma = 6$
Source: Cairns et al. (2006, Fig. 5)

in addition to being an investment asset. In countries with stable political systems, a house has generally been a very attractive investment in terms of long-term capital growth, although housing markets are nevertheless subject to periodic slumps (as in the United Kingdom in the early 1990s and later 2000s, for example). The desire to own a house can influence the age at which a pension plan begins, the amount contributed and the plan's asset allocation. Many people in countries such as the United Kingdom, where the housing market has experienced long-term capital growth, have started to see their house as an important source of income in retirement. The bottom line is that housing adds another complex dimension to lifetime portfolio allocations, and ideally this should be taken into account when designing the investment strategy of a DC pension plan.

Turning now to entrepreneurial risk, Heaton and Lucas (2000) show that individuals with high and variable proprietary business income (for example, from entrepreneurial ventures) hold less wealth in equity than similarly wealthy individuals. Such individuals are typically classed as self-employed, and self-employed individuals often treat their businesses as their pension. Naturally, this should be taken into account in the investment strategies of the DC plans held by such individuals. Given that entrepreneurs typically have a high net worth, a DC plan can be tailored better to their needs than is the case for poorer people.

10.4.2.5 The practical implementation of the accumulation stage investment strategy

These investment strategies are clearly very complex, and their full implications are still poorly understood. They are also very information-intensive, in the sense that they require constantly updated information about factors such as labour income, human capital and housing wealth. They are therefore very difficult to implement, and one has to consider simpler strategies that are easier to implement.

Blake et al. (2001) consider some simplified investment strategies that either approximate the optimal dynamic asset allocation –given in Equations (10.14)–(10.16) – or protect the downside risk from investing in equities and hence increase the likelihood of achieving the goal of an adequate targeted pension in retirement. These are

- *Deterministic lifestyling.* This strategy begins with 100% equity weighting and then linearly switches into bonds or cash in the five or ten years prior to retirement. The intention is to reduce the impact of a large fall in equity returns and hence fund value in the period leading up to retirement. If the intention is to purchase an annuity on the retirement date, the strategy will switch into 100% bonds by the retirement date. If, as is permissible in some jurisdictions, such as the United Kingdom, where 25% of the accumulated pension fund can be taken as a tax-free lump sum, the strategy will switch 75% into bonds and 25% into cash by the retirement date. The strategy could be modified to replicate a stochastic lifestyling strategy.
- *Threshold* (or *funded status* or *return banking*) strategy. This is 100% invested in equities if the fund is below a lower threshold and 100% invested in the bonds if the fund is above an upper threshold, with linear switching in between these thresholds. The thresholds are set in relation to the fund size needed to deliver the target DC pension, such as a lower threshold of 20% and an upper threshold of 80%. The idea is to invest in risky assets when the fund is doing badly, but to lock in returns and switch to lower risk assets when the fund is doing well.
- *Portfolio insurance.* This is the mirror image of the threshold strategy and involves buying more equities according to pre-set rules when equities are performing well and selling equities and buying bonds when equities are declining.

The investment strategy is a critical ingredient of the pension plan, and involves a complex set of trade-offs between contributions, asset allocation, and asset risk. Conservative investment strategies will lead either to low pensions or require high compensating contribution rates. In contrast, a heavy equity component to the asset allocation will raise both the expected return on the portfolio and its risk: the first factor will have the effect of lowering the average required contribution rate, while the second will raise the *short-fall risk* (of ending up with a pension below the target pension), unless more conservative investment strategies are adopted as the retirement date approaches or the plan member is prepared to work longer or make additional contributions in the period just before retirement, in the case in which a shortfall is likely to emerge. These trade-offs are not well explained to plan members, and given the very high degree of risk aversion reported by most of them, they will typically choose conservative investment strategies unsuited to a long-term investment horizon. However, most current plan providers will be unconcerned by this, because they have no contractual obligation to deliver any particular fund size on the retirement date.

10.4.3 The retirement decision and the option to retire

For many people, the decision to retire is not made by them but by their employer, and this typically happens at the company's normal retirement age. Increasingly, however, and more so as both age discrimination legislation and DC plans become more widespread, individuals have more choice over when to retire. The retirement decision can be quite complex and can depend on such factors as the accumulated amount of DC wealth and the size of the pension annuity it will purchase; other pension wealth, especially social security wealth; other wealth, especially housing and financial wealth; the employment status of the member, for example, self-employed people tend to retire later than employees, in some cases because they enjoy work, while others cannot afford to retire because their accumulated pension is inadequate and their business does not have saleable assets; the health status of the member (this might either advance annuitization in the case of very ill health or delay annuitization in order to have cash to pay medical expenses); and the member's partner's retirement, financial and health statuses.

One way to examine the retirement decision is suggested by Stock and Wise (1990). They model the work-retirement decision in terms of the option value of continued work or equivalently the option to retire at a later date. An individual decides to retire when the expected value of continuing to work falls below the expected value of retiring.

10.4.4 The decumulation stage

An important decision that every plan member has to make is the form in which the income is drawn: should the member keep the pension fund invested in return-generating assets and draw an income from the fund (this is known as income drawdown or systematic withdrawal) or should the pension fund assets be sold and the proceeds used to purchase a life annuity? In some jurisdictions (for example, the United States, Germany, Italy, Australia and Japan), plan members are free to select whatever choice suits them. In others (for example, Sweden), there is a legal requirement to purchase a life annuity by a certain age. Plan members therefore have an option to annuitize some or all of their pension wealth, either at any age or before a legally set age.

10.4.4.1 The value of annuitization

There are good theoretical reasons for individuals to eventually annuitize all their pension wealth and, indeed, their entire financial wealth. Annuitization means that individuals are fully protected from outliving their resources (Yaari, 1965). This is an essential feature of a proper pension plan, namely a plan to provide retirement income security for however long the plan member lives (Bodie, 1990). Consequently, we would argue that unless a pension plan requires the member to purchase an annuity with the accumulated assets at some stage in the life of the plan, it is not a pension plan in the true sense of the term, but merely an asset accumulation or long-term savings plan.

An annuity can be a valuable investment asset, especially when it is purchased at higher ages. An annuity is an asset with both an age-dependent and survival-dependent return. Each surviving annuitant gets a return at age x that exceeds the risk-free rate by a survival credit $(q_x/(1-q_x))$. This is equal to the percentage of the population of a given age that is expected to die within the next year. We can regard the survival credit as a bonus paid to those who survive by those who die. The survival credit increases with age because the survival probability declines with age. To illustrate, the one-year survival credit for a 65-year-old UK male pensioner is 1.2%, but the survival credit for an 85-year-old UK male is 12.1%.

Nonetheless, the original Yaari argument that one should eventually annuitize all one's financial wealth depends on certain assumptions, and some of these are quite severe. Amongst these are the assumptions that the only source of risk is longevity risk (that is, the risk of running out of resources before dying), that annuities are fairly priced and that the individual has no bequest motive. Fortunately, Davidoff et al. (2005) show that Yaari's recommendation would hold under much less restrictive assumptions than he assumed. They show that it is optimal for an individual to eventually annuitize all financial wealth if there is no bequest motive, if the return on the annuity exceeds other assets, such as equities, and if the market is complete in the sense that all future risks can be completely hedged using currently available assets. And, when there is a bequest motive or when the market is not complete, partial annuitization becomes optimal at some stage. Thus, despite the intrinsic value of an annuity, it might not be optimal to annuitize *all* the accrued pension fund *at a single point in time*, such as the retirement date. This is in part because, by annuitizing all pension wealth on, say, the retirement date, the plan member is converting it into an investment that is linked to the return on bonds and hence foregoes the equity premium available by keeping the accumulated fund invested in equities.

This consideration suggests that we need to treat the decision about *when* to annuitize separately from the decision about *how much* to annuitize. Clearly, the possibility of delaying annuitization is only open to those with alternative resources to live off in the meantime.

10.4.4.2 The option to annuitize: When?

The decision about when to annuitize can be thought of as an option and will depend on the survival credit, the degree of risk aversion, annuity income risk, and the fund size. One of the earliest studies analysing this option is Milevsky (1998). He proposed a simple rule for determining the optimal time to annuitize: in the absence of a bequest motive, it is optimal to switch fully into annuities when the survival credit just begins to exceed the equity premium. However, Milevsky ignored risk aversion and his decision rule is not optimal when the prospective annuitant is risk averse.

Furthermore, the optimal annuitization decision is not once and for all, but gradual (Milevsky and Young, 2007, and Horneff et al. 2006a,b). This is because there is a trade-off between the illiquidity of annuities and the longevity risk insurance they provide. Although the longevity risk insurance from annuities is valuable, the purchase decision is irreversible, so that annuities are a very illiquid asset. In option terminology, the illiquidity of annuities creates a value for the option to delay annuitization. Milevsky and Young (2007) show that the optimal age to annuitize is when the option to delay has zero time value. They argue that the option value from waiting is valuable at younger ages, and this explains why gradual annuitization is preferable.

The annuitization timing decision also depends on the presence of annuity income risk. In order to hedge the risk of buying an annuity at an unfavourable point in the interest rate cycle, when interest rates are low, and hence being locked into a low annuity amount, Horneff et al. (2006a) show that it is optimal to spread the purchases over time, a strategy known as phased annuity purchases. Horneff et al. (2006a) show that it is optimal to begin to annuitize from as early as age 20. The rising survival credit first crowds out bonds (at around age 50) and eventually equities (by age 79).

Finally, the annuitization timing decision depends on the evolution over time of the fund size, that is, it is path-dependent (Blake et al., 2003). Figure 10.4 shows some possible outcomes from an income drawdown programme at selected levels of relative risk aversion (γ), beginning with an initial fund size of £100,000; shown besides the γ value is the associated optimal asset allocation for the pension fund prior to annuitization. In each graph, the dots show how the plan member's fund value would change over time if he had opted at age 65 for a life annuity. This gives a useful reference point for comparing the fund size under a drawdown programme at different ages. The dashed lines show the stochastic trajectories of the residual fund for a

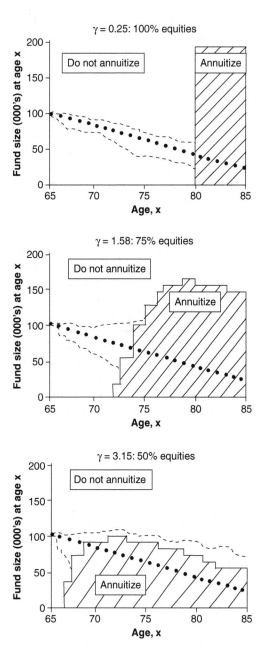

Figure 10.4 Relationship between the annuitization decision and the plan member's age and fund size for different levels of risk aversion

Source: Blake et al. (2003, Fig. 6)

drawdown programme under two particular realizations of asset returns. We can also observe that, for any given age and γ, annuitization will either (a) not be optimal for any fund size, (b) be optimal for all fund sizes or (c) be optimal for low fund sizes, but not for fund sizes above some threshold.

For example, with $\gamma = 1.58$ and a drawdown programme invested 75% in equities (second panel of Figure 10.4), we can see that annuitization is likely to occur sometime between the ages of 72 (if equities perform poorly) and 80 (if equities perform moderately well). However, if equities perform sufficiently well, then the fund-age trajectory will lie above the shaded region and annuitization might only take place when it is compulsory to do so (which in the case of Figure 10.4 is assumed to be at age 85). In the third panel, where $\gamma = 3.15$ and the drawdown programme is invested 50% in equities, the shaded annuitization 'hill' is somewhat lower, implying that some of the stochastic trajectories of W_t will avoid hitting the hill (and so avoid annuitization) at ages below 85. On the other hand, if W_t is going to hit the hill, it will probably do so within the first three or four years after retirement: this case is more likely given that an income must be drawn from the fund to pay for retirement consumption.

We can infer from these observations that in some (that is, low γ) cases, the option to delay annuitization will not add much value (the plan member will choose to annuitize at around age 80 regardless). However, in other (high γ) cases, the shape and height of the annuitization hill are such that many stochastic fund-age trajectories cross over the hill without hitting it, and this suggests that the option to delay annuitization is a valuable feature.

It is also interesting to note that at very low levels of γ (first panel of Figure 10.4), the optimal annuitization age of 80 is close to the age we would get (namely, 79) by applying Milevsky's (1998) rule, which specifies that we switch at the point at which the survival credit equals the equity premium. This should not be surprising as the analysis in Blake et al. (2003) shows that the Milevsky rule matches the optimal strategy presented in Figure 10.4 only for a plan member who is close to risk neutral. The latter's more general analysis demonstrates that the optimal annuitization decision is much more complex than the Milevsky rule suggests. Their analysis also tends to confirm Milevsky and Young (2007)'s finding that the higher the degree of risk aversion, the lower the age of annuitization.

10.4.4.3 The option to annuitize: How much?

There is also the option of *how much* to annuitize. An examination of recent literature suggests that the optimal degree of annuitization is reduced if (a) state pensions are high, since these crowd out private annuitization (Bernheim, 1991); (b) risk pooling within the family is efficient, especially if adverse selection and the transactions costs of entering the formal annuities market are high and married couples behave as a two-person annuity market; (c) risk aversion is low, since such individuals prefer equity investments (Milevsky and Young, 2002); (d) the equity premium is sufficiently high (Horneff et al., 2007); (e) investment volatility is low (Milevsky and Young, 2007); (f) the member is in poor health (Milevsky and Young, 2002; in such a case, an impaired life annuity will be optimal); (g) the member is male rather than female, given their shorter life expectancy (Milevsky and Young, 2007); and (h) there is a bequest motive.

It is clear from the above analysis that the options of when and how much to annuitize make the optimal decumulation investment strategy, like the optimal accumulation investment strategy, both highly complex and very information-intensive.

10.4.4.4 *Optimal retirement-income programmes*

What type of annuity or drawdown programme should plan members choose? The answer depends on their desired income, and hence consumption profile, in retirement. Most individuals prefer an upward sloping income and consumption profile. Annuity providers have responded to this declaration of preferences by introducing various types of *investment-linked retirement-income programmes* (ILRIPs), the principal examples being income drawdown and investment-linked annuities with a substantial equity component in order to benefit from the equity premium. Individuals preferring a flat profile in real terms can achieve this using an index-linked or real annuity or drawdown programme. Those preferring a falling profile can get this using a nominal annuity or drawdown programme that generates declining real income over time. Both inflation-linked annuities and investment-linked (or variable) annuities provide an important hedge when there is inflation risk and time-varying risk premia, respectively (Koijen et al., 2006).

Blake et al. (2003) investigated the following distribution programmes for a male plan member retiring at age 65 and having some investment flexibility until the age of 75, at which age, assuming he lives that long, he must buy an index-linked life annuity with the residual fund. With the exception of the first programme listed below, each programme comes in two variations: (a) an income drawdown variation, in which the residual fund is paid as a *bequest* to the plan member's estate if he dies before age 75, and (b) an annuity variation, in which the residual fund reverts to the insurer, in return for which the insurer agrees to pay a *survival credit* at the start of each year while the plan member is still alive:

- *Programme 1 – Purchased life annuity* (PLA): The plan member transfers his pension fund immediately on retirement at age 65 to the insurer in return for an index-linked pension. No bequest is payable at the time of death of the plan member. Instead a survival credit is implicitly payable throughout the duration of the policy. This is the benchmark programme against which all the ILRIPs listed below are compared.

- *Programme 2 – Fixed income programme* (FIX) with a life annuity purchased at age 75: In this case, the plan member transfers his retirement fund to a managed fund (which invests in a mixture of equities and bonds) when he retires at age 65. He then withdraws a fixed income each year equal to that which he would have obtained had he purchased an annuity at age 65 (if there are sufficient monies in his fund). At age 75, assuming he lives that long, he uses whatever fund remains to purchase a life annuity. There is a possibility that the fund will be exhausted before 75 (and, in the case of a 100% equity investment, there is something like a 10% chance that this will happen).[6]

- *Programme 3 – Flexible income programme* (FLX) with a life annuity purchased at age 75: In this case, it is not possible to run out of money before age 75, because if the fund falls in value, the income received has to fall in tandem. The outcome will be similar to that of the flexible unit-linked programme described below, and identical in the case where a survival credit is payable. We consider four cases with different levels of equity exposure in the managed fund: 25%, 50%, 75% and 100%.

- *Programme 4 – Flexible income programme with a deferred annuity* (DEF) purchased at retirement age and payable at age 75: In this case, the plan member purchases a deferred annuity at age 65 which will provide an income from age 75 equal to that which would be payable at that age from an immediate annuity bought at age 65. He invests the remaining monies at age 65 in a managed fund. He then draws an income from the fund on the same basis as the flexible income programme above up to age 75, when the deferred annuity comes into payment. On death before age 75, the value of the deferred annuity policy is lost. Other things being equal, it is cheaper to purchase at age 65 a deferred annuity that comes into payment at age 75 than to wait to purchase the annuity at age 75;[7] this is because there is some chance that the purchaser will not live long enough to receive the annuity payments, and this is reflected in the deferred annuity price.

- *Programme 5– Unit-linked programme* (UNI) with a life annuity purchased at age 75: In this case, the plan member uses his retirement fund to purchase a fixed number of units in a managed fund at age 65. The number of units received will depend on the forecasts for mortality made at age 65. Each year a number of units are sold and the plan member's income will change in line with changes in the price of these units. At age 75, assuming he lives that long, he uses the residual fund to purchase a life annuity.

- *Programme 6 – Collared income programme* (COL) with a life annuity purchased at age 75: This programme is similar to the flexible income programme, but involves a smoothing out of investment returns. Instead of investing solely in a managed portfolio, the fund invests in a mixed portfolio of equities, put and call options with the aim of achieving significant protection against downside equity risk. For each equity unit held, the portfolio is long one at-the-money put option and short one call option. The strike price of the call option is chosen so that the prices of the put and call options are equal. This means that the net cost of the resulting *collar* is zero. As a result, we have 100% participation in equity returns subject to the cap and floor. This is one way of selling some of the upside potential to pay for downside protection. The resulting smoothing of investment returns is similar in some respects to a with-profits policy, although in the present case the smoothing method is much more explicit.

- *Programme 7 – Floored income programme* (FLR) with a life annuity purchased at age 75: Like the collared income programme, this programme involves foregoing some upside potential to pay for downside protection. The plan member is guaranteed to get a minimum return of zero (that is, holds an implicit at-the-money put option), and pays for this by selling off a proportion of the equity performance above 0%. He will get some proportion (say, k) of the rise in the value of equities, with the difference of $(1-k)$ being used to 'pay for' the put. In effect, a fraction $(1-k)$ of an at-the-money call option is sold to pay for the put option. This annual return structure can also be achieved in a more simple way by investing in cash plus k at-the-money call options. This programme is also sometimes known as a participating-equity or guaranteed-equity programme.

Blake et al. (2003) show that the programmes with the highest expected discounted utility are Programme 3 (with 100% equities) and Programme 5. These are the flexible income and unit-linked annuities paying survival credits. For the particular plan member considered, a high level of equity investment is valued, but the possibility of making a bequest is not. An investor with a higher risk aversion would choose a lower equity weighting, whereas an investor with a higher bequest intensity would choose an income drawdown programme involving a bequest.

The approach set out here is an invaluable aid for helping DC pension plan members select the right retirement product for them, once the desired income and consumption profile in retirement is known. A highly complex set of choices can be reduced to just two: finding the plan member's risk aversion parameter and his bequest intensity.

10.4.5 Summary

We can summarize this section as follows: A well-designed DC plan will look very much like a defined benefit plan, offering a promised retirement pension, but without the guarantees implicit in the DB promise. In other words, a well-designed DC plan will try to target a particular pension by generating the lump sum on the retirement date needed to deliver that pension in the form of a life annuity, although it will not be able to guarantee delivery of that target pension. This is because guarantees over long investment horizons are very expensive to secure. Surveys suggest that individuals in retirement prefer consumption profiles that rise smoothly in real terms. They do not like to experience large cuts in consumption. Contributions into the pension plan during the accumulation stage must be sufficient to generate the fund size needed to purchase the annuity that can finance this consumption profile. The investment strategy during the accumulation stage should take into account the plan member's degree of risk aversion, the riskiness of his labour income and hence human capital, and possibly other background risks as well. When human capital is taken into account, the weight of the portfolio in equities is higher for any given degree of risk aversion. This is because individuals, especially when they are young, 'own' a lot of human capital and very little equity capital, and to compensate for this they will increase the proportion of equities held in their pension plan. Over time, as the weight of human capital to financial capital falls, the weight of equities in the pension fund also falls and the weight in bonds rises. One investment strategy for doing this is called stochastic lifestyling. In practice, however, investment strategies such as stochastic lifestyling are expensive to implement and manage in terms of information requirements. From an implementation perspective, there is, therefore, a premium on simpler-to-implement strategies that include deterministic lifestyling, threshold, and portfolio insurance.

For many people, the decision to retire is not made by them but by their employer, and this typically happens at the company's normal retirement age. Increasingly, however, individuals have some choice (that is, have an option) over when to retire. This choice will depend on such factors as the size of the pension annuity from the DC plan, the level of social security payments and the health status of the individual. Similarly, for many people, the decision to begin drawing an income from the plan is made at the same time as the decision to retire. In general, the income can be in the form of an annuity or in the form of income drawdown or systematic withdrawal (with the fund remaining invested in return-generating assets). Annuities are valuable, but illiquid, investments. They generate survival credits which increase with age, so long as the plan member continues to live. Eventually, the return on an annuity exceeds that on equities. The annuitization-timing decision depends on the degree of risk aversion: higher levels of risk aversion lead to lower annuitization ages. The optimal annuitization decision is not once and for all, but gradual. This is because of the trade-off between the illiquidity of annuities and the longevity risk insurance they provide. In order to hedge the risk of buying an annuity at an unfavourable point in the interest rate cycle, it is optimal to spread the purchases over time, a strategy known as phased annuity purchases. Individuals with low degrees of risk aversion might consider an investment-linked retirement-income programme, such as a unit-linked programme, where the plan member uses his retirement fund to purchase a fixed number of units in a managed fund at retirement (say at age 65). The number of units received will depend on the forecasts for mortality made at the time of retirement. Each year a number of units are sold and the plan member's income will change in line with changes in the price of these units. Eventually (say at age 75), assuming he lives that long, he uses the residual fund to purchase a life annuity. Each programme comes in two variations: (a) an income drawdown variation, in which the residual fund is paid as a bequest to the plan member's estate if he dies before, say, age 75, and (b) an annuity variation, in which the residual fund reverts to the insurer, in return for which the insurer agrees to pay a survival credit at the start of each year while the plan member is still alive. However, for many, if not most, people, the range of choices discussed above will not be relevant, because the fund they have accumulated will not be large enough to give value to these choices. In such cases, a simplified DC plan would involve a deterministic lifestyling investment strategy during the accumulation stage and an index-linked life annuity purchased with the accumulated fund on the retirement date.

10.5   The role of the regulator

Until now, we have assumed that the individuals involved in pension planning over their life cycle are well-informed, rational economic agents who make decisions in a way that maximizes their utility or welfare. Such individuals are assumed to be able to 'interpret and weigh information presented regarding options offered by employers and governments, appropriately evaluate and balance these choices, and then make an informed decision based on a weighing of the alternatives' (Mitchell and Utkus, 2004b, p. 3).

Few would dispute the claim that there is little need for regulation when consumers are well informed and are able to exercise and enforce their rights in a competitive market place. Unfortunately, when it comes to financial matters, and especially financial products extending over long periods of time, many consumers are clearly not well informed or well educated. In this case, there may be a role for some kind of guide or supervisor to act on behalf of members as a surrogate 'intelligent consumer'. As regards pensions, this role might be filled by pension regulators.

One key task of such a regulator is to recognize certain behavioural biases in individual decision-making. In terms of pension planning, the principal ones are the contribution puzzle, the investment puzzles and the annuity puzzle.

Due to the difficulty in forecasting lifetime earnings, asset returns, interest rates, tax rates, inflation and longevity and the required level of retirement savings, many people experience a significant fall in living standards after they retire. Behaviouralists (social scientists working in the fields of behavioural psychology) explain this inadequate preparation for retirement in terms of lack of willpower. People might want to save for retirement, but are unable to do so (Thaler and Shefrin, 1981).

To explain this behaviour, behaviouralists argue that decision-making has two dimensions: a primitive or emotional dimension and an advanced or cerebral one (Weber, 2004). Correspondingly, there are two dimensions to risk: *dread risk*, the fear of a catastrophe, and *uncertainty risk*, the fear of the new or unknown. Retirement risks are low in these two dimensions: there is neither a sufficient sense of catastrophe nor enough sense of great uncertainty to frighten most people into preparing for retirement and overcoming their inadequate self-control.

To overcome this problem, individuals need to employ *commitment devices* that support permanent changes in behaviour (cf. Laibson, 1997, Laibson et al., 1998). Two simple examples that encourage long-term savings behaviour are auto-enrolment in a pension plan[8] and payroll deduction of contributions. Another is the 'save more tomorrow' concept of Thaler and Benartzi (2004), which exploits the behavioural traits of *inertia* and *procrastination*, whereby the plan member agrees to start or increase savings on a regular basis not now, but on a future significant date, such as the date of the next pay rise, or the anniversary date of joining the company.

Then there are the investment puzzles: studies of real world investor behaviour show that there is little evidence that pension plan holders invest rationally. The median US investor holds a portfolio containing just two securities, whilst amongst the richest investors, the median holding is just 15 securities – far fewer than is needed to eliminate diversifiable risk (Polkovnichenko, 2003).

Behaviouralists have put forward a number of reasons for these puzzles: When presented with a choice of investment strategies, pension plan members appear to have relatively weak preferences for the asset portfolio they choose (Benartzi and Thaler, 2002). In an experiment in which members were given a choice between holding their own current portfolio, the portfolio of the median member of their plan, and the portfolio of the average member, 80% preferred the median to their own and many would have been happy with the average portfolio. Only 21% still preferred their own portfolio. This indicates a herding instinct in investment behaviour in which it is comforting to be at or near the average of the peer group of comembers.

Investment decisions are also affected by framing effects. Experiments conducted on the effect of investment menu design on investment choices made in DC pension plans show that the menu design has a bigger influence on investment choice than the actual risk and return characteristics of the investments themselves.

For example, Benartzi and Thaler (2001) conducted an experiment in which pension plan members were invited to choose an investment mix from a choice of two different funds. One group was offered a choice between a stock fund and a bond fund, a second group was offered a choice between a stock fund and a balanced fund, and a third group offered a choice between a bond fund and a balanced fund. The most common strategy for all groups was to select an equal 50:50 mix of the two funds offered. Yet the underlying asset allocation and risk characteristics of this mix were dramatically different for each group: the equity weightings for the three groups were 54%, 73% and 35%, respectively. As the number of funds offered in the experiment increased, a *1/N rule* seemed to emerge, with allocations spread equally across the number of funds offered, irrespective of the risk characteristics. Other experiments suggest that plan members follow the *naïve heuristic* of picking the middle option and avoiding extremes, instead of selecting on the basis of the return and risk characteristics of the underlying investments themselves.

Investment decision-making is also affected by anchoring effects (Mitchell and Utkus, 2004b). *Anchoring* is the idea that the initial conditions used to justify a decision remain important over time, however irrational this decision might be. This behaviour is also consistent with the significant *inertia* and *procrastination* in investment decision-making by pension plan members.

Mitchell and Utkus (2003) report that 11 million 401(k) plan members in the US hold at least 20% of their fund in their own company's shares, and 5 million hold at least 60%. This clearly violates the investment principle of good risk diversification, although it is sometimes argued that employers encourage this to provide an incentive for employees to work harder.

From a behavioural viewpoint, these large concentrations in company shares are the result not only of incentive effects, but also of computational or behavioural errors. Employees appear to suffer from *risk myopia* in respect of their own company's shares. Another anomaly is that asset allocations in DC pension plans tend to be driven by past performance rather than by expected future returns and risks. Plan members tend to forecast returns by extrapolating their company's shares' historic performance. Good past performance led to the pension fund being overweight in the employer's shares and vice versa. Two behavioural factors have been put forward to explain this behaviour. The first is the *representativeness heuristic* identified by Tversky and Kahneman (1974). For example, if they are offered a short series of random numbers, individuals will often try to identify a pattern in these numbers.

This representativeness heuristic might be caused by a framing effect. Rather than use a wide frame to assess skill versus luck, such as the population of all mutual fund managers, the individual investor might adopt a narrow frame, such as the three-year track record of a single fund manager. This leads to random outcomes being incorrectly interpreted as logical sequences.

The second is the *availability heuristic*. Confronted with a complex decision, individuals often use whatever information is readily at hand. In the example above, investors rely on past performance probably because it is freely available from newspapers and websites and is used despite the small print warning that 'past performance is no guide to future performance'.

These two heuristics might help to explain the *return-chasing phenomenon* observed in mutual fund purchase decisions (Patel et al., 1991). This is where mutual fund investors rush into funds whose recent past performance has been exceptional, irrespective of these funds' future prospects.

There is also some reason to suspect that individuals do not, in practice, maximize expected utility. According to *prospect theory* developed by Kahneman and Tversky (1979), individuals maximize a nonlinear value function. This optimization problem differs from expected utility maximization in two important respects. First, individuals judge how their decisions affect incremental gains and losses to their wealth, rather than how they affect their total wealth (as required by standard utility theory). In addition, individuals treat gains and losses asymmetrically: losses have a much more negative impact on welfare than the same dollar gain has on improving welfare. The *gain function* (to the right of the origin) is concave, but the *loss function* (to the left of the origin) is convex and has a much steeper slope to begin with. In experiments, Kahneman and Tversky found that the index of loss-aversion is about 2.5. This implies that a typical individual would not be willing to take part in a fair game unless the potential gain was 2.5 times the potential loss.

Prospect theory has powerful implications for investment behaviour. Investors will be risk averse for a realized gain and will act to lock in this gain prematurely, an effect called the *disposition effect* by Shefrin and Statman (1985).[9] When it comes to losses, a *break-even effect* operates. Recognizing that they face a certain loss, many investors take on additional risk in an attempt to recover their investment and breakeven. This is particularly so in falling stock markets, where losses are perceived as temporary and another bet will enable the losses to be recovered. By contrast, rational economic behaviour predicts that realized losses should be ignored on the grounds that they are sunk costs. Kahneman (2003) argues that prospect theory is important for understanding investment decision-making in three ways: it leads to overconfidence in the domain of gains, combined with premature realization of investment gains; it leads to a policy of loss avoidance in the domain of losses; and it leads to these features being magnified by narrow framing effects.

A key finding of behavioural economics is the tendency for individuals to be overconfident about the future and to make excessively optimistic forecasts.

Loss aversion explains why investors are reluctant to 'cut their losses', and keep loss-making positions in the hope that they will recover their original investment. For example, Odean (1998) reports that investors who hold on to loss-making positions underperform the market in the following year by 1%. He also found that investors sold their winning positions too quickly, that is, failed to 'run their profits', and subsequently underperformed the market over the next year by 2%. The net effect of these two behavioural traits was therefore 3% p.a.

Small-scale risk aversion seems to result from a tendency to assess risk in isolation rather than in a broader context (that is, the investor is 'thinking small'). If small-scale, better-than-fair gambles were assessed in a broader context, individuals would be more likely to accept them. Many individuals refuse to accept a coin-tossing gamble where heads wins $200 and tails looses $100. However, if the gamble is rephrased in terms of a $200 increase in the individual's housing equity if the coin shows heads and a $100 reduction if tails, then more people are likely to take part (Rabin and Thaler, 2001).

As Benarzi and Thaler (1995) discovered, loss-averse investors can act myopically in evaluating sequences of investment opportunities, and this leads to myopic loss aversion (MLA). A feature of MLA is excessive monitoring of the investment performance of the investment programme, even by long-term investors, and evidence suggests that the more frequently returns are evaluated, the more risk averse investors will be (Gneezy and Potters, 1997). Another symptom of MLA is over insurance against small-scale, low-risk events, such as extended warranties on household appliances (Rabin and Thaler, 2001).

Benarzi and Thaler (1995) also showed that, while a MLA investor would reject a single small-scale, better-than-fair gamble such as the coin-tossing gamble of $200 winnings versus a $100 loss, he would be prepared to engage in a series of such gambles (that is, the investor switches to 'thinking big'), so long as each gamble in the sequence was not individually monitored. To avoid the risk that the investor withdraws from the sequence of gambles in response to early losses, a commitment device is needed. An example would be a standing order for the premiums to a personal pension plan, rather than an annual invitation to send a cheque to the plan provider. The plan provider should also report the performance of the plan's assets to the plan member no more frequently than annually. This would help to sustain commitment and help to avoid the overconfidence that would emerge in the investor if the early sequence of gambles fortuitously showed net winnings.

Overconfidence and loss-aversion are also exacerbated by *narrow framing* effects, also known as *mental accounting*. Mental accounting plays a key role in understanding investor attitude and response to risk. Mental accounting is the set of cognitive operations individuals seem to use to keep track of financial transactions and evaluate them (Kahneman and Tversky, 1984, 2000; Thaler, 1985, 1999; Barberis and Huang, 2001). One feature of mental accounting is the assignment of specific activities to specific accounts. For instance, expenditures are grouped into categories (housing, food, holiday savings and so forth) and spending in these categories is often limited by implicit or explicit budget constraints.

Finally, there is the question of the annuity puzzle. Despite the benefits of annuitization, very few people choose to annuitize their pension wealth unless the rules of their plan oblige them to do so. In countries such as the United States, Germany, Australia and Japan, there is no mandatory requirement to purchase an annuity at any stage during the life of a DC plan, and very few plan members voluntarily do so. In a few countries, the key examples being Sweden and the United Kingdom, most DC plan members are required to purchase an annuity. Indeed, more than half the world's life annuities are sold in the United Kingdom (300,000 in 2005, with premiums of £8bn[10]) and most of these are level annuities that do not adjust for inflation. The global market in life annuities is currently tiny in comparison with what we would have expected it to be.

The possible behavioural explanations for why people choose the lump sum over the annuity are (a) overconfidence: many people underestimate how much they need to live on after retirement; (b) lack of self-control: some people actually spend all their retirement savings within a few years of retirement; (c) the framing effect: choices can be framed in a way that causes people to overvalue the 'large' lump sum and undervalue the 'small' annuity; and (d) poor financial literacy: most people are not sufficiently competent to manage the drawdown of their investments in old age.

Pension plan members who do not purchase annuities leave themselves exposed to a number of risks: longevity and health risks, inflation risk and capital market risks.

As we have seen, longevity risk can be eliminated by purchasing a life annuity at retirement. Nevertheless, most DC plan members, given the choice, do not choose to buy annuities with their accumulated lump sums. Similarly, in the case of DB plans in the United States, most (75%) of company pension payouts now take the form of lump sum payments (McGill et al., 2005), whereas previously they took the form of a retirement pensions. This means that increasing numbers of people are failing to hedge their own longevity risk, that is, the risk that they will live longer than anticipated.

A number of explanations have been offered to explain this phenomenon:

- People tend to underestimate how long they will live after retirement.
- People usually have a state pension, which implies some insurance against longevity risk.
- In a world of low interest rates, annuity rates are also low, so annuities appear to offer poor value for money.

- The cost loading of the annuity provider reduces the return compared with a pure investment.
- People might have a strong bequest motive. Individuals are concerned that they might die shortly after buying the annuity, in which case the lump sum used to buy the annuity would no longer be available to make bequests.
- People might also be concerned about future long-term care costs. Individuals tend to retain large holdings of assets until very late in life, in contrast with the predictions of the life cycle model. To address concerns about future long-term care costs, some insurers offer annuities combined with life assurance, long-term care and disability benefits.
- Adverse selection and the asymmetric information between the annuity buyer and seller. Individuals hold private information about their health status which it is hard for an annuity provider to identify. It is therefore optimal for healthy individuals to purchase annuities before the annuity provider discovers their true health status. Aware that healthy individuals are more likely to purchase annuities voluntarily than unhealthy individuals (adverse selection), the annuity provider will raise the price of annuities to protect itself. This reduces the value of annuities to average individuals and hence lowers their demand for them (Brugiavini, 1993).

Inflation reduces the real value of investments paying fixed income returns, such as level annuities. Inflation risk can be hedged by purchasing index-linked annuities. However, if inflation is expected to be 3% p.a., an indexed annuity will have a starting payment that is 30% below that of a level annuity. It will take 11 years for the cash payments on the two annuities to equalize, and 19 years in total for the total payments on the indexed annuity to exceed those of the level annuity. Given the choice, few people choose the indexed over the level annuity.

The existence of behavioural biases suggests a possible task for those charged with looking after or regulating pension schemes: these pension regulators should aim to ensure that pension plans are designed to minimize the effects of behavioural biases.

Mitchell and Utkus (2004b) suggest that we should learn the following lessons:

- *Behavioural research challenges some of the most central assumptions of decision-making:* Contrary to the expected utility maximization model, behavioural research suggests that workers are not rational life-cycle financial planners in respect of their pension plans. There are a number of reasons for this, including self-control problems over savings, a divergence between desire and action, or a poor understanding of risk.

- *Plan design drives participant decision:* The combination of default, framing and inertia effects means that investment and saving decisions are heavily influenced by the design of the pension plan.
- *The current design of DC plans does not encourage pension savings:* This follows because workers are told in effect that saving is optional, the need to increase saving is optional and risk is a bad thing rather something that is a necessary feature of a balanced investment portfolio.
- *Current work-place financial education is inappropriate:* The current model of providing work-place information to employees assumes that workers are rational economic planners, but this is not the case. An alternative model is that desired behaviour must come about before education (Selnow, 2004). The defaults are needed to induce the 'correct' behaviour, and then education is used to explain the defaults. In other words, behavioural economics suggest a reversal in the education-behaviour causality link.

These lessons have some major implications for plan design choices:

- *Much depends on the default choices in defined contribution plans:* Behavioural traits such as inertia, procrastination, and lack of decision-making willpower can be used constructively to increase pension saving. This is how 'save more tomorrow' plans work: automatic enrolment of all workers, planned annual contribution increases, and default funds that constitute optimal portfolio choices, for example, balanced portfolios with age-related switching to bonds as retirement approaches (that is, stochastic or deterministic lifestyling). The passive decisionmaker can then depend on the plan design to achieve a good pension outcome. At the same time, if they wish to, financially skilled workers can reject the defaults and make their own preferred choices.
- *Simplified menu design in retirement plans could be very useful:* It is clear that 'choice overload' in investment menus can have a negative impact on plan participation: what is needed is a limited menu of core choices, and, separate from the main menu, an expanded range of options for more sophisticated investors.
- *New approaches are needed to help workers and retirees better manage company stock risk:* Suggestions include a possible need to limit the level of self-investment.
- *Sensible plan design includes default choices at retirement:* Behavioural research suggests that the framing of the annuity versus lump sum decision can be improved, and there is a good argument that the annuity should automatically be the default option in DC plans, as it is in DB plans. The worker's understanding of mortality and investment risks should also be taken into account.

Furthermore, pension regulators should insist that there are governance structures in place that ensure: effective targets for fund managers during the accumulation stage and for annuity providers during the decumulation stage; the safe custody of contributions and accumulating assets; and charges that are not excessive and strike an appropriate balance between cost and efficiency.

10.6 Conclusions

Two key conclusions are glaringly obvious from the above analysis. The first is that there is strong evidence that individuals cannot be regarded as 'intelligent consumers' when it comes to understanding and assessing different investment strategies for their pension plans. The second is that DC pension plans and their investment strategies are currently in a very primitive stage of development.

While the authorities (for example, the UK Office of Fair Trading, 1997, 1997) are becoming aware of the poor standards of financial literacy, it is likely to be a long, slow process to raise standards of financial literacy to the level needed both to protect DC pension plan members and to get them to fully understand how to invest their pension assets (OECD, 2005; Financial Literacy and Education Commission, 2006; Thoresen, 2007).

It is the role of the regulator to ensure that all this happens by acting as an 'intelligent consumer' on behalf of plan members. A third conclusion is that flexibility in the design of DC pension plans is valuable only above a certain minimal fund size. Examples of flexibility include choice over accumulation-stage investment strategy, retirement date, and choice over pension annuity or drawdown programme. For poorer individuals, such choice flexibility will not be feasible. In fact, to avoid the potential moral hazard problem of individuals consuming their retirement pot too quickly and falling back on the state for support, there needs to be a minimum annuitization fund accumulated before any investment flexibility post-retirement should be safely permitted. Members with accumulated funds below the minimum annuitization fund level needed to keep them off further state support should be required to purchase an index-linked life annuity with their accumulated fund.

Acknowledgement

We are grateful to Dr. Katharina Schwaiger for preparing this chapter. The chapter is based on a longer working paper that can be found here: www. pensions-institute.org/workingpapers/wp0806.pdf.

Notes

1. It is generally the case that individuals with a high degree of risk aversion also have a low IES and vice versa. In the case of individuals with a power utility function (as

in Section 3.2 below), the coefficient of relative risk aversion (γ) is the inverse of the IES (see, e.g., Blake (2006, pp. 94–95)).

2. This was one of the empirical observations that led to the development of the life cycle model.

3. As v tends to zero, the labour supplied becomes fixed independent of the real wage and $\beta_w = \rho$ and $\beta_z = (1-\rho)$ and (10.11) approaches (10.9). As v tends to infinity, the labour supplied becomes infinitely elastic and $\beta_w = 0$ and $\beta_z = (1/\gamma)$.

4. These funds are dominated by equities, bonds and cash, respectively, but each fund contains some of the other assets in order to hedge intertemporal shifts in investment opportunities, interest rate volatility and correlation with labour income. For example, the 'equities' fund is an efficient portfolio of equities (mainly), bonds and cash, with the weights in the risky assets depending on the ratios of the assets' risk premium to return variance in the standard fashion; the weights are then adjusted to account for the correlation between asset returns and labour income. For more details, see Cairns et al. (2006). More sophisticated versions of the 'equities' fund might involve *diversified growth* or *new balanced funds*. These are funds that invest across a range of traditional and generally noncorrelated alternative asset classes, such as private equity, commodities and infrastructure. This asset allocation, which aims to reduce risk and volatility, contrasts with 'old' balanced funds, which typically have approximately 80%–85% invested in listed equities. For more details, see Byrne et al. (2007).

5. This will be proportional to human capital if the contribution rate is constant.

6. As discussed above, high returns can never fully compensate for poor returns if the fund also has to pay a fixed income stream, regardless of realized investment performance. Programme 2 is therefore not a genuine pension programme, but is included for completeness.

7. This might not be the case in the presence of longevity risk, however (Blake et al. 2008).

8. This is the concept in which the individual has to actively make the decision to opt out of the pension plan, rather than what happens at present in most plans, in which the individual has to make the active decision to opt in.

9. However, many investors switch from risk-averse to risk-seeking behaviour if they feel they are risking someone else's money (for example, accumulated earnings from prior bets). This is known as the *house money effect*.

10. H M Treasury (2006).

References

Ando, A., and Modigliani, F. (1963) The Life Cycle Hypothesis of Saving: Aggregate Implications and Tests, *American Economic Review*, 53, 55–84.

Balvers, R., Wu, Y., and Gilliand, E. (2000) Mean Reversion across National Stock Markets and Parametric Contrarian Investment Strategies, *Journal of Finance*, 55, 745–772.

Barberis, N. (2000) Investing for the Long-Run when Returns Are Predictable, *Journal of Finance*, 55, 225–264.

Barberis, N., and Huang, M. (2001) Mental Accounting, Loss Aversion, and Individual Stock Returns, *Journal of Finance*, 56, 1247–1292.

Benartzi, S., and Thaler, R. (1995) Myopic Loss Aversion and the Equity Premium Puzzle, *Quarterly Journal of Economics*, 110, 73–92.

Benartzi, S., and Thaler, R. (2001) Naive Diversification Strategies in Retirement Saving Plans, *American Economic Review*, 91, 79–98.

Benartzi, S., and Thaler, R. (2002) How Much Is Investor Autonomy Worth?, *Journal of Finance*, 57, 1593–1616.

Bernheim, B. D. (1991) How Strong Are Bequest Motives? Evidence Based on Estimates of the Demand for Life Insurance and Annuities, *Journal of Political Economics*, 99, 899–927.

Blake, D. (1996) Efficiency, Risk Aversion and Portfolio Insurance: An Analysis of Financial Asset Portfolios held by Investors in the United Kingdom, *Economic Journal*, 106, 1175–1192.

Blake, D. (2006) *Pension Economics*, Wiley, Chichester.

Blake, D., Cairns, A. J. G., and Dowd, K. (2001) Pensionmetrics: Stochastic Pension Plan Design and Value-at-Risk during the Accumulation Phase, *Insurance: Mathematics & Economics*, 29, 187–215.

Blake, D., Cairns, A. J. G., and Dowd, K. (2003) PensionMetrics 2: Stochastic Pension Plan Design during the Distribution Phase, *Insurance: Mathematics & Economics*, 33, 29–47.

Blake, D., Cairns, A. J. G., and Dowd, K. (2007) The Impact of Occupation and Gender on the Pensions from Defined Contribution Plans, *Geneva Papers on Risk & Insurance*, 32, 458–482.

Blake, D., Cairns, A. J. G., and Dowd, K. (2008) Longevity Risk and the Grim Reaper's Toxic Tail: The Survivor Fan Charts, *Insurance: Mathematics & Economics*, 42, 1062–1066.

Blake, D., Lehmann, B., and Timmermann, A. (1999) Asset Allocation Dynamics and Pension Fund Performance, *Journal of Business*, 72, 429–462.

Blake, D., Lehmann, B., and Timmermann, A. (2002) Performance Clustering and Incentives in the UK Pension Fund Industry, *Journal of Asset Management*, 3, 173–194.

Blake, D., and Timmermann, A. (2005) Returns from Active Management in International Equity Markets: Evidence from a Panel of UK Pension Funds, *Journal of Asset Management*, 6, 5–20.

Bodie, Z. (1990) Pensions as Retirement Income Insurance, *Journal of Economic Literature*, 28, 28–49, 75.

Bodie, Z., Merton, R., and Samuelson, W. (1992) Labour Supply Flexibility and Portfolio Choice in a Lifecycle Model, *Journal of Economic Dynamics and Control*, 16, 427–449.

Brinson, G. P., Hood, L. R., and Beebower, G. L. (1986) Determinants of Portfolio Performance, *Financial Analysts Journal*, July–August, 39–48.

Brinson, G., Singer, B., and Beebower, G. (1991) Determinants of Portfolio Performance II: An Update, *Financial Analysts Journal*, May–June, 40–48.

Brugiavini, A. (1993) Uncertainty Resolution and the Timing of Annuity Purchases, *Journal of Public Economics*, 50, 31–62.

Byrne, A., Harrison, D., and Blake, D. (2007) *Dealing with the Reluctant Investor: Innovation and Governance in DC Pension Investment*, Pensions Institute Report, London, April.

Cairns, A. J. G., Blake, D., and Dowd, K. (2006) Stochastic Lifestyling: Optimal Dynamic Asset Allocation for Defined Contribution Pension Plans, *Journal of Economic Dynamics & Control*, 30, 843–877.

Campbell, J., and Viceira, L. (1999) Consumption and Portfolio Decisions when Expected Returns Are Time-Varying, *Quarterly Journal of Economics*, 114, 433–495.

Campbell, J., and Viceira, L. (2002) *Strategic Asset Allocation: Portfolio Choice for Long-Term Investors*, Oxford University Press, Oxford.

Chacko, G., and Viceira, L. (2005) Dynamic Consumption and Portfolio Choice with Stochastic Volatility in Incomplete Markets, *Review of Financial Studies*, 18, 1369–1402.

Davidoff, T., Brown, J., and Diamond, P. (2005) Annuities and Individual Welfare, *American Economic Review*, 95, 1573–1590.

Fama, E., and French, K. (1988) Permanent and Temporary Components of Stock Prices, *Journal of Political Economy*, 96, 246–273.

Financial Literacy and Education Commission (2006) *Taking Ownership of the Future: The National Strategy for Financial Literacy 2006*, US Department of the Treasury, Washington, DC.

Frank, R., and Hutchens, R. (1993) Wages, Seniority and the Demand for Rising Consumption Sequences, *Journal of Economic Behavior and Organization*, 21, 251–276.

French, K., Schwert, G., and Stambaugh, R. (1987) Expected Stock Returns and Volatility, *Journal of Financial Economics*, 19, 3–29.

Ghysels, E., Harvey, A. C., and Renault, E. (1996) Stochastic Volatility, chapter 14 in Maddala, G., and Rao, C. (eds), *Handbook of Statistics*, Vol. 14, North-Holland, Amsterdam.

Gneezy, U, and Potters, J (1997) An Experiment on Risk Taking and Evaluation Periods, *Quarterly Journal of Economics*, 112, 631–645.

Gollier, C. (2004) Optimal Dynamic Portfolio Risk with First-Order and Second-Order Predictability, *Contributions to Theoretical Economics*, 4:1, Article 4, 1–33.

H M Treasury (2006) *The Annuities Market 2006*, H M Treasury, London.

Heaton, J., and Lucas, D. (2000) Portfolio Choice and Asset Prices: The Importance of Entrepreneurial Risk, *Journal of Finance*, 55, 1163–1198.

Horneff, W., Maurer, R., and Stamos, M. (2006a) Life-Cycle Asset Allocation with Annuity Markets: Is Longevity Insurance a Good Deal? Working Paper WP2006-146, Michigan Retirement Research Centre, December.

Horneff, W., Maurer, R., and Stamos, M. (2006b) Optimal Gradual Annuitization: Quantifying the Costs of Switching to Annuities, Working Paper, Goethe University, Frankfurt, April.

Horneff, W., Maurer, R., Mitchell, O., and Stamos, M. (2007) Money in Motion: Dynamic Portfolio Choice in Retirement, National Bureau of Economic Research Working Paper 12942, February.

Kahneman, D. (2003) The Psychology of Risky Choices, Address before the Investment Company Institute, May 2003, Washington, DC.

Kahneman, D. and Tversky, A. (1979) Prospect Theory: An Analysis of Decision Under Risk, *Econometrica*, 47, 263–291.

Kahneman, D., and Tversky, A. (1984) Choices, Values and Frames, *American Psychologist*, 39, 341–350.

Kahneman, D., and Tversky, A. (2000) *Choices, Values and Frames*, Russell Sage Foundation and Cambridge University Press, Cambridge, MA.

Keasey, K., Summers, B., Duxbury, D., and Hudson, R. (2006) Angst about Annuities? An Exploration of Individuals' Evaluations of Annuities, Leeds University Business School Working Paper.

Koijen, R., Nijman, T., and Werker, B. (2006) Dynamic Asset Allocation and Annuity Risk, Working Paper, Tilburg University, April.

Kosowski, R., Timmermann, A., Wermers, R., and White, H. (2006) Can Mutual Fund 'Stars' Really Pick Stocks? New Evidence from a Bootstrap Analysis, *Journal of Finance*, 61, 2551–2595.

Laibson, D. (1997) Golden Eggs and Hyperbolic Discounting, *Quarterly Journal of Economics*, 112, 443–478.

Laibson, D., Repetto, A., and Tobacman, J. (1998), Self Control and Saving for Retirement, *Brookings Papers on Economic Activity* I, 91–196.

Matsumo D., Peecher, M. E., and Rich, J. S., (2000) Evaluations of Outcome Sequences, *Organizational Behavior and Human Decision Processes*, 83, 331–352.

McGill, D., Brown, K., Haley, J., and Schieber, S. (2005) *Fundamentals of Private Pensions*, 8th ed., Oxford University Press, Oxford.

Merton, R. C. (1969) Lifetime Portfolio Selection under Uncertainty: The Continuous Time Case, *Review of Economics and Statistics*, 51, 247–257.

Merton, R. C. (1971) Optimum Consumption and Portfolio Rules in a Continuous Time Model, *Journal of Economic Theory*, 3, 373–413.

Merton, R. C. (1973) An Intertemporal Capital Asset Pricing Model, *Econometrica*, 41, 867–887.

Milevsky, M. (1998) Optimal Asset Allocation towards the End of the Life Cycle: To Annuitize or Not to Annuitize? *Journal of Risk and Insurance*, 65, 401–426.

Milevsky, M., and Young, V. (2002) Optimal Asset Allocation and the Real Option to Delay Annuitization: It's Not Now or Never, Working Paper, Schulich School of Business, York University, April.

Milevsky, M., and Young, V. (2007) Annuitization and Asset Allocation, *Journal of Economic Dynamics and Control*, 31, 3138-3177.

Mitchell, O., and Utkus, S. (2003) Company Stock and Retirement Plan Diversification, in Olivia S. Mitchell and Kent Smetters (eds.) *The Pension Challenge: Risk Transfers and Retirement Income Security*, Oxford University Press, Oxford, 81.

Mitchell, O., and Utkus, S. (eds.) (2004a) *Pension Design and Structure: New Lessons from Behavioural Finance*, Oxford University Press, Oxford.

Mitchell, O., and Utkus, S. (2004b) Lessons from Behavioural Finance for Retirement Plan Design, in Mitchell, O., and Utkus, S. (eds.), *Pension Design and Structure: New Lessons from Behavioural Finance*, Oxford University Press, Oxford.

OECD (2005) *Improving Financial Literacy: Principle, Programmes, Good Practices*, Organization for Economic Co-operation and Development, Paris.

Odean, T. (1998) Are Investors Reluctant to Realize Their Losses?, *Journal of Finance*, 53, 1775–1798.

Office of Fair Trading (1997) *Consumer Detriment under Conditions of Imperfect Information*, Research Paper 11, London.

Office of Fair Trading (1999) *Vulnerable Consumers and Financial Services*, Report 255, London.

Patel, J., Zeckhauser, R., and Hendricks, D. (1991) The Rationality Struggle: Illustrations from Financial Markets, *American Economic Review*, 81, 232–236.

Polkovnichenko, V. (2003) Household Portfolio Diversification, presentation at Rodney White Center for Financial Research conference on Household Portfolio Choice and Financial Decision-Making, March.

Poterba, J., and Summers, L. (1988) Mean Reversion in Stock Returns: Evidence and Implications, *Journal of Financial Economics*, 22, 27–60.

Rabin, M., and Thaler, R. (2001) Anomolies: Risk Aversion, *Journal of Economic Perspectives*, 15, 219–232.

Samuelson, P. A. (1969) Lifetime Portfolio Selection by Dynamic Stochastic Programming, *Review of Economics and Statistics*, 51, 239–246.

Selnow, G. (2004) Motivating Retirement Planning: Problems and Solutions, in Mitchell, O., and Utkus, S. (eds.). *Pension Design and Structure: New Lessons from Behavioural Finance*, Oxford University Press, Oxford.

Shefrin, H., and Statman, M. (1985) The Disposition to Sell Winners Too Early and Ride Losers Too Long: Theory and Evidence, *Journal of Finance*, 40, 777–790.

Siegel, J. (1997) *Stocks for the Long Term*. Richard D. Irwin, New York.

Stock, J., and Wise, D. (1990) Pensions, the Option Value of Work and Retirement, *Econometrica*, 58, 1151–1180.

Thaler, R. (1985) Mental Accounting and Consumer Choice, *Marketing Science*, 4, 199–214.

Thaler, R. (1999) Mental Accounting Matters, *Journal of Behavioural Decision Making*, 12, 183–206.

Thaler, R., and Bernartzi, S. (1999) Risk Aversion or Myopia? Choices in Repeated Gambles and Retirement Investments, *Management Science*, 45, 364–381.

Thaler, R., and Bernartzi, S. (2004) Save More Tomorrow: Using Behavioural Economics to Increase Employee Saving, *Journal of Political Economy*, 112, S164–S187.

Thaler, R. and Shefrin, H. (1981) An Economic Theory of Self-Control, *Journal of Political Economy*, 89, 392–406.

Thoresen, O. (2007) *Financial Capability: The Government's Long-term Approach*, H M Treasury, London.

Timmermann, A., and Blake, D. (2005) International Asset Allocation with Time-Varying Investment Opportunities, *Journal of Business*, 78, 71–98.

Tversky, A., and Kahneman, D., (1974) Judgment Under Uncertainty: Heuristics and Biases, *Science*,185, 1124–1131.

Vasicek, O. (1977) An Equilibrium Characterisation of the Term Structure, *Journal of Financial Economics*, 5, 177–188

Weber, E. (2004) Who's Afraid of a Poor Old Age? Risk Perception and Risk Management Decisions, in Mitchell, O., and Utkus, S. (eds.), *Pension Design and Structure: New Lessons from Behavioural Finance*, Oxford University Press, Oxford, 84.

Yaari, M. (1965) Uncertain Lifetime, Life Insurance, and the Theory of the Consumer, *Review of Economic Studies*, 32, 137–150.

11
Duration-Enhancing Overlay Strategies for Defined Benefit Pension Plans

John M. Mulvey, Woo Chang Kim and Yi Ma

11.1 Introduction

In many countries, there is a concern about demographic trends associated with providing adequate pensions to retired workers. For example, the work-force in Japan is expected to shrink from 84 million to 74 million, while the number of retirees will increase from 26 million to 36 million by 2030. In Europe, the population aged 65 years and older, as a ratio of the working-age population, will increase from 25 per cent in 2008 to 53 per cent in 2060. Given these headwinds, companies who sponsor pension trusts will benefit from improving their investment performance.

Subsequently, there has been a trend to modify defined benefit (DB) pension plans. First, pension plans have lost their surpluses since the 2001–2002 drop in equity markets and the commensurate decrease in interest rates. Second, changes in regulation in the United States have increased the penalty for pension deficits. Third, the bankruptcy of a number of large firms over the past few years has shown that traditional pension valuations may be too optimistic when a firm experiences financial distress.

In this article, we show that a specialized version of overlay strategies can help DB pensions to achieve their financial goals more efficiently. In addition to empirical tests using historical data, we adopt a forward-looking model under the asset liability management (ALM) framework[1] that integrates assets and liabilities in stochastic simulations.

11.2 Two approaches in core portfolio management for DB pension plans

In defined pension plans, liabilities can be understood as a form of a fixed-income security. Retirees are guaranteed to receive a pre-determined amount of money in the future from the pension plan. Therefore, a major source of risk involves the discount rate because of changes in interest rates. Thus, it is natural to construct the core portfolios (traditional assets such as equities and bonds) to hedge interest rate risks by matching duration of assets with liabilities. Owing to the nature of pensions, duration on liabilities is rather long. For instance, a typical pension plan possesses roughly 12.6 years duration.[2] Therefore, in order to match or immunize these liabilities, the core portfolios are mainly composed of long-term fixed-income securities, such as long-dated zero-coupon bonds. As mentioned, this type of conservative pension plan management scheme prioritizes duration matching (immunization) to replicate the future cash outflows, so the portfolios have usually higher weights on long-term bonds.

However, there is a downside to these conservative approaches. In particular, long-term bonds have lower expected returns than equities; therefore, these strategies will give rise to expected contributions from the sponsoring company. Historically, fixed-income securities have underperformed compared to other investment vehicles such as stocks, so the portfolios mainly formed with bonds would have lower returns. Thus, they are unlikely to provide high growth rate in the core portfolios enough to cover the growth in liabilities, which will force high contributions. With the changes in demographic trends of lower birth rates and extended life expectancies in most of the developed countries, poor performance in core assets will burden sponsoring companies more as time goes on. Further, there could be macro impacts on the economy if a large number of pension plans move their asset allocation to fixed-income categories. Considering the size of pension plans, for example, their concentration on the bond market will decrease returns.

In contrast to the conservative matching approaches, another approach puts more emphasis on the performance of the core portfolios. Under this framework, the core portfolios are mainly constructed with investment vehicles with relatively high performance, such as stocks, private equities, hedge funds and so on. Owing to higher expected performance, it could ease the burden of large future contributions by the sponsoring companies. However, as the core assets are less correlated to the liabilities as compared to the conservative approaches because of the duration mismatch, future contributions become more volatile. In other words, although the performance-oriented approach might reduce the contributions on average, the worst case over shorter time periods will be more significant to the sponsoring companies than that of the duration matching approach. The main source of risk arises from the shorter duration on core assets, as duration of non-fixed income securities is relatively short, if not zero.

11.3   Duration-enhancing overlay strategies

For large DB pensions, the traditional approach is to hire an outside manager, such as commodity trading advisor. The manager can develop and implement an overlay strategy. Herein, traditional assets in the core portfolio are employed as margin capital for targeted positions in the futures/forward markets. Overlay strategies have been popular with institutional investors in several areas including managing currencies. Mulvey *et al* (2006) and Mulvey *et al* (2007) show the benefits of general overlay strategies within asset allocation and ALM. These strategies seek to widen diversification of the portfolio, while generating higher growth rates. Popular strategies employ three general domains: commodities, fixed income and currencies. In each case, trading volume in the futures market is large enough so that investors can quickly rebalance the portfolio mix as conditions warrant.

Importantly, these types of overlay strategies must be implemented in conjunction with careful risk management. There are examples of organizations that experienced severe difficulties as they were either unaware of possible risks in their positions, or did not take adequate action to protect their capital. A prime example occurred in 1994 involving Orange County, California. The treasurer Edward Citron wished to increase returns for the county. He managed to take on a substantial bet on long-dated interest rates through swaps and related investments, and a short bet on short-term interest rates. The drop in his position in 1994 because of a structural shift in the yield curve was not foreseen. Subsequently, Orange County declared bankruptcy.

In this article, we focus on a specialized type of overlay called duration-enhancing overlay (DEO) in order to improve the performance of defined benefit pension plans. The basic idea is straightforward: it is a zero-investment strategy constructed by taking long future positions in long-dated treasury bonds, while taking opposite positions in shorter-term treasury securities.

Here, we evaluate the fixed-percentage DEO strategy. It provides a special case of the longstanding fixed-mix rule. The investor modifies her portfolio over time in order to enforce a constant percentage target. For example, an investor might select 75 per cent as a target for DEO. This investor will reset the portfolio values on a recurring basis. Fixed-mix rules have been shown to be optimal for long-term investors. For example, see the early work by Samuelson (1969) and Merton (1969); also see Fernholz and Shay (1982), Luenberger (1998) and Mulvey *et al* (2005).

The logic for employing DEO for DB pension plans is intuitive. Suppose the core portfolio is constructed from various investment vehicles and DEO will be employed in addition to the traditional assets. Then, the DEO strategy works similar to other levered investments, as long-term bonds will generally have higher returns than cash. Therefore, in traditional portfolio management contexts, the asset values can be written as in the following equation.

$$w_{t+1} = w_t \left[1 + \sum x_{i,t} r_{i,t} + x_{\text{DEO},t} r_{\text{DEO},t} \right],$$

where W_t: wealth at t; $x_{i,t}$: weight on asset i at t; $r_{i,t}$: return on asset i at t; $x_{\text{DEO},t}$: weight on DEO at t; $r_{\text{DEO},t}$: return on DEO at t.

As DEO is implemented independently to the core assets, the sum of the weights on core assets ($\sum x_{i,t}$) is 1. Under the performance-oriented approach, the effects of employing DEO depend on the trade-off between the diversification benefits from the low correlation between DEO and the core portfolio and increased risks because of the position on DEO, if the asset-only aspect is considered.

However, when the pension plan is considered as an integrated system of asset and liability, DEO can provide benefits beyond enhanced asset performance. The answer lies with increased duration. Assuming linearity, the duration of core assets with DEO is

$$D_{Asset,t} = \sum x_{i,t} D_{i,t} + x_{\text{DEO},t} D_{\text{DEO},t},$$

where $D_{Asset,t}$: duration of core assets at t; $x_{i,t}$: weight on asset i at t; $D_{i,t}$: duration on asset i at t; $x_{\text{DEO},t}$: weight on DEO at t; $D_{\text{DEO},t}$: duration on DEO at t.

In general,

$$D_{\text{DEO},t} \approx D_{LongBond,t} - D_{Cash,t} > 0.$$

As DEO adds duration to the asset portfolio, the performance pattern of core assets would become more similar to that of liabilities as the interest rate changes over time. This gives investors more room to invest in high performance securities with low duration while controlling exposure to the interest risk at a reasonable level. In the long run, the approach improves investment performance for long-term investors, causing healthier plans and lower contributions.

11.4   Empirical results with historical data

This section describes a set of empirical results of applying the specialized overlay strategy over the 26-year period (1982–2007). In particular, we evaluate the duration-based strategy presented in the previous section with a focus on potentials to extend the duration of core assets. To keep the discussion relatively simple, we focus on asset allocation decisions only and ignore contribution and payout decisions. The next section will take up the full pension plan environment.

To analyze the impact of the DEO strategies, we apply two standard fixed-mix rules: 60–40 (60 per cent equities and 40 per cent bonds) and 70–30 (70 per cent equities and 30 per cent bonds). We employ the S&P 500 index and the US 10-year government bond index as proxies for equities and bonds, respectively. Under the fixed-mix approach, the investor must rebalance her portfolio at the beginning of each period (monthly in our empirical tests) to the target percentages (60–40 or 70–30). Thus, stocks must be sold (bought) if they outperform (underperform) bonds over the previous time period. The Towers-Perrin liability index[3] is employed as a proxy on liabilities to replicate the long duration of the liability properly.[4] In addition, as mentioned, DEO is modeled by taking long position on 10-year bonds and short position on 3-month T-bills. Although DEO should be constructed within the futures market, we adopt spot returns on 10-year bonds and T-bills to keep the analysis relatively simple. See Table 11.1 for the performance of the six main ingredients.

Several points should be addressed in Table 11.1. First, although the historical performance of the two benchmark strategies (70–30 and 60–40) are good (Sharpe ratios above 0.6), they have relatively low correlations to the liabilities (0.537 and 0.459, respectively). When duration of core assets and liabilities are well matched, changes in their wealth because of a parallel shift in the yield

Table 11.1   Performance of the key strategies

	Liability	Equity	Bond	T-bill	60–40	70–30	DEO
Panel A: Asset-only performance measures							
Annual geometric mean return (%)	8.15	13.06	10.24	5.38	12.26	12.50	4.63
Volatility (%)	10.39	14.66	8.38	0.70	9.88	10.93	8.33
Maximal drawdown (%)	24.35	44.73	11.64	0.00	20.80	27.45	19.06
Sharpe ratio	0.267	0.524	0.584	NA	0.699	0.653	−0.090
Excess return/maximal drawdown	0.114	0.172	0.418	NA	0.331	0.259	−0.039
Panel B: Short-term risk measures							
Mean return for 5% worst month (%)	−5.81	−8.98	−4.09	0.08	−5.12	−6.03	−4.55
Mean return for 1% worst month (%)	−8.24	−14.00	−5.33	0.08	−7.56	−9.00	−5.77
Return for worst month (%)	−10.00	−21.53	−6.71	0.07	−10.45	−13.22	−6.79
Panel C: Relative performance measures							
Correlation to liability	1.000	0.284	0.840	0.043	0.537	0.459	0.841
Tracking error (%)	0.00	4.90	2.09	−2.77	4.11	4.35	−3.52
Std (tracking error) (%)	0.00	15.37	5.65	10.38	9.76	11.10	5.63
Information ratio	NA	0.319	0.370	−0.267	0.421	0.392	−0.625

Notes: The performance of liability, equity, bonds, 60/40, T-bills and DEO over the time period January 1982 − December 2007 is listed. The historical performance of the two benchmark strategies (70–30 and 60–40) is good (Sharpe ratios above 0.6), whereas their correlations to the liabilities are relatively low. On the other hand, the standalone performance of DEO has been moderate (Sharpe ratio: −0.09 and Information ratio: −0.625) and the level of risk exposure is relatively high, but the returns from DEO are highly correlated to the liabilities. Also, equities are the best performing assets (13 per cent per annum), yet one of the least correlated assets to liability (0.284). NA=Not applicable.

curve are similar. Thus, as the duration mismatch declines, asset returns and liability growth rates become more correlated. In this sense, the correlation between monthly returns of liabilities and strategies can be employed as an indirect measure for a level of duration matching. Therefore, low correlations between returns of benchmark strategies and liabilities imply that the conventional approaches have suffered from the short core portfolio duration. All of the investment vehicles employed in this section generally possess lower duration than liabilities. The main issue is to lengthen the core asset duration.

Next, as a standalone investment vehicle, the performance of DEO has been rather poor (Sharpe ratio: −0.09, Information ratio: −0.625), whereas the level of risk exposure is relatively high. Especially, short-term risk measures possess similar values to those of benchmark strategies. Nevertheless, the returns from DEO are highly correlated to the liabilities, implying that it could potentially be a useful tool to modify the return pattern and duration of the core portfolio. An important observation is that equities are the best performing asset (13 per cent per annum), yet one of the least correlated assets to liability (0.284). Therefore, the key to the successful DB pension plan management is to add duration while properly utilizing high performance assets, such as equities.

Table 11.2 depicts the summary statistics for benchmark strategies (Panel A: 60–40, Panel B: 70–30) after applying several levels of DEO (0–200 per cent). Note that weights on DEO are relative to the wealth on core assets. For instance, when 100 per cent DEO is employed, the investor should take a long position on the long-term bond worth the current core assets' wealth, and a short position on a T-bill worth the same amount. The portfolios of benchmark strategies and DEO are rebalanced at the beginning of every month to ensure the desired level of the DEO at every juncture.

Table 11.2 Performance of key strategies after applying DEO

DEO (%)	0	25	50	75	100	125	150	175	200
Panel A: 60–40									
1. Asset performance measures									
Annual return (%)	12.2	13.5	14.7	15.8	16.9	18.0	19.1	20.1	21.0
Volatility (%)	9.8	11.0	12.4	13.9	15.6	17.4	19.2	21.1	23.0
Maximal drawdown (%)	20.8	16.8	16.5	20.6	25.0	29.1	33.1	36.9	40.6
Sharpe ratio	0.69	0.73	0.75	0.75	0.74	0.73	0.71	0.69	0.68
Excess return/maximal drawdown	0.33	0.48	0.56	0.50	0.46	0.43	0.41	0.39	0.38
2. Short-term risk measures									
Return for 5% worst month (%)	−5.1	−5.4	−6.1	−6.9	−7.8	−8.9	−10.0	−11.1	−12.2
Return for 1% worst month (%)	−7.5	−7.6	−8.1	−9.0	−10.0	−11.2	−12.5	−13.8	−15.1
Return for worst month (%)	−10.4	−9.0	−8.8	−10.4	−12.1	−13.7	−15.3	−16.9	−18.6
3. Relative performance measures									
Correlation to liability	0.53	0.64	0.71	0.75	0.78	0.80	0.82	0.83	0.83
Tracking error (%)	4.1	5.3	6.5	7.7	8.8	9.9	10.9	11.9	12.9

Continued

Table 11.2 Continued

DEO (%)	0	25	50	75	100	125	150	175	200
Std (tracking error) (%)	9.7	9.0	8.8	9.1	9.8	10.9	12.2	13.7	15.3
Information ratio	0.42	0.58	0.73	0.84	0.89	0.91	0.89	0.87	0.84
Panel B: 70–30									
1. Asset performance measures									
Annual return (%)	12.5	13.7	14.9	16.1	17.3	18.4	19.4	20.4	21.4
Volatility (%)	10.9	11.8	13.0	14.4	16.0	17.6	19.4	21.2	23.0
Maximal drawdown (%)	27.4	23.4	19.6	20.1	24.4	28.6	32.6	36.4	40.1
Sharpe ratio	0.65	0.70	0.73	0.74	0.74	0.73	0.72	0.71	0.69
Excess return/maximal drawdown	0.25	0.35	0.48	0.53	0.48	0.45	0.43	0.41	0.40
2. Short-term risk measures									
Return for 5% worst month (%)	−6.0	−6.1	−6.5	−7.1	−8.0	−8.9	−9.9	−11.0	−12.1
Return for 1% worst month (%)	−9.0	−8.8	−9.1	−9.5	−10.4	−11.4	−12.5	−13.8	−15.0
Return for worst month (%)	−13.2	−11.7	−10.3	−10.4	−12.0	−13.7	−15.3	−16.9	−18.5
3. Relative performance measures									
Correlation to liability	0.45	0.57	0.65	0.71	0.75	0.78	0.80	0.81	0.82
Tracking error (%)	4.3	5.6	6.8	8.0	9.1	10.2	11.3	12.3	13.3
Std (tracking error) (%)	11.1	10.3	10.0	10.1	10.6	11.5	12.7	14.1	15.6
Information ratio	0.39	0.53	0.67	0.78	0.85	0.88	0.88	0.87	0.85

Notes: The summary statistics for benchmark strategies (Panel A: 60–40, Panel B: 70–30) after applying several levels of DEO (0–200 per cent) are illustrated. Applying DEO improves the correlation significantly, implying that it is a useful tool to increase the duration on core assets. However, it becomes less efficient after a certain level (100 per cent). As the DEO is employed more than 100 per cent level, the short-term risks increase significantly, whereas the performance enhancement is less so.

Indeed, adding the DEO increases correlations of core asset portfolios to the liability significantly. For instance, applying 100 per cent DEO improves the correlation from 0.54 to 0.79 for 60–40 and from 0.46 to 0.75 for 70–30. As the level of the DEO strategies increases, the returns and the information ratios get higher, in addition to the increment of correlations.

The test results also indicate that investors should be careful while applying DEO above a certain level. For instance, for the 70–30 strategy, the expected shortfall at 5 per cent level (mean return for 5 per cent worst month) increases only by 2 per cent for the first 100 per cent of DEO, but it is 4 per cent for the next 100 per cent. Also, the maximal drawdown gets even better when the DEO is employed up to 100 per cent, whereas it worsens significantly (24.5 per cent → 40 per cent) for the next 100 per cent. Note that the relative performance measures, such as correlations to liability, should be prioritized to asset-only measures, as the main issue in the DB pension plan management is to match the future out stream of the cash flows of the liability with the core assets. However, short-term risk measures should be carefully considered along with the relative measures to achieve investment goals. See Figure 11.1 for the trend of performance changes because of different levels of the DEO strategies.

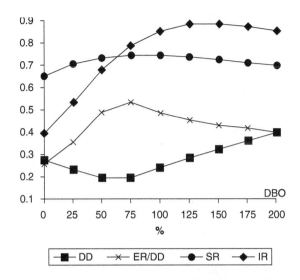

Figure 11.1 Comparisons on portfolio performance at different levels of DEO

Note: DD: maximal drawdown, ER: excess return, SR: Sharpe ratio, IR: information ratio. Several performance measures wi th different DEO levels are depicted. It illustrates that the DEO is an efficient investment tool only up to a certain level (100 per cent). When it is employed excessively, it increases risks more than performance.

The implications are clear. The DEO strategies can help pension plans to reduce their exposure to interest rate risk factors. However, they should be implemented only at a modest level (roughly up to 100 per cent) in order to avoid another Orange County incident.

11.5 Empirical results with a forward-looking scenario generator (cap:link)

Next, we evaluate the DEO strategies under the ALM context. The ALM models have been implemented in numerous pension and insurance studies (Dert, 1995; Peskin, 1997; Boender *et al*, 1998; Hilli *et al*, 2007; Ryan and Fabozzi, 2003; Ziemba, 2003; Olson, 2005; Mulvey *et al*, forthcoming). In these models, there are three basic ingredients: a system for generating future scenarios, a set of rules for significant decisions at each time period and an algorithm for selecting the best set of decisions.

We employ the CAP:Link scenario generator for the empirical tests. This system has been employed widely throughout the world over the past 15 years (Mulvey *et al*, 2000). The generator employs a cascade structure in which a set of economic factors are modeled at the highest level (interest rates, GDP and so on) with stochastic equations. Returns of assets are modeled as functions of

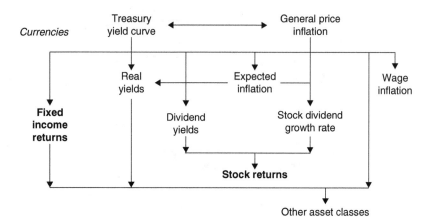

Figure 11.2   CAP:Link – cascade of stochastic processes

Note: The CAP:LINK system models the returns of assets as functions of economic factors at each time period under each scenario. Its cascade structure can guarantee a consistent relationship between interest rates and asset returns.

the economic factors at each time period for each scenario (Figure 11.2). This approach guarantees a consistent relationship between interest rates needed for discounting liabilities and asset returns, including bond categories.

We assume that the investment mix is rebalanced to a target asset mix at the beginning of each period. The fixed-mix rule has become a norm in the DB pension plan management domain. For instance, it is now common for large pension plans, such as Teachers Insurance and Annuity Association – College Retirement Equities Fund (TIAA-CREF), to rebalance portfolios back to the chosen weights at the client's requests. A simple and intuitive explanation on the benefits of the fixed-mix rules can be found in Luenberger (1998).

Let's assume that there are n stocks whose mean return is $r \in R^n$ and covariance matrix $\Sigma \in R^{n \times n}$. With a normality assumption, the return of the fixed-mix portfolio with weight w follows

$$N\left(w^T r + \frac{1}{2}\sum_{i=1}^{n} w_i \sigma_i^2, -\frac{1}{2}\sigma_p^2, \quad \sigma_p^2\right) \equiv N\left(w^T r + \frac{1}{2}\sum_{i=1}^{n} w_i \sigma_i^2 - \frac{1}{2}w^T \sum w, w^T \sum w\right).$$

The extra term in the expected return compared to the Markowitz model, $\frac{\sum_{i=1}^{n} w_i \sigma_i^2 - \sigma_p^2}{2}$, which is often called rebalancing gains or volatility pumping, illustrates the benefits of the fixed-mix rule. For simplicity, suppose all stocks have the same expected return (r) and volatility (σ), and the correlation is ρ for any given pair. Then, the rebalancing gain for an equal-weighted portfolio becomes

$$\frac{1}{2}\left\{ \sum_{i=1}^{n} \frac{1}{n}\sigma^2 - \left(\frac{1}{n}\cdots\frac{1}{n}\right)\Sigma\left(\frac{1}{n}\cdots\frac{1}{n}\right)^{T} \right\} = \frac{(n-1)\sigma^2(1-\rho)}{2n}.$$

whose value is always positive, unless all stocks are perfectly correlated.

The best decision variables are selected via multi-period optimization techniques. Given the set of scenarios generated from CAP:LINK and the fixed-mix rule, we optimize the multi-period portfolio models taking into account the initial investments and the rebalancing decisions at the beginning of each time period. In general, these models cannot be formulated as a convex program,[5] so we solve each problem several thousand times with different initial solutions.[6] This procedure is repeated with several risk aversion levels to generate efficient frontiers.

11.5.1 Data summary and problem settings

The number of the generated scenarios (paths) is equal to 500 for the empirical tests. In each scenario, annual returns for ten core assets with one DEO strategy are generated for the 10-year sample period. Liabilities and benefit payments are also generated accordingly. Table 11.3 summarizes the data generated by the CAP:LINK system.

Several points are noteworthy. First, compared to the historical data, the DEO strategy is modeled in a more conservative fashion. Its average return is a mere 1.3 per cent, whereas the historical return is almost four times greater (4.6 per cent). Also, the DEO risk measures (volatility: 3.5 per cent, drawdown: 11.6 per cent) are almost the half the historical values (volatility: 8.3 per cent, drawdown: 19.1 per cent). Next, expected annual returns of fixed income securities are lower than the liability growth rate (7.3 per cent) by 1.4–2.6 per cent, respectively. Equities (large-cap and mid-small cap stock indices) are the only asset class whose expected returns exceed the liability growth rate. However, non-fixed income securities are assumed to have zero duration causing relatively low correlations to the liabilities. The data generated by the CAP:LINK system reflect the current DB pension plan projections: high performance assets have shorter durations, and long duration assets have lower performance.

Regulatory issues are modeled to approximate actuarial practice. Each year, the sponsoring company must contribute a pre-determined amount of money to the pension plan under certain conditions. To replicate the current 6-year smoothing rule,[7] we adopt the following contribution rules[8]:

if $A \geq L\left(or\, FR \geq 1\right),$ then contribution $= 0,$

$$\textit{if } 0.8L \le A < L \left(\textit{or } 0.8 \le FR < 1\right), \text{then contribution} = \frac{L-A}{6}$$

$$\textit{if } A < 0.8L \left(\textit{or } FR < 0.8\right), \text{then contribution} = \left(0.8L - A\right) + \frac{0.2L}{6},$$

where A : asset; L : liability and FR : funding ratio $= \dfrac{A}{L}$

Also, we assume the following payout schedules.

1. Benefit payments are paid to retirees at the end of each year.
2. The contributions are made based on the Funding ratio (FR) right after benefit payments.
3. During the following year, the wealth will change according to performance.

Table 11.3 Summary statistics of data generated by CAP:LINK

Core asset classes (10 Assets)	Return (%)	Volatility (%)	Drawdown (%)	Duration	Correlation to liability
Panel A: Core assets and DEO strategies					
LB Agg. bond index	5.66	2.97	3.31	4.59	0.80
Long HQ bond	5.85	5.96	21.34	11.53	0.95
10-year tips	5.20	3.15	5.38	6.68	0.54
Large-cap stock index	8.20	12.81	28.61	0.00	0.40
Cash equivalent	4.33	3.80	0.00	0.25	−0.08
Hi-yield bond index	6.45	11.69	17.47	6.03	0.45
Real estate index	7.03	18.10	21.83	0.00	0.02
Mid-small stock index	8.20	17.22	39.03	0.00	0.34
25-year zero-coupon bond	4.68	12.59	79.01	25.00	0.87
10-year T-bond	5.28	3.69	10.53	8.00	0.81
Duration-based overlay Long-short (agg. bond − cash)	1.32	3.45	11.58	4.34	0.83
Net growth rate (%)	Benefit payments to outstanding liability (%)	Gross liability growth rate (%)	Duration		
Panel B: Liabilities					
1.19	6.06	7.26	12.13		

Notes: Summary statistics of the data generated from CAP:LINK are illustrated (Panel A: core assets and DEO, Panel B: liability). Compared to the historical data, the DEO strategy is modeled in a more conservative manner (return: 1.3 per cent, volatility: 3.5 per cent, drawdown: 11.6 per cent). In addition, expected annual returns of fixed-income securities are lower than the liability growth rate (7.3 per cent) by 1.4–2.6 per cent, respectively. The data generated by the CAP:LINK system reflect current issues of the DB pension plan management properly: high performance assets have shorter durations, and long duration assets have lower performance.

Table 11.4 List of performance-risk measures of ALM model

Performance measures	Associated risk measures
Expected return	Volatility, Drawdown, Semi-deviation and Expected Shortfall
Funding ratio (FR)	Volatility, Min FR, VaR, Expected Shortfall and Semi-deviation
Wealth	Volatility, VaR, Expected Shortfall and Semi-deviation
Surplus	Volatility, VaR, Expected Shortfall and Semi-deviation
Contribution	Volatility and Maximum Contribution
Economic value	Volatility, VaR, Expected Shortfall and Semi-deviation

The optimal asset allocations are obtained by solving the following types of optimization problems.[9]

Maximize

$$W\left(x_{asset}, x_{\mathrm{DEO}}\right) - \lambda R\left(x_{asset}, x_{\mathrm{DEO}}\right)$$

subject to $\quad 0 \le x_{\mathrm{DEO}} \le \gamma x_{asset} \ge 0$

where W: performance measures; R: risk measures; $x$asset: fixed-mix weights on core assets; x_{DEO}: fixed-mix weight on DEO; λ: risk-aversion factor and γ: maximum DEO.

Several popular performance and risk measures are employed for W and R (Table 11.4). Efficient frontiers are generated by changing values of λ, and the effect of DEO is evaluated by observing its outcomes with different values of γ.

11.5.2 Applying DEO strategies within an ALM model

To illustrate the advantages of DEO, we provide an example of the ALM models with typical conditions of current DB pension plans in the United States. The plan is assumed to be modestly underfunded at the beginning of the sample period (initial FR = 0.9). The objective is to maximize the economic value at the end of the horizon ($T = 10$), while controlling the risk of the worst cases. Thus, the ALM model is formulated as follows:

Maximize $\quad$ Econ val$\left(x_{asset}, x_{DEO}\right) - \lambda \cdot ES_{5\%}\left(\text{Econ val}\left(x_{asset}, x_{DEO}\right)\right)$

subject to $\quad 0 \le x_{DEO} \le \gamma x_{asset} \ge 0$

where EconVal = Present value (Final surplus − Total contributions); $ES_{5\%}(\cdot)$ = Expected shortfall at 5 per cent level.

Economic value provides a natural objective function for a DB pension plan. It combines the health of the plan and the level of contribution over the planning horizon. Owing to the wide set of stakeholders, there are numerous other objective functions for a DB pension plan. Appendix B lists the impact of DEO on several of these objectives. In a similar fashion, DEO strategies improve the overall performance.

By maximizing the economic values, we can achieve a healthier plan while reducing excessive contributions to sponsoring companies. Also, as the expected shortfall of the economic value is penalized, the decision rules tend to be more conservative, causing more robust outcomes. Six different levels of maximal DEO (γ =0, 50, 100, 150, 200 and 250 per cent) are employed to evaluate its effects.

The outcomes from the model are depicted in Figure 11.3 and Table 11.5. Indeed, introducing DEO improves performance for the investors possessing long-term goals. As the allowed level of DEO strategies increases, the efficient frontiers in Figure 11.3 shift to north-west, implying that it is the dominant strategy to apply the DEO. Also, other performance measures can be enhanced

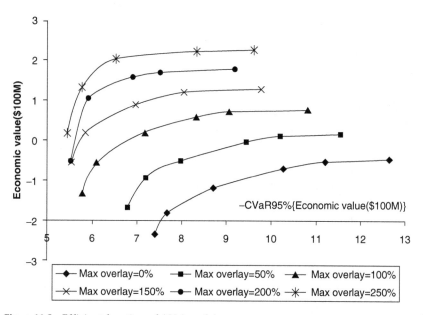

Figure 11.3   Efficient frontiers of ALM models

Note: An example of ALM models with different levels of DEO strategies (0–250 per cent) is illustrated. The economic value (Final Surplus – Total Contributions) and its expected shortfall at 95 per cent level are employed as the performance-risk measure pair. Numbers in red next to the points on efficient frontiers are the duration match ratios. Consistent with the historical test results, applying 100–150 per cent of DEO can increase the duration of core assets enough to match that of the liability.

Table 11.5 Performance-risk measures of ALM models

DM (%)	Max overlay=0%				Max overlay=100%				Max overlay=200%			
	← aggressive conservative →				← aggressive conservative →				← aggressive conservative →			
	−100	−38	−7	13	−47	−12	26	35	13	3	37	37
Investment on assets (%)												
E[R]	8.2	8	7.5	7.1	9.3	9.1	8.5	7.9	10.2	10.3	9.8	8.6
Vol	20.2	16.9	17.9	19.2	22.3	19.6	20.5	20.1	25.1	21	21.6	19.6
DD	38.1	26.2	28.9	33.4	40.5	32.6	36.5	36	49.5	35.3	39.2	33.9
SD	13.7	11.4	11.7	12.3	15.1	13.3	13.6	13.1	17.1	14.5	14.7	13
Funding ratio (%)												
FR	141	113	103	98	149	125	113	105	158	144	133	112
Vol	69	32	21	16	69	37	25	19	72	51	40	23
VaR95%	76	79	80	79	79	81	83	82	83	84	84	83
ES95%	68	74	75	75	71	75	76	77	73	75	76	78
SD	35	17	11	9	36	21	15	11	39	30	24	14
Min FR	77	82	83	82	79	83	84	84	80	83	84	85
Contribution ($100 million)												
Ctbn	3.07	2.04	1.91	2.02	2.48	1.66	1.53	1.58	2.12	1.53	1.43	1.38
Vol	2.89	1.72	1.39	1.24	2.43	1.48	1.16	1.01	2.11	1.48	1.27	1.01
Max	1.45	0.81	0.67	0.66	1.19	0.73	0.62	0.57	1.09	0.76	0.69	0.54
Wealth ($100 million)												
Wealth	27.6	22.3	20.6	19.6	29.3	24.7	22.6	20.9	31.4	28.4	26.4	22.2
Vol	13.4	7.4	6.3	5.8	14.7	9	7.4	6.3	16.2	11.4	9.9	6.8
VaR95%	11.7	12.1	11.6	11	12.5	12.8	12.1	11.8	13.3	13.9	13.3	12.6
ES95%	10.3	10.7	9.8	9.2	10.8	11	9.9	9.4	10.9	11.7	11	10
SD	7.4	4.7	4.1	3.9	8.1	5.6	4.8	4.2	9.1	7	6.2	4.5
Surplus ($100 million)												
Surplus	3.4	1	0.1	−0.3	4.2	2.1	1	0.3	5.2	3.8	2.8	0.9
Vol	5.7	2.5	1.7	1.4	6.1	3.2	2.2	1.6	6.7	4.4	3.5	2
Economic value ($100 million)												
EV	−0.4	−1.2	−1.8	−2.3	0.8	0.2	−0.5	−1.3	1.8	1.6	1.1	−0.5
Vol	5.8	3.3	2.6	2.2	5.6	3.5	2.7	2.2	5.5	4.1	3.5	2.5
VaR95%	−10.0	−6.9	−6.3	−5.9	−8.2	−5.7	−5.0	−4.9	−6.9	−5.2	−4.6	−4.6
ES95%	−12.6	−8.7	−7.7	−7.4	−10.8	−7.2	−6.1	−5.8	−9.2	−6.9	−5.9	−5.5

Abbreviations: DM: Duration matching ratio; E[R]: Expected return; FR: Funding ratio; Ctbn: Contribution; Vol: Volatility; DD: Max drawdown; SD: Semi-deviation.

by the DEO (Table 11.5). For instance, as the risk tolerance parameter becomes higher, the final FR increases significantly without causing the rising volatility of the FR.

Another important feature is the increasing weighted duration match ratio (DM). The weighed DM ratio is defined as follows:

$$DM\left(x_{asset}, x_{DEO}\right) = \frac{\text{Funding ratio} \times D_{asset} - D_{liability}}{D_{liability}}$$

As the change of fixed-income security returns because of a parallel yield curve shift is $-$Duration$\cdot\Delta$ Yield, the change in wealth is $-$Duration$\cdot\Delta$ Yield$\cdot$Wealth. Thus, by controlling DM close to 0, investors can make the change in the total wealth of the core assets from yield changes similar to that of the liability. Similarly, they can control the volatilities on the contributions, which is an importance risk measure for the sponsoring companies.

As pensions adopting the ALM framework typically suffer from short duration on their core portfolios than liabilities, their main issue is to increase DM. The test results indicate that DEO could increase DM without compromising other performance measures. When reasonably conservative risk aversion factors are adopted, the DM values of core assets with 100 per cent to 150 per cent of DEO are similar to or greater than that of liability (Table 11.5). It is consistent with the historical test results provided in the previous section; a modest level of DEO strategies can significantly add duration to the core assets. See Appendix B2, B4 and B5 for ALM models that constrain DM explicitly in the problem formulation.

The DEO strategies can help ALM models under many circumstances, yet the details can vary greatly. Also, the CAP:LINK system is designed for long-term risk management. Thus, short-term risk exposures from sharp yield curve changes are not addressed as the system focuses mainly on the long-term investment analytics. As mentioned, the historical data show that an excessive use of DEO can lead to undesirable consequences, especially over short-time periods. Therefore, careful analysis procedures should be preceded before implementation. See Appendix B for more test results with different risk measures and settings.

11.6   Conclusions and future research

We have shown that for investors possessing a set of long-term liabilities and future contributions such as DB pension plans, there is much to gain by implementing specialized overlay strategies (in careful doses). Both the empirical evidence with historical returns and forward-looking tests illustrate the advantages of these concepts. The added duration reduces contribution risks, whereas it increases expected portfolio performance.

What are possible next steps? First, in order to distinguish the effects of DEO from the traditional leverage, the ALM model should consider the practical issues upon implementing them, such as fees for leverage, limits on overlay based on the core portfolio characteristics and so on. Although the traditional leverage could be less efficient because of the liquidity and the transaction costs, it would be meaningful to identify the usefulness of DEO over the leverage.

Second, short-term effects of DEO should be more carefully analyzed. The main weakness comes from the potential disruption of core asset performance because of the yield curve changes, which typically occurs in relatively short time periods, so further analysis via high-frequency data is essential. The recent turmoil in the global financial market could provide a good data source for the empirical tests. Ideally, a dynamic strategy can be developed to improve both short-term and long-term results. To this end, the investor must be able to execute the overlay strategy in a timely fashion. Other duration enhancing strategies should be evaluated beyond the fixed-mix and duration matching rules, which have been tested in this report.

Another topic involves combining the duration-based strategy with overlays in other domains, for example commodities and currencies. Previous research has shown the advantages of diverse overlays (Mulvey *et al*, 2007). The goal in these studies is to improve risk-adjusted performance by increasing diversification for the asset portfolios and the ALM portfolios. Wide diversification can lead to higher returns, especially for long-term investors. Again, it is important to implement the strategies with highly liquid assets so that rebalancing can be accomplished efficaciously in concert with careful risk management.

Notes

1. See Consigli and Dempster (1998), Mulvey and Ziemba (1998), Muralidhar and van der Wouden (1999), Ziemba (2003), Fabozzi *et al* (2004) and Zenios and Ziemba (2006).
2. Towers-Perrin liability index has a duration of 12.6 years.
3. For the period of 1982–2000, the liability growth rates are extrapolated based on the Towers-Perrin liability construction rules. Growth rates for 2001–2007 are directed obtained from the Towers-Perrin liability index.
4. We also conduct the same tests employing the 30-year government bond index as a different proxy for the liability. The tests yield similar results as the tests with Towers-Perrin liability index (see Appendix A).
5. Two issues arise upon formulating the model into a convex problem. First, as we employ the fixed-mix rule under multi-period setting ($n=5$, 10), the final wealth becomes a polynomial of order n, which is a non-convex function. Second, most of the problems include constraints related to funding ratio. As it is defined as the ratio of wealth to outstanding liability, the problems become non-convex.
6. We employ OptQuest as the solver, which is embedded in the Crystal Ball software package.
7. When the funding ratio falls below a threshold level, the sponsoring company is generally obliged to make contributions to make up for the deficit within the following 6-year period.
8. This is to ensure that the funding ratio is always above 0.8.
9. In most cases, DB pension plans do not take short positions on core assets except via hedge funds and related asset categories.

References

Boender, G.E.C., van Aalst, P.C. and Heemskerk, F. (1998) Modelling and management of assets and liabilities of pension plans in the Netherlands. In: W.T. Ziemba and J.M. Mulvey (eds.) *Worldwide Asset and Liability Modeling.* UK: Cambridge University Press, pp. 561–580.

Consigli, G. and Dempster, M.A.H. (1998) Dynamic stochastic programming for asset-liability management. *Annals of Operations Research* 81: 131–162.

Dert, C.L. (1995) Asset liability management for pension funds. PhD thesis, Erasmus University, Rotterdam, the Netherlands.

Fabozzi, F.J., Focardi, S. and Jonas, C. (2004) Can Modeling Help Deal with the Pension Funding Crisis? The Intertek Group. Working Paper.

Fernholz, R. and Shay, B. (1982) Stochastic portfolio theory and stock market equilibrium. *The Journal of Finance* 37: 615–624.

Hilli, P., Koivu, M., Pennanen, T. and Ranne, A. (2007) A stochastic programming model for asset liability management of a Finnish pension company. *Annals of Operations Research* 152(1): 115–139.

Luenberger, D. (1998) *Investment Science.* New York: Oxford University Press.

Merton, R.C. (1969) Lifetime portfolio selection under uncertainty: The continuous-time case. *Review of Economics Statistics* 51: 247–257.

Mulvey, J.M. and Ziemba, W. (1998) Asset and liability management systems for long-term investors. In: W.T. Ziemba and J.M. Mulvey (eds.) *Worldwide Asset and Liability Modeling.* UK: Cambridge University Press, pp. 3–38.

Mulvey, J.M., Gould, G. and Morgan, C. (2000) An asset and liability management system for towers Perrin-Tillinghast. *Interfaces* 30: 96–114.

Mulvey, J.M., Simsek, K. and Zhang, Z. (2006) Improving investment performance for pension plans. *Journal of Asset Management* 7: 99–108.

Mulvey, J.M., Ural, C. and Zhang, Z. (2007) Improving performance for long-term investors: Wide diversification, leverage, and overlay strategies. *Quantitative Finance* 7: 175–187.

Mulvey, J.M., Simsek, K., Zhang, Z. and Fabozzi, F. (2008) Assisting defined-benefit pension plans. *Operations Research* 56(5): 1066–1078.

Mulvey, J.M., Fabozzi, F.J., Pauling, B., Simsek, K.D. and Zhang, Z. (2005a) Modernizing the defined-benefit pension system. *Journal of Portfolio Management* 31: 73–82.

Muralidhar, A.S. and van der Wouden, R.J.P. (1999) Optimal ALM strategies for defined benefit pension plans. *The Journal of Risk* 2(2): 47–69.

Olson, R.L. (2005) *The School of Hard Knocks: The Evolution of Pension Investing at Eastman Kodak.* Rochester, NY: RIT Cary Graphic Arts Press.

Peskin, M.W. (1997) Asset allocation and funding policy for corporate-sponsored defined-benefit pension plans. *Journal of Portfolio Management* 23: 66–73.

Ryan, R. and Fabozzi, F.J. (2003) Pension fund crisis revealed. *Journal of Investing* 12: 43–48.

Samuelson, P.A. (1969) Lifetime portfolio selection by dynamic stochastic programming. *Review of Economics Statistics* 51: 239–246.

Zenios, S.A. and Ziemba, W.T. (2006) *Handbook of Asset and Liability Modeling.* Amsterdam, the Netherlands: North-Holland.

Ziemba, W.T. (2003) *The Stochastic Programming Approach to Asset-liability and Wealth Management.* AIMR-Blackwell.

Appendix A

Test results with 30-year government bond index as a proxy for liabilities

See Tables 11A1–11A3.

Table 11.A1 Performance of key strategies over 1982–2007 with 30-year bond index as liability

	Liability	Equity	Bond	Tbill	60–40	70–30	DEO
1. Asset-only performance measures							
Annual return (%)	10.02	13.06	10.24	5.38	12.26	12.50	4.63
Volatility(%)	11.13	14.66	8.38	0.70	9.88	10.93	8.33
Maximal drawdown(%)	18.44	44.73	11.64	0.00	20.80	27.45	19.06
Sharpe ratio	0.418	0.524	0.584	N/A	0.699	0.653	−0.090
Excess return/drawdown	0.252	0.172	0.418	N/A	0.331	0.259	−0.039
2. Short-term risk measures							
Expected shortfall at 5% level (%)	−5.84	−8.98	−4.09	0.08	−5.12	−6.03	−4.55
Expected shortfall at 1% level (%)	−7.69	−14.00	−5.33	0.08	−7.56	−9.00	−5.77
Return for worst month (%)	−10.99	−21.53	−6.71	0.07	−10.45	−13.22	−6.79
3. Relative performance measures							
Correlation to liability	1.000	0.159	0.947	0.065	0.462	0.367	0.947
Tracking error (%)	0.00	3.03	0.22	−4.64	2.24	2.48	−5.39
Std (tracking error) (%)	0.00	16.94	4.19	11.11	10.95	12.42	4.21
Information ratio	NA	0.179	0.052	−0.418	0.204	0.200	−1.280

NA: Not applicable.

Table 11.A2 Performance of 60–40 strategies after applying DEO with 30-year bond index as liability

DEO (%)	0	25	50	75	100	125	150	175	200
1. Asset performance measures									
Annual return (%)	12.2	13.5	14.7	15.8	16.9	18.0	19.1	20.1	21.0
Volatility (%)	9.8	11.0	12.4	13.9	15.6	17.4	19.2	21.1	23.0
Maximal drawdown (%)	20.8	16.8	16.5	20.6	25.0	29.1	33.1	36.9	40.6
Sharpe ratio	0.69	0.73	0.75	0.75	0.74	0.73	0.71	0.69	0.68
Excess return/maximal drawdown	0.33	0.48	0.56	0.50	0.46	0.43	0.41	0.39	0.38
2. Short-term risk measures									
Return for 5% worst month (%)	−5.1	−5.4	−6.1	−6.9	−7.8	−8.9	−10.0	−11.1	−12.2
Return for 1% worst month (%)	−7.5	−7.6	−8.1	−9.0	−10.0	−11.2	−12.5	−13.8	−15.1
Return for worst month (%)	−10.5	−9.0	−8.8	−10.4	−12.1	−13.7	−15.3	−16.9	−18.6
3. Relative performance measures									
Correlation to liability	0.46	0.54	0.68	0.75	0.79	0.82	0.85	0.87	0.88
Tracking error (%)	2.2	3.4	4.6	5.8	6.9	8.0	9.0	10.1	11.0
Std (tracking error) (%)	10.9	9.9	9.3	9.2	9.5	10.2	11.3	12.6	14.2
Information ratio	0.20	0.34	0.49	0.63	0.72	0.78	0.80	0.79	0.77

Table 11.A3 Performance of 70–30 strategies after applying DEO with 30-year bond index as liability

DEO (%)	0	25	50	75	100	125	150	175	200
1. Asset performance measures									
Annual return (%)	12.5	13.7	14.9	16.1	17.3	18.4	19.4	20.4	21.4
Volatility (%)	10.9	11.8	13.0	14.4	16.0	17.6	19.4	21.2	23.0
Maximal drawdown (%)	27.4	23.4	19.6	20.1	24.4	28.6	32.6	36.4	40.1
Sharpe ratio	0.65	0.70	0.73	0.74	0.74	0.73	0.72	0.71	0.69
Excess return/maximal drawdown	0.25	0.35	0.48	0.53	0.48	0.45	0.43	0.41	0.40
2. Short-term risk measures									
Return for 5% worst month (%)	−6.0	−6.1	−6.5	−7.1	−8.0	−8.9	−9.9	−11.0	−12.1
Return for 1% worst month (%)	−9.0	−8.8	−9.1	−9.5	−10.4	−11.4	−12.5	−13.8	−15.0
Return for worst month (%)	−13.2	−11.7	−10.3	−10.4	−12.0	−13.7	−15.3	−16.9	−18.5
3. Relative performance measures									
Correlation to liability	0.36	0.50	0.60	0.68	0.74	0.78	0.81	0.84	0.85
Tracking error (%)	2.4	3.7	4.9	6.1	7.2	8.3	9.4	10.4	11.4
Std (tracking error) (%)	12.4	11.4	10.8	10.5	10.7	11.2	12.1	13.3	14.6
Information ratio	0.20	0.32	0.45	0.57	0.67	0.74	0.77	0.78	0.78

Appendix B

Additional results on empirical tests with ALM models

We discuss the positive effects of DEO using various performance-risk measures. The main results indicate that employing a moderate level of DEO can improve the perform-ance-risk trade-off as in 'Empirical results with a forward-looking scenario generator (CAP:Link)' section.

Importantly, institutional managers tend to focus on short-term performance as their performance is evaluated based on short- to mid-term investment outcomes, although the ultimate objective is to achieve long-term goals. Therefore, in order to ensure a suc-cessful implementation of DEO in practice, it is imperative to examine the investment outcomes with a shorter time horizon as well. Fortunately, the test results show that one can still achieve superior investment performance by applying a moderate level of DEO for a shorter time horizon ($T = 5$).

Additional ALM model (1)

The return and the volatility of core assets are employed as the performance-risk meas-ure pair. Numbers in red next to the points on efficient frontiers are the DM values (see Figure 11B1 and Table 11B1).

Additional ALM model (2)

The return and the volatility of core assets are employed as the performance-risk meas-ure pair. A constraint on duration matching ratio is introduced (DM≥0.9). Numbers in red next to the points on efficient frontiers are the DM values (see Figure 11B2 and Table 11B2).

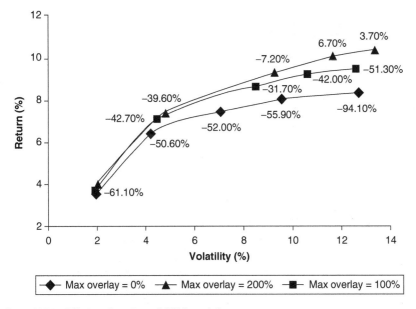

Figure 11.B1 Efficient frontiers of ALM models

Table 11.B1 Performance-risk measures for ALM models

	Max overlay=0%				Max overlay=100%				Max overlay=200%			
	← aggressive conservative→				← aggressive conservative →				← aggressive conservative →			
Investment on assets (%)												
E[R]	8.3	7.4	6.4	3.6	9.5	8.6	7.1	3.6	10.3	9.2	7.4	4
Vol	16	11.8	8.4	4.4	17.4	13.8	9	3.9	20	15.8	9.9	4.5
DD	24.4	13.4	7.3	3.5	25.2	16.9	8.1	2.3	31.8	21.6	9.7	2.9
SD	11	8	5.7	3	12	9.5	6.1	2.6	13.8	10.9	6.7	3
Funding ratio (%)												
FR	128	104	95	87	136	115	99	88	145	121	101	88
Vol	54	34	27	19	54	35	24	19	55	34	24	19
VaR$_{95\%}$	77	78	77	72	79	81	79	71	82	81	79	72
ES$_{95\%}$	71	75	75	69	74	76	76	68	75	78	76	69
SD	26	13	9	7	28	17	10	8	31	19	11	8
Min FR	80	84	82	74	82	85	83	74	83	85	84	75
Contribution ($100 million)												
Ctbn	2.46	1.97	2.51	4.97	1.85	1.53	2.10	4.93	1.52	1.34	1.95	4.57
Vol	2.29	1.57	1.70	2.56	1.82	1.35	1.56	2.61	1.50	1.17	1.50	2.53
Max	1.14	0.62	0.72	1.58	0.85	0.55	0.65	1.62	0.72	0.51	0.58	1.49

Continued

Table 11.B1   Continued

	Max overlay=0% ← aggressive conservative→				Max overlay=100% ← aggressive conservative →				Max overlay=200% ← aggressive conservative →			
Wealth ($100 million)												
Wealth	24.9	20	18.4	17.1	26.5	22.3	19.2	17.2	28.4	23.6	19.5	17.3
Vol	9.2	4.8	3.9	4.2	10	6	3.9	4.2	11.6	6.8	3.9	4.2
VaR$_{95\%}$	13.1	13.1	12.9	10.8	13.3	13.7	13.6	10.8	13.8	14	13.8	11.2
ES$_{95\%}$	11.2	11.8	11.9	10	11.8	12.4	12.5	10.2	11.8	12	12.6	10.5
SD	5.6	3.1	2.5	2.8	6	3.9	2.6	2.8	7	4.4	2.6	2.7
Surplus ($100 million)												
Surplus	2.1	−0.1	−0.9	−1.5	2.9	0.9	−0.5	−1.4	3.8	1.5	−0.4	−1.4
Vol	3.7	1.7	1.3	1.3	4.1	2.2	1.4	1.3	4.6	2.5	1.5	1.3
Economic value ($100 million)												
EV	−0.7	−2.1	−3.4	−6.5	0.5	−0.7	−2.6	−6.4	1.6	0.1	−2.3	−6.0
Vol	4.4	2.9	2.7	3.4	4.3	3.0	2.7	3.5	4.2	3.1	2.7	3.4
VaR$_{95\%}$	−8.0	−6.9	−8.1	−12.0	−6.8	−5.7	−7.2	−12.2	−5.5	−4.9	−7.0	−11.6
ES$_{95\%}$	−10.6	−8.6	−9.9	−14.7	−8.8	−7.4	−9.2	−14.8	−7.4	−6.5	−8.9	−14.2

Abbreviations: E[R]: Expected return; FR: Funding ratio; Ctbn: Contribution; Vol: Volatility; DD: Max drawdown; SD: Semi-deviation.

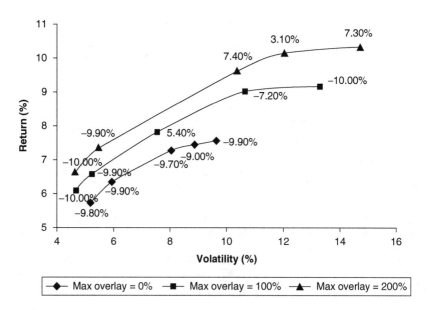

Figure 11.B2   Efficient frontiers of ALM models

Table 11.B2 Performance-risk measures for ALM models

	Max overlay=0%				Max overlay=100%				Max overlay=200%			
	← aggressive conservative →				← aggressive conservative →				← aggressive conservative →			
Investment on assets (%)												
E[R]	7.6	7.3	6.3	5.7	9.2	7.8	6.6	6.1	10.3	9.6	7.4	6.7
Vol	17.7	16.1	13.2	12.5	20.3	15	11.9	11.5	20.7	17.1	12	11.1
DD	28.5	23.7	17.4	16.9	34	20.8	14.5	14.5	33.6	24.9	14.8	13.5
SD	11.6	10.4	8.5	8.1	13.7	9.9	7.8	7.6	14.1	11.8	8.2	7.5
Funding ratio (%)												
FR	104	98	91	87	131	102	92	90	150	127	98	95
Vol	21	18	12	11	45	20	15	11	65	37	17	15
VaR$_{95\%}$	79	80	78	77	80	80	79	77	81	82	80	78
ES$_{95\%}$	75	77	76	75	75	77	76	74	74	78	77	75
SD	12	9	6	5	25	11	7	6	35	22	9	8
Min FR	83	84	83	82	82	86	84	82	82	85	85	82
Contribution ($100 million)												
Ctbn	1.83	1.78	2.26	2.67	1.84	1.57	2.17	2.51	1.72	1.31	1.79	2.27
Vol	1.34	1.17	1.23	1.35	1.74	1.13	1.29	1.37	1.75	1.17	1.21	1.44
Max	0.64	0.49	0.53	0.56	0.82	0.44	0.51	0.63	0.81	0.54	0.50	0.67
Wealth ($100 million)												
Wealth	20.6	19.4	17.9	17.3	25.9	20.1	18.1	17.7	29.4	24.8	19.2	18.6
Vol	6.3	5.2	4.5	4.2	10.4	5.1	4.2	4.2	13.2	8	4.3	4.2
VaR$_{95\%}$	11.6	11.5	11	11.3	13	12.7	11.8	11.7	13.8	13.7	12.9	12.5
ES$_{95\%}$	9.9	10.1	9.5	9.4	11	10.4	10.2	9.7	11.5	11.8	11.1	10.7
SD	4.1	3.5	3	2.8	6.2	3.4	2.8	2.8	7.6	5.1	2.9	2.8
Surplus ($100 million)												
Surplus	0.2	−0.4	−1.1	−1.4	2.6	−0.1	−1	−1.2	4.2	2.1	−0.5	−0.8
Vol	1.8	1.4	1	1	4	1.6	1.1	1.1	5.5	2.9	1.3	1.3
Economic value ($100 million)												
EV	−1.7	−2.2	−3.3	−4.1	0.4	−1.7	−3.2	−3.7	1.6	0.6	−2.3	−3.1
Vol	2.6	2.2	2.1	2.2	4.2	2.4	2.2	2.2	4.8	3.2	2.3	2.4
VaR$_{95\%}$	−6.0	−6.0	−6.6	−7.5	−6.3	−5.5	−6.8	−7.5	−6.3	−4.6	−5.9	−6.9
ES$_{95\%}$	−7.4	−7.4	−8.4	−9.4	−8.4	−7.2	−8.7	−9.4	−8.6	−6.2	−7.9	−9.2

Abbreviations: E[R]: Expected return; FR: Funding ratio; Ctbn: Contribution; Vol: Volatility; DD: Max drawdown; SD: Semi-deviation.

Additional ALM model (3)

The funding ratio and its volatility are employed as the performance-risk measure pair. Numbers in red next to the points on efficient frontiers are the DM values (see Figure 11B3 and Table 11B3).

Additional ALM model (4)

The funding ratio and its volatility are employed as the performance-risk measure pair. A constraint on duration matching ratio is introduced (DM ≥ 0.9). Numbers in red next to the points on efficient frontiers are the DM values (see Figure 11B4 and Table 11B4).

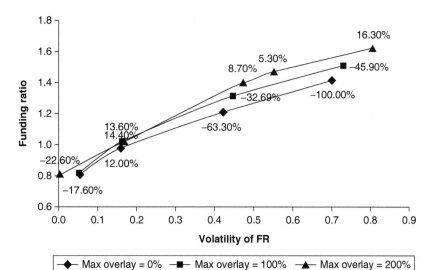

Figure 11.B3   Efficient frontiers of ALM models

Table 11.B3   Performance-risk measures for ALM models

	Max overlay=0%				Max overlay=100%				Max overlay=200%			
	← aggressive conservative →				← aggressive conservative →				← aggressive conservative →			
Investment on assets (%)												
E[R]	8.2	8.2	7.1	2.4	9.3	9.3	7.8	3.3	10.1	10.1	7.9	2.6
Vol	20.5	16.9	19	11.4	22.8	19.7	17.5	12.2	26.1	21.4	17.3	10.8
DD	39	26.5	33	24	42.5	32.7	27.8	24.2	53.5	37.4	27.2	22.3
SD	13.9	11.6	12.2	7.2	15.5	13.5	11.6	7.9	17.7	14.8	11.5	7.1
Funding ratio (%)												
FR	142	121	98	81	151	132	102	82	163	140	103	81
Vol	70	42	16	5	73	45	16	5	81	47	17	5
VaR$_{95\%}$	75	78	79	74	78	80	81	75	80	83	82	74
ES$_{95\%}$	67	72	75	72	70	74	78	74	72	75	78	73
SD	36	22	9	3	38	25	10	3	42	28	10	3
Min FR	77	81	82	76	79	82	85	78	79	83	85	76
Contribution ($100 million)												
Ctbn	3.14	2.20	1.93	5.67	2.59	1.83	1.52	4.81	2.35	1.54	1.49	5.52
Vol	3.00	2.01	1.13	2.10	2.58	1.71	1.00	1.95	2.37	1.44	0.99	2.25
Max	1.49	0.97	0.62	1.18	1.25	0.84	0.48	0.96	1.20	0.76	0.47	1.12
Wealth ($100 million)												
Wealth	27.8	23.8	19.6	16.2	29.8	26	20.3	16.4	32.4	27.8	20.4	16.3
Vol	13.7	8.6	5.8	4.4	15.5	10.1	5.8	4.4	18.1	11	5.8	4.4

Continued

Table 11.B3   Continued

	Max overlay=0%				Max overlay=100%				Max overlay=200%		
	← aggressive conservative →				← aggressive conservative →				← aggressive conservative →		
VaR₉₅%	11.7	12.4	11.2	9.7	12.6	13	11.7	9.7	13.2	13.4	11.9	9.7
ES₉₅%	10.2	11.1	9.2	7.8	10.6	11.4	9.7	8	10.7	11.5	9.8	7.9
SD	7.5	5.2	3.9	2.9	8.4	6.2	3.9	3	9.7	6.8	3.9	2.9
Surplus ($100 M)												
Surplus	3.5	1.6	−0.3	−1.9	4.4	2.6	0	−1.8	5.6	3.5	0.1	−1.9
Vol	5.8	3.2	1.4	0.9	6.5	3.8	1.4	0.9	7.6	4.1	1.4	0.9
Economic value ($100 million)												
EV	−0.5	−0.8	−2.3	−7.6	0.8	0.5	−1.5	−6.6	1.8	1.4	−1.4	−7.4
Vol	5.9	4.0	2.1	2.8	5.9	4.0	2.1	2.7	6.1	3.9	2.1	3.0
VaR₉₅%	−10.3	−7.4	−5.8	−12.0	−8.5	−6.0	−5.0	−10.8	−7.4	−5.1	−4.9	−12.0
ES₉₅%	−12.8	−9.5	−6.8	−14.2	−11.2	−8.0	−6.0	−13.0	−10.1	−6.7	−6.0	−14.4

Abbreviations: E[R]: Expected return; FR: Funding ratio; Ctbn: Contribution; Vol: Volatility; DD: Max drawdown; SD: Semi-deviation.

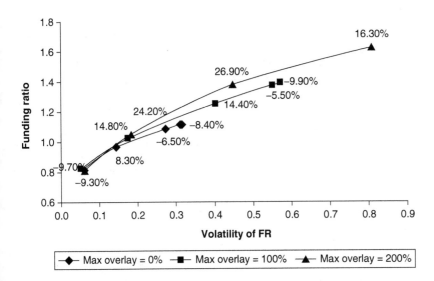

Figure 11.B4   Efficient frontiers of ALM models

Table 11.B4   Performance-risk measures for ALM models

	Max overlay=0%				Max overlay=100%				Max overlay=200%			
	← aggressive conservative →				← aggressive conservative →				← aggressive conservative →			
Investment on assets (%)												
E[R]	7.7	7.6	7	3.6	9.1	8.9	7.8	3.4	10.1	9.9	8.2	2.4
Vol	19	18.4	18.3	13.6	22.2	21.4	19	13.2	26.1	22.5	17.3	12.7
DD	32	30.2	30.7	26.6	40.5	38.2	32.4	26.2	53.5	41.7	27.6	30.9
SD	12.4	12	11.7	8.6	14.9	14.3	12.5	8.4	17.7	15.4	11.6	8.5
Funding ratio (%)												
FR	112	109	97	82	137	126	102	82	163	138	105	82
Vol	31	28	15	6	55	40	18	6	81	45	19	6
VaR$_{95\%}$	77	78	79	75	80	81	81	75	80	83	82	73
ES$_{95\%}$	74	74	76	74	73	75	77	74	72	75	79	71
SD	17	15	8	3	30	23	10	3	42	26	11	4
Min FR	82	82	83	78	81	82	84	78	79	83	85	76
Contribution ($100 million)												
Ctbn	2.13	2.08	1.92	4.52	2.19	1.84	1.59	4.70	2.35	1.57	1.40	5.66
Vol	1.80	1.69	1.10	1.81	2.12	1.67	1.05	1.87	2.37	1.43	0.96	2.40
Max	0.82	0.76	0.59	0.90	1.00	0.80	0.51	0.94	1.20	0.78	0.46	1.19
Wealth ($100 million)												
Wealth	22.3	21.6	19.3	16.5	27.3	25.1	20.4	16.4	32.4	27.5	20.9	16.4
Vol	8	7.3	5.6	4.4	12.7	10.1	5.9	4.4	18.1	11.1	5.8	4.4
VaR$_{95\%}$	11.8	11.6	11.3	9.9	12.4	12.5	11.6	9.9	13.2	13	12.3	9.5
ES$_{95\%}$	10	9.9	9.2	8	10.5	10.4	9.8	8	10.7	11	10	7.9
SD	4.9	4.6	3.7	3	7.2	6	3.9	3	9.7	6.8	3.9	3
Surplus ($100 million)												
Surplus	0.9	0.6	−0.4	−1.8	3.3	2.2	0	−1.8	5.6	3.3	0.3	−1.8
Vol	2.7	2.4	1.3	0.9	5	3.7	1.5	0.9	7.6	4.1	1.6	1
Economic value ($100 million)												
EV	−1.3	−1.5	−2.4	−6.3	0.4	0.1	−1.6	−6.5	1.8	1.3	−1.1	−7.5
Vol	3.6	3.4	2.0	2.5	4.9	4.0	2.2	2.6	6.1	3.9	2.2	3.1
VaR$_{95\%}$	−7.0	−6.8	−5.8	−10.3	−7.4	−6.2	−5.2	−10.6	−7.4	−5.2	−4.8	−12.6
ES$_{95\%}$	−9.1	−8.8	−6.9	−12.2	−9.7	−8.1	−6.2	−12.6	−10.1	−6.5	−5.8	−14.8

Abbreviations: E[R]: Expected return; FR: Funding ratio; Ctbn: Contribution; Vol: Volatility; DD: Max drawdown; SD: Semi-deviation.

Additional ALM model (5)

The economic value (Final Surplus – Total Contributions) and its expected shortfall at 95 per cent level are employed as the performance-risk measure pair. A constraint on duration matching ratio is introduced (DM≥0.9). Numbers in red next to the points on efficient frontiers are the DM values (see Figure 11B5 and Table 11B5).

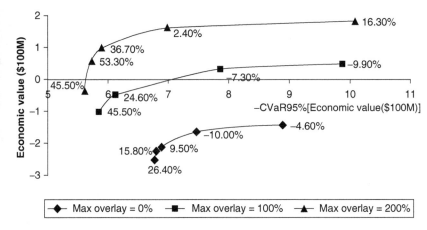

Figure 11.B5 Efficient frontiers of ALM models

Table 11.B5 Performance-risk measures for ALM models

	Max overlay=0%				Max overlay=100%				Max overlay=200%			
	← aggressive conservative →				← aggressive conservative →				← aggressive conservative →			
Investment on assets (%)												
E[R]	7.7	7.2	7	6.8	9.1	8.5	7.9	7.4	10.1	9.8	9.3	8.7
Vol	18.9	19.1	19.6	20.5	22.2	20.5	21	17.6	26.1	20.8	22.5	20.4
DD	31.9	33	34.9	38.4	40.5	36.2	38.8	28.1	53.5	36.4	43.3	37
SD	12.4	12.3	12.5	13	15	13.6	13.6	11.4	17.7	14.1	15.1	13.6
Funding ratio (%)												
FR	110	99	98	97	139	113	107	100	163	131	126	114
Vol	29	17	16	16	57	25	21	18	81	39	34	25
VaR$_{95\%}$	78	79	79	78	79	83	81	79	80	85	84	83
ES$_{95\%}$	74	75	75	74	73	76	76	76	72	77	76	77
SD	16	10	9	9	31	15	12	10	42	23	21	15
Min FR	82	82	82	81	80	84	83	84	79	84	83	84
Contribution ($100 million)												
Ctbn	2.10	1.91	1.97	2.10	2.23	1.53	1.65	1.77	2.35	1.37	1.48	1.41
Vol	1.74	1.17	1.13	1.08	2.18	1.16	1.10	1.17	2.37	1.22	1.24	1.06
Max	0.79	0.64	0.65	0.69	1.03	0.62	0.62	0.56	1.20	0.64	0.70	0.58
Wealth ($100 million)												
Wealth	21.9	19.8	19.7	19.5	27.6	22.6	21.3	20	32.4	26	25.1	22.6
Vol	7.6	5.9	5.9	5.8	13	7.5	6.7	5.8	18.1	9.4	9	7.1
VaR$_{95\%}$	11.7	11.3	11	10.9	12.4	12.1	11.8	11.7	13.2	13.4	13	12.6
ES$_{95\%}$	10	9.3	9.1	8.8	10.5	10	9.4	9.8	10.7	11	10.3	10.1
SD	4.7	4	3.9	3.9	7.3	4.9	4.4	3.8	9.7	6	5.8	4.7

Continued

Table 11.B5   Continued

	Max overlay=0%				Max overlay=100%				Max overlay=200%			
	← aggressive conservative →				← aggressive conservative →				← aggressive conservative →			
Surplus ($100 million)												
Surplus	0.8	−0.2	−0.3	−0.4	3.4	1.1	0.5	−0.2	5.6	2.7	2.2	1.1
Vol	2.6	1.5	1.4	1.4	5.2	2.2	1.8	1.5	7.6	3.4	3	2.1
Economic value ($100 million)												
EV	−1.4	−2.1	−2.3	−2.5	0.5	−0.5	−1.0	−1.0	1.8	1.0	0.6	−0.4
Vol	3.5	2.2	2.1	1.9	5.1	2.7	2.3	2.2	6.1	3.4	3.2	2.6
$VaR_{95\%}$	−6.9	−5.6	−5.6	−5.8	−7.5	−4.9	−5.0	−5.6	−7.4	−4.6	−4.6	−4.8
$ES_{95\%}$	−8.9	−6.9	−6.8	−6.8	−9.9	−6.1	−5.9	−5.8	−10.1	−5.9	−5.7	−5.6

Abbreviations: E[R]: Expected return; FR: Funding ratio; Ctbn: Contribution; Vol: Volatility; DD: Max drawdown; SD: Semi-deviation.

Additional ALM model (6)

An example of ALM models with different levels of DEO strategies (0–250 per cent) is illustrated for a shorter time period ($T=5$). The economic value (Final Surplus – Total Contributions) and its expected shortfall at 95 per cent level are employed as the performance-risk measure pair. Numbers in red next to the points on efficient frontiers are the DM values. Consistent with the historical test results with a long–term horizon, applying 100–150 per cent of DEO can increase the duration of core assets enough to match that of the liability for a shorter period (see Figure 11B6 and Table 11B6).

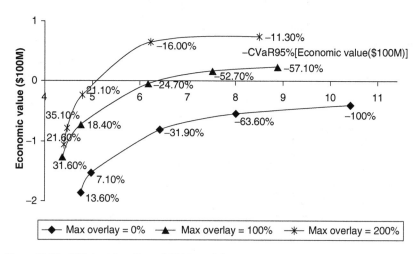

Figure 11.B6   Efficient frontiers of ALM models

Table 11.B6 Performance-risk measures for ALM models

	Max overlay=0%				Max overlay=100%				Max overlay=200%			
	← aggressive conservative →				← aggressive conservative →				← aggressive conservative →			
Investment on assets (%)												
E[R]	8.46	7.77	6.68	6.21	9.33	8.88	7.81	7.03	9.94	8.58	7.73	7.35
Vol	18.7	16.5	17.8	17.6	20.9	18.4	19.5	19.5	24.7	19.4	20	19.6
DD	18.9	14.2	16.7	16.8	21.3	16.4	18.6	19.4	28.3	18	19.8	19.4
SD	11.9	10.4	10.8	10.7	13.3	11.7	12	11.9	15.7	12.1	12.4	12.1
Funding ratio (%)												
FR	118	104	96	94	120	110	102	98	124	106	101	99
Vol	36	17	9	7	34	20	12	9	37	14	11	10
VaR$_{95\%}$	1	1	1	1	1	1	1	1	1	1	1	1
ES$_{95\%}$	1	1	1	1	1	1	1	1	1	1	1	1
SD	0	0	0	0	0	0	0	0	0	0	0	0
Min FR	81	86	87	87	83	86	87	87	82	87	87	87
Contribution ($100 million)												
Ctbn	1.90	1.16	1.04	1.09	1.59	1.10	0.94	0.98	1.55	0.90	0.94	0.95
Vol	1.96	0.97	0.54	0.44	1.64	0.99	0.62	0.48	1.61	0.64	0.56	0.50
Max	1.10	0.53	0.38	0.35	0.91	0.56	0.41	0.38	0.92	0.43	0.41	0.39
Wealth ($100 million)												
Wealth	20.2	18	16.7	16.3	20.7	19.1	17.8	17	21.7	18.4	17.7	17.3
Vol	6.48	4.37	3.83	3.61	7.07	5.11	4.44	4	8.32	4.59	4.27	4.08
VaR$_{95\%}$	12	11.4	10.6	10.5	11.8	11.6	11	10.9	11.1	11.4	11.3	11.2
ES$_{95\%}$	10.7	10.5	9.49	9.42	10.5	10.5	9.55	9.44	9.92	9.97	9.6	9.55
SD	3.86	2.89	2.62	2.49	4.22	3.31	3	2.76	4.9	3.11	2.93	2.82
Surplus ($100 million)												
Surplus	1.89	0.37	−0.5	−0.8	2.25	1.13	0.22	−0.3	2.88	0.67	0.15	−0.1
Vol	3.94	1.96	1.08	0.89	4.02	2.39	1.43	1.03	4.62	1.66	1.28	1.12
Economic value ($100 million)												
EV	−0.4	−0.8	−1.5	−1.9	0.2	0.0	−0.7	−1.3	0.7	−0.2	−0.8	−1.1
Vol	4.5	2.6	1.5	1.2	4.2	2.9	1.8	1.3	4.5	2.1	1.6	1.4
VaR$_{95\%}$	−7.8	−5.0	−3.9	−3.7	−6.7	−4.8	−3.8	−3.5	−6.3	−3.6	−3.6	−3.5
ES$_{95\%}$	−10.0	−6.0	−4.6	−4.4	−8.5	−5.8	−4.3	−4.0	−8.1	−4.4	−4.1	−4.0

Abbreviations: E[R]: Expected return; FR: Funding ratio; Ctbn: Contribution; Vol: Volatility; DD: Max drawdown; SD: Semi-deviation.

12

A Robust Optimization Approach to Pension Fund Management

Garud Iyengar and Alfred Ka Chun Ma

12.1 Introduction

Pension plans in the United States come in two varieties. Defined contribution pension plans specify the contribution of the corporation. The employees have the right to invest the corporation's contribution and their own contribution in a limited set of funds. The participants in a defined contribution pension plan are responsible for making all the investment decisions and bear all the risks associated with these decisions; thus, the benefit to the participants is uncertain. In contrast, defined benefit pension plans specify the benefits due to plan participants. The plan sponsor, that is the corporation, makes all the investment decisions in a defined benefit pension plan and bears all the investment risk. Defined benefit plans have been in the news in the past few years because some firms face the prospect of bankruptcy over severely underfunded pension plans. Consequently, there is a need to develop models that account for uncertainty in future market conditions and plan accordingly.

Pension fund management is an instance of the asset-liability management problem (see, for example, Consigli and Dempster, 1998; Klaassen, 1998; Drijver *et al*, 2000; Sodhi, 2005) in which the goal of the decision maker is to manage the capital invested into a set of assets in order to meet obligations at the minimum possible cost. The typical modeling paradigm adopted in the literature is to model the uncertainty in market conditions as random variables with a known distribution, formulate the asset-liability management problem (and, hence, also the specific case of the pension fund management problem) as a stochastic program, and solve the problem by sampling the market conditions from the given distributions. All sampling-based methods suffer from the curse-of-dimensionality and become intractable as the number of decisions increases, that is either the number of assets in the portfolio or the number of decision epoch increases. In this article, we propose a robust optimization-based approach as an alternative to the stochastic programming based-methods.

Robust optimization is a methodology for explicitly incorporating the effect of parameter uncertainty in optimization problems (Ben-Tal *et al*, 2000; Ben-Tal and Nemirovski, 2001). In this approach, the parameter values are assumed to belong to known and bounded uncertainty sets, and the solution is computed assuming the worst-case behavior of the parameters. Thus, robust solutions are conservative. This is particularly appropriate for pension fund management. Typically, the uncertainty sets correspond to confidence regions around point estimates of the parameters; consequently, one is able to provide probabilistic guarantees on the performance of the robust solution. For a very large class of uncertainty sets, the computational effort required to solve the robust optimization problem is polynomial in the size of the problem (Ben-Tal and Nemirovski, 2001; Goldfarb and Iyengar, 2003) – in contrast, the computational complexity of the stochastic programming-based methods is exponential in the problem size. Consequently, robust methods are likely to become a computationally tractable alternative to stochastic programming-based methods.

A pension fund management problem involves optimizing a given objective, for example minimizing the discounted value of all contributions, while ensuring that the fund is always able to meet its liabilities. In addition, the fund's holdings must also satisfy regulatory requirements. We assume that the parameters of the financial markets of relevance to pension fund management, for example the yield curve, the expected return and volatility on an equity index and so on, are described by factors that evolve according to a stochastic differential equation. In this setting, we show that the pension fund management problem can be formulated as a chance-constrained optimization problem. However, the random variables in the chance constraints are nonlinear functions of the underlying factors. We use the Itô-Taylor expansion to linearize the nonlinear chance constraints and show that the linearized chance constraints can be approximated by second-order cone (SOC) constraints. Thus, the pension fund management problem can be approximated by a second-order cone program (SOCP). This implies that very large-scale problems can be solved efficiently both in theory (Alizadeh and Goldfarb, 2003) and in practice (Andersen and Andersen, 2006). Moreover, as a number of commercial solvers, such as MOSEK, CPLEX and Frontline System (supplier of EXCEL SOLVER), provide the capability for solving SOCPs in a numerically robust manner, we expect the robust approach to become the method of choice for solving large-scale pension fund problems.

The rest of the article is organized as follows. In the section 'Robust pension fund management', we show how to use linearization and robust optimization techniques to formulate general pension fund management problems as a SOCPs. In the section 'Numerical example', we report the results of our numerical experiments with a frozen fund and illustrate the robustness of the robust optimization solution. In the 'Concluding remarks' section, we include some concluding remarks.

12.2   Robust pension fund management

In this section, we present a robust optimization-based framework for pension fund management. As pension funds evaluate and re-balance their portfolio holdings at best on a quarterly basis, we work with a discrete time model. In this section, we discuss a general framework for approximating the typical constraints and objectives by second-order constraints; we consider a concrete example in the 'Numerical example' section.

12.2.1   Constraints

At each decision epoch $t \in \{0, 1, ..., T\}$, the pension manager has to make two decisions: select a new portfolio of traded assets and decide the amount of fresh capital to be injected into the fund. Let $\mathbf{x}_t$ denote the number of shares of the traded assets held by the pension fund from time t to time $t+1$, that is over period t, let w_t denote the fresh capital injected into the fund at time t, and let l_t denote the random liability of the pension fund at time t. Then, assuming that the trading costs are negligible, we must have:

$$\tilde{\mathbf{p}}_t^T \left(\mathbf{x}_{t-1} - \mathbf{x}_t \right) + w_t - \tilde{l}_t \geq 0, \tag{12.1}$$

where $\tilde{\mathbf{p}}_t$ denotes the random prices for the traded assets at time t. As the price $\tilde{\mathbf{p}}_t$ is random, and typically has support on the entire positive orthant, one has to ascribe a proper meaning to the uncertain constraint (12.1). In this article, we approximate the uncertain liability constraint (12.1) at time t by the chance constraint

$$\mathrm{P}(\tilde{\mathbf{p}}_t^T \left(\mathbf{x}_{t-1} - \mathbf{x}_t \right) + w_t - \tilde{l}_t \geq 0) \geq 1 - \varepsilon, \tag{12.2}$$

where P denotes the probability measure conditioned on all available information and $\varepsilon > 0$ is the constraint violation probability. Note that we are implicitly assuming that when the event $\tilde{\mathbf{p}}_t^T(\mathbf{x}_{t-1} - \mathbf{x}_t) + w_t < \tilde{l}_t$ occurs, the fund sponsor is able to meet the shortfall using earnings or raising debt. We discuss this in greater detail in the next section on pension fund objectives.

In addition to the budget constraint (12.1), pension fund holding must also satisfy some regulatory requirements. These requirements typically impose constraints of the form

$$\tilde{\mathbf{p}}_t^T \mathbf{x}_t \geq \beta \left(\sum_{\tau > t} \frac{\tilde{l}_\tau}{(1 + \tilde{d})^\tau} \right),$$

where $\tilde{d}$ denotes the (possibly stochastic) nominal interest rate set by the regulatory body and β is a specified funding level. We approximate this uncertain constraint by the chance constraint

$$P\left(\tilde{\mathbf{p}}_t^T \, \mathbf{x}_t \geq \beta \left(\sum_{\tau > t} \frac{\tilde{l}_\tau}{(1+\tilde{d})^\tau} \right) \right) \geq 1-\varepsilon.$$

Thus, the generic chance constraint encountered in the pension fund management problem is of the form

$$P(\tilde{\mathbf{a}}_t^T \mathbf{y}_t \geq d_t) \geq 1 - \varepsilon, \tag{12.3}$$

where $\tilde{\mathbf{a}}_t$ denotes stochastic parameters such as the prices of assets, liabilities, discount factors and so on, and $\mathbf{y}_t$ and d_t are affine functions of the decision variables $\{(\mathbf{x}_t, w_t)\}_{t=1}^T$.

We assume that the stochastic parameters are described by a factor model:

$$\tilde{\mathbf{a}}_t = f(\mathbf{Z}_t), \tag{12.4}$$

where f is a sufficiently smooth function mapping the m stochastic factors $\mathbf{Z}_t \in \Re^m$ into the random coefficients $\tilde{\mathbf{a}}_t$, and the m-dimensional vector of factors $\mathbf{Z}_t \in \Re^m$ evolves according to the stochastic differential equation

$$d\mathbf{Z}_t = \boldsymbol{\mu}(t, \mathbf{Z}_t)dt + \Sigma(t, \mathbf{Z}t)\, d\mathbf{W}_t, \tag{12.5}$$

where $\boldsymbol{\mu}(t, \mathbf{Z}_t) \in \Re^{m \times n}$, and $\Sigma(t, \mathbf{Z}_t) \in \Re^{m \times n}$, and n denotes the length of the vector of standard Brownian motions $\mathbf{W}_t$. Most popular financial models in the literature satisfy (12.4)–(12.5). For example, it is easy to show that when the universe of assets is a set of treasury bonds and the equity index, the short rates are given by the Hull–White model (Hull and White, 1990), and the equity index evolves according to a geometric Brownian motion, then the price process $\tilde{\mathbf{p}}_t$ for the asset satisfies (12.4)–(12.5).

12.2.2 Objective

The most obvious objective for managing a pension fund is to minimize the net present value of all the future contributions:

$$\min \sum_t w_t B_{0,t}, \tag{12.6}$$

where $B_{0,t}$ denotes the price at time 0 of a zero-coupon bond with face value $F=1$ maturing at time t. Defined benefit pension funds most often use this objective.

The objective (12.6) does not account for the impact of the pension contributions on the fund's sponsor. There is evidence that pension contributions

w_t have a serious impact on the stock price of the sponsor (Jin *et al*, 2006). We next discuss an objective that explicitly accounts for the impact of the pension fund on the sponsor. The Myers and Majluf pecking order hypothesis (Myers and Majluf, 1984) suggests that the sponsor would first use earnings, and then use debt to finance the pension contributions $\{w_t\}$. We assume that the firm will not be able to issue equity for the purpose of meeting its pension obligations. Suppose w_t^e denotes the portion of the pension fund contribution wt that is financed directly from the firm's earnings C_t before interest and tax (EBIT). We assume that the earnings C_0 at time $t = 0$ are known and the portion of the earnings invested in the firm grows at a rate r_e. Thus,

$$C_{t+1} = (Ct - w_t^e)(1 + r_e). \tag{12.7}$$

We also impose the additional constraint that $w_t^e \le uC_t$, where $u \in [0, 1]$ indicates the maximum fraction of the earnings that can be used for funding pension obligations.

Let w_t^d denote the amount raised in the debt market at time t. We assume that this debt has maturity $D = 1$. Thus, at time $t + 1$, the firm has to repay $(1 + (s_{t,1} + P))w_d$, where $st, 1$ denotes the spot risk-free interest rate at time t for maturity $D = 1$ and P denotes the spread over the risk-free rate that the sponsoring firm needs to pay to raise capital. As interest payments are tax deductible, the effective cost incurred by the firm at time $t + 1$ is $(1 + (1 - \alpha_T)(s_{t,1} + P))w_d$, where α_T denotes the marginal tax rate of the firm. Thus, the discounted cost $c_t^d(P)$ of raising an amount w_t^d in the debt market is given by

$$
\begin{aligned}
C_t^d(P) &= \left(1 + (1 - \alpha_T)(s_{t,1} + P)\right) B_{0,t+1} \, w_t^d \\
&= \left((1 - \alpha_T)(1 + s_{t,1}) B_{0,t+1} + ((1 - \alpha_T)P + \alpha_T) B_{0,t+1}\right) w_t^d \\
&= \left((1 - \alpha_T) B_{0,t} + ((1 - \alpha_T) \times P + \alpha_T) B_{0,t+1}\right) w_t^d,
\end{aligned}
\tag{12.8}
$$

where we have used the identify $B_{0,t+1}(1 + s_{t,1}) = B_{0,t}$.

The spread P is not a constant – it is a function of the credit rating of the sponsoring firm. Therefore, in order to use $c_t^d(P)$ to model the cost of debt, we have to ensure that the credit rating of the firm remains above a certain level. We assume that the credit rating of the firm is a function of the interest coverage (*IC*), and a firm has a credit rating Q provided $IC \in [\alpha(Q), \beta(Q)]$ and in this case the spread is given by $P(Q)$ (Damodaran, 2004). We also assume that the function mapping interest coverage *IC* to the credit rating Q is fixed over time. As we assume that each debt offering has a duration $D = 1$, it follows that the interest coverage IC_t is given by

$$IC_t = \frac{C_t}{(s_{t,1} + P) w_t^d}.$$

Suppose the firm maintains a debt rating $Q \geq \underline{Q}$, then the spread $P \leq P(\underline{Q})$, and we can use $c_t^d(P(\underline{Q}))$ to estimate the cost of debt. The chance constraint

$$P(\alpha(\underline{Q})\,(s_{t,1}(\mathbf{Z}_t + P(\underline{Q}))\,W_t^d \leq C_t) \geq 1 - \varepsilon, \tag{12.9}$$

where we write $s_{t,1}(\mathbf{Z}_t)$ to emphasize that $s_{t,1}$ is a function of the factors $\mathbf{Z}_t$, ensures that $Q \geq \underline{Q}$ with high probability and we can use $c_t^d(P(\underline{Q}))$ to approximate the cost of debt. The constraint (12.9) also belongs to the general class of chance constraints described in (12.3).

We adopt $c_t^d(P(\underline{Q}))$ defined in (12.8) as the objective. Thus, the pension fund management optimization problem is given by the chance-constrained problem

$$\min \sum_t c_t^d \left(P(\underline{Q}) \right)$$

s.t. $\qquad\qquad\qquad\qquad\qquad\qquad\qquad\qquad\qquad (12.10)$

$$P\left(\tilde{\mathbf{a}}_t^T \mathbf{y}_t \geq d_t,\ t = 1,\ldots,T \right) \geq 1 - \varepsilon,$$

In general, chance-constrained optimization problems are difficult to solve. In most cases, the problem is non-convex. Except for a few special cases, one has to resort to sampling to solve chance-constrained problems. Consequently, the complexity of solving chance-constrained problems is exponential in the problem dimension. In the next section, we construct a tractable approximation to (12.10).

12.2.3 Linearization and robust constraints

Let $\mathbf{f} = (f_1,\ldots,f_l): \mathfrak{R}^m \to \mathfrak{R}^l$ denote the function that defines the stochastic parameters $\mathbf{a}_t$ in terms of the factors $\mathbf{Z}_t$ at time t. By Itô's lemma (see Chang (2004) for example),

$$d\mathbf{f}_t(\mathbf{Z}) = \boldsymbol{\mu}^f(t,\mathbf{Z})dt + \boldsymbol{\Sigma}^f(t,\mathbf{Z})d\mathbf{W}_t, \tag{12.11}$$

where

$$\boldsymbol{\mu}^f(t,\mathbf{Z}) = \mathbf{J}_f(\mathbf{Z})\boldsymbol{\mu}(t,\mathbf{Z}) + \frac{1}{2}\boldsymbol{\eta}_f\,\boldsymbol{\Sigma}^f(t,\mathbf{Z})$$

$$= \mathbf{J}_f(\mathbf{Z})\boldsymbol{\Sigma}(t,\mathbf{Z})d\mathbf{W}_t,$$

$$\boldsymbol{\eta}_f = \left[\mathrm{tr}\left(\boldsymbol{\Sigma}(t,\mathbf{Z})\boldsymbol{\Sigma}(t,\mathbf{Z})^T \mathbf{H}_1(\mathbf{Z})\right),\ldots,\mathrm{tr}\left(\boldsymbol{\Sigma}(t,\mathbf{Z})\boldsymbol{\Sigma}(t,\mathbf{Z})^T \mathbf{H}_l(\mathbf{Z})\right) \right]^T,$$

$\mathbf{J}_f(\mathbf{Z})$ denotes the Jacobian matrix of $\mathbf{f}$, $\mathbf{H}_i(\mathbf{Z})$ denotes the Hessian matrix of f_i with respect to the factors, and $\mathrm{tr}(\cdot)$ denotes the trace of a matrix. We approximate

$$\mathbf{f}_t \approx \mathbf{f}_0 + \boldsymbol{\mu}_0^f t + \boldsymbol{\Sigma}_0^f \mathbf{W}_t, \tag{12.12}$$

where

$$\mu_0^f = J_f(Z)\mu(t,Z) + \frac{1}{2}\eta_f\bigg|_{Z=Z_0},$$
$$\Sigma_0^f = J_f(Z)\Sigma(t,Z)\big|_{Z=Z_0},$$

that is, we evaluate the coefficients at time $t=0$ and then let f_t evolve according to a Gaussian process. Thus, $f_t \sim N(f_0 + t\mu_0^f, t\Sigma_0^f)$. We discuss the impact of this approximation in the section 'Numerical example'.

We can now approximate the generic chance constraint (12.3) by

$$P\left(\left(f_0 + \mu_0^f t + \Sigma_0^f W t\right)^T y_t \geq d_t\right) \geq 1 - \varepsilon. \tag{12.13}$$

Let $\Phi(\cdot)$ denote the cumulative density function of the standard normal random variable. Then $P(\|W_t\| \leq t\,\Phi^{-1}(1-\varepsilon)) = 1-\varepsilon$, and it follows that (12.13) holds if

$$\left(f_0 + \mu_0^f t + \Sigma_0^f w\right)^T y_t \geq d_t \quad \textit{for all} \quad \|w\| \leq \sqrt{t}\Phi^{-1}(1-\varepsilon). \tag{12.14}$$

A constraint of the form (12.14) is called a robust constraint (Ben-Tal and Nemirovski, 2002). Note that the robust constraint (12.14) is a conservative approximation for the chance constraint. Using the Cauchy–Schwarz inequality, (12.14) can be written as

$$\left(f_0 + \mu_0^f t\right)^T y_t - d_t \geq \sqrt{t}\Phi^{-1}(1-\varepsilon) \times \left\|\Sigma_0^f y_t\right\|_2, \tag{12.15}$$

where $\|x\|_2 = \sqrt{x^T x}$ denote the L_2-norm. The constraint (12.15) is of the form

$$\|Bx - a\|_2 \leq d^T x + c,$$

where B, a, d, and c are constants and x is the decision variable. Constraints of this form are called SOC constraints.

12.2.4   SOC programming approximation for pension fund management

In a pension fund management problem, we have at least one constraint of the form (12.3) at each decision epoch t. Suppose we have K chance constraints in total. We want to guarantee that all the chance constraints hold with probability at least η. We set $\varepsilon = \eta/K$ for each chance constraint of the form $P(C_i) \geq 1 - \varepsilon, i=1,...,K$. The Bonferroni inequality (see for example Boros and Prékopa, 1989) implies that

$$P\left(\bigcap_{i=1}^{K} C_i\right) \geq 1 - \sum_{i=1}^{K}\left(1 - P(C_i)\right) \geq 1 - \sum_{i=1}^{K}\frac{\eta}{K} = 1 - \eta, \tag{12.16}$$

that is, by setting a more conservative target for each chance constraint, the Bonferroni inequality guarantees that all the chance constraints hold simultaneously. We use $\varepsilon = \eta/K$ in constraints of the form (12.15) to approximate each chance constraint by an SOC constraint. Thus, the resulting optimization problem is of the form

$$\min \sum_t c_t^d \left(P(\underline{Q})\right)$$

s.t. $\tag{12.17}$

$$\|B_i y - a_i\|_2 \leq d_i^T x + c_i, \quad i = 1,...,K,$$

that is, it has one linear objective and several SOC constraints. Such an optimization problem is called an SOCP.

Very large-scale SOCPs can be solved efficiently both in theory (Alizadeh and Goldfarb, 2003) and in practice (Andersen and Andersen, 2006). Moreover, a number of commercial solvers, such as MOSEK, CPLEX and Frontline System (supplier of EXCEL SOLVER), provide the capability for solving SOCPs in a numerically robust manner. As the approximation (12.12) implies that the pension fund management problem can be approximated by an SOCP, the approach proposed in this article can be used to solve very large-scale pension fund management problems.

12.3 Numerical example

In this section, we consider a specific example and formulate the optimization problem that computes the optimal contribution schedule and portfolio holdings for a frozen pension fund using the general framework described in the section 'Robust pension fund management'. A frozen fund is a fund in which all the liabilities l_t are fixed; therefore, there is no actuarial risk and the only risk in the problem is financial risk.

12.3.1 Assets, liabilities and dynamics

We assume that a pension fund invests in an equity index and zero-coupon bonds with face value 1 and maturities up to M years. Thus, the holdings of the fund at time t can be described by the vector

$$\mathbf{x}_t = \begin{bmatrix} \text{Number of shares of } 1 - \text{year bond} \\ \vdots \\ \text{Number of shares of M} - \text{year bond} \\ \text{Number of shares of equity} \end{bmatrix} \in \mathfrak{R}^{M+1}.$$

Note that, if the equity investment is specified as a broad market index, we can use the index to denote price even if it is not possible to invest in the market index directly. As long as the index is used consistently over time, the investment returns can still be correctly calculated in the model. At time $t+1$, all the bonds in the portfolio have a maturity that is 1 year shorter (the bond with 1-year maturity is now available as cash). Thus, the holding $\mathbf{x}_{t+1}$ before any trading at time $t+1$ is given by

$$\hat{\mathbf{x}}_{t+1} = \mathbf{D}\mathbf{x}_t,$$

and $\mathbf{d}^T\mathbf{x}_t$ is available as cash, where

$$D = \begin{bmatrix} 0 & 1 & 0 & 0 & \cdots & 0 \\ 0 & 0 & 1 & 0 & \cdots & 0 \\ \vdots & \ddots & \ddots & \ddots & \ddots & \vdots \\ 0 & 0 & \cdots & 0 & 1 & 0 \\ 0 & 0 & \cdots & 0 & 0 & 0 \\ 0 & 0 & \cdots & 0 & 0 & 1 \end{bmatrix}, \text{ and } \mathbf{d} = \mathbf{e}_1 = \begin{bmatrix} 1 \\ 0 \\ \vdots \\ 0 \end{bmatrix}.$$

The value of the portfolio $\mathbf{x}_t$ at time $t+1$ is given by $\mathbf{p}_{t+1}^T\mathbf{D}\mathbf{x}_t + \mathbf{d}^T\mathbf{x}_t$.

The liability of the pension fund at time t is denoted by l_t and time $t = 0,1,\dots,T$, that is, the time horizon for the pension fund problem is T. We assume that at time $t = 0$, all the future payments l_t, $t = 0,1,\dots,T$, are deterministic as in the case of frozen pension funds, that is, the uncertainty in the model is only from the changing financial conditions.

12.3.2 Bond prices and the yield curve

We follow Nelson and Siegel (1987) and assume that the short rates

$$s_{t,j} - Z_t^1 + Z_t^2\left[\frac{1-\exp(-j/\tau)}{j/\tau}\right] + Z_t^3\left[\frac{1-\exp(-j/\tau)}{j/\tau} - \exp(-j/\tau)\right], \tag{12.18}$$

where the factors Z_t^1, Z_t^2 and Z_t^3 refer, respectively, to level, slope and curvature of the yield curve and τ is a constant. We use the Nelson–Siegel model because this model ensures non-negative spot rates $s_{t,j}$ for large $t \gg 1$. This is necessary in our setting as we need to discount liabilities with very long durations.

In the Nelson–Siegel model, the price $B_{t,j}$ at time t of a zero-coupon bond with face value $F = 1$ and maturing at time $t + j$ is given by

$$
\begin{aligned}
B_{t,j} &= \frac{1}{\left(1 + s_{t,j}\right)^j} \\
&= \left(1 + Z_t^1 + Z_t^2 \left[\frac{1 - \exp(-j/\tau)}{j/\tau}\right] + Z_t^3 \left[\frac{1 - \exp(-j/\tau)}{j/\tau} - \exp(-j/\tau)\right]\right)^{-j}.
\end{aligned} \tag{12.19}
$$

Thus, $B_{t,j}$ is a highly nonlinear function of the factors $\mathbf{Z}$. We chose the Nelson–Siegel model to illustrate our framework because a highly nonlinear yield curve is a good test for the linearization technique introduced in the section 'Robust pension fund management'.

We denote the value of the equity index by q_t. We assume that the equity index q_t and the factors $\{Z_t^i : i = 1, ..., 3\}$ driving the yield curve (12.18) evolve according to the stochastic differential equation

$$
\begin{bmatrix} dZ_t^1 \\ dZ_t^2 \\ dZ_t^3 \\ \dfrac{dq_t}{q_t} \end{bmatrix} = \begin{bmatrix} \left(m_1 - Z_t^1\right) \\ \left(m_2 - Z_t^2\right) \\ \left(m_3 - Z_t^3\right) \\ \mu \end{bmatrix} dt + A d\mathbf{W}_t, \tag{12.20}
$$

where $\mathbf{W}_t = (W_t^1, W_t^2, W_t^3, W_t^4)^T$, $\{W_t^i\}\, t \geq 0$, $i = 1, 2, 3, 4$, are independent standard Brownian motions, and the lower triangular matrix $A \in \Re^{4 \times 4}$ denotes the Cholesky decomposition of the covariance matrix $V \in \Re^{4 \times 4}$ of the vector $(Z_t^1, ..., Z_t^3, q_t)$. The dynamics in (12.20) imply that each of the factors Z_t^i is an Ornstein–Uhlenbeck process and the equity index q_t is a geometric Brownian motion. The yield curve dynamics given by (12.20) is similar to the one considered in Fabozzi *et al* (2005). With the above definitions, the price vector is given by

$$
\mathbf{p}_t = (B_{t,1, ...,} B_{t, M, q_t})^T.
$$

Note that the price vector and the stochastic differential equations (12.20) conform to the general framework described in the section 'Robust pension fund management'.

12.3.3 Optimization problem

We assume that at time $t = 0$, we determine the contribution w_t and the portfolio x_t for $t = 0, ..., \overline{T} \leq T$. We expect that the pension fund problem will be solved on a rolling-horizon basis, that is, at time $t = 1$, we will recompute the optimal portfolio for the horizon $t = 0, ..., \bar{T} + 1$. The horizon $\bar{T}$ is chosen to be long enough so that the impact of the liabilities $l_t, t > \bar{T}$, is minimal.

Let Ψ denote the initial holdings of the fund, that is the holdings before rebalancing at time 0. We require that the portfolio x_0 must satisfy

$$\mathbf{p}_0^T \Psi + w_0 - l_0 = \mathbf{p}_0^T \mathbf{x}_0, \tag{12.21}$$

that is, the total value of the portfolio x_0 must equal the difference between the available capital $(\mathbf{p}_0^T \Psi + w_0)$ and the liability l_0. Note that (12.21) implicitly assumes that rebalancing does not incur any transaction costs. Therefore, we can assume, without loss of generality, that the portfolio Ψ is held in cash.

The constraint for time $t \geq 1$ is

$$P\left(\mathbf{p}_t^T \mathbf{D} \mathbf{x}_{t-1} + \mathbf{d}^T \mathbf{x}_{t-1} + w_t - l_t \geq \mathbf{p}_t^T \mathbf{x}_t\right) \geq 1 - \varepsilon, \quad t = 1, ..., \bar{T} - 1, \tag{12.22}$$

where P denotes the probability measure conditioned on the information available at time $t = 0$. We also require the following target funding level constraint

$$P\left(\mathbf{p}_{\bar{T}}^T \mathbf{D} \mathbf{x}_{\bar{T}-1} + \mathbf{d}^T \mathbf{x}_{\bar{T}-1} + w_{\bar{T}} \geq l_{\bar{T}} + \beta L_{\bar{T}}\right) \geq 1 - \varepsilon, \tag{12.23}$$

to set the target funding level at time $\bar{T}$ to be a fraction β of the future liabilities, where L_t denote the net present value at time t of the entire set of future liability at a fixed discount rate d, that is

$$L_t = \sum_{\tau=t+1}^{T} \frac{l_\tau}{(1+d)^{\tau-1}},$$

and the discount rate d is chosen by the plan sponsor subject to some regulatory constraints. The funding level of a pension fund at time t is defined to be the ratio of the total spot value $\mathbf{p}_t^T \mathbf{x}_t$ of the assets of fund to L_t.

In addition, one may have to impose other constraints that meet regulatory requirements. For example, in the US, pension funds need to maintain a funding level of $\gamma = 90$ per cent and the sponsor is required to contribute if the funding level drops below γ. Such a regularity requirement can be met by imposing constraints of the form:

$$\mathbf{p}_0^T \mathbf{x}_0 \geq \gamma L_0, \tag{12.24}$$

and

$$P\left(\mathbf{p}_t^T \mathbf{x}_t \geq \gamma L_t\right) \geq 1 - \varepsilon, \quad t = 1, ..., \bar{T} - 1 \tag{12.25}$$

See Fabozzi *et al* (2004) for a summary of regulations on pension funds in different countries.

Collecting together all the constraints and using the objective incorporating the corporate structure of the plan sponsor given as an example in the section 'Linearization and robust constraints', we solve the following optimization problem

$$\min \sum_{t=0}^{\bar{T}} \left((1-\alpha_T) B_{0,t} + \left((1-\alpha_T) P(\underline{Q}) + \alpha_T \right) B_{0,t+1} \right) w_t^d$$

subject to $(21), (22), (23), (24), (25), (7)$ and (9).

(12.26)

In the Appendix section, we discuss how to use the general results in section 'Robust pension fund management' to reformulate (12.26) into an SOCP.

12.3.4   Discussion

Typically, the pension fund manager only chooses capital allocation to asset classes. The tactical decisions of the particular assets to purchase within each asset class are left to asset managers who are specialists in a particular asset classes. We consider two asset classes – equity and treasury bonds. The solution of the pension fund problem (12.26) guides the fraction of capital that should be allocated to an asset manager specializing in equity market for tactical asset allocation, and the fraction that should be given to an asset manager specializing in fixed income market. Therefore, the bond portfolio is only a proxy for total fixed income holdings.

We want our robust optimization-based approach to produce conservative portfolios. In constructing (12.26), we linearize the nonlinear factor dynamics, but then we use Bonferroni's inequality (see (12.16)), to impose a very conservative chance constraint. It is not immediately clear that the net outcome is a conservative portfolio. We show in the section 'Stationary portfolio selection' that the robust solution is indeed conservative when the risk is measured by the Value-at-Risk (VaR) and the Conditional Value-at-Risk (CVaR).

12.3.5   Problem parameters

Following Fabozzi *et al* (2005) (see also Barrett *et al*, 1995), we set $\tau = 3$. The other parameters used in the example are:

$$Z_0^1 = 4.5794, Z_0^2 = -0.3443,$$
$$Z_0^3 = -0.2767, q_{0,} = 1248.29,$$
$$\mu = 0.0783, m_1 = 6.1694,$$
$$m_2 = -2.4183, m_3 = 0.4244,$$

the covariance matrix

$$\mathbf{V} = \begin{bmatrix} 2.1775 & -4.5778 & 19.3399 & -0.1201 \\ -4.5778 & 15.6181 & -43.6039 & 0.2679 \\ 19.3399 & -43.6039 & 179.7153 & -1.0094 \\ -0.1201 & 0.2679 & -1.0094 & 0.0078 \end{bmatrix},$$

and the correlation matrix

$$\boldsymbol{\rho} = \begin{bmatrix} 1.0000 & -0.2178 & 0.5685 & -0.4008 \\ -0.2178 & 1.0000 & -0.4452 & 0.0945 \\ 0.5685 & -0.4452 & 1.0000 & -0.1149 \\ -0.4008 & 0.0945 & -0.1149 & 1.0000 \end{bmatrix}.$$

Thus, the Cholesky decomposition $\mathbf{A}$ of $\mathbf{V}$ is given by

$$\mathbf{A} = \begin{bmatrix} 1.4756 & 0 & 0 & 0 \\ -3.1023 & 2.4482 & 0 & 0 \\ 13.1063 & -1.2027 & 2.5485 & 0 \\ -0.0814 & 0.0063 & 0.0255 & 0.0212 \end{bmatrix}.$$

These parameter estimates result in the current yield curve displayed in Figure 12.1. The number of maturities M is set to $M = 10$ in our numerical experiments.

The liability stream used in our numerical experiments is shown in Figure 12.2. The liability stream ends in year $T = 85$. We obtained these data for a frozen pension fund from Goldman Sachs. We set the value of initial holding

$$\mathbf{p}_0^T \boldsymbol{\Psi} = 0.8 (L_0 + l_0),$$

Other parameters for this numerical example are set as follows:

(i) We consider the optimal plan for the first 4 years, that is $\bar{T} = 4$.
(ii) The regulation mandated minimum funding level γ is set to $\gamma = 0.9$. Thus, the fund is *underfunded* at time $t = 0$.
(iii) The target funding level β that controls the influence of liabilities beyond $\bar{T}$ is set to $\beta = 0.9$.
(iv) The liabilities are discounted at a nominal discount rate $d = 6$ per cent.
(v) The violation probability $\eta = 1$ per cent (see (12.16)), that is, all chance constraints in (12.26) are satisfied with $1 - \eta = 99$ per cent probability.

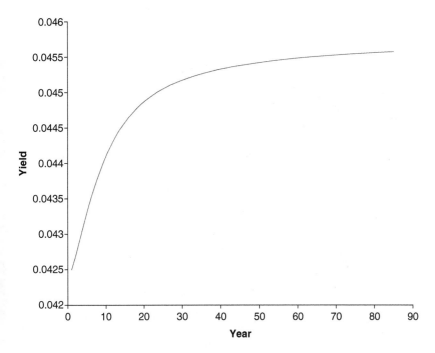

Figure 12.1   Current yield curve

(vi) The earnings $C_0 = 500$ and $u = 0.2$, that is, we impose a limit that at most 20 per cent of the earnings can be used to fund the pension plan. We set $r_e = 0.05$.

(vii) The marginal tax rate $\alpha_T = 0.35$ and we assume that the company wants to maintain a credit rating $Q =$ 'A+', that is, $\alpha(Q) = 5.5$ and $P(Q) = 0.008$ (Damodaran, 2004).

We summarize the values for the parameters as follows.

Parameter	Value
$\bar{T}$	4
γ	0.9
β	0.9
d	6%
η	1%
C_0	500
u	0.2
α_T	0.35
$\alpha(Q)$	5.5
$P(Q)$	0.008

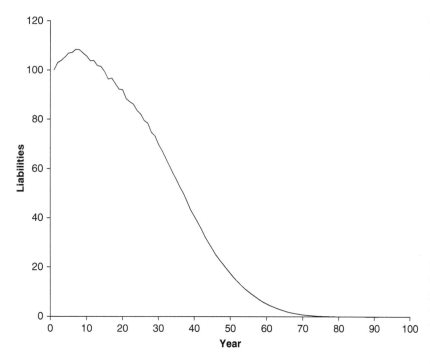

Figure 12.2 Liability as a function of time

12.3.6 Stationary portfolio selection

We consider optimal portfolio selection over $\bar{T}=4$ for a liability stream with time horizon $T = 85$. We consider this setting for simpler presentation and evaluation of the solution. As $\bar{T} \ll T$, we require that portfolio x_t $t = 1,...,\bar{T}$ be stationary, that is, $x_0 = x_1 = x_2 = x_3$. In order to investigate the impact of the equity ratio, that is the fraction of the total capital of the fund that is invested in equity, we impose the constraint

$$\left(B_{1,1},...,B_{1,M}\right)\left(x_0\left(1\right),...,x_0\left(M\right)\right)^T = \rho q' x_0\left(M+1\right)$$

that sets the equity ratio of the initial portfolio x_0 to $1/(1+\rho)$. We compute x_0 and $\{w_k\}_{k=0}^{\bar{T}}$ by solving

$$\min \sum_{t=0}^{\bar{T}}\left(\left(1-\alpha_t\right)B_{0,t}+\left(\left(1-\alpha_t\right)P\left(\underline{Q}\right)+\alpha_t\right)B_{0,t+1}\right)w_t^d$$

subject to $\quad x_0 = x_1 = x_2 = x_3,$

$$\left(B_{1,1},...,B_{1,M}\right)\left(x_0\left(1\right),...,x_0\left(M\right)\right)^T = \rho q' x_0\left(M+1\right),$$

$$(7), (21), (24), (34), (35), (36), \text{ and } (37).$$

(12.27)

Table 12.1   Worst-case contribution as a function of equity ratio

Equity ratio	w_0	w_1	w_2	w_3	$\sum_{t=0}^{\bar{T}} B_{0,t} w_t$
0.2	239.90	125.00	155.60	180.41	683.69
0.4	283.96	120.04	143.91	163.44	697.36
0.6	348.05	114.88	131.76	145.81	729.92

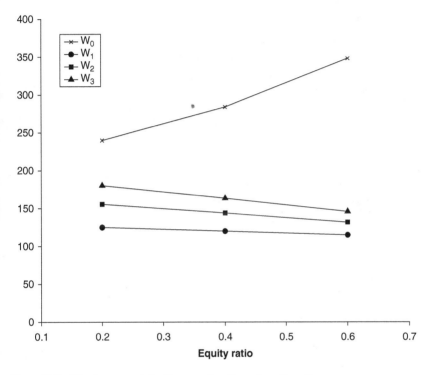

Figure 12.3   Worst-case contribution as a function of equity ratio

Table 12.1 and Figure 12.3 shows the worst-case payments as a function of the equity ratio $1/(1+\rho)$ with the probability of constraint satisfaction fixed at $1-\eta=0.99$. The contribution $w0$ increases with increasing equity ratio while the contributions (w_1, w_2, w_3) all decrease with the increase in the equity ratio. The total discounted payment, however, increases with the increase in the equity ratio.

In Table 12.2 we display the worst-case payments as a function of the probability of constraint satisfaction with the equity ratio $1/(1+\rho)$ fixed at 0.4. As expected, the worst-case contribution decreases with a decrease in constraint satisfaction.

Table 12.2   Worst-case contribution as a function of time

Probability	w_0	w_1	w_2	w_3	$\sum_{t=0}^{\bar{T}} B_{0,t} w_t$
0.99	283.96	120.04	143.91	163.44	697.36
0.95	244.27	111.20	130.97	147.34	622.91
0.90	230.03	107.11	125.01	139.95	592.79

12.3.7   Conditional VaR

In this section, we test the effect of linearizing the dynamics by stress-testing the pension fund portfolio using the VaR and CVaR measures.

We simulate the asset prices using the dynamics described by (12.18)–(12.20) (that is, we do not linearize the dynamics) and compute the real (as opposed to the worst-case) payments $\bar{w}_t$ required to finance the portfolio strategy. From the constraints (12.21), (12.22), (12.23), (12.24) and (12.25), it follows that

$$\bar{w}_t = \begin{cases} \max\left(l_t + \mathbf{p}_t^T \mathbf{x}_t - \alpha_{t-1}\left(\mathbf{p}_t^T \mathbf{D} \mathbf{x}_{t-1} + \mathbf{d}^T \mathbf{x}_{t-1}\right), \gamma L_t - \mathbf{p}_t^T \mathbf{x}_t, 0\right) \\ \text{if } 1 \le t \le \bar{T}, \\ \max\left(l_t + \beta L_t - \alpha_{t-1}\left(\mathbf{p}_t^T \mathbf{D} \mathbf{x}_{t-1} + \mathbf{d}^T \mathbf{x}_{t-1}\right), 0\right) \\ \text{if } t = \bar{T}, \end{cases} \tag{12.28}$$

where

$$\alpha_t = \max\left(\frac{\gamma L_t}{\mathbf{p}_t^T \mathbf{x}_t}, 1\right). \tag{12.29}$$

The variable α_t keeps track of whether the payment $\bar{w}_t$ is needed to maintain the regulation requirement $\gamma L_t / \mathbf{p}_t^T \mathbf{x}_t \le 1$, and the value of the portfolio in the next period will increase or remain unchanged accordingly. Note that, in our numerical experiments, $\mathbf{x}_t$ is fixed over time.

We generated $K = 100\,000$ independent sample paths and set the shortfall probability

$$\bar{\eta} = \frac{\sum_{k=1}^{K} \max_{0 \le t \le 3} \mathbf{1}\left(w_t < \bar{w}_t^{(k)}\right)}{K},$$

where $\{\bar{w}_t^{(k)}\}$ denotes the real payments on the k-th simulation run and $\mathbf{1}(\cdot)$ is the indicator function that takes the value 1 when the argument is true and 0 otherwise. Thus, $\bar{\eta}$ is the empirical probability that the real payment

$\overline{w}_t$ is larger than the worst case payment w_t. The expected net shortfall $\overline{W}$ was defined as follows.

$$\overline{W} = \frac{\displaystyle\sum_{k=0}^{K} \sum_{t=0}^{\overline{T}} B_{0,t} \left(\overline{w}_t^{(k)} - w_t \right)^+}{\displaystyle\sum_{k=0}^{K} \mathbf{1}\left(\sum_{t=0}^{\overline{T}} B_{0,t} \left(\overline{w}_t^{(k)} - w_t \right)^+ > 0 \right)}, \tag{12.30}$$

that is $\overline{W}$ is the expected shortfall conditioned on their being a shortfall. We define the Value-at-Risk (VaR$_p$) at probability p of the discounted total real payment as

$$\text{VaR}_p = \sup_{x \geq 0} \left\{ \sum_k \mathbf{1}\left(\sum_{t=0}^{\overline{T}} B_{0,t} \overline{w}_t^{(k)} \geq x \right) \geq (1-p) K \right\}$$

and Conditional Value-at-Risk (CVaR$_p$) of the discounted total real payment $\sum_{t=0}^{\overline{T}} B_{0,t} \overline{w}_t$ as

$$\text{CvaR}_p = \frac{1}{1-p} \left(\sum_{k=1}^{K} \left(\sum_{t=0}^{\overline{T}} B_{0,t} \overline{w}_t^{(k)} \right) \times \mathbf{1}\left(\sum_{t=0}^{\overline{T}} B_{0,t} \overline{w}_t^{(k)} \geq \text{VaR}_p \right) \right).$$

Table 12.3 plots the shortfall probability $\overline{p}$, the expected shortfall $\overline{W}$, the VaR and CVaR as a function of the probability p. From the numerical results, we can conclude that the linearized robust problem (12.27) does produce a conservative solution for the true nonlinear problem (note that, this is not guaranteed). In all cases, the empirical shortfall probability is at least an order of magnitude lower than that guaranteed by the robust problem. This result confirms our initial hypothesis that linearizing the dynamics should not result in a significant deterioration in performance.

For a fixed p, let $\tilde{p}$ denote the probability such that the corresponding shortfall probability $\overline{p} \approx 1 - p$. For example, for $p = 0.98$, $\tilde{p} = 0.85$ as the

Table 12.3 Simulation results

p	$\overline{p}$	$\overline{w}$	$\sum_{t=0}^{\overline{T}} B_{0,t} w_t$	VaR	CVaR
0.99	0.0014	5.98	697.36	537.40	546.96
0.98	0.0027	5.07	667.48	511.58	521.73
0.97	0.0039	5.41	644.63	496.18	506.83
0.96	0.0050	5.34	632.27	487.12	498.22
0.95	0.0063	5.43	622.91	479.91	491.22
0.90	0.0126	5.64	592.79	456.23	496.00
0.85	0.0182	5.99	574.24	441.90	455.63
0.80	0.0235	6.08	560.48	430.38	445.12

corresponding shortfall probability $\bar{\tilde{p}} \approx 0.0182 \approx 1 - p = 0.02$. Another such pair is $(p, \tilde{p}) = (0.99, 0.90)$. Then total discounted worst-case payment corresponding to p is approximately equal to the CVaR_p – note that, this is in spite of the fact that the robust problem does *not* minimize the total discounted payment.

12.3.8 Computational efficiency

All numerical computations reported in this work were conducted using Matlab 6.5 and MOSEK 4.0 (Andersen and Andersen, 2006). We used a Windows/32-X86 platform with Intel-PM. A typical portfolio problem had less than 100 constraints and 100 variables and it took no longer than a second for MOSEK to solve the portfolio problem.

12.4   Concluding remarks

In this article, we introduce a robust optimization framework for pension fund management that minimizes the worst-case pension contributions of the sponsoring firm. The illustrated model is able to account for some aspects of the corporate structure of the firm, for example cost of debt. The optimal pension plan from the proposed framework is computed by solving an SOCP and is, therefore, very efficient both in theory and in practice. In addition, we show that the framework is very versatile in that it allows us to compute both the optimal plan and also stress test any existing pension plans. The solution to the pension fund management problem is shown to be robust and conservative in the stress testing result.

There are fundamental differences between the robust approach and the stochastic programming approach. In the stochastic programming approach, the evolution of the stochastic parameters is approximated by a tree and one computes an optimal portfolio for each node in the tree taking the evolving information into account. As the tree can be constructed for any stochastic model, the stochastic programming approach is extremely versatile. However, a tree has zero probability and the stochastic programming approach is not able to provide any worst-case guarantees. Moreover, the complexity of the associated optimization problem is exponential in the time horizon and number of assets. In the robust optimization approach, one is able to provide a worst-case probabilistic guarantee; however, the portfolio selection cannot take advantage of evolving information (adjustable robust optimization somewhat mitigates this objection (Ben-Tal *et al*, 2004)). The computational complexity of the robust approach is polynomial in the time horizon and the number of assets. Both of these approaches cannot be implemented in an open-loop manner, and a new optimization problem has to be solved at each decision epoch. In summary, neither of these two approaches are clear winners; however, robust methods are very well suited for solving large-scale pension fund management problems.

Appendix

Derivation

The Itô-Taylor expansion applied to (12.19) at time 0 using (12.18) and (12.20) implies that

$$
B_{t,j} \approx B_{0,j} + \left(\sum_{i=1}^{3} (m_i - Z_0^i) \frac{\partial B_{s,j}}{\partial Z_s^i}\bigg|_{s=0} + \frac{1}{2} \sum_{i,l=1}^{3} \rho_{il} \frac{\partial^2 B_{s,j}}{\partial(Z_s^i)\partial(Z_s^l)}\bigg|_{s=0} \right) t
$$
$$
+ \sum_{i=1}^{3} \frac{\partial B_{s,j}}{\partial Z_s^i}\bigg|_{s=0} \sum_{k=1}^{4} \nu_{ik} W_t^k, \tag{A.1}
$$

where $\rho_{il} = \sum_{k=1}^{4} \nu_{ik}\nu_{kl}$ and $\mathbf{A} = [\nu_{ij}]$ is the covariance matrix of the factor vector $(W_t^1, \dots, W_t^4)$. Similarly, for the equity index q_t, we have

$$
q_t \approx q_0 + q_0\mu t + q_0 \sum_{k=1}^{4} \nu_{4k} W_t^k. \tag{A.2}
$$

Thus,

$$
\mathbf{p}_t \approx \mathbf{p}_0 + \mu_0^p t + \sum{}_0^p W_t, \tag{A.3}
$$

where

$$
\mu_0^p = \begin{bmatrix} \sum_{i=1}^{3}(m_i - Z_0^i)\frac{\partial B_{s,1}}{\partial Z_s^i}\bigg|_{s=0} + \frac{1}{2}\sum_{i,l=1}^{3}\rho_{il}\frac{\partial^2 B_{s,1}}{\partial(Z_s^i)\partial(Z_s^l)}\bigg|_{s=0} \\ \vdots \\ \sum_{i=1}^{3}(m_i - Z_0^i)\frac{\partial B_{s,M}}{\partial Z_s^i}\bigg|_{s=0} + \frac{1}{2}\sum_{i,l=1}^{3}\rho_{il}\frac{\partial^2 B_{s,M}}{\partial(Z_s^i)\partial(Z_s^l)}\bigg|_{s=0} \\ q_0\mu \end{bmatrix} \in \Re^{M+1},
$$

and

$$
\sum{}_0^p = \begin{bmatrix} \frac{\partial B_{s,1}}{\partial Z_s^1}\bigg|_{s=0} & \frac{\partial B_{s,1}}{\partial Z_s^2}\bigg|_{s=0} & \frac{\partial B_{s,1}}{\partial Z_s^3}\bigg|_{s=0} & \frac{\partial B_{s,1}}{\partial q_s}\bigg|_{s=0} \\ \vdots & \vdots & \vdots & \vdots \\ \frac{\partial B_{s,M}}{\partial Z_s^1}\bigg|_{s=0} & \frac{\partial B_{s,M}}{\partial Z_s^2}\bigg|_{s=0} & \frac{\partial B_{s,M}}{\partial Z_s^3}\bigg|_{s=0} & \frac{\partial B_{s,M}}{\partial q_s}\bigg|_{s=0} \\ 0 & 0 & 0 & q_0 \end{bmatrix} \cdot \mathbf{A} \in \Re^{(M+1)\times 4}.
$$

It then follows that for all $t = 1, ..., \bar{T}-1$,

$$
\begin{aligned}
&P\left(\mathbf{p}_t^T \mathbf{D} \mathbf{x}_{t-1} + \mathbf{d}^T \mathbf{x}_{t-1} + w_t - l_t \geq \mathbf{p}_t^T \mathbf{x}_t\right) \\
&= P\left(\mathbf{p}_t^T \left(\mathbf{D} \mathbf{x}_{t-1} - \mathbf{x}_t\right) + \mathbf{d}^T \mathbf{x}_{t-1} + w_t - l_t \geq 0\right) \\
&= P\left(\left(\mathbf{p}_0 + \mu_0^p t\right)^T \left(\mathbf{D} \mathbf{x}_{t-1} - \mathbf{x}_t\right) + \mathbf{d}^T \mathbf{x}_{t-1} t + w_t - l_t \geq \left(\mathbf{D} \mathbf{x}_{t-1} - \mathbf{x}_t\right)^T \textstyle\sum_0^p W_t\right)
\end{aligned}
$$

Since $-\left(\mathbf{D} \mathbf{x}_{t-1} - \mathbf{x}_t\right)^T \sum_0^p W^t \sim N \times \left(0, \ \left\|\left(\mathbf{D} \mathbf{x}_{t-1} - \mathbf{x}_t\right)^T \sum_0^p\right\|_2^2 t\right)$ if $\varepsilon < 0.5$, we have

$$
\begin{aligned}
&\left(\mathbf{p}_0 + \mu_0^p t\right)^T \left(\mathbf{D} \mathbf{x}_{t-1} - \mathbf{x}_t\right) + \mathbf{d}^T \mathbf{x}_{t-1} + w_t - l_t \\
&\geq \sqrt{t} \Phi^{-1}(1-\varepsilon) \left\|\left(\mathbf{D} \mathbf{x}_{t-1} - \mathbf{x}_t\right)^T \textstyle\sum_0^p\right\|_2 \\
&\Downarrow \\
&P\left(\mathbf{p}_t^T \mathbf{D} \mathbf{x}_{t-1} + \mathbf{d}^T \mathbf{x}_{t-1} + w_t - l_t \geq \mathbf{p}_t^T \mathbf{x}_t\right) \geq (1-\varepsilon),
\end{aligned} \tag{A.4}
$$

where $\Phi(\cdot)$ denotes cumulative density function of the standard normal random variable.

Using an analysis similar to the one employed above, the constraint (12.23) can be reformulated as the SOC constraint

$$
\begin{aligned}
&\left(\mathbf{p}_0 + \mu_0^p \bar{T}\right)^T \mathbf{D} \mathbf{x}_{\bar{T}-1} + \mathbf{d}^T \mathbf{x}_{\bar{T}-1} + w_{\bar{T}} - l_{\bar{T}} - \beta L_{\bar{T}} \\
&\geq \sqrt{\bar{T}} \Phi^{-1}(1-\varepsilon) \left\|\left(\mathbf{D} \mathbf{x}_{\bar{T}-1}\right)^T \textstyle\sum_0^p\right\|_2,
\end{aligned} \tag{A.5}
$$

and the regulation constraint (12.25) can be reformulated as the SOC constraint

$$
\left(\mathbf{p}_0 + \mu_0^p t\right)^T \mathbf{x}_t - \gamma L_t \geq \Phi^{-1}(1-\varepsilon) \sqrt{t} \left\|x_t^T \textstyle\sum_0^p\right\|_2 \tag{A.6}
$$

As the short rates $s_{t,1}$ are described by a Ornstein–Uhlenbeck process whose marginal distribution is normal, it follows that the interest-coverage constraint (12.9) is equivalent to the linear constraint

$$
\alpha\!\left(\underline{Q}\right)\!\left(E\!\left(s_{t,1}\right) + \sqrt{\operatorname{var}\!\left[s_{t,1}\right]}\,\Phi^{-1}(1-\varepsilon) + P\!\left(\underline{Q}\right)\right) w_t^d \leq C_t, \quad t = 1,2,...,\bar{T}, \tag{A.7}
$$

where $\operatorname{var}[s_{t,1}]$ denotes the variance of $s_{t,1}$.

Finally, we can solve the following SOCP

$$
\min \sum_{t=0}^{\bar{T}} \left((1-\alpha_T) B_{0,t} + \left((1-\alpha_T) \times P\!\left(\underline{Q}\right) + \alpha_T\right) B_{0,t+1}\right) w_t^d \tag{A.8}
$$

subject to (21), (34), (35), (24), and (36), (7), and (37).

Acknowledgements

We thank Mr Armen Avanessians of Goldman Sachs for a gift that helped support this research. We also thank Professor Donald Goldfarb and Dr Erol Hakanoglu for constructive comments. This research was partially supported by NSF grants CCR-00–09972, DMS- 01–04282, DMS 06–06712, ONR grant N000140310514 and DOE grant GE-FG01–92ER-25126.

References

Alizadeh, F. and Goldfarb, D. (2003) Second-order cone programming. *Mathematical Programming* 95: 3–51.

Andersen, E.D. and Andersen, K.D. (2006) The MOSEK optimization toolbox for MATLAB manual Version 4.0, http://www.mosek.com/products/40/tools/help/index. html.

Barrett, W.B., Gosnell, T. and Heuson, A. (1995) Yield curve shifts and the selection of immunization strategies. *Journal of Fixed Income* 5(2): 53–64.

Ben-Tal, A. and Nemirovski, A. (2001) *Lectures on Modern Convex Optimization: Analysis, Algorithms, and Engineering Applications.* Philadelphia, USA: Society for Industrial & Applied Math.

Ben-Tal, A. and Nemirovski, A. (2002) Robust optimization – Methodology and applications. *Mathematical Programming* 92(3): 453–480.

Ben-Tal, A., Margalit, T. and Nemirovski, A. (2000) Robust modeling of multi-stage portfolio problems. In: H. Frenk (ed.) *High Performance Optimization.* Dordrecht, The Netherlands: Kluwer Academic Publishers, pp. 303–328.

Ben-Tal, A., Goryashko, A., Guslitzer, E. and Nemirovski, A. (2004) Adjustable robust solutions of uncertain linear programs. *Mathematical Programming* 99(2): 351–376.

Boros, E. and Prékopa, A. (1989) Closed form two-sided bounds for probabilities that at least r and exactly r out of n events occur. *Mathematics of Operations Research* 14(2): 317–342.

Chang, F. (2004) *Stochastic Optimization in Continuous Time.* Cambridge, UK: Cambridge University Press.

Consigli, G. and Dempster, M. (1998) Dynamic stochastic programming for asset-liability management. *Annals of Operations Research* 81: 131–161.

Damodaran, A. (2004) *Applied Corporate Finance: A User's Manual,* 2nd edn. Hoboken, NJ: Wiley.

Drijver, S., Haneveld, W. and Vlerk, M. (2000) Asset Liability Management Modeling Using Multistage Mixed-integer Stochastic Programming. University of Groningen. Technical Report.

Fabozzi, F., Focardi, S. and Jonas, C. (2004) *Can Modeling Help Deal with the Pension Funding Crisis.* Houston, TX: The Intertek Group.

Fabozzi, F., Martellini, L. and Priaulet, P. (2005) Predictability in the shape of the term structure of interest rates. *Journal of Fixed Income* 15(1): 40–53.

Goldfarb, D. and Iyengar, G. (2003) Robust convex quadratically constrained programs. *Mathematical Programming Ser B* 97(3): 495–515.

Hull, J. and White, A. (1990) Pricing interest rate derivative securities. *Review of Financial Studies* 3(4): 573–592.

Jin, L., Merton, R. and Bodie, Z. (2006) Do a firm's equity returns reflect the risk of its pension plan? *Journal of Financial Economics* 81(1): 1–26.

Klaassen, P. (1998) Financial asset-pricing theory and stochastic programming models for asset/liability management: A synthesis. *Management Science* 44(1): 31–48.

Myers, S. and Majluf, N. (1984) Corporate financing and investment decisions when firms have information that investors do not have. *Journal of Financial Economics* 13(2): 155–295.

Nelson, C. and Siegel, A. (1987) Parsimonious modeling of yield curves. *Journal of Business* 60(4): 473–489.

Sodhi, M. (2005) LP modeling for asset-liability management: A survey of choices and simplifications. *Operations Research* 53(2): 181–196.

13
Alternative Decision Models for Liability-Driven Investment

Katharina Schwaiger, Cormac Lucas and Gautam Mitra

13.1 Introduction and background

Traditional Asset and Liability Management (ALM) models have been recently recast as Liability-Driven Investment (LDI) models for making integrated financial decisions in pension schemes investment: matching and outperforming liabilities. LDI has become extremely popular as the decision tool of choice for pension funds. The last decade experienced a fall in the equity markets, while bond yields reached low levels. The UK Accounting standard FRS17 (since 2001, replacing SSAP24) requires the assets to be measured by their market value and liabilities to be measured by a projected unit method and a discount rate reflecting the market yields then available on AA rated corporate bonds of appropriate currency and term. When these new regulations were introduced, liabilities became harder to meet. In the case of a deficit, the pension fund trustees and employers have to agree on extra contributions to fill the deficit within 10 years time. Furthermore, deficit or surplus has to be fully included on the balance sheet of the sponsoring company. In the Netherlands and the Nordic countries, LDI models have become established (see C. Dert, 1995 and Drijver, 2005); the United Kingdom, Italy and a few other European countries are close followers of this trend. Traditionally, assets and liabilities were considered separate. In asset management, the aim was to maximize return for a given risk level. However, the matching of the liabilities was not taken into consideration. The main argument was that assets should be made to grow faster than liabilities. The modern integrated approach to LDI considers the cash flow streams for invested assets of fixed-income portfolios enhanced by interest rate swaps and in some cases of swaptions.

We present an ALM problem for LDI formulated as four alternative decision models: a deterministic expected value linear programming (EVLP) model, a two-stage stochastic programming (SP) model with recourse, a chance-constrained SP model and an integrated chance-constrained SP model. In the deterministic model, we look at the relationship between *PV*01 matching and the required funding, where *PV*01 is the (sterling) change in the net present value of a bond due to a 0.01 per cent (one basis point) positive parallel shift in the yield curve; this is an industry-accepted measure of sensitivity analysis. In the SP model, we have two sources of randomness: liabilities and interest rates. We generate interest rate scenarios, look at the relationship between funding requirements and minimize the deviation of the present value (PV) matching of the assets and liabilities over time. In the chance-constrained programming (CCP) model, we limit the number of future deficit events by introducing binary variables and a user-specified reliability level. The last model has integrated chance constraints (ICC), which not only limits the events of underfunding but also the amount of underfunding relative to the liabilities. Since the mid 1980s, the use of SP models for the ALM problem have been widely advocated and it has been applied in banks (see Kusy and Ziemba, 1986), insurance companies (Carino *et al*, 1998), hedge and mutual funds (Ziemba, 2003), university endowments (Merton, 1993), wealthy individuals (Medova *et al*, 2008) and pension funds (Consigli and Dempster, 1998 and Mulvey *et al*, 2000). In the late 1990s, case studies and applications were described in a book by Ziemba *et al* (2003). SP models are classified as single-stage optimization models, two-stage optimization models, multi-stage optimization models and chance-constrained optimization models. The most frequently used mean-variance approach falls under the single-stage model category. A recent survey by Fabozzi *et al* (2007) and its update (2008) showed that quantitative fund management is now widely used in the industry. Although optimization is used, the most applied is mean-variance optimization; with SP being applied only in one case out of 36 survey participants. Measuring risk is also widely employed, but variance and value at risk (VaR) are the most frequently used measures, with conditional value at risk (CVaR) being one of the least used techniques. We note in this context that scenario-based SP models allow the inclusion of VaR and CVaR constraints.

This article is structured as follows: In the next section, four different approaches for LDI using deterministic linear programming (LP), two-stage SP, CCP and integrated chance-constrained programming (ICCP) are introduced. In the subsequent section, computational results, details and backtests are given. The last section presents a discussion of the results and concludes the article.

13.2   The decision models

As economic and business environments change, all pension funds experience some continued deviation between assets and liabilities. The central decision problem in ALM is to construct a portfolio of fixed-income securities for a pension fund, which takes into account the future outflows (liabilities) of the pension scheme and a set of other constraints and determines the optimum trade-off between initial injected cash from member benefits and the sponsoring company and deviations between assets and liabilities. These decision problems are essentially *ex-ante* decision problems in which the evolution of time and uncertainty are taken into consideration.

13.2.1 LP model

The first decision model proposed is the EVLP model; it uses an immunization technique: *PV01* matching. *PV01* matching attempts to match the interest rate sensitivity of the bond portfolio with the interest rate sensitivity of the liability stream. The indices are the time buckets $t = 1,..., T$ and bond b from a set of bonds B. In reality, b is a function of the quadruplet i, j, k and l, which is defined by the set $\{(i, j, k, l) \mid i \in Ratingclass, j \in Sectors, k \in Country, l \in Issuer\}$. Decisions about borrowing and lending are made at the beginning of the new time point. The asset classes include corporate and government bonds, both UK and foreign. Time intervals can be represented as T time buckets. A time bucket consists of several time points. The initial set of time buckets are defined over a short time period (for example, 3 months), whereas the later set of time buckets are defined over longer time periods (for example, 1 or 2 years).

The model indices are:

b	bond from a bond set B
t	time horizon $1,..., T$

Define the model parameters using these indices:

L_t	liability value at time t
$LPV01_t$	*PV01* value of the liability at time t
$BPV01_t^b$	*PV01* value of bond b at time t
c_t^b	cash flow stream of bond b at time t
P_b	trading price of bond t
α	transaction cost involved when bonds are sold or bought
O_b	opening position of bond b at the initial time period
M_t	maximum amount of money allowed to be borrowed
r_t	interest rate at time t

Define the decision variables, which are constrained to be non-negative:

x_b	amount of bond b purchased
y_b	amount of bond b sold
z_b	amount of bond b held
d_t	amount borrowed at time period t; limited to be $\leq M_t \; \forall_t$

s_t amount lent at time period t

C   initial available cash.

Furthermore, we introduce the two sets of non-negative decision variables, which measure the deviation of the assets' *PV01* and the liabilities' *PV01*:

$devo_t$ measurement of over deviation at time t

$devu_t$ measurement of under deviation at time t.

The set of constraints include some typical constructs of portfolio planning: these are the cash-flow accounting equation and the inventory balance constraints. The cash-flow accounting equation initializes the new asset portfolio by liquidating the old asset allocation and including the available cash C:

$$\sum_{b=1}^{B}(1+\alpha)P_b x_b \le C + \sum_{b=1}^{B}(1-\alpha)P_b y_b. \tag{13.1}$$

The inventory balance constraint assures that the holding of bond b is made up of the opening position of the same bond including the amount bought minus the amount sold:

$$z_b = O_b + x_b - y_b \quad \forall b. \tag{13.2}$$

The following constraints match the bonds cash flows with the liabilities stream, having the possibility to borrow from the bank or to reinvest spare cash with it. At the final time period, there is no opportunity to borrow from the bank.

$$\sum_{b=1}^{B} c_1^b z_b + d_1 = L_1 + s_1 \tag{13.3}$$

$$\sum_{b=1}^{B} c_t^b z_b + d_t - (1+r_t)d_{t-1} = L_t + s_t - (1+r_t)s_{t-1} \quad t:2 \le t \le T \tag{13.4}$$

$$\sum_{b=1}^{B} c_T^b z_b - (1+r_T)d_{t-1} = L_T + s_T - (1+r_T)s_{t-1}. \tag{13.5}$$

Furthermore, we define the behaviour of the variables $devo_t$ and $devu_t$ with the following constraint that binds them to the difference of the assets and liabilities *PV01* values:

$$\sum_{b=1}^{B} BPV01_t^b z_b = devo_t - devu_t + LPV01_t, \quad \forall t. \tag{13.6}$$

If we include the minimum and maximum amount of bonds in the portfolio within a specific rating class, say AAA rating, specified by the pension fund, we get the following user-specific constraints:

$$MinInRatingclassAAA \leq \sum_{b=1}^{B} z_{b(i=AAA,\cdot,\cdot,\cdot)} \leq MaxInRatingclassAAA. \tag{13.7}$$

Similar limits are imposed in respect of other bond characteristic, that is country, issuer and sector. Equation (13.6) is also called a goal constraint, where any under- and over-deviations are penalized in the objective function.

13.2.1.1   Two objective functions

The decision model we consider has two objective functions and the direction of optimization is minimization.

The pension fund has to operate efficiently and this is achieved by keeping its contributions (employees' plus employers') low. An increased need of initial cash means an increase in the active members' contributions. The first objective function is the initial cash, which has to be injected in advance to achieve a (feasible) match between assets and liabilities:

$$\phi_1(C, d_t) = \text{Minimize}\left(C + \sum_{t=1}^{T} d_t \right). \tag{13.8}$$

The second objective function is the total deviation of assets and liabilities; there are other suitable objective functions we might consider depending on the decision values required. This linear objective function minimizes the total *PV*01 deviations of assets and liabilities:

$$\phi_2(devo_t, devu_t) = \text{Minimize}\sum_{t=1}^{T}\left(devo_t + devu_t \right), \tag{13.9}$$

where $devo_t$ and $devu_t$ are the over- and under-deviations between the portfolios *PV*01 and the liabilities *PV*01 at time t, which are restricted to be non-negative. These values are determined by equation (13.6) and the above objective function minimizes the absolute deviation to zero or as close to zero as possible.

13.2.2   SP model

The deterministic LP model can be extended to various SP models that take into account uncertainty around the interest rate. Instead of matching *PV*01 values of the assets and liabilities, the stochastic models match the PVs of the assets and liabilities. Three SP models are formulated: a two-stage SP model,

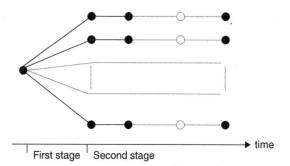

Figure 13.1   Scenario tree

which is first extended to include chance constraints and then ICC. The decision models determine the optimum allocation in bonds for the pension fund, whose liability stream is matched by the bonds' coupon and principal cash flows, taking into account the additional cash that needs to be raised.

We begin by considering the two-stage SP model and introduce an index set of scenarios S. Each scenario represents possible future outcomes; and with each scenario s, we also associate a probability π_s of occurrence. The model will determine an optimal decision by using past information and anticipating future events. Uncertainty is only resolved between Stage 1 and Stage 2. Figure 13.1 illustrates this. Although we have multiple time stages, the model uses a degenerated (multi-time period) tree structure with a single branching point. The resulting model is thus a two-stage recourse model.

This model has the same indices as the EVLP model plus an additional set, which represents the scenarios:

b bond from a bond set B
t time horizon $1,...,T$
s scenarios $1,...,S$

The following parameters are affected by uncertainty:

L_t^s liability value at time t under scenario s
r_t^s uncertain interest rate at time t
π_s probability of scenario s occurring.

We replace the *PV*01 notation by using PVs:

LPV_t^s uncertain PV of the liability at time t
$BPV_t^{b,s}$ uncertain PV of bond b at time t

The following are the stochastic decision variables:

dt^s uncertain amount borrowed at time period t; limited to be $\leq M_t \; \forall_t$

PVd_t^s PV of the uncertain amount borrowed at time period t; limited to be $\leq M_t \; \forall_t$

s_t^s uncertain amount lent at time period t

PVs_t^s PV of the uncertain amount lent at time period t

$devo_t^s$ measurement of over deviation at time t at scenario s

$devu_t^s$ measurement of under deviation at time t at scenario s

Decisions about borrowing and lending are made before each time period. The restrictions (constraints) are comparable to the EVLP problem described earlier. Wherever appropriate, uncertain parameters and decision variables are included. Thus, the revised constraints of the two-stage SP model are:

Matching equations for all time periods:

$$\sum_{b=1}^{B} c_1^b z_b + d_1^s = L_1^s + s_1^s \quad \forall \, s \tag{13.10}$$

$$\sum_{b=1}^{B} c_t^b z_b + d_t^s - (1+r_t) d_{t-1}^s = L_t^s + s_t^s - (1+r_t) s_{t-1}^s \quad \forall \, s, t \geq 2 \tag{13.11}$$

$$\sum_{b=1}^{B} c_T^b z_b - (1+r_T) d_{T-1}^s = L_T^s + s_T^s - (1+r_T) s_{T-1}^s \quad \forall \, s. \tag{13.12}$$

PV matching of assets and liabilities:

$$\sum_{b=1}^{B} BPV_t^{b,s} z_b + PVs_t^s = devo_t^s - devu_t^s + LPV_t^s + PVd_t^s \quad \forall \, s,t. \tag{13.13}$$

Non-anticipativity constraints:

$$d_1^s = d_1^1 \quad s = 2,..., S \tag{13.14}$$

$$s_1^s = s_1^1 \quad s = 2,..., S. \tag{13.15}$$

The cash-flow accounting equation and the inventory balance equation are the same as for the LP model. Equation (13.13) is also called a goal constraint with stochasticity: any over- and under-deviations are penalized in the objective function. Non-anticipativity constraints (equations (13.14) and (13.15)) are required to ensure that the sets of initial feasible decisions coincide and do not depend on future scenario realizations.

13.2.2.1   Two objective functions

Similar to the first model, there are two objective functions and the direction of optimization is minimization. Taking into consideration all possible future outcomes, the first objective function involves the injected initial cash to meet expected future liabilities:

$$\phi_3\left(C, d_t^s\right) = \text{Minimize}\left(C + \sum_{t=1}^{T}\sum_{s=1}^{S} \pi_s d_t^s\right). \tag{13.16}$$

The second objective function is the expected total deviation of bonds' and liabilities' PVs and becomes:

$$\phi_4\left(devo_t^s, devu_t^s\right) = \text{Minimize}\sum_{t=1}^{T}\sum_{s=1}^{S} \pi_s \left(devo_t^s + devu_t^s\right). \tag{13.17}$$

13.2.3   CCP model

We define a reliability level β, $0 \le \beta \le 1$ for the chance constraints, which is the probability of their satisfaction. As in Van der Vlerk (2003), we introduce a scalar γ, that is the level on which liabilities are to be met to satisfy the constraints. If $\gamma = 1$, we are trying to meet the liabilities precisely; if $\gamma = 1$, we force more inflows than outflows. The value of the liability at time t under scenario s is denoted by L_t^s and the value of the asset portfolio at time t under scenario s is denoted by A_t^s to yield:

$$P\left\{A_{t+1}^s - \gamma L_{t+1}^s \ge 0 \middle| (t,s)\right\} \ge \beta_t, \quad t = 1,\dots,T-1. \tag{13.18}$$

This constraint applies for all time periods t across all scenarios s, which means that there is a chance constraint in every time period of the scenario tree. In each period, only a predefined number of scenarios can have underfunding. The ratio between the total number of scenarios and the number of scenarios in which underfunding can occur is the specified β_t.

The CCP model has the same sets, parameters, decision variables, constraints and objective functions as discussed in the previous SP model.

We add new parameters:

γ_t weight of liabilities with respect to the asset value at time t; likely to be > 1; can be user defined with high values at the earlier time points and then decreasing with time

β_t reliability level at time t; likely to be >0; can be user defined or assumed to be constant over time

N sufficiently large number for the chance constraint (maximum value the investment portfolio is likely to reach)

A new decision variable:

δ_t^s binary variable, which takes the value of 1 if there is any underfunding.

The chance constraints are formulated as follows:

$$P\left\{\sum_{b=1}^{B} BPV_{b,t+1}^{S}zb + PVs_{t+1}^{s} - \gamma LPV_{t+1}^{s} - \gamma PVd_{t+1}^{s} \geq 0 \middle| (t,s)\right\} \geq \beta_t$$
$$\forall t = 1,\ldots,T-1 \tag{13.19}$$

$$N\delta_{t+1}^{s} \geq \gamma LPV_{t+1}^{s} + \gamma PVd_{t+1}^{s} - \sum_{b=1}^{B} BPV_{b,t+1}^{S}zb - PVs_{t+1}^{s}c \quad t = 1,\ldots,T-1 \tag{13.20}$$

$$N\left(1-\delta_{t+1}^{s}\right) - \frac{1}{N} \geq BPV_{b,t+1}^{S}zb + PVs_{t+1}^{s} - \gamma LPV_{t+1}^{s} - \gamma PVd_{t+1}^{s}$$
$$\forall s,t = 1,\ldots,T-1 \tag{13.21}$$

$$\pi_s \sum_{s=1}^{s} \delta_{t+1}^{s} \leq 1 - \beta_t \quad t = 1,\ldots,T-1 \tag{13.22}$$

$$\delta_t^s \varepsilon \{0,1\} \forall t, \tag{13.23}$$

where the shortfall probability is measured for all scenarios and is constrained at a reliability level. This is a direct way of modelling risk and incorporating risk aversion. For different time periods, different reliability levels for β_t can be set. It makes sense to set a high value (close to 1) for β_t in the earlier time periods, whereas lowering the level of β_t through time. The more distant the time period is from today, the more the world will probably differ from the forecast scenarios; therefore, in the later time periods, it is very likely that the model will be rerun with added knowledge of the world and the planned actions changed accordingly. High reliability levels in early time periods still ensure the fund resulting in a surplus. This may be considered as a form of future discounting using β_t, which determines the tightness of the constraints. Equation (13.20) ensures that δ is forced to become 1 if there is any underfunding, that is when the portfolio's PV is lower than the liabilities' PV. Equation (13.21) ensures that δ is forced to become 0 if there is overfunding, that is if the portfolio's PV is higher than the liabilities' PV.

13.2.4   ICCP model

Another way of incorporating risk of underfunding is to use ICC, introduced by Haneveld (1985), see also Van der Vlerk (2003). The idea behind ICC is that both the probability of underfunding and the amount of underfunding are considered. ICC are closely related to constraints on conditional surplus at risk, which is a variant of CVaR. We have seen that the chance constraints are qualitative; they measure the probability of a deficit, but the amount of the deficit is not considered. The ICC, however, are quantitative, which take into account the amount of the underfunding. VaR is closely related to chance constraints and CVaR constraints are closely related to ICC. The only difference is that, in the ICCP model, the new decision variable *shortage* is limited to a user pre-specified level, that is the level of deficit it is not allowed to exceed. Using CVaR constraints, however, limits the average level of deficit above the α confidence level, which is then incorporated into the optimization stage and the model is optimized to meet that CVaR target.

The ICCP model has the same sets, parameters and variables as the SP model. A new parameter λ_t is introduced, with $0 \leq \lambda_t \leq 1$. Multiplied by the liabilities, it represents the maximum allowed shortage at each time period. Another new decision variable is *shortage$_t^s$* that measures the amount of underfunding at each time period in each scenario.

The ICC can be included as:

$$\sum_{b-1}^{B} BPV_{b,t}^s zb + PVs_t^s - \gamma LPV_t^s - \gamma PVd_t^s + shortage_t^s \geq 0 \ \forall t,s \tag{13.24}$$

$$\pi \sum_{s=1}^{s} shortage_t^s \leq \lambda_t * \max_s \left(LPV_t^s \right) \forall t. \tag{13.25}$$

Our formulation of ICC does not require the use of binary variables, which reduces the central processing unit (CPU) time compared to the CCP.

The chance-constrained and integrated chance-constrained formulation can be compared to the recent work of Dempster *et al* (2006), in which the expected average shortfall (EAS) or the expected maximum shortfall (EMS) is limited for a long-term nominal minimum guaranteed return plan suitable for pension schemes. The EAS limits the number of times the portfolio wealth drops below a pre-specified barrier, whereas the EMS limits any substantial shortfall.

13.3 Computational investigation

13.3.1 The experimental set-up

The models are solved for a time period of 45 years, with 150 interest rate scenarios and a set of 376 bonds to choose from. The liabilities of a defined benefit pension fund are long dated and need to be projected far into the future. The liability stream is generated using a typical closed pension scheme population (only today's members have the right on future retirement benefits of today's pension fund) and UK mortality tables for the subsequent scheme population. Entry age is 21 years, retirement age is 65 years and no differences between male and female are assumed. As it is a defined benefit scheme, final salary estimates are generated taking into account merit salary scales, productivity rates and inflation to construct an expected liability stream. In the SP models, this expected liability stream is discounted using stochastic interest rates making the liability stream stochastic, too. For further details, the reader is referred to Schwaiger (2009) or to textbooks such as Winklevoss' (1993).

All models are written in AMPL (Fourer *et al*, 2002) and solved using ILOG CPLEX 11.0 on a P4 3.0 GHz machine. The LP model has 633 constraints, 1243 linear variables and its CPU time is 0.0625 seconds. The SP model has 66 306 constraints, 34 128 linear variables and solves in 28.7656 seconds. The CCP model has 53 750 constraints, 6750 binary variables, 13 877 linear variables

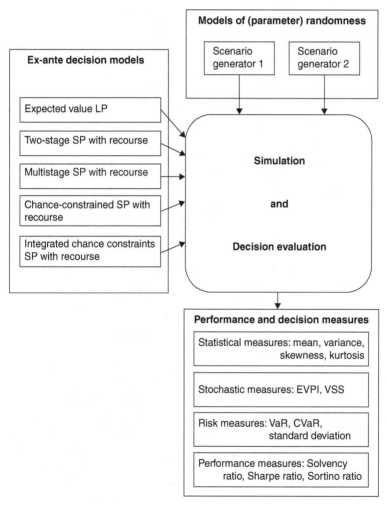

Figure 13.2 Information flow and simulation

and solves in 1022.23 seconds. The ICCP model has 66 201 constraints, 34 128 linear variables and solves in 56.7344 seconds. Our formulation of ICC does not require the use of binary variables, which reduces the CPU time compared to that of CCP. The family of models were originally investigated using AMPL and processed by the CPLEX solver adopted to solve deterministic equivalent models or scenario-based chance constrained models. For additional discussion, the reader is referred to Schwaiger (2009). The authors and the researchers in the CARISMA team are focused on developing and improving SP tools; ALM/LDI is an important and key application of SP. At the beginning of the project, considerable effort was deployed towards the computational platform that uses CPLEX and is reported here. Subsequently, this family of models have been developed and implemented in the stochastic AMPL (SAMPL, see Valente *et al*, 2005) environment utilizing the stochastic programming integrated environment (SPInE) (see Valente *et al*, 2009) platform. The model instances are processed using the FortSP solver, which has been recently enhanced to process large instances of SP models (Zverovich *et al*, 2008). A particularly attractive feature of the enhanced SPInE is that two-stage SP, CCP and ICCP models can be formulated and processed by the FortSP solver. In addition, the systems architecture supports the analysis in the ex-post investigation of optimum decisions. An outline of the modelling architecture of SPInE is shown in Figure 13.2, which illustrates how alternative SP decisions can be put through a central simulator connected to alternative scenario generators (see Di Domenica *et al*, 2007).

13.3.2   The efficient frontier

The efficient frontier in deviation-initial cash space is plotted for the LP, SP, CCP and ICCP models. Equidistant initial cash and total deviations are fixed and then total deviations and initial cash are minimized, respectively. For high initial cash amounts, an increase in cash will not reduce the total deviations between assets and liabilities as much as it would in the more nonlinear part of the trade off in which an increase in initial cash decreases the total deviations between assets and liabilities more drastically.

In Figure 13.3, the red points give the deviation values for the equidistant initial cash values and the blue points give the initial cash values for the equally spaced deviations. From the graph, we see a concave efficient frontier: lower amount of initial cash increase the deviation and higher amount of initial cash decrease the deviation. Figure 13.4 compares the deviation-budget trade-off of the SP model with the CCP model with $\gamma = 1.05$ and $\beta = 0.875$ for three time periods. The thick green line is the efficient frontier of the CCP model and the blue points are the efficient frontier points of the SP model. The CCP model requires more initial cash for the same deviations to assure that only a pre-specified percentage of scenarios are allowed to go underfunded. Figure 13.5

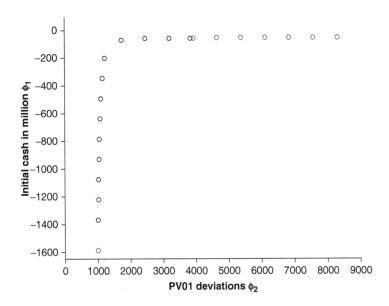

Figure 13.3   PV01 deviation-budget trade-off

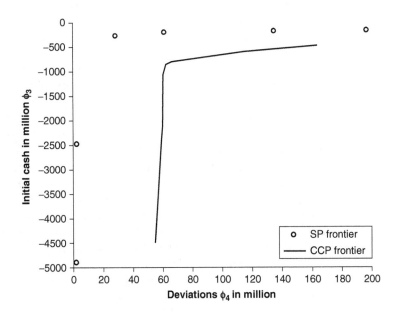

Figure 13.4   SP versus CCP deviation-budget trade-off

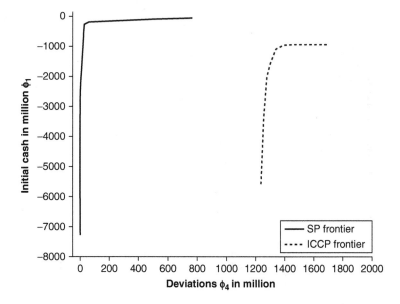

Figure 13.5 SP versus ICCP deviation-budget trade-off

shows the ICCP results in comparison with the SP results, with $\gamma = 1.05$ and $\lambda = 0.01$ for all time periods. The ICCP is more expensive in terms of initial injected cash for the same total deviations, but, at the same time, the deficit is only limited to be 1 per cent of the maximum allowed liabilities. The SP frontier dominates the CCP and ICCP model frontiers; this is simply explained by the fact that the CCP and ICCP models include the corresponding constraints of the SP formulation.

Figure 13.6 shows different β values and the corresponding initial required cash. A constant γ of 1.05 has been used and the chance constraints were only forced for the first three time periods. As expected, for a higher reliability level β, more initial cash is required. The shape of the graph can be explained as follows: It is not a straight line because of the relationship of β, δ and the total number of scenarios. If β is changed by 0.1, then the sum of allowed δ_s in equation (13.22) will also change by 10 per cent of the total number of scenarios; it is already, as such, 'expensive' to assure that the probability of underfunding events is restricted, an increase of 10 per cent in that probability might be even more expensive in terms of initial injected cash. For the case of a low probability of total underfunding events, it might not be expensive to increase that probability. For example, it is as expensive to have a β of 0.75 as having a β of 0.825, but there is a higher increase of initial cash from $\beta = 0.9$ to $\beta = 1$ than from $\beta = 0.8$ to $\beta = 0.9$.

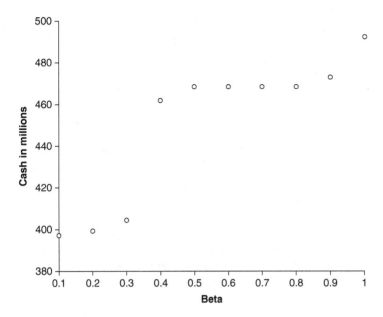

Figure 13.6   CCP beta-budget trade-off

13.3.3   Historical backtests

Each model exhibits a different efficient frontier; the SP models require higher initial cash to reach an optimal decision that makes them expensive for the pension fund to implement, but also means that less deficit is expected. Therefore, it is difficult to compare the models' optimal decisions with each other from a practical viewpoint. A good way is to perform a backtest and look at the resulting wealth states of the pension fund. During backtesting, the models are estimated with past data and their recommendations to out-of-sample historical data. Thus, a closer look can be taken at what would have happened had the decisions suggested by the models been implemented in the past. Using data from 2000 onwards is especially important, since in that period pension funds were experiencing higher deficits. Optimal decisions are taken at time t and the surplus/deficit of the pension fund at time $t+1,...,T$ is recorded using historical data. From then onwards, the models are rolled forward: the scenario generator uses historical data up to $t+1$ and generates interest rate scenarios until T. At each time period, the models are rerun with the newly generated scenarios. The liabilities and bond maturities are reduced in a telescopic manner, that is from $t,...,T$ to $t+1,...,T$ and so on.

The following backtest results use this multi-period simulation approach. In order to conduct the backtesting simulations, the data set is manipulated and processed for this purpose over the period 1997–2007. For each backtesting year, 150 interest rate scenarios were generated using the Cox, Ingersoll and Ross model calibrated to historical data. The liability profile was shortened after each year and the bonds were repriced every year.

Figure 13.7 shows the cash-deviation trade off of the LP, SP, CCP and ICCP models as of 1997. The CCP and ICCP trade-offs are dominated by the SP trade-off, with a focus on over-deviations to assure a limited number of events/amount of deficit.

Figure 13.8(a) shows the performance of the SP model during the backtesting period 1997–2006, the model is rerun every year and the corresponding profit/loss over the planning horizon is plotted. At the end of the planning horizon, the SP model leads the pension fund to a surplus; however, in the earlier time periods, there are deficit occurrences. Figure 13.8(b) shows the performance of the CCP model during the backtesting period 1997–2006. At the later time points, the model underperforms, which is because of the fact that the model has its chance constraints not run for the whole time horizon, but only for the next seven time periods. The model still outperforms for longer

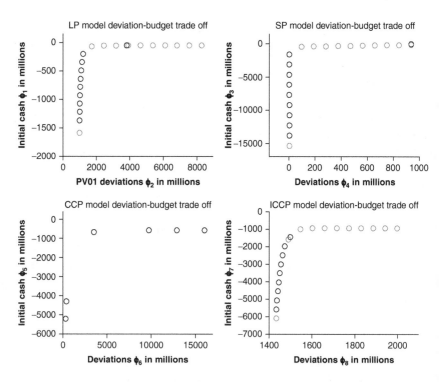

Figure 13.7 Budget-deviation trade-offs of the LP, SP, CCP and ICCP models 1997

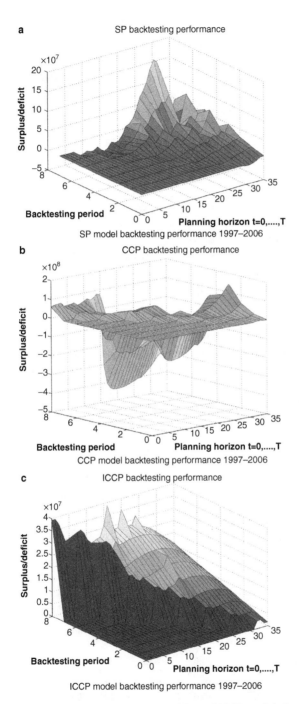

a   SP backtesting performance

SP model backtesting performance 1997–2006

b   CCP backtesting performance

CCP model backtesting performance 1997–2006

c   ICCP backtesting performance

ICCP model backtesting performance 1997–2006

Figure 13.8   Backtesting performance of the SP, CCP and ICCP models from 1997–2006

than seven time periods, which leads the pension fund, especially in the last years, to a surplus. Figure 13.8(c) plots the profit/loss of the ICCP model during backtesting. Compared to the previous models, it outperforms in terms of matching the assets with the liabilities and never leading the pension fund into deficit. In terms of outperformance, the ICCP model generates much less surplus than the SP at some time points. As expected, both the CCP and ICCP models restrict the event/amount of underfunding and they both satisfy the objective of minimizing deviations between assets and liabilities more than the SP model. From a pension fund perspective, the ICCP is the most suitable model: it guarantees fewer deficit events and does not lead the pension fund to overfunding.

Table 13.1 shows the bond rating allocation of the SP, CCP and ICCP during the backtesting period of 1998–2005, where the models were rerun every year. For all the models, it can be said that the shorter the planning horizon, the more conservative the asset allocation, which can be explained by the reduced risk, coupled with less uncertain return, associated with this policy. In the case of a pension fund, this behavior is reasonable as a generated deficit is more damaging in later times than earlier ones, where closing the deficit can still be achieved.

Figure 13.9 shows the Solvency ratio (see for example Koivu *et al*, 2005) and the Sortino ratio (see Sortino and Price, 1994) for the SP, CCP and ICCP models. The higher these ratios, the better; but in case of matching, in which the liabilities are the benchmark and outperformance is penalized, both these ratios reflect good results when they are close to zero.

Table 13.1   Bond rating allocation during backtest for SP, CCP and ICCP models

	Bond rating allocation in percentage from 1998–2005							
	1998	1999	2000	2001	2002	2003	2004	2005
SP								
A	0.01	0	8.27	0	13.84	3.34	17.35	23.41
AA	99.95	4.73	29.66	0.26	6.39	14.81	19.16	25.76
AAA	0.04	94.76	62.07	99.74	79.77	81.84	63.49	50.84
BBB	0	0.5	0	0	0	0	0	0
CCP								
A	0.57	2.15	45.85	3.01	0	23.97	6.59	10.64
AA	2.31	14.61	0	12.83	18.02	71.96	3.09	44.84
AAA	4.19	19.86	54.15	83.73	79.92	4.08	86.96	39.94
BBB	92.93	63.38	0	0.43	0.14	0	3.36	4.57
ICCP								
A	12.03	37.44	28.62	7.15	29.13	14.65	22.95	11.86
AA	64.36	12.47	6.43	3	4.17	25.11	0	0
AAA	18.65	46.58	46.37	89.85	60.28	39.77	77.05	88.11
BBB	4.96	3.52	18.59	0	6.42	20.46	0	0

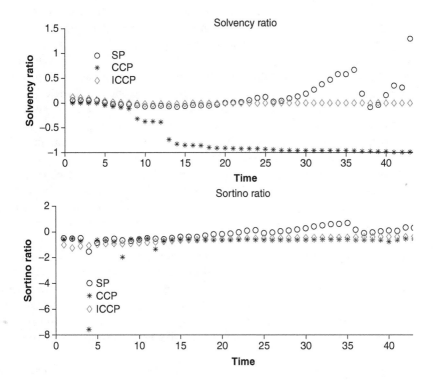

Figure 13.9 Solvency and Sortino ratios for the SP, CCP and ICCP models

From Figure 13.9, it can be seen that the SP model has a Solvency ratio close to zero for half the time periods and then it increases in the other half; the CCP has a downward sloping Solvency ratio, which means that the liabilities are growing faster than the assets; and, finally, the ICCP model has a very smooth Solvency ratio close to zero for all time periods, which means that the assets match the liabilities nearly perfectly. The second graph explains a bit more: the SP model has an upward sloping Sortino ratio, which means that above zero the risk of making big losses gets smaller and that the assets outperform the liabilities; the CCP model has, at some points in time, a high risk of making a big loss when looking at its Sortino ratio; whereas, again, the ICCP is close to zero as it is closely matches the liabilities.

13.4 Conclusions

In the current financial climate, model-based decision making is becoming increasingly important for pension funds. Owing to increases in computer power and access to better quality data, quantitative models are gaining acceptance and are providing superior results. In this article, we have introduced four different mathematical programming models that variously address the pension fund problem. A possible advantage of the SP model lies in dealing with uncertainty and hedging against possible future deficits. The extended SP models, the chance-constrained and ICCP models take into account the event of underfunding and the amount of underfunding explicitly. The ICCP model, being a model with quantitative constraints, allows the user to restrict not only the events of possible underfunding but also the amount of the deficit. From a computational perspective, the ICCP model does not use binary variables and thus it can be solved within a reasonable time.

The next step is to test the models via further simulations and decision evaluations such as stress tests using extreme events such as low interest rate scenarios. In a compendium paper (Schwaiger *et al*, 2008), we report our investigation of LDI decisions via simulation and decision evaluation. As set out earlier (see computation investigation section: Figure 13.2), the SPInE environment has been specially developed to support such evaluation. Readers are also referred to the tools and components of STOCHASTICS by Dempster *et al* (2005).

The LDI asset allocation strategy involves investing in fixed-income instruments and cash; extended models could also invest in equities and make use of overlay strategies. If other investments are included, new decision variables may be introduced for recourse actions that enable the pension fund to change its asset position over time.

Although the SP models are more costly to implement, they guarantee the model to be less exposed to a deficit. Fund managers can easily run the LP, SP and ICCP models with a large asset universe and long time horizon within a reasonable time.

References

Carino, D., Myers, D. and Ziemba, W. (1998) Concepts, technical issues, and uses of the Russell-Yasuda Kasai financial planning model. *Operations Research* 46(4): 450–462.

Consigli, G. and Dempster, M. (1998) Dynamic stochastic programming for asset-liability management. *Annals of Operations Research* 81: 131–162.

Dempster, M., Germano, M., Medova, E., Rietbergen, M., Sandrini, F. and Scrowston, M. (2006) Managing guarantees. *Journal of Portfolio Management* 32(2): 51–61.

Dempster, M., Scott, J. and Thompson, G. (2005) Stochastic modeling and optimization using STOCHASTICS. In: S.W. Wallace and W.T. Ziemba (eds.) *Applications of Stochastic Programming*. USA: Society for Industrial Mathematics, pp. 131–150.

Dert, C. (1995) Asset liability management for pension funds. A multistage chance-constrained programming approach. PhD thesis, Erasmus University, Rotterdam, The Netherlands.

Di Domenica, N., Mitra, G., Valente, P. and Birbilis, G. (2007) Stochastic programming and scenario generation within a simulation framework: An information systems perspective. *Decision Support Systems* 42(4): 2197–2218.

Drijver, S. (2005) Asset liability management for pension funds using multistage mixed-integer stochastic programming. PhD thesis, University Library Groningen Host.

Fabozzi, F., Focardi, S. and Jonas, C. (2007) Trends in quantitative equity management: Survey results. *Quantitative Finance* 7(2): 115–122.

Fabozzi, F., Focardi, S. and Jonas, C. (2008) On the challenges in quantitative equity management. *Quantitative Finance* 8(7): 647–665.

Fourer, R., Gay, D. and Kernighan, B. (2002) *The AMPL Book*: Pacific Grove, CA: Duxbury Press.

Haneveld, W.K.K. (1985) *Duality in Stochastic Linear and Dynamic Programming. LN in Economics and Math. Systems* Vol. 274. Berlin: Springer.

Koivu, M., Pennanen, T. and Ranne, A. (2005) Modeling assets and liabilities of a Finnish pension insurance company: A VEqC approach. *Scandinavian Actuarial Journal* 2005(1): 46–76.

Kusy, M. and Ziemba, W. (1986) A bank asset and liability management model. *Operations Research* 34(3): 356–376.

Medova, E., Murphy, J., Owen, A. and Rehman, K. (2008) Individual asset liability management. Quantitative Finance 8(6): 547–560.

Merton, R. (1993) Optimal investment strategies for university endowment funds. In: C.T. Clotfelter and M. Rothschild (eds.) *Studies of Supply and Demand in Higher Education*. USA: NBER, pp. 211–236.

Mulvey, J., Gould, G. and Morgan, C. (2000) An asset and liability management system for towers Perrin-Tillinghast. *Interfaces* 30(1): 96–114.

Schwaiger, K. (2009) Asset and liability management under uncertainty: Models for decision making and evaluation. PhD thesis, CARISMA, Brunel University.

Schwaiger, K., Mitra, G. and Lucas, C. (2008) Evaluation and Simulation of Liability Determined Investment Models. CARISMA, Brunel University. Report.

Sortino, F. and Price, L. (1994) Performance measurement in a downside risk framework. *The Journal of Investing* 3(3): 59–64.

Valente, C., Mitra, G., Sadki, M. and Fourer, R. (2009) Extending algebraic modelling languages for stochastic programming. *INFORMS Journal on Computing* 21(1): 107–122.

Valente, P., Mitra, G. and Poojari, C.A. (2005) A Stochastic Programming Integrated Environment (SPInE). In: Wallac S.W. and Ziemba W.T. (eds.) *Applications of Stochastic Programming*. USA: Society for Industrial Mathematics, pp. 115–136.

Van der Vlerk, M. (2003) *Integrated Chance Constraints in an ALM Model for Pension Funds*. University of Groningen; University Library Groningen Host, The Netherlands.

Winklevoss, H. (1993) *Pension Mathematics with Numerical Illustrations*. Philadelphia, PA: Pension Research Council and University of Pennsylvania Press, Philadelphia, USA.

Ziemba, W. (2003) *The Stochastic Programming Approach to Asset, Liability, and Wealth Management*. USA: CFA Institute, USA.

Zverovich, V., Fabian, C., Ellison, F. and Mitra, G. (2008) A Computational Study of a Solver System for Processing Two-stage Stochastic Linear Programming Problems. CARISMA, Brunel University. Report.

14
A Liability-Relative Drawdown Approach to Pension Asset Liability Management

Arjan Berkelaar and Roy Kouwenberg

14.1 Introduction

In recent years, the traditional investment philosophy of defined benefit pension funds has come under pressure. Before the collapse of the tech bubble in 2000 and 2001, pension funds generally invested a large chunk of their portfolio in equities (in some countries as much as 70 per cent) with little regard to the underlying liabilities that they are ultimately funding. When the equity bubble popped and the central banks aggressively cut interest rates, pension funds experienced what has been labeled 'the perfect pension storm'. Funded ratios of pension funds generally dropped by 40 per cent. Initially, the pension storm led to an awakening in the pension industry. Regulators and accounting boards embraced the practice of marking to market pension liabilities based on the prevailing term structure of interest rates. Some pension funds, particularly in Europe, adopted a liability-driven investment approach to replace the traditional asset-only approach. However, the recovery in global stock markets and the low level of interest rates from 2003 to 2006 led to complacency. Many pension funds were reluctant to fully implement a liability-driven approach in the view that interest rates were too low and that it would be too costly to hedge the interest rate risk in liabilities at such levels. Unfortunately, the subprime crisis of 2007, that turned into a global financial crisis in 2008, caused another pension storm. Interest rates fell lower still and global equity markets registered one of their worst years on record. US pension funds have seen funded ratios drop on average by about 30 per cent in 2008.

To help pension funds weather future extreme market events, we propose a liability-driven asset allocation approach based on drawdown risk measures in this article, which explicitly takes into account worst-case scenarios. Defined benefit pension schemes accumulate assets with the ultimate objective of honoring their obligation to the beneficiaries. Liabilities should be at the center of designing investment policies and serve as the ultimate reference point for evaluating and allocating risks and measuring performance. The goal of the investment policy should be to maximize expected excess returns over liabilities subject to an acceptable level of risk relative to liabilities. For risk measurement, we propose a liability-relative drawdown (LRDD) approach that focuses on the most difficult periods for the pension plan in a large set of long-term scenarios for asset returns and interest rates. For example, the maximum LRDD measures the worst-case drop in the funded ratio of a pension plan. Given the pension storm from 2000 to 2002 and the recent turmoil in financial markets, we believe that LRDD is a more meaningful and intuitive measure of risk for pension funds than a simple measure like the volatility of asset returns. An advantage of maximum drawdown is that this risk measure is also applicable when returns are serially correlated and exhibit skewed and fat-tailed distributions as is the case for many asset classes.

To construct optimal drawdown portfolios, we cannot simply rely on historical data only. Some asset classes might not have sufficient historical data, forcing us to truncate other data series. Maximum drawdown is also sensitive to the time period chosen for the analysis. Instead of relying on historical returns, we need a framework for modeling and simulating asset and liability returns. We use a vector autoregressive (VAR) process for asset returns, predictive state variables and the yield curve. This process is an extension of the standard models used in studies on return predictability by, for example, Barberis (2000), Campbell *et al* (2003), Campbell and Viceira (2005) and others. Our asset return modeling approach is similar to that of Hoevenaars *et al* (2008). We use the VAR model to simulate asset returns and yield curves and to calculate liability returns.

On the basis of the simulated asset and liability returns, we construct optimal portfolios that maximize expected utility over the funded ratio at the end of the investment horizon subject to a limit on the worst-case drop in the funded ratio over the investment horizon. We also use 90 per cent conditional drawdown at risk (CDaR) as an alternative LRDD risk measure for constructing portfolios. We compare these optimal drawdown risk portfolios with surplus optimal and mean-variance optimal portfolios. The mean variance portfolios are quite risky and inefficient when evaluated against liabilities and expose investors to significant tail events (the maximum LRDD of these portfolios is typically in excess of 100 per cent). Both the optimal surplus and optimal drawdown portfolios allocate a significant portion to long-term Treasuries to hedge the interest rate risk in liabilities through a synthetic duration overlay portfolio (short cash/long long-term bonds). Optimal drawdown portfolios display strong horizon effects, whereas the surplus optimal portfolios are less influenced by the length of the investment horizon. Compared to surplus optimal portfolios, drawdown optimal portfolios have a larger allocation to long-dated Treasuries, lower overall allocation to government bonds and are less equity centric and have a higher allocation to commodities, real estate and hedge funds. On the basis of our forward-looking expected returns, drawdown optimal portfolios outperform surplus optimal portfolios by approximately 30–60 bps per year for the same maximum LRDD level. Overall drawdown optimal portfolios are better balanced and provide better downside protection to pension funds.

Drawdown optimization was first studied by Grossman and Zhou (1993) in a continuous-time setting with one risky and one riskless asset. Grossman and Zhou (1993) derive a closed-form solution for the optimal dynamic portfolio weights under the assumption of log-normality for the risky asset returns. Reveiz and Leon (2008) and Chekhlov *et al* (2005) study drawdown optimization in a discrete-time setting using numerical methods. Reveiz and Leon (2008) find that drawdown optimization may help overcome some of the shortcomings of traditional mean-variance optimization and argue that it is more appropriate for constructing optimal portfolios for long-term investors. They also show that maximum drawdown is a coherent risk measure in the sense of Artzner *et al* (1998). Reveiz and Leon (2008) resort to nonlinear optimization techniques to solve the drawdown optimization problem. Chekhlov *et al* (2005) introduce the notion of CDaR and show that maximum drawdown is a special case of this class of risk measures. CDaR is simply the conditional value at risk of the distribution of drawdowns. They show that portfolio optimization problems with CDaR constraints can be reformulated as linear programming problems by introducing auxiliary variables. They also discuss various theoretical properties of this class of risk measures.

In deriving optimal portfolios, we assume that the portfolio weights are constant over time. In recent years, several advances have been made to solve dynamic portfolio optimization problems. Dynamic portfolio choice problems can be solved using dynamic programming techniques or stochastic programming methods. Recent examples of dynamic programming approaches to dynamic portfolio choice problems can be found in Campbell and Viceira (2002) and Brandt (2009). Examples of stochastic programming approaches to dynamic portfolio choice problems can be found in Kusy and Ziemba (1986), Carino *et al* (1994), Mulvey and Vladimirou (1992), Zenios (1995), Consigli and Dempster (1998), Kouwenberg (2001) and Kouwenberg and Zenios (2006). Stochastic programming approaches rely on discrete distributions also referred to as scenarios. One of the main advantages of stochastic programming methods is that they allow for an enormous amount of flexibility in specifying the return-generating process – unlike dynamic programming in which more structure is typically required. The drawdown portfolio optimization approach, that we adopt in this article, could easily be reformulated as a stochastic programming problem with time-varying portfolio weights.

This article is organized as follows. The next section introduces the portfolio optimization problem of defined benefit pension funds and discusses LRDD risk. In the subsequent section, we discuss our approach to modeling and simulating asset and liability returns and describe the data that is used in estimating the model. The penultimate section describes the portfolio optimization results and contrasts surplus optimal portfolios with drawdown optimal portfolios. The final section concludes the article and offers some avenues for further research.

14.2 Liability-relative portfolio optimization

Modern portfolio theory assumes that investors trade-off risk and reward. The main workhorse for portfolio construction is mean-variance optimization developed by Markowitz (1952). In mean-variance analysis, investors trade-off variance and expected return. The optimal portfolios lie on the so-called mean-variance efficient frontier and the investor chooses the portfolio with the highest expected return for a given level of variance. Sharpe and Tint (1990) extended the mean-variance framework to incorporate liabilities. In their model, investors make a trade-off between variance of surplus returns (asset returns minus liability returns) and expected surplus returns. The investor chooses the portfolio with the highest expected surplus return for a given level of surplus variance. Sharpe and Tint (1990) find that the investor is willing to accept lower expected asset returns in exchange for hedging some of the risk in liabilities. The 'risk-free' asset for a pension fund is the portfolio that minimizes risk relative to liabilities, that is the portfolio that best mimics the liabilities. It should be noted that this portfolio is the minimum risk position for a pension fund but not truly a riskless position.[1]

In this article, we consider optimal portfolios based on both the surplus variance approach of Sharpe and Tint (1990) and a maximum LRDD approach that constrains the worst-case drop of the funded ratio. We assume that the investor wants to maximize expected utility over the terminal funded ratio (the ratio of assets to liabilities) subject to either a constraint on the variance of the log funded ratio at the end of the investment horizon or a constraint on the maximum drawdown of asset returns relative to liabilities over the investment horizon. We denote assets at time t by A_t and liabilities at time t by L_t. The funded ratio is denoted by $F_t = A_t / L_t$. The initial funded ratio is assumed to be equal to one. The vector of log asset returns at time t is denoted by $\mathbf{r}_t$ and log liability returns are given by r_t^L. Portfolio weights, denoted by the vector $\mathbf{w}$, are assumed to be constant over the investment horizon and sum up to one. Assets and liabilities evolve according to the following equations:

$$A_{t+1} = A_t \exp\left(\mathbf{r}'_{t+1}\mathbf{w}\right),$$
$$L_{t+1} = L_t \exp\left(r_{t+1}^L\right).$$

The investor maximizes expected utility over the funded ratio – the ratio of assets to liabilities – at the end of the investment horizon T subject to a constraint on risk relative to liabilities.[2] We assume that the investor has a log utility function. Solving for the funded ratio recursively, expected log utility over the terminal funded ratio can be expressed as:

$$\mathbb{E}U(F_T) = \mathbb{E}\left(\sum_{t=1}^{T}\left(\mathbf{r}_t'\mathbf{w} - r_t^L\right)\right).$$

We consider two measures of liability-relative risk: the variance of the log funded ratio at the end of the investment horizon and maximum LRDD over the investment horizon. We will refer to the variance of the log funded ratio as surplus variance. The surplus variance of the terminal funded ratio can be expressed as the variance of cumulative excess asset returns over liabilities:

$$\mathrm{Var}\left(\log\left(F_T\right)\right) = \mathrm{Var}\left(\sum_{t=1}^{T}\left(\mathbf{r}_t'\mathbf{w} - r_t^L\right)\right) = \mathbf{w}'\boldsymbol{\Omega}_{AL}\mathbf{w},$$

where $\boldsymbol{\Omega}_{AL}$ denotes the covariance matrix of cumulative excess returns over liabilities. Maximizing expected log utility subject to a constraint on the surplus variance can be written as the following optimization problem:

$$\max_{\mathbf{w}}\mathbb{E}\left(\sum_{t=1}^{T}\left(\mathbf{r}_t'\mathbf{w} - r_t^L\right)\right)\mathbf{w}'\boldsymbol{\Omega}_{AL}\mathbf{w} \leq V_{\max} \quad \mathbf{e}'\mathbf{w} = 1, \quad \mathbf{b}_l \leq \mathbf{w} \leq \mathbf{b}_u$$

where $V_{\max}$ denotes the maximum allowable surplus variance, $\mathbf{b}_l$ and $\mathbf{b}_u$ are vectors with lower and upper bounds on the portfolio weights and $\mathbf{e}$ is a vector of ones. Solving this optimization problem for different levels of surplus variance determines the surplus efficient frontier: all portfolios that maximize expected cumulative excess return for a given level of surplus variance. These efficient portfolios will be referred to as surplus optimal portfolios. The efficient portfolio with the lowest surplus variance will be referred to as the minimum surplus variance portfolio.

To introduce LRDD risk, we first need to define the drawdown concept. The drawdown at time t for a time series of returns is defined as:

$$DD_t = \max_{0\leq\tau\leq t} R_\tau - R_t, \quad t = 1, 2, \ldots, T \tag{14.1}$$

where $R_0 = 0$, R_t is the cumulative log return defined by $R_t = \sum_{\tau=1}^{t} r_\tau$ for $t = 1, 2, \ldots, T$ and r_τ the periodic log return at time τ. The maximum drawdown is simply the maximum of the time series of drawdowns: $\max(DD_1, DD_2, ..., DD_T)$. Note that drawdown risk, by definition, increases with the investment horizon. Liability-relative maximum drawdown is the maximum drawdown of excess asset returns over liability returns, that is $\mathbf{r}_t'\mathbf{w} - r_t^L$. In other words, maximum LRDD measures the worst possible drop in the funded ratio over the investment horizon. An LRDD of 40 per cent means that the funded ratio drops by about 40 percentage points. For example, during the perfect pension storm of 2000 to 2002, the funded ratio of US pension funds dropped on average from 120 per cent to 80 per cent – this translates into an LRDD of $\log(0.8) - \log(1.2) = -40.5$ per cent. Such large drawdowns typically require plan sponsors to contribute significantly to the pension fund at precisely the wrong times – when stock markets are down and the economy is in a recession. In our view, managing against a worst-case LRDD is therefore more important for pension funds than managing surplus variance or the volatility of asset returns.

We can now formulate the LRDD portfolio optimization problem as follows:

$$\max_{\mathbf{w}} \mathbb{E}\left(\sum_{t=1}^{T}\left(\mathbf{r}_t'\mathbf{w} - r_t^L\right)\right) \max\left(DD_1, DD_2, ..., DD_T\right) \le D_{\max} \mathbf{e}'\mathbf{w} = 1, \quad \mathbf{b}_l \le \mathbf{w} \le \mathbf{b}_u$$

where $D_{\max}$ denotes the maximum allowable LRDD. Solving this optimization problem for different levels of maximum LRDD determines the efficient frontier. In this case, the efficient frontier represents all portfolios that maximize the expected cumulative excess return for a given maximum LRDD. These efficient portfolios will be referred to as drawdown optimal portfolios. The efficient portfolio with the lowest maximum LRDD will be referred to as the minimum drawdown-risk portfolio.

In this article, all stochastic variables will be represented by a finite set of sample paths (scenarios) indexed by $s = 1, ..., S$. The maximum drawdown of a portfolio is a nonlinear function of the portfolio weights. However, Chekhlov *et al* (2005) show that the maximum drawdown constraint can be reformulated as a set of linear constraints by introducing auxiliary variables. This allows us to rewrite the optimization problem as a linear optimization problem:

$$\max_{\mathbf{w},u} \frac{1}{ST} \sum_{s=1}^{S}\sum_{t=1}^{T}\left(\mathbf{r}_{st}'\mathbf{w} - r_{st}^L\right) u_{st} - u_{s,t-1} + \mathbf{r}_{st}'\mathbf{w} - r_{st}^L \ge 0, \quad \forall_t, \forall_s$$

$$0 \le u_{st} \le D_{\max}, \quad \forall_t, \forall_s \qquad \mathbf{e}'\mathbf{w} = 1, \quad \mathbf{b}_l \le \mathbf{w} \le \mathbf{b}_u$$

where u_{st} is an auxiliary variable used to linearize the drawdown constraint (see Chekhlov *et al* (2005) for details). The drawdown optimization problem above is a large-scale optimization problem. With nine assets, 40 periods and 500 scenarios, the number of constraints is 40 010 and the number of variables is 20 009. We use Matlab with the commercial optimization package Mosek to solve these large-scale optimization problems.

Note that the maximum drawdown constraint is enforced over all sample paths (scenarios). The optimal portfolio will protect the investor against a worst-case drop in the funded ratio over the investment horizon in the most adverse scenario. Chekhlov *et al* (2005) have introduced a new class of risk measures called CDaR. Instead of constraining the maximum drawdown, the investor could alternatively decide to constrain the average 10 per cent worst drawdowns (the 90 per cent CDaR). In this article, we will not only focus on worst-case drawdown, but also solve for optimal portfolios with a constraint on the 90 per cent CDaR. We refer to Chekhlov *et al* (2005) for a linear formulation of the CDaR constraint.

In constructing optimal portfolios, we allow the investor to short cash up to 100 per cent and invest the proceeds in long-term bonds to emulate the implementation of a liability hedging overlay program. For example, a portfolio that is 100 per cent short cash and 100 per cent long in long-term bonds with the same duration as the liabilities can be interpreted as a duration overlay that is implemented through a total return swap. Allowing for such overlay portfolios is important, as pension funds want to be able to hedge the interest rate risk in liabilities, while pursuing return generation. Some pension funds have, in fact, recently adopted an investment approach with two portfolios: a liability hedging portfolio that is implemented through derivatives (typically using swaps) and a return-generating portfolio that seeks to maximize expected returns for a given level of risk. Using a liability hedging and a return-generating portfolio allows pension funds to both hedge interest-rate risk and seek returns rather than being forced to settle for a compromise that neither hedges all of the interest rate risk in the liabilities nor maximizes the expected return.

In the next section, we discuss the simulation approach that is used to construct future asset and liability returns.

14.3   Asset and liability modeling framework

To understand and evaluate the future financial position of a pension fund, we need to know the future path of a number of economic variables. These include, among others, the term structure of interest rates and asset returns for each of the asset classes that the fund is invested in. Rather than trying to predict the exact future realization of each of these variables, we generate a large number of scenarios using a stochastic time series model. This allows us to derive probability distributions for several key statistics of the pension plan. In generating scenarios, we are interested in realistically modeling the key relationships between the relevant financial and economic variables over time and at any point in time. The objective is to build a credible set of possible evolutions of the future. We need the term structure of interest rates to value pension liabilities and model bond returns. For this purpose, we use the so-called Nelson–Siegel yield curve model. Asset returns will be modeled using a VAR process with state variables, building on the works of Campbell and Viceira (2005) and Hoevenaars *et al* (2008). Finally, we use a simple model based on projected cash flows and future pension accruals to simulate pension liabilities into the future.

14.3.1 Data

We consider five asset classes: bonds, stocks, commodities, real estate and hedge funds. We use six state variables that have been found to have predictive power for stocks and bonds in the literature: the level, slope and curvature of the yield curve, the dividend yield, the default spread, and the consumption–wealth ratio (CAY). Our analysis is based on quarterly US data. Most of the data series start in 1952:Q1 and all series end in 2008:Q3. The starting date 1952:Q1 comes shortly after the Fed-Treasury Accord that allowed short-term nominal interest rates to freely fluctuate. Returns for commodities, listed real estate and hedge funds, however, are available for a shorter history only. Commodity returns start in 1970:Q1, listed real estate returns start in 1972:Q1 and hedge fund returns start in 1990:Q1. Commodity returns are based on the Goldman Sachs Commodities Total Return Index. Listed real estate returns are from the National Association of Real Estate Investment Trusts (NAREIT).[3] Hedge fund returns are based on the Hedge Fund Research Inc. (HFRI) Index.[4] All return series are in logarithmic form and expressed as excess return over 3-month Treasury bills.

The level, slope and curvature of the yield curve are estimated using the Nelson–Siegel model. We use zero yields with maturities: 3 months, 1 year, 2 years, 3 years, 4 years, 5 years, 7 years and 10 years. The zero yields are spliced from zero yield data from McCulloch and Kwon (1993) for the period 1952:Q1–1990:Q4, from Bliss (1997) for the period 1991:Q1–1997:Q4 and Huston McCulloch's website[5] for the period 1998:Q1–2008:Q3. The default spread is the difference between the Moody's Baa and Aaa corporate bond yields. The corporate bond yield data is obtained from the Federal Reserve Economic Data (FRED) website at the Federal Reserve Bank of St Louis.[6] Data on stock returns and the dividend yield are based on the S&P composite and obtained from Shiller (2000).[7] CAY is from Lettau and Ludvigson (2001).[8]

Table 14.1 shows summary statistics for equity log excess returns (Equity), commodity log excess returns (Comm), listed real estate log excess returns (REITs) and hedge fund log excess returns (HF). Hedge funds have historically provided the best excess returns over cash – almost 2 per cent on a quarterly basis.[9] Commodity returns have historically been the most volatile asset class

Table 14.1   Summary statistics

	Mean	SD	Min	Max	Skew	Xkurt	SC (1)	Max. DD	Start date
Excess returns									
Equity	1.31	7.12	−28.7	21.56	−1.00	2.51	0.11	62.42	1952:Q1
Comm	1.31	10.00	−34.1	41.97	0.00	1.97	−0.06	75.36	1970:Q1
REITs	0.91	8.37	−30.6	28.93	−0.36	1.66	0.09	100.61	1972:Q1
HF	1.93	4.14	−10.5	12.70	−0.56	0.94	0.08	13.01	1990:Q1
State variables									
Level	6.50	2.59	2.6	14.1	0.78	0.17	0.98	−	1952:Q1
Slope	−1.45	1.70	−5.4	5.4	0.09	0.55	0.82	−	1952:Q1
Curv	−0.05	1.95	−5.1	7.2	0.08	1.22	0.66	−	1952:Q1
DivYld	3.26	1.20	1.1	6.1	0.26	−0.44	0.98	−	1952:Q1
DefSpr	0.95	0.41	0.3	2.7	1.40	2.13	0.91	−	1952:Q1
CAY	0.00	1.43	−2.8	3.8	0.31	−0.34	0.88	−	1952:Q1

This table shows the summary statistics of the quarterly log excess returns over 90-day Treasury bill returns for US equities (Equity), commodities (Comm), listed real estate (REITs), hedge funds (HF) as well as several state variables, from the start date in the last column through 2008:Q3. The level, slope and curvature state variables are time series of the three factors of the Nelson–Siegel yield curve model. Note that the slope of the yield curve is expressed as the difference between short- and long-term rates – a negative sign means that the slope of the curve is positive. Dividend yields (DivYld) are calculated for the S&P500 index. The default spread (DefSpr) is the difference between Moody's BAA and AAA yields. The consumption–wealth ratio (CAY) is from Lettau and Ludvigson.

with a quarterly standard deviation of 10 per cent. Listed real estate has experienced the largest maximum drawdown (highest cumulative loss from top to bottom) of slightly over 100 per cent. Equity returns and hedge fund returns are slightly negatively skewed. All asset class returns exhibit slightly fatter tails than a normal distribution. Equities have the highest excess kurtosis of about 2.5 followed by commodities with an excess kurtosis of almost 2. There is little serial correlation in quarterly returns. Hedge fund returns are typically serially correlated on a monthly basis, but this effect disappears when sampling returns quarterly. State variables, however, exhibit significant serial correlation, ranging from 0.98 for the level of the yield curve and dividend yield, to 0.66 for the curvature of the yield curve. The historical level of the yield curve was about 6.5 per cent with a slope of about 1.5 per cent. Dividend yields have been 3.26 per cent on average and ranged between a low of 1.1 per cent and a high of 6.1 per cent. The default spread has been 95 basis points on average but has widened significantly in the recent past.

14.3.2   Nelson–Siegel yield curve model

To value and model pension liabilities, we need a yield curve model. Diebold and Li (2006) have introduced a simple, yet elegant framework for simulating future yield curves. They rely on the so-called Nelson–Siegel model (Nelson and Siegel, 1987), which represents the yield curve using three factors at each point in time. The three factors are the level, slope and curvature of the yield curve. Diebold and Li (2006) assume that the three parameters of the Nelson–Siegel model are latent factors that follow a VAR process. The model can be estimated using Kalman filtering techniques. An interesting extension of the model with regime shifts can be found in Bernadell *et al* (2005). In this article, we will use the Diebold–Li approach to simulate future yield curves.

Although Nelson and Siegel (1987) originally specified a functional form for the forward curve, the Nelson–Siegel yield curve is more commonly expressed in terms of the spot curve:

$$Y_n(t) = \beta_{1t} + \beta_{2t}\left(\frac{1 - e^{-\lambda n}}{\lambda n}\right) + \beta_{3t}\left(\frac{1 - e^{-\lambda n}}{\lambda n} - e^{-\lambda n}\right), \qquad (14.2)$$

where n denotes maturity and $Y_n(t)$ is the spot rate (zero-coupon rate) for maturity n at time t. The first term is a level factor, the second term is the negative of the slope and the third term represents the curvature. This can be seen

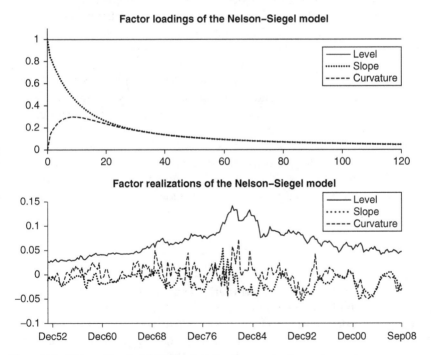

Figure 14.1   Nelson–Siegel yield curve factors

from the limit behavior of the yield curve model. Long-term yields, as $n \to \infty$, approach β_1. Short-term yields, as $n \to 0$, approach $\beta_1 + \beta_2$ (that is, long-term yield plus the negative of the slope). Finally, the loading of the third factor approaches its maximum for intermediate maturities, whereas it is zero at both very short and very long maturities; representing curvature. Finally, the parameter λ is an exponential decay rate; small values of λ result in slow decay, whereas large values result in fast decay. The parameter λ also governs where the curvature loading achieves its maximum. Figure 14.1 shows the factor loadings for $\lambda = 0.18$ with maturity n expressed in quarters.

The spot curve can be estimated at every point in time (for example, monthly or quarterly), producing time series for each of the parameters. Following Diebold and Li (2006), we assume that the parameter λ is constant over time and fix λ at 0.18.[10] We estimate the parameters β_t using quarterly US zero yields from 1952:Q1 to 2008:Q4 at maturities (in quarters) $n = (1, 4, 8, 12, 16, 20, 28, 40)$. Figure 14.1 shows the estimated factor realizations from 1952 to 2008.

14.3.3   Modeling asset returns

Econometricians have developed several tools and models to describe financial and economic time series. These tools include time series models with time-varying means – such as VAR models and vector error correction models – and time series models with time-varying volatilities and correlations – such as conditional volatility models (GARCH) and regime switching models. In this article, we build on the works of Campbell *et al* (2003), Campbell and Viceira (2005) and Hoevenaars *et al* (2008) and use VAR models. One difference between the VAR models used in Campbell and Viceira (2005) and Hoevenaars *et al* (2008) is that we exclude excess bond returns from the VAR estimation. Instead, we use the Nelson–Siegel yield curve factors and calculate bond returns directly from the simulated yield curves.

We denote the vector of all time series by $\mathbf{X}_{t+1}$. We split this vector in two parts $\mathbf{X}_{t+1} = (\mathbf{X}_{1,t+1}, \mathbf{X}_{2,t+1})$, where the vector $\mathbf{X}_1$ contains the long time series (the quarterly log excess return on stocks and each of the six state variables), and the vector $\mathbf{X}_2$ contains the shorter time series. The first-order VAR process for $\mathbf{X}_{1,t+1}$ is:

$$\mathbf{X}_{1,t+1} = \boldsymbol{\Phi} + \boldsymbol{\Psi}\mathbf{X}_{1,t} + \boldsymbol{\Gamma}\boldsymbol{\varepsilon}_{t+1}, \tag{14.3}$$

where $\boldsymbol{\varepsilon}_{t+1} \sim N(0, \mathbf{I})$, and $\boldsymbol{\Gamma}$ is a lower triangular matrix with $\boldsymbol{\Gamma}\boldsymbol{\Gamma}' = \mathbf{C}$. The stationarity condition for a VAR(1) model requires that the roots of the characteristic equation $|\mathbf{I} - \lambda\boldsymbol{\Psi}| = 0$ lie outside the unit circle (that is, have a modulus greater than one). This condition is equivalent to the requirement that all eigenvalues of the companion matrix $\boldsymbol{\Psi}$ are less than one in absolute value. If the

stationarity condition is satisfied, the unconditional mean and variance of the
VAR model are given by:

$$\bar{\mathbf{X}}_1 = (\mathbf{I} - \mathbf{\Psi})^{-1}\mathbf{\Phi}$$
$$\text{vec}(\text{Var}(\mathbf{X}_1)) = (\mathbf{I} - \mathbf{\Psi} \otimes \mathbf{\Psi})^{-1}\text{vec}(\mathbf{C})$$

where $\otimes$ is the Kronecker product operator and vec the operator for converting
a $(m \times n)$ matrix into a column vector of size mn. As a p-th order VAR model can
always be reformulated as a first-order VAR process by introducing additional
variables, we only consider VAR(1) models in this article.

Table 14.2 shows the parameter estimates, t-statistics and R^2 for a VAR(1)
model for the core variables with a long history. Note that the R^2 is quite high
for almost every equation, ranging from about 97 per cent for the level of the
yield curve and dividend yields to 13.6 per cent for equity returns. The low
R^2 for equity returns is in line with findings in the literature. Excess equity
returns are partially explained by the level of the yield curve, the dividend
yield, the default spread and CAY. These variables have also been found to be
statistically significant by others (Lettau and Ludvigson, 2001; Campbell *et al*,
2003; Campbell and Diebold, 2009). Given the high serial correlation in the
state variables, it is not surprising that the parameter coefficients on their own
lagged values are statistically significant.

We follow the approach advocated by Hoevenaars *et al* (2008) to include time
series of different length in the estimation of the VAR model. The approach of
Hoevenaars *et al* (2008) is an extension of the method discussed in Stambaugh

Table 14.2 Parameter estimates of VAR(1) model for core variables

	Equity	Level	Slope	Curv	DivYld	DefSpr	CAY	R^2
Equity	0.078	−0.969	−0.157	−0.142	0.928	4.526	1.390	0.136
	(1.21)	(−3.49)	(−0.50)	(−0.54)	(2.17)	(2.57)	(3.73)	–
Level	0.001	0.955	0.072	−0.027	0.012	0.276	0.023	0.970
	(0.16)	(50.89)	(3.35)	(−1.49)	(0.41)	(2.32)	(0.90)	–
Slope	0.019	0.061	0.737	0.062	0.041	−0.815	−0.172	0.709
	(2.13)	(1.58)	(16.79)	(1.69)	(0.69)	(−3.35)	(−3.33)	–
Curv	0.020	0.138	0.170	0.554	0.167	−0.526	−0.040	0.476
	(1.45)	(2.33)	(2.50)	(9.74)	(1.82)	(−1.40)	(−0.50)	–
DivYld	−0.003	0.040	0.009	−0.000	0.969	−0.239	−0.048	0.959
	(−1.43)	(3.94)	(0.77)	(−0.03)	(62.15)	(−3.73)	(−3.55)	–
DefSpr	−0.009	0.019	0.016	0.003	0.008	0.833	−0.007	0.868
	(−5.84)	(2.95)	(2.15)	(0.53)	(0.79)	(20.89)	(−0.84)	–
CAY	−0.007	0.037	−0.024	0.015	0.015	−0.208	0.851	0.775
	(−0.99)	(1.31)	(−0.74)	(0.57)	(0.35)	(−1.15)	(22.31)	–

This table shows the parameter estimates of a vector autoregressive model of order 1 for the core
variables with long data series. The t-statistics are shown in brackets. Equations are displayed hori-
zontally with the columns representing the parameter coefficients on the lagged variables.

(1997) for estimating covariance matrices with time series of different length. We assume that the shorter time series $X_{2,t+1}$ follows the process:

$$X_{2,t+1} = a + B_0 X_{1,t+1} + B_1 X_{1,t} + H X_{2,t} + S\eta_{t+1}, \qquad (14.4)$$

where H is a diagonal matrix, the shocks η_t have zero mean and covariance matrix $V = SS'$, and the covariance between η_t and ε_t is zero. Contemporaneous covariances between $X_{1,t}$ and $X_{2,t}$ are captured through the matrix B_0. Combining (14.3) and (14.4), $X_t = (X_{1,t}, X_{2,t})'$ follows a VAR(1) process:

$$X_{t+1} = c + \Phi X_t + \sum u_{t+1},$$

Where

$$c = \begin{pmatrix} \Phi \\ a + B_0\Phi \end{pmatrix}, \quad \Phi = \begin{pmatrix} \Psi & 0 \\ B_1 + B_0\Psi & H \end{pmatrix}$$

and the covariance matrix of u_t, $\Omega = \Sigma\Sigma'$ is given by:

$$\Omega = \begin{pmatrix} C & CB_0' \\ B_0 C & V + B_0 CB_0' \end{pmatrix}.$$

The same approach can be applied when there are more than two sets of time series with different length (see, for example, Kouwenberg *et al*, 2009).

Table 14.3 shows the parameter estimates and R^2 for equation (14.4) for the short series. The R^2 for listed real estate and hedge fund returns is relatively high because of the fact that we regress these returns on contemporaneous equity returns and both series have a relatively high correlation with equity returns. The historical correlation of listed real estate with US stock returns is almost 0.6, whereas the historical correlation of hedge funds with US stock returns is about 0.75. Commodities, on the other hand, exhibit negative correlation with US stock returns of about -0.20. The R^2 for commodities is 13.3 per cent, similar to that of equities.

In contrast to an unconditional normal distribution, volatilities and correlations are a function of the investment horizon in a VAR process. As shown by Campbell and Viceira (2005), the term structures of volatilities and correlations for each variable in a VAR model can be calculated analytically. Figure 14.2 shows the term structure of annualized volatility for equities, commodities, real estate and hedge funds for investment horizons ranging from 1 quarter to

Table 14.3   Parameter estimates for short time series

	Comm(t)		REITs(t)		HF(t)	
	Parameters	t-statistics	Parameters	t-statistics	Parameters	t-statistics
Equity(t)	0.06	0.21	0.31	1.56	0.17	1.15
Level(t)	0.64	0.37	−2.48	−2.15	2.14	1.89
Slope(t)	−0.38	−0.45	−1.61	−2.97	0.92	1.05
Curv(t)	−0.31	−0.56	−0.75	−2.00	−0.40	−1.15
DivYld(t)	9.19	1.10	−8.69	−1.59	−6.88	−1.05
DefSpr(t)	−7.90	−1.52	−5.89	−1.73	−3.99	−1.30
CAY(t)	0.38	0.30	−0.62	−0.75	−1.44	−2.93
Equity($t-1$)	0.09	0.71	−0.04	−0.40	−0.10	−1.31
Level($t-1$)	−1.23	−0.69	2.22	1.89	−1.26	−1.11
Slope($t-1$)	−0.03	−0.03	0.95	1.67	−0.24	−0.35
Curv($t-1$)	0.54	0.99	0.39	1.09	−0.55	−1.54
DivYld($t-1$)	−7.72	−0.91	9.53	1.70	6.69	0.99
DefSpr($t-1$)	3.17	0.61	5.75	1.67	2.01	0.63
CAY($t-1$)	−1.42	−1.09	0.06	0.07	1.50	3.12
Comm($t-1$)	−0.09	−0.98	−0.05	−0.77	0.00	−0.04
REITs($t-1$)	–	–	0.01	0.11	−0.02	−0.42
HF($t-1$)	–	–	–	–	0.14	1.09
Comm(t)	–	–	−0.07	−1.31	0.03	1.05
REITs(t)	–	–	–	–	0.09	1.78
R^2	0.133	–	0.510	–	0.753	–

This table shows the parameter estimates of equation (14.4) for the short series.

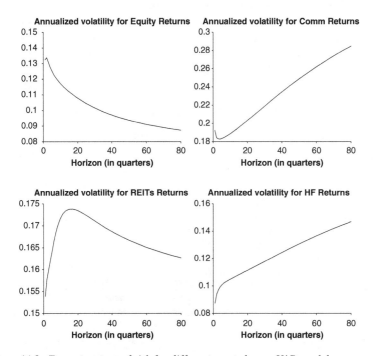

Figure 14.2   Term structure of risk for different asset classes: VAR model

80 quarters (20 years). The volatility of equities decreases with the investment horizon from about 13.25 per cent to 8.75 per cent. This finding is consistent with the results of Campbell and Viceira (2005) and Hoevenaars *et al* (2008) and is caused by mean reversion in stock returns. The annualized volatility of listed real estate is hump shaped. The annualized volatility is about 15.4 per cent for one quarter, rises to about 17.4 per cent for a 5-year investment horizon and then drops again to about 16.3 per cent for an investment horizon of 20 years. This hump shape for the term structure of volatility of real estate returns is also observed by Hoevenaars *et al* (2008). The volatility of both commodities and hedge funds, on the other hand, increases with the investment horizon. The annualized volatility of commodities rises from about 19.2 per cent for one quarter to 28.5 per cent for an investment horizon of 20 years. The annualized volatility of hedge funds rises from about 8.75 per cent for one quarter to over 14.5 per cent for 20 years. In contrast, Hoevenaars *et al* (2008) find that the term structure of volatilities for commodities and hedge funds is flat. Note that we use a slightly different set of variables and also include CAY as state variable. This variable has predictive power for equities and hedge funds. We also use different time series for hedge fund returns. We use the HFRI hedge fund index, whereas Hoevenaars *et al* (2008) use the HFRI conservative fund of funds index. Finally, we include all parameter estimates, whereas Hoevenaars *et al* (2008) set the insignificant coefficients to zero.

Figure 14.3 shows the term structure of correlations for commodities, real estate and hedge funds with equity returns. Equities and commodities are

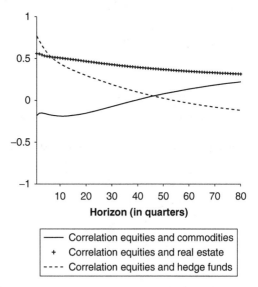

Horizon (in quarters)

```
——   Correlation equities and commodities
 +    Correlation equities and real estate
----  Correlation equities and hedge funds
```

Figure 14.3   Term structure of correlations for different asset classes: VAR model

virtually uncorrelated across all investment horizons (although the correlation slightly increases with the investment horizon). This is consistent with the findings of Hoevenaars *et al* (2008) and Gorton and Rouwenhorst (2006). Gorton and Rouwenhorst (2006) have found that stocks and commodities behave quite differently over the business cycle, resulting in a low or even negative correlation. Commodities therefore provide strong diversification benefits to a portfolio of stocks. The correlation between real estate and equities and between hedge funds and equities decreases with the investment hxorizon. The correlation between real estate and equities decreases from approximately 0.56 for quarterly returns to 0.32 over an investment horizon of 20 years. The correlation between hedge funds and equities drops significantly as the investment horizon lengthens from 0.77 for quarterly returns to −0.11 over a 20-year investment horizon. Note that the volatilities and correlations in Figures 14.2 and 14.3 are based on excess asset returns over 3-month T-bills.

14.3.4 Modeling liabilities

We model pension liabilities using the projected benefit obligation (PBO) method, which only considers pension entitlements that have been earned by employees up to the current date. Liabilities are the present value of current expected benefit payments discounted at the term structure of nominal Treasury rates. We assume that the liabilities are non-indexed. This is commonly the case for US corporate pension funds. Expected benefit payments from t to $t+1$, under the PBO method, typically increase because of the accrual of additional pension rights by current employees and potentially inflow of new employees. Ignoring these additional accruals would underestimate the growth rate in pension liabilities. Hence, when calculating the change in liabilities in future time-periods, we also discount the expected costs of new accruals because of additional pension right of current employees (while assuming no inflow of new employees).

Figure 14.4 shows expected benefit payments and the cost of new accruals for the next 100 years. Using these data together with the simulated yield curve, we construct liability returns. The average interest rate duration of the liabilities falls from approximately 16.3 to 13.3 over the next 10 years. A portfolio of long-dated Treasuries should provide a reasonable hedge against the interest rate risk of the liabilities. Owing to the accrual of additional pension rights from year to year, however, the total return on long-dated Treasuries is lower than the growth rate in liabilities. The liabilities in our case outgrow long-term Treasuries by approximately 1.5–2.0 per cent per year. A fully hedged portfolio would therefore result in a drop of 1.5–2.0 per cent in the funded ratio per year. New accruals should partially be funded by contributions from the plan sponsor and partially from the expected return on plan assets. In the remainder, we

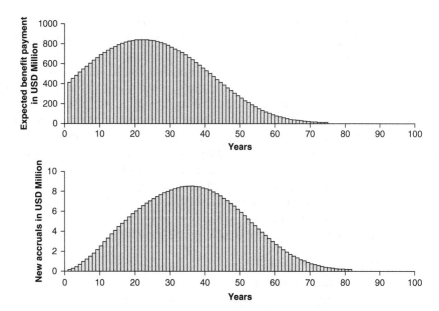

Figure 14.4   Expected benefit payments and cost of new accruals

assume that there are no contributions to the fund. As a result, the expected return on the strategic asset allocation should exceed long-term Treasuries by approximately 1.5–2.0 per cent per year to maintain the current funded status. Pension liabilities are exposed to other risks such as longevity risk, changes in the demographics of a pension fund and labor income risk. Currently, these risks cannot be hedged with financial instruments and we do not account for them in this article. The additional uncertainty from these risk exposures may, however, provide an additional rationale to seek excess returns.

14.4   Portfolio optimization results

The investor can invest in five broad asset classes: US Treasuries, US stocks, commodities, listed real estate and hedge funds. Returns on US Treasuries are calculated using the Nelson–Siegel yield curve model. We construct bond returns following Campbell *et al* (1997):

$$r_{n,t+1} \approx \frac{1}{4}\gamma_{n-1,t+1} - D_{n,t}(\gamma_{n-1,t+1} - \gamma_{n,t}),$$

where n is the maturity of the bond, the bond yield is Y_{nt}, the log bond yield is

$\gamma_{n,t} = \log(1+Y_{nt})$ and $D_{n,t}$ is the bond duration. Duration at time t is calculated as

$$D_{n,t} \approx \frac{1-(1+\gamma_{nt})^{-n}}{1-(1+\gamma_{nt})^{-1}}.$$

The bond yield Y_{nt} is calculated from equation (14.2).

We calculate returns on 3-month Treasury bills, 2-year Treasury notes, 5-year Treasury notes, 10-year Treasury bonds and 20-year Treasury bonds. In total, the investor can allocate fun ds across nine asset classes. We allow short sales in 3-month Treasury bills and the proceeds can be invested in Treasuries (but not in risky assets), to mimic total return swaps on long-dated Treasuries for increasing the duration of the asset portfolio. We simulate 500 sample paths of quarterly asset and liability returns using the estimated VAR process discussed in the previous section.[11] Total returns on each of the asset classes are calculated by adding 3-month Treasury bill returns to the excess returns on stocks, commodities, real estate and hedge funds.

It is important to anchor the simulated values of the VAR process around forward-looking assumptions. For several of the variables in the VAR model, it would be unrealistic to assume that they revert to their long-term historical average because of structural shifts in the economy. We impose forward-looking expected values for the returns on the risky asset classes and the state variables by modifying the intercept of the VAR process:

$$\bar{\mathbf{c}} = (\mathbf{I} - \mathbf{\Phi})\mathbf{\mu}_{LT},$$

where $\mathbf{\mu}_{LT}$ denotes the vector of forward-looking long-term expectations. As an example, we use the forward-looking return expectations used at the World Bank pension fund. These estimates are derived from a proprietary building-block approach for capital market assumptions. The long-term expected equity risk premium is 4.0 per cent (annualized). The long-term expected risk premia for commodities, real estate and hedge funds are 2.5 per cent, 3.5 per cent and 3.5 per cent, respectively. The level of the yield curve is assumed to revert to 5.5 per cent, with a slope of 1.5 per cent. The long-term expected dividend yield is 2.5 per cent and the expected default spread is 1.5 per cent, which is somewhat higher than the long-term historical average. The long-term values for the curvature of the yield curve and CAY are set to 0 per cent. The VAR process produces horizon dependent expected returns. Table 14.4 shows the annualized expected total return and excess return over liabilities for investment horizons of 5, 10 and 20 years. Over a 5-year investment horizon, 10-year and 20-year Treasuries provide slightly higher expected returns compared to 5-year Treasuries. This is reversed over a 20-year investment horizon. Commodities

Table 14.4   Expected annualized total and surplus returns for each asset class

	T = 5		T = 10		T = 20	
	Exp. ret.	Surplus ret.	Exp. ret.	Surplus ret.	Exp. ret.	Surplus ret.
Cash	2.4	23.3	2.8	22.7	3.2	22.0
UST 2-yr	3.0	−2.7	3.4	−2.1	3.9	−1.3
UST 5-yr	3.4	−2.3	3.7	−1.8	4.1	−1.1
UST 10-yr	3.7	−1.9	3.7	−1.8	4.0	−1.2
UST 20-yr	4.2	−1.5	3.7	−1.8	3.8	−1.5
US equities	8.7	3.0	7.7	2.2	7.6	2.4
Commodities	6.4	0.7	7.3	1.8	7.5	2.3
REITs	8.9	3.2	7.4	1.9	7.1	1.9
Hedge funds	6.8	1.2	6.1	0.6	6.2	1.0

provide slightly higher expected returns as the investment horizon increases, whereas the expected return on equities, real estate and hedge funds goes down as the horizon increases. We observe, in Table 14.4, that the expected returns have not yet converged to the long-term steady state after 20 years. Convergence takes long because of the long-term memory in the state variables, which have a systematic influence on the asset returns in the estimated VAR model.

As discussed in the section 'Liability-relative portfolio optimization', we consider both surplus optimal portfolios and drawdown optimal portfolios and compare the results with standard mean-variance optimal portfolios. Surplus optimal portfolios are those portfolios that maximize expected utility over the funded ratio at the end of the investment horizon for a given level of surplus variance (that is, the variance of the terminal log funded ratio). Maximum drawdown optimal portfolios are those portfolios that maximize expected utility over the funded ratio at the end of the investment horizon for a given acceptable worst-case drop in the funded ratio over the investment horizon. Optimal 90 per cent CDaR portfolios are derived similarly, but under a restriction on the expected decline in funded ratio in the 10 per cent worst-case scenarios for the fund. We consider investment horizons of 5, 10 and 20 years.

Of particular interest are the minimum risk portfolio and the portfolio that maximizes the risk-adjusted expected return. The minimum risk portfolio in the case of standard mean-variance analysis is the portfolio with the lowest variance in cumulative asset returns at the end of the investment horizon. The minimum surplus-risk portfolio is the portfolio with the lowest surplus variance (variance of asset returns over liability returns) at the end of the investment horizon. Finally, the minimum drawdown portfolio is the portfolio with the lowest liability-relative maximum drawdown ($LRDD_{100\%}$) in the worst-case scenario, whereas the minimum 90 per cent CDaR portfolio has the lowest expected LRDD in the 10 per cent most adverse scenarios ($LRDD_{90\%}$).

The portfolios that maximize risk-adjusted expected return are respectively those that maximize the Sharpe ratio, the ratio of expected surplus return over surplus standard deviation (the so-called liability-adjusted Sharpe ratio – or LASR), the ratio of expected (cumulative) surplus return over maximum liability relative drawdown (we will refer to this as the liability-adjusted Calmar ratio – or $LACR_{100\%}$) and the ratio of expected surplus return to the 90 per cent CDaR measure ($LACR_{90\%}$).[12]

Figure 14.5 shows the efficient liability-relative maximum drawdown frontier. The vertical axis shows the expected annualized surplus return, whereas the maximum LRDD ($LRDD_{100\%}$) is shown on the horizontal axis. The solid line shows all the optimal portfolios along the efficient maximum LRDD frontier. The solid line with circles shows the optimal 90 per cent CDaR portfolios. The dashed line shows the surplus optimal portfolios. Clearly, the maximum drawdown optimal portfolios are superior – outperforming the surplus optimal portfolios by approximately 40–80 bps for the same level of maximum drawdown risk. We also show a 100 per cent equity allocation and the typical pension portfolio with 40 per cent in 5-year bonds and 60 per cent in equities. These portfolios are extremely inefficient in an LRDD sense. Both portfolios would expose investors to significant tail risk – the maximum LRDD for

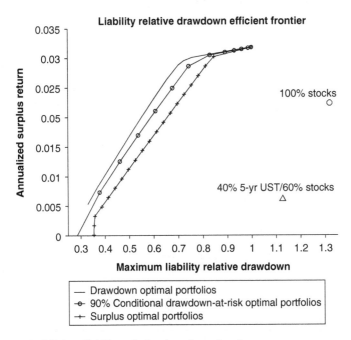

Figure 14.5 Efficient liability-relative drawdown frontier

these portfolios is 113 per cent and 132 per cent, respectively. On average, these portfolios do reasonably well – the median of the LRDDs over all scenarios is 43 per cent and 52 per cent, respectively. These portfolios, however, expose pension funds to an adverse scenario that could wipe out the pension fund. In fact, mean-variance optimal portfolios are extremely risky for pension funds. The maximum LRDD for all such portfolios is in excess of 100 per cent. Note that maximum drawdown is a tail risk measure that calculates the maximum drawdown in the worst of all possible scenarios. Our simulated scenario set includes more extreme scenarios than what we have observed in history (so far). Our maximum drawdown estimates are therefore higher than historical estimates. On the basis of historical data for asset and liability returns from 1952:Q1 to 2008:Q3, the maximum LRDD of a 100 per cent equity allocation was 71 per cent and for a 40/60 bond/equity portfolio about 40 per cent.

Table 14.5 shows the minimum risk portfolios at different investment horizons. The minimum variance portfolios have a significant allocation to cash and 10-year Treasuries. The allocation to cash decreases, whereas the allocation to 10-year Treasuries increases with the investment horizon. This suggests that cash is not an attractive asset class for long-term investors. The minimum variance portfolios also have an increasing allocation to risky assets from 6 per cent for a 5-year investment horizon to almost 25 per cent for a 20-year investment horizon. Minimum variance portfolios are quite risky and inefficient when evaluated against liabilities. For example, the minimum variance portfolio for a 10-year investment horizon has an annualized volatility of only 2.6 per cent,

Table 14.5 Minimum risk portfolios

	Min Var			Min S-Var			Min LRDD$_{100\%}$			Min LRDD$_{90\%}$		
	$T=5$	$T=10$	$T=20$	$T=5$	$T=10$	$T=20$	$T=5$	$T=10$	$T=20$	$T=5$	$T=10$	$T=20$
Exp. Ret.	3.2	3.9	4.8	4.7	4.1	4.3	5.0	5.2	5.6	5.4	5.4	5.7
Volatility	1.6	2.6	4.2	12.5	7.9	6.5	12.9	9.2	7.5	12.4	8.9	6.2
Surplus ret.	−2.5	−1.6	−0.4	−0.9	−1.4	−0.9	−0.6	−0.3	0.4	−0.2	−0.1	0.5
Surplus vol.	11.9	7.5	3.6	0.9	1.1	1.3	1.1	2.3	2.5	1.5	2.2	2.4
Max. LRDD	146.4	125.8	106.2	17.8	37.1	45.1	12.6	23.8	34.0	14.0	27.7	43.3
Cash	60.7	36.2	6.2	−31.5	−18.5	−21.4	−38.7	−91.6	−100.0	−68.8	−100.0	−100.0
UST 2-yr	0	0	0	0	0	0	0	53.7	49.0	26.2	54.6	14.6
UST 5-yr	0	0	0	0	0	0	0	0	38.6	0	26.9	78.6
UST 10-yr	33.2	49.3	69.3	29.1	13.1	43.5	31.9	17.1	0	28.5	0	24.3
UST 20-yr	0	0	0	100.0	100.0	69.6	100.0	96.9	81.5	100.0	92.5	53.2
Total UST	93.9	85.5	75.5	97.6	94.6	91.7	93.2	76.1	69.2	85.9	74.0	70.7
Stocks	1.4	3.8	10.7	1.2	2.0	4.4	5.0	8.1	13.5	4.6	11.5	14.6
Commodities	1.6	4.5	10.9	1.3	2.0	3.6	1.8	8.3	8.8	4.1	7.3	7.5
Real estate	3.2	6.2	2.9	0	1.4	0.4	0	0	1.3	0	0.9	0.5
Hedge funds	0	0	0	0	0	0	0	7.5	7.3	5.4	6.3	6.8

Note: UST = U.S. Treasury bonds.

but an annualized surplus volatility of 7.5 per cent while underperforming liabilities by 1.6 per cent per annum. The maximum LRDD for this portfolio is almost 126 per cent. In other words, in an extreme scenario, the top to bottom drop in the logarithm of the funded ratio could be as high as 126 per cent. This is mostly driven by the significant duration mismatch between assets and liabilities in the minimum variance portfolio. Note that the maximum drawdown in the case of multiple sample paths is the maximum drawdown of the worst-case scenario. Figure 14.6 shows the histogram of maximum drawdowns based on the 500 simulated sample paths and an investment horizon of 10 years for the minimum variance portfolio, the minimum surplus variance portfolio and the minimum drawdown-risk portfolios. Note that the drawdown histogram of the minimum variance portfolio is highly skewed to the right. Although the minimum variance portfolio performs reasonably well in most scenarios (the median LRDD is about 40 per cent), it can result in disastrous outcomes in some states of the world.

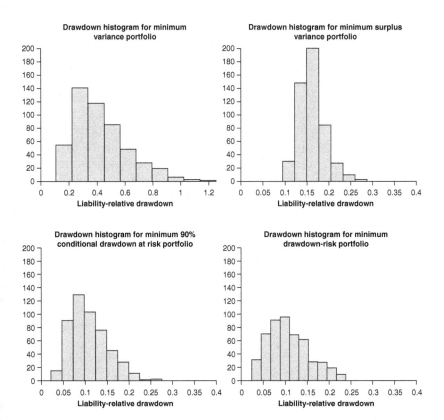

Figure 14.6 Histogram of liability-relative drawdowns for minimum risk portfolios

In contrast to the minimum variance portfolios, the minimum surplus variance and the minimum drawdown-risk portfolios have significant positions in 10-year and 20-year US Treasuries and short positions in cash. These positions can be interpreted as synthetic duration overlay portfolios. A portfolio that is short cash and long the same amount in, for example, 10-year or 20-year Treasuries mimics a total return swap on long-dated Treasuries. For investment horizons of 10 and 20 years, the minimum drawdown-risk portfolios also allocate considerably to 2-year and 5-year US Treasuries to reduce the drawdown risk of the portfolio. Although the minimum drawdown-risk portfolios are significantly more levered than the minimum surplus variance portfolios, the overall LRDD risk is lower. As in the case of the minimum variance portfolios, there are strong horizon effects for the minimum drawdown-risk portfolios. The allocation to risky assets in the minimum drawdown-risk portfolios increases from about 10 per cent for a 5-year investment horizon to over 30 per cent for a 20-year investment horizon. This horizon effect is less pronounced for the minimum surplus variance portfolios in which the overall allocation to US Treasuries remains above 90 per cent for a 5-, 10- and 20-year investment horizons.

The minimum drawdown-risk portfolios are riskier in terms of surplus volatility but provide better downside protection (lower maximum drawdown) while offering higher expected surplus returns. For example, when the investment horizon is 10 years, the minimum drawdown-risk portfolio LRDD$_{100\%}$ has an annualized volatility of 9.2 per cent and an annualized surplus volatility of 2.3 per cent, whereas the minimum surplus variance portfolio has an annualized volatility of only 7.9 per cent and a surplus volatility of 1.1 per cent. The minimum drawdown-risk portfolio, however, has a lower maximum LRDD of 24 per cent compared to 37 per cent for the minimum surplus variance portfolio. The minimum drawdown-risk portfolio LRDD$_{100\%}$ also outperforms the minimum variance portfolio both in terms of expected total return (5.2 per cent versus 4.1 per cent) and in terms of expected surplus return (-0.3 per cent versus -1.4 per cent). The optimal CDaR portfolio LRDD$_{90\%}$ performs even better, with an expected return of 5.4 per cent and a surplus return of -0.1 per cent, while having a maximum drawdown that is only moderately higher (27.7 per cent versus 23.8 per cent for LRDD$_{100\%}$). Overall, the two minimum drawdown-risk portfolios have a lower overall allocation to US Treasuries and a higher allocation to risky assets (US stocks, commodities, real estate and hedge funds).

Figure 14.6 shows the drawdown histograms for each of the minimum risk portfolios over a 10-year investment horizon. Investors would likely prefer the drawdown profile of the minimum drawdown-risk portfolios versus that of the minimum surplus variance portfolio. The minimum drawdown-risk portfolios are more balanced across scenarios and less exposed to extreme scenarios.

The median drawdown for the minimum surplus variance portfolio is about 16 per cent versus 10 per cent for the minimum drawdown-risk portfolio $LRDD_{100\%}$. The drawdown profile of the minimum surplus variance portfolio is also more skewed (skewness of 1.2 versus 0.6) and has fatter tails (excess kurtosis of 5.1 versus -0.2) compared to the drawdown profile of the minimum draw-down-risk portfolio. The drawdown histogram for the minimum 90 per cent CDaR portfolio ($LRDD_{90\%}$) is very similar to the maximum drawdown case ($LRDD_{100\%}$), and it has comparable favorable properties. Overall, minimum drawdown-risk portfolios provide better protection against adverse scenarios.

Table 14.6 shows the portfolios with the highest risk-adjusted returns over different investment horizons. Both the maximum Sharpe ratio and the max-imum LACR portfolios display strong horizon effects. The allocation to fixed income decreases from 65 per cent to 2.4 per cent, as the investment horizon lengthens for the maximum Sharpe ratio portfolio. Most of this decrease is offset by an increase in the equity allocation. In contrast, the drawdown opti-mal portfolios are fully levered and have a higher allocation to commodities, real estate and hedge funds. The horizon effects for the maximum drawdown measure ($LACR_{100\%}$ portfolios) are complex: the allocation to equities goes from 54 per cent to 25 per cent and then increases again to 37 per cent as the invest-ment horizon is lengthened. Similarly, the allocation to hedge funds falls from 21 per cent to 2 per cent and then increases again to 38 per cent. Given that maximum drawdown optimal portfolios put more emphasis on outliers, the optimal portfolio weights are more sensitive to the investment horizon and the

Table 14.6   Maximum risk-adjusted return portfolios

	Max SR			**LASR**			**LACR$_{100\%}$**			**LACR$_{90\%}$**		
	$T=5$	$T=10$	$T=20$	$T=5$	$T=10$	$T=20$	$T=5$	$T=10$	$T=20$	$T=5$	$T=10$	$T=20$
Exp. ret.	5.0	6.7	8.1	10.1	8.5	8.2	9.7	8.4	7.8	9.6	8.4	8.1
Volatility	2.8	4.5	6.5	16.3	10.7	8.0	14.8	14.0	8.6	14.8	11.4	7.6
Surplus ret.	-0.7	1.2	2.9	4.4	3.0	3.0	4.1	2.9	2.6	4.0	2.9	2.9
Surplus vol.	11.7	7.6	5.8	7.6	6.0	5.4	7.3	9.0	6.3	7.3	6.5	6.2
Max. LRDD	133.2	110.0	107.5	51.1	84.6	109.6	41.5	69.9	75.6	46.6	74.4	100.0
Cash	-35.2	-73.6	-100.0	-100.0	-100.0	-100.0	-100.0	-100.0	-100.0	-100.0	-100.0	-100.0
UST 2-yr	100.0	100.0	49.9	3.5	0	0	0	0	0	0	0	0
UST 5-yr	0	4.4	52.5	0	4.8	76.8	0	0	0	0	0	0
UST 10-yr	0	0	0	0	95.2	24.3	0.8	82.0	70.8	1.4	36.8	100.0
UST 20-yr	0	0	0	96.5	0	0	100.0	18.0	29.2	100.0	63.2	0
Total UST	64.8	30.8	2.4	0	0	1.1	0.8	0	0	1.4	0	0
Stocks	18.8	36.8	60.2	63.8	64.2	62.7	53.7	25.2	37.0	45.0	50.8	53.6
Commodities	6.1	11.9	15.7	13.3	14.4	10.7	16.0	37.5	25.3	22.0	24.6	20.5
Real estate	6.3	15.5	12.4	17.4	19.5	14.0	8.6	35.2	0	17.5	15.2	13.6
Hedge funds	4.0	4.9	9.3	5.6	2.0	11.5	20.9	2.1	37.7	14.1	9.4	12.3

Note: UST = U.S. Treasury bonds.

simulated sample paths. Maximum drawdown optimization therefore requires care in constructing a large and realistic scenario set for asset and liability returns. The stability of the solution clearly improves by using 90 per cent CDaR as the target risk measure. CDaR does not focus on a single worst-case scenario for the pension fund, but takes the average of the α per cent worst outcomes below a given threshold ($\alpha = 10$ per cent in this example). The equity portfolio weight of the LACR$_{90\%}$ portfolios steadily increases from 45 per cent to 54 per cent as the investment horizon lengthens from 5 to 20 years, whereas the total weight of alternative asset classes decreases.

Horizon effects are much less pronounced for the maximum LASR portfolio. Although the weights to the various Treasury segments change with the investment horizon, the allocation to equities, commodities, real estate and hedge funds is virtually identical across investment horizons. As the investment horizon increases, the overall duration of the minimum surplus variance portfolios decreases to take advantage of the slightly higher return on 5-year Treasuries versus 10- and 20-year Treasuries (over a 20-year investment horizon 5-year Treasuries outperform 10-year Treasuries by about 8 bps and 20-year Treasuries by about 35 bps). Both the surplus optimal and the drawdown optimal portfolios employ a duration overlay strategy with a short position of 100 per cent in cash and a long position in long-dated Treasuries. The total allocation to fixed income for these portfolios is relatively low compared to the maximum Sharpe ratio portfolios. This is one of the advantages of employing a duration overlay strategy – it allows investors to hedge the interest rate risk in their liabilities while pursuing return maximization. Asset-only portfolios are grossly inferior when evaluated against liabilities exposing investors not only to greater surplus volatility but also to extreme events. Over a 5-year investment horizon, the worst-case LRDD for the optimal Sharpe ratio portfolio is 133 per cent compared to 51.1 per cent for the optimal LASR portfolio and only 41.5 per cent for the optimal LACR$_{100\%}$ portfolio. Interestingly, as the investment horizon lengthens, the optimal Sharpe ratio portfolio converges to the optimal LASR portfolio. The main difference between the optimal Sharpe ratio and the optimal LASR portfolio, for an investment horizon of 20 years, is the allocation to the various Treasury segments. The allocation to equities, commodities, real estate and hedge funds is virtually the same, but the optimal LASR portfolio has a slightly higher duration compared to the optimal Sharpe ratio portfolio.

The portfolios that maximize the LACR are less equity centric and have a higher allocation to commodities and hedge funds compared to maximum Sharpe ratio and LASR portfolios. These portfolios have a higher surplus volatility but a significantly lower maximum LRDD with only a slighter lower expected surplus return compared to the maximum LASR portfolios. Table 14.7 compares surplus optimal and drawdown optimal portfolios for

Table 14.7 Optimal surplus and drawdown portfolios for various maximum drawdown levels for a 10-year investment horizon (VAR process)

	DD = 40%			DD = 50%			DD = 60%		
	Surplus	Drawdown	90% CDaR	Surplus	Drawdown	90% CDaR	Surplus	Drawdown	90% CDaR
Expected surplus return	0.55	1.01	0.87	1.13	1.66	1.47	1.68	2.31	2.06
Surplus volatility	2.60	4.73	3.53	3.30	6.06	4.33	4.04	7.45	5.19
Expected return	6.05	6.51	6.38	6.63	7.16	6.97	7.18	7.81	7.56
Maximum LRDD	40.0	40.0	40.0	50.0	50.0	50.0	60.0	60.0	60.0
Median LRDD	15.2	15.1	13.2	18.2	17.4	16.3	21.6	21.4	19.7
Cash	-100.0	-100.0	-100.0	-100.0	-100.0	-100.0	-100.0	-100.0	-100.0
UST 2-yr	37.5	0.0	0.0	0.0	0.0	0.0	0.0	0.0	0.0
UST 5-yr	58.8	0.0	25.4	99.7	0.0	0.0	83.9	0.0	0.0
UST 10-yr	0.1	94.7	74.6	0.0	25.8	89.3	4.8	4.0	60.9
UST 20-yr	63.6	45.8	50.7	47.8	96.0	45.4	44.4	100.0	57.7
Total UST	60.0	40.4	50.7	47.4	21.8	34.7	33.1	4.0	18.6
Stocks	25.1	1.1	21.2	33.2	7.0	28.4	41.6	10.1	35.2
Commodities	6.7	19.1	13.2	8.5	25.5	16.8	10.4	32.5	20.2
Real estate	7.3	13.7	3.5	9.4	17.4	7.0	12.5	24.3	11.0
Hedge funds	0.9	25.6	11.4	1.5	28.3	13.3	2.5	29.1	15.0

different maximum LRDD levels when the investment horizon is 10 years. For a drawdown level of 50 per cent, the maximum drawdown portfolio invests 78 per cent in risky assets (equities, commodities, real estate and hedge funds), whereas the surplus optimal portfolio only invests 53 per cent in risky assets. In addition, the maximum drawdown optimal portfolio invests a larger proportion in 20-year Treasuries compared to the surplus optimal portfolio. The optimal 90 per cent CDaR portfolio has a risk profile that lies in between the other two portfolios, with a risky asset weight of 65 per cent and a large allocation to 10-year Treasuries.

Overall, the drawdown optimal portfolios have a higher allocation to long-term Treasuries, a lower total allocation to fixed income and are less equity centric (and consequently have a higher allocation to commodities, real estate and hedge funds) compared to the surplus optimal portfolios. The drawdown optimal portfolios outperform the surplus optimal portfolios by approximately 30–60 bps per year based on our forward looking assumptions. This is achieved at the expense of a higher surplus volatility.

14.5   Conclusions

In this article, we have studied the optimal long-term investment policy for defined benefit pension funds while taking pension liabilities explicitly into account. We have utilized a VAR process to model asset returns and predictive state variables following Campbell and Viceira (2005) and Hoevenaars *et al* (2008). Bond returns and liability returns are derived using the Nelson–Siegel yield curve model. The three factors of the Nelson–Siegel yield curve model (level, slope and curvature) are included as variables in the VAR process. On the basis of simulated asset and liability returns, we construct optimal portfolios. We argue that LRDD risk is a more meaningful risk measure for pension funds than return or surplus volatility. The optimal surplus and optimal drawdown portfolios differ substantially from the standard mean-variance optimal portfolios. These portfolios have a significant allocation to long-duration bonds (and are short cash) to offset the interest rate risk in liabilities. Drawdown optimal portfolios display strong horizon effects. These effects are virtually absent for surplus optimal portfolios. The drawdown optimal portfolios have a larger allocation to long-dated Treasuries, lower overall allocation to government bonds and are less equity centric and have a higher allocation to commodities, real estate and hedge funds. On the basis of our forward-looking expected return assumptions, drawdown optimal portfolios outperform the surplus optimal portfolios by approximately 30–60 bps per year for the same maximum LRDD level. In our view, drawdown optimization produces portfolios that are better balanced and less exposed to extreme events. This is particularly true when comparing the results to mean-variance optimal portfolios.

Among the two measures of drawdown risk considered, maximum drawdown and 90 per cent CDaR, the latter measure is less sensitive to extreme values in the scenarios and leads to more stable optimal portfolios.

There are several possible directions for future research. First, additional state variables could be included in the VAR model, which have some predictive power for real estate returns and commodity futures returns. Possible candidates are, for example, hedging pressures in commodity markets (see for example, Basu *et al* (2006)) and cap yields for real estate. The menu of asset classes could also be expanded to include, for example, small- and large-cap stocks and corporate bonds. Another interesting extension is to incorporate regime switches in the VAR process, where the regimes could be related to the business cycle. Guidolin and Timmermann (2006) and Guidolin and Timmermann (2007) consider regime switching VAR models for stock and bond returns with predictive variables. They find that four regimes are necessary to capture the joint distribution of stock and bond returns. They also find that the optimal asset allocations vary considerably across these regimes. Our VAR model can readily be extended to incorporate Markov regime switching. Regime switching models can also help describe fat tails and skewness in asset returns. However, the use of regime switching VAR processes does increase the number of parameters significantly. It would also be worth exploring the impact of parameter uncertainty. We conjecture that this would make investors more conservative and result in larger allocations to fixed income. Finally, as mentioned in the introduction, the drawdown optimization problem can be extended to allow for dynamic portfolio weights and optimal rebalancing. Stochastic programming techniques could be used to solve the resulting dynamic optimization problem.

One clear message from the results in this article is that an asset-only approach is far inferior to an asset liability approach. Asset-only optimal portfolios expose pension funds to extreme adverse scenarios. Although we believe that a LRDD approach is preferable, even a surplus optimization approach would result in marked improvement compared to the asset-only approach that pension funds traditionally have employed. Fully adopting a liability-driven investment philosophy requires an important shift in view point for Boards and investment officers. Liabilities should be at the center of the investment decision-making process and performance and risk should be measured relative to liabilities. Pension funds should move away from the obsession with short-term asset-only performance. Changing the traditional paradigm is hard, but absolutely necessary if pension funds are going to be able to meet the retirement needs of millions of workers in the future.

Acknowledgements

We thank two anonymous referees for valuable comments and suggestions.

Notes

1. Some of the uncertainty embedded in pension liabilities, such as mortality risk and wage growth uncertainty, cannot (currently) be hedged away.
2. Maximizing expected utility over the funded ratio is closely related to maximizing the expected utility of the fund surplus $(A_T - L_T)$, as in Rudolf and Ziemba (2004), as the funded ratio is equal to the value of the fund surplus scaled by the value of the liabilities: $F_T = (A_T - L_T)/L_T + 1$. An advantage of the funded ratio is that it is nonnegative by definition and therefore more suited for traditional power utility functions (including logarithmic utility).
3. www.nareit.com.
4. www.hedgefundresearch.com.
5. www.econ.ohio-state.edu/jhm/jhm.html.
6. research.stlouisfed.org/fred2/.
7. www.econ.yale.edu/shiller/.
8. www.econ.nyu.edu/user/ludvigsons/.
9. Several studies have shown that historical hedge fund returns are biased upwards because of survivorship bias and other reporting biases. Estimates of survivorship bias in hedge fund returns range from about 1.8 per cent to 2.4 per cent per annum.
10. For quarterly data, we find that setting λ equal to 0.18 produces the best overall fit to the yield curve data. A value of 0.18 on a quarterly basis is identical to $\lambda = 0.06$ on a monthly basis, as used by Diebold and Li (2006).
11. Starting values for the VAR process in the simulation are the latest observed values in our sample (2008:Q3). We use antithetic sampling from the error distribution to generate the scenarios.
12. The original Calmar ratio is the ratio of compound annualized return to maximum drawdown.

References

Artzner, P., Delbaen, F., Eber, J. and Heath, D. (1998) Coherent measures of risk. *Mathematical Finance* 9: 203–228.
Barberis, N. (2000) Investing for the long run when returns are predictable. *Journal of Finance* 55: 225–264.
Basu, D., Oomen, R. and Stremme, A. (2006) How to Time the Commodity Market. Cass Business School. Technical report.
Bernadell, C., Coche, J. and Nyholm, K. (2005) Yield Curve Prediction for the Strategic Investor. European Central Bank, No. 472. Technical report.
Bliss, R. (1997) Testing term structure estimation methods. *Advances in Futures and Options Research* 9: 197–231.
Brandt, M. (2009) Portfolio choice problems. In: Y. Ait-Sahalia and L. Hansen (eds.) *Handbook of Financial Econometrics*. Amsterdam: North-Holland Publishers, pp. 269–336.
Campbell, J., Chan, Y. and Viceira, L. (2003) A multivariate model of strategic asset-allocation. *Journal of Financial Economics* 67: 41–80.
Campbell, J., Lo, A. and MacKinlay, G. (1997) *The Econometrics of Financial Markets*. Princeton, NJ: Princeton University Press.
Campbell, J. and Viceira, L. (2002) *Strategic Asset Allocation*. Oxford: Oxford University Press.
Campbell, J. and Viceira, L. (2005) The term structure of the risk-return trade-off. *Financial Analysts Journal* 61: 34–44.

Campbell, S. and Diebold, F. (2009) Stock returns and expected business conditions: Half a century of direct evidence. *Journal of Business and Economic Statistics* 27: 266–278.

Carino, D. *et al* (1994) The Russell-Yasuda Kasai model: An asset/liability model for a Japanese insurance company using multistage stochastic programming. *Interfaces* 24: 29–49, Reprinted in Ziemba, W.T. and Mulvey, J.M. (eds.) (1998) *World Wide Asset and Liability Modeling*, Chapter 24. Cambridge University Press, pp. 609–633.

Chekhlov, A., Uryasev, S. and Zabarankin, M. (2005) Drawdown measure in portfolio optimization. *International Journal of Theoretical and Applied Finance* 8: 13–58.

Consigli, G. and Dempster, M. (1998) Dynamic stochastic programming for asset-liability management. *Annals of Operations Research* 81: 131–162.

Diebold, F. and Li, C. (2006) Forecasting the term structure of government bond yields. *Journal of Econometrics* 130: 337–364.

Gorton, G. and Rouwenhorst, K. (2006) Facts and fantasies about commodity futures. *Financial Analyst Journal* 62: 47–68.

Grossman, S. and Zhou, Z. (1993) Optimal investment strategies for controlling drawdowns. *Mathematical Finance* 3: 241–276.

Guidolin, M. and Timmermann, A. (2006) An econometric model of nonlinear dynamics in the joint distribution of stock and bond returns. *Journal of Applied Econometrics* 21: 1–22.

Guidolin, M. and Timmermann, A. (2007) Asset allocation under multivariate regime switching. *Journal of Economic Dynamics and Control* 31: 3503–3544.

Hoevenaars, R.P., Molenaar, R.D., Schotman, P.C. and Steenkamp, T.B. (2008) Strategic asset allocation with liabilities: Beyond stocks and bonds. *Journal of Economic Dynamics and Control* 32(9): 2939–2970.

Kouwenberg, R. (2001) Scenario generation and stochastic programming models for asset liability management. *European Journal of Operational Research* 134: 51–64.

Kouwenberg, R., Mentink, A., Schouten, M. and Sonnenberg, R. (2009) Estimating value-at-risk of institutional portfolios with alternative asset classes. In: G. Gregoriou (ed.) *The VaR Modeling Handbook: Practical Applications in Alternative Investing, Banking, Insurance, and Portfolio Management.* New York: McGraw Hill, pp. 33–54.

Kouwenberg, R. and Zenios, S. (2006) Stochastic programming models for asset liability management. In: S. Zenios and W. Ziemba (eds.) *Handbook of Asset and Liability Management.* Amsterdam: North-Holland Publishers, pp. 253–303.

Kusy, M. and Ziemba, W. (1986) A bank asset and liability management model. *Operations Research* 34(3): 356–376.

Lettau, M. and Ludvigson, S. (2001) Consumption, aggregate wealth and expected stock returns. *Journal of Finance* 56: 815–849.

Markowitz, H. (1952) Portfolio selection. *Journal of Finance* 7: 77–91.

McCulloch, J. and Kwon, H. (1993) US Term Structure Data 1947–1991. Ohio State University. Technical Report 93–6.

Mulvey, J. and Vladimirou, H. (1992) Stochastic network programming for financial planning problems. *Management Science* 38: 1642–1664.

Nelson, C. R. and Siegel, A. F. (1987) Parsimonious modelling of yield curves. *Journal of Business* 60: 473–489.

Reveiz, A. and Leon, C. (2008) Efficient Portfolio Optimization in the Wealth Creation and Maximum Drawdown Space. Banco de la Republica de Colombia. Technical report.

Rudolf, M. and Ziemba, W. (2004) Intertemporal surplus management. *Journal of Economic Dynamics and Control* 28: 975–990.

Sharpe, W. and Tint, L. (1990) Liabilities – A new approach. *Journal of Portfolio Management* 16(Winter): 5–10.

Shiller, R. (2000) *Irrational Exuberance*. Princeton, NJ: Princeton University Press.

Stambaugh, R. (1997) Analyzing investments whose histories differ in length. *Journal of Financial Economics* 45: 285–331.

Zenios, S. (1995) Asset/liability management under uncertainty for fixed-income. *Annals of Operations Research* 59: 77–97.

15

Asset-Liability Management in Defined Contribution Pensions: A Stochastic Model with reference to Auto Choice Portfolios in the New Pension System in India

Hira Sadhak and Steward Doss

15.1 Introduction

The recently witnessed global financial crises forced banks, insurance companies, pension funds and other financial companies – which manage the financial assets of others – to look again into the way assets are managed and liabilities are valued. The Indian financial services industry, which has been opened up in the recent past, could withstand the onslaught of global turmoil to a great extent. However, it is not fully insulated now – and in the future would be more prone to global development – and needs to take long-term strategic decisions to protect itself from the devastating economic consequences originating from the changing business cycle, market volatility and system failure. Institutional investors such as life insurance companies and pension funds need to be more alarmed, since their investment horizon is much longer than that of others and they deal with public money, meaning personal financial risk management (life insurance) and retirement income (pension funds). The health of the fund management business depends to a large extent on understanding changing national and global economies, the movement of the business cycle, potential risks associated with the market and the ability to design an appropriate investment strategy to capture these changes and absorb the untimely adverse developments.

Pension funds are institutional investors having twin objectives: to provide the maximum risk-adjusted return and at the same time to ensure that the capital base remains intact. In a defined benefit plan, funding is a critical problem; but that is the responsibility of pension providers, and thus investment risks are borne by the employers/pension providers. However, in a funded defined contribution plan, the investment risks are transferred to the members (investors). Contractually, the fund managers have no obligations. Yet it is a business responsibility of the pension fund managers to protect the capital and ensure maximum possible returns. Furthermore, in a sense, DC fund managers need to be more concerned than DB fund managers about the investment returns and market consequences, since no guaranteed pension provision is available to the members of the funds. Risk management thus becomes a very crucial strategic issue in fund management under the defined contribution pension system. Asset-liability management (ALM) is a dynamic concept and an important tool of risk management, and also an integral part of strategic investment management.

Asset-liability management (ALM) is an overall risk management technique for pension funds, which in a defined benefit pension plan seeks to provide guidance to risk management, an asset allocation strategy which enables the pension providers and fund managers to minimize the asset and liability mismatch in order to fulfil pension obligations. ALM also plays an important role in DC pension funds by providing guidance to appropriate strategic asset allocation and managing long-term risk at the accumulation phase. ALM plays a more important role in the payout phase.

Secondly, most of the developed markets are moving towards a risk-based capital regime; India is also transitioning towards the same. It is essential that everyone re-examine their (deterministic) ALM models and resulting investment strategies, and more importantly, move towards a more dynamic and realistic ALM approach, such as stochastic modelling or dynamic financial modelling. The primary objective of developing ALM is to minimize all possible financial risks resulting from a mismatch of assets and liabilities, including systemic and reinvestment risks, with a view to ensuring that the life or annuity fund is statutorily solvent in most, if not all, future years, subject to current investment limits as specified by the regulator. This chapter focuses on developing a stochastic ALM for a pension fund in an Indian context. The simple spreadsheet-based ALM model developed here includes not only fixed income assets, but also equity, cash and treasury bills for a pension fund under present Indian market conditions.

The New Pension System (NPS), effective as of 1 January 2004, is a defined contribution system, the accumulation and investment of pension assets being managed by fund managers approved by the pension fund regulator (PFRDA). Insurance companies will manage the payout in NPS, since a part of accumulated wealth (at least 40%) needs to be used for purchasing an annuity policy. Thus in NPS, fund managers should be more concerned about risk management and how to provide the maximum risk-adjusted return, which will enhance investment value and enable the investors to purchase an annuity that would provide regular income to maintain the same standard of living. In the payout phase, investment management by life insurance companies needs to focus more on the liability side and to keep the liability obligation arising out of annuity contract in mind when designing the investment strategy. This chapter, however, attempts to examine the issues in risk management, the environment and instruments necessary for managing long-term risks, and the applicability of ALM in NPS. We will also attempt to provide guidance to fund managers in the design of risk management strategies that ensure capital protection, while at the same time earning maximum risk-adjusted returns at the accumulation phase, and to provide guidance to on investment management at the payout phase to maintain liability obligation.

Although our discussions are based on NPS and the prevailing market environment in India, it should have general appeal among fund managers and policy makers in any emerging market, since they all experience similar institutional constraints at the initial stage of pension reforms, and the market environments are more or less similar in emerging markets.

15.2 The salient features of the New Pension System (NPS)

The New Pension System, introduced by the government of India and regulated by the Pension Fund Regulatory and Development Authority (PFRDA), is a fully funded defined contribution (DC) pension, which is a very low cost retirement saving system with many attractive features. NPS was operationalized in two phases. Initially, mandatory NPS was opened to the employees of the central government (excluding the armed forces), effective as of 1 January 2004. Subsequently, 22 state governments also joined the mandatory NPS. In the second phase, the NPS was opened to all citizens, effective as of 1 May 2009.

While joining the NPS is mandatory for employees of central government and for employees of the state governments which have opted for NPS, it is voluntary for all others (All Citizens). There are three fund managers for management of government sector pension assets under NPS, while there are six fund managers selected for managing funds under the All Citizens' scheme. Subscribers can choose from multiple pension fund managers and from the multiple schemes. There is no implicit or explicit assurance of benefits except market-based return. Every subscriber is issued a unique Permanent Retirement Account Number (PRAN) by the Central Record-Keeping Agency (CRA), which can be used for monitoring fund performance, accumulation of assets, status of contributions and so forth.

Under the NPS, pension fund managers offer multiple schemes to subscribers: the fund manager will offer two schemes to the government servants and three schemes for the All Citizens' scheme, according to the risk tolerance level of the investors. The NPS is portable, and the members will have the option to transfer individual pension accounts in case of change of employment or change of residence. Subscribers to the NPS will be entitled to switch over from one scheme to another, as well as from one fund manager to another.

There is a provision of mandatory annuitisation in NPS. All members, at the time of exit at age 60, or at superannuation are required to use at least 40% of their pension wealth to purchase an annuity (from an IRDA-regulated life insurance company). Individual members of the NPS have the flexibility to leave the pension system prior to age 60, but in that case, the mandatory annuitisation is 80% of the pension wealth.

15.2.1　Investment regulation in NPS

The PFRDA has issued two different investment guidelines – one for the mandatory NPS for government employees and another for the voluntary NPS for All Citizens. While there are two investment options for the members in the NPS for government employees, there are three investment options in NPS for All Citizens. However, asset allocations in both the schemes are heavily tilted towards debt instruments, though it is more so in the NPS for government employees. Maximum equity investment in government scheme is 15%, while that in the All Citizens' scheme is 50%.

15.2.1.1　Asset allocation in central and state government funds

There are two investment options under the NPS for the government employees, and the pattern of asset allocation differs accordingly.

15.2.1.1.1　Investment option I.

- Investment in Government Bonds: According to investment regulations, a maximum of 55% of funds can be invested in central and state government securities and units of mutual funds set up as dedicated funds for investment in government securities, regulated by the SEBI.
- Investment in Corporate Bonds: Up to 40 % of funds can be invested in debt securities with maturity of not less than three years tenure, issued by bodies corporate, including banks and public financial institutions.
- Investment in Equity and Equity Mutual Funds: Up to 15% of funds can be invested in shares of companies on which derivatives are available on the Bombay Stock Exchange or National Stock Exchange, or equity linked schemes of mutual funds regulated by the Securities and Exchange Board of India.
- Investment in Money Market Instruments: Up to 5% of funds can be invested in money market instruments, including units of money market mutual funds.

15.2.1.1.2　Investment option II.　Investment under this option is fully oriented towards government securities, that is, 100% investment in central government and state government securities. Furthermore, up to 10% of the total portfolio

at the end of the preceding financial year can be treated as tradeable and may be used for active management. The tradeable portfolio of government securities shall be marked-to–market, and mutual funds shall be valued at the net asset value at the close of the financial year.

15.2.1.2 *Investment and asset allocation in funds for all citizens*

The investment guidelines issued by PFRDA for the New Pension System for all citizens of India, other than government employees covered by NPS, detail various investment options and portfolio composition of asset classes. Under this scheme, two options are available to the investors, namely, active choice and auto choice (default option):

15.2.1.2.1 *Asset allocation under the active choice portfolio.* Investors under the active choice can select a portfolio of their choice. The PFRDA has allowed three separate schemes, each investing in a different asset class, identified as asset class E, asset class G and asset class C. Asset class E consists of equity market instruments, restricted to up to 50% of portfolio assets, and the funds will be invested in index funds that replicate the portfolio of either BSE Sensitive index or NSE Nifty 50 index. Asset class G consists of government securities, and funds will be invested in central government bonds and state government bonds. The C asset class consists of fixed income instruments, other than bonds, issued by any entity other than central and state government.

15.2.1.2.2 *Asset allocation under auto choice portfolio.* Investors who are unable to select any fund or who do not want to exercise active choice, can opt for auto choice, which is a predetermined default option, and funds will be invested depending on the age of the investors. This is a life cycle fund and the investment is age-based – the lower the age, the higher the investment in equities – which automatically changes with the changes in age profile. Asset portfolios of investors up to the age of 35 will consist of 50% in equity asset class, 30% in asset class C (corporate bonds) and 20% in asset class G (government bonds). At the age of 45, the portfolio changes to favour to government bonds – with 20% investment in equities, 15% investment in corporate bonds and 65% investment in government bonds. Furthermore, the portfolios virtually become government bond funds at the age of 55, having 10% investment in equity, 10% investment in corporate bonds and 80% investment in government bonds.

15.3 The NPS and risk management

There are a number of risks directly and indirectly affecting fund management operation, since operational objectives are basically a futuristic function. The future is uncertain and mostly unpredictable; a part of that uncertainty may be predicted, and precautionary initiatives can be taken. Pension fund managers operate within the given regulatory framework and the changing market environment in an uncertain future. However, scientific prediction and projection of probable changes may, to some extent, mitigate the risks associated with fund management, capital protection and future provision of annuities to the members. We outline here some of such risks associated with funded pension fund management.

15.3.1 Investment management risk

In an unfunded pension scheme, fund managers are expected to attain twin objectives, namely protecting capital and ensuring reasonable risk-adjusted returns for the members of the scheme. Return enhancement becomes crucial, because the investor defers present consumption for future consumption, with an expectation of increased and regular payments for future consumption. Risk management, therefore, becomes a critical operational concern. Risk is an important component of return, and needs careful understanding of the nature of risks and its dimension. Risk elimination is never possible. A portion of investment risk may be handled through diversification of portfolio asset allocation, while some portion of risk is nondiversifiable. Therefore, there are two components of investment risk – diversifiable and nondiversifiable. Risk elements in investment may be reduced through portfolio diversification by investing in various financial instruments, such as equity, debt and money market instruments, within the given regulatory framework. Some regulators also allow alternative investments such as real estate, commodities and so forth. Furthermore, a liberal investment regulation regime may also allow investment of pension assets in foreign equity and debt.

15.3.1.1 The nondiversifiable portion of risks composed of capital risk, reinvestment risk, inflation risk and so forth

Capital risk arises when the value of a portfolio declines due to declines in the price of equity, market value of debt instruments or default. Interest rate changes have a significant impact on the portfolio value since the increased interest rate adversely impacts the value of the existing debt portfolio. Increased inflationary trends also adversely impact the portfolio value.

Reinvestment risks arise due to changing interest rate regimes; for example, banks in India offered fixed interest rates ranging from 10% to 11.5% in 2008 and 2009, but the rate declined to 6.5% to 7.25% in early 2009. Maturity proceeds received from early investment will earn very low interest, causing erosion in the portfolio value. Inflation risk is accompanied by changes in macroeconomic factors, and monetary policy cannot be avoided over a long period of time. However, the adverse impact of changes in the inflation factor can be hedged by investing in long-term inflation protected bonds.

15.3.1.2 Mortality risk

Mortality risk is not of a concern for fund managers in the accumulation stage of a funded DC pension system, but becomes an important risk factor in the payout stage of DC systems and in defined benefit plans. Mortality risk arises out of a longer life expectancy than estimated. In an annuity contract between a pensioner and the annuity provider (normally a life insurance company) the annuity provider may underestimate the longevity and ends up providing more annuity benefits than the purchase price. This may happen due to obsolete mortality tables, absence of mortality research and irregular updating of mortality data.

15.4 Capital markets in India

A pension provider is primarily an asset management company, and the investment performances and risk management activities are significantly influenced by the country's capital market and economic policies. In view of this, we need to provide an outline of the current situation of India's capital market – both opportunities and constraints for fund managers. India's capital market has experienced sweeping changes in the last decades. A large number of reform initiatives have been made by the government and regulators of financial service authorities to open up the market, improve market infrastructure, real-time trading and delivery systems, disclosure systems, corporate governance, and so forth. Reforms have paid handsomely, as in 2007, when India's debt market as a percentage of GDP was 41.6% (ADB, 2007) and equity market capitalisation as a percentage of GDP was 155% (World Bank, 2008). These are comparable with other emerging economies, in which equity market capitalization is around 130% of GDP. However, lack of depth in the debt market, and particularly in the corporate segments, is a matter of concern for fund managers. A broad outline is thus provided below, particularly in respect to equity and debt markets.

15.4.1 Equities market

The Indian securities market has made enormous progress during the last few years in developing a sophisticated automated market mechanism. The market regulator, the Securities and Exchange Board of India (SEBI), is an independent regulator and has put in place a sound regulatory system with respect to market intermediaries, risk management, take-overs, corporate governance, trading mechanisms, settlement cycles and derivative trading. There has been a significant spurt in market capitalization and turnover in the equity security market. Market capitalization increased from USD 135,295 million in 1998–1999, to USD 1,288,392 million in 2007–2009, but declined to USD 607,061 million in 2008–2009. At the same time, the market turnover went up from USD 241,191 million in 1998–1999 to USD 1,283,667 million in 2007–2008, but declined to USD 756,054 million in 2008–2009. The market capitalization ratio (a measure to understand the importance of equity markets in relation to GDP), which was 109.3% in 2007–2008, declined to 58.12% in 2008–2009, yet compares well with other emerging markets (NSE 200) (see Figure 15.1).

15.4.1.1   Market volatility

Market volatility has a significant impact on the stability of return and is one of the concerns for pension fund managers, as it affects the return. Market volatility is measured by the standard deviation of daily volatility; however, increased for sensex stocks while the same declined for Nifty stocks in 2009. Volatility of weekly returns on BSE Sensex increased from 4.57 in 2008 to 5.12 in 2009 while the same for the Top 50 Nifty declined from 4.30 to 3.89 during the same period. (Economic Survey 2009–2010). The volatilatility has further reflected in movement BSE index. Movement in BSE Index as shown below (Table 15.1) shows that during 2004–2005 to 2007–2008, there was a steady climb up but in 2008-2009, there was a drastic decline in average, high and low. Capital inflows, holding pattern of equity, etc., influences the market volatility. India has become an attractive destination for portfolio investment. Net capital inflow, which reached all time of USD 107 billion in 2007–2008, declined to USD 7 billion in 2008–2009, but then increased substantially to 50 billion in 2009–2010. Capital inflow is a welcome development for equity market growth, but some regulation is required to avoid its volatility impact.

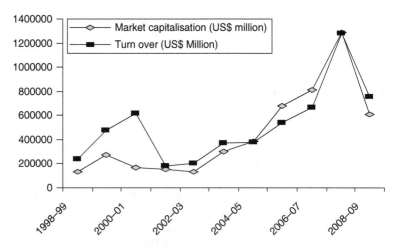

Figure 15.1   Equity market capitalisation and turn-over in USD

Table 15.1 Movement in BSE index

Year	Average	High	Low
2004–2005	5741	6915	4505
2005–2006	8280	11307	6135
2006–2007	12278	14652	8929
2007–2008	16569	20873	12455
2008–2009	12366	17600	8160

Source: Annual Report 2008–2009, Reserve Bank of India, Mumbai.

Another factor contributing to volatility and creating liquidity constraints in the equity market is the poor quantity of floating stocks.

A study of stocks listed in NSE at the end of June 2009 indicates that, on average, the promoters held 57.90% of the total share, while nonpromoters held the other 42.10%. Individual and institutional investors held 13.05% and 12.49%, respectively.

15.4.2 Debt market

Although the Indian equity market has become one of the most vibrant markets among the emerging markets, the Indian debt market is still lagging far behind the many developing markets in Asia. The bond market as a percentage of the GDP in India was substantially behind other Asian emerging markets. The bond market of India as a percentage of GDP was only 41.6%, as against 136% of Korea and 71.5% of Singapore. The corporate bond market is especially poorly developed. As against 38.3% of the government debt market, the corporate debt market as a percentage of GDP was only 3.2%, as against 58.3% in Korea and 30.8% in Singapore (ADB, 2008). According to the investment guidelines issued by PFRDA, 55% of funds can be invested in government papers, and up to 40% of funds can be invested in corporate papers. However, the current debt market does not provide any comfort to pension fund managers, due to several structural deficiencies, namely, short supply of papers, particularly long duration paper, absence of inflation protected bonds, lack of trading and liquidity and concentrated holding.

15.4.2.1 *Demand supply gap in government securities*

The growing demand for government securities and increased demand supply gap can be further assessed in terms of bids received and bids accepted by the Reserve Bank of India in auction of central and state government securities. Let us now consider this in terms of (1) notified amount minus bids received as an indication of the extent of excess demand and (2) bids received minus bids accepted as an indication of the extent of the supply shortage in government securities. As per the Reserve Bank of India, Annual Report 2008–2009, in the year 2008–2009 auction of central government securities bids were received in the amount of Rs 645,934.18, but bids were accepted in the amount of Rs 250,226.55; therefore, there was a short supply of Rs 395,707.63 crore of central government securities. Similarly, demand also exceeded the supply of state government securities. During 2008–2009, the gap between bids received and accepted was to the tune of Rs 70,424.00 (bids received amounted to Rs 98,565.00 crore; bids accepted 28,141.00 crore). Therefore, supply of government securities is approximately 70% of demand, though it is to some extent better in respect to central government securities.

The market is still not able to catch up to the growing demand of long-term debt instruments, as required for long-term investment and hedging by the financial institutions, such as pension funds and life insurance companies. Furthermore, the government securities market is still underdeveloped in terms of trading volume. There is a huge demand supply gap in the government securities market, creating critical concern for the pension fund industry. A short supply of government securities is not the only constraint for efficient investment risk management for institutions like pension funds, provident funds or life insurance companies, but the problem is further compounded by the virtual absence of long-term government securities for hedging long-term risk and asset-liability management.

15.4.2.2   Decline in supply of long-term central government securities

The problems of short supply have been further compounded by the decline in the supply of long-term government securities. In India, the average tenor of central government dated securities has been declining for the past few years. Maturity distribution of long-term central government dated securities over ten years has declined from 74% in 2005–2006 to 39% in 2008–2009, while medium-term securities of five to ten years more than doubled (26% to 55%) during the same period. There is a severe shortage in supply of long-term securities over 30 years. It was only 23.37% of all central government dated securities, while 51.35% securities had a maturity below 15 years. This makes long-term hedging and risk management difficult for pension funds, provident funds and life insurance companies. Risk management is a critical function for these institutions, and that function can be successfully carried out with help of long-term debt instruments.

15.4.2.3   Concentrated holding of government securities

Commercial banks and the Life Insurance Corporation hold the bulk of government securities in India. While all the commercial banks together held 46.93% of all central and state government securities, the Life Insurance Corporation held 22.76% of such securities in 2007. Therefore, ownership is primarily concentrated, which adversely reduces the trading volume, since the Life Insurance

Corporation is a long-term investor and prefers to retain such securities on a held-to-maturity basis. Furthermore, the Employees' Provident Coal Miners' Provident Fund, and others involved in long-term investment, would prefer to buy and hold government securities, thus creating scarcity and widening the demand supply gap in the government securities market. Concentration has its impact on market liquidity and prices, which are disadvantageous for the newly entrant institutional investors like pension funds.

15.4.2.4 *Depressed secondary debt market and liquidity constraint*

A vibrant debt market to support long-term investors must have an active secondary market, allowing the long-term institutional investors to buy and sell securities. This would, however, depend on the transparent liquid and active secondary market. However, the secondary market for central and state government securities is not as active as required. Absence of trading in the secondary market forces fund managers to invest through negotiated deals. Since negotiated deals depend on the supply demand situation, as well as the bargaining power of buyers and sellers, sometimes the risk content in such investment may be higher than when purchasing such instruments through government auction. This may adversely affect the long-term return and risk management mechanism.

According to an NSE Study, trading in non-repo government securities has been declining considerably since 2004–2005. The aggregate trading volumes in central and state government dated securities on SGL declined from Rs 398,988 million (USD 91,374 million) in 2006–2007 to Rs 5,003,047 million (USD 125,170) million in 2007–2008.

Furthermore, whatever liquidity there is is concentrated in a few bonds. According to the Clearing Corporation of India, trading is highly concentrated in ten-year bonds maturing in 2016–2017, which comprises 50% of all trading. Next were five-year bonds maturing in 2010–2012, which constituted 20% of all trading. In 2007, 35 bonds were not traded at all, while 22 bonds traded less than 25 days, 11 bonds were traded 25 to 50 days, 15 bonds were traded 50 to 99 days and 13 bonds were traded 100 to 149 days.

15.4.2.5 *Corporate debt market*

The corporate debt market, at 3% of GDP, is not only very undeveloped, but also very illiquid and thinly traded, which is a cause of concern for the fund. According to an ADB study, India's corporate turnover is quite high at 61%, comparing favourably with most other emerging Asian corporate bond markets.

15.4.2.6 *Lower return and higher risk*

A short supply of long-term government securities not only makes risk management difficult, but also adversely impacts the long-term investment return of funds. In general, the long-term yield on government securities is higher than that on the short-term securities. A shortage in long-term securities forces fund managers to invest in short-term low-yield securities, as a result of which long-term returns remain low. Alternatively, fund managers seeking competitive returns may invest in high yielding risky corporate debt, which may not be in the interest of pension funds and their members. According to RBI (Annual Report, 2008–2009), yield on nine-year, three-month central government securities was 5.44%, while that of nine-year, eight-month securities was 9.14% in 2008–2009. For the long-term bond, this was slightly higher – yield on 26-year, eight-month securities was 6.52%, while the same on 23-year, seven-month securities was 10.03%. This further indicates that the longer-term yield was depressed.

15.5   Asset liability model for NPS auto choice fund

Capital market constraints, as indicated above, are a serious concern for fund managers in the NPS system. They need to find a way to minimize risks and maximize returns, which should at least be above some guaranteed return provided by Employees' Provident Organisation (EPFO) in India, and that is possible if an appropriate investment strategy, backed by the fund management skill, is in place. An asset liability model designed with the help of simulation techniques may be of great use in estimating the expected liability of a portfolio and in deciding the asset allocation and reallocation strategy. Keeping this in view, we have made an attempt to work out an ALM model for the auto choice option (default option) for NPS.

15.5.1   Outline of the model

This simplified model highlights the purposes of ALM to understand the implications of various assets and liabilities arising out of an auto choice life-cycle-based (age-risk-adjusted) pension model. This chapter also describes the major steps necessary to build the ALM model. A description of a sample default model is also developed, with certain assumptions. First, to determine the cash available for investment, cash flows of all the income and expenses (including liabilities) were modelled using available data from the Indian market. Second, the stochastic models for each selected asset class are developed under dynamic market conditions. The asset classes include cash, short-term deposits or treasury bills, long-term bonds, and equity. Each asset class is modelled using its respective (assumed or validated) distribution. Next, the liability and asset cash flows are to be combined in order to determine available cash for investment. Then, each of the modelled parameters of each asset and liability class is further validated through Monte Carlo simulation under different market conditions. The derived results of the stochastic simulation are incorporated in the estimation of the future value of the capital fund and cash payouts. The simulation results using portfolio investment returns at the lower tail of 5% and the upper tail of 95% are also obtained, to study the implication of the suggested asset-liability model under two extreme conditions, using both positive and negative scenarios. Finally, we discuss the relevant strategies for better management of the asset-liability model under the current market conditions with a view to maintaining the required solvency of the fund.

15.5.1.1 Limitations

We do not discuss here management issues in the asset-liability management of a company. The proposed ALM model is based on the existing contribution flow and does not consider the new risk-based capital regime. The asset classes to be modelled will be limited to selected asset classes such as cash, equity, bonds and treasury bills, and it does not include others, such as property, gold, commodity or exchange derivatives. The first step in building the ALM model is to specify the proposed annuity product life-cycle-based auto choice model.

15.5.1.2 Specification of the proposed portfolio

This section describes the product features of a life-cycle-based auto choice model available in the Indian market. This model is a default model in which customers do not need to specify their investment choices. The model has an inbuilt option in which the contributions of customers are invested, in certain specified percentages, in G class assets (government securities), E class assets (equity) and C class assets, which are mainly short-term securities such as cash deposits and treasury bills. Initially, when a customer is young (below age 35) the maximum contribution amount is invested in equity (maximum 50%), while 20% is invested in G class assets and the remaining 30% in C class securities. As the customer ages, the equity exposure decreases and investment in G class assets increases, while balancing the C class securities with other short-term securities. Ultimately, when the customer reaches age 55, nearly 80% of his or her contribution is kept in government securities, with just a minimum of 10% in equity and 10% in other short-term securities. The vesting age for annuities is 55. If the customer withdraws before age 55, then he or she can withdraw only 20% of the accumulated capital fund, while the other 80% is to be used for purchasing an annuity from any of the approved institutions. After age 55, the customer is allowed to withdraw 60% of the fund, until the age of 70. If the annuitant dies before reaching the vested age, then the entire accumulated capital fund is provided to his or her dependant or nominee. The given pricing assumptions and the corresponding reserve and solvency margin are based on certain assumed reserve and solvency margins of the selected insurance company. The methodology used in this chapter is valid in any reserve regime.

15.5.1.3   Liability assumptions

- Entry Age: 18 Years
- Minimum monthly contribution: Rs 1000
- Expense: Fund management fee of .0009%, CRA charges of Rs 500 P.A.
- Investment Return: 8%

15.5.2   Overview of the asset models

The returns on the G class assets, consisting of government securities (SGL), and C class assets, consisting of short-term deposit rates and treasury bills, were generated using the Cox Ingersoll Ross (CIR) Model with term structure, looking upon the dynamics of interest-rate movements considering the following:

1. Volatility of yields at different maturity periods.
2. Interest rates may in the long run revert to their long-term mean.
3. Rates at different maturities are positively correlated.
4. Interest rates should not be allowed to become negative.

Hence, the interest rates were modelled using the CIR formula:

$$r_t = r_{t-1} + a(b - r_{t-1}) + s\sqrt{r_{t-1}}\, zt$$

where

r_t = the interest rate at the beginning of the year (t)
r_{t-1} = the interest rate at the preceding day
b = long term mean
a = constant that determines the speed of reversion of the interest rate towards its long-term mean (b)
s = volatility of the interest rate
zt = the standard normal variates from the distribution N (0, 1)

Thus, the calculated rates were simulated using Monte Carlo simulation with the Box-Mueller algorithm.

The simulated trend of SGL returns in the long run indicates an average return of 10% with a standard deviation of 2%.

15.5.2.1   Inflation model

Inflation (denoted by inf) is assumed to follow the one-factor Vasicek model. The expected level of future inflation is a weighted average between the most recent value of inflation (inf$t$) and a mean reversion level of inflation, μinf. The speed of reversion is determined by the parameter κinf. The change in

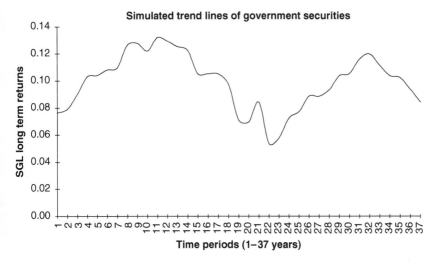

Figure 15.2   Simulated return of SGL securities (1–37 year forecast)

Brownian motion is represented by εinf. The uncertainty is scaled by the parameter σinf, which affects the magnitude of the volatility associated with the inflation process.

The futurist trend of inflation for the next 30 years seems to indicate our past 30 years historical inflation rate of 6% to 8%.

15.5.2.2   Real interest rates model

Real interest rates (CPI Index Rate – BLR) are assumed to follow the Cox Ingersoll Ross (CIR) model with term structure with the assumption that the short-term real interest rate (s) reverts to a long-term real interest rate (l). Both rates are stochastic. In the long run, l reverts to a deterministic average mean reversion level μl. The parameters of this distribution with mu and sigma values were simulated using the Box-Mueller algorithm. Figure 15.4 describes the future trend of simulated real interest rate for the next 30 years.

Figure 15.4 confirms the earlier study result of an average 6% return in the long run.

15.5.2.3   Nominal interest rates model

Inflation rates are added back to the short-term and long-term real interest rates to obtain the nominal short-term and long-term interest rates, respectively. Here again, the mean and standard deviation of the historical values were simulated with 1000 runs. Chart 15.6 provides the simulated trend of bank deposits with a nominal interest rate.

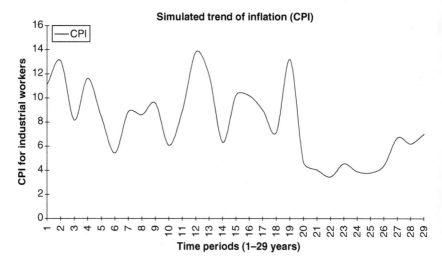

Figure 15.3   Simulated trend of inflation (1–29 years forecast)

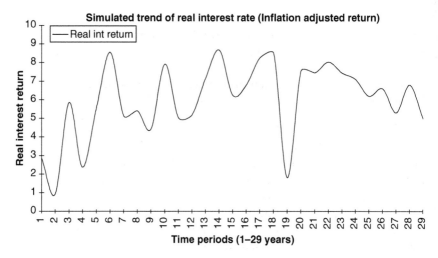

Figure 15.4   Simulated trend of real interest rate

The simulated trend of bank deposits seems to indicate a mean return of 8% with 2% standard deviation.

15.5.2.4   *Equity model*

The equity model is assumed to follow a log normal (LN) model. The equity market is assumed to behave in two states, one state being lowly volatile and

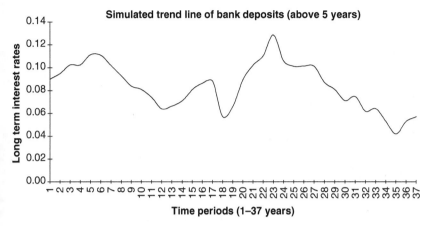

Figure 15.5 Simulated return of short-term securities (1–37 years forecast)

high average return, and the other being highly volatile and low or negative average return. Within each state of the regime, the equity returns are assumed to follow a simple log normal distribution with a fixed volatility that is state dependent.

Let St be the stock price at time t, ρt denote the regime applying in the interval t, t + 1 where $\rho t = 1$ or 2, $\mu \rho t$ be the mean and $\sigma \rho t$ be the standard deviation. The simulated stock returns were split into two groups: Upper Quartile (top 25% stock return) and Lower Quartile (bottom 25% stock return). The Upper Quartile reflects the increasing trend of the equity market with high average return value, while Lower Quartile indicates the downward or decreasing trend of the stock market. The mean and standard deviation of these two distributions are simulated using the Box-Mueller algorithm with 1000 runs. Figure 15.6 shows the simulated stock trends for the next 37 years.

The simulated stock return provides a mean return of 12% with 13% standard deviation, which almost conforms to the view that the stock return, in the long run of over 30 years, will revert back to the mean return of government securities (SGL) or bond rates.

15.5.3 Monte Carlo simulation for projecting the future returns

The main part of this analysis is to develop a simulation model to examine the relative performance of the proposed default life cycle portfolio models with different asset allocation options. Secondly, to estimate the future accumulated pension fund values at different periods of time (at the end of 10, 20, 30 and 35 years), it is necessary to generate the future return values of all the important parameters (yield on SGL, stock return, long-term bank deposit rates, and Consumer Price Index (CPI) values for industrial workers). Accordingly, the

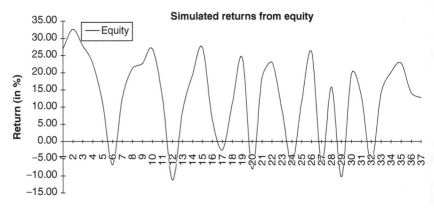

Figure 15.6 Simulated return of equity (1–37 years forecast)

future return values of these parameters were generated using the past trend of their distribution with the necessary model parameters, using Monte Carlo simulation with 1000 runs. Furthermore, the simulated values are validated by examining the descriptive statistical values of these parameters as well as the visual plots of their respective distribution. All these measures indicate that the simulated future returns of these parameters significantly represent the past trend of their respective distributions (see Figures 15.2, 15.4, 15.5 and 15.6).

Table 15.2 exhibits the future forecasted return values for the selected parameters at different periods of time (year 1 to 37) as well as their mean return values and the standard deviations. All these values again conform to the long-term average return values of these parameters, as suggested in the earlier studies. Simulated returns of SGL l, equity and other securities (1–37 years) are shown in Table 15.2.

15.5.3.1 Estimation of accumulated capital fund value for the life-cycle-based portfolio

The following life cycle model is built with the assumption that the customer enters the scheme at the age of 18 with a monthly contribution of Rs 1000. This model is a default model in which the customer does not need to specify his or her investment choices. The model has an inbuilt option in which a certain specified percentage of the customer's contribution is invested in G class assets (government securities), E class assets (equity) and C class assets, which are mainly short-term securities such as cash deposits and treasury bills. Initially, when the customer is young (under age 35) the maximum amount

Table 15.2 Simulated returns of SGL1, equity and other securities (1–37 years)

Simulated returns Of SGL, equity and other securities (1–37 years):

Years	SGL	Equity (%)	Others
1	0.08	26.94	0.09
2	0.08	32.64	0.09
3	0.09	27.83	0.10
4	0.10	22.72	0.10
5	0.10	11.33	0.11
6	0.11	−6.72	0.11
7	0.11	12.73	0.10
8	0.13	21.15	0.09
9	0.13	22.63	0.08
10	0.12	26.94	0.08
11	0.13	12.64	0.07
12	0.13	−11.21	0.06
13	0.13	8.90	0.07
14	0.12	19.39	0.07
15	0.11	27.34	0.08
16	0.11	6.22	0.09
17	0.11	−2.47	0.09
18	0.10	11.33	0.06
19	0.07	24.22	0.07
20	0.07	−7.96	0.09
21	0.08	18.69	0.10
22	0.05	23.04	0.11
23	0.06	9.18	0.13
24	0.07	−6.27	0.11
25	0.08	11.71	0.10
26	0.09	25.94	0.10
27	0.09	−6.36	0.10
28	0.09	15.86	0.09
29	0.10	−10.21	0.08
30	0.11	19.63	0.07
31	0.12	13.14	0.07
32	0.12	−6.00	0.06
33	0.11	14.19	0.06
34	0.10	20.19	0.05
35	0.10	22.78	0.04
36	0.09	14.19	0.05
37	0.08	12.78	0.06
Mean	0.10	12.95	0.08
St Dev	0.02	12.37	0.02

of his or her contribution is invested in equity (maximum 50%) with 20% in G class assets and the remaining 30% in C class securities. As the age of the customer increases, the equity exposure decreases and investment in G class assets increases, while balancing the C class securities with other short-term securities.

Table 15.3 Auto choice model: age-risk-adjusted lifecycle portfolio (accumulated fund value before adjusting for all possible liabilities)

Monthly contribution = (Rs 1000)		Assumed annual return =8%	
Annual compounded value =		12533	

Age groups	Asset distribution			Cumulative fund value
	SGL	Equity	Others	
Annual contribution	2507	6266	3760	12533
18–35 YRS	123815	794874	151528	1070217
(The Fund is invested for 17 years)		(The fund value at the end of 17 years)		
(Accumulated value + contribution)	249033	519720	313998	1082750
Value at the end of 36 years	273323	578622	331950	1183895
	311071	550357	335000	1196428
Value at the end of 37 years	333117	683648	357157	1373923
	402072	610040	374343	1386456
Value at the end of 38 years	430036	561504	407772	1399312
	451790	592975	367080	1411844
Value at the end of 39 years	489862	703818	404558	1598238
	563770	644309	402693	1610771
Value at the end of 40 years	594062	792768	447131	1833961
	701668	701668	443159	1846494
Value at the end of 41 years	742250	766076	500199	2008525
	828634	727581	464843	2021058
Value at the end of 42 years	888640	681954	513997	2084590
	922734	713022	461367	2097123
Value at the end of 43 years	994026	796550	508051	2298627
	1086245	739571	485344	2311160
Value at the end of 44 years	1182562	931421	534557	2648540
	1330537	798322	532215	2661073
Value at the end of 45 years	1448545	747546	586117	2782207
	1481212	782527	531001	2794740
Value at the end of 46 years	1619518	906597	577277	3103392
	1744918	810140	560866	3115925
Value at the end of 47 years	1926006	727420	606297	3259723
	1930631	785341	552022	3267995
Value at the end of 48 years	2134011	939539	591298	3664849
	2279977	809024	584371	3673371
Value at the end of 49 years	2544347	915342	628028	4087717
	2665162	820050	615037	4100250
Value at the end of 50 years	2984331	770814	653048	4408193
	3006094	795731	618902	4420726
Value at the end of 51 years	3340744	908681	658603	4908028
	3493598	787290	639673	4920561
Value at the end of 52 years	3856316	946265	673480	5476061
	4061559	768403	658631	5488594
Value at the end of 53 years	4477399	943420	686263	6107082
	4712103	734354	673158	6119615
Value at the end of 54 years	5154209	838579	708734	6701522
	5371244	671406	671406	6714055
Value at the end of 55 years	5824492	757189	709645	7291325

Ultimately when the customer reaches the age of 55, nearly 80% of the contribution is kept in government securities, with just a minimum of 10% in equity and 10% other short-term securities. The vesting age for annuities is 55. The accumulated fund value has been estimated only with the simulated return values for those assets discussed above (government securities, bank deposits, stocks, and so forth). The capital fund value does not consider liabilities such as expenses, lapsation or surrender rate, or future annuity payouts. The accumulated fund value before adjusting for all possible liabilities in an auto choice model, age-risk-adjusted (life cycle) portfolio is shown in Table 15.3.

15.5.4 Projected liability cash flows

This analysis highlights the summary of the projected liability outflows which fund managers need to assume while estimating the future accumulated capital. These liabilities vary in accordance with the type and nature of the contributory fund flow available to fund managers and the possible changes in the investment assumptions specified earlier. The possible liabilities are deficit or low-fund management charges, increasing transaction costs, custodian charges, and expected withdrawals of the annuitants in the midway, through lapsation or surrenders, annuity payouts, or the return of the accumulated capital fund, either on death or after the 15 years of annuity payments. All these liabilities need to be deducted from the accumulated capital fund, and the difference will indicate the solvency of the pension fund. The possible impact of some of these liabilities on the projected accumulated capital fund needs to be highlighted. The following sections briefly discusses these implications.

15.5.4.1 *Average withdrawal rate*

Since NPS is a very young scheme and no record of withdrawal is available, we have made an attempt to estimate such withdrawal following the Samuel H. Cox, Yijia Lin and Jifeng Yu, model for policy surrender (see Figure 15.7).

We can infer from Figure 15.7 that as the policy duration increases, the surrender rate tends to increase, and it reaches a peak (14%) at the eighth year of the policy duration. The median surrender rate is around 8%. Hence, we have considered the median surrender rate of 8% as our average surrender liability. Although the surrender rate of annuitants may not have direct major implications for fund managers, they have significant indirect impact due to the reduced fund flow and the increasing concern for earning higher returns to match the expected returns assumed in the projected capital fund.

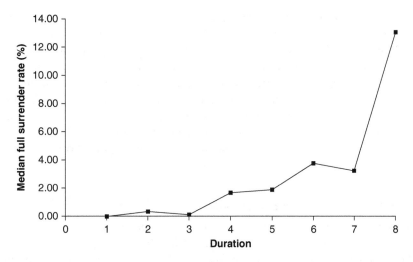

Figure 15.7   Median surrender rate versus policy duration
Source: Modeling surrender rate by Samuel H. Cox, Yijia Lin and Jifeng Yu.

15.5.4.2   Low fund management fee

It is quite reasonable for fund mangers to expect that the fee they receive should enable them to recover at least their cost of fund management. Very low or negligible fees may increase their cost of fund management, causing significant capital strains as well as lack of motivation to earn higher returns.

15.5.4.3   Early withdrawals of annuitant's capital fund

Fund managers make certain assumptions about the time horizon of their investment while estimating the projected capital fund. Early withdrawal of capital funds by the annuitants upsets the projected calculations and causes enormous capital strains for fund mangers.

15.5.4.4   Mortality and longevity risks

Decreasing mortality and increasing longevity causes a huge responsibility for fund mangers to earn increasingly higher returns in shorter investment horizons. Though mortality and longevity are the primary concern of a life insurance company or pension company, in reality they are transferred to the fund managers, necessitating appropriate hedging through suitable securities.

Following the above assumptions, an estimate has been made to find out the accumulated capital fund value after adjusting the above liabilities as shown in Table 15.4.

Table 15.4 Auto choice model: age-risk-adjusted lifecycle portfolio (accumulated fund value after adjusting for all possible liabilities)

Monthly contribution = Rs. 900	Assumed annual return = 8%		
Annual compounded value =	11280		

Age groups	Asset distribution			Cumulative fund value
	SGL	Equity	Others	
Annual contribution	2256	5640	3384	12533
18–35 years	111434	715387	136375	963196
(The Fund is invested for 17 years)	(The Fund value at the end of 17 years)			
(Accumulated value + contribution)	224129	467748	282598	974476
Value at the end of 36 years	245991	520760	298755	1065506
	279964	495321	301500	1076786
Value at the end of 37 years	299806	615284	321441	1236531
	361865	549037	336909	1247811
Value at the end of 38 years	387033	505354	366995	1259381
	406611	533678	330372	1270661
Value at the end of 39 years	440876	633437	364103	1438415
	507393	579878	362424	1449695
Value at the end of 40 years	534656	713492	402419	1650566
	631501	631501	398843	1661846
Value at the end of 41 years	668025	689469	450179	1807673
	745771	654823	418359	1818953
Value at the end of 42 years	799776	613759	462598	1876133
	830462	641720	415231	1887413
Value at the end of 43 years	894625	716896	457246	2068766
	977622	665615	436810	2080046
Value at the end of 44 years	1064307	838279	481102	2383689
	1197484	718490	478994	2394968
Value at the end of 45 years	1303691	672792	527506	2503989
	1333093	704275	477901	2515269
Value at the end of 46 years	1457568	815939	519549	2793056
	1570428	729127	504780	2804335
Value at the end of 47 years	1733408	654679	545668	2933754
	1737570	706808	496821	2941199
Value at the end of 48 years	1920613	845586	532169	3298368
	2051982	728122	525934	3306038
Value at the end of 49 years	2289915	823809	565226	3678949
	2398649	738046	553534	3690229
Value at the end of 50 years	2685901	693734	587744	3967379
	2705488	716158	557012	3978658
Value at the end of 51 YRS	3006674	817814	592744	4417231
	3144243	708562	575706	4428511
Value at the end of 52 YRS	3470689	851640	606132	4928461
	3655408	691564	592769	4939741
Value at the end of 53 YRS	4029664	849079	617638	5496381
	4240899	660919	605843	5507661
Value at the end of 54 YRS	4638795	754722	637861	6031378
	4834126	604266	604266	6042658
Value at the end of 55 YRS	5242050	681471	638681	6562202

15.6   Policy implications

We have made an attempt to project the future returns on a life cycle portfolio in NPS with the help of Monte Carlo simulation. Estimated accumulated capital fund value and projected liability cash flows for the life-cycle-based portfolio will be of great help to fund managers in designing an appropriate asset allocation and risk manage strategy.

However, the market risks cannot be eliminated or minimized by the allocation strategy, which needs to be supported by the economic and market environments. Stability in economic policy, realistic monitory policy, interest rate policy and so forth are fundamental to pension fund performance.

Debt markets of the country have an important role to play in pension fund management, since they depend heavily on debt investments. As we have noted, the debt market development is very slow and the corporate debt market is poorly developed and constrained by lack of liquidity, necessitating concerted efforts to increase the supply of quality debt instruments in government and corporate bond markets.

Inflation and interest rate risk has an immense impact on pension fund return and risk, which can be effectively managed by long-term inflation index bonds. However, no such instrument is available on the Indian market, and fund managers are therefore handicapped. Though some attempts were made in the past to introduce capital protection bonds, they could not attract investors, since those bonds were linked to the wholesale price index (WPI) instead of the Consumer Price Index (CPI). We need to introduce such bonds for hedging future risks in pension investment.

References

Securities Market in India and Abroad – Overview, NSE, www.nseindia.com.
World Development Indicators, 2008, World Bank.
Asia Bond Monitor, 2008, Asian Development Bank, asianbondsonline.adb.org.

Part IV

ALM Models Applied to
Other Areas of Financial Planning

16
Planning for Retirement: Asset Liability Management for Individuals

Michael Dempster and Elena Medova

16.1 Introduction

Pension systems are in crisis. Every day brings dire warnings of future poverty across the globe for large numbers of older people. Governments and corporations are pushing the responsibility for pensions and health care back to individuals. With current demographic trends, the present workforce will be faced with the problem of significant 'pension gaps' which, unless somehow covered, will force drastic changes in their post-retirement lifestyles. The relatively affluent are no exception. For the last few years, even before the crisis, *Fortune* magazine has devoted an annual special issue to the problem, with subtitles like 'Take control of your future'. For example, the July 2006 issue begins: 'Traditional pensions are melting away ...'. By and large, however, the asset management industry remains focussed on asset returns measured by relative performance and treats individuals' liabilities, at best, in aggregate in terms of asset return goals. Financial planning and wealth management advice for individuals sorely needs innovation.

16.1.1 Global pensions crisis

From 1975 to the present day, the global *dependency ratio* – the ratio between retirees and workers – has been on the increase. The Organisation for Economic Co-operation and Development (OECD) forecasts that this ratio will continue to rise for OECD countries in total from 22% in 2000 to 47% in 2050 (OECD, 2009a). In the developed world, this is largely because, due to rising affluence and advances in health care, people are living longer. For example, life expectancy in the United Kingdom has risen from 76.7 to 80.2 in the past 20 years and is forecast by Towers Watson to rise to 84.7 in the next 20 years. According to McKinsey and Company, the number of people aged 60 or older is projected to double in the first half of this century, from

12.2 million in 2000 to 20.4 million in 2040, and their share of personal financial assets in the United Kingdom to rise from 68% to 76% in the same period. This has forced governments to progressively reduce planned state retirement benefits across the developed world, nevertheless resulting in significant government expenditures forecast to range from 5% to 22% of GDP at their peaks around 2040 (McKinsey & Company, 2005). These forecasts may seem optimistic after the financial crisis of 2007–2009, which hit pension funds heavily with significant real losses, for example, amounting to 37.5% of capital in Ireland and 26.2% in the United States in 2008 (OECD, 2009b).

In Europe there are currently about 45 million people in the baby boomer generation, now aged between 40 and 60, and another 45 million aged 60 or over. But, as is well known, the habits and lifestyle of these two groups are very different. Baby boomers are healthy, better-educated and more affluent, while subscribing to liberal, individualistic and even counterculture values, and remaining proactive and participatory in politics and society generally. The over 60s, although adapting to the Web culture, are much more conservative and less inquisitive, tending to be more traditional and considerate of their children, for example, with regard to bequests. They tend to have a significantly greater propensity than baby boomers to continue to save in retirement, keep assets aside for inheritance and to store assets against a rainy day. On the other hand, as a by-product of globalisation, baby boomers are more likely to travel extensively and spend extensive periods, or even move, abroad.

The possible effects of the pensions crisis on personal lifestyles for both groups may be significant – with savings and pensions eaten by inflation in a prolonged period of poor financial returns, together with reduced state pensions – but few households have the ability to mitigate these risks. A similar situation applies to household health and mortality risks, such as need for long-term care and the risk of outliving current wealth, but these contingencies are even more difficult to manage without professional help.

16.1.2   Financial planning

The best of current financial planning advice is based on investment portfolio optimization, introduced by the Nobel Laureate Harry Markowitz nearly 60 years ago, which is applicable only to short time horizons. Investment risk is measured by variability of returns, and clients are advised to make risky investments, that is, with much higher equity components, while they are young and become more risk averse, that is, hold more bonds and cash, as they approach retirement. Much effort is expended to derive an investor's attitude to risk. Lifestyle goals such as retirement, children's education, weddings, second houses, boats, cars, and so forth (when not simply aggregated) are treated in terms of separate investment pots with relative priorities reflected by contribution rates. All such funds are balanced only in terms of current market conditions and clients' 'risk appetites', and no account is taken of random events in life, like sickness or death, uncertain future incomes and costs, or varying priorities over time. As a result, the investment strategies proposed tend generally to be overoptimistic.

A number of software tools using this portfolio optimization approach are now available for individual household use with PC's or over the Internet, but no joined-up view of a household's financial requirements in terms of income, asset and liability cash flows is given. Hoevengars et al. (2009) and Amenc et al. (2009, 2010) try to take account of forward household liabilities by applying the best practice approach described above to a funding ratio variable, but even in the institutional pension fund setting from which it comes this is best handled by explicit cash flow matching (Dempster et al., 2009). See also Wilcox and Fabozzi (2009) who account for the uncertain present value of future liabilities using a Bayesian discretionary wealth approach, which derives risk aversion from surplus and uses the joint posterior distribution of both investor and investment attributes as a basis for scenario based optimal asset allocation in a Markowitz framework.

Does the current best-of-breed advice accord with practical client reality? A Bank of Italy (2005) survey of investors suggests the answer is no. For example, the young were found to hold less equity, not more, and in fact the 65–74 age group held the highest equity proportion (25%). In general, the survey showed that attitudes to risk depend on many factors other than age. These findings accord with common sense, and the survey identified human capital (lifetime future earning capacity), family structure, wealth base and housing needs as most critical to household investment choices.

Naturally, factors affecting portfolio choices change with age at a pace unique to the individual. Uncertainty about the future is highest when householders are young and reduces with age. Traditional advice and products link risk with the age. Depending on household circumstances, such advice may incorrectly limit exposure to risky assets approaching retirement, just when more certainty about future lifestyle could allow more investment risk-taking. In general, a particular household is *not* a *static* entity; it may represent different types of household over time as desired lifestyles and circumstances change. The recent financial crisis hit individual households severely – loss of real estate equity, reduction in pension benefits, loss of savings value, increased unemployment rates and many other factors – all showing that the current state of financial planning and wealth management advice for individuals needs new innovative approaches (Kahneman, 2009).

16.1.3   Chapter overview

In this chapter we describe the recently developed *individual* Asset Liability Management (*i*ALM) system for support of lifestyle planning through lifelong savings and asset allocation which has been designed to meet this challenge.

Our exposition is directed to a broad audience and avoids the highly technical details of the mathematical model underlying *i*ALM. Here we focus on a few new ideas underlying our system which we illustrate by creating financial plans for a middle-class UK household in Section 16.3. Section 16.2 first gives a high level description of the system, its use and its extensive testing, while Section 16.4 concludes.

16.2 Lifestyle planning with *i*ALM

The *i*ALM system is a decision support tool for individual household financial planning based on stochastic programming theory and a state of art software implementation.

16.2.1 Approach and methodology

A mathematical model description and some details of implementation are given in Medova et al. (2008) and Dempster and Medova (2010). The main features of the dynamic stochastic programming implementation are, in brief, modelling and simulation of stochastic returns for financial assets, economic factors and liabilities; the household input dependent formulation of the stochastic optimization problem, with major decision points corresponding to the times of expected significant changes in the household's balance sheet; and the solution of a large scale equivalent piece-wise linear deterministic problem. Such an *individual* asset liability management (*i*ALM) problem is a large-scale risk-managed optimal resource allocation problem over linked networks of various household cash flows in order to satisfy consumption and other goal based demands.

All cash flows, such as projected incomes, forecast returns on investments, and existing and future liabilities, are specified by household spending on desired goals and are simultaneously simulated forward to the time of the expected death of the household head(s). The objective is to achieve the desirable amount of spending on specified lifestyle goals according to the households chosen priorities and subject to the availability of resources. The balance between assets and liabilities sets the requirements for the portfolio return from investments, and therefore forms the household's dynamic attitude to risk. The first-year portfolio allocation is to be implemented, and all other decisions are generated in the form of 'what-if scenarios' which are summarised in various graphs over household lifetime. There are many submodels and software modules involved in the creation of the overall *i*ALM model (for a detailed description of this *meta* model, see Dempster and Medova, 2010).

We would like to point out that management of the personal finances of a household of any wealth is very different from the asset liability management of institutional funds. This is because the events connected with individual liabilities cannot be smoothed out by diversification over a large number of investors, pensioners or events. We do not share view of some other authors that proxies like TIPS or a real estate index can replace individual liabilities (see, for example, Amenc et al., 2010, Chapter 18 of this ALM Handbook). Personal liabilities are sharp and often occur at fixed points in time (children's education, weddings) or are discretionary (house purchase, retirement) or highly uncertain (future income, redundancy, illness, death, need for long-term care). This imposes technical requirements on lifetime planning which are further complicated by the practical requirement of accommodating very different life-styles and wealth over an uncertain planning horizon depending upon the ages of the individuals involved.

On the asset side of the *i*ALM model, there is much more similarity with institutional fund management models. The asset returns are represented by indices, and portfolio allocation is at the level of preselected asset classes. Some of the asset-return models used in *i*ALM are described in our previous publications, Dempster et al. (2007, 2009). For UK investors, the investment universe is given by nine assets:

1. bank cash
2. Treasury bills (3 month)
3. gilts (10 years)
4. AA corporate bonds (10 years)
5. domestic equities
6. international equities
7. alternatives
8. real estate
9. commodities.

The US version of *i*ALM includes all of the above plus TIPS (US indexed gilts) and municipal bonds.

In summary, the *i*ALM mathematical formulation involves the modelling of economic factors and market asset returns, individuals' liabilities in terms of both random discrete events and continuous processes, random lifetimes of individuals from different age groups and highly individual preferences for goal-oriented consumption, savings and investment. The optimization objectives are framed in terms of the risk-adjusted expected present value of lifetime household spending.

16.2.2   Implementation

The current version of the *i*ALM model includes 20 random processes that vary over a client's lifetime (up to 90 years forward) and around 200 mathematically formulated conditions (constraints). A typical household problem might involve a half a million variables and a similar number of constraints. Such a complex problem can only be formulated and solved efficiently with the *STOCHASTICS*™ suite software developed specifically for stochastic programming applications and used previously for institutional fund management applications (Dempster et al., 2006, 2007, 2008, 2009).

The behavioural characteristics of an individual client household can be revealed to an advisor through an interactive dialogue by generating alternative versions of the financial plan, each of which requires just a few minutes on an average desktop or laptop computer. The client may analyse retirement and savings alternatives by changing their preferences on goals and goal priorities. This is what behavioural finance views as an essential feature of any advisory tool. Other findings in behavioural finance show that investors often under-diversify their portfolios due to irrationally heavy discounting of the future. Depending on temperament, people also tend to overestimate their financial prospects to varying degrees, which results in unrealistic discretionary allocations for spending on goals. This behaviour is controlled by iALM's risk management, which imposes discretionary limits on asset class allocations and *portfolio drawdown* on each scenario.

The *i*ALM system's feature is its unique ability to determine optimum values for many decision variables – spending, borrowing, saving, investment, and so forth – across time and simultaneously for multiple future scenarios of random processes and events representing uncertain markets and life circumstances. This optimal plan contains spending and portfolio recommendations both for now and for the current view of future decisions. All aspects of the client's forward financial plan can be examined on all scenarios in 'what if' mode. There are many visual tools available in the system which aid analysis of the generated optimal financial plan in terms of cash flow and wealth evolution, balance sheets, goal achievement likelihoods, and so forth. The task of assembling many pieces of information about individuals' incomes, liabilities and discretionary spending, to say nothing of forecasting returns on available investments, has been a challenge from the point of view of software development, and all effort has been made to simplify the process – from initial household data entry to presenting lifetime summaries as comprehensively as possible.

Each *i*ALM plan is expected to be updated periodically, or at the occurrence of major lifestyle events, to correct for imperfect forecasts and to take account of unforeseen events which cannot be statistically modelled. The implemented *i*ALM portfolio allocation decisions are at the strategic level by virtue of taking a long-term view of individual circumstances. The system is designed to be used in conjunction with a short-term (annual) tactical allocation which can exploit the financial advisor's knowledge at the level of individual investments in funds or financial instruments. Both levels must, of course, consider the appropriate legal and institutional framework regarding taxation and pension regulations specific to each jurisdiction, and these aspects are modularized within the *i*ALM system.

16.2.3   System evaluation

The *i*ALM system has undergone extensive testing on profiles of US investors, including careful reviews of client needs. The behavioural aspects of the system's design recommendations have been tested using its ability to analyse the relationships between current wealth, future earnings, savings and desirable consumption in constructing dynamic portfolios with lifestyle enabling returns. In addition *i*ALM's performance has been successfully back-tested over a ten year period of market conditions, including the internet bubble and crash, and favourably compared to top financial advisor's client recommendations and short-term Markowitz mean variance portfolio composition.

The UK version of the model has been analysed using information about various households from the weekly Money sections of the *Financial Times* (2005–2007).

This collection of household profiles has been augmented with household profiles supplied by a few independent financial advisers and with private client data from a UK bank.

In all evaluations it has been observed that the interactive use of the *i*ALM helps to build the relationship between financial adviser and client. A client's reaction to the possible outcomes (for example, projected wealth at the time of retirement given by the generated financial plan) may require 'readjustment' of inputs (for example, reducing the desirable standard of living after retirement to a lower level). Through interactive learning, the system provides a final version of the financial plan which emphasizes regret avoidance and is suitable to the client's individual choices regarding risks.

16.3   Case study

In this section we will illustrate the use of iALM on an example UK family. Our aim is to demonstrate to the reader that financial advice embraces much more than the generation of a financial plan based on a single data input. It is rather a process of discussion between the client and a professional who helps to analyse a variety of outcomes of personal circumstances and preferences, the result of which is the choice of the most appropriate investment decisions for immediate implementation, consistent with a long view of household resources and personal abilities. To accommodate this aim we will use in the sequel as many views as possible from the graphical user interface (GUI) of the system, selecting appropriate input screens and output graphs.

16.3.1   Household information and assumptions

We start with the basic household information of Jim and Caroline Jones, which is summarised in Figure 16.1.

All information needed for financial plan generation is classified in categories: personal data, cash inflows and outflows, starting assets. The position limits and modelling assumptions are data which can be edited by the financial adviser.

In this example, the goal is spending on general consumption over household lifetime, that is, pre- and post-retirement annual spending within limits specified by the household. Each specifies acceptable and desirable levels. In a situation in which there are many goals, each goal may have a different priority. These goals are merely objectives whose probability of achievement are unknown to the household. Their personal attitudes and sociological make-up may greatly overestimate or underestimate these values. The purpose of useful financial advice is therefore to 'readjust' household expectations to the objective reality of their current and prospective resources. Figure 16.2 details the input data for liabilities and goals. Figure 16.3 shows projected salaries and other inflows.

Profile Summary for Jones, Jim

Personal Data

- H1 was born in 1966 and is now 43 years old and would like to retire at 65.
- H2 was born in 1964 and is now 45 years old and would like to retire at 65.
- 2 dependents.

Starting Assets Data

Non Qualified Asset Account TOTAL: £62,000

Carolyn's Cash Account	Cash, Taxable	£10,000
Joint Account	Cash, Taxable	£5,000
HSBC	Cash, Taxable	£10,000
Bonds	Fixed Income - Long Duration Bonds	£5,000
Childrens Accounts	Cash, Taxable	£2,000
National Savings	Cash, Taxable	£5,000
Equities	Equities - Domestic	£25,000

SIPP Account TOTAL: £15,000

SIPP Account	Cash, Taxable	£15,000

ISA Account TOTAL: £35,000

ISA Family Account	Cash, Taxable	£35,000

Tangible Assets TOTAL: £300,000

Family Home	£300,000

Figure 16.1   Household profile summary

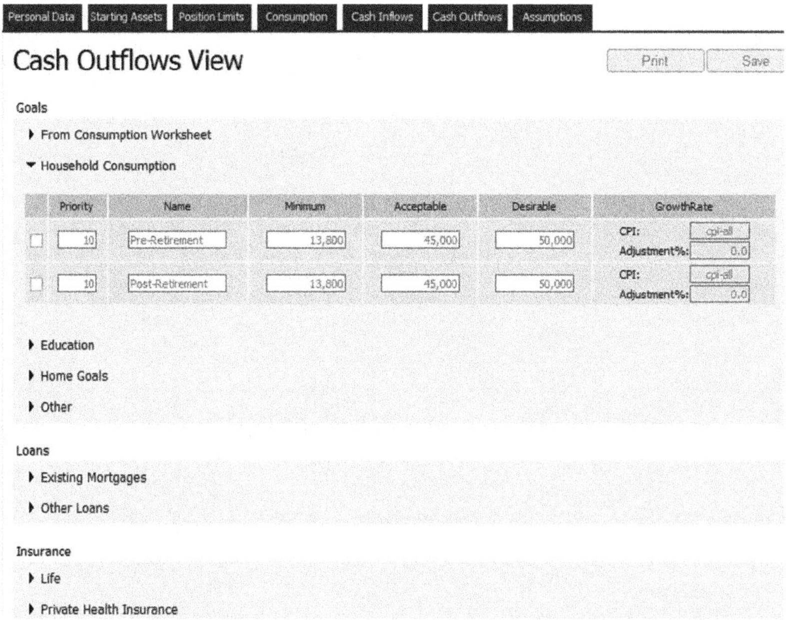

Figure 16.2   Range of household consumption pre- and post-retirement

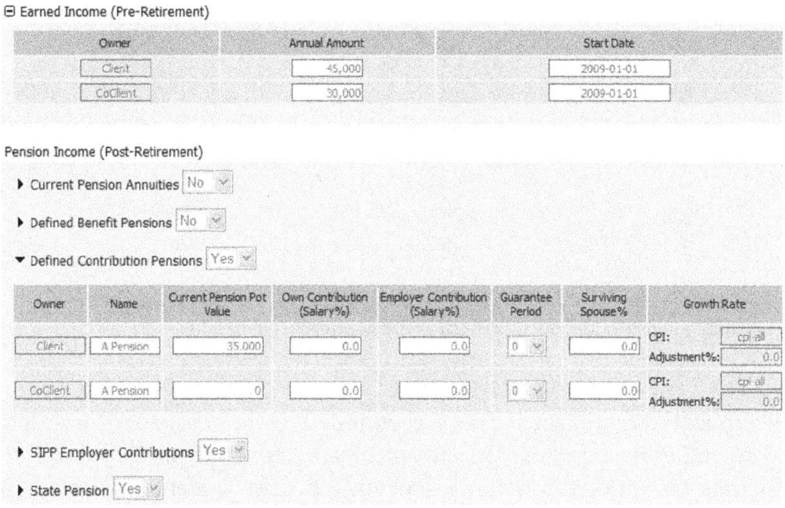

Figure 16.3   Household income and pensions

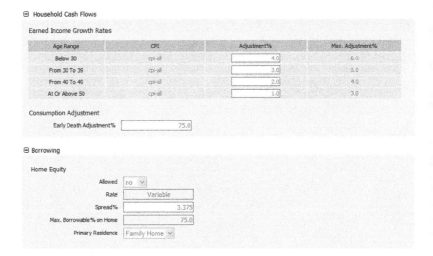

Figure 16.4 Salary growth and borrowing restrictions

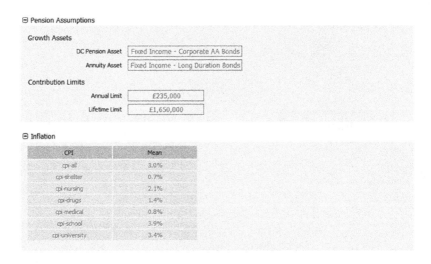

Figure 16.5 Pension and specific item inflation spreads over CPI

To model and simulate various economic factors, we made the simplifying assumptions regarding the growth of salaries shown in Figure 16.4. The scenarios for various cash flows, including salaries, are abruptly stopped by the occurrence of the death of the last head of household. Because the *i*ALM problem is formulated for the household (not at the level of individual heads of the family unless only one is specified at input), we assume that the level of total

⊟ Investment Assumptions

Risk Tolerance

Portfolio Loss Tolerance%	15.0

Transaction Costs

Asset Class	Buy%	Sell%
Equities - Domestic	1.5	1.5
Equities - International	1.5	1.5
Fixed Income - Long Duration Bonds	1.0	1.0
Fixed Income - Corporate AA Bonds	1.0	1.0
Commodities	1.0	1.0
Property	1.0	1.0
Alternatives - Hedge Funds of Funds	1.0	1.0
Cash, Taxable	0.0	0.0

Managed Account Fees

AssetClass	Fraction%
Equities - Domestic	0.75
Equities - International	1.0
Fixed Income - Long Duration Bonds	0.35
Fixed Income - Corporate AA Bonds	0.35

Figure 16.6 Investment assumptions

⊟ Taxes and Contributions

Income Tax Rates (Per Person)

Income From	Income To	Income Tax Rates
£0	£6,035	0.0%
£6,036	£40,635	20.0%
£40,636	Unlimited	40.0%

National Insurance Rates (Earned Income Only)

Income From	Income To	National Insurance Rates
£0	£4,680	0.0%
£4,681	£40,040	11.0%
£40,041	Unlimited	1.0%

Allowances

Capital Gains Allowance	£9,600
ISA Annual Allowance	£7,200

Figure 16.7 Tax and national insurance contribution assumptions

consumption is reduced for a surviving head by a certain percentage, in this example by 25%.

To allow more financial flexibility, any household (particularly a young one) may opt to borrow against their equity in their house.[1] We impose limits on the maximum amount of borrowing, with the cost given by a specified spread over the short-term rate (the three month interest rate termed the Treasury bill rate above). These assumptions are shown in Figure 16.4.

Our principal economic stochastic factor is the consumer price index (CPI).[2] A variety of spreads to price the specific liabilities are shown in Figure 16.5, together with the assumptions regarding the growth of pensions and the current limits on pension contributions.[3]

Other 'rule-based' assumptions regarding investments and taxes are shown in Figures 16.6 and 16.7, which are self-explanatory. Note that 'Risk tolerance' in Figure 16.6 is expressed by the discretionary limits on annual portfolio drawdown applied to each generated scenario.[4]

Equipped with this information, which is minimal to specify a financial plan for the household, we proceed to the analysis of the first such plan generated by optimizing the *i*ALM meta model.

16.3.2   Analysis of household lifetime optimal plans

As we said above, the resulting solution gives the optimum value for many decision variables across all generated scenarios and for each time interval, that is, annually. Therefore, there is an enormous amount of information available for analysis. In the iALM graphical user interface (GUI) this information is classified by category and presented by a variety of visual tools – graphs over household life time, tables, balance sheets for selected dates, views of main scenarios, and so on. Figure 16.8 shows the classes of optimal decisions and Figure 16.9 gives a summary of goal achievement in this first version of the Jones' financial plan.[5]

The portfolio allocation for the current year to be implemented in the first year of the plan is shown in Figure 16.10. As is seen from total portfolio return

Figure 16.8.   Optimal decision classes for analysis (with goals highlighted)

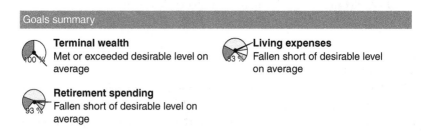

Figure 16.9   Probabilities of acceptable goal achievement (%)

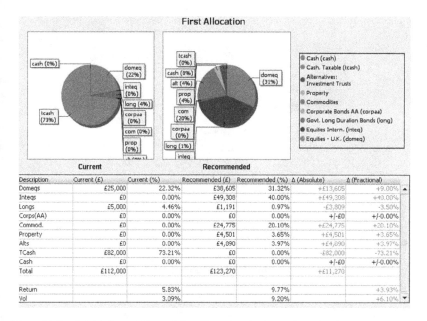

Figure 16.10 Initial financial portfolio allocation for immediate implementation

and its volatility shown, the investment risk is high, and as a consequence, the probability of goal achievement shown above is low.

The histograms in Figure 16.11 show that the distribution of spending values across all scenarios is very disperse. The expected annual spending on 'living' is lower than the acceptable value. Similarly, while the acceptable post-retirement spending is just barely achieved in expectation, its histogram has a heavy left tail with a few scenarios having very low values.

Analysis of this plan shows that the household' s expectations for a comfortable lifestyle are overly optimistic, and therefore we should consider either reducing consumption or prolonging retirement for few years, or both.

We opt to change the household heads' retirement age to 67, leaving all other information as in the previous version of the Jones' financial plan. This new instance of the plan requires about two minutes solution time (on an i5 laptop) with selected results analysed below.

First we look at the goal achievement histograms in Figure 16.12.

Now both pre- and post-retirement spending on alternative scenarios mainly concentrates between acceptable and desirable levels, although there are still some post-retirement values on low scenarios that correspond to the dire prognostications of the pension crisis. The expected value of consumption per annum prior to retirement is £46,517 (in current pounds) with 75% of

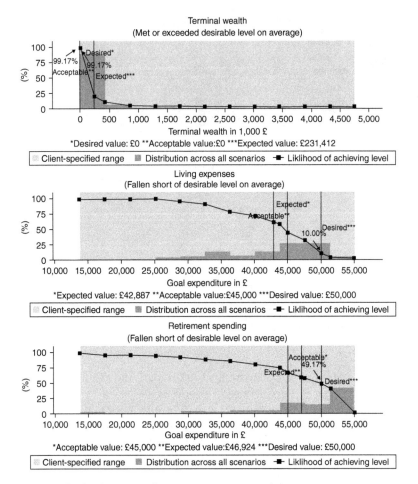

Figure 16.11   Goal achievement histograms across scenarios

scenarios having at least the acceptable value. The post-retirement consumption expectation is now higher, with expected spending of £48,246 per annum, but more variation, with nevertheless 65% of the scenarios at or above the acceptable level of spending.

The Jones household can accept this plan as the one they will follow. Figures 16.13 through 16.16 show various recommended decisions over the household lifetime for this plan. These graphs present averages over many generated scenarios.

The evolution of expected wealth depicted in Figure 16.15 adheres to the (Modigliani) life cycle theory – wealth accumulation to retirement (date

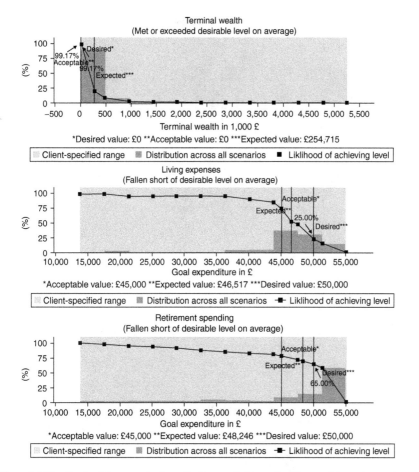

Figure 16.12 Goal achievement when the Joneses' planned retirement is postponed

indicated by the vertical red line in the graph) and wealth decumulation thereafter to household expiry.[6]

A selected view of three main wealth scenarios is shown in Figure 16.16, which illustrates that projected wealth is affected greatly not only by asset returns, but also by household length of life and related liabilities. The four scenarios are sorted by household expected total lifetime spending on goals in current pounds.

16.3.3 Further considerations

Evaluation of additional goals is important in developing an acceptable family financial plan. Our preferred approach is to solve iALM with respect to all

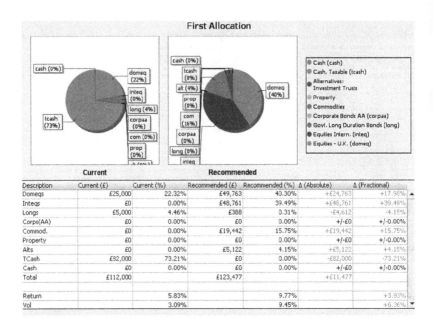

Description	Current (£)	Current (%)	Recommended (£)	Recommended (%)	Δ (Absolute)	Δ (Fractional)
Domeqs	£25,000	22.32%	£49,763	40.30%	+£24,763	+17.98%
Inteqs	£0	0.00%	£48,761	39.49%	+£48,761	+39.49%
Longs	£5,000	4.46%	£388	0.31%	-£4,612	-4.15%
Corps(AA)	£0	0.00%	£0	0.00%	+/-£0	+/-0.00%
Commod.	£0	0.00%	£19,442	15.75%	+£19,442	+15.75%
Property	£0	0.00%	£0	0.00%	+/-£0	+/-0.00%
Alts	£0	0.00%	£5,122	4.15%	+£5,122	+4.15%
TCash	£82,000	73.21%	£0	0.00%	-£82,000	-73.21%
Cash	£0	0.00%	£0	0.00%	+/-£0	+/-0.00%
Total	£112,000		£123,477		+£11,477	
Return		5.83%		9.77%		+3.93%
Vol		3.09%		9.45%		+6.36%

Figure 16.13   Portfolio implementation for the Joneses' deferred retirement plan

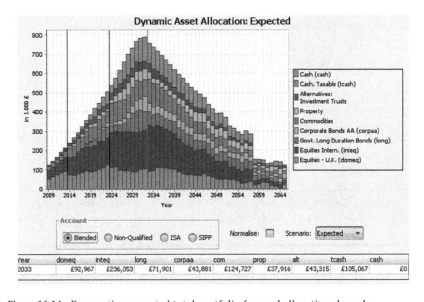

Figure 16.14   Prospective expected total portfolio forward allocations by value

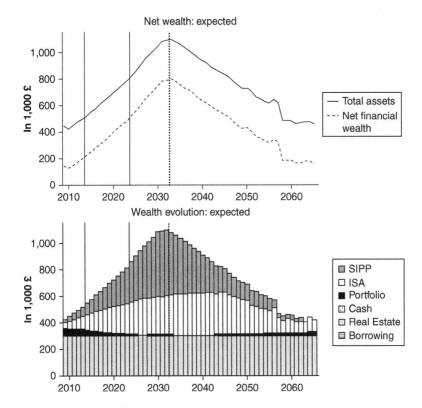

Figure 16.15   Prospective lifetime evolution of Jones family's expected wealth

goals under consideration, according to priorities (preferences) expressed by the household – some would prefer to provide to their children education at the expense of a comfortable retirement.

The usual current practice approach of planners and wealth managers is to create separate funds for each goal. This is far from optimal, as the initial allocation of wealth to goals must be arbitrary when no prospective decisions or circumstances are accounted for. Using *i*ALM, annual savings are prospectively allocated to financial portfolios to enable optimal forward-goal achievement at minimal risk.

Another related feature of *i*ALM is its prospective annual optimal use of tax-shielded accounts over a household's lifetime to provide an important active management component of savings.

Without further comment we introduce one more version of the Jones' financial plan with the additional goals specified in Figure 16.17. We assume

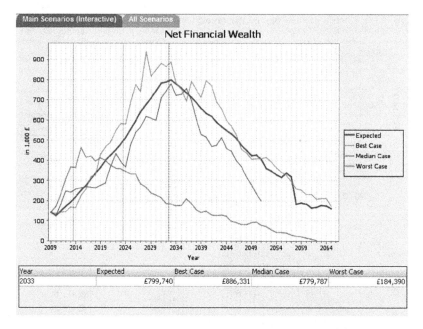

Figure 16.16   Alternative prospective household wealth scenarios

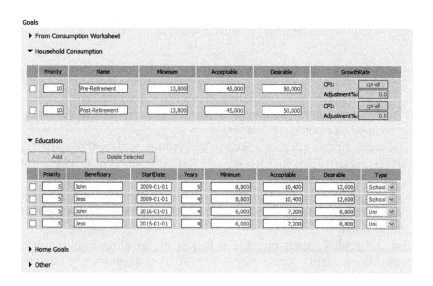

Figure 16.17   Additional children's educational goal specification

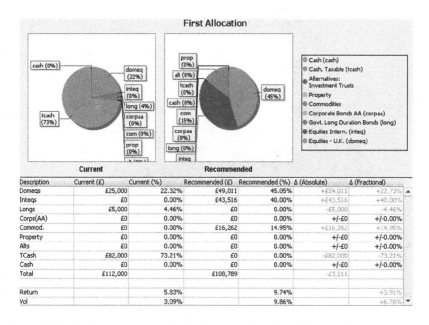

Description	Current (£)	Current (%)	Recommended (£)	Recommended (%)	Δ (Absolute)	Δ (Fractional)
Domeqs	£25,000	22.32%	£49,011	45.05%	+£24,011	+22.73%
Inteqs	£0	0.00%	£43,516	40.00%	+£43,516	+40.00%
Longs	£5,000	4.46%	£0	0.00%	-£5,000	-4.46%
Corps(AA)	£0	0.00%	£0	0.00%	+/-£0	+/-0.00%
Commod.	£0	0.00%	£16,262	14.95%	+£16,262	+14.95%
Property	£0	0.00%	£0	0.00%	+/-£0	+/-0.00%
Alts	£0	0.00%	£0	0.00%	+/-£0	+/-0.00%
TCash	£82,000	73.21%	£0	0.00%	-£82,000	-73.21%
Cash	£0	0.00%	£0	0.00%	+/-£0	+/-0.00%
Total	£112,000		£108,789		-£3,211	
Return		5.83%		9.74%		+3.91%
Vol		3.09%		9.86%		+6.76%

Figure 16.18   Implemented portfolio recommendation with children's education

that all other inputs are as in the previous version of the plan with household heads retiring at age 67.

Figure 16.8 and Figure 16.9 show the implemented portfolio recommendation with children's education, the expected asset allocation and expected wealth evolution over time. Figures 16.20 through 16.22 emphasize the potential sacrifices a family makes for the education of its children. In the worst case scenario, in Figure 16.20 the Jones' family wealth is exhausted when Jim is 76, only nine years after retirement, although he and Carolyn live into their 90s.[7] Although Figure 16.21 shows that the household's educational goals for both children are achieved at acceptable levels with over 70% probability, all have fallen short of acceptability in expectation, even though the expected household consumption levels have been reduced only slightly from the previous plan; compare Figures 16.22 and 16.11.

16.4   Conclusion

This chapter discusses a user-friendly tool for lifestyle life cycle planning called *i*ALM (individual asset liability manager) which has been developed to help financial advisors, planners and wealth managers engage in creative dialogue with individual households. The sophisticated technology employed in iALM

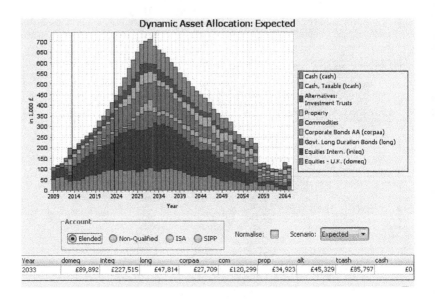

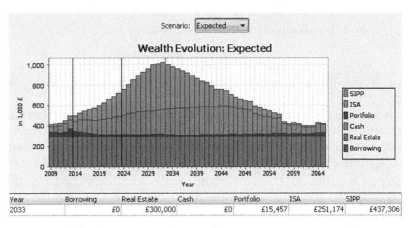

Figure 16.19 Expected portfolio value and wealth evolution with education goals

is a reality today, but a focus on consumer education and a change in the organization of financial services will be required to bring such systems into widespread use in the future. There is evidence that preparations to meet these requirements, involving both opportunities and threats, are currently being made by leading players, both commercial and governmental. Otherwise, the consequences of the coming pensions crisis will be more severe than they need be for middle-class people everywhere.

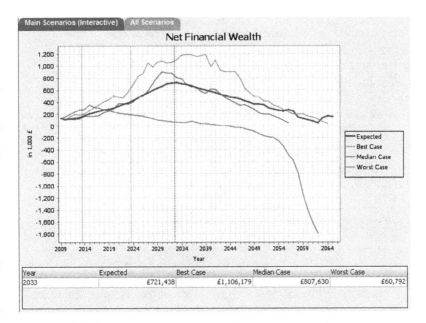

Figure 16.20   Prospective alternative scenarios with educational goals

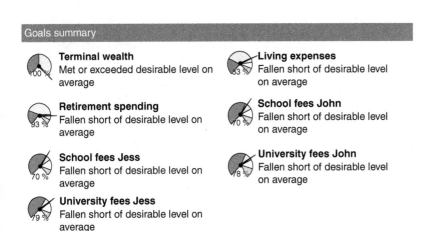

Figure 16.21   Probabilities of acceptable goal achievement with education goals

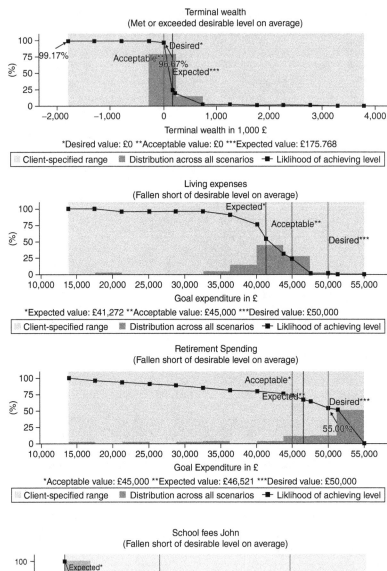

Terminal wealth
(Met or exceeded desirable level on average)

*Desired value: £0 **Acceptable value: £0 ***Expected value: £175.768

Client-specified range   Distribution across all scenarios   Liklihood of achieving level

Living expenses
(Fallen short of desirable level on average)

*Expected value: £41,272 **Acceptable value: £45,000 ***Desired value: £50,000

Client-specified range   Distribution across all scenarios   Liklihood of achieving level

Retirement Spending
(Fallen short of desirable level on average)

*Acceptable value: £45,000 **Expected value: £46,521 ***Desired value: £50,000

Client-specified range   Distribution across all scenarios   Liklihood of achieving level

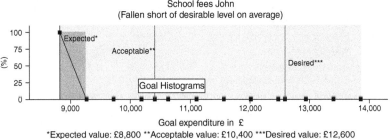

School fees John
(Fallen short of desirable level on average)

*Expected value: £8,800 **Acceptable value: £10,400 ***Desired value: £12,600

Client-specified range   Distribution across all scenarios   Liklihood of achieving level

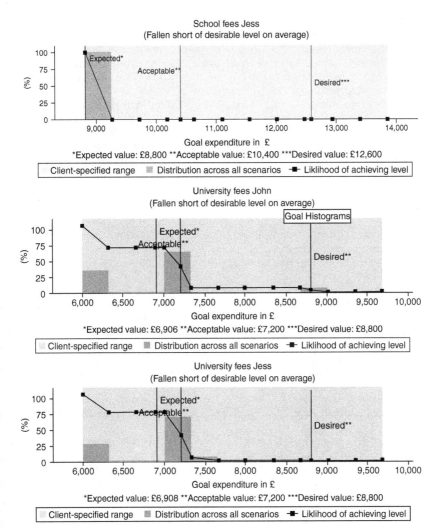

Figure 16.22 Histograms of goal achievement with educational goals

Notes

1. Households are also allowed to borrow against total salary income within specified limits.
2. CPI is modelled as a mean reverting (geometric Ornstein Uhlenbeck) process with parameters estimated over the past ten years up to 2009 (Dempster and Medova, 2010).
3. The pension assumptions are UK tax and pension 2009 regulations (HMRC, 2009).

4. Portfolio risk can also be controlled by discretionary limits on each asset class allocation, expressed in maximum fractions of portfolio wealth.
5. Here 'Terminal Wealth' is the remaining wealth at the time of death of last head of
   household. It is not a household 'goal' unless one is specified in 'cash outflow' as a
   bequest at a specified date. In this example there is no requirement for a bequest goal
   and hence terminal wealth is not optimized.
6. This is a typical middle class phenomenon not exhibited by the wealth evolution of
   higher net worth individuals.
7. We have not here considered either the possibility of borrowing against their home
   equity or the purchase of an annuity soon after retirement, although in practice both
   avenues would be open to the Jones family, and the consequences could be explored
   with *i*ALM.

References

Amenc, N., L. Martinelli, V. Milhau and V. Ziemann (2009). Asset-liability management
in private wealth management. *Journal of Portfolio Management* 36.1, 100–120.

Bank of Italy (2005). Presentation at Pioneer Investments Annual Conference, Paris,
February 2006.

Dempster, M. A. H., M. Germano, E. A. Medova, M. Rietbergen, F. Sandrini and M. Scrowston
(2006). Managing guarantees. *Journal of Portfolio Management* 32.2, 51–61.

Dempster, M. A. H., M. Germano, E. A. Medova, M. Rietbergen, F. Sandrini and
M. Scrowston (2007). Designing minimum guaranteed return funds. *Quantitative
Finance* 7.2, 245–256.

Dempster, M. A. H., M. Germano, E. A. Medova, J. K. Murphy and F. Sandrini (2009).
Risk profiling defined benefit pension schemes. *Journal of Portfolio Management* 35.4,
76–93.

Dempster, M. A. H., G. Mitra and G. Plug, eds. (2008). *Quantitative Fund Management*.
Chapman and Hall / CRC Series in Mathematical Finance, Taylor and Francis, Boca
Raton, FL.

Dempster, M. A. H. and E. A. Medova (2011). Asset liability management for individual
households. *British Actuarial Journal*.

HMRC (2008). Pension Schemes Services. HM Revenue & Customs. Available online: at
www.hmrc.gov.uk/PENSIONS SCHEMES, accessed date August 2010.

Hoevenaars R., R. Molenar, P. Schotman and T. Steenkamp (2009). Strategic asset allocation with liabilities: Beyond stocks and bonds. *Journal of Economic Dynamics and
Control* 32.9, 2939–2970.

Kahneman, D. (2009). The myth of risk attitudes. *Journal of Portfolio Management* 36.1, 1.

McKinsey & Company (2005). The coming demographic deficit. Available online at:
www. mckinsey.com, accessed date August 2010.

Medova, E. A., J. K. Murphy, A. P. Owen and K. Rehman (2008). Individual asset liability
management. *Quantitative Finance* 8.6, 547–560.

OECD (2009a). Aging: Population pyramids 2000 & 2050. Available online at: www.
oecd.org, accessed date August 2010.

OECD (2009b). Pensions at a glance 2009: Retirement-income systems in OECD countries. Available online at: www.oecd.org, accessed date August 2010.

Wilcox, J. and F. J. Fabozzi (2009). A discretionary wealth approach for investment
policy. *Journal of Portfolio Management* 36.1, 46–59.

17
The Discretionary Wealth Hypothesis in an Arbitrage-Free Term Structure Approach to Asset-Liability Management

Dan diBartolomeo

17.1 Introduction

Traditional approaches to asset-liability management have evolved substantially in recent years. Unfortunately, even the sophisticated, multi-period approaches in common use neglect important features of the underlying economic problem. This chapter describes a new approach to asset-liability management that combines four key elements, one of which is quite new to the finance literature.

There are several key benefits to this technique. First, it estimates the present value of future consumption liabilities in a fashion that is consistent with current market conditions, is arbitrage-free, and yet does not imply an absolute guarantee of liability fulfilment in cases in which no such guarantee is desired. The second key benefit of this technique is that it dynamically reallocates assets over time in a sensible way, based on the 'Discretionary Wealth Hypothesis' of Wilcox (2003), and yet is mean-variance optimal, as defined in Markowitz (1952), at each moment in time. This approach maximizes the median, rather than the expected, value of surplus in a way that more realistically represents investor utility. Finally, we will show that our combined technique is equally suitable as an ALM technique for both institutions and households.

This technique also explicitly addresses the existence of transaction costs and other frictions within the multi-period process, as opposed to the single-period assumptions underlying Markowitz.

17.2 Key elements of the method

Our approach uses a number of building blocks. The first is to use the binomial tree approach from diBartolomeo (1997) to forecast the entire distribution of the surplus between assets and liabilities for all future periods. Each node of the binomial tree represents a potential future state for discount rates and expected returns on assets, and hence the expected value of the surplus. In each of these possible future states, we use the 'Discretionary Wealth Hypothesis' from Wilcox (2003) to determine the optimal degree of mean-variance risk aversion for the investor. With our determined level of risk aversion, we can apply traditional Markowitz mean-variance optimization to find the optimal asset allocation for each future state, both across time and across the path-dependent scenarios within the binomial tree. To account for the multi-period nature of the process we will introduce a new approximation to modify the 'single-period' assumption in Markowitz and to more precisely incorporate transaction costs in a multi-period Markowitz approach.

Traditional actuarial procedures assumed a single rate for discounting future cash outflows to present value. The discount rate is usually set as equal to the expected investment on assets. Conversely, asset cash flows are priced in financial markets by a 'yield curve' or term structure of interest rates that reflects investor preferences for maturities and expectations about future changes in interest rates. Due to this conflict of methods, an entity can have riskless incoming cash flows that would *exactly meet all required outflows* but still appear to have a substantial surplus or deficit. Accounting standards for corporations generally embody the concept of the market value of liabilities (i.e., FASB 87), while standards for units of governments often retain the traditional approach, as described by Minahan (2010). In addition, the potential correlation between asset values and the present value of liabilities is often ignored or addressed in a primitive fashion by assuming some fixed statistical correlation.

Our preference is to assume a lognormal interest rate process in discrete time and model the evolution of short-term interest rates in a binomial tree. A convenient model of this type is provided in Fabozzi and Dattatreya (1989). Within this model, the discount rate for any event subsequent to any point (node) in the tree can be calculated as the average interest rate over all possible future paths. At any point in the tree the forward (in time) present value of any subsequent cash flow can be calculated by discounting the cash flow over all possible future paths. The 'tree' nature of the model allows us to separately consider the present values of assets, liabilities and surplus as probability distributions in their own right.

A key step is to calibrate the tree to an arbitrage-free condition. This can be done by 'bending' the branches of the tree using a backward induction procedure, until all riskless bonds (i.e., Treasuries) have a present value at the root of the tree equal to the market value. Alternatively, at each node we can change the relative probability of an upward or downward movement in the short-term interest rate, as in Black, Derman and Toy (1990).

It should be noted that creating an arbitrage-free term structure as a basis for our process does not imply that the market value of liability cash flows must be discounted at risk-free interest rates. We can simply define our discount rates for a given cash flow to be as determined within the tree structure plus a spread (e.g., +1%, +2%, etc.). Each possible value of the spread corresponds to a likelihood of not fulfilling the future obligation when required. In the context of personal financial planning, we might choose to discount liabilities associated with future retirement income by the risk-free rate, while using a higher (risky) discount rate for a desirable but nonessential consumption event, such as making a future charitable donation.

For defined benefit pension funds, we can use the tree to solve for the spread that would equate the present value of liabilities and assets, or equate the present value of liabilities with the present value of liabilities as calculated by whatever actuarial standard is currently employed. We can then convert the resulting spreads to estimate the probability that pension obligations will not be met in full without additional financial contributions from the sponsoring entity.

It should be noted that, while the ability to add a spread over the risk-free rate across the interest rate tree is a convenient way to reconcile our approach with conventional actuarial or personal financial planning practice, there is a practical danger that unrealistically high discount rates will be used to disguise the reality that many retirement plans, whether collective or individual, are seriously underfunded.

To complete our basic model, we will represent the prices process for assets as a second binomial tree that is correlated with the interest rate process. Asset returns in each period are the sum of a drift term (risk premium), an effect from correlation with the interest rate process and a noise term. The required estimation is typically done using vector auto-regression techniques as used in Campbell and Viciera (1999). The correlation of the two trees can be represented geometrically as in Margrabe (1978).

Assuming a fixed asset allocation, we can now get an expected value for surplus at any particular node of the tree, and hence the expected value of the surplus distribution at any point in time. What if the asset allocation were not fixed? Since we can project asset returns all along the binomial tree, we can change the asset allocation at each node of the tree with no loss of generality. We just have to start projecting asset values at the root of the tree and work outward, just as we work from the branches inward to estimate the present value of liabilities. We propose to change asset allocation dynamically over time, using Markowitz mean-variance optimization, *but allowing state-dependent risk aversion that varies with both time and the relationship between assets and liabilities.* One key assumption is that all investment assets may be liquidated to fund consumption, but are subject to nonzero transaction costs. We propose that the general concepts of Markowitz mean-variance efficiency be adhered to, but modified slightly to reflect a multi-period process in discrete time.

The Markowitz Modern Portfolio Theory (MPT) says that an investor can form an *efficient frontier* of differently composed portfolios. Each portfolio on the frontier has the maximum return for a given level of risk and also has the minimum risk for a given level of return. The time dimension of the process is defined as a single period of indefinite length. However, the theory itself says nothing about how an investor should go about choosing which portfolio on the efficient frontier to actually hold.

Most finance literature assumes that investors have some form of quadratic or log-wealth utility function, as described in Levy and Markowitz (1979):

$$U = \alpha - \lambda\sigma^2$$

where

U = investor utility
α = expected periodic returns
σ = expected standard deviation of periodic returns
λ = investor risk aversion

A financial professional might do well to ponder the problematic nature of asking a passerby on the street, 'What is your risk tolerance parameter in mean-variance space?' Investors constantly use terms of art such as 'conservative' or 'aggressive' to describe their posture without any quantification of what that means. This ambiguity results muddles the reason why investors change their portfolio composition over time. A portfolio might change because expectations have changed about the future returns or risks of available assets, or because the investor's risk aversion has changed, probably without being recognized or consciously done.

17.3   Discretionary wealth

One old adage regarding the management of financial risk says simply that investors should not put more money at risk than they can afford to lose. A useful formalization of this idea is provided in the 'Discretionary Wealth Hypothesis' from Wilcox (2003). This concept is equally applicable to the asset-liability concerns of both institutions and households.

Financial institutions such as insurers and defined benefit pension schemes have long thought in terms of assets, the present value of liabilities and surplus. For households, it is more novel to think of your life as a *balance sheet*, including implied assets such as the present value of future savings, and the present value of the liability for expected consumption expenditures. It should be noted that for pension schemes, the inclusion of implied assets (discounted at a risky rate) in this framework can help mediate how the 'going concern' value of the future contributions from the sponsoring entity can be accommodated. See Keating (2010) for further discussion on this issue.

Wilcox then derives that the optimal value for λ, the Levy-Markowitz mean-variance aversion for an investor, is equal to one-half times the ratio of total assets divided by net worth (surplus). For private wealth, Wilcox recommends the use of 'investable' assets rather than total assets in the numerator, as a way to convey that some assets, such as a personal residence, might be considered unavailable for liquidation to fund future consumption.

$$\lambda^* = \text{Total Assets} / [2^* (\text{Total Assets} - \text{Present Value of Liabilities})]$$

where

λ^* = the optimal risk aversion

Given that our tree structure can provide us with expected values for assets and liabilities at each node, we can calculate the expectation of λ^* for each future moment in time. An intuitive way to think of this is that the optimal degree of risk aversion will vary through time for both predictable reasons (e.g., getting close to retirement age) and unpredictable reasons (e.g., market volatility).

The important outcome of this process is that allowing time variation in λ maximizes the expected median of future wealth, rather than the mean. The effect is a dynamic asset allocation process, somewhat similar to a strategy of portfolio insurance. A good overview of portfolio insurance strategies can be found in Bouye (2009). You are increasing aggressiveness when you can afford to do so and taking a more conservative posture when you must as a matter of prudence. Note that these changes only impact your risk aversion level. Actual changes in portfolio composition must also reflect changes in capital market expectations and expected trading costs.

It is important to highlight that dynamic asset allocation strategies do introduce path dependence into terminal wealth values. Under the approach presented here, if investors experience a period of positive returns followed by a period of negative returns, the resulting wealth will generally be different than if the sequence had been negative returns followed by positive returns. However, the introduction of path dependence is nothing new for individuals. We all live our lives by waiting to cross a street when a car is coming, carrying an umbrella when it's raining, or buying a little extra when a favourite food is unexpectedly on sale at the market.

Also, this form of dynamic allocation may be pro-cyclical, in that investors will normally switch from high-risk assets (stocks) to low-risk assets (bonds, cash) when the stock market declines. Such induced selling of stocks may increase the volatility of equity markets, if carried out by large institutions. It is less likely that even widespread action by retail investors would have a significant effect.

The discretionary wealth approach can also incorporate uncertainty in the balance sheet formation using the Bayesian logic provided in Wilcox and Fabozzi (2009). For example, as individuals, we don't know how long we'll live or whether our children will require financial support for education. Institutions might choose to examine the impact of inflation on future outgoing cash flows in this way, or incorporate such concerns directly in my tree structure.

17.4   A walk through the algorithm

Assuming we have our two calibrated trees and our asset return equation, we can go forward with the process. For discussion purposes, we'll use one-year time blocks.

1. Start at the root of the interest rate tree (today). Move forward randomly through the tree until you reach the other end at a time equalling 30 years from now. This will give us a series of 30 one-year interest rate scenarios which we might experience.
2. We now discount the newly projected series cash flow liabilities using the series of 30 interest rates along our time path. Note that the projected 'then' present value of subsequent liabilities is forecast for each year in the 30-year series. Save this series of 30 projected present values of subsequent liabilities.
3. Now follow the same path along the asset pricing tree, using our return equation to project returns for each year period for each asset class.
4. We now go back to the root of the tree and calculate our initial surplus as the difference between current value of assets and the present value of liabilities. Following the discretionary wealth approach, we calculate the value of λ* Using this value and our return expectations for each asset class, we can calculate the initial Markowitz optimal portfolio.
5. We now move to the second point along our interest rate tree and estimate the value of assets at this node of the tree. This value would be previous asset value plus the change in value due to the first period return, inclusive of both the expected return and a random noise component. We can also subtract any cash outflows from asset values to represent assets that would have to be liquidated to fund consumption.

6. Once we have the asset value at the second node on the path, we can calculate a new value for λ^*. With this input and our return expectations at the second node, we can rebalance the asset weights in the portfolio, subject to transaction costs. We repeat this process for nodes 3 through 30 of the path.
7. Go back and start again at step number 1. Recall that since many of the steps in the analysis assume random movements and returns, each trip through the tree represents a different sequence of events. Repeat the entire procedure a large number of times (as many as necessary) to reach the desired confidence interval around the estimates of the parameters of the resultant probability distributions.

As in most matters of random sampling, the standard errors on the parameter estimates are inversely proportional to the square root of the number of trials. Depending on how far into the future we choose to project and how precise a result we wish to obtain, a larger number of trials may be required. While this is not usually a problem with today's fast computers, methodologies for reducing the required number of sample paths are presented in Ho (1992) and Beaglehole (1997).

Assuming that we repeated this procedure 1000 times, we would have 1000 series of projected funding surpluses (deficits), each series containing 30 separate projections for each of the next 30 years. If we look at each year, we can assess the **probability distribution** of funding surpluses (deficits) at that future moment in time.

17.5 Moving Markowitz optimization to a multi-period process

Our multi-period approach requires a change to the traditional Markowitz assumption of a time being a single, long period. If we know that our portfolio will be changing over time, and those changes require transaction costs, we need to weigh the benefits of improvements in expected utility against the trading costs in the right way.

Traditional optimization procedures that assume a single period can be substantially improved by incorporating a simple approximation.

The approximation herein is a cruder form of the multi-period optimization heuristic (MvD) presented in Markowitz and Van Dijk (2003), but is computationally much more tractable. In Kritzman, Mygren and Paige (2007), the authors are able to test the efficiency of MvD against full dynamic programming for cases up to only five assets, as dynamic programming becomes computationally too burdensome. They are able to extend the MvD method to 100 assets. The technique presented is routinely used for portfolios of many thousands of assets.

Imagine we have a portfolio, P_1 with return α (net of fees and expenses) and standard deviation σ. Our usual utility function would say

$$U_1 = \alpha - \lambda\sigma^2$$

Now let's imagine that another portfolio, P_2, has a higher utility, because either the return is higher or the standard deviation is lower. This portfolio has completely different positions than the initial portfolio. Let's assume that this portfolio has a higher return by positive increment Δ, so

$$U_2 = (\alpha + \Delta) - \lambda\sigma^2$$

Since U_2 is greater than U_1, we should be willing to pay some transaction costs to switch from P_1 to P_2. Now let's consider a different way to improve our returns. We go back to the manager of Portfolio 1 and ask him or her to reduce the fees by Δ, so now our revised utility on P_1 is U_{1L} for 'lowered fees'.

Notice that U_{1L} and U_2 are equal. So if we invest our money in either P_2 or P_{1L} (after lowering the fees), the expected value of wealth at the end time is the same. This suggests that we should be willing to pay the manager an upfront fee to lower ongoing management costs equal to the trading costs we would be willing to pay to switch from the initial portfolio P_1 to P_2. *As long as conditions never change, this is valid.*

However, since P_2 and P_{1L} have different securities, the performance will be different from month to month, even if the long-term average return and volatility are identical. So over any finite time horizon, we cannot be sure which of the portfolios will perform better. On the other hand, P_{1L} will always perform better than P_1 over all time horizons, because it is the same portfolio with lower fees. For P_{1L}, the probability of outperforming P_1 is always one. P_2 is guaranteed to be better than P_1 in the long run if conditions don't change, but the probability that P_2 will actually outperform P_1 over any finite horizon is between one-half and one. We call this probability value the 'probability of realization' of the utility increase.

17.6   Implementation of multi-period optimization

A typical way of accounting for transaction costs in an optimization is to deduct these costs from the objective function, amortizing the expected costs over the expected holding period of the investment.

$$U_1 = \alpha - \lambda\sigma^2 - \{\Sigma_j =_{1 \text{ to } N}[\text{abs}(W_{ij} - W_{fj}) * K_j] * M\}$$

where

N = the number of assets in the portfolio
W_{ij} = the initial weight of asset J
W_{fj} = the optimal weight of asset J
K_j = the unit cost of trading asset J
M = the amortization constant for portfolio turnover

Amortizing transaction costs over a single period is equivalent to assuming that the probability of realization is always one. Let's assume a single period optimization for a strategy with expected turnover of M% per annum. Put differently, the expected holding period is just 100%/M%. In our multi-period world, we want to amortize by M divided by the probability that the revised portfolio will actually realize a better risk-adjusted return over the finite holding period. That is

$$M^* = M/Z$$

where

M^* = the adjusted amortization rate
Z = the probability of realization

To calculate Z we can use the tracking error (expected volatility of the return differences) between any two portfolios as a standard error on the expected differences in utility. We obtain the tracking error value from whatever model we are using to estimate σ in our utility function. We can then calculate a T-statistic on the expected difference in utility and calculate Z under a one-tailed test and our choice of probability distribution.

In the example above, the value of Z is one for the incremental utility of P_{1L} relative to P_1. This is because the tracking error between P_1 and P_{1L} is zero, as they are the same portfolio with different fee structures.

17.7   Conclusions

Traditional asset-liability management for both institutions and households has substantial limitations arising from the distortions caused by overly simplistic methods for discounting liabilities. Our approach resolves several of these issues. By combining the arbitrage-free discounting process with the Discretionary Wealth Hypothesis, we allow investors to sensibly employ Markowitz mean-variance analysis over time in a way that both anticipates and responds optimally to changes in surplus. We also provide a required adjustment to the usual mean-variance treatment for trading costs to reflect the multi-period nature of the problem.

References

Beaglehole, David, Philip Dybvig and Guofu Zhou. 'Going to Extremes: Correcting Simulation Bias in Exotic Option Valuation', *Financial Analyst Journal*, January 1997.

Black, Fischer, Emanuel Derman and William Toy. 'A One-Factor Model of Interest Rates and Its Application to Treasury Bond Options', *Financial Analysts Journal*, Jan – Feb 1990, 33–39.

Bouye, Eric. 'Portfolio Insurance: A Short Introduction', University of Warwick Working Paper, 2009.

Campbell, John Y. and Luis M. Viceira. 'Consumption and Portfolio Decisions When Expected Returns Are Time Varying', *The Quarterly Journal of Economics*, 114(2), May 1999, 433–495.

diBartolomeo, Dan. 'Investment Performance Measurement and the Probability Distribution of Pension Assets, Liabilities and Surplus', *Journal of Performance Measurement*, 1(3), Spring 1997.

Dattatreya, Ravi and Frank Fabozzi. 'A Simplified Model for Valuing Debt Options', *Journal of Portfolio Management*, 15(3), 64–72, 1989.

Ho, Thomas. 'Managing Illiquid Bonds and the Linear Path Space', *Journal of Fixed Income*, June 1992.

Keating, Con. 'Pensions, Covenants and Insurance', Mitra & Schwaiger, Asset and Liability Management Handbook, Palgrave, 2011.

Kritzman, Mark, Simon Mygren and Sebastien Page. 'Optimal Rebalancing: A Scalable Solution', (February 9, 2009). *Journal Of Investment Management*, First Quarter 2009. Available at SSRN: http://ssrn.com/abstract=1340013.

Levy, Haim and Harry Markowitz. 'Approximating Investor Utility with a Function of the Mean and Variance', *American Economic Review*, 69(3), 308–317,1979.

Margrabe, W. 'The Value of an Option to Exchange One Asset for Another', *Journal of Finance*, 33(1), 177–186, 1978.

Markowitz, Harry. 'Portfolio Selection', *Journal of Finance*, 7(1), 1952, 77–91.

Markowitz, Harry M. and Erik L. van Dijk. 'Single-Period Mean-Variance Analysis in a Changing World', *Financial Analysts Journal*, 59(2), March/April 2003, 30–44.

Minahan, John. 'Valuing and Funding Public Pension Liabilities', New England Pension Consultants Working Paper, February 2010.

Wilcox, Jarrod. 'Harry Markowitz and the Discretionary Wealth Hypothesis', *Journal of Portfolio Management*, 29(3), 58–65, 2003.

Wilcox, Jarrod and Frank Fabozzi. 'A Discretionary Wealth Approach to Investment Policy', *Journal of Portfolio Management*, (March 9, 2009).

Yale ICF Working Paper No. 09–03. Available at SSRN: http://ssrn.com/abstract=1355922, Fall 2009.

18

Exploiting Asset-Liability Management Concepts in Private Wealth Management

Noël Amenc, Lionel Martellini, Vincent Milhau and Volker Ziemann

18.1 Introduction

Asset and liability management (ALM) has traditionally been applied to banks, insurance companies and pension funds. In this chapter we will introduce a new application area of ALM: private wealth management. Over the past decade, private wealth management has become a profitable business for banks and asset managers around the globe. According to the private banking and wealth management survey conducted by Euromoney (2008), global private banking assets rose to USD 7.6 trillion in 2008, from USD 3.3 trillion the year before. This increase is currently driving a growth in the wealth management market, creating greater opportunities for wealth advisors to leverage new technology to acquire new clients and grow profits. As a result, competition among wealth advisory firms is increasing for new ways to improve existing client relationships and provide new tools to improve advisor effectiveness. While the private banking industry is, in general, relatively well equipped on the tax-planning side, with tools that can potentially allow private bankers to analyze the situation of high net worth individuals operating offshore or across multiple tax jurisdictions, the software packages used on the financial simulation side typically suffer from significant limitations and cannot satisfy the needs of a sophisticated clientele.

In fact, most existing financial software packages used by private bankers to generate asset allocation recommendations rely on single-period mean-variance asset portfolio optimization, which cannot yield a proper strategic allocation for at least two reasons. First, optimization parameters (expected returns, volatilities and correlations) are defined as constant across time, a practice which is contradicted by empirical observation and does not allow for taking into account the length of the investment horizon. Second, and most importantly perhaps, liability constraints and risk factors affecting them, such as inflation risk on targeted spending, are neither modeled nor explicitly taken into account in the portfolio construction process. Overall, the process of dealing with a private client typically leads to a detailed analysis of the client's objectives, constraints, and risk-aversion parameters, sometimes on the basis of rather sophisticated approaches. Yet, it is striking that once this information has been collected, and sometimes formalized, very little is done in terms of customizing a portfolio solution to the benefit of the specific needs of the client. Typically, the approach consists in providing several profiles expressed in terms of volatility or drawdown levels with, in some instances, a distinction in how the capital will eventually be accessed (annuities or lump-sum payment), but the client's specific objectives, constraints and associated risk factors are simply not taken into account in the design of the optimal allocation. While some industry players have recently developed planning tools that model assets in a multi-period stochastic framework, asset-liability matching for individuals remains an area for exploration. In this chapter, we shed some light into new forms of welfare-improving financial innovation inspired by the use of asset-liability management techniques, originally introduced in the context of institutional money management, within a private wealth management context.

Asset-Liability Management (ALM) denotes the adaptation of the portfolio management process in order to handle the presence of various constraints relating to the commitments that represent the liabilities of an investor. In what follows, we argue that it would be useful to transpose suitable extensions of portfolio optimization techniques used by institutional investors, for example, pension funds, to the context of private wealth management, because they have been precisely engineered to allow for the incorporation in the portfolio construction process of an investor's specific constraints, objectives and horizon, all of which may be summarized in terms of a single state variable, the value of the 'liability' portfolio. While ours is obviously a fairly stylized model, and while important effects such as taxes or mortality risk are not explicitly taken into account at this stage, we believe it represents a significant first normative step towards a better understanding of private wealth management decisions. In this context, our chapter can be regarded as an attempt to provide a first step towards a rational framework for private investors' financial decisions that extends standard portfolio optimization techniques in recognizing that the presence of the various aforementioned factors seriously affects the optimal allocation decision.

We show that a significant fraction of the complexity of optimal asset allocation decisions for private investors can conveniently be captured through the introduction of a single additional state variable, the liability value, which can account in a parsimonious way for investors' specific constraints and objectives.

It should be noted at this stage that within the framework of private wealth management, we use a broad definition of 'liabilities', which encompasses any commitment or spending objective, typically self-imposed (as opposed to exogenously imposed, as in a pension fund context), that an investor is facing. For example, an investor committed to a real estate acquisition will perceive such an expense as a future commitment or soft liability for which money should be available when needed. Overall, it is not the performance of a particular fund nor that of a given asset class that will be the determinant factor in the ability to meet a private investor's expectations. The success or failure of the satisfaction of the investor's long-term objectives is fundamentally dependent on an ALM exercise that aims at determining the proper strategic interclasses allocation as a function of the investor's specific objectives and constraints, in addition to the investor's time horizon. In other words, what will prove to be the decisive factor is the ability to design an asset allocation solution that is a function of the kinds of particular risks to which the investor is exposed, as opposed to the market as a whole. Similarly, the very concept of a risk-free asset is a function of the household time-horizon, but is also objective. Hence a five-year zero-coupon Treasury bond will not prove a perfectly safe investment for a private investor interested in a real estate acquisition in five years. The actual risk-free asset in this context (which we call below the *liability-hedging portfolio*) would instead be an asset perfectly correlated with real estate prices. More generally, an investor whose objective is related to the acquisition of a property would accept low and even negative returns in situations when real estate prices significantly decrease, but will not be satisfied with relatively high returns if such high returns are not sufficient to meet a dramatic increase in real estate prices. In such circumstances, a long-term investment in stocks and bonds, with a performance weakly correlated with real estate prices, would not be the right investment solution. In a similar way, in a pension context, an absolute return performance, often perceived as a natural choice in the context of private wealth management, would not be a satisfactory response to the needs of a private investor facing long-term inflation risk, for which the concern is capital preservation in real, as opposed to nominal, terms. In other words, the first benefit of the ALM approach is perhaps through an impact on the menu of asset classes, with a focus on including an asset that exhibits the highest possible correlation with the liability portfolio.

This chapter is related to the literature on long-term financial decisions, which starts with the seminal work of Merton (1969), Merton (1971) and was further specialized to encompass either uncertain interest rates (for example, Viceira (2001), Brennan and Xia (2002), Wachter (2003)), uncertain risk premia, (Kim and Omberg (1996), Campbell and Viceira (1999)), or both (Brennan, Schwartz and Lagnado (1997), Lynch (2001), Campbell, Chan and Viceira (2003)). These early papers highlight some important aspects of life-cycle investing, including, for example, the usefulness of real bonds for inflation hedging purposes. On the other hand, they mostly abstract away from some of the key complexities of private financial decisions. A large number of more recent papers have subsequently focused on integrating various useful salient features of private wealth management, including the impact of human capital (see, for example, Bodie, Merton and Samuelson (1992), Viceira (2001), Cocco, Gomes and Maenhout (2005)), illiquid real estate allocation or borrowing constraints on optimal allocation decisions. However, because they typically rely on standard expected utility maximization of terminal wealth, these papers fail to integrate a key dimension of private wealth management, namely, the fact that investment decisions should be designed to help investors achieve certain predetermined objectives, such as preparing for retirement or, earlier in the life cycle, preparing for real estate acquisition. In a nutshell, we argue that existing literature on household finance has mostly taken an asset management perspective, as opposed to an asset-liability management perspective. In parallel, several authors have attempted to extend intertemporal selection analysis to account for the presence of liability constraints in the asset allocation policy. A first attempt towards the introduction of liability constraints in optimal portfolio selection theory has been made by Merton (1993), who studies the allocation decision of a university that manages an endowment fund. As a couple of examples among many other papers falling into this particular strand of the finance literature, one may mention Rudolf and Ziemba (2004), who have formulated a continuous-time dynamic programming model of pension fund management in the presence of a time-varying opportunity set, or Sundaresan and Zapatero (1997), which also involves an endogenous retirement decision.

Our chapter can be seen as an attempt to merge these two somewhat separate strands of the literature, namely the literature on long-term financial decisions for private investors, which has mostly focused on an asset-only perspective, and the literature on asset-liability management decisions, which have been mostly analyzed from an institutional perspective (pension funds, insurance companies, or endowments). We do so by casting the long-horizon life cycle investment problem within an asset-liability management framework suitable for the private wealth management context, which allows us to show that pursuing an asset-only strategy involves, in general, a substantial opportunity cost. Broadly speaking, adopting an ALM approach leads to defining risk and return in relative terms with respect to the liability portfolio, which is a critical improvement over asset-only asset allocation models that fail to account for the presence of various investment or consumption goals and objectives, such as preparing for retirement or preparing for a real estate acquisition. As a result, adopting an ALM approach leads to a focus on liability-hedging properties of various asset classes, a focus that would, by definition, be absent from an asset-only perspective.

This chapter is organized as follows: In Section 18.2, we introduce a formal, stylized model of asset-liability management for household financial decisions. In Section 18.3, we present a series of illustrations of the usefulness of asset-liability management techniques within a household finance context, with a focus on a pension objective. A conclusion and suggestions for further research can be found in Section 18.4.

18.2   A formal model of asset-liability management in private wealth management

In what follows, we introduce a formal model of asset-liability management, and discuss its application within a private wealth management context. This analytical approach to ALM is appealing, in spite of its highly stylized nature, because it leads to a tractable solution, allowing one to fully and explicitly understand the various mechanisms affecting the optimal allocation strategy. In particular, we argue that the three-fund separation theorem we obtain, typical of optimal asset allocation decisions in the presence of stochastic state variables, is a parsimonious way to capture some of the complexity involved in private wealth management decisions.

18.2.1   Stochastic Model for risk factors impacting asset and liability values

Based on a suitable econometric model, we provide estimates for the short- and long-term dependencies between the return on a set of asset classes and factors impacting liability values. For this, we rely on a stationary vector-autoregressive (VAR) approach for modeling the joint asset and liability return dynamic distributions, similar to Campbell, Chan and Viceira (2003), and Campbell and Viceira (2005), extended to an asset-liability management (see also Hoevenaars et al. (2008) or Berkelaar and Kouwenberg (2010)):

$$\mathbf{z}_{t+1} = \mathbf{\Phi}_0 + \mathbf{\Phi}_1 \mathbf{z}_t + \mathbf{\varepsilon}_t \tag{18.1}$$

with $\mathbf{z}_t$ being a vector of risk factors impacting asset and liability values, and $\mathbf{\varepsilon}_t$ is an error term which distribution needs to be specified.

More specifically, on the asset side, our empirical analysis focuses on a set of traditional and alternative asset classes. Stock returns are represented by the CRSP value-weighted stock index. Commodities are proxied by the S&P Goldman Sachs Commodity index (GSCI). Real estate investments are represented by the FTSE NAREIT real estate index, which is a value-weighted basket of REITs listed on NYSE, AMEX and NASDAQ. We thus limit the opportunity set to liquid and publicly traded assets. Finally, we add a 20-year constant maturity bond return and the 3-month US Treasury Bills, both from the CRSP database.

Following the evidence from the extensive literature on return predictability (see Stock and Watson (1999), among others), we also add potential predictive economic variables to the set of endogenous variables. We introduce the dividend yield (see, for example, Campbell and Shiller (1988), Hodrick (1992) or Campbell and Viceira (2002)), the credit spread (computed as the difference between Moody's Seasoned Baa Corporate Bond Yield and the 10-year Treasury Constant Maturity Rate), as well as the term spread (obtained from the difference between the 10-year Treasury Constant Maturity Rate and the 3-month T-Bill rate). The dividend series for the value-weighted stock index are obtained from CRSP and the dividend yield is reconstituted as the cumulated dividends perceived over the preceding four quarters, divided by the current price. All other economic variables were obtained from Datastream.

On the liability side, we consider two main examples in what follows. The first example relates to a pension objective, with a focus on maintaining a target level of purchasing power after retirement. As far as this objective is concerned, the natural proxy for liability returns is the return on a treasury inflation protected security (TIPS), since the payoff of the TIPS is given by the cumulative inflation over the time-horizon. Unfortunately, an empirical time series with a sufficiently long history is not available for TIPS. We therefore construct a time series for a constant maturity treasury inflation protected bond by using the following ingredients: constant maturity nominal bond returns from CRSP (r^b), the median inflation forecast ($\widehat{\pi}$) from the Survey Research Center (University of Michigan) and realized inflation (π) as proxied by the US Consumer Price Index. The return on the TIPS portfolio is denoted by r_t^r and given by

$$r_t^r = r_t^b - \widehat{\pi}_t + \pi_t - \Lambda_\pi \tag{18.2}$$

where Λ_π denotes the inflation risk premia that we assume at 50 annual basis points, which is consistent with Kothari and Shanken (2004). Note that the constructed nominal return incorporates an interest rate risk premium since the nominal bond return r^b accounts for the presence of a term spread. The constant time-to-maturity for the bond is set to five years and, consistently, the five-year ahead inflation forecast is used from the inflation survey.[1] The second example relates to real estate acquisition. In this case, we assume that the liability return exactly coincides with the return on the FTSE NAREIT index. Obviously, this is a simplification, since the value of a given piece of property that a private investor considers acquiring will not be perfectly correlated with the return on a broad REIT index, which is well known to contain equity market exposure in addition to real estate market exposure. The reason why we choose to use an investable proxy for real estate returns is because it will prove

Table 18.1 Summary statistics

	Average return	Volatility	Sharpe ratio
Stocks	11.36	17.50	0.65
CPI	−0.92	1.69	−0.54
3M T-Bill	6.67	1.50	−

Note: Summary statistics are calculated from quarterly log-returns from 1962.Q1 through 2005.Q4 for stocks, bonds and T-Bills, from 1970.Q2 through 2005.Q4 for commodities, from 1972.Q2 through 2005.Q4 for real estate and from 1979.Q2 through 2005.Q4 for TIPS. All returns are in excess of T-Bills except for the T-Bill returns. Average returns and volatilities are corrected for Jensen's inequality and in annualized percentage numbers.

useful in the empirical section to analyze a complete market setting, where risk factors in liability returns are entirely spanned by existing securities.

In total, the vector of endogenous variables $\mathbf{z}$ in Formula (18.1) contains ten elements. Table 18.1 presents summary statistics of the corresponding time series of quarterly returns from 1962.Q1 through 2005.Q4. We see that Sharpe ratios for all asset classes are somewhat similar over the sample period, to the notable exception of long bonds, which are dominated on a risk-adjusted basis. It is important to note that these summary statistics refer to arithmetic averages over the empirical sample, while the analysis that follows is designed to derive horizon dependent moments for the different asset classes.

To estimate the VAR model, we follow the procedure of Hoevenaars et al. (2008), who impose restrictions on the parameters. We first define a core system of equations in the VAR: consider the sub-vector $\mathbf{z}_1$ containing the excess returns on the stock, the long bond, the return on the T-Bill, the inflation rate, the credit spread, the term spread and the dividend yield. We estimate an unrestricted VAR model for $\mathbf{z}_1$:

$$\mathbf{z}_{1,t+1} = \mathbf{\Phi}_{0,1} + \mathbf{\Phi}_{1,1}\mathbf{z}_{1,t} + \mathbf{\varepsilon}_{1,t}$$

As a consequence, the variables that are not contained in the core model have no impact on core variables. We then define $\mathbf{z}_2$ as the complement of $\mathbf{z}_1$: $\mathbf{z}_2$ thus contains the excess returns on commodities, real estate and the TIPS. We then estimate the following regression system:

$$\mathbf{z}_{2,t+1} = \mathbf{\Phi}_{0,2} + \mathbf{A}\mathbf{z}_{1,t+1} + \mathbf{B}\mathbf{z}_{1,t} + \mathbf{\Phi}_{1,2}\mathbf{z}_{2,t} + \mathbf{\varepsilon}_{2,t}$$

where the matrix $\mathbf{\Phi}_{1,2}$ is restricted to be diagonal and so is the covariance matrix of the error term $\mathbf{\varepsilon}_2$. These restrictions imply that non-core variables have no effect on each other and that their innovations are independent. The matrices **A** and **B** are not restricted. In particular, **A** accounts for contemporaneous correlations between non-core variables and core variables, so that we can assume that the error terms ε_1 and ε_2 are uncorrelated. Finally, we can write the restricted parameters of the VAR system (18.1) as:

$$
\boldsymbol{\Phi}_0 = \begin{pmatrix} \boldsymbol{\Phi}_{0,1} \\ \boldsymbol{\Phi}_{0,2} \end{pmatrix}, \quad
\boldsymbol{\Phi}_1 = \begin{pmatrix} \boldsymbol{\Phi}_{1,1} & 0 \\ \mathbf{B} + \mathbf{A}\boldsymbol{\Phi}_{1,1} & \boldsymbol{\Phi}_{1,2} \end{pmatrix}, \quad
\boldsymbol{\Sigma}_\varepsilon = \begin{pmatrix} \boldsymbol{\Sigma}_{\varepsilon,1} & \boldsymbol{\Sigma}_{\varepsilon,1}\mathbf{A}' \\ \mathbf{A}\boldsymbol{\Sigma}_{\varepsilon,1} & \boldsymbol{\Sigma}_{\varepsilon,2} + \mathbf{A}\boldsymbol{\Sigma}_{\varepsilon,1}\mathbf{A}' \end{pmatrix}
$$

These restrictions allow us to make use of the full history for core variables, which covers the period from 1962.Q1 through 2005.Q4, even if the sample for non-core variables is much smaller. Indeed, our series of returns on commodities starts in 1970.Q2, while the series of returns on real estate starts in 1972. Q2, and the series for the TIPS starts in 1979.Q2.

We present the estimated matrix $\boldsymbol{\Phi}_1$ in Table 18.2 and the residual correlations in Table 18.3. The VAR-implied dynamics for asset and liability returns are, indeed, governed by these two parameter matrices. The VAR modeling framework is particularly convenient in a portfolio context, since it generates analytic expressions for time-dependent variances and expected returns. The model implied first and second moments of compounded returns can in fact be written as

$$
E_t\left(\sum_{k=1}^T \mathbf{H}\mathbf{z}_{t+k}\right) = \begin{pmatrix} \boldsymbol{\mu}_T^A \\ \boldsymbol{\mu}_T^L \end{pmatrix} = \left[\sum_{k=0}^{T-1}(T-k)\mathbf{H}\widehat{\boldsymbol{\Phi}_1^k}\right]\boldsymbol{\Phi}_0 + \left[\sum_{k=1}^T \mathbf{H}\widehat{\boldsymbol{\Phi}_1^k}\right]\mathbf{z}_t \tag{18.3}
$$

$$
V_t\left(\sum_{k=1}^T \mathbf{H}\mathbf{z}_{t+k}\right) = \begin{pmatrix} \boldsymbol{\Sigma}_T^A & \boldsymbol{\sigma}_T^{AL} \\ \boldsymbol{\sigma}_T^{AL'} & \boldsymbol{\sigma}_T^L \end{pmatrix} = \sum_{k=1}^T \left[\left(\sum_{i=1}^{k-1}\mathbf{H}\widehat{\boldsymbol{\Phi}_1^i}\right)\boldsymbol{\Sigma}_\varepsilon\left(\sum_{i=1}^{k-1}\mathbf{H}\widehat{\boldsymbol{\Phi}_1^i}\right)'\right] \tag{18.4}
$$

Table 18.2   Estimated VAR – $\boldsymbol{\Phi}_1$

		1	2	3	4	5	6	7	8	9	10
1	Stocks	−0.06	0.17	−1.74	−0.71	1.40	0.28	0.06			
2	20Y bond	−0.05	−0.07	0.55	0.44	−0.89	1.64	−0.02			
3	3M T-Bill	−0.00	−0.03	0.76	0.01	0.07	−0.11	0.00			
4	CPI	0.00	−0.03	0.00	0.26	0.24	−0.22	0.01			
5	Credit spread	−0.00	−0.01	0.14	0.07	0.81	0.06	−0.00			
6	Term spread	−0.01	−0.01	−0.11	−0.00	0.46	0.70	0.00			
7	Dividend yield	−1.09	0.03	−0.94	0.20	−0.89	0.25	1.00			
8	Commodities	−0.01	0.01	−4.55	0.11	−1.76	−1.40	0.04	−0.03		
9	Real estate	−0.06	−0.06	−0.14	0.57	3.53	1.60	0.01		−0.04	
10	TIPS	−0.06	−0.03	0.89	−0.39	−0.20	0.62	−0.01			−0.28

Note: Quarterly returns from 1962-Q1 to 2005-Q4 are fitted to the VAR system (18.1). Blank elements are zero by construction of the VAR. All returns related to tradable assets 1, 2, 8, 9 and 10 are in excess of T-Bills.

Table 18.3 Correlation matrix of residuals ε

		1	2	3	4	5	6	7	8	9	10
1	Stocks	0.08									
2	20Y bond	0.20	0.05								
3	3M T-Bill	−0.12	0.28	0.00							
4	CPI	−0.27	−0.34	0.06	0.01						
5	Credit spread	−0.00	0.67	0.22	−0.17	0.00					
6	Term spread	0.00	0.07	0.23	−0.17	−0.03	0.01				
7	Dividend yield	−0.02	−0.08	0.02	0.27	−0.13	−0.15	0.02			
8	Commodities	0.11	0.00	−0.16	−0.22	−0.06	0.06	−0.02	0.09		
9	Real estate	0.05	0.10	0.11	0.02	0.09	0.07	0.03	−0.02	0.08	
10	TIPS	−0.18	−0.00	0.12	0.18	−0.05	0.01	−0.14	−0.06	−0.00	0.03

Note: Quarterly returns from 1962-Q1 to 2005-Q4 are fitted to the VAR system (18.1). Off-diagonal elements are correlations, and diagonal elements are standard deviations. All returns related to tradable assets 1, 2, 8, 9 and 10 are in excess of T-Bills.

Here μ_T^A is the vector of expected returns on assets, μ_T^L is the (scalar) return on the liability portfolio (either inflation-linked or real-estate related) for a horizon equal to T years. Σ_T^A is the asset covariance matrix for the T-year horizon, σ_T^{AL} is the vector of covariances between the asset classes and the liability portfolio, and σ_T^L is the liability variance for a horizon equal to T years as well. Σ_ε denotes the residual covariance matrix. Finally, $\mathbf{H}$ is a matrix that selects the vector of excess returns on the assets and the liability from the state vector $\mathbf{z}$.

Figure 18.1 depicts the horizon-dependent annualized volatilities as derived from the fitted parameters and implied by the VAR system (see Formula 18.4). Consistent with the findings in Campbell and Viceira (2001), we find that equity markets are less risky for the long term. This effect is explained by the presence of implied mean-reversion in stock returns. Indeed, dividend yields are widely documented to exhibit significant predicting power for stock returns (see, for example, Campbell and Viceira (2001)). On the one hand, innovations to dividend yields and stock returns are negatively correlated (see Table 18.3). On the other hand, lagged dividend yields are positively correlated with contemporaneous stock returns (see Table 18.2), which leads to a smoothing effect of the past innovations. In contrast, we find that investing in T-Bills generates a higher annualized volatility as the investment horizon increases, which is due to the uncertainty involved in rolling over short-term debt in the presence of stochastic interest rates. Figure 18.1 shows that the term structure of volatilities implied by the VAR model is also upward-sloping for real estate and commodity investments.

Figure 18.2 displays the correlations of the various asset classes with the Consumer Price Index as functions of time-horizon. It appears that the inflation-hedging properties of the various asset classes depend on the horizon. For instance, T-Bills have negative correlation with realized inflation over short

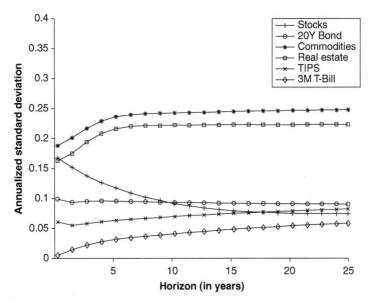

Figure 18.1   Term structure of risk

Note: This figure plots the volatility implied by the VAR model of the nominal return on each asset class, as a function of investment horizon.

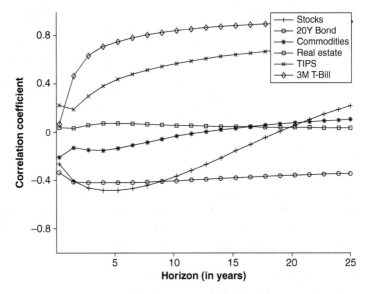

Figure 18.2   Term structure of correlations with realized inflation

Note: This figure plots the correlation implied by the VAR model between nominal returns on the asset classes and the realized inflation, as a function of investment horizon.

horizons, but this correlation becomes positive, and relatively high, over horizons exceeding ten years. In addition, we find that stocks display negative correlation with inflation in the short run, but they have good inflation hedging properties over horizons that exceed 20 years. Our finding of a negative short-term relationship between expected stock returns and expected inflation is consistent with previous empirical findings on the subject (see Fama and Schwert (1977), Gultekin (1983) and Kaul (1987), among others) and is also consistent with the intuition that higher inflation leads to lower economic activity, thus depressing stock returns (for example, Fama (1981)). On the other hand, higher future inflation leads to higher dividends and thus higher returns on stocks (for example, Campbell and Shiller (1988)), and thus equity investments should offer significant inflation protection over longer horizons, a fact that also has been confirmed by a number of recent empirical academic studies (Boudoukh and Richardson (1993) or Schotman and Schweitzer (2000)).

Overall, these findings suggest that utilizing a standard one-period optimization model, as is typically done in private wealth management, is a severe simplification which does not allow investors to benefit from life-cycle effects induced by time-varying opportunity sets. In what follows, we will formally confirm that optimal allocation decisions are a function of time-horizon, a fact that cannot be captured in the context of a static portfolio optimization exercise. We will also argue that not taking into account the presence of liabilities leads to a substantial opportunity cost.

18.2.2   Life-cycle investment decisions in asset-liability management

In a dynamic asset allocation model, it is customary to assume that the preferences of the investor are expressed in terms of expected utility of terminal asset value:

$$\max_{\omega} E[u(A_T)] \qquad (18.5)$$

where T is the investor's time-horizon. One key problem with this objective is precisely that it fails to recognize that targeted (liability) payments are scheduled beyond the horizon T. One natural approach to tackle this problem consists of recognizing that terminal wealth at date T is made of a long position in the asset portfolio with value A_T, but also involves a short position in the liability portfolio with value L_T. Another related approach to account for the presence of liability payments beyond the horizon consists of introducing a related state variable, the funding ratio, defined as the ratio of assets to liabilities:

$$F_t \equiv \frac{A_t}{L_t} \qquad (18.6)$$

which is well-defined as long as L_t is not zero. This quantity is commonly used in pension fund practice, in which a fund is said to be overfunded when the funding ratio is greater than 100%, to be fully funded when the funding ratio equals 100%, and to be underfunded when the funding ratio is lower than 100%. From an interpretation standpoint, focusing on the funding ratio amounts to using the liability value process $(L_t)_{t\geq0}$, as opposed to the bank account, as a numeraire, which we adopt in this chapter.

In what follows we take u to be the constant relative risk aversion (CRRA) utility function, defined as

$$u(x) = \frac{x^{1-\gamma}}{1-\gamma} \qquad \text{for x} > 0$$
$$u(x) = -\infty \qquad \text{for x} \leq 0$$

where γ lies in $[1,\infty]$. If $\gamma = 1$ we obtain the logarithmic utility function.

If one makes the additional assumption of log-normal return distributions, the portfolio choice model collapses into a mean-variance problem:

$$\max_{\omega}\left\{E\left[\frac{F_T^{1-\gamma}}{1-\gamma}\right]\right\} \Rightarrow \max_{\omega}\left\{E\left[r_T^F\right] + \frac{1-\gamma}{2}V\left[r_T^F\right]\right\} \qquad (18.7)$$

with r_T^F the T-period forward-looking log-funding-ratio return such that $F_T = \exp(r_T^F)$ and γ the level of relative risk aversion. In the absence of log-normal returns, this approach can also be justified by a second-order approximation (see Campbell (1993), Campbell (1996) or Campbell, Chan and Viceira (2003) for details).

Analyzing the above program for different levels of relative risk aversion coincides with analyzing the mean-variance efficient frontier of the terminal funding ratio or the T-period funding ratio return. Portfolios on the efficient frontier are thus the solutions to the following program:

$$\min_{\omega} \frac{1}{2}V\left(r_T^F\right) \qquad (18.8)$$
$$\text{s.t.} \quad E\left(r_T^F\right) = \mu_T^F$$

where μ_T^F is an achievable target funding ratio return. The Lagrangian for this program is given as

$$L = \frac{1}{2}V\left(r_T^F\right) - \lambda\left(E\left(r_T^F\right) - \mu_T^F\right) \qquad (18.9)$$

As is transparent from Equations (18.3) and (18.4), first and second moments in (18.9) can be derived from the VAR model, and exhibit an explicit dependency with respect to time-horizon. Assuming a fixed-mix allocation $\boldsymbol{\omega}$ for a given time-to-maturity T, and discretizing Ito's lemma (see details in Campbell, Chan and Viceira (2003)), we can write the log-funding ratio return as

$$r_T^F = \boldsymbol{\omega}' \left(\mathbf{r}_T^A + \frac{1}{2}\boldsymbol{\sigma}_T^A \right) - \frac{1}{2}\boldsymbol{\omega}'\boldsymbol{\Sigma}_T^A\boldsymbol{\omega} - r_T^L \tag{18.10}$$

with $\boldsymbol{\Sigma}_T^A$ the covariance matrix, $\boldsymbol{\sigma}_T^A$ its diagonal, $\mathbf{r}_T^A$ the vector of the asset log-returns, r_T^L the log-liability return and $\boldsymbol{\omega}$ denotes the vector of the asset portfolio weights.[2] All returns here are expressed as excess returns over the T-Bills.

Using (18.10) we obtain the VAR-implied annualized expected funding ratio returns:

$$E\left(r_T^F\right) = \frac{1}{T}\left[\boldsymbol{\omega}' \left(\boldsymbol{\mu}_T^A + \frac{1}{2}\boldsymbol{\sigma}_T^A \right) - \frac{1}{2}\boldsymbol{\omega}'\boldsymbol{\Sigma}_T^A\boldsymbol{\omega} - \mu_T^L \right] \tag{18.11}$$

where $\boldsymbol{\sigma}_T^A \equiv \mathrm{diag}(\boldsymbol{\Sigma}_T^A)$. Furthermore, noting that $r_T^F = \begin{pmatrix} \boldsymbol{\omega} \\ -1 \end{pmatrix}' \mathbf{Hz}_T$, we derive from (18.4) the annualized funding ratio return variance as

$$V\left(r_T^F\right) = \frac{1}{T}\left[\boldsymbol{\omega}'\boldsymbol{\Sigma}_T^A\boldsymbol{\omega} - 2\boldsymbol{\omega}'\boldsymbol{\sigma}_T^{AL} + \sigma_T^L \right] \tag{18.12}$$

Substituting (18.11) and (18.12) in (18.9), we obtain the VAR-implied Lagrangian equation for mean-variance ALM efficient portfolios:

$$L(\boldsymbol{\omega},\lambda) = \frac{1}{2}\boldsymbol{\omega}'\boldsymbol{\Sigma}_T^A\boldsymbol{\omega} - \boldsymbol{\omega}'\boldsymbol{\sigma}_T^{AL} + \frac{1}{2}\sigma_T^L - \lambda\left(\boldsymbol{\omega}'\left(\boldsymbol{\mu}_T^A + \frac{1}{2}\boldsymbol{\sigma}_T^A \right) - \frac{1}{2}\boldsymbol{\omega}'\boldsymbol{\Sigma}_T^A\boldsymbol{\omega} - \mu_T^L - \mu_T^F \right) \tag{18.13}$$

The first-order condition leads to the following description of mean-variance efficient portfolio weights:

$$\boldsymbol{\omega} = \alpha(\boldsymbol{\Sigma}_T^A)^{-1}\left(\boldsymbol{\mu}_T^A + \frac{1}{2}\boldsymbol{\sigma}_T^A \right) + (1-\alpha)(\boldsymbol{\Sigma}_T^A)^{-1}\boldsymbol{\sigma}_T^{AL} \tag{18.14}$$

with $\alpha = \lambda/(1+\lambda)$. Given that $\lambda \geq 0$, this result implies that $\alpha \in [0,1]$. We thus obtain a fund separation theorem, dictating to allocate a fraction α of the wealth to the performance seeking portfolio (PSP) and another fraction $1-\alpha$ to the liability hedging portfolio (LHP).[3] The efficient frontier can than be drawn by letting α vary between zero (which generates 100% investment to the LHP) and one (which generates 100% investment to the PSP) and plugging (18.14) in (18.11) and (18.12) in order to derive implied expected returns and implied volatilities, respectively.

We may compare these portfolio allocations to mean-variance efficient portfolios of an asset-only investor who does not take the presence of liability streams into account. As a consequence, the investor focuses on asset return only, and r_T^F in (18.10) becomes

$$r_T = \omega'\left(\mathbf{r}_T^A + \frac{1}{2}\sigma_T^A\right) - \frac{1}{2}\omega'\Sigma_T^A\omega + r_T^R \tag{18.15}$$

with r^R the return of the risk-free asset (T-Bills in this setting). The expectation in (18.11) thus becomes

$$E(r_T) = \omega'\left(\mathbf{r}_T^A + \frac{1}{2}\sigma_T^A\right) - \frac{1}{2}\omega'\Sigma_T^A\omega + \mu_T^R \tag{18.16}$$

while the variance in (18.12) is now given by

$$V(r_T) = \omega'\Sigma_T^A\omega + 2\omega'\sigma_T^{AR} + \sigma_T^R \tag{18.17}$$

where σ_T^{AR} is the covariance vector of the assets with the risk-free asset at horizon T and μ_T^R and σ_T^R the corresponding mean and variance of the risk-free asset. Accordingly, we can solve the Lagrangian for the asset-only problem and obtain the set of mean-variance efficient portfolios $\widetilde{\omega}$ as

$$\widetilde{\omega} = \alpha(\Sigma_T^A)^{-1}\left(\mu_T^A + \frac{1}{2}\sigma_T^A\right) - (1-\alpha)(\Sigma_T^A)^{-1}\sigma_T^{AR} \tag{18.18}$$

Again, we obtain a separation result involving the performance-seeking portfolio and also a portfolio capturing a hedging demand against unexpected changes in interest rate levels; this is the second term in the right side of (18.18). Such a demand was not present in (18.14): indeed, the funding ratio is defined as the ratio of asset over liability, so that the impacts of changes in interest-rate level on the numerator and the denominator cancel out, as can be seen from the fact that the risk-free rate does not appear in (18.10). In Section 18.3, we shall study the behaviour of sub-optimal strategies (both in the AM and in the ALM sense) in which the hedging demand in (18.18) is simply ignored, so as to analyze the opportunity costs involved in following a purely myopic portfolio strategy. It should also be noted that the portfolios in (18.18), while efficient in an asset-management sense, will not be efficient in the ALM space, and we will provide in Section 18.3 ample evidence of the efficiency/opportunity cost of not taking the presence of liabilities into account in a private wealth management context.

As argued before, our analysis of the life-cycle component of long-term investment decisions consists in allowing the asset allocation decisions to be dependent upon the investor's time-horizon, a dimension that can not be captured by standard static optimization problems. While a significant improvement, this approach, which directly follows the seminal work by Campbell, Chan and Viceira (2003), does not provide the most general form of asset allocation strategies. There are, in fact, three different levels of extensions of standard static portfolio allocation models, which consist respectively in (1) allowing for time-horizon dependencies, (2) allowing for (purely deterministic) time dependencies, and (3) allowing for time- and state-dependencies. These advances have been made possible by the pioneering work of Merton (1969), Merton (1971), who has opened a world of opportunities for more subtle dynamic asset allocation decisions, involving intertemporal adjustments to the asset mix as time goes by. The calculation of optimal intertemporal portfolios is, however, typically very challenging to handle, whether analytically or numerically, as soon as the number of state variables exceeds one or two. In this chapter, we therefore stick to the first level of extension for simplicity and tractability, and focus on allowing investors with different time-horizons to hold different optimal portfolios. It should be noted that the second level of extension (time-dependency without state-dependency), while seeming to offer a good compromise between the conflicting objectives of generality versus tractability, and while often used in the context of so-called target-date funds, simply cannot be rationalized within a formal asset allocation model (see, for example, Viceira and Field (2007)).

18.3   Empirical illustrations of the benefits of an ALM approach in private wealth management

In the empirical applications, we distinguish between a pension-related objective and a real estate acquisition objective. The idea of this distinction is to highlight the importance of properly identifying the appropriate benchmark liability and its impact on optimal portfolios. It is worthwhile to note that the nature of the liability stream raises the question of whether a perfect hedge against unexpected shocks in the liability asset is available and how to model the liabilities. In the case of a pension-related objective, it is appropriate to assume that the contractual pension is written in real terms with an actual payment indexed with respect to inflation. As far as the case of an acquisition of real estate is concerned, several real estate related indices are suitable candidates for the liability benchmark. So as to explicitly distinguish between the complete and the incomplete market case, we choose (as explained above) to proxy real estate prices by an investable real estate investment trust index.

The illustrations that follow are highly stylized in nature, and a number of additional dimensions would have to be addressed in the context of a real-world application of the framework discussed in this chapter. Among these additional dimensions, one stands out in particular: the necessity to account for the presence of various tax schedules for different forms of investment. It is expected that accounting for differential tax treatment will impact the optimal allocation decisions in a complex manner. It would also be desirable to account for the presence of a variety of constraints (for example, maximum drawdown limits) and objectives (for example, bequest motives) that extend beyond the standard expected utility maximization framework used in this chapter, and which have been found to be relevant to private investors. Finally, one would also need to take into account the presence of *flexible* contribution as well as consumption schedules, as opposed to assuming, as is done below, one or several *pre-defined* contributions and withdrawals. Designing a very general asset allocation model incorporating a realistic tax treatment, a variety of risk budgets and also flexible endogenous contribution and liability schedules would certainly be a very desirable objective, but not one that could be achieved in the context of an analytical model such as the one discussed in this chapter. While our results are derived under a number of simplifying assumptions, a number of useful insights can still be learnt from this stylized analysis, in particular related to the fact that failing to adopt an ALM approach to long-term investment decisions, and sticking to the sub-optimal asset-only perspective, will generate very substantial opportunity costs for the private investor.

18.3.1   Computational investigation

In this section, we focus on a pension objective, and consider a 65-year-old wealthy individual who is already retired. This person's goal is to ensure inflation-protected pension payments, which we normalized at 100 with no loss of generality, at a given horizon date T (in what follows we consider $T = 1, 5,$ 10 and 25 years, respectively). To achieve this goal the individual is prepared to invest a fixed amount of money, and we assume that the funding ratio at retirement date is 100%. For each given time-horizon, we will derive four different efficient frontiers corresponding to (1) the AM objective in (18.18), in which we assume that the menu of asset classes does not include the perfect liability-hedging asset, the investor mistakenly uses a short-term one-year horizon while the actual horizon is T years and the investor ignores the hedging demand against interest-rate risk (a case we denote by 'AM SH' and to which we refer as 'AM with short horizon'); (2) the AM objective in (18.18), in which we still assume that the menu of asset classes does not include the perfect liability-hedging asset (a case we denote by 'AM LH' and to which we refer as 'AM with long horizon'), but the investor uses the true horizon T when computing the parameters; (3) the ALM objective (18.14), with a proper treatment of the horizon T, but without the perfect liability-hedging asset in the menu of asset classes (a case denoted by 'ALM$-$' and to which we refer as the 'incomplete market case'); and (4) the ALM objective (18.14) with a proper treatment of the horizon T and with the perfect liability-hedging asset (in this case an inflation-linked bond) in the menu of asset classes (we denote this case by 'ALM$+$' and we refer to it as the 'complete market case' since the menu of tradable assets is sufficiently rich to allow for a perfect hedge of liability risk). The outcomes are drawn from Amenc et al. (2009).

The first asset-only approach is consistent with the static approach used in standard asset allocation exercises. The second efficient frontier represents an improvement based on allowing for time-horizon dependencies, but still fails to account for the presence of liabilities. The third efficient frontier depicts the case in which both the time-horizon and the presence of liabilities are taken into account, but without an effort towards the integration of new asset classes with specific liability-hedging properties. The fourth efficient frontier corresponds to the final improvement, with an asset allocation decision that takes into account time-horizon effects and the presence of liabilities, and with a specific liability-hedging asset introduced in the asset mix. Analyzing separately the ALM$-$ and ALM$+$ portfolios allows us to disentangle the two main benefits of the ALM approach, namely, the benefits due to assessing risk and return with respect to the liability benchmark, on the one hand, and the benefits related to the introduction of a liability-hedging instrument, on the other hand.

We first focus on the benefits obtained by taking into account the investment horizon, as opposed to using a standard static model in an asset-only context. To do this, we compute for allocations (1) and (2) the expected value and the variance of the log return on the asset portfolio, following (18.16) and (18.17), respectively. We then let α vary over the interval [0,1], so as to obtain a representation of these strategies in the AM space, as shown in Figure 18.3. By definition, the AM LH strategy dominates the AM SH strategy in the mean-variance sense, except, of course, for the case of a one-year time-to-horizon, in which they are mathematically equivalent. In fact, for $T = 5$ or 10 years, the performance of the AM strategy with short-horizon is quite similar to that of the AM strategy with long horizon. On the other hand, when the horizon is very long ($T = 25$ years), the opportunity cost of using a static optimization model with a short-term objective is quite substantial.

We then move on to the analysis of the additional benefits induced by accounting for the presence of liabilities, in addition to the investment horizon. To do this, we obtain expected (log) funding ratios according to (18.11) and variances for (log) funding ratios from (18.12) for each set of efficient

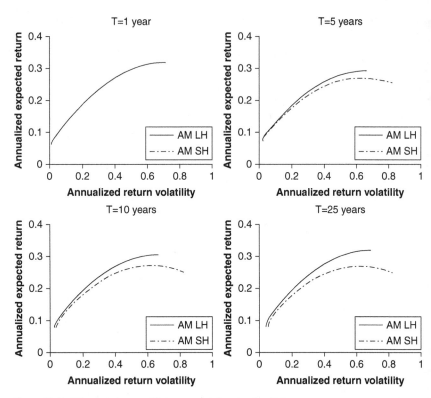

Figure 18.3 Mean-variance efficient portfolios in the AM space

Note: This figure plots the efficient frontiers in the $(E[r_T], \sigma[r_T])$-diagram, where r_T denotes the return on the asset portfolio after T years, as computed in (18.16) and (18.17). These frontiers are obtained by letting α vary from 0 to 1 in (18.18). In the "ALM LH" situation, the investor has a "long-term" horizon equal to T years, while in the "AM SH" case she applies (18.18) by mistakenly assuming that $T = 1$ year.

portfolios corresponding to the situations (2), (3) and (4). Assuming normality of the log-returns in the system (18.1) and denoting $\mu^F=E(r^F)$ and $\sigma^F=V(r^F)$, we can derive the expected value and the variance of the funding ratio as

$$E(FR) = e^{\mu^F + \frac{1}{2}\sigma^F} \tag{18.19}$$

$$V(FR) = \left(e^{\sigma^F} - 1\right)\left(e^{2\mu^F + \sigma^F}\right) \tag{18.20}$$

We let α vary in (18.14) and (18.18) from zero to one and use (18.19) and (18.20) to plot the efficient frontiers for various investment horizons. Figure 18.4 shows

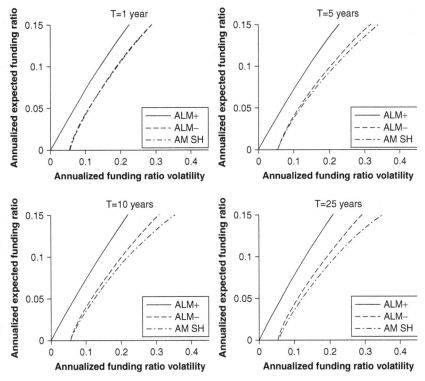

Figure 18.4   Mean-variance efficient portfolios in the ALM space: CPI indexed returns

Note: This figure plots the efficient frontiers in the $(E[r_T^F], \sigma[r_T^F])$-diagram, where $E[r_T^F]$ and $\sigma[r_T^F]$ denote respectively the annualized expected value and standard deviation of the log funding ratio after T years, as computed in (18.11) and (18.12). "ALM+" and "ALM–" are obtained by letting α vary from 0 to 1 in (18.14). "ALM+" refers to the complete market case where TIPS are available for trading, while "ALM–" refers to the incomplete market setting. "AM SH" is obtained by mistakenly assuming that $T = 1$ year and letting α vary from 0 to 1 in the myopic portfolio rule.

the three frontiers (ALM with TIPS, ALM without TIPS, and AM SH – without TIPS) when the investor goal is based on pension payments related to the consumer price index, and this for four different time-horizons (one year, five years, ten years and 25 years). As can be seen from the Figure 18.4, the myopic strategy 'AM SH' is strongly dominated by ALM-efficient portfolios, especially when the menu of asset classes available to the ALM investor includes inflation-linked bonds. To get a better sense of the magnitude of the outperformance of ALM-efficient portfolios with respect to asset-only efficient portfolios, Table 18.4 presents summary statistics for three portfolios on the efficient frontiers, corresponding to low, medium and high target expected returns, respectively. Precisely, we consider three levels of annualized expected

Table 18.4   Efficient portfolios (CPI indexed returns): summary statistics

Horizon (years)		Low			Medium			High		
		ALM+	ALM−	AM SH	ALM+	ALM−	AM SH	ALM+	ALM−	AM SH
1	$E[r_T^F]$	5.00	5.00	5.00	10.00	10.00	10.00	15.00	15.00	15.00
	$\sigma[r_T^F]$	6.71	10.89	10.98	14.12	18.90	18.99	22.46	28.88	28.90
	$P(FR<1)$	22.77	32.32	32.43	23.91	29.86	29.90	25.22	30.18	30.19
	ES	3.76	6.71	6.77	7.76	10.88	10.93	12.06	15.90	15.92
5	$E[r_T^F]$	5.00	5.00	5.00	10.00	10.00	10.00	15.00	15.00	15.00
	$\sigma[r_T^F]$	6.83	11.64	12.21	14.42	20.53	21.81	23.01	31.89	34.86
	$P(FR<1)$	23.18	33.38	34.15	24.36	31.29	32.35	25.72	31.91	33.35
	ES	3.85	7.23	7.62	7.96	11.91	12.72	12.40	17.63	19.29
10	$E[r_T^F]$	5.00	5.00	5.00	10.00	10.00	10.00	15.00	15.00	15.00
	$\sigma[r_T^F]$	6.57	11.48	12.32	13.85	19.98	22.06	22.00	30.78	35.29
	$P(FR<1)$	22.41	33.16	34.23	23.51	30.87	32.50	24.78	31.29	33.55
	ES	3.67	7.12	7.69	7.58	11.57	12.87	11.78	17.00	19.52
25	$E[r_T^F]$	5.00	5.00	5.00	10.00	10.00	10.00	15.00	15.00	15.00
	$\sigma[r_T^F]$	6.43	11.23	12.30	13.43	19.40	22.07	21.16	29.49	35.49
	$P(FR<1)$	21.72	32.85	34.26	22.76	30.30	32.55	23.95	30.53	33.62
	ES	3.56	6.95	7.69	7.30	11.19	12.88	11.26	16.26	19.63

Note: Expected returns $E[r_T^F]$ and returns volatilities $\sigma[r_T^F]$ are annualized percentage values. Shortfall probabilities $P(FR<1)$ and expected shortfalls ES are derived from closed form formulas presented in (18.21) and (18.23) and are expressed as percentage values. Nine different setups are studied. "ALM+" refers to the ALM objective function under complete market conditions. "ALM−" denotes the same objective function in incomplete markets, that is, without TIPS, and "AM SH" relates to a situation in which the investor chooses the weights following the myopic portfolio rule, assumes that $T=1$ year and ignores the presence of a liability. Low, Medium and High refer to ex ante fixed annualized expected returns on funding ratio of 5%, 10% and 15% respectively.

return on the funding ratio, namely 5%, 10% and 15%. Shortfall probabilities $P(FR<1)$ are simply derived from the relation $P(FR<1) = P(r^F<0)$, which under the assumption of Gaussian returns can also be written as

$$P(r^F < 0) = \Phi\left(-\frac{\mu^F}{\sqrt{\sigma^F}}\right) \qquad (18.21)$$

with Φ being the cumulative density function of the standard normal distribution. Expected shortfalls can, in fact, be derived in analytical form from the Black-Scholes formula as follows.[4] First, we can decompose the expression for the put price as

$$E\left[e^{-rT}\max(K-S_T,0)\right] = e^{-rT}KP(S_T<K) - e^{-rT}E\left(S_T 1_{\{S_T<K\}}\right)$$
$$= e^{-rT}K\Phi(-d_2) - S_0\Phi(-d_1) \qquad (18.22)$$

Second, we know that the expected shortfall ES can be written as

$$ES = 1 - E\left(S_T \mid S_T < K\right) = 1 - \frac{E\left(S_T 1_{\{S_T < K\}}\right)}{P(S_T < K)} \qquad (18.23)$$

Noting that μ^F and σ^F are annualized parameters and setting

$$S_T \equiv FR, \ S_0 \equiv 1, \ K \equiv 1, \ r \equiv \mu^F + \frac{1}{2}\sigma^F, \ T \equiv 1,$$

we obtain the expected annualized shortfalls from (18.22) and (18.23) as

$$ES = 1 - E\left(FR \mid FR < 1\right) = 1 - \frac{e^{\mu^F + \frac{1}{2}\sigma^F}\Phi(-d_1)}{\Phi(-d_2)} \qquad (18.24)$$

with

$$d_1 = \frac{\mu^F + \sigma^F}{\sqrt{\sigma^F}}; \qquad d_2 = \frac{\mu^F}{\sqrt{\sigma^F}}. \qquad (18.25)$$

Table 18.4 shows that for given expected funding ratio, the optimal allocation from the ALM sense dominates optimal allocations from an AM sense in terms of the risk perspective, and this holds whether risk is measured in terms of funding ratio volatility, expected shortfall or probability of a shortfall. This result is more pronounced for the more risk-averse investor, which is not surprising, given that an AM perspective cannot deliver a sound risk minimization strategy with respect to the liability benchmark. We also obtain that the effect is more pronounced for longer horizons, which is the typical case in a pension-related context. We confirm that ALM strategies in complete market environments (for example, when the inflation-linked bonds are included in the asset mix) strongly dominate the corresponding ALM strategies in the absence of a perfect liability-hedging instrument. For example, in case of a 25-year horizon and a high (15%) expected return target, the volatility of the funding ratio is 21.16% for the ALM strategy in complete markets, versus 29.49% in an incomplete market setting, and 35.49% for the AM strategy.

Table 18.5 gives the composition of the efficient portfolios for the three strategies ALM+, ALM− and AM SH, when the target expected funding ratio is low, high or medium. Overall, we find a substantial amount of leverage in some cases, an effect which is larger when a high expected funding ratio is targeted, implying a more aggressive strategy. When comparing the ALM− and AM SH allocations, we find that the allocation to stocks is smaller in ALM− than in AM SH for the short horizon $T = 1$ year. This is in line with the findings of Figure 18.2, which suggest that stocks have poor hedging properties against inflation on the short run, while having substantial volatility (see Figure 18.1). Overall, this makes them relatively undesirable in the liability-hedging portfolio. In contrast, when the horizon lengthens, the inflation-hedging properties of stock investment improve while the annualized volatility decreases, which makes the allocation to stocks higher in ALM− compared to AM SH. This effect is most visible for the longest horizon ($T = 25$ years) and the least risk-averse investor, for which the weight allocated to stocks is multiplied by three.

Table 18.5 Efficient portfolios (CPI indexed returns): allocations

Horizon (years)		Low			Medium			High		
		ALM+	ALM−	AM SH	ALM+	ALM−	AM SH	ALM+	ALM−	AM SH
1	Stocks	0.16	0.07	0.14	0.33	0.22	0.28	0.53	0.40	0.45
	Long bond	0.09	0.28	0.20	0.20	0.46	0.39	0.32	0.68	0.62
	Commodities	0.30	0.43	0.41	0.63	0.83	0.81	0.99	1.30	1.29
	Real estate	0.04	0.08	0.07	0.09	0.14	0.13	0.14	0.22	0.21
	TIPS	1.50	0.00	0.00	2.06	0.00	0.00	2.69	0.00	0.00
	T-Bills	−1.09	0.14	0.18	−2.30	−0.65	−0.62	−3.66	−1.59	−1.56
5	Stocks	0.25	0.17	0.14	0.52	0.44	0.28	0.84	0.76	0.47
	Long bond	−0.08	0.09	0.19	−0.18	0.07	0.39	−0.28	0.05	0.65
	Commodities	0.25	0.38	0.40	0.53	0.74	0.81	0.85	1.18	1.34
	Real estate	0.11	0.22	0.06	0.23	0.41	0.13	0.36	0.63	0.21
	TIPS	1.63	0.00	0.00	2.32	0.00	0.00	3.11	0.00	0.00
	T-Bills	−1.15	0.13	0.20	−2.43	−0.65	−0.61	−3.88	−1.62	−1.66
10	Stocks	0.32	0.26	0.14	0.67	0.61	0.28	1.07	1.04	0.47
	Long bond	−0.12	0.01	0.19	−0.25	−0.08	0.39	−0.40	−0.18	0.65
	Commodities	0.23	0.36	0.40	0.49	0.69	0.81	0.79	1.09	1.34
	Real estate	0.11	0.23	0.06	0.23	0.42	0.13	0.37	0.64	0.21
	TIPS	1.62	0.00	0.00	2.31	0.00	0.00	3.09	0.00	0.00
	T-Bills	−1.16	0.14	0.20	−2.46	−0.64	−0.61	−3.90	−1.60	−1.66
25	Stocks	0.43	0.42	0.14	0.91	0.92	0.28	1.43	1.52	0.47
	Long bond	−0.11	−0.03	0.19	−0.24	−0.13	0.39	−0.37	−0.25	0.65
	Commodities	0.22	0.32	0.40	0.45	0.62	0.81	0.71	0.98	1.34
	Real estate	0.11	0.23	0.06	0.23	0.41	0.13	0.37	0.63	0.22
	TIPS	1.61	0.00	0.00	2.27	0.00	0.00	3.00	0.00	0.00
	T-Bills	−1.26	0.06	0.20	−2.63	−0.82	−0.61	−4.14	−1.88	−1.68

Note: This table displays the optimal weights allocated to the various asset classes in different contexts. Low, Medium and High refer respectively to a target annualized expected return of 5%, 10% and 15%. "ALM+" refers to the complete market case, in which the investor chooses the weights according to Formula (18.14) and has access to TIPS as an asset class only in the hedging part of his or her portfolio, "ALM−" refers to the incomplete market case, in which the investor chooses the weights according to the same formula but has no access to TIPS, and "AM SH" refers to the case in which the investor chooses the weights following the myopic portfolio rule, assumes that $T = 1$ year and cannot trade in TIPS.

It should be noted again that these results are likely to underestimate the inflation-hedging properties of various asset classes, such as stocks for example, and quite different results would be obtained in the context of a more general model allowing for the presence of long-term co-integration relationships. Using a vector error correction model (VECM), Amenc et al. (2009) actually show that novel forms of investment solutions, including equities, commodities and real estate, in addition to inflation-linked securities, can be designed so as to decrease the cost of inflation insurance for long-horizon investors. As a result, it is important to emphasize that investing in inflation-linked instruments is neither the only nor necessarily the most cost-efficient manner to obtain protection with respect to inflation uncertainty. The capacity of the inflation-linked securities market is not sufficient to meet the collective demand of institutional and private investors. Furthermore, the OTC inflation derivatives market, which is used in institutional money management, is probably not a natural alternative to inflation-linked bonds for private investors. Additionally, real returns on inflation-protected securities, negatively impacted by the presence of a significant inflation risk premium, are typically very low, which implies that investing in inflation-linked securities, when feasible, is a costly option for pension hedging motives.

Overall, our results strongly suggest that failing to adopt an ALM approach to long-term investment decisions involves a strong opportunity cost. They also suggest that a focus on introducing investment vehicles that enjoy attractive liability-hedging properties in the menu of asset classes is of high relevance.

A second example with a real estate acquisition objective can be found in Amenc et al. (2009).

18.4   Conclusion

We have shown that a significant fraction of the complexity inherent to optimal asset allocation decisions in private wealth management can conveniently be addressed through the introduction of a single additional state variable, the value of the household liability portfolio, which accounts in a parsimonious and tractable way for investors' specific constraints and objectives. We have also presented a series of numerical illustrations suggesting that the model explained in this chapter could be applied in a variety of different situations typical to private wealth management problems.

Our analysis has important potential implications for the wealth management industry. It has indeed often been argued that the proximity to investors is the main *raison d'être* and a key source of competitive advantage for private wealth management. Building on this proximity, private bankers should be ideally placed to better account for their clients' specific liability constraints when engineering an investment solution for them. Most private bankers implicitly promote an ALM approach to wealth management. In particular, they claim to account for the investor's goals and constraints. The technical tools involved, however, are often nonexistent or ill-adapted. While the private client is routinely asked all kinds of questions regarding current situation, goals, preferences, constraints, and so forth, the resulting service and product offerings mostly boil down to a rather basic classification in terms of risk profiles. We have described a framework suggesting that asset-liability management is an essential improvement in private wealth management that allows private bankers to provide their clients investment solutions and asset allocation advice that truly meet their needs.

Broadly speaking, our analysis has shown that adopting an ALM perspective to private wealth management generates two main benefits. First, adopting an ALM approach has a direct impact on the selection of asset classes. In particular, it leads to a focus on liability-hedging properties of various asset classes, a focus that would, by definition, be absent from an asset-only perspective. Second, adopting an ALM approach leads to defining risk and return in relative, as opposed to absolute, terms, with the liability portfolio used as a benchmark or numeraire. This is a critical improvement over asset-only asset allocation models, which fail to recognize that changes to asset values have to be analyzed in comparison to changes in liability values. In other words, private investors do not have utility over terminal wealth per se, but instead over the purchasing power of terminal wealth expressed in terms of various investment or consumption goals and objectives, such as preparing for retirement or preparing for a real estate acquisition.

Our research can be extended in a number of directions. It would be desirable to incorporate the impact of taxes in the analysis of optimal asset allocation decisions. While tax optimization is arguably currently one of the key sources of added value in private wealth management, it is typically very challenging to account for the detailed features of tax regulations that significantly vary across countries in the context of a formal optimal allocation model, especially given that tax treatment can depend on trading behavior and portfolio turnover in a complex manner.[5] Other previously mentioned elements that are left for further research are the introduction of flexible contribution/withdrawal decisions and the extension of the asset allocation model to more general forms of state-dependent optimal allocation strategies. Finally, and perhaps more importantly, it would be interesting to try to cast the ALM approach to private wealth management in a context in which the investor has a behavioural objective. One challenge here is that recent advances in behavioural finance, while providing very useful insights into investors' behaviour, do not provide much guidance towards the design of a formal normative analysis of optimal asset allocation decisions. A possible approach would be capturing some of this complexity by introducing a set of suitably specified investor-dependent goals and constraints within the standard expected utility maximization paradigm.

Notes

Lionel Martellini is the author for correspondence. He can be reached at the following address: EDHEC-Risk Institute, 392 Promenade des Anglais, BP 3116, 06202 Nice Cedex 3, France; email: lionel.martellini@edhec.edu. We acknowledge financial support from ORTEC, the sponsor of the Research Chair in Asset-Liability Management in Private Wealth Management at EDHEC-Risk Institute. We also would like to thank Hens Steehouwer, as well as seminar participants at the EDHEC-ORTEC Geneva and Zurich seminars on ALM in PWM, for useful comments.

1. Using a constant maturity approach in modeling TIPS returns is consistent with various investment horizons if the real yield curve is flat.
2. Note that we omit the time-index t since we assume a stationary system.
3. With our choice of notation, the weights allocated to risky assets in the PSP and LHP portfolios have not been normalized and do not add up to 100%, with the remainder invested in cash. Hence the separation theorem we obtain is a three-funds, involving the PSP and the LHP, but also the risk-free asset.
4. One key difference is that probabilities are taken under the risk-adjusted measure in an option pricing context, while they are taken under the historical measure in the context of risk parameter estimation.
5. Moreover, most industrialized and developing countries have tax incentives to encourage retirement savings. Examples of countries that offer tax-advantaged savings accounts include Australia, Canada, Germany, Italy, the Netherlands, and the United Kingdom, and most of these countries permit tax-deductible contributions.

References

Amenc, N., Martellini, L., Milhau, V. and Ziemann, V. Asset-liability management in private wealth management. *The Journal of Portfolio Management*, 36(1):100–120, 2009.

Amenc, N., Martellini, L. and Ziemann, V. Inflation-hedging properties of real assets and implications for asset-liability decisions. *The Journal of Portfolio Management*, 35(4): 94–110, 2009.

Berkelaar, A. and Kouwenberg, R. A Liability-Relative Drawdown Approach to Pension Asset Liability Management. *Journal of Asset Management: Special Issue on ALM*, this volume, 2010.

Bodie, Z., Merton, R. C. and Samuelson, W. Labor Supply Flexibility and Portfolio Choice in a Life Cycle Model. *Journal of Economic Dynamics and Control*, 16:427–449, 1992.

Boudoukh, J. and Richardson, M. Stock Returns and Inflation: A Long-Horizon Perspective. *The American Economic Review*, 83(5):1346–1355, 1993.

Brennan, M. J., Schwartz, E. S. and Lagnado, R. Strategic Asset Allocation. *Journal of Economic Dynamics and Control*, 21(8/9):1377–1403, 1997.

Brennan, M. J. and Xia, Y. Dynamic Asset Allocation under Inflation. *Journal of Finance*, 57(3):1201–1238, 2002.

Campbell, J. Y. Intertemporal asset pricing without consumption data. *The American Economic Review*, 83(3):487–512, 1993.

Campbell, J. Y. Understanding risk and return. *Journal of Political Economy*, 104(2): 298–345, 1996.

Campbell, J. Y., Chan, Y. L. and Viceira, L. M. A Multivariate Model of Strategic Asset Allocation. *Journal of Financial Economics*, 67(1):41–80, 2003.

Campbell, J. Y. and Shiller, R. J. Stock prices, earnings, and expected dividends. *Journal of Finance*, 43(3):661–676, 1988.

Campbell, J. Y. and Viceira, L. M. Consumption and Portfolio Decisions When Expected Returns are Time Varying. *Quarterly Journal of Economics*, 114(2):433–495, 1999.

Campbell, J. Y. and Viceira, L. M. *Strategic Asset Allocation: Portfolio Choice for Long-Term Investors*, Oxford University Press Inc, New York, 2002.

Campbell, J. Y. and Viceira, L. M. Who Should Buy Long-Term Bonds? *American Economic Review*, 91(1):99–127, 2001.

Campbell, J. Y. and Viceira, L. M. The Term Structure of the Risk-Return Trade-Off. *Financial Analysts Journal*, 1(1):34–44, 2005.

Cocco, J. F., Gomes, F. J. and Maenhout, P. J. Consumption and Portfolio Choice over the Life Cycle. *Review of Financial Studies*, 18(2):491–533, 2005.

Fama, E. F. Stock Returns, Real Activity, Inflation, and Money. *The American Economic Review*, 71(4):545–565, 1981.

Fama, E. F. and Schwert, G. W. Asset Returns and Inflation. *Journal of Financial Economics*, 5(2):115–146, 1977.

Gultekin, N. B. Stock Market Returns and Inflation Forecasts. *Journal of Finance*, 38(3):663–673, 1983.

Hodrick, R. J. Dividend Yields and Expected Stock Returns: Alternative Procedures for Inference and Measurement. *Review of Financial studies*, 5(3):357, 1992.

Hoevenaars, R. P. M. M., Molenaar, R. D. J., Schotman, P. C. and Steenkamp, T. B. M. Strategic Asset Allocation with Liabilities: Beyond Stocks and Bonds. *Journal of Economic Dynamics and Control*, 32(9):2939–2970, 2008.

Kaul, G. Stock Returns and Inflation: The Role of the Monetary Sector. *Journal of Financial Economics*, 18(2):253–276, 1987.

Kim, T. S. and Omberg, E. Dynamic Nonmyopic Portfolio Behavior. *Review of Financial Studies*, 9(1):141–161, 1996.

Kothari, S. P. and Shanken, J. Asset Allocation with Inflation-Protected Bonds. *Financial Analysts Journal*, 60(1):54–70, 2004.

Lynch, A. W. Portfolio Choice and Equity Characteristics: Characterizing the Hedging Demands Induced By Return Predictability. *Journal of Financial Economics*, 62(1): 67–130, 2001.

Merton, R. Optimal Portfolio and Consumption Rules in a Continuous-Time Model. *Journal of Economic Theory*, 3(4):373–413, 1971.

Merton, R. C. Lifetime Portfolio Selection under Uncertainty: The Continuous-Time Case. *Review of Economics and Statistics*, 51(3):247–257, 1969.

Merton, Robert. *Continuous-Time Finance*, Blackwell Publishing Ltd, Oxford, 649–675, 1993.

Rudolf, M. and Ziemba, W. T. Intertemporal Surplus Management. *Journal of Economic Dynamics and Control*, 28(5):975–990, 2004.

Schotman, P. C. and Schweitzer, M. Horizon sensitivity of the inflation hedge of stocks. *Journal of Empirical Finance*, 7(3/4):301–315, 2000.

Stock, J. H. and Watson, M. W. *Forecasting Inflation. Journal of Monetary Economics*, 44(2):293–335, 1999.

Sundaresan, S. and Zapatero, F. Valuation, Optimal Asset Allocation and Retirement Incentives of Pension Plans. *Review of Financial Studies*, 10(3):631–660, 1997.

Viceira, L. M. Optimal Portfolio Choice for Long-Horizon Investors with Nontradable Labor Income. *Journal of Finance*, 56(2):433–470, 2001.

Viceira, L. M. and Field, S. *Life-Cycle Funds*. 2008, chapter 5 in 'Overcoming the Saving Slump: How to Increase the Effectiveness of Financial Education and Saving Programs', edited by Annamaria Lusardi and published by University of Chicago Press.

Wachter, J. A. Risk Aversion and Allocation to Long-Term Bonds. *Journal of Economic Theory*, 112(2):325–333, 2003.

19
Backtesting Short-Term Treasury Management Strategies Based on Multi-Stage Stochastic Programming

Robert Ferstl and Alexander Weissensteiner

19.1 Introduction

Baumol (1952) applies well-known results from inventory control problems to treasury management, in which an individual facing a transaction demand for cash chooses to hold his liquid funds partly in cash and partly in bonds. An analytical solution is derived under very restrictive assumptions. To focus on more practically relevant settings, dynamic stochastic programming techniques started to make their way into applications in quantitative asset management. Early approaches using linear programming for financial planning tasks with multiple assets and stages are proposed by Charnes *et al* (1959); Chambers and Charnes (1961); Cohen and Hammer (1967). These models still use a deterministic framework. Since then many extensions were proposed. Dempster *et al* (2009) give an extensive overview of the state-of-the-art methods for financial planning under uncertainty.

Our work emanates from a literature stream that deals with bond portfolio management problems using scenario trees generated from an interest rate model. Let us briefly discuss the most important contributions. Bradley and Crane (1972) present a multi-stage decision model for bond portfolio management in discrete time. They develop a decomposition algorithm for linear programming, which allows an efficient, recursive solution of sub-problems in the general portfolio model. Optimal global solutions are found by iterating between the sub-problems and the master program. Mulvey and Zenios (1994) and Golub *et al* (1995) propose to include interest rate risk scenarios by using the no-arbitrage Black–Derman–Toy (BDT) model (Black *et al*, 1990), which can be calibrated to the current term structure of interest rates and their volatilities. They use an option-adjusted spread to equate the market price of interest-sensitive securities with the fair price obtained by applying the expectation hypothesis. Their objective function maximises the expected utility of final wealth.

Dupacova (2000) analyses the stability and sensitivity of the bond portfolio management problem for small changes in the coefficients. The stability results given in various proofs are valid for the optimal value and also for the first-stage solutions. This theoretical paper is complemented by simulation studies in Bertocchi *et al* (2000), who quantify the behaviour of the model with respect to random movements in the yield curve. One of their conclusions is that stability in the optimal solution can be achieved only for a very small magnitude of perturbations in the short rate.

Dupacova and Bertocchi (2001) solve a bond portfolio management problem with a data set of Italian government coupon bonds in the BDT context. They provide simulation results for different scenarios that are sampled from the fitted BDT lattice. Liabilities are not considered in this context. Bertocchi *et al* (2006) analyse further the sensitivity of the solution of the resulting large-scale mathematical program with respect to the model inputs and to different interval lengths between the two decision stages.

Although there is much literature on long-term asset liability management (ALM) for pension funds and insurance companies (see for example Kusy and Ziemba, 1986; Gondzio and Kouwenberg, 2001; Dempster *et al*, 2003), only a few papers consider short-term cash or treasury management problems. Volosov *et al* (2005) propose a stochastic programming model to compute currency hedging strategies and provide a backtest with a rolling horizon. Castro (2007) implements a cash management model for automatic teller machines and for compensation of credit card transactions.

In Ferstl and Weissensteiner (2010), we use the standard ALM setting based on the BDT model (in line with the papers above). As a contribution to the existing literature, we extend the bond portfolio management strategy in several ways to make it applicable for short- to medium-term treasury management problems. First, after using the interest rate model under the risk-neutral measure $\mathbb{Q}$ for fair bond pricing, we explicitly estimate the market price of risk (MPR) from historical data to switch to the objective measure $\mathbb{P}$ for the purpose of portfolio optimisation. Most of the current literature ignores this point, implicitly assuming a constant MPR equal to zero. This contradicts recent findings in the finance literature (see for example Stanton, 1997; Bernaschi *et al*, 2007), which stress that investors also require a compensation for bearing interest rate risk. Although Jobst and Zenios (2005), Jobst *et al* (2006) and Dempster *et al* (2007) mention the importance of this change of measure, Ferstl and Weissensteiner (2010) is the first paper to use an empirically estimated MPR to modify the conditional probabilities in the scenario tree. Second, in contrast to the current literature, which uses no-arbitrage interest rate models for scenario generation, we also allow for the inclusion of an equity investment. This gives the company in our treasury management problem the opportunity to reach a higher expected final wealth by taking additional risk. A large domestic index is used to represent the equity investment. We extend the scenario tree to match the first four moments of the corresponding return distribution, while taking into account the empirically observed correlation between interest rates and equity returns.

This article complements the methodological work in Ferstl and Weissensteiner (2010) by an *out-of-sample* backtest. As is well known in finance, many different theoretically sound algorithms give questionable results when applied in practice using real market data: strong sensitivity to the input parameters and – as a consequence – high portfolio turnover, heavily leveraged or corner solutions in many assets and poor *out-of-sample* performance (see for example Michaud, 2003). Therefore, to study the behaviour of our approach, we base our backtest on historical data to calibrate the no-arbitrage interest rate model to simulate equity returns, to derive the investment policy and to evaluate ex post the performance using real (out-of-sample) market returns. Similar to Bertocchi *et al* (2006), we analyse the stability of the first-stage solutions under realistic assumptions for the input parameters. In contrast to the earlier approach of sampling from the scenario tree, we use the full binomial lattice of the BDT model to rule out arbitrage opportunities and account for the empirically estimated MPR. Sensitivity tests are performed for the major input parameters: parallel shifts in the yield curve, changes in the equity returns and modification of the cash flows. We compare the performance to various alternative strategies. Similar to Topaloglou *et al* (2008), who optimise Conditional Value at Risk (*CVaR*) for an international bond portfolio in a multi-stage context, we also find a well diversified and stable asset allocation. Further, our stochastic linear programming (SLP) SLP strategy realises an attractive performance (in terms of aggregate risk measures) compared to the naive and myopic alternatives. Sensitivities to changes in the input parameters are rather low and follow economic intuition.

The plan of the article is as follows. The next section defines the multi-stage stochastic programming model for cash management and the subsequent section describes the scenario generation. In the section after that, we explain the set-up of the backtest, the alternative strategies and the data set. The penultimate section discusses the numerical results and the final section concludes the article.

19.2 Model

We consider the cash management model introduced in Ferstl and Weissensteiner (2010), which is formulated as a multi-stage stochastic linear program with recourse. The asset allocation decisions are taken at discrete time stages $t = 0,..., T$, where the investor can choose between a riskless asset (cash), J different bonds and an equity investment. The uncertainty in the model is represented with scenarios $s = 0,..., S$. We construct a scenario tree consisting of the stochastic interest rates r_t^s and equity returns r_{et}^s. The interest rate scenarios are based on the one-factor interest rate model proposed by Black *et al* (1990), which is calibrated to the current term structure of interest rates and their volatilities. Furthermore, we perform an estimation of the MPR and correct the scenario tree as proposed in Ferstl and Weissensteiner (2010). A detailed description of the scenario generation procedure follows in the section 'Scenario generation'.

The variables ζ_{jt}^s, ζ_{et}^s denote the purchasing prices and ξ_{jt}^s, ξ_{et}^s the selling prices of the bonds and the equity investment. Transaction costs tc_b, tc_e are included by adding/subtracting them from the fair bond prices P_{jt}^s and the fair equity prices P_{et}^s. The maximum weight of equity holdings u_e in the total portfolio (excluding cash) can be restricted to a certain percentage amount. The holdings of bonds and equities are indicated by the variable z, whereas purchases and sales are given by the non-negative decision variables x and y.

In the objective function, we minimise *CVaR* of final wealth. The linear programming formulation follows Pflug (2000) and Rockafellar and Uryasev (2000, 2002):

$$\phi + \frac{1}{1-\alpha} \sum_{s=1}^{S} p^s \psi_T^{+s} \rightarrow \min \tag{19.1}$$

subject to:

$$y_{j0} + z_{j0} = b_j + x_{j0} \quad \forall j \tag{19.2}$$

$$y_{e0} + z_{e0} = b_e + x_{e0} \tag{19.3}$$

$$y_0^+ + \sum_{j=1}^{J} \zeta_{j0} x_{j0} + \zeta_{e0} x_{e0} = b_0 + \sum_{j=1}^{J} \xi_{j0} y_{j0} + \xi_{e0} y_{e0} \tag{19.4}$$

$$z_{jt}^s + y_{jt}^s = z_{j,t-1}^s + x_{jt}^s \quad \forall j, s, \quad 1 \leq t \leq T \tag{19.5}$$

$$z_{et}^s + y_{et}^s = z_{e,t-1}^s + x_{et}^s \quad \forall s, \quad 1 \leq t \leq T \tag{19.6}$$

$$\sum_{j=1}^{J} \xi_{jt}^s y_{jt}^s + \xi_{et}^s y_{et}^s + \sum_{j=1}^{J} f_{jt}^s z_{j,t-1}^s + (1 - \delta_1 + r_{t-1}^s) y_{t-1}^{+s} + y_t^{-s}$$

$$= L_t^s + \sum_{j=1}^{J} \zeta_{jt}^s x_{jt}^s + \zeta_{et}^s x_{et}^s + (1 + \delta_2 + r_{t-1}^s) y_{t-1}^{-s} + y_t^{+s} \quad \forall j, s, \quad 1 \leq t \leq T \tag{19.7}$$

$$\left(z_{e0} P_{e0} + \sum_{j=1}^{J} z_{j0} P_{j0} \right) u_e \geq z_{e0} P_{e0} \tag{19.8}$$

$$\left(z_{et}^s P_{et}^s + \sum_{j=1}^{J} z_{jt}^s P_{jt}^s \right) u_e \geq z_{et}^s P_{et}^s \quad \forall j, s, \quad 1 \leq t \leq T \tag{19.9}$$

$$y_T^s = y_T^{+s} - y_T^{-s} \quad \forall s \tag{19.10}$$

$$\psi_T^{+s} = -y_T^s - \phi + \psi_T^{-s} \quad \forall s \quad \sum_{s=1}^{S} p^s y_T^s \geq \beta \tag{19.11}$$

$$x_{jt}^s = x_{jt}^{s'}, \quad x_{et}^s = x_{et}^{s'}, \quad y_{jt}^s = y_{jt}^{s'}, \quad y_{et}^s = y_{et}^{s'}, \quad \forall j, s \quad 0 \leq t \leq T - 1, \tag{19.12}$$

$$\forall s, \quad s' \text{ with identical past up to time } t \tag{19.13}$$

Although the Value at Risk (*VaR*) of the optimal solution is represented by ϕ, the second term accounts for the expected shortfall below the *VaR* for a given confidence level α. The probabilities of the different scenarios are given by p^s.

The first-stage decision variables have to fulfil the inventory equations (19.2)–(19.3), forcing the final holdings of each asset to equal the initial holdings plus purchases minus sales. This must also hold in monetary terms leading to the first-stage budget equation in (19.4). The variable y_0^+ denotes the lending amount after the first-stage decision, where no borrowing is allowed. δ_1 is the spread subtracted from the riskless interest rate for a positive bank account balance and δ_2 denotes the spread added for borrowing cash. Multiplying the quantities of asset purchases and sales by their corresponding prices yields the respective turnover. Linear transaction costs tc_b and tc_e are included for purchases and sales of bonds and stocks.

Depending on the revealed uncertainty, optimal second-stage decisions are calculated. Although these variables have to fulfil the inventory equations (19.5)–(19.6), the budget equation (19.4) is extended for interest rate payments on the cash account, coupon payments on bond holdings denoted by f_{jt}^s and external cash outflows or inflows L_t^s. The liabilities are negative for net cash inflows. A company is typically facing stochastic cash flows, which are influenced by various factors, for example development of exchange rates, changes in customer demands, payment delays. In such a case, the evolution of the stochastic L_t^s should be included in the scenario generation (see section 'Backtest'). However, to focus on the main purpose of our article, that is backtesting the impact of the change of measure and comparing the results to alternative strategies, we assume deterministic cash flows in our numerical example.

Constraint (19.7) states that coupons are paid exactly at the discrete decision stages. We assume that coupon payments between two decision stages are reinvested at the current (scenario-dependent) interest rate (minus the spread δ_1) until the next stage. The maximum weight of equities in the portfolio holdings for first- and second-stage decision variables is restricted by (19.8)–(19.9). On the left-hand side, the market value of the portfolio (excluding cash) is multiplied by the maximum weight of total portfolio holdings u_e. This must be greater than or equal to the market value of the equity investment at each stage on the right-hand side. Given the final balance on the bank account at stage T in (19.10), the portfolio shortfall in excess of VaR[1] used in the objective function is $\psi_T^{+s} = \max[0, -y_T^s - \phi]$. To determine the value of the maximum operator in the linear programming formulation, we introduce two non-negative auxiliary variables ψ_T^{+s} and ψ_T^{-s}. The portfolio shortfall in excess of *VaR* in (19.11) is used in the objective function (19.1) for the calculation of *CVaR*. We define β as a lower bound on the portfolio's expected wealth at the final stage T (see (19.12)). In the section 'Backtest', we explain how we set β in each time step of the backtest application. Further, the so-called 'non-anticipativity constraints' are imposed in (19.13) to guarantee that a decision made at a specific node is identical for all scenarios leaving that node. The stochastic optimisation problem in (19.1)–(19.13) is a multi-stage stochastic linear program with recourse, using a split variable formulation of the deterministic equivalent.

19.3   Scenario generation

In this section, we give an overview on the scenario generation method proposed in Ferstl and Weissensteiner (2010). The four-step procedure results in a scenario tree that captures the uncertainty in interest rates and equity returns under the objective measure.

19.3.1   Calibration of the no-arbitrage interest rate model

We calibrate the Black *et al* (1990) model to the zero-coupon yield curve and the term structure of volatilities observed on the market by the implied Black volatilities of caplets with different expiry dates. The resulting binomial tree of future interest rates allows for the pricing of all available coupon and zero-coupon bonds. The interest rate r_t^s is valid for the period t to $t+1$. The set N_t^s consists of the immediate successor nodes, where $\nu \in N_t^s$ in stage $t+1$ of the node represented by scenario s at stage t. $\mathbf{r}(N_t^s)$ is the set of interest rates $r_t^{s\nu}$ for the subsequent stage with conditional probability $q_t^{s\nu} > 0$ under the martingale measure $\mathbb{Q}$ and $p_t^{s\nu} > 0$ under the objective measure $\mathbb{P}$, with $\nu \in N_t^s$.

The scenario-dependent fair price of any bond P_{jt}^s is calculated as the risk-neutral expectation using backward induction on the tree (see (19.14)). As the probabilities $q_t^{s\nu}$ for conditional successor interest rates of r_t^s are given under the martingale measure $\mathbb{Q}$, the expected value (taking conditional coupon payments $f_{jt}^{s\nu}$ and future bond prices $P_{jt}^{s\nu}$ into account) can be discounted by the risk-free spot rate r_t^s.

$$P_{jt}^s = \left(1 + r_t^s\right)^{-1} \sum_{\nu \in N_s^t} q_t^{s\nu} \left(f_{jt}^{s\nu} + P_{jt}^{s\nu}\right) \tag{19.14}$$

Figure 19.1 shows an example of the first branch of the calibrated interest rate tree along with the fair prices of two bonds used in the backtest in the section 'Backtest'.

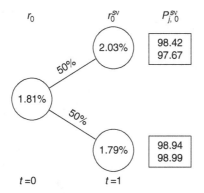

Figure 19.1   Sample scenario tree under the martingale measure $\mathbb{Q}$

In addition to coupon bonds, the Black *et al* (1990) model allows for the pricing of other interest rate-sensitive securities such as options on Treasury bonds or interest rate derivatives using the backward induction algorithm (see (19.14)). However, the BDT one-factor model is not appropriate for products in which the payoff depends on the joint distribution of interest rates with different maturities, for example swaptions. To price derivatives that depend on the short rate and some other factors, the joint evolution has to be modelled within the scenario tree.

19.3.2   MPR estimation

In the previous step, we used the short rate process under the martingale measure $\mathbb{Q}$ for fair bond pricing. As we have to solve the portfolio optimisation problem in (19.1)–(19.13) under the physical measure $\mathbb{P}$ (that is, the real-world probabilities), we must change the probability measure from $\mathbb{Q}$ to $\mathbb{P}$ accounting for the so-called *market price of risk*.

MPR λ represents the excess return over the riskless rate per unit volatility. Following Stanton (1997), we use a kernel-density estimation to calculate it as a function of the current level of the short rate r_t giving:

$$\lambda(r_t) = \frac{\mathbb{E}_t^{\mathbb{P}}\left[R^{(i)}\right] - r_t}{\sigma^{(i)}(r_t)},$$

where $\mathbb{E}_t^{\mathbb{P}}[R^{(i)}]$ and $\sigma^{(i)}(r_t)$ denote the percentage quantities for the drift and the volatility of bond i.[2]

The resulting MPR is time-homogeneous and can be used for any one-factor interest rate model without any parametric assumptions on the form of the

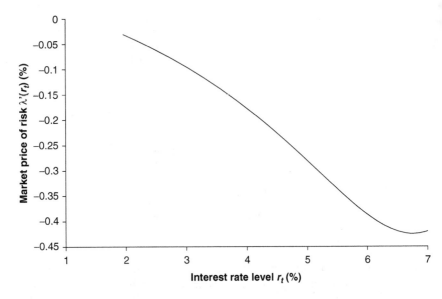

Figure 19.2   Estimated market price of interest rate risk

drift and the diffusion. Stanton (1997) defines the approximated absolute excess return after removing the scaling for volatility by:

$$\lambda'(r_t) = \frac{\sigma(r_t)}{\Delta(\sigma^{(1)}(r_t) - \sigma^{(2)}(r_t))} \times \mathbb{E}_t^{\mathbb{P}}\left[R_{t,t+\Delta}^{(1)} - R_{t,t+\Delta}^{(2)} \right] + \mathcal{O}(\Delta). \tag{19.15}$$

Figure 19.2 shows the function for the MPR used in the backtest, which we estimated from a data set of daily, 3-month and 6-month EURIBOR/FIBOR rates. Note that MPR is clearly different from zero and negative values, which indicate a positive premium for taking interest rate risk.

19.3.3   Change of measure

The third step in our scenario generation procedure involves changing the risk-neutral probabilities q_t^{sv} to account for the estimated MPR and to simulate equity returns. As described above, the BDT interest rate model represents the potential evolution of future spot rates by a recombining binomial tree, in which the probabilities of both successor nodes equal 50 per cent (see Figure 19.1). For the purpose of portfolio optimisation, we use the estimated MPR to switch

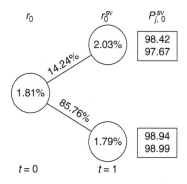

r_0 r_0^{sv} $P_{j,0}^{sv}$

2.03%

| 98.42 |
| 97.67 |

14.24%

1.81%

85.76%

1.79%

| 98.94 |
| 98.99 |

$t = 0$ $t = 1$

Figure 19.3   Sample scenario tree under the objective measure $\mathbb{P}$

to the objective measure $\mathbb{P}$ by modifying the conditional probabilities of the successor nodes to p_t^{sv} such that the following equation holds:

$$\mathbb{E}^{\mathbb{Q}}(\mathbf{r}_t^{sv}) + \lambda'(r_t^{s}) = \mathbb{E}^{\mathbb{P}}(\mathbf{r}_t^{sv}). \tag{19.16}$$

The probability measure is changed in such a way that the expectation of the interest rate under $\mathbb{P}$ is equal to the expectation under $\mathbb{Q}$ plus the expected excess return from (19.15). The fair bond prices calculated from the calibrated interest rate tree in Figure 19.1 are unaffected by this change of measure. Therefore, we modify only the probabilities of the interest and price scenarios, whereas r_0^{sv}, $P_{1,0}^{sv}$ and $P_{2,0}^{sv}$ remain the same (see also Figure 19.3).

19.3.4   Equity return generation

Finally, we extend the scenario tree to allow for the second source of uncertainty in our model, that is the evolution of equity returns. They are characterised by the first four moments of their distribution and correlation with the spot rate. The binomial structure of the scenario tree used to model the interest rate uncertainty leads to a lack of degrees of freedom, making it impossible to match all four moments of the equity return distribution. To resolve this shortcoming, we duplicate the successor nodes of each unique predecessor node in the original scenario tree, so that the branching factor is increased to four. We use a nonlinear optimiser to change the equity returns r_{e0}^{sv} and the probabilities p_0^{sv} in Figure 19.4 in such a way that they match the moments of the empirical equity return distribution and the correlation with the spot rate. Simultaneously, we force the probabilities of the duplicated successor nodes (that is the first two and the last two nodes in Figure 19.4) to sum up to the original probabilities in Figure 19.3.

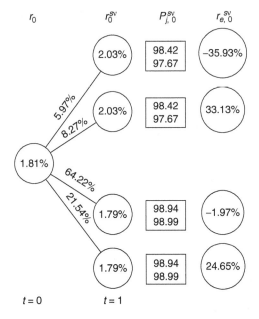

Figure 19.4   Sample scenario tree including simulated equity returns

We apply the procedure proposed by Klaassen (2002) to generate equity returns in such a way that arbitrage opportunities are ruled out, as these would be exploited by the optimisation algorithm.

19.4   Backtest

It is well known from the literature that not all theoretical concepts for asset allocation decisions are well suited for their practical out-of-sample implementation. For example, the classical Markowitz mean-variance optimisation may lead to large short positions in many assets when no bounds are imposed on the problem. When constraints rule out short positions, the models often prescribe 'corner' solutions with zero weights in many assets. Furthermore, the result is highly sensitive to small changes in the input parameters, leading to large portfolio turnovers when applying this concept repeatedly over time. These limitations have (a) contributed to a lack of acceptance of this model by practitioners and (b) strengthened – as a consequence – the efforts in academia to overcome these drawbacks (see for example Michaud, 2003). For these reasons, we perform a backtest of our dynamic stochastic optimisation model based on a real market data set from 1999 to 2008. This includes an analysis of the evolution of the asset allocation under different market constellations and sensitivity tests for changes in the major input parameters. The performance of our model is compared to several alternative strategies.

19.4.1 Test setting

We consider a company that updates its business plan, that is the projected cash in- and outflows $L_{t+\tau}$ for the next 2.5 years, using a rolling planning horizon of 6 months. Repeatedly solving the stochastic optimisation problem in (19.1)–(19.13) leads to a sequence of first-stage asset allocations (see Figure 19.5).

The firm can invest in different (coupon bearing) bonds j and in a broad equity index (that is the German DAX). As proposed in Dempster *et al* (2003), the model is re-calibrated and re-solved on each such 'planning update', taking into account real market returns on initial holdings in cash and assets. We parametrise the lower bound on the portfolio's expected value at the end of the planning horizon β in (19.12) by:

$$\beta = (MP_t - PVL_t)(1 + r_{t,T} + \delta_3)^T, \qquad (19.17)$$

where MP_t is the market value of the portfolio at stage t, that is including the value of the cash account plus interest rates received/paid, the market value of the asset holdings, the cash flows generated by the bonds and the external in- and outflows indicated by $L_{t+\tau}$; PVL_t is the present value of all future in- and outflows $L_{t+\tau}$ with $\tau \in \{0.5, 1,..., 2.5\}$ using the corresponding spot rates $r_{t,t+\tau}$ at stage t;[3] and δ_3 is a required surplus over the risk-free spot rate, defining the risk aversion of the company. If δ_3 is set equal to zero, then β simply corresponds to the accumulated wealth calculated with the spot rate for the planning horizon.

The starting date of the backtest is 4 January 1999 with an initial cash endowment $b_0 = 100$. No bonds and equities are held at this date, so that $b_j = 0$ $\forall j$ and $b_e = 0$. The company anticipates the external cash in- and outflows $L_{t+\tau}$

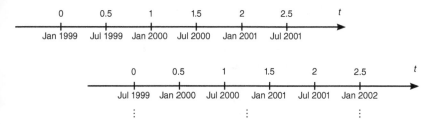

Figure 19.5 Overview of backtest methodology

as shown in Table 19.1. The cash flows used for the asset allocation on January 1999 are indicated by the first row. Six months later, on 1 July 1999, the first cash outflow with an amount of eight is paid, and all other future cash flows shift – as expected – one period to the left. The last value in the second row is the new unanticipated information arriving before updating the business plan. We set this new value by convention equal to the cash flow just paid/ received.

A branching factor of four and the five time intervals (6 month each) leads to a tree with $1024 \, (= 4^5)$ scenarios. The critical probability level α is set to 95 per cent. An example of the corresponding market data to calibrate the scenario tree is given in Table 19.2. At each rebalancing stage, we re-estimate the spot rate curve, the term structure of caplet volatilities and the higher moments of the equity returns. To calculate volatility, skewness and kurtosis, we use a 10-year rolling window.

The expected equity return follows the capital asset pricing model:

$$\mathbb{E}^{\mathbb{P}}(\mathbf{r}_{e,t}^{s\nu}) = r_t^s + \left(\mathbb{E}^{\mathbb{P}}(\mathbf{r}_{M,t}^{s\nu}) - r_t^s \right) \times \frac{\sigma_{M,e}}{\sigma_M^2}, \tag{19.18}$$

where the expected return of the equity investment under the physical measure is given by the (scenario-dependent) risk-free rate plus the risk premium (or

Table 19.1 Evolution of liabilities

Rebalancing date	Liabilities $L_{t+\tau}$				
	0.5	1	1.5	2	2.5
Jan 1999	8	19	−22	20	−20
Jul 1999	19	−22	20	−20	8
Jan 2000	−22	20	−20	8	19
⋮		⋮			

Table 19.2 Market data on 4 January 1999

	Term structure		Equities (German DAX)	
τ	Spot rates (%)	Caplet volatilities (%)		
0.5	3.20	20.00	Excess return % p.a.	4.80
1	3.17	21.07	Volatility % p.a.	23.17
1.5	3.18	22.13	Skewness	−0.08
2	3.20	22.40	Kurtosis	2.70
2.5	3.24	23.00	Correlation with r	−0.01

expected excess return) of the market portfolio ($\mathbb{E}^{\mathbb{P}}(\mathbf{r}_{M,t}^{s\nu})-r_t^s$) weighted by $\sigma_{M,e}/\sigma_M^2$ (the so-called 'beta' of the equity e with the market portfolio M). This fraction is set equal to one because our broad equity index is a proxy for the market portfolio. Further, we assume that the expected excess return is constant and equal to the historical outperformance of the German DAX index over the German bond index (REX 01 Yr) for the 20-year period between 1 January 1979 and the starting date of our optimisation model on 1 January 1999, that is equal to 4.80 per cent p.a. in Table 19.2.

Therefore, the expected equity return of immediate successor nodes under the real-world probability measure $\mathbb{P}$ is set equal to the (time-scaled) risk premium plus the scenario-dependent risk-free rate of the predecessor node (see (19.18)). In this way, we can guarantee that in states of the world with high nominal interest rates, high equity returns can also be expected, and vice versa. Further, the *ex ante* expected return of equities is always positive and above the risk-free rate, that is investors receive a premium to bear market risks.

In addition to the first four moments, a correlation between equity returns and interest rates is required to generate equity scenarios as illustrated in the section 'Backtest'. We set this parameter equal to the long-run correlation between the 3-month EURIBOR/FIBOR rate and DAX, that is equal to -0.01 in Table 19.2. It is well known that correlations change over time, not only in size but also in sign, and that the expectations on these are judgmental (see Høyland and Wallace, 2007). Therefore, real-world applications use scenario-dependent correlation matrices to model regime shifts (see for example, Geyer and Ziemba, 2008).

The transaction costs included in the purchasing and selling prices are $tc_b = 0.40$ per cent for bonds and $tc_e = 0.50$ per cent for equities.[4] Cash can be invested with a spread of $\delta_1 = 0.30$ per cent and borrowed with a spread of $\delta_2 = 0.60$ per cent. Owing to these costs for our company, we set the target in a prudent way by choosing $\delta_3 = -0.15$ per cent (which is half of δ_1).

At the beginning, the company can choose to invest money, aside from the equity index, in two bonds with maturities of 1.5 and 2.5 years, as indicated in Table 19.3. Their prices are uncertain and depend on the evolution of the future interest rates (see section 'Scenario generation'). As the time to maturity of the bonds becomes shorter when moving forward in time, we can also take

Table 19.3 Available bonds on 4 January 1999

Bonds	Coupon (%)	Maturity	Coupon frequency
Bond 1	5.0	1 Jul 2000	Semi-annually
Bond 2	0.0	1 Jul 2001	Annually

into account the so-called 'pull to par' effect. Whenever a bond expires, we replace it with a new bond having the same characteristics (coupon, coupon frequency and time to maturity) as the original ones in Table 19.3.

To study the impact of the changing market data and cash flows, we decided to solve the problem without restricting the maximum weight in the portfolio holdings by (19.8) and (19.9).

19.4.2   Data for scenario generation

To calibrate the scenario tree, we use daily data of the EUR swap term structure and the volatility curve of at-the-money EUR interest rate caps from Thomson Datastream. We calculate the spot rate curve from the swap rates by bootstrapping. With these spot rates, we can compute forward rates and, as the price of a cap is the sum of the prices of the individual caplets, we can use the Black market formula (Black, 1976) to strip the volatility term structure for caplets from the volatility term structure of caps (see Brigo and Mercurio, 2006). These caplet volatilities, also known as spot volatilities, are normally hump shaped with a peak at about 2–3 years. The results are shown in Figure 19.6.

As described in (Rebonato, 2004, p. 677), we find two main regimes for the evolution of the term structure of volatilities: the 'normal' and the 'excited' shapes. When the first regime prevails, the overall structural features tend to be very constant over time; whereas for the second regime, the uncertainty about the short end of the yield curve can dramatically increase. By using these data,

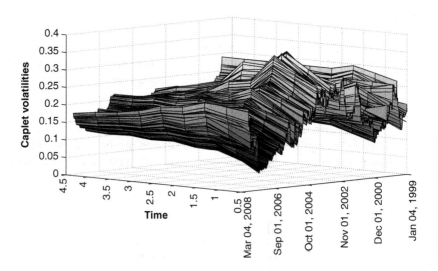

Figure 19.6   Term structure of caplet volatilities (from 1999 to 2008)

we are able to include the 'correct' (market) expectation of the term structure of volatilities in our scenario tree following the algorithm by Black *et al* (1990) (see section 'Scenario generation').

19.4.3 Alternative strategies

To compare the results of the proposed cash management model, we implement two alternative strategies: a pure cash investment and a 'duration matching' approach. In the first case, all wealth is invested in the interest-bearing bank account. The uncertainty is only given by the evolution of the short rate. In the second case, we calculate the dollar duration of the liabilities $L_{t+\tau}$ in the next 2.5 years. As we define cash outflows with a positive sign, a positive (negative) dollar duration indicates that increasing interest rates reduce (increase) the present value of our cash flows, and vice versa. When short selling assets is not allowed, a bond investment can be used to hedge against the risk of a falling term structure when the dollar duration of the cash flow is negative. To allow for a more meaningful comparison between this approach (duration matching) and the SLP results, in terms of aggregate risk measures, we also invest a constant fraction of the wealth in the equity. This is set to 5.67 per cent, that is the mean equity allocation in our SLP strategy (see Table 19.4).

Table 19.4 First-stage asset allocation with and without liabilities L_t

Date	With cash flows						No cash flows					
	B1 (%)	B2 (%)	E (%)	C (%)	CVaR	Δ(%)	B1 (%)	B2 (%)	E (%)	C (%)	CVaR	Δ(%)
Jan 1999	0.00	90.07	1.23	8.70	101.28	–	0.00	99.66	0.34	0.00	107.77	–
Jul 1999	0.00	97.57	2.43	0.00	94.03	17.40	0.00	99.10	0.90	0.00	108.55	1.12
Jan 2000	0.00	91.76	8.24	0.00	75.46	11.62	0.00	94.70	5.30	0.00	108.87	8.80
Jul 2000	15.44	71.31	13.25	0.00	98.98	40.89	0.00	84.11	15.89	0.00	109.81	21.18
Jan 2001	19.18	64.22	16.60	0.00	79.29	14.18	0.00	85.35	14.65	0.00	110.28	2.48
Jul 2001	15.24	83.14	1.61	0.00	104.09	37.84	0.00	98.94	1.06	0.00	116.62	27.18
Jan 2002	0.00	90.63	2.26	7.11	97.02	30.49	0.00	99.51	0.49	0.00	117.73	1.15
Jul 2002	0.00	92.68	7.32	0.00	78.08	14.22	0.00	95.15	4.85	0.00	118.41	8.71
Jan 2003	0.00	74.86	4.29	20.85	96.77	41.70	0.00	95.36	4.64	0.00	114.94	0.41
Jul 2003	1.83	93.08	5.10	0.00	77.49	41.70	0.93	94.95	4.12	0.00	115.86	1.86
Jan 2004	11.03	80.50	1.20	7.27	103.43	32.95	0.73	98.82	0.45	0.00	124.03	7.74
Jul 2004	11.62	87.04	1.34	0.00	96.18	14.54	0.71	98.88	0.41	0.00	124.93	0.12
Jan 2005	0.00	95.23	4.77	0.00	76.65	23.24	0.00	97.24	2.76	0.00	124.41	4.69
Jul 2005	0.00	75.07	4.16	20.76	98.84	41.52	0.00	95.45	4.55	0.00	124.10	3.57
Jan 2006	0.00	90.33	9.67	0.00	80.40	41.52	0.00	91.69	8.31	0.00	126.18	7.53
Jul 2006	0.00	90.90	1.42	7.68	108.04	16.50	0.00	99.27	0.73	0.00	137.19	15.18
Jan 2007	0.00	95.85	4.15	0.00	100.44	15.37	0.00	96.73	3.27	0.00	137.72	5.09
Jul 2007	0.00	86.96	13.04	0.00	81.46	17.78	0.00	90.94	9.06	0.00	138.02	11.59
Mean	4.13	86.18	5.67	4.02	91.55	26.68	0.13	95.32	4.54	0.00	120.30	7.55

19.5   Results

The scenario generation procedure was implemented in MATLAB and we formulated the optimisation problem in AMPL. The solution time on a MacBook Pro 2.4 GHz Intel Core 2 Duo, 4 GB RAM with MOSEK was approximately 25 seconds in each time step with the interior-point solver.

In Figure 19.7, we illustrate the evolution of the first-stage asset allocation and the corresponding portfolio values, applying our cash management strategy on the rolling horizon window. It shows that, compared to other quantitative asset allocation models (for example Markowitz mean-variance optimisation), *CVaR*-optimisation leads to a 'smoothly' diversified evolution in the asset allocation, avoiding excessive portfolio turnovers. Reallocations depend both on changes in the market variables (for example, the term structure of interest rates, the higher moments of the equity returns) and on planned cash in- and outflows. To separate these effects, we solve the optimisation problem also without cash flows. The results are given in Table 19.4.

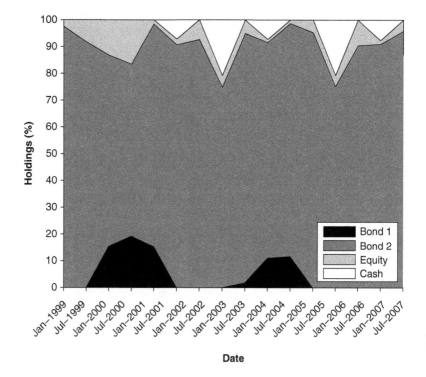

Figure 19.7   First-stage asset allocation

The column $\Delta(\%)$ defines the sum of the absolute percentage changes in the first-stage asset allocation. Without external cash flows, the mean of $\Delta(\%)$ is equal to 7.55 per cent. This value is solely because of the changing market variables. The obtained strategy reflects pure asset management. Including also the external cash flows (see Table 19.1), $\Delta(\%)$ increases to 26.68 per cent, that is most of the additional trading activity is related to the integrated asset- and liability management. In both cases, the major fraction of wealth is invested in Bond 2 and equities. However, in the integrated asset liability case, under the *CVaR*-optimisation, more is invested in equities and some amount of wealth is held in cash to account for cash outflows.

Figure 19.8 shows the evolution of the portfolio values and Figure 19.9 compares the realised (out-of-sample) portfolio returns of our model to the alternative strategies. No strategy (first order) dominates the others for the chosen time interval. However, the stochastic programming approach – suggesting equity investments – suffers in the first few years, whereas it generally benefits later from a rising equity market. The largest breakdowns in the equity index

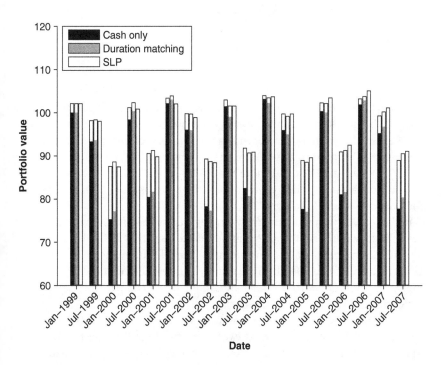

Figure 19.8   Portfolio values of alternative strategies

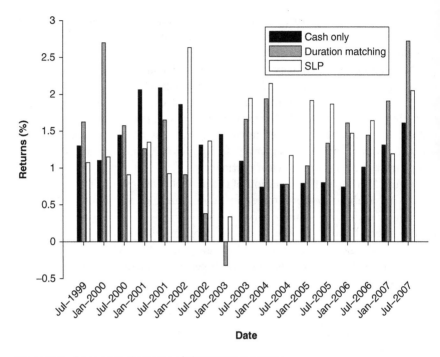

Figure 19.9   Semi-annual returns of alternative strategies

occurred during the years 2001–2002. In this period, the SLP approach outperformed the duration matching strategy for two reasons: The fraction held in
equities was lower than the one in the duration matching approach (see first-
stage asset allocation in July 2001 and January 2002). During the second half
of 2002, when the DAX lost more than 33 per cent of its value, our strategy
gained from a sharply falling term structure of interest rates (a large amount of
the portfolio was held in Bond 2).

In Table 19.5, we report the following aggregate risk measures for our strategies: final wealth W, mean $\bar{R}$ and standard deviation $\sigma(R)$ of semi-annual
returns, Sharpe ratio SR, the minimum and maximum realised return as well
as aggregated returns AR. The SLP strategy realises a higher final wealth and a
higher mean return with a lower standard deviation compared to the duration
matching and the cash-only approach.

In the next three subsections, we analyse the sensitivity of the first-stage
asset allocations on the expected excess return of equities, on parallel shifts
in the term structure of interest rates and on deferring the starting date of our
optimisation in a comparative static way.

Table 19.5 Aggregate risk measures

	W	R̄ (%)	σ (R) (%)	SR	min(R) (%)	max(R) (%)	AR (%)
Cash only	77.76	1.26	0.45	−0.67	0.74	2.09	23.80
Duration matching	80.42	1.42	0.75	−0.19	−0.32	2.72	27.10
SLP	81.38	1.48	0.56	−0.15	0.35	2.64	28.32

19.5.1 Sensitivity of equity holdings to changes in equity excess return

Despite the fact that the analysis of return predictability and its impact on asset allocation decisions has found considerable attention in the literature (see for example Barberis, 2000; Wachter, 2002; Brandt *et al*, 2005; Cochrane, 2008), the empirical evidence for practical asset management is not unambiguous (see for example Ang and Bekaert, 2007). A deep discussion of this topic is far beyond the scope of this contribution. However, estimating higher moments of asset returns from past data and adding a constant excess return to the short rate to determine the expected return of the equity investment, induces (implicitly) time-varying investment opportunities in our backtest. On the basis of these parameters, our model calculates asset allocations on a rolling horizon window, considering realised market returns and interest rates 6 months later. As is well known in the finance literature, estimating the *future* excess return of an equity investment is not an easy task. Assuming risk-averse market participants in a market equilibrium implies an *ex ante* positive expected excess return.

We used data from 1 January 1979 to 1 January 1999 to estimate an average excess return for the DAX of 4.80 per cent, as indicated in Table 19.2. Obviously, this value and the corresponding investment strategy depend on the chosen time interval. Therefore, we conduct a sensitivity analysis of the first-stage asset allocation with respect to changes in this parameter. Using a *CVaR* minimisation under the constraint of a given target wealth (see (19.1) and (19.12)) we find effects that are normally known from Giffen or inferior goods as described in Poulsen and Rasmussen (2008): the higher the expected return, the lower the fraction of wealth invested in equities. This is illustrated in Figure 19.10, in which the expected excess return is changed to 4.4 per cent and 5.2 per cent p.a.

The effect can be explained by our constrained optimisation. Although equity investments are interesting for their higher expected return and their diversification benefits, they imply a higher volatility. This negatively affects the objective function value. An increase in the expected return requires less risk-taking to fulfil the expected target wealth in (19.12).

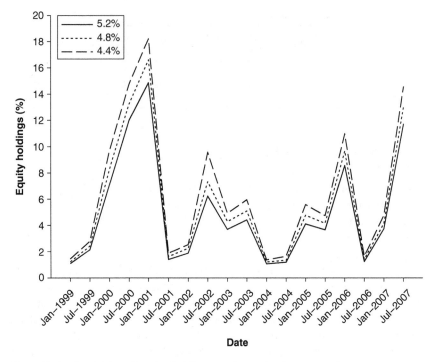

Figure 19.10   Sensitivity of equity holdings to change in the expected excess return

19.5.2   Sensitivity to parallel shifts in the term structure of interest rates

In our setting, many parameters depend on the future evolution of the term structure of interest rates, for example the prices of traded bonds, the short rate received/paid on the bank account, the target wealth or the expected equity return. All these effects are interrelated and the final outcome under a constrained *CVaR* optimisation is not obvious. Therefore, we analyse the effects of parallel shifts in the term structure of + 50 and + 100 Basis points on the evolution of the first-stage asset allocation. Major changes are observable for the equity and the Bond 2 investment, their corresponding wealth fractions are shown in Figure 19.11.

The effects of parallel shifts in the term structure of interest rates are not as clear as in the case of the expected excess returns. For small changes, we observe an increasing fraction invested in equities and a decline in the Bond 2 expenditures. This is the result of two opposite effects: higher expected returns of all assets versus a higher target wealth (see (19.17)). Although the

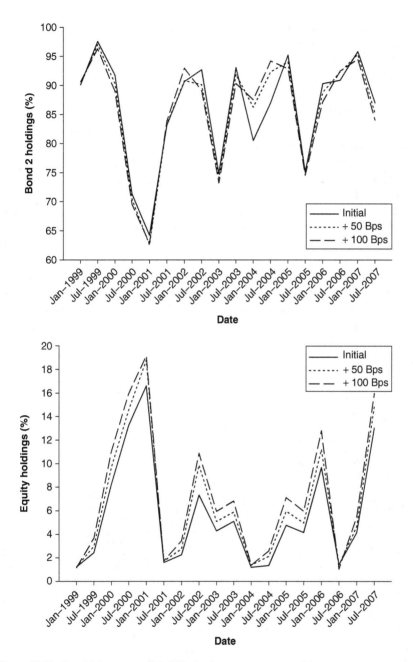

Figure 19.11   Sensitivity to parallel shifts in the term structure of interest rates

impact on the asset allocation is rather small, both effects do not cancel each other out. We explain this by the fact that some parameters are related to interest rates in a nonlinear way, for example price–yield relationship of bonds.

19.5.3   Sensitivity to the starting date

In the previous sections, we illustrated the first-stage asset allocation of a company starting the optimisation on January 1999 with semi-annual rebalancing, and analysed the sensitivity with respect to the expected equity return and parallel shifts in the term structure of interest rates. We showed that the portfolio turnover is modest and that a large part of portfolio rebalancing is because of changes in the business plan of the company. However, one might ask for the sensitivity of the results to a time shift in the starting month without changing other input parameters. In Table 19.6, we show the evolution of first-stage asset allocations when starting our backtest on February 1999 and on March 1999, while deferring also the external cash flows for 1 or 2 months. Differences to the left panel of Table 19.4 are because of changes in the market variables between the shifted starting dates. We can verify that the asset allocation is quite insensitive with respect to small time shifts, again confirming in this way the smooth evolution of our optimal policy.

Table 19.6   First-stage asset allocation with different starting dates

Starting date	Feb 1999					Mar 1999				
Date	B1 (%)	B2 (%)	E (%)	C (%)	CVaR	B1 (%)	B2 (%)	E (%)	C (%)	CVaR
Feb/Mar 1999	0.00	80.31	1.48	18.21	100.87	0.00	88.18	1.17	10.65	101.58
Aug/Sep 1999	0.00	87.16	3.17	9.67	94.25	0.00	97.66	1.92	0.42	95.04
Feb/Mar 2000	0.00	93.01	6.99	0.00	76.32	0.00	90.21	9.79	0.00	78.04
Aug/Sep 2000	14.27	72.01	13.72	0.00	99.39	17.53	70.39	12.07	0.00	100.62
Feb/Mar 2001	17.71	66.35	15.95	0.00	80.48	22.02	62.02	15.97	0.00	79.26
Aug/Sep 2001	14.21	84.44	1.35	0.00	103.15	17.69	80.79	1.52	0.00	100.90
Feb/Mar 2002	0.00	91.94	3.19	4.87	96.21	0.00	87.95	3.27	8.78	94.18
Aug/Sep 2002	0.00	92.12	7.88	0.00	76.39	0.00	86.61	13.39	0.00	74.04
Feb/Mar 2003	0.00	73.49	4.76	21.75	96.67	0.00	74.41	4.03	21.56	92.40
Aug/Sep 2003	1.53	90.71	7.76	0.00	78.95	3.60	92.50	3.90	0.00	74.63
Feb/Mar 2004	16.09	75.19	1.17	7.55	103.20	16.47	74.89	0.93	7.71	97.99
Aug/Sep 2004	16.97	82.05	0.98	0.00	96.08	16.67	81.59	1.74	0.00	90.92
Feb/Mar 2005	0.00	94.96	5.04	0.00	76.93	0.00	94.70	5.30	0.00	71.36
Aug/Sep 2005	0.00	74.50	4.84	20.66	99.17	0.00	73.41	5.04	21.55	93.65
Feb/Mar 2006	0.00	89.84	10.16	0.00	80.84	0.00	88.71	11.29	0.00	75.49
Aug/Sep 2006	0.00	90.74	1.04	8.22	107.31	0.00	90.37	1.27	8.36	101.87
Feb/Mar 2007	0.00	96.09	3.91	0.00	99.66	0.00	96.09	3.91	0.00	94.13
Aug/Sep 2007	0.00	86.50	13.50	0.00	80.25	0.00	85.92	14.08	0.00	75.07
Mean	4.49	84.52	5.94	5.05	91.45	5.22	84.24	6.14	4.39	88.40

19.6 Conclusion

We considered a short- to medium-term treasury management optimisation task for a risk-averse company, which is faced with projected cash in- and out-flows for a rolling planning horizon. The investment opportunity set was given by several bonds, a cash account and an equity index. We used real market data to perform a backtest of the model and demonstrated its practical viability with an evaluation of the out-of-sample performance and various sensitivity analyses.

In a multi-stage stochastic programming formulation, we minimised the coherent risk measure *CVaR*. To generate the scenarios for our optimisation, we calibrated a no-arbitrage interest rate model (to the observed term structure of interest rates and volatilities) and performed the change of measure by taking into account the empirically estimated MPR. To further include the asymmetric and leptokurtic distribution observed for historical equity returns in the decision problem, we use a moment-matching approach. For all our scenarios, the no-arbitrage condition holds. In each time step, we marked to market the portfolio with the realised (out-of-sample) returns using the optimal (in-sample) asset allocation from the previous stage.

The results indicate an attractive performance of our stochastic programming model. Compared to alternative approaches, our strategy shows a better risk-return trade-off for different aggregate risk measures. Further, the optimal portfolio weights adapt smoothly over time to the real market data during the backtest. Major changes in the asset allocation are because of the incorporation of the external cash flows.

Several sensitivity tests lead to the following findings: An increase in the equity return causes a decrease in the corresponding portfolio weight. We show that for a parallel upward shift in the term structure of interest rates several interrelated effects are present. For small changes, we observe an increase in the equity holdings and a decrease in the bond. Modifying the starting date with a rolling window approach does not lead to notable differences in the asset allocation.

We conclude that the conducted backtest confirms the performance and the stability of our short-term treasury management model. In our opinion, the approach offers a reasonable trade-off between the computational complexity and the required accuracy for a practical implementation.

Acknowledgements

We gratefully acknowledge helpful comments by Michael Hanke, Josef Hayden and two anonymous referees. We thank the Austrian National Bank for financial support under Jubiläumsfondsprojekt 13054.

Notes

1. Note that VaR and $CVaR$ are defined as positive values.
2. For easy comparability, our notation follows that in Stanton (1997). There, the dependence of the bond's return on the short rate is also omitted for the sake of brevity.
3. In section 'Model', we use for notation brevity rt as one-period interest rate (paid at $t+0.5$, that is 6 months later) instead of $r_{t,t+0.5}$.
4. Owing to a comparison of our dynamic SLP strategy with a pure 'cash holding' in the section 'Results', we propose a conservative setting with high costs here. Clearly, lower transaction costs will make bond and equity investments even more attractive, improving in this way our SLP results.

References

Ang, A. and Bekaert, G. (2007) Stock return predictability: Is it there? *The Review of Financial Studies* 20: 651–707.

Barberis, N.C. (2000) Investing for the long run when returns are predictable. *The Journal of Finance* 55: 225–264.

Baumol, W.J. (1952) The transactions demand for cash: An inventory theoretic approach. *The Quarterly Journal of Economics* 66(4): 545–556.

Bernaschi, M., Torosantucci, L. and Uboldi, A. (2007) Empirical evaluation of the market price of risk using the CIR model. *Physica A: Statistical and Theoretical Physics* 376: 543–554.

Bertocchi, M., Moriggia, V. and Dupacova, J. (2000) Sensitivity of bond portfolio's behavior with respect to random movements in yield curve: A simulation study. *Annals of Operations Research* 99(1–4): 267–286.

Bertocchi, M., Moriggia, V. and Dupacova, J. (2006) Horizon and stages in applications of stochastic programming in finance. *Annals of Operations Research* 142(1): 63–78.

Black, F. (1976) The pricing of commodity contracts. *Journal of Financial Economics* 3: 167–179.

Black, F., Derman, E. and Toy, W. (1990) A one-factor model of interest rates and its applications to treasury bond options. *Financial Analysts' Journal* 46: 33–39.

Bradley, S.P. and Crane, D.B. (1972) A dynamic model for bond portfolio management. *Management Science* 19(2): 139–151.

Brandt, M.W., Goyal, A., Santa-Clara, P. and Stroud, J.R. (2005) A simulation approach to dynamic portfolio choice with an application to learning about return predictability. *The Review of Financial Studies* 18(3): 831–873.

Brigo, D. and Mercurio, F. (2006) *Interest Rate Models – Theory and Practice: With Smile, Inflation and Credit*, 2nd edn., Springer Finance. New York: Springer.

Castro, J. (2007) A stochastic programming approach to cash management in banking. *European Journal of Operational Research* 192(3): 963–974.

Chambers, D. and Charnes, A. (1961) Inter-temporal analysis and optimization of bank portfolios. *Management Science* 7(4): 393–410.

Charnes, A., Cooper, W.W. and Miller, M.II. (1959) Application of linear programming to financial budgeting and the costing of funds. *The Journal of Business* 32(1): 20–46.

Cochrane, J.H. (2008) The dog that did not bark: A defense of return predictability. *The Review of Financial Studies* 21: 1533–1575.

Cohen, K.J. and Hammer, F.S. (1967) Linear programming and optimal bank asset management decisions. *The Journal of Finance* 22(2): 147–165.

Dempster, M., Pflug, G. and Mitra, G. (2009) *Quantitative Fund Management*, Financial Mathematics Series. Boca Raton, FL: Chapman & Hall/CRC.

Dempster, M.A.H., Germano, M., Medova, E.A., Rietbergen, M.I., Sandrini, F. and Scrowston, M. (2007) Designing minimum guaranteed return funds. *Quantitative Finance* 7(2): 245–256.

Dempster, M.A.H., Germano, M., Medova, E.A. and Villaverde, M. (2003) Global asset liability management. *British Actuarial Journal* 9(1): 137–195.

Dupacova, J. (2000) Stability properties of a bond portfolio management problem. *Annals of Operations Research* 99(1–4): 251–265.

Dupacova, J. and Bertocchi, M. (2001) From data to model and back to data: A bond portfolio management problem. *European Journal of Operational Research* 134(2): 261–278.

Ferstl, R. and Weissensteiner, A. (2010) Cash management using multi-stage stochastic programming. *Quantitative Finance* 10(2): 209–219.

Geyer, A. and Ziemba, W.T. (2008) The innovest Austrian pension fund financial planning model InnoALM. *Operations Research* 56(4): 797–810.

Golub, B., Holmer, M., McKendall, R., Pohlman, L. and Zenios, S.A. (1995) A stochastic programming model for money management. *European Journal of Operational Research* 85(2): 282–296.

Gondzio, J. and Kouwenberg, R. (2001) High-performance computing for asset-liability management. *Operations Research* 49(6): 879–891.

Høyland, K. and Wallace, S.W. (2007) Chapter 13: Stochastic programming models for strategic and tactical asset allocation – A study from Norwegian life insurance. In: S.A. Zenios and W.T. Ziemba (eds.) *Handbook of Asset and Liability Management, Volume 2: Applications and Case Studies*. Amsterdam, Netherlands: Elsevier, pp. 591–625.

Jobst, N.J., Mitra, G. and Zenios, S.A. (2006) Integrating market and credit risk: A simulation and optimisation perspective. *Journal of Banking & Finance* 30(2): 717–742.

Jobst, N.J. and Zenios, S.A. (2005) On the simulation of portfolios of interest rate and credit risk sensitive securities. *European Journal of Operational Research* 161(2): 298–324.

Klaassen, P. (2002) Comment on 'generating scenario trees for multistage decision problems'. *Management Science* 48: 1512–1516.

Kusy, M.I. and Ziemba, W.T. (1986) A bank asset and liability management model. *Operations Research* 34(3): 356–376.

Michaud, R.O. (2003) A practical framework for portfolio choice. *Journal of Investment Management* 1(2): 14–29.

Mulvey, J.M. and Zenios, S.A. (1994) Capturing the correlations of fixed-income instruments. *Management Science* 40(10): 1329–1342.

Pflug, G.C. (2000) Some remarks on the value-at-risk and the conditional value-at-risk. In: S.P. Uryasev (ed.) *Probabilistic Constrained Optimization – Methodology and Applications*. Dordrecht, Netherlands: Kluwer Academic Publishers, pp. 272–281.

Poulsen, R. and Rasmussen, K.M. (2008) Financial Giffen goods: Examples and counterexamples. *European Journal of Operational Research* 191(2): 572–576.

Rebonato, R. (2004) *Volatility and Correlation in the Pricing of Equity, FX and Interest-Rate Options*. West Sussex, England: John Wiley & Sons.

Rockafellar, R.T. and Uryasev, S. (2000) Optimization of conditional value-at-risk. *Journal of Risk* 2(3): 21–41.

Rockafellar, R.T. and Uryasev, S. (2002) Conditional value-at-risk for general loss distributions. *Journal of Banking & Finance* 26(7): 1443–1471.

Stanton, R. (1997) A nonparametric model of term structure dynamics and the market price of interest rate risk. *The Journal of Finance* 52(5): 1973–2002.

Topaloglou, N., Vladimirou, H. and Zenios, S.A. (2008) A dynamic stochastic programming model for international portfolio management. *European Journal of Operational Research* 185(3): 1501–1524.

Volosov, K., Mitra, G., Spagnolo, F. and Lucas, C. (2005) Treasury management model with foreign exchange exposure. *Computational Optimization and Applications* 32: 179–207.

Wachter, J. (2002) Portfolio and consumption decisions under mean-reverting returns: An exact solution. *Journal of Financial and Quantitative Analysis* 37(1): 63–91.

Service Provider Directory

Current Providers

Axioma, Inc.
Barrie and Hibbert
Cambridge Systems Associates Limited
Cardano
The Chartered Institute for Securities & Investment
d-fine GmbH
Ehrentreich LDI Consulting & Research, LLC
Fraunhofer Institute for Industrial Mathematics ITWM
Institute for Operations Research and Computational Finance of the University of
   St. Gallen
Northfield Information Services, Inc.
OptiRisk Systems
ORFIVAL
Pensions Institute
Redington Ltd

Company Name: Axioma, Inc.

Head Office: New York, NY

Other sites: London, Hong Kong, Singapore, Atlanta, San Francisco
CEO: Sebastian Ceria, PhD
VP, Global Sales and Client Services: Jon Underhill
VP, Research: Robert Stubbs, PhD
CTO: Stefan Schmieta, PhD

Tools/Services:
Axioma Portfolio™ Optimizer
Axioma Portfolio – Backtester
Axioma Portfolio – Performance Attribution
Axioma Robust Risk Model™ Suite
(Global, Emerging Markets, Europe, Australia, Canada, Japan, Taiwan, United Kingdom, United States)
Axioma Portfolio – Risk Analytics

Tools/Services Description:
Founded in 1998, Axioma offers a suite of analytic tools, including modules for portfolio optimization, backtesting, performance attribution and risk analysis, along with a comprehensive suite of multi-country and single country risk models. Axioma's risk models include fundamental and statistical model variants, with all risk model components updated daily. Axioma's Client Services staff offers extensive training and custom implementation services. Axioma services seven out of the top ten worldwide institutional money managers, based on assets under management, and is relied upon by hundreds of users globally, managing trillions of dollars every day.

Axioma's analytic tools are available as a desktop application (GUI) and API, can be used within Matlab and R and are available via FactSet. They constitute an open platform which may be used with Axioma's risk models and market data or any internal or third party data source.

Contact: sales@axioma.com
Axioma Portfolio, Axioma Backtester and Axioma Robust Risk Model are trademarks of Axioma, Inc.

Company Name: **barrie hibbert**

Head Office:
Barrie & Hibbert Ltd
7 Exchange Crescent
Conference Square
Edinburgh
EH3 8RD
Tel: +44(0) 131 625 0203
www.barrhibb.com

Other Sites:
Barrie & Hibbert Limited 41 Lothbury London EC2R 7HG
Barrie & Hibbert Inc. 1515 Broadway, 11th Floor New York, New York 10036
Barrie & Hibbert Asia Limited Level 19, Two International Finance Center Central Hong Kong
Chief Executive: Andy Frepp

Tools/Services:
Barrie & Hibbert provides a wide range of products and services. The core modelling platform, the Economic Scenario Generator, bespoke calibrations, calibration tools, liquidity premium estimation, consultancy on variance reduction techniques, pension modelling, variable annuity pricing and hedging strategies, product risk, design and governance and asset allocation services.

Tools/Services Description:
The Barrie & Hibbert ESG, a multi-period, multi-risk-factor model, provides a consistent framework for use across multiple applications such as market consistent valuation of technical provisions and the one-year real world projection required for calculating the SCR. It includes a variety of modelling options from the simple and easy to understand to the cutting edge risk factor models that may be required for certain risk profiles allowing users to choose the appropriate level of sophistication. The ESG and associated calibration services cover a broad coverage of applications, asset classes and economies.

Solvency II means that it is more important than ever for a company to demonstrate understanding of their ESG and ownership of the key assumptions. Both the ESG software and our calibration services come with comprehensive documentation and training targeted at different levels, from the CRO to technical expert users. The ESG also gives full user control of risk factor structure and parameter values, so that users can test sensitivities and their own key assumptions.

The ESG includes flexible output formats and API functionality to allow easy integration with ALM and ERM software. It also offers a range of multi-core and grid processing options to help with ever more onerous reporting deadlines.

Available by annual subscription covering full technical support, training, quarterly calibrations, free upgrades and access to our knowledge base, which gives full details of our models and methods.

Contact: Shailendra Jain
Barrie & Hibbert Limited 41 Lothbury London EC2R 7HG
Tel: +44(0)203 170 6145
Price: Determined by individual client requirements.

Company Name: Cambridge Systems Associates Limited

Founded in 1996, CSA is an innovative financial consultancy and software developer, whose technology leverages more than 25 years of dedicated research in probability, optimization and quantitative finance. Our creative international team, all holding advanced qualifications, applies cutting edge ideas to real-world problems.

CSA's principals founded the Centre for Financial Research at the Judge Business School in the University of Cambridge, and the company maintains strong links with the international academic community. Its senior personnel are regularly involved globally with financial services conferences and executive education in quantitative finance.

Our clients are leading financial institutions, consultants, corporations and governments. We have pioneered the introduction of dynamic stochastic optimization techniques to practical risk-managed long-term asset-liability problems in banking, insurance and pension fund management, for clients such as Towers Watson, Swiss Re, Frank Russell and Pioneer Investments, as well as tactical strategies for mutual and hedge funds.

Head Office: Cambridge, UK
Managing Directors: Professor Michael Dempster and Dr Elena Medova

Tools/Services:

* STOCHASTICS™ Suite
* GSPL™
* GNBS™
* iALM™
* Consulting services employing these and other tools

Tools/Services Description:
The STOCHASTICS™ Suite is a full model development system, written in C++, for the construction and maintenance of stochastic optimization models of strategic and tactical fund management problems, especially involving explicitly modelled liabilities and risk management. It consists of a variety of simulators for asset class returns of equities, commodities, fixed income, credit, and so forth, a modelling language (General Stochastic Programming Language, GSPL™) and various optimizers based on problem decomposition (General Nested Benders Decomposition, GNBS™). This software has been purposely built for the large-scale dynamic stochastic problems which are involved in long-term commercial asset-liability management (ALM) and it incorporates sophisticated stochastic problem pre-processing. International patents on the system are pending.

In addition to being employed for client problems, STOCHASTICS™ has been used to construct our user-friendly iALM™ system, which applies institutional techniques for the support of financial advice to individual households by financial advisors, private bankers and wealth managers. iALM™ is a full cash-flow-based life cycle lifestyle planning system, accounting for client goals, taxes, pensions, insurance and annuities, for which US and UK versions are currently available.

Contact:
The Administrator
Cambridge Systems Associates Limited
5–7 Portugal Place
Cambridge CB5 8AF
UK
admin@cambridge-systems.com
www.cambridge-systems.com
+44 (0)1223 557640 (tel)
+44 (0)1223 557641 (fax)

Company Name: Cardano

Head Office: Rotterdam, The Netherlands
Other Sites: London
Managing Director: Theo Kocken, CEO
Marketing and Sales Director: Richard Dowell (UK), Bart Oldenkamp (NL)
Chief Technology Officer/Director: Roger Lord (UK), Vincent van Antwerpen (NL)

Tools/Services:
Cardano offers strategic risk management services to medium and large European pension funds and insurance companies. Cardano's services are supported from its Dutch and UK office, currently employing over 80 professionals. Cardano helps institutional investors to reach their long-term strategic objectives with more certainty. Our services include both advisory and implementation using a wide range of investment instruments, ranging from Over The Counter (OTC) interest rate, equity and inflation derivatives, as well as the underlying investment portfolio.

Tools/Services Description:
Our risk management services include both (1) strategic advice to arrive at an effective investment and derivative overlay strategy, meeting long-term objectives while satisfying shorter-term risk constraints, and (2) the implementation and management of derivative overlay strategies. We execute well over EUR 40bn notional in derivatives on an annual basis.

Over the last ten years, Cardano has developed a software library of tools which we employ to integrate risk management and valuation of OTC derivatives into our clients' ALM software and portfolio management and operational support systems. We cover derivatives on the most relevant underlying economic variables, such as interest and inflation rates and equities.

Cardano has extensive experience in modelling the risk-neutral environment required for pricing and risk management of derivatives, in alignment with the 'real world' stochastic models typically used to describe the economic environment and financial markets in existing ALM software. In addition, we focus on stress testing and implementation issues, such as liquidity, secondary markets and counterparty risk management. As a result, our clients benefit from derivatives strategies which are robust against a wide range of different economic scenarios, as well as easy and transparent to maintain in terms of risks, benefits and pricing.

Contact: Bart Oldenkamp (b.oldenkamp@cardano.com)
Price: On request

Company Name: The Chartered Institute for Securities & Investment

"To set standards of professional excellence and integrity for the securities and investment industry, providing qualifications and promoting the highest level of competence to our members, other individuals and firms." Formerly the Securities & Investment Institute (SII), and originally founded by members of the London Stock exchange in 1992, the Institute is the leading examining, membership and awarding body for the securities and investment industry. It was awarded a royal charter in October 2009, becoming the Chartered Institute for Securities & Investment (CISI).

The CISI currently has around 40,000 members, who benefit from a programme of professional and social events, with continuing professional development (CPD) and the promotion of integrity, very much at the heart of everything the organization does.

With ever-increasing regulatory focus on both individuals' and firms' commitments to competence and compliance, the Institute assists companies as well as practitioners to demonstrate their commitment to CPD and professionalism. The core values of the Institute are to

- set standards of integrity and competence for those working in the financial services industry. Ultimately, these standards are for the benefit of investors.
- be the centre of excellence for the design, maintenance and delivery of qualifications, both in the United Kingdom and abroad.
- provide members' forums to highlight, share and influence changes in the financial services industry.
- recognise and actively promote the importance of continuing professional development.
- offer appropriate qualifications of the highest calibre, relevance and quality.

The Institute is approved as an awarding body by Ofqual, the UK regulator in education. Its qualifications feature prominently on the Financial Services Skills Council (FSSC) lists of appropriate and recommended exams.

It provides a range of relevant qualifications which attract over 42,000 exam entries each year, delivered in more than 50 countries. The Institute continues to develop its qualifications to meet the demands of the changing financial services industry.

The CISI is committed to assisting individuals to attain and maintain competence and to promoting trust and integrity.

Membership
CISI membership brings together thousands of practitioners from all parts of a diverse and complex industry into a single effective network. Membership of the CISI is the hallmark of professional recognition and signifies that individuals have attained a high standard in their chosen field. This visibly demonstrates an individual's competence and professionalism to employers, colleagues and clients.

All new exam candidates automatically become student members of the CISI, at no extra cost, to assist them from the outset of their studies. Once candidates pass a benchmark qualification (for example, the Investment Administration Qualification) they are eligible to progress to Associate (ACSI) membership. Full Membership (MCSI) is achieved by attaining a higher-level CISI or other relevant professional qualification. It can also be achieved by having very substantial expertise and seniority in the industry.

Members also have the opportunity to become personally chartered. To achieve this they have to meet a number of criteria, including a number of years successfully logged CPD through the CISI scheme (which requires 35 hours of CPD logged across four learning types on an annual basis) and an A/B pass in Integrity Matters.

For those members achieving the full CISI Diploma or the CISI Masters Programme (Wealth Management), this ultimately leads to Chartered Fellowship (FCSI) of the Institute.

Members are experienced and qualified practitioners in securities, derivatives, corporate finance, investment management, private wealth management and other related areas. All categories of membership must adhere to both the letter and the spirit of the Institute's Code of Conduct and its Principles.

More information? To learn more about the CISI or any aspect of the organization's work or to contact us, please visit cisi.org/contactus or call +44 (0)20 7645 0600.

Company Name: d-fine GmbH

Head Office:
Opernplatz 2
60313 Frankfurt
Germany

Other Sites: Munich, London, Hong Kong
Managing Director:
Marketing Director:
Chief Technology Officer/Director:

Tools/Services:

- Consulting in business needs in ALM and liquidity risk management – frameworks as well as special topics
- Advice in the different regulatory requirements, for example, liquidity risk controlling
- Development of models for internal management and regulatory reporting, conceptual and bespoke software
- Quick Check or comprehensive review of existing implementations, theoretical models and processes by experienced experts
- Lead-through or assistance in the selection processes for suitable analysis and reporting software
- Implementation of models and customization of ALM Software in the clients' system architecture
- Design and Setup of integrated reporting systems
- Trainings, workshops and presentations on best practices

Tools/Services Description: The ALM section of d-fine offers consultancy in business as well as technical aspects of ALM such as the following:

- Development and setup of
  - internal liquidity risk models
  - basic and advanced analyses for classical ALM (interest rate risk, interest income) and liquidity (risk) management covering gap analyses, durations and PV changes, liquidity (value) at risk calculations and others
  - FTP mechanisms including costs for liquidity (risk)
- Review and validation of existing frameworks and models for ALM and liquidity (risk) management

Within these tasks we provide our continuously extended and updated knowledge on special topics such as the following:

- statistic and stochastic models for nondeterministic products
- modelling of customer behaviour, for example, prepayments or cancellation rights
- definition of appropriate scenarios for stress testing, taking into account different risk drivers

- design of possible funding strategies, including new business depending on, for example, prospective market data
- adequate pricing of liquidity reserves
- design of liquidity limit systems

From the technical perspective our services cover, among others

- Implementation of ALM systems, such as Kamakura, SunGard Focus ALM, FRSGlobal riskpro, Fermat, and so forth, including the conceptual design of interfaces and systematic testing for all analyses and products
- development of bespoke software solutions
- setup of back testing facilities and adequate, flexible and integrated reporting
- implementation of processes and procedures

Contact: Dr Oliver Hein, Phone: +49 69 90737–324, E-Mail: info@d-fine.de

Company Name: Ehrentreich LDI Consulting & Research, LLC

Head Office:
4146 Sheridan Ave N.
Minneapolis, MN 55412
USA

Other Sites: www.ldi-research.com
Managing Director: Dr. Norman Ehrentreich
Marketing Director:
Chief Technology Officer/Director:

Tools/Services:

- LDI-Optimizer: Creation of customized liability indices, levered / unlevered, pooled & separate accounts
- Multi-Period Asset Allocation Algorithm that takes liabilities and financing constraints into account

Tools/Services Description:
Ehrentreich LDI Consulting & Research provides consulting services on asset allocation and LDI strategies to corporate and public DB plan sponsors, investment managers, and other consulting companies.

We have developed an integrated suite of LDI solutions for a variety of DB pension plans. We employ a proprietary optimization procedure to create customized liability indices. They are designed to minimize funding status volatility, no matter the plan's size, funding status, duration, and cash flow structure.

For asset allocation decisions, we use a multi-period algorithm that takes liabilities, pension regulations, and financing constraints of plan sponsors into account. Our research suggests the widespread existence of an Asset Return–Funding Cost Paradox and the possibility of a risk-penalty relationship for DB pension plans instead of the well-known risk-reward trade-off of the CAPM. According to this paradox, lower-returning LDI strategies are more likely to result in lower funding costs than higher returning equity-based investment strategies. Because of pension regulations in most developed economies, the requirements to convert an eventual equity risk premium into lower funding costs are generally violated. Our multi-period allocation algorithm regularly results in lower equity allocations than those obtained through a one-period CAPM.

Contact: Ehrentreich@ldi-research.com, [p] +1–612-706–7819, [c] +1–763-360–9538
Price: Upon request

Company Name: Fraunhofer Institute for Industrial Mathematics ITWM

Head Office:
Fraunhofer ITWM,
Financial Mathematics Department
Fraunhofer Platz 1, 67663 Kaiserslautern, Germany

Other Sites:
Managing Director:
Director of the Institute: Prof. Dr Dieter Praetzel-Wolters
Head of the Financial Mathematics Department: Prof. Dr Ralf Korn
Marketing Director: Ilka Blauth
Chief Technology Officer/Director:

Tools/Services:
2-Factor Generic Interest Rate Product Pricer
ALMSim

Tools/Services Description:
The 2-Factor Generic Interest Rate Product Pricer uses a new HJM-G2++ model of the short rate for the calibration of the term structure and efficient pricing of a wide range of structured interest rate derivatives. It is based on an Excel interface with underlying C++ code. The generic concept allows an easy extension to new products. The pricer is already in use by a German asset management company. Consulting and support are provided by Fraunhofer ITWM. Target clients are insurance companies and banks.

ALMSim is a scenario generator for the simulation of both the asset and the liability side of an insurance company. It allows an individual modelling of the assets and liabilities and a coupling between them. It is designed in a special form that is based on a direct modelling language that is supported by a parser that generates C++ code. ALMSim is successfully used by Swedish pension funds. Consulting and support are provided by Fraunhofer ITWM. Target clients are insurance companies and pension funds.

Contact:
Dr Joerg Wenzel (joerg.wenzel@itwm.fraunhofer.de)
Prof. Dr Ralf Korn (ralf.korn@itwm.fraunhofer.de)
Price: Depends on the extent of the support and functionality provided for both products.

Company Name: Institute for Operations Research and Computational Finance of the University of St. Gallen

Head Office: Bodanstr. 6, CH-9000 St. Gallen, Switzerland
Managing Director: Prof. Dr. Karl Frauendorfer
Product Manager: Dr. Michael Schuerle
Chief Technology Officer: Claus Liebenberger

Tools / Services:
DEVA/ DEVA+ : Dynamic Expectation Variance Analysis
MO: Margin Optimizer

Tool / Services Description:
DEVA / DEVA+
The diversification potential of an allocation decision depends mainly on the risk/ return structure of the international capital markets. Estimating profits, return, and their interdependency structures still represents a major challenge. The ior/ cf-HSG supports institutional investors with the developed software DEVA Market: in respond to the dynamic volatilities and correlations, it uses a 'regime switch approach' to explain the dynamics, i.e. return, risk and interdependency structure, based on historical time series. Integrating DEVA Market, DEVA+ addresses the strategic and tactical asset allocation. It takes into account important aspects like market frictions, stochastic volatilities, and portfolio rebalancing. Furthermore, it supports a liability-based asset management and tracking a given benchmark.

MO: Margin Optimizer
Margin Optimizer is a software for the control and quantification of the potential risk of non-maturing assets and liabilities in a bank's balance. By analyzing a large number of representative scenarios for the evolution of future interest rates and volumes, the application calculates dynamic replicating portfolios that take into account the risk inherent to changes in these factors. Compared to static approaches that are currently still standard in the banking industry, this dynamic replication approach allows a substantial increase and stabilization of the margins of variable positions.

Contact: Dr. Michael Schürle; Michael.Schuerle@unisg.ch; +41–71-224 3055
Price: Offer on request

Company Name: Northfield Information Services, Inc.

Founded in 1985, Northfield has developed open, analytical models to identify, measure and control risk. These risk models cover most marketable securities traded worldwide. Based upon sound investment theory, Northfield's products and services have stood the test of time from users within the global institutional investment community.

With over 250 clients worldwide and offices in Boston, London and Tokyo, Northfield strives to be a preferred partner for institutional investors and asset managers.

Head Office: Boston, MA
Other Sites: London and Tokyo
Managing Director: Dan DiBartolomeo, President
Marketing and Sales Director: Nick Cutler
Chief Technology Officer/Director: Anrei Bunin

Tools/Services:

Risk Models

- Everything Everywhere
- US Fundamental Equity
- US Macroeconomic Equity
- US Short Term Equity
- Global Equity Risk
- US REIT
- Single Country & Regional Equity
- Global FTSE EPRA/NAREIT REIT
- Adaptive Near Horizon
- Transaction Costs

Analytical Tools

- Optimizer Service
- Performance Attribution Service
- Allocation Research Toolkit Service ("ART")
- Managed Account Rebalancing Service ("MARS")

Tools/Services Description:
Our risk models and analytical tools are used by investment professionals globally to better forecast portfolio risk versus a given market benchmark (relative risk) or in the case of absolute risk, cash. Our models cover all the major global asset classes; equities, sovereign debt, corporates, convertibles, fx, basic commodities, structured fixed income, US mortgage backed and US munis. In addition, we provide the user the ability to model illiquids, such as real estate, private equity and hedge funds, along with private placement securities and derivatives.

Our client type ranges from the largest buy side asset managers and plan sponsors, who use our analytical services to assess risk across the entire enterprise, to individual portfolio managers and analysts who employ our analytics one portfolio at a time, to the large end retail institutions, who private label Northfield analytics into their various high net worth platforms.

Company Name: OptiRisk Systems

OptiRisk Systems is a UK-based company with a global reach that provides products and services for Optimization and Risk Management solutions. OptiRisk serves customers across a number of business sectors, including finance, defence, transportation and supply chain logistics.

OptiRisk Systems offers products and services in the area of Optimization, Risk Modelling, Portfolio Planning, Asset and Liability Management, Supply Chain Management, Strategic and Tactical Management, and Scheduling of Transport Assets.

Head Office: Greater London, UK
Other Sites: Chennai, Gurgaon, India
Managing Director: Professor Gautam Mitra, President
Marketing and Sales Director: Dr. Michael(Xiaochen) Sun
Chief Technology Officer/Director: Professor Gautam Mitra, President; Dr. Cormac Lucas

Tools/Services:

- Asset and Liability Management:
- LDIOpt
- Bespoke solutions

Modelling Tools

- AMPL
- AMPL Studio
- AMPL COM
- SPInE/SAMPL

Solver Systems

- FortMP
- FortMP-MEX
- FortSP
- MOSEK
- MOPS
- GUROBI

Tools/Services Description:
Products:
OptiRisk Systems offers an extensive range of software for Optimization and Risk applications. These include both our own products and third party products. Our software range includes Modelling Systems for Mathematical Programming, Optimization Tools, and a number of Optimization Software Suites. Whether you are an analyst, developer, or an optimization specialist, we have the software to match your requirement.

Our state-of-the-art mathematical programming modelling systems all have seamless database connections. The optimization inference engines are embedded, and include Linear, Integer, Quadratic, and Integer Quadratic programming features. Our modelling systems are suitable for developing business analytics through rapid prototyping.

Services:
As a technology leader in the domain of optimization and risk analytics, we offer software solutions and consultancy in the areas of:

Portfolio Planning
Asset and Liability Management
Uncertainty and Risk Analysis/Modelling
News Analytics in Finance
Supply Chain Planning
In addition, we offer services of rapid prototyping and training in the areas of:
Algebraic Modelling Systems
Asset and Liability Management
Decision Analysis
Decision Support
News Analytics in Finance
Optimization (Linear/Integer/Quadratic and Stochastic)
Databases/Data Management
Scenario Generation and Simulation
Logistics Planning and Supply Chain Management

Furthermore, our competency and service offerings include:
Customized Software development
Quality Assurance and Benchmark Testing

Contact: info@optirisk-systems.com
         www.optirisk-systems.com
         www.optiriskindia.com
Price: Depends on service

Company Name: ORFIVAL

Head Office:
ORFIVAL SA
Avenue J.E. Lenoir 2
1348 Louvain-la-Neuve
Belgium

Other Sites:
ORFIVAL France
Rue de Paradis, 50 75010 Paris
France
ORFIVAL UK
City Tower 40 Basinghall Street London EC2V 5DE
England
Managing Director: Philippe Grégoire
Marketing Director: Philippe Vandooren
Chief Technology Officer/Director: Isabelle Platten

Tools/Services:

- Asset and Liability Management
- Portfolio Analytics
- Portfolio Management System

Tools/Services Description:
GPMS ALM is a valuable tool for any life insurance company or pension fund wishing to adopt a proactive ALM approach based on the principle of 'economic value'. The general features of the software are the following:

- A set of inter-correlated risk factors (financial, credit, underwriting) can be specified by the user.
- On the liability side, analysis can be performed at the policy level or by using model points.
- The approach can be varied according to deterministic or stochastic scenarios.
- Integration in GPMS allows easy linking with portfolios of financial assets and calibration of models parameters.
- The equation writer offers total flexibility to develop the user's own solutions.
- A high performance reporting tool can be adapted to the customer's needs.
- The data warehouse features allow for control and validation of the results.

Due to its high level of transparency and flexibility, GPMS ALM is perfectly suited for companies wishing to adopt an internal approach to the ALM risk. In addition, predefined functions allow for direct computation of the SCR in the Solvency II framework.

We ensure the services of a staff of the highest calibre during the progress of the initial implementation, or in the development of new functionalities as they are required by the market. We therefore make our clients' satisfaction our primary goal.

Contact: herve.vanoppens@orfival.be
Price: Annual licence: 30,000–150,000 EUR, depending on the number of users and the complexity

Company Name: Pensions Institute

Head Office:
106 Bunhill Row
London, EC1Y 8TZ
United Kingdom
Director: Professor David Blake

Tools/Services Description:
The Pensions Institute is unique in bringing together internationally renowned experts from across many different disciplines – including economics, finance, insurance, actuarial science, accounting, corporate governance, law and regulation. This interdisciplinary approach enhances strategic thinking towards the development of new solutions to the complex pension challenges facing states, corporations and individuals, and fosters research and knowledge-sharing.

Aims:
The Pensions Institute aims to

- undertake high quality research in all fields related to pensions
- communicate research results to academics, practitioners and policy makers
- contribute to and develop international networks of pension experts from a variety of disciplines
- provide expert advice to the pension industry and government

Key Research and Consultancy Fields:
The Pensions Institute has developed a global reputation for its research and consultancy in:

- pension fund management and performance, both for occupational and personal pension plans
- pension funding and valuation, covering actuarial and insurance issues including funding, risk management, asset-liability management, plan design, annuities and guarantes
- stochastic mortality modelling and longevity risk management

http://www.pensions-institute.org/

Company Name: Redington Ltd

Redington's 'fusion investment consulting' model blends capital market and investment banking expertise with traditional actuarial analysis. We provide clients with clear, directional, articulate advice, to help them better understand and manage risk. The firm has over 185 years of combined 'hands-on' experience in derivatives and capital markets, alongside a deep understanding of traditional asset classes and the pension industry. Redington has in excess of £150bn of assets under consulting, on behalf of more than 30 clients across the United Kingdom, Europe, and North America – including five of the 25 largest UK defined benefit pension schemes. We continue to expand our client base within the pension and insurance industries, both domestically and overseas.

Head Office:
Redington Ltd
13–15 Mallow Street
London
EC1Y 8RD

Other Sites: n/a
Managing Director: Robert Gardner – Co-Chief Executive; Dawid Konotey-Ahulu – Co-Chief Executive
Marketing Director: Stuart Breyer
Chief Technology Officer/Director: Stuart Dillon

Tools/Services:
Investment strategy analysis and design
Asset/liability optimization
Portfolio construction
Deficit funding
Derivative overlays
Manager research, selection and monitoring
Incorporating longevity risk into an overall risk framework
Alternative investment selection
Implementation
Portfolio solvency monitoring

Tools/Services Description:
Redington's founders executed the first holistic interest rate and inflation risk management transaction for the Friends Provident Pension Scheme in 2003. Redington remains at the cutting edge of LDI developments, and in the challenging market conditions of 2009 we helped clients hedge over £10bn of liability exposure to interest rates and inflation.

We provide investment advice that sets clear goals in a structured form by working with stakeholders to gain a full understanding of their objectives and constraints and, if required, adapt the governance structure to facilitate it.

To support our investment advice we employ our ALM analytics to assess any proposed asset allocation or risk management strategy; this helps to determine the most efficient risk/return profile for the client, and doesn't rely on a single and potentially misleading figure.

Using this information, we construct a Flight Plan to full funding, against which all subsequent analysis and strategies are benchmarked. The Flight Plan projects the expected funding level and outlines the path to its objectives under a given investment strategy. We then work together with all stakeholders to implement and execute strategic decisions around key objectives and devise solutions to encourage ongoing efficiency.

Contact: Stuart Breyer

Index

CPSIA information can be obtained
at www.ICGtesting.com
Printed in the USA
LVHW081240270221
679585LV00020B/22

9 780230 277779